THE PSYCHOLOGY OF ADOPTION

THE PSYCHOLOGY
OF ADOPTION

Edited by

DAVID M. BRODZINSKY

MARSHALL D. SCHECHTER

New York   Oxford
OXFORD UNIVERSITY PRESS

Oxford University Press

Oxford New York Toronto
Delhi Bombay Calcutta Madras Karachi
Kuala Lumpur Singapore Hong Kong Tokyo
Nairobi Dar es Salaam Cape Town
Melbourne Auckland

and associated companies in
Berlin Ibadan

Copyright © 1990 by Oxford University Press

First published in 1990 by Oxford University Press, Inc.,
198 Madison Avenue, New York, New York 10016-4314

First issued as an Oxford University Press paperback in 1993

Oxford is a registered trademark of Oxford University Press

Library of Congress Cataloging-in-Publication Data
The Psychology of Adoption /
David M. Brodzinsky, Marshall D. Schechter, editors.
p. cm. Bibliography: p. Includes indexes.
ISBN 0-19-504892-X   ISBN 0-19-508273-7 (pbk.)
1. Adoption—United States—Psychological aspects.
2. Children, Adopted—United States—Psychology.
I. Brodzinsky, David. II. Schechter, Marshall D.
[DNLM: 1. Adoption. WS 105.5F2 P974]
HV875.55.P79 1989
362.7'34'019—dc19
DNLM/DLC   89-2902

10 9 8 7 6 5 4

Printed in the United States of America

Dedicated to all those affected
by the profound influences of adoption

Foreword

Those of us who have become professionally involved in the field of adoption have often yearned for a comprehensive text to guide us through the many vicissitudes of the adopting process. This book provides us with some workable models—psycho-biological, psychoanalytical, and psychosocial—that should help us to conceptualize daily experiences with such cases, to become more deeply perceptive of the familiar reactions of the adopted child to being "different," to being unsure of his identity, to being told of his actual status (with its cumulative significance) and to having his sense of being and becoming undermined by the endless uncertainties of belonging.

The type of research included in this book is highly relevant to the questions that professionals and practitioners in this area often ask themselves about these children. What part does environment play in the outcome of their development? What can the family do to make the future more promising? What strains do large differences—for example, ethnic ones—impose on adaptation? Is disruption inevitable in the circumstances of adoption? Even the beginnings of some answers to these complex inquiries will add a needed confidence to our approach and thus facilitate the long-term management of the poorly adjusted child. Of particular value is the treatment section with its focus on the disorders that erupt in these families.

Moreover, those whose job it is to work with adoption on a social and organizational level will be pleased to find a group of chapters dedicated to this stage in the adoption process. Even in this context, it is heartwarming that a place has been found for the struggles the birthmother must undergo in giving up her baby to strangers. Unfortunately, the infant or child during the selection process may pass through a succession of transitional mothers and may reach the adopting parents only after growing wary of relationships and emotional commitments.

The contributions to this book remind us that these are children at risk with a more than ten-to-one chance for psychosocial maldevelopment as compared with offspring raised entirely by their own parents within their own families. Although human resilience, both genetic and acquired, questions the overall casualty rate among adoptees, there is often a price exacted by the process, with the parents having to maintain their steadiness under crisis until the child is able to bounce back. Parents and children both may need support from the practitioner whose hopefulness may help the troubled family focus on normative developments rather than endless conflicts.

The thought of being unwanted and the experience of being unconnected remain a haunting background to the inner life and prime the individual for all future rejections. At different times, the past may weigh heavily but unconsciously on the adoptee's mind, affecting his internal vision of intimacies and likenesses that come into play in later human relationships. On one occasion I recall asking a disturbed 8-year-old adopted girl why she failed to get on with her mother, and her response was: "I expect it's because I was never close inside her to her heart," revealing the type of mystique that develops in these children's minds. At another time, I put the same question to a 14-year-old girl engaged in endless battles with her adopting mother, and her reply was: "I don't know how you can expect us to get on. We're so different. She probably would have got on much better with someone like herself. We adopted kids should be chosen when we are old enough to be ourselves, and then they could match us with parents who are the same as us." To this I said: "So you would want your parents to be like you, rather than you should become like them as you grow up with them?" "Of course! Why do we have to change ourselves completely to be like them? I would always feel a phoney if I did that."

Added to these basic feelings of being unconnected and different are the feelings of being unwanted and of being unwanted because of "badnesses" inside oneself. The theme of being unwanted leads inevitably to thoughts of not belonging and perhaps eventually to thoughts of not wanting to belong. "I care for nobody, no, not I, and nobody cares for me." There is nothing to hold one to people, places, or pursuits, and one may remain tenuously connected in day-to-day dealings with people. Both parents and therapists may be determined to transform unwantedness into wantedness, but their good intentions are often wrecked by the adoptee's determination to defeat them and to be unaware that they are defeating themselves. The sense of "badness" may stem from unconscious thoughts. For example, "My birthmother got rid of me. Everyone gets rid of dirty things. I am sometimes dirty. I was gotten rid of because of my dirtiness." Or another case: "If something makes you mad, you don't like it. If you don't like it, you want to get rid of it. But if you don't want it, no one else wants it, although they may pretend to want it." Such internal logic can set up chronic insecurities, acute sensitivities, suspiciousness, secretiveness, mournfulness, and the need to act out rage.

I have pointed to some of the complexities in the adoption process to indicate what a challenging field this is and to point out how much the reader stands to gain from acquainting himself with the rich information provided in this volume.

August 1989

E. James Anthony, M.D.
Director, Child and Adolescent Psychotherapy
Chestnut Lodge Hospital

Preface

Since recorded history, adoption has been practiced either formally, through established laws or rules (e.g., Code of Hammurabi, the Napoleonic Code, English common law), or informally by social custom, and has long been seen as an acceptable way of incorporating new members into a family.

In contemporary society, adoption is a widely accepted solution for the care and rearing of children whose biological parents could not or would not provide for them (Boswell, 1988). In this context, the practice of adoption is geared primarily toward meeting the physical, emotional, social, and educational needs of the child; however, this "best interests of the child" philosophy has a rather recent origin (see Goldstein, Freud, & Solnit, 1973). In the past, adoption was primarily a vehicle for serving the needs of childless adults rather than the needs of homeless children. From the time of antiquity, adoption has been a means of securing heirs, satisfying political requirements, meeting religious needs, securing additional labor for the family, and building family alliances. Rather than being a rare, emergency measure, historically, adoption was a common social practice, particularly among preliterate societies (see Dunning, 1962; Lowie, 1930; Weckler, 1953).

It was not until the industrial revolution that attention slowly began to shift toward the needs and welfare of homeless children (Presser, 1972). But even then, social service practice seldom matched prevailing rhetoric. Although the emergence of "modern" child welfare services at the turn of this century promised permanence in the lives of homeless children, it often was not achieved, especially for children beyond the infancy years. For these latter youngsters, a life of institutional care or long-term foster care too often was the outcome (Wiltse, 1985).

In the past two decades, however, a remarkable transformation has begun to take place in the child welfare system. Fueled by the civil rights movement, and a number of significant changes in demographic trends, family structure, gender roles, and societal values, adoption policy and practice has entered a new era, one characterized by a strong commitment to permanency planning for all children (Cole, 1985). These changes have given rise to a new interest in and perspective on the well-being of adopted children, not only among social service personnel, but also among mental health professionals.

Historically, mental health professionals have paid little attention to adoption. After all, adoption was seen as a rather successful social service solution to the problems confronting all three parties of the adoption triangle—that is, the problem of an unwanted pregnancy for the birthparents, the problem of infertility and childlessness for the prospective adoptive parents, and the problem of a state of home-lessness for the child. With the placement of the child in the adoptive family, it was generally assumed that the various parties of the adoption triangle would simply go on their way to live "happily ever after." But how valid was this assumption? Does adoption solve the problems of these individuals, or does the experience of adoption itself or factors related to adoption place these individuals, especially the child, at risk for various psychological problems?

During the first half of this century, these questions and others slowly began to attract the attention of the mental health community due to the development of psychoanalytic theory with its emphasis on the role of early childhood experience (Clothier, 1939, 1943). Research on the adverse effects of institutionalizaton and separation from attachment figures (often described in the context of maternal deprivation) also sensitized professionals to the potential risks associated with adoption (Bowlby, 1951; Bowlby, Ainsworth, Boston, & Rosenbluth, 1956). Still, interest in the psychology of adoption remained quite limited until the 1960s when two important contributions were made to the literature. The first was an empirical contribution by Marshall Schechter and his colleagues. In two papers, these clinical researchers noted that although nonblood related adopted children constituted approximately 1 to 2% of the population of children in the United States under 18 years of age, they accounted for a far greater percentage of those individuals seeking mental health services in outpatient settings (Schechter, 1960; Schechter et al., 1964). These papers stimulated much debate among the professional community and led to a series of epidemiological studies addressing the incidence and prevalence of adoptees in clinical settings, as well as a host of studies on the clinical symptomatology of outpatient and inpatient adoptees. They also raised many questions regarding the appropriate timing for disclosing adoption information to children.

The second contribution was theoretical in nature. In 1964, H. David Kirk published *Shared Fate,* a sociological examination of adoptive family relationships. At the heart of Kirk's theory was the assumption that adoptive family life exposes parents and children to a host of tasks, challenges, and dilemmas that must be resolved before satisfactory adjustment can be achieved. For example, do adoptive parents see themselves in the same way as biological parents, or as somehow different? Do they acknowledge the differences of adoptive family life to their children as they integrate them into the family, or are these differences downplayed or ignored? What about the child's past? Do parents attempt to recall background information about the child and bring it into their family life, or do they display ignorance of the child's birthparents and origins? As Kirk noted, these dilemmas and others combine to create a number of role handicaps for adoptive parents and their children. He further suggested that parents who were more willing to acknowledge the inherent differences in adoptive family life would be in a better position to help their children adjust to their adoptive status. Conversely, families who denied their differences in origin (from biologically formed families) were thought to be at greater risk for difficulties in the future.

Although Kirk's theory has been criticized, both conceptually and in terms of its empirical support (Brodzinsky, 1987; D. Brodzinsky, Chapter 1; Kaye, Chapter 7), its importance cannot be denied. For one thing, it represented the first major theoretical effort to conceptualize adoptive family life, in contrast to earlier psychoanalytic writings on adoption which generally focused on the individual dynamics of children and parents. It also helped to normalize many of the adjustment difficulties among adoptees and adoptive parents. Finally, the theory was of critical importance in opening up the adoption process. *Shared Fate* promoted greater openness and honesty in placement practices (e.g., sharing of background information with adoptive parents), as well as greater openness in the adoptive parent–child relationship, especially with regard to the "telling process." In fact, recent trends related to unsealing closed adoption records and to the development of open adoption placements (Baran & Pannor, Chapter 17) clearly have been influenced by the ideas set forth in Kirk's now classic book.

Over the past two decades or so, a great deal has been written about adoption. And yet our understanding of the impact of this arrangement on children and parents (both adoptive parents and relinquishing parents) remains quite limited. Until recently, much research in this area was difficult to interpret because of its atheoretical nature. Furthermore, the heavy focus of research on clinical populations restricted the generalizability of the findings to the broader nonclinical adoption community.

Another complication in understanding the impact of adoption on members of the adoption triangle is that the practice of adoption itself is changing. In the first half of this century, adoption typically involved the placement of an infant with a childless, infertile couple of the same race (and often of the same religious background). Today adoption is much more complex. Relative to the total number of adoptions each year, traditional infant adoptions are on the decline. This trend reflects the increased availability of contraception and abortion, as well as the increasing number of young women who are choosing to parent their children out-of-wedlock rather than placing them for adoption (Cole, 1985; Resnick, 1984). With fewer babies available for adoption, more and more couples are now choosing other adoption options—that is, children of a different race or from a foreign country, older children, sibling groups, physically and emotionally handicapped children, and other so-called "special needs" children. Still other couples who are determined to adopt a baby rather than an older child or a special needs child are choosing independent (nonagency) adoption, either through an intermediary (e.g., a lawyer) or through direct placement of the child by the biological parents. In addition, the new reproductive technologies (artificial insemination by donor, in vitro and in vivo fertilization, surrogacy, etc.) have offered nonfecund couples opportunities for creating a family with direct blood ties with one or both of the parents.

The nature of those who adopt children also is changing. In the past, most adopters in this country were white, infertile, middle-class couples. Although this group still comprises the largest number of adoptive parents, today a much wider range of adults are seeking to build families through adoption—for example, fertile couples (with or without biological children of their own), minority couples, single adults, foster parents, and working class couples. The increased number of divorces and remarriages presently occurring also has added to the number of adoptive parents, as individuals have legally adopted the offspring brought into the marriage by their new spouse. In fact, stepparent adoptions and other forms of relative adoptions (e.g., adoptions within the extended biological family) constitute the largest percentage of adoptions in the United States.

Finally, the trend toward greater openness in adoption (see Sorosky, Baran, &

Pannor, 1978; Baran & Pannor, Chapter 17) also has had a profound impact on the face of adoption today. There is perhaps no area in adoption that stimulates as much intense debate and in which there is more diverse opinion than open adoption, including not only the issue of open adoption placements, but also breaking sealed adoption records, and facilitating the search by adoptees and birthparents for one another.

Thus, it is clear that adoption is a complex and, at times, confusing form of family life. The changes that have taken place in this field have had a significant impact on the lives of adoptees, adoptive parents, and birthparents, as well as adoption agency personnel, the legal profession, and the mental health practitioners who work with members of the adoption triangle. Researchers too have been affected by these changes. The degree of complexity in adoption often appears to overwhelm them in their attempt to understand this family pattern.

For too long, adoption has been seen as an area of concern only for social service personnel. In turn, this attitude has made it difficult to generate interest in this area among professionals from other disciplines. And yet, the very complexity of adoption, especially in current times, demands an interdisciplinary approach if we are to foster greater understanding of this form of family life. Fortunately, the situation appears to be changing. Interest in adoption is widespread and touches numerous disciplines, including not only social work, but also psychology, psychiatry, clinical medicine, fetology, sociology, special education, genetics, clinical nursing, and the legal and judicial systems.

It was with an appreciation for the broad-based interest in adoption that the current volume was planned. Professionals from a variety of disciplines (e.g., psychology, psychiatry, social work, sociology, behavioral genetics) in the United States and in Europe were asked to contribute to the project. Our goal was to provide an overview of current work in adoption, with a focus primarily on mental health issues. Toward this end, four sections were conceptualized.[1] Part I involves an overview of various theoretical approaches to adoption adjustment. In Chapter 1, D. Brodzinsky examines children's adjustment to adoption within the context of current theories of stress and coping. This is followed in Chapter 2 by Cadoret's review of the genetic contribution to various forms of psychopathology and the possible implications of this data for adopted children's adjustment. In Chapter 3, Brinich presents an overview of psychoanalytic perspectives on the adjustment of adoptees, adoptive parents, and birthparents. Finally, in Chapter 4, Schechter and Bertocci examine the phenomenon of search behavior among adoptees, also from a psychodynamic perspective.

Part II involves a series of chapters dealing with empirical issues in adoption adjustment. Chapters 5 and 6, by Bohman and Sigvardsson, and Triseliotis and Hill, respectively, provide valuable longitudinal perspectives on adoption adjustment. Chapter 7, by Kaye, presents original data examining H. David Kirk's hypothesis regarding family communication patterns (i.e., acknowledgment- versus rejection-of-differences) and children's adjustment. This contribution is followed in Chapter 8 by a review of the literature on identity development among adoptees by Hoopes. Factors associated with the adjustment of residentially placed adolescent adoptees is examined by Grotevant and McRoy in Chapter 9, followed in Chapter 10 by a review of the literature on interracial adoption by Silverman and Feigelman. Finally, in Chapter 11, Festinger reviews the data on the rates and correlates of adoption disruption.

Part III focuses on clinical issues in adoptees and their families. Hartman and Laird, in Chapter 12, describe a number of common themes seen in postadoption family treatment with adoptees and their parents. In Chapter 13, Lindstrom and Schaffer describe the application of a brief, solution-focused family therapy model to many of these same clinical issues. This is followed in Chapter 14 by Goodrich and his colleague's examination of the characteristics and clinical issues of more seriously disturbed adolescent adoptees in inpatient mental health settings.

The final section of the book, Part IV, focuses on selected social policy and casework issues. Cole and Donley, in Chapter 15, describe the history, values, and placement policy underlying modern child welfare services to members of the adoption triangle. Chapter 16, by A. Brodzinsky, presents a historical and empirical review of the literature on the plight of relinquishing mothers, as well as an examination of the casework and clinical needs of these individuals. This is followed in Chapter 17 by Baran and Pannor's analysis of one of the most controversial areas in this field—open adoption. Finally, the book closes with a sociolegal examination by Derdeyn of recent trends affecting foster parent adoption.

Although this book covers a wide range of topics dealing with mental health issues in adoption, it is by no means comprehensive. We acknowledge that many important areas have been covered only tangentially, or not at all. Nevertheless, as editors of this book, we hope that readers will find much of interest, a great deal of practical value, and perhaps some areas for debate—all of which should lead to further studies and dialogue on this profound area of the human condition.

D.M.B.
M.D.S.

NOTE

1. In many chapters of the book, authors have used case vignettes to highlight important clinical and casework issues. To protect the confidentiality of the individuals described, names and circumstances occasionally have been altered.

Contents

Contributors

Annette Baran, M.S.W., A.C.S.W., L.C.S.W.
Private Practice
Los Angeles, California

Linda Beth Berman, M.A.
Research Institute
Chestnut Lodge
Rockville, Maryland

Doris Bertocci, M.S.W., A.C.S.W.
Columbia University Health Services
Columbia University
New York, New York

Paul Brinich, Ph.D.
Department of Psychiatry
University Hospitals of Cleveland
Cleveland, Ohio

Anne B. Brodzinsky, M.A.
Doctoral Candidate, Department
  of Counseling Psychology
New York University
New York, New York

David M. Brodzinsky, Ph.D.
Department of Psychology
Rutgers University
New Brunswick, New Jersey

Michael Bohman, M.D.
Department of Child
  and Adolescent Psychiatry
University of Umeå
Umeå, Sweden

Remi J. Cadoret, M.D.
Department of Psychiatry
University of Iowa School of Medicine
Iowa City, Iowa

Elizabeth S. Cole, M.S.W., A.C.S.W.
Elizabeth S. Cole Associates
New Hope, Pennsylvania

Andre Derdeyn, M.D.
Department of Psychiatry
University of Virginia Medical Center,
  Blue Ridge Division
Charlottesville, Virginia

Kathryn S. Donley, M.S.W., A.C.S.W.
National Resource Center on Special Needs
  Adoption
Chelsea, Michigan

William Feigelman, Ph.D.
Department of Sociology
Nassau Community College
Garden City, New York

Trudy Festinger, D.S.W.
Department of Social Work
New York University
New York, New York

Carol S. Fullerton, Ph.D.
Department of Psychiatry
Uniformed Services University of the Health
  Sciences
Bethesda, Maryland

Wells Goodrich, M.D.,
Adolescent and Child Research
Chestnut Lodge
Rockville, Maryland

Harold D. Grotevant, Ph.D.
Department of Home Economics
  and Psychology
University of Texas
Austin, Texas

Ann Hartman, D.S.W.
Department of Social Work
Smith College
Northampton, Massachusetts

Malcolm Hill, Ph.D.
Department of Social Work
University of Edinburgh
Edinburgh, Scotland

Janet Hoopes, Ph.D.
Department of Human Development
Bryn Mawr College
Bryn Mawr, Pennsylvania

Kenneth Kaye, Ph.D.
Department of Clinical Psychiatry
Northwestern University School of Medicine
Chicago, Illinois

Joan Laird, D.S.W.
Department of Social Work
Smith College
Northampton, Massachusetts

Christina Lindstrom, Ph.D.
The Center for Adoptive Families
New York, New York

Ruth G. McRoy, Ph.D.
Department of Social Work
University of Texas
Austin, Texas

Reuben Pannor, M.S.W., A.C.S.W.,
    L.C.S.W.
Private Practice
Los Angeles, California

Judith Schaffer, M.A.
The Center for Adoptive Families
New York, New York

Marshall D. Schechter, M.D.
Child and Adolescent Psychiatry
University of Pennsylvania School
    of Medicine
Philadelphia, Pennsylvania

Sören Sigvardsson, Ph.D.
Department of Behavior Genetics
University of Umeå
Umeå, Sweden

Arnold Silverman, Ph.D.
Department of Sociology
Nassasu Community College
Garden City, New York

John Triseliotis, Ph.D.
Department of Social Work
University of Edinburgh
Edinburgh, Scotland

Brian T. Yates, Ph.D.
Department of Psychology
American University
Washington, D.C.

I

THEORETICAL PERSPECTIVES ON ADOPTION ADJUSTMENT

1

A Stress and Coping Model
of Adoption Adjustment

DAVID M. BRODZINSKY

In the past two decades, social casework personnel, clinicians, and researchers alike have begun to pay increased attention to the psychological complications associated with adoption. Their attention has been prompted by numerous reports of high rates of referral of adopted children and youth to outpatient and inpatient mental health facilities. For example, although adopted children constitute approximately 2% of the total population of children in the United States (Zill, 1985), they represent between 4 and 5% of the children referred to outpatient mental health facilities (Kadushin, 1980; Mech, 1973) and between 10 and 15% of the children in residential care facilities (R. Colburn, personal communication, 1986; K. Donley, personal communication, 1986). Research on the symptomatology presented by the children referred to clinics also indicates that adoptees are more likely than their nonadopted counterparts to display a variety of acting-out problems (e.g., aggression, stealing, lying, oppositional behavior, running away, hyperactivity), low self-esteem, and a host of learning difficulties (Dalby, Fox, & Haslam, 1982; Deutsch et al 1982; Fullerton, Goodrich, & Berman, 1986; Kenny, Baldwin, & Mackie, 1967; Lifshitz, Baum, Balgur, & Cohen, 1975; Menlove, 1965; Offord, Aponte, & Cross, 1969; Schechter, Carlson, Simmons, & Work, 1964; Silver, 1970; Simon & Senturia, 1966; Taichert & Harvin, 1975). Even research with nonclinical, community-based samples suggests somewhat greater psychological vulnerability for adopted children as compared to nonadopted children (Bohman, 1970; Brodzinsky, Radice, Huffman, & Merkler, 1987; Brodzinsky, Schechter, Braff, & Singer, 1984; Hoopes, 1982; Lindholm & Touliatos, 1980; Seglow, Pringle, & Wedge, 1972; Ternay, Wilborn, & Day, 1985; Zill, 1985), although admittedly, the data are less consistent for these types of studies (see Marquis & Detweiler, 1985; Stein & Hoopes, 1985). Moreover, the increased vulnerability of adopted children generally does not emerge until the elementary school years (Brodzinsky, 1987).

Assuming that adopted children are at increased risk for various psychological and academic problems, the obvious question that needs to be addressed is the basis for their vulnerability. Mental health professionals have offered a variety of theoretical explanations for the problems manifested by adoptees. Psychodynamic theorists, on the one hand, have focused their attention on those aspects of the adoption experience that complicate coping with object loss, the resolution of the oedipal conflict, and the development of a mature and stable ego identity (Blum, 1983; Brinich, 1980; Brodzinsky, 1987; Easson, 1973; Nickman, 1985; Sants, 1964; Schechter, 1960; Sorosky, Baran, & Pannor, 1975). Kirk's (1964) social role theory of adoption adjustment links the problems of adoptees to the failure of their adoptive parents to handle effectively various "role handicaps" that are an inherent part of adoptive family life (see Brodzinsky, 1987). Cognitive-developmental factors have also been offered as components of the adoption-adjustment process, particularly as they relate to the child's growing awareness of the meaning of adoption (Brodzinsky, 1984, 1987; Brodzinsky, Braff, & Singer, 1980; Brodzinsky, Schechter, & Brodzinsky, 1986; Brodzinsky, Singer, & Braff, 1984). In addition, ethological theory has emphasized the importance of the attachment-separation-loss process as fundamental to the problems of many adoptees, particularly those individuals who are placed beyond the infancy years (Bowlby, 1951; Bowlby, Ainsworth, Boston, & Rosenbluth, 1956; Steinhauer, 1983; Yarrow & Goodwin, 1973; Yarrow, Goodwin, Manheimer, & Milowe, 1973). Finally, various researchers have suggested that the problems of the adopted child may have a biological source associated either with increased genetic vulnerability or prenatal and reproductive complications (Bohman, 1970; Cadoret, 1978, Chapter 2; Deutsch et al., 1982; Loehlin, Willerman, & Horn, 1982; Losbough, 1965; Schechter et al., 1964).

Although many different perspectives have been offered on the adjustment problems of adopted children and their families, a common thread can be found running through most of them—namely, that adoption is experienced as *stressful* by many children and parents and, consequently, results in a variety of coping efforts, some of which are successful in handling the stress and others which are not. In light of this common theme and the growing acceptance of the role of stress and coping in mediating physical and psychological well-being (see Garmezy & Rutter, 1983; Lazarus & Folkman, 1984), the remainder of this chapter examines the adjustment process of adopted children (and to a lesser extent, their adoptive parents) in terms of a stress and coping model. For an analysis of the adjustment problems of birthparents, see A. Brodzinsky (Chapter 16) and Winkler and Van Keppel (1984).

ADOPTION AND THE EXPERIENCE OF STRESS

The idea that adoption is a stressful experience runs counter to many prevailing myths and stereotypes about this family life situation. In fact, adoption typically has been viewed as a societal solution for the stress confronting all three parties of the adoption triangle—that is, the stress associated with (1) an unwanted pregnancy on the part of birthparents, (2) infertility and childlessness on the part of adoptive parents, and (3) a state of homelessness and a sense of insecurity on the part of prospective adopted children. With the placement of the child in the adoptive family, it has often been assumed that the various parties of the adoption triangle simply go on their way to live "happily ever after." Although many members of the adoption triangle do seem to adjust quite well to their adoption-related experiences, we now know that a sizable percentage of them continue to have a stressful time in dealing with adoption issues in the postplacement period (see Lifton, 1979; Sorosky, Baran, & Pannor, 1978). Before describing why adoption is experienced as stressful by many adopted children and their parents, it is important to first define what is meant by stress and understand its relationship to adaptational outcomes.

Stress and Adaptational Outcomes

The concept of stress has been the center of considerable controversy for some time, and numerous definitions of this construct have been offered. Some theorists have focused on stress as a stimulus or stressor (Holmes & Rahe, 1967). In this context, stress is equated with environmental events that produce undesirable consequences for the individual. Natural disasters and manmade catastrophes (e.g., war), family disruption such as death and divorce, loss of a job, and so on, are all examples of stressors within this perspective. As Lazarus and Folkman (1984) have noted, however, this approach is rather narrow, since it tends to ignore individual differences in vulnerability to such events. Moreover, it also tends to equate stressors with major life events and thus avoids dealing with chronic stressors or with the "daily hassles" that are known to irritate and distress many people and that have been shown to be very important in adaptation and health (see DeLongis, Coyne, Dakof, Folkman, & Lazarus, 1982; Lazarus & Folkman, 1984).

A second approach to defining stress, which typically has been associated with biology and medicine, has focused on response or outcome variables (Selye, 1950, 1976). From this perspective, something is stressful if it produces a characteristic physiological outcome (e.g., increased heartrate and respiration, elevated corticosteroids, etc.). Like the stimulus-oriented definition, this approach also suffers from various shortcomings. Lazarus and Folkman (1984) note that this perspective ignores the fact that the same type of response (e.g., elevated heartrate) can occur for different reasons. Thus without reference to a specific stimulus, it is difficult to know whether a particular response should be judged as a psychological stress reaction. Furthermore, these authors also point out that this approach restricts our ability to define stress prospectively. In other words, we can never know ahead of time whether something will be stressful or not. We must await the individual's reaction to the event to determine whether it is stressful.

A more useful approach to understanding stress has been offered by Lazarus and his colleagues (Lazarus, DeLongis, Folkman, & Gruen, 1985; Lazarus & Folkman, 1984). This approach not only considers the interaction of stimulus and response components of stress, but also incorporates cognitive appraisal processes, coping style and defense mechanisms, and the social context into a comprehensive model of the role of stress in the development of physical and psychological illness. Although it is beyond the scope of this chapter to describe this model in detail, a brief overview is warranted since it forms the basis for the model of adoption adjustment presented here.

Lazarus and his colleagues have placed considerable importance on the role of cognitive appraisal in understanding the link between stress and adaptational outcomes. Two forms of cognitive appraisal have been described by these investigators. Primary appraisal refers to the evaluation of the potential impact of the event on the individual. Three kinds of evaluations have been distinguished: (1) the event is *irrel-*

evant to one's well-being; (2) the event is *benign-positive* to one's well-being; and (3) the event is *stressful* (i.e., viewed as representing harm or loss, threat, or challenge) and, therefore, is potentially damaging to one's well-being. By contrast, secondary appraisal refers to judgments concerning possible steps that can be taken to meet the demands of the stressful event. In other words, this form of appraisal involves a subjective evaluation of the individual's coping options.

In addition to cognitive appraisal, Lazarus and his co-workers also have emphasized the role of coping strategies in mediating adaptational outcomes. These investigators have defined coping as "constantly changing cognitive and behavioral efforts to manage specific external and/or internal demands that are appraised as taxing or exceeding the resources of the person" (Lazarus & Folkman, 1984, p. 141). From this perspective, coping is viewed as a process—one that can either facilitate or impede successful adaptational outcomes. Two forms of coping are differentiated. Problem-focused coping strategies are directed at managing or altering the problem causing the distress. These strategies are similar to those used in more general forms of problem solving and involve such efforts as altering environmental pressures, barriers, resources, and the like. In addition, problem-focused coping also can be directed inward in an attempt to produce motivational or cognitive changes such as altering one's level of aspiration, reducing one's ego involvement, or developing new standards of behavior. By contrast, emotion-focused coping strategies are directed at regulating emotional response to the problem at hand. These strategies can involve attempts to *reduce* emotional distress by such means as avoidance, minimization, distancing, selective attention, positive comparison, and so on; or the strategies can *increase* emotional distress as a way of mobilizing oneself for action. Furthermore, certain emotion-focused coping strategies are directed at bringing about a change in the meaning of the stressful event. In such a case, coping involves a reappraisal or redefinition of the event as less threatening than was first thought.

Finally, Lazarus and his colleagues argue that cognitive appraisal processes and coping strategies are highly influenced by a host of person variables and environmental variables. For example, the individual's values, commitments, goals, and general beliefs—including self-esteem, mastery, sense of control, and interpersonal trust—are assumed to interact with various environmental demands, constraints, and resources (e.g., social support) to produce divergent appraisals as to whether the stimulus event in question is potentially stressful and, if so, what the person can do to cope with it. Thus in integrating person variables with the environmental conditions being faced, cognitive appraisal processes provide the bases of individual differences in response to psychological stress reactions (Lazarus et al., 1985).

Loss as a Source of Stress in Adoption

A primary assumption of this chapter is that adoption involves loss, which, in turn, creates stress for the child and thereby increases his or her vulnerability for emotional and behavioral problems (see Brodzinsky, 1987). Although this idea certainly is not new, in the past it has been associated primarily with adoption placements involving the separation of an older child from a caregiver (i.e., biological parent or foster parent) with whom he or she has an attachment relationship (Bowlby, 1969; Fahlberg, 1979; Jewett, 1978; Steinhauer, 1983). Here the concept of loss is incorporated into a model of adjustment for children who are placed for adoption during the first few months of their life (i.e., what has been called traditional adoption), prior to the time when they have developed primary attachments.

The experience of loss among adopted children placed as infants has often gone unrecognized by mental health professionals and laypersons alike. Too often, it has been assumed that adopted children cannot feel loss for individuals (i.e., biological parents) they have never known. In recent years, though, adoption specialists have come to appreciate the unique role played by loss in the psychological adjustment of even those children given homes when they were infants (see Brinich, 1980; Brodzinsky, 1987; Nickman, 1985). This is not to suggest, however, that the experience of loss among early- and late-placed adopted children is the same. To be sure, loss due to separation from an attachment figure is not only more "overt" (Nickman, 1985), but is assumed to be more traumatic, thereby creating greater stress and vulnerability for the child. Moreover, to the extent that the child experiences multiple separations from attachment figures as he or she moves through the foster care system, this form of loss probably can be considered a *provoking agent* that contributes directly to the development of psychopathology (Brown & Harris, 1978; Costello, 1982). Conversely, loss associated with early adoption placement is "covert" (Nickman, 1985) and subtle, and emerges slowly with time in conjunction with the child's growing awareness of the meaning and implications of having been adopted (Brodzinsky, 1987). Moreover, this form of loss, being less traumatic, is not as likely to lead to psychopathology, by itself, but increases the child's vulnerability to other pathogenic experiences (Brown & Harris, 1978; Costello, 1982).

In stating that adoption involves loss, let us be clear about what exactly this sense of loss entails. Simply put, adopted children, once they come to realize the implications of being adopted, not only experience a loss of their biological parents and origins, but also a loss of stability in the relationship to their adoptive parents (Brinich, 1980; Brodzinsky, 1987; Nickman, 1985). In addition, there is loss of self (Brodzinsky, 1987) and genealogical continuity (Sants, 1964). Adopted children also experience "status loss" associated with being different (Kirk, 1964; Nickman, 1985). These various losses often leave the adoptee feeling incomplete, alienated, disconnected, abandoned, or unwanted. Furthermore, the sense of loss typically leads to a characteristic pattern of emotional and behavioral reactions commonly associated with grieving (see Bowlby, 1973, 1980). In fact, Brodzinsky (1987) has suggested that much of what has been called pathogenic in the adopted child's behavior is nothing more than the unrecognized manifestation of an adaptive grieving process.

Comparing Loss in Adoption, Parental Divorce, and Parental Death

The significance of loss as a central factor underlying children's adjustment is certainly not restricted to adoption. In fact, loss has been conceptualized as a fundamental explanatory construct in children's adjustment to many forms of family distruption and life transitions (see Bloom-Feshbach & Bloom-Feshbach, 1987). This is not to suggest, however, that the experience of loss is the same in reaction to different life circumstances—for clearly it is not. As a stressor, loss associated with family disruption and life transitions varies along a number of dimensions, including degree of acuteness, pervasiveness, permanence, universality, public recognition of loss, and so on. In an attempt to provide a clearer picture of the role of loss in the adjustment of adopted children, it is instructive to compare it with the experience of loss associated with other, more common, forms of family disruption—parental divorce and parental death (see Wallerstein, 1983, for a similar comparison of these two forms of family disruption).

Adoption, parental divorce, and parental death differ on at least six dimensions. Consider first the dimension of *universality*. Death is a universal experience. Not only will we all die, but in the process of growing up it is inevitable that we will be exposed to the death of significant others—grandparents, parents, friends, acquaintances, and so on. As Wallerstein (1983) notes, "Each person finds both terror and comfort in the recognition that the same fate awaits us all" (p. 273). By contrast, divorce and adoption, like most other losses, are not universal experiences. Nowadays divorce is so common in our society that nearly all children whose parents separate and eventually divorce know others who have had similar experiences. This is often not the case in adoption. Because relatively few children in our society are adopted, there is a greater likelihood that adoptees will feel more alone with their losses. In turn, this may well foster feelings of "differentness" that can undermine self-esteem and psychological well-being.

Adoption and divorce also differ from parental death in terms of its *permanence*. On the one hand, loss due to death is final—that is, irreversible. Although young children do not understand this aspect of death, by the time they reach the early elementary school years they generally have mastered it (Speece & Brent, 1984). On the other hand, most children recognize that loss due to divorce and adoption are at least potentially reversible—for, in fact, the noncustodial parent (in divorce) and the "surrendering" parents (in adoption) usually are alive. Certainly, hope of reunion with the lost person is a theme of much of the fantasy life of children who experience divorce and adoption. In divorce, this hope (which typically includes a desire for parental reunification) often is reinforced by the ongoing contact between the child and the noncustodial parent (Wallerstein, 1983). Although such contact can make it difficult at first for the child to acknowledge the reality of the divorce, in the long run it typically fosters healthier adjustment on the child's part than in cases where the child has little, if any, contact with the noncustodial parent. Adopted children also fantasize about "undoing" their loss. Fantasies about reunions with birthparents (and birthsiblings) are extremely common among adopted children as they are growing up. The fact that these fantasies potentially can come true—which is reinforced by the well-publicized search efforts of adult adoptees and birthparents—may well serve to impede the resolution of loss among many adopted individuals.

A third dimension differentiating adoption, divorce, and death is the child's *relationship with the lost person or persons*. Children who experience parental death generally have a history of interaction with these individuals. Consequently, there are memories of the parent and of their shared experiences, as well as memories of the circumstances surrounding the parent's death that can be drawn on in coming to terms with the loss. In divorce, too, there typically is a history of a relationship with the lost parent, as well as a history of experiencing various conditions of family life that may have contributed to parental divorce. These experiences, along with the possibility of an ongoing relationship with the noncustodial parent, can make it easier for the child to understand the basis of the loss—and, therefore, how to come to terms with it. Adopted children, in contrast, are at a disadvantage in comparison to other children who have lost parents. Because the original relinquishment typically occurs in infancy, adoptees seldom have memories of their birthparents and the circumstances surrounding their adoptive placement. They also are frequently prevented from gaining greater insight into their past because of the adoptive parents' anxiety in discussing the relinquishment, as well as the reluctance of adoption agencies to share relevant information with the adoptive family. Thus that which is lost to the adopted child is often unknown. This lack of knowledge tends to foster misperceptions and distortions of the birthparents and the circumstances of the relinquishment. As a result, the lost birthparents often linger as "ghosts" in the mental and emotional life of adopted persons, and prevent them from achieving some satisfactory resolution of their loss.

The issue of whether the loss was the result of *voluntary versus involuntary* circumstances also is a dimension that differentiates these various forms of family disruption. Adoption and divorce, unlike death, involve presumed voluntary decisions on the part of the parents. As Wallerstein (1983) notes, this knowledge can be a burden for the child, and foster feelings of intense anger toward the parents. It also can be the basis of considerable guilt and self-blame (e.g., "If only I were good, daddy wouldn't have left" or "If only I were good, my birthparents wouldn't have given me up for adoption"). Although anger and guilt are also seen in children's response to parental death, these reactions usually are less intense and less prolonged probably because they are not reinforced by the very real possibility of restoration represented by living parents.

Although adoption, divorce, and death all involve loss, the *extent of the loss* is greater in adoption. In death, there is a permanent loss of a single parent. Divorce, too, involves the loss of a single parent, although this loss typically is not permanent and may be partially "undone" through regular visitation. Furthermore, it is common for children who experience parental death and divorce to feel some sense of family loss, although the presence of the surviving parent or the custodial parent, as well as siblings and other extended family, helps to offset this feeling. In adoption, the loss is more pervasive, although perhaps less obvious. Not only do adopted children experience the loss of birthparents and the extended birth family as well as the loss of cultural and genealogical heritage, but for many adoptees there is a loss of a sense of permanence in, and connectedness to, their adoptive family, as well as a loss of self and social status.

A final dimension differentiating these forms of family disruption concerns the extent of *societal and community acknowledgment of loss and the support offered to the bereaved person.* Death is a universally recognized loss. Every society and culture not only acknowledges the loss involved in death, but provides a variety of rituals and supports (e.g., funerals, wakes, burials, religious ceremonies, etc.) to help the individual both acknowledge and mourn the loss. By contrast, mental health professionals have noted the lack of readily available supports to help the child (and adults) deal with divorce-related losses (Wallerstein, 1983; Wallerstein & Kelly, 1980). In a similar vein, those individuals who experience loss because of adoption are often lacking in the necessary rituals and emotional support that would help them move through the mourning process. In fact, I would argue that public recognition and acceptance of loss in adoption (at least traditional adoption involving placement in infancy) is even less than in the case of divorce. The consequence of this diminished support is that it makes it more difficult for adoptees to consciously acknowledge to themselves their sense of loss, as well as find effective ways of coping with their sorrow and loneliness.

To summarize, although adoption, parental divorce, and parental death all involve significant loss for the child, the nature of the loss differs considerably in each of these circumstances. In my clinical experience, the pervasiveness of loss in adoption, coupled with the diminished societal recognition and support for this loss, as well as the realization that restoration of a relationship with the lost individuals is a possibility, combine to complicate the grieving process for the adoptee.

A MODEL OF STRESS AND COPING IN ADOPTION

Figure 1.1 presents a schematic representation of our current thinking about adoption adjustment in terms of a stress and coping model. Before describing the various components of the model and elaborating on a number of them, two points must be made. First, the present model, as noted earlier, draws heavily on the work of Lazarus and his colleagues (DeLongis et al., 1982; Lazarus et al., 1985; Lazarus & Folkman, 1984), as well as our own previous work on cognitive-developmental and psychosocial factors in adoption adjustment (Brodzinsky, 1984, 1987; Brodzinsky et al., 1980; Brodzinsky & Huffman, 1988; Brodzinsky, Singer, & Braff, 1984; Brodzinsky et al., 1986). Second, although the current model is believed to have substantial integrative and generative value, it still must be considered speculative and most certainly incomplete, given the paucity of research on children's adoption adjustment.

As noted earlier, a primary assumption of the present model is that adoption leads to an experience of loss on the part of the child. Although this is believed to be universal among adoptees, the extent to which the loss is experienced as stressful obviously varies from child to child. Whereas some children are severely distressed over the loss of birthparents, origins, and so on, others show minimal reactions to these losses. Explaining the wide array of reactions to the experience of adoption-related losses constitutes the primary challenge for any model of adoption adjustment.

At the heart of the current model is the assumption that children's adjustment to adoption (both short-term and long-term outcome) is mediated by various cognitive-appraisal processes and coping efforts. Cognitive appraisal includes both the child's interpretation of the meaning of being adopted, including its potential as a stressor, as well as a subjective evaluation of the options available to the child for dealing with the conflict, demands, challenges, and so on that are part of the adoption experience. Coping efforts include a variety of strategies that are activated in response to the perceived stress of adoption. Some of these strategies are thought to be problem focused (e.g., instrumental action, negotiation, mobilizing support, information seeking, altering one's aspirations or expectations, and exercising restraint) and others are thought to be emotion focused (e.g., minimization, denial, escapism, distancing, self-blame, and redefinition). Impacting on the cognitive-appraisal process are a host of person-related variables. Among the more important of these variables are

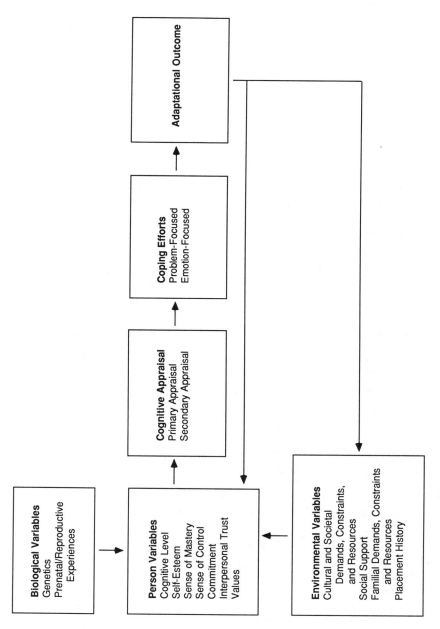

Figure 1.1 A stress and coping model of children's adoption adjustment.

the child's self-esteem, sense of mastery and control, interpersonal trust, values, and level of cognitive functioning. In addition, two sets of background variables are also posited as influencing the adoption adjustment process. These include biological factors, such as the child's genetic endowment and prenatal and reproductive experiences, as well as various environmental factors such as general familial and peer socialization experiences, and various cultural and situational demands, constraints, and resources specifically associated with adoption. Finally, it should be noted that the current model is recursive in nature. As such, it is assumed that short-term adaptational outcomes influence various person variables directly as well as indirectly through their impact on more general environmental experiences.

Having outlined the basics of the model, let us turn now to some of its specifics. In previous work, my colleagues and I have emphasized the role of cognitive-developmental factors in children's knowledge of, and reactions to, their adoptive status (Brodzinsky, 1984, 1987; Brodzinsky et al., 1980; Brodzinsky, Singer, & Braff, 1984; Brodzinsky et al., 1986). We have argued that adopted children's adjustment is mediated, in part, by their emerging comprehension of the meaning of adoption—including their awareness of adoption-related losses and their evaluation of the basis for their relinquishment. This assumption places a great deal of emphasis on the interface between person variables (e.g., level of cognitive functioning) and appraisal and coping processes. It also incorporates the stress and coping model into a developmental framework. Because of its centrality within the present model, we turn now to the role of cognitive-developmental factors in children's sensitivity to, and appraisal of, adoption-related losses.

Appraisal of Loss Among Adopted Children: Developmental Changes

The relinquishment of a young baby by a biological mother and the subsequent placement of that child with an adoptive couple does not, by itself, produce a sense of loss in the experience of the newly placed infant. In traditional adoption (i.e., placement in infancy), where the child's primary attachments are formed in the adoptive family, the emergence of a sense of loss grows slowly and typically does not appear until the elementary school years. This developmental pattern has been well documented in recent research by the author and his co-workers (Brodzinsky, 1984, 1987; Brodzinsky et al., 1980; Brodzinsky, Singer, & Braff, 1984; Brodzinsky et al., 1986).

In the preschool years, when most adoptive couples begin to disclose adoption information to their children, there is little evidence of any immediate, adverse reaction to the information. In fact, young adopted children often have a very positive view of adoption (Singer, Brodzinsky, & Braff, 1982). Their initial reaction to their family status is based on two factors. First, they generally are told about being adopted in the context of a warm, loving, and protective family environment. Thus the emotional climate surrounding the telling process is one which fosters acceptance and positive self-regard.

A second and very important factor in the young child's positive attitude about adoption is his or her limited cognitive ability. Our research suggests that most children do not understand the meaning of being adopted until 5 to 7 years of age, and even then their understanding is quite limited (Brodzinsky, Singer, & Braff, 1984). Although younger children may well be able to describe the events leading to their adoption (e.g., having been born to another woman; flying in an airplane to the United States from Korea and meeting their new mommy and daddy), in most cases, these descriptions mask a conspicuous absence of knowledge. The young child's verbal report typically represents little more than an ability to repeat, often with considerable accuracy, the adoption story presented by parents. Thus it is understandable that young adopted children show little distress regarding their adoptive family status. The combination of a warm emotional climate surrounding the initial telling process and the young child's cognitive limitations almost assures that the adoption information received by the child will be accepted in a positive light.

As children enter the elementary school years, however, a number of important changes occur that impact significantly on adoption adjustment. During this developmental period, which roughly corresponds to Piaget's concrete operational stage, children are becoming increasingly reflective, analytic, planful, and logical in their approach to the world (Braine & Rumain, 1983; Brown, Bransford, Ferrara, & Campione, 1983; Gelman & Baillargeon, 1983; Kogan, 1983; Shantz, 1983). As part of this growth in cognitive and social-cognitive reasoning, children's knowledge of adoption also undergoes important changes. Not only do children clearly differentiate between adoption and birth as alternative ways of entering a family, but they gain new insights into the implications of being adopted. For example, whereas preschool children tend to define a family in terms of the people who live together, by the elementary school years, most children view family members as individuals who share a blood (i.e., biological) relationship (Pederson & Gilby, 1986; Piaget 1964). This new way of looking at the family fosters increased recognition and appreciation of the lack of biological connectedness between the child and the adoptive parents, which, in turn, often creates confusion and stress on the part of the child, and undermines his or her sense of security and permanence in the family (Brodzinsky, Singer, & Braff, 1984; Brodzinsky et al., 1986).

Another new insight into adoption that emerges at this time is the child's recognition of relinquishment. Preschool age children tend to focus primarily on being adopted by their parents—that is, being incorporated into their new family. This focus parallels the nature of the story presented by most adoptive parents which emphasizes aspects of family building and minimizes aspects concerning the birthmothers's surrender of the child. As children mature cognitively, however, their capacity for understanding logical reciprocity leads them to a profound insight—to be adopted, one first must be relinquished or surrendered. *Thus in the elementary school years, children view adoption not only in terms of family building, but also in terms of family loss.*

The child's sense of loss associated with adoption is accompanied by many behavioral, emotional, and attitudinal changes. To begin with, children no longer view adoption in such a positive light. Singer et al. (1982) reported that by eight years of age, most adopted children experience considerable ambivalence about being adopted. In addition to this attitudinal change, numerous professionals have commented on the increase in anger, aggression, oppositional behavioral, uncommunicativeness, depression, and self-image problems that emerge during this time among many adoptees (Brinich, 1980); Brodzinsky, 1987; Nickman, 1985). Brodzinsky (1987) has suggested that this behavioral and emotional pattern reflects a process of adaptive grieving—a response to the recognition that one has lost something significant. Moreover, as the individual moves into adolescence, this sense of loss may deepen. No longer is the experience of loss restricted primarily to one's birthparents. With the development of higher order cognitive functions, adolescents begin to re-evaluate the loss in terms of their emerging identity. At this time, a loss of self often is experienced as well as a loss of connectedness to a genealogical line. These new losses contribute to the behavioral and emotional reactions associated with the grieving process.

To summarize, the present model assumes that adopted children's adjustment is determined, in part, by their appraisal of adoption-related losses, which, in turn, is mediated by the gradual emergence of various cognitive and social-cognitive capabilities. In other words, until adopted children have reached the stage where they are cognitively mature enough to reflect on their unknown past and their unknown parents—until their origins and the circumstances surrounding the relinquishment take on a reality within a well-developed representational system—there is little basis for expecting that they will experience adoption-related losses and the subsequent behavioral and emotional reactions of the grieving process. (Similar points have been made by other writers who have emphasized the role of mental processes in children's development and maintenance of attachment relationships and their subsequent response to separation and loss—Bloom-Feshbach & Bloom-Feshbach, 1987; Bowlby, 1969, 1973, 1980; Main, Kaplan, & Cassidy, 1985).

Other Person Variables Impacting on Appraisal and Adjustment

Besides level of cognitive functioning, there are a number of other person variables that are assumed to influence the child's adjustment to adoption. Self-esteem, self-efficacy, and the child's sense of control are three variables commonly associated with one another that are believed to mediate the adoption appraisal and coping process. Clinical experience suggests that children with low self-esteem, low feelings of efficacy, and a diminished sense of personal control tend to evaluate their adoption experience more negatively and utilize coping strategies that produce less satisfying adaptational outcomes. In particular, it is quite common to find these children engaging in self-blame for their relinquishment, which, in turn, often produces depressive affect, withdrawal, and uncommunicative behavior. Conversely, other children with problems in self-esteem, self-efficacy, or perceived control project blame outward, either toward the birthparents or the adoptive parents. In this case, difficulties in adaptational outcome tend to be more externalizing in nature—for example, anger, aggression, oppositional behavior, lying, stealing, and so on (see Brodzinsky, 1987).

Two other person variables also need to be mentioned. The child's sense of interpersonal trust and the degree of commitment to the adoptive family are believed to be powerful forces shaping the appraisal and coping process. These two variables are part of the more general process of attachment, which numerous writers have discussed in the context of adoption adjustment (Brodzinsky, 1987; Fahlberg, 1979; Singer, Brodzinsky, Ramsay, Steir, & Waters, 1985; Steinhauer, 1983; Yarrow & Goodwin, 1973; Yarrow, Goodwin, Manheimer, & Milowe, 1973). Although to date, we know very little about the role of interpersonal trust and family commitment in the adopted child's adjustment, clinical experience suggests that children who have little trust, in or commitment to, their adoptive family members are likely to appraise the adoption experience more negatively, feel a greater sense of adoption-related loss, and utilize coping strategies that produce less satisfying patterns of adjustment. This point is well illustrated by Karen, a 15-year-old who was seen in individual therapy by the author.

> Adopted in infancy, Karen appeared to adjust reasonably well until the early elementary school years. Around 8 to 9 years of age, however, as her understanding of adoption grew, Karen began to feel disconnected from her parents, especially her father who was a rather demanding and critical person. With time, Karen's sense of trust in, and commitment to, her adoptive parents lessened. At the same time, she displayed an intensely positive attachment to her fantasized biological mother with whom she strongly identified. In her attempts to resolve the loss of her birthmother, Karen began to display serious oppositional behavior at home and indiscriminate sexual behavior among her peers. With regard to the latter behavior, Karen was quite conscious of her motives to recreate the conditions of her own relinquishment so as to achieve a more satisfactory solution. She acknowledged having frequent fantasies of getting pregnant and caring for her baby, and in so doing, experiencing a sense of nurturance denied her by her birthmother. Over the course of therapy, Karen has been able to find more effective coping strategies to resolve her sense of loss. One strategy, in particular, has been quite beneficial for her—namely, an active search for her birthmother. This search, which still has not achieved her goal of a reunion, has increased Karen's self-esteem and sense of control, and greatly improved her relationship with her adoptive parents. It also has resulted in more responsible sexual behavior.

Finally, a clarification of the causal link between children's adaptational outcome and various person variables is warranted. Although it has been suggested that children's self-esteem, sense of personal control, interpersonal trust, and so forth, mediate their appraisal of adoption-related loss, and their subsequent adoption adjustment, it is also recognized that short-term adaptational outcomes invariably impact on children's self-esteem and other aspects of their personality. In other words, adjustment to adoption is viewed as a transactional process in which person variables, appraisal and coping processes, and adaptational outcomes are assumed to have an ongoing interactive influence on one another (see Figure 1.1).

Background Variables

Having described the link between various person variables and the child's adoption appraisal and coping efforts, let us turn now to two sets of background variables that are assumed to influence the adoption adjustment process.

Biological Variables

As noted earlier, the child's adjustment to adoption is believed to be influenced by his or her genetic endowment as well as by prenatal and reproductive experiences. Recently, several writers have argued that the psychological and academic problems of adopted children may have a genetic basis (see Chapter 2; Deutsch et al., 1982). This assumption is tied to the frequently reported finding that psychopathology in adoptees is more strongly related to psychopathology in the biological parents as opposed to the adoptive parents (see Chapter 2 for a review of the literature). Furthermore, at least one study (Horn, Green, Carney, & Erickson, 1975) found that unwed mothers whose children were placed for adoption scored higher on a number of clinical scales on the Minnesota Multiphasic Personality Inventory (MMPI) than did the adoptive parents of these children. To the extent that the problems measured by these scales have a genetic component (as the authors suggest), it could be argued, on the one hand, that the findings support the position that adoptees come from a less optimal hereditary background than their nonadopted counterparts. Although this argument has a certain compelling quality to it, it should be noted that a more recent follow-up study to the Horn et al. (1975) investigation found that the more disturbed unwed mothers produced children who were calmer and more secure in their adoptive homes (Loehlin, Willerman, & Horn, 1982). This finding is directly opposed to predictions made by any traditional gene-based explanation of adoption adjustment. On the other hand, according to the investigators, it does fit a gene-environment interaction model, whereby the genetic-based vulnerabilities of the child are suppressed and other more favorable qualities are encouraged within the warm and supportive adoptive family environment.

Like genetic endowment, the child's prenatal and reproductive experiences are also assumed to play an important role in adoption adjustment. This assumption is based on the substantial literature documenting the negative impact of prenatal and reproductive complications on postnatal development (Kopp, 1983). Since many of these complications are commonly found among young, unwed mothers (e.g., poor nutrition, poor medical care, substance abuse, high levels of psychological stress, etc.), and since this group of women accounts for a sizable percentage of children placed for adoption, it is reasonable to expect that prenatal and reproductive experiences may be important for explaining subsequent developmental problems among adoptees. In support of this assumption, it should be noted that in several studies (Bohman, 1970; Everett & Schechter, 1971; Losbough, 1965), adoptees have been found to have poorer prenatal histories compared to nonadopted control groups.

At present, there is relatively little information available concerning the extent and the way in which biological factors influence children's adoption adjustment. Within the current model, neither of these factors are assumed to manifest themselves directly. Instead, genetic vulnerabilities and prenatal or reproductive complications are assumed to interact in complex, and currently unknown, ways with a variety of postnatal environmental factors to produce specific patterns of adoption adjustment. Although this statement must seem passé within the Zeitgeist of current psychological theory, it needs to be emphasized since the role of biological factors (either acting alone or in concert with environmental factors) has received scant attention as a basis for the adjustment problems of adopted children (see Chapter 2). In light of the growing evidence of a genetic basis for a variety of psychopathological conditions, future researchers would do well to focus their attention on the role of biological factors in the adjustment of adopted children. As a case in point, consider the findings of Deutsch et al. (1982), who reported that adoptees are significantly overrepresented among children diagnosed as having attention deficit disorder (ADD). Their data indicated that there was a 32 to 36% chance that a male adoptee would exhibit symptoms of ADD; the comparable figure for female adoptees was 6 to 14%. In attempting to explain the high incidence of ADD among adopted children, the authors noted the substantial amount of alcoholism, sociopathy or psychopathy, and hysteria found among the biological relatives of hyperactive adoptees (see Cantwell,

1975). They further noted that ADD, which has a moderate genetic component (Cantwell, 1975), often persists into adulthood and contributes to the development of sociopathy or psychopathy (Cantwell, 1978). The authors argued that these data, together with the finding of increased psychopathic tendencies in unwed mothers who give up their children for adoption (Horn et al., 1975), provide strong indirect evidence of a genetic basis for the high incidence of ADD among adoptees.

Environmental Variables

Within the current model, a number of environmental variables are assumed to have a significant influence on the adjustment of adopted children. Among these variables are a host of demands, constraints, and resources associated with cultural attitudes and practices concerning adoption, as well as with the individual's specific interpersonal adoption experiences within and outside of the family. The child's placement history also is assumed to influence subsequent adoption adjustment.

   Cultural Factors. To begin with, consider cultural attitudes concerning adoption. Although adoption is a widely accepted form of substitute care for children whose biological parents could not or would not care for them, there still is a feeling within most cultural groups that it is a "second best route to parenthood" and a "second best way of entering a family" (see Kirk, 1964, 1981; Lifton, 1979; Sorosky et al., 1978). This attitude is most clearly seen in such comments as, "Isn't it too bad you couldn't have a child of your own" or "You are so courageous to raise someone else's child. I don't think I could do it." Comparable remarks made to adopted children include "Who are your real parents?", "Do you mind being adopted?", and "You sure are lucky to have been adopted." Adoptive parents and their children report that these insensitive, albeit well meaning, comments, which can come not only from relative strangers, but from friends and family members, tend to reinforce in them a sense of being different—of somehow not fitting in, of even being defective. Thus to be part of an adoptive family is to be exposed continually to the challenge represented by society's ambivalent attitude about adoption—a challenge that can create considerable stress among adoptive family members.

   Cultural attitudes and beliefs concerning adoption also play a role in the child's adjustment process through the standards, rules, and regulations governing adoption practice. For example, in this day and age, adoption remains primarily a closed system. At the time of legal finalization, the original birth record is sealed, thereby preventing the adoptee from knowing the truth about his or her origins. Although adoption agencies are beginning to recognize the importance of providing detailed information about birthparents (and their families) to the adoptive family, there still is considerable resistence among adoption professionals to opening up the whole adoption process (see Chapter 17 for an analysis of the closed versus open adoption controversy). As an example of the difficulties engendered by current societal attitudes and standards concerning adoption, consider the case of Amy, a 14-year-old, adopted privately (nonagency placement) in infancy from a small southern town.

> Amy was brought for psychological consultation by her parents because of depression, social withdrawal, oppositional behavior, and school failure. Amy's parents reported that when she was first told about being adopted—around 4 years of age—she showed little interest in the topic. During third grade, however, she began to question her parents about the reasons for her relinquishment. These questions intensified over the next few years,

and included a desire to know more about her birthmother's family, background, physical characteristics, interests, etc. Amy's parents, who had little information about the birth family except some very general descriptive information and what they believed was the birthmother's last name, agreed to contact the physician through whom the placement was made in order to get any additional information he might have. Although the parents were successful in contacting the physician, he made it clear that he would not provide additional information—even nonidentifying information. He stated that to do so would violate the trust placed in him by the birthmother. As might be expected, Amy's response to this roadblock was frustration, anger, and depression. However, her ability to cope remained strong, at least for a while. With the help of her parents, she continued to search for information about her background. A private detective was even hired to locate families with the same name as the one they believed belonged to the birthmother. They also petitioned the court to require the physician to open his records on the case. Unfortunately, all efforts proved unsuccessful. After two frustrating years of searching, Amy's coping efforts weakened. She became more depressed, began to withdraw from her peers and her school studies, and projected much of her anger on to her adoptive parents—who became the symbol of her relinquishment by her birthmother. Although Amy progressed well in therapy, she still struggles with a sense of emptiness within herself, as well as considerable anger and resentment at the adoption system which has prevented her from developing a fuller sense of who she is.

Interpersonal Factors. Probably the most important interpersonal factors influencing the adopted child's adjustment are the experiences he or she has with family members. These experiences are related to the general quality of the caregiving environment, the adjustment of adoptive parents, and the way in which adoption issues are communicated between parents and children. In a review of adoption outcome research, Kadushin (1980) noted that children's successful adjustment to adoption is related to two general factors—parental attitudes toward the child and adoption, and the nature of the parent-child relationship. Specifically, acceptance of and satisfaction in adoptive parenthood coupled with a warm and accepting attitude toward the child was generally predictive of positive adoption adjustment. By contrasts, parental rejection of the child as well as parental dissatisfaction with adoptive parenthood typically were related to poor adjustment on the part of children. Similar findings have been reported in a recent longitudinal study on the adjustment of adopted children by Hoopes (1982). These findings, of course, parallel the role of parental caregiving characteristics in the development and adjustment of nonadopted children (see Maccoby & Martin, 1983).

Other research has implicated the role of adoptive parent adjustment (and the stability of the adoptive family) in the well-being of adopted children. For example, a number of studies have noted that the biological vulnerabilities of adopted children, which were mentioned earlier in the chapter, are more likely to manifest themselves when one or both adoptive parents suffer from psychopathology, or when there is a history of death, divorce, or desertion within the adoptive family (see Chapter 2; Schechter, 1970).

In addition to the issue of general parental adjustment, the well-being of adopted children is also assumed to be influenced by the parents' response to *specific* adoption-related issues. Kirk (1964) and, more recently, Brodzinsky and his colleagues (1987; Brodzinsky & Huffman, 1988) have suggested that children's adjustment to adoption is mediated by a host of factors associated with the transition to adoptive parenthood.

For example, infertility, the uncertainty of the timing of the adoption process, the intrusiveness of the home study, the stigma associated with adoptive parenthood, and the lack of readily available role models, among other factors, are viewed by these authors as additional stresses confronting adoptive couples in their transition to parenthood—stresses which could very well have a negative impact on the parent-child relationship in the early years of the family life cycle. Moreover, as children get older, other adoption-related issues confront the family, including telling the child of his or her adoptive status, helping the child cope with a sense of loss, fostering a positive self-image as an adopted person, supporting the child's curiosity and need for information about the birthparents and his or her origins, and potentially handling the issue of searching for birthparents. As Brodzinsky (1987) has noted, these tasks provide the adoptive family with additional challenges that interact with and complicate the more universal tasks of family life. To the extent that adoptive parents are able to confront these issues openly and honestly, it is expected that they will be in a better position to foster more positive adjustment among their children.

Related to these tasks of adoptive parenthood is the way in which parents and children communicate about adoption-related issues. Kirk's (1964) classic social role theory of adoption adjustment suggests that a fundamental issue for adoptive families is the way they handle the inherent differences of adoptive family life. By differences, Kirk means the unique tasks, challenges, and conflicts such as those outlined above that differentiate adoptive from nonadoptive families (see also Brodzinsky, 1987). According to Kirk, some couples in reacting to the role handicaps of adoptive parenthood try to take the "sting" out of adoption by simulating nonadoptive family life as closely as possible. In their interactions with their child, they communicate the importance of forgetting about being adopted, and all that goes with it—as they, themselves, try to do. This pattern of behavior has been labelled *rejection-of-difference* (RD). By contrast, other parents openly confront the differences associated with adoption. These individuals seek to resolve the challenges and conflicts of adoptive family life by more active and direct involvement with the issues. They allow themselves and their children the freedom and opportunity to explore the feelings of being different that occasionally arise in the course of life experiences. Kirk has labeled this pattern *acknowledgment-of-difference* (AD).

Within Kirk's theory, these two patterns represent a continuum of attitudes and communicative behavior, with the acknowledgment-of-difference pole more closely associated with optimal adjustment among family members and the rejection-of-difference pole more often tied to problems in adjustment. Thus Kirk suggests that rejection-of-difference behavior tends to inhibit the development of an accepting and trusting family atmosphere—an atmosphere conducive to open and honest exploration of adoption-related issues. He also suggests that this communicative pattern tends to reinforce in the child the idea that to feel different is to be deviant. In turn, both of these consequences can have a significant impact on the self-esteem and general adjustment of the adopted child. For example, consider the case of Tony, an 11-year-old Korean boy, adopted at 4 years by his Caucasian family.

> Tony was referred for treatment because of uncommunicativeness, mild depression, self-esteem problems, and academic underachievement. In the initial family session it became immediately clear that Tony's parents had difficulty discussing the issue of adoption, especially in his presence. They indicated that their family was no different from any

other family and that adoption played little, or no, role in Tony's difficulties. To support their belief, they stated that Tony seldom questioned them about being adopted and showed no interest in his origins. They believed he had made an excellent adjustment to their family, and to being adopted. When I expressed surprise that Tony was so uninterested in such an important part of his life, he began to fidget and appeared quite uncomfortable. This behavior was pointed out both to his parents and to him. When asked what it might mean, his mother indicated that I was putting ideas into his head and making him uncomfortable—that is, I was suggesting that adoption should be important to him when it was not. At this point, Tony was asked directly to comment on his mother's interpretation. With some hesitancy, he stated that being adopted was important to him—that it always had been. With encouragement, he was able to acknowledge that he thought a great deal about his previous life in Korea, what it would be like to still live there, where his birth parents were, and if they ever thought of him. Needless to say, Tony's comments were a surprise and revelation to his parents. With support, though, they gradually were able to accept the reality and normality of Tony's feelings. This led to a more open, flexible, and less conflict-ridden pattern of communication in the family which, in turn, facilitated a freer expression of grief on Tony's part (for all that he had lost), as well as a greater sense of connectedness to his adoptive parents.

Although Kirk (1964) has suggested a linear relationship between the continuum of acknowledgment-of-difference and the psychological well-being of adoptive family members, Brodzinsky (1987) has recently argued that the relationship actually is curvilinear. That is, parents who adopt extreme views at either end of the belief continuum are assumed to foster poorer adjustment among their adopted children. For example, in clinical settings, the author has worked with numerous families who have been characterized by an *insistence-of-difference* (ID) coping pattern. In these families, parents (and occasionally children) not only acknowledge the inherent differences of adoptive family life, but emphasize the differences to such an extent that they become the major focus of the family. In turn, this pattern often leads family members to view adoption as the basis for family disharmony and disconnectedness. Moreover, in such cases, it is quite common for parents to promote an unfavorable view of the biological parents (and their background), and consequently resort to "bad seed" or genetic explanations for the child's behavioral and emotional problems—thereby, allowing the parents to avoid their own share of the responsibility for the family's difficulties.

To date, attempts to test Kirk's theory of adoption adjustment have yielded mixed results. In his original work, Kirk (1964) reported that parents who were characterized by an AD pattern were more likely to be empathic to their child's feelings, to think more often about the child's birthparents, to feel greater satisfaction as adoptive parents, and to communicate more openly with their children. No measures of the child's adjustment, however, were included in the study. Carroll (1968) also examined the relationship between adoptive parents' coping strategies and aspects of their personal adjustment. He noted that prospective adoptive parents who tended to use an AD coping strategy were more likely to report dissatisfaction with selective aspects of their self concept compared with individuals who used an RD strategy. Although this result would appear to contradict Kirk's position, Carroll argued that "the intensity and scope of their [AD subjects] expressed self dissatisfactions . . . were well within the limits of 'normality' and seemed logically to reflect a more realistic and genuine self appraisal'' (p. 114). Thus Carroll interpreted these results as supportive of Kirk's social-role theory of adoption adjustment.

Several recent studies have examined the relationship between adoptive parent coping strategies and children's adjustment. For example, Brodzinsky and Reeves (1987) found that adoptive mothers who displayed an ID coping pattern had children who were rated lower in social competence and higher in behavior problems than children whose mothers adopted either an AD, RD, or mixed AD-RD pattern. Furthermore, mothers who adopted an ID pattern also rated their children, as well as themselves and their spouses, as less well-adjusted to adoption than mothers who displayed the other three coping styles. Interestingly, an insistence-of-difference pattern was also associated with greater emphasis on heredity as opposed to environment as an explanation for children's personality and adjustment. Finally, mothers who displayed an RD pattern scored higher on the Crowne-Marlowe social desirability scale than mothers who displayed either an AD or an ID pattern—thereby suggesting that rejection-of-difference may be part of a more global defensiveness pattern within certain adoptive parents rather than a pattern that is specific to adoption-related matters. In related research, Kaye (see Chapter 7) also failed to support Kirk's position regarding the detrimental effect of an RD coping pattern, and conversely, the beneficial effect of an AD pattern. This observational study of adoptive family interaction suggested, in fact, that rejection-of-difference, at least in certain families, may actually reflect the absence of serious family problems, whereas acknowledgment-of-difference may indicate their existence. This finding must be viewed cautiously, however, particularly in light of the fact that the subject sample was skewed toward an upper-middle-class population.

How are we to reconcile the findings of Brodzinsky and Reeves (1987) and Kaye (Chapter 7) with Kirk's theory of adoption adjustment? If the findings of these two studies are valid, then it appears that rejection-of-difference is not necessarily a detrimental coping pattern. In fact, it may well be a beneficial one, at least under certain conditions. One possible resolution to this dilemma lies in the relationship between an RD coping pattern and the process of denial which is assumed to covary with it. Lazarus and Folkman (1984) note that although denial generally is considered to be an ineffective coping response, under certain conditions it does lead to adaptive outcomes. For example, when there is nothing constructive that can been done to overcome the harm or threat—that is, when the situation is perceived as unchangeable—denial can be useful for alleviating the person's distress. Furthermore, they state that denial may be adaptive for certain aspects of the problem, but not for the whole. In addition, the timing of denial may be significant in determining its usefulness. These researchers argued that in the early stages of a crisis when the situation cannot yet be faced, at least in its entirety, denial may be beneficial. By contrast, this same coping process may become detrimental to the person if it persists beyond a certain point in time. In line with this last point, Brodzinsky (1987) suggested that the effectiveness of the adoptive parents' coping efforts must be viewed within the context of family life cycle tasks. In the initial stages of the family life cycle, when children are still very young, an RD coping pattern may serve the family well by supporting the primary socialization goals of building family unity, connectedness, and interpersonal trust. However, in later stages of the family life cycle, when children are struggling to understand the meaning of being adopted and the basis of their relinquishment, an RD coping pattern may well interfere with open and honest parent-child communication, thereby leading to detrimental outcomes. Support for family life cycle changes in adoptive parent coping patterns has been reported by Brodzinsky and Jackiewicz (1987). These researchers found that although an RD coping pattern was quite common among parents who had infants and toddlers, it decreased in intensity among parents who had older children. By contrast, parents with preschool and school age children tended to adopt an AD or mixed AD-RD coping pattern. Finally, an ID pattern was seldom observable except in families with adolescents.

In summary, although the present model suggests that adoptive parent coping strategies (and the communicative patterns that follow from them) are particularly important in understanding children's adoption adjustment, it still is unclear just how, when, and under what conditions, these coping strategies impact on children's adaptational outcomes. It remains for future research to unravel these complex relationships.

Children's Coping Efforts

Having outlined the developmental implications of the interface between children's appraisal of adoption and various person-related variables, as well as the potential impact of biological and environmental factors on this interface, let us return to the issue of the specific coping efforts displayed by children in their adjustment to adoption. As noted earlier, Lazarus and Folkman (1984) have identified two broad categories of coping behaviors: (1) problem-focused efforts which are geared toward managing or altering the problem causing the distress, and (2) emotion-focused efforts which are geared toward regulating the individual's emotional response to the problem at hand.

Although clinical experience suggests that children manifest a wide range of coping behaviors in dealing with their adoption experiences, to date, there has been no systematic empirical work in this area. In fact, examination of developmental trends in children's coping behavior in areas other than adoption has only recently been undertaken (see Band & Weisz, 1988; Curry & Russ, 1985; Wertlieb, Weigel, & Feldstein, 1987). This research suggests that children as young as six years are aware of stress in their lives and are able to report on specific efforts to cope with it. The data also indicates that children more often utilize problem-solving rather than emotion-management strategies, as well as those strategies involving overt and direct modes of action. Conversely, as children get older there is increased use of emotion-management and intrapsychic modes of coping. Not surprising, the findings also suggest that the use of coping strategies varies considerably from one situation to another (see Band & Weisz, 1988).

The results of this research are in line with clinical observations of the coping behavior of adopted children. When children are first informed of their adoptive status, there is much question asking. Information regarding the birthparents and the reasons for the relinquishment typically are sought from the adoptive parents. In addition, children often seek emotional support from their parents. By contrast, strategies for regulating or managing emotions are less often seen in this early phase of adoption adjustment. As children enter middle childhood, however, there is a gradual increase in emotion-focused coping. Denial, avoidance, minimization, cognitive reappraisal, and so forth are just some of the strategies commonly employed by children in their effort to cope with adoption-related stresses. To a great extent, this increase in emotion-focused coping probably reflects a growing recognition on the part of the child that little can be done to change or modify the circumstances represented by their adoptive status (see Lazarus & Folkman, 1984).

Although the use of emotion–management strategies appears to increase with age, clinical observations suggest that problem-focused strategies continue to play an important role in the adjustment of older adopted children. The nature of these latter coping strategies, however, may well change with age. Whereas preschool and early school age children typically engage in direct action such as information seeking and support mobilization, older school age children frequently display inhibition of action. That is, they often purposely hold back or otherwise limit actions, impulses, or behaviors in an effort to cope with adoption-related stress. For example, it is quite common for children who were once very curious about their adoption to appear now as uninvolved or disinterested in this aspect of their life. This change is reflected in the decline in adoption-related questions commonly reported by parents of older school age children. A more dramatic example of inhibition of action is represented by the case of Cindy, a 12-year-old child adopted at the age of 16 months.

> After two years of pressuring her parents to allow her to search for her birth family (including two known birth siblings), Cindy repeatedly sabotaged the search process-thereby reducing her level of anxiety—by her own lack of action when the adoptive parents finally agreed to assist her.

Although it is obvious from clinical experience that children display a wide range of coping behaviors in response to adoption-related stresses, the nature of the relationship between their cognitive appraisal of adoption and the use of specific coping strategies remains elusive. So too, does the relationship between specific coping behaviors and various adaptational outcomes. These issues, and others, such as developmental trends in adopted children's coping, represent priorities for future research.

SUMMARY AND CONCLUSIONS

A brief review of the research literature suggests that adopted children are at increased risk for psychological and academic problems in comparison to their non-adopted counterparts. These problems, however, generally do not manifest themselves until the elementary school age years. Furthermore, it is clear that adopted children display a wide range of adjustment patterns, with only a minority presenting evidence of clinically significant symptomatology. Indeed, most adopted children appear to cope quite well with the challenges, conflicts, and demands of adoptive family life.

In attempting to explain the individual variation in adopted children's behavior and development, a new model of adoption adjustment was presented. The model represents an integration of the work of Lazarus and his colleagues in the area of stress and coping, and our own work on cognitive–developmental and psychosocial factors in adoption adjustment. At the core of the model is the assumption that children's adjustment to adoption rests on their appraisal of, and efforts to cope with, a host of subtle, but pervasive, adoption-related losses.

To date, the majority of our knowledge about the development of adopted children rests on casework and clinical observation, and a small body of atheoretical research. Each of these sources of data, however, are unsatisfactory—casework and clinical data because of problems in generalizability and lack of observer objectivity; and atheoretical research because of the lack of a conceptual context within which to interpret the findings. In contrast, the present model offers the investigator a clear theoretical context, with substantial generative power, to guide his or her empirical endeavors. Whether or not the model has integrative and explanatory power, however, remains to be seen. It is much too early to evaluate how well the model "fits" the data. It is the hope of the author, though, that this model, and others like it, may help to bridge the historical (and conceptual) gap that exists between social service fields, which traditionally have dominated adoption (and foster care), and more research-based disciplines such as psychology, psychiatry, and sociology. Until the boundaries between these fields and disciplines can be made more flexible and a productive level of cross-fertilization of ideas and objectives can be achieved, our understanding of the adjustment problems of adopted children and our capacity to meet their casework and clinical needs will surely be inadequate.

2

Biologic Perspectives
of Adoptee Adjustment

REMI J. CADORET

Human behavior has had no lack of apologists and explanations since time imme-
morial, including such diverse explanatory schemes as phrenology and astrology.
Scientific explanations of the vagaries of human character have been more recent
additions to a long list of "whys" of behavior. Toward the end of the last century
there was an organized effort to study factors influencing personality and human
abilities with the avowed goal of using this information to improve the race. The
eugenic movement, as it came to be called, stemmed largely from the lifework of a
British genius, Sir Francis Galton. Galton, whose life spanned almost a century (1822–
1911), was fascinated by the tremendous individual variation found in human social
status, intellectual abilities, and temperament. He conceived two categories of factors
responsible for this variation: nature, or what was physically inherited from parents
through the procreative process; and nurture, or what was transmitted through culture, upbringing, and other environmental conditions. In order to measure "nature"
and "nurture," Galton devised ingenious techniques used today in the study of inheritance. These approaches include the family study, the twin method, and statistical
devices such as regression. Using these techniques Galton came to the conclusion
that nature was more important than nurture where human abilities, social success,
and temperament were concerned. In 1875 in *History of Twins, as a Criterion of the
Relative Powers of Nature and Nurture*, he wrote:

> There is no escape from the conclusion that nature prevails enormously over nurture when
> the differences in nurture do not exceed what is commonly to be found among persons of
> the same rank of society in the same country. My only fear is that my evidence seems to
> prove too much, and may be discredited on that account, as it seems contrary to all
> expectation that nurture should go for so little. But experience is often fallacious in as-
> cribing great effects to trying circumstances. Many a person has amused himself by throwing
> bits of stick into a brook and watching their progress; how they are arrested, first by one
> chance obstacle, then by another, and again, how their onward course is facilitated by a
> combination of circumstances. He might ascribe much importance to each of these events,
> and think how largely the destiny of the stick has been governed by a series of trifling
> accidents. Nevertheless, all the sticks succeed in passing down the current, and they
> travel, in the long run, at nearly the same rate. So it is with life, in respect to the several

accidents which seem to have had a great effect upon our careers. The one element, which varies in different individuals, but is constant for each of them is the natural tendency; it corresponds to the current in the stream, and inevitably asserts itself. (Pearson, 1914, p. 8)

In one way Galton foresaw how adoptees could help in sorting out the relative importance of nature or nurture. In his wide-ranging search for evidence on this point he cited an example of adoption in nature. Consider the cuckoo, he stated, which is raised exclusively by foster parents (the mother cuckoo lays her egg in other species' nests and leaves it to be hatched and reared by an alien parent)—neither its song, habits, or sympathies are influenced by those of its foster parents.

Since Galton's time there has been lively debate and frequent acrimony as to the relative importance of nature or nurture. This debate continues to the present, especially with regard to the heritability of IQ (Lewontin, Rose, & Kamin, 1986; Scarr, 1981). Over the years debate has focused at times on the importance of nature to the exclusion of nurture, or at other periods has focused on nurture to the exclusion of nature. In part, theoretical positions prescribed by such disciplines as psychodynamic psychiatry led to one-sided assessments in the nature–nurture controversy (Cadoret, 1986). However in recent years there has been more reliance on empirical studies rather than theoretical positions so that a more balanced view of nature and nurture is emerging. Many of these empirical study designs used today date back to the time of Galton. One of the earliest was developed by Galton himself: the family study. In this approach pedigrees were prepared of families starting with a proband or member of a family with a behavior of interest (e.g., alcohol abuse). When classical genetics came into the picture in the early years of this century the pedigree was studied to see if the pattern of transmission followed known genetic mechanisms such as the dominant gene transmission seen in Huntington's chorea. The family study was also used to determine whether familial transmission of behavior occurred. Pedigrees of families selected on the basis of certain proband behaviors were compared to control families (selected by matching probands without the behavior in question). If the incidence of relatives with the target behavior is higher in the proband families than the control then familial transmission is demonstrated. For example, studies of families of alcoholics almost invariably show higher rates of alcoholism in relatives than are found in relatives of control probands (Cotton, 1979). The difference could be due to genetic or environmental factors—the family study merely indicates that one or the other (or both) factors are likely involved.

In order to isolate and measure separately the effects of genes from those of the environment, special techniques have been developed. The oldest, again introduced by Francis Galton, is the comparison of monozygotic with dizygotic twin pairs. Since monozygotic twins share the same genes but dizygotic have only half their genes in common, differences in concordance for behaviors reflect this genetic difference. Twin studies have been and remain a very important tool in delineating the importance of genetic and environmental variables in determining human behavior.

In order to separate further the effects of genes from those of the environment, studies have been done of twins, separated early in life. The separation design has been used most effectively in the case of adoptees. The natural prototype of this design is the case in nature where an individual from one species is raised by a member of a different species as seen in the example of the cuckoo. The use of human adoptees to separate nature from nurture was first suggested by L. F. Richardson (1912–13). During the early decades of the century, interest in adoptees first centered around the question of nature and nurture in human intelligence, which was stimulated in part by the development at that time of tests to measure intelligence. The adoption strategy involved a study of adoptees, their biologic parents, and their adoptive parents. As adoptions developed in the early years of this century, children generally separated at birth from biologic parents and their birth environment were placed with nonrelatives who legally adopted and raised the children. In nature–nurture studies the focus of the investigation was usually a trait, behavior, or other characteristic—as in the early studies during the teens and twenties of this century when the focus was on intelligence. The crux of the technique involves comparisons between adoptees and both sets of parents, biologic and adoptive. The resemblance in behavior between adopted children and their biologic parents estimated the genetic aspects of inheritance, while the resemblance between adopted children and their adoptive parents (or some other aspect of their adoptive environment) measured environmental transmission. As will be seen later in this chapter, this technique has been applied to a wide variety of human behaviors ranging from intelligence to psychopathology.

Recently mathematical models are being increasingly used in human inheritance to measure the relative importance of genes, environment, and the interaction of the two. Some of the modeling is designed to show whether a trait is inherited by dominant, recessive, or multigenic transmission (Cloninger, Rue, & Reigh, 1979). With other types of statistical models it is possible to measure the interaction of genetic factors with those of the environment (Plomin, Defries, & Loehlin, 1977). Gene-environment interaction is a potentially important factor in human behavior (Cadoret & Cain, 1982). Interaction is the process whereby certain environments markedly enhance or decrease the likelihood of certain genetically determined behaviors—significantly more so than would be expected if the genetic factors and the environmental factors acted independently. Such a finding in human behavior has been reported by the author who found that adoptees from an antisocial biologic background when placed in adoptive homes where another family member had a psychiatric or behavior disturbance demonstrated far higher numbers than expected of different antisocial behaviors in adolescence (Cadoret, 1985; Cadoret & Cain, 1982). Gene-environment interaction, therefore, is of considerable importance to the adoption process. If there are environments in which genetically determined behaviors are markedly enhanced, or markedly diminished, then selective placement of adoptees in adoptive homes could affect dramatically the manifestation of these behaviors. In the past it has not been the practice to use information about gene-environment interaction in adoption placement decisions, but as more facts are available for specific behaviors this practice might become more important.

More recent developments in the field of genetics have led to additional powerful techniques to determine the involvement of genes in behavior and even to determine where on a particular chromosome a gene encoding for behavioral abnormality might be located. For a number of years, a technique known as linkage analysis has been used by geneticists to demonstrate that a particular behavior has a genetic basis. In linkage analysis, a trait known to be genetic (such as a blood group, blood serum protein, etc.) is traced through a family pedigree and its appearance with a target behavior noted. If the gene causing the trait—known as the marker—is located physically close to the gene causing the target behavior, the marker and the behavior will segregate or "travel together," so that the marker and the behavior will occur in the same individual and be transmitted to offspring in predictable ways. Conversely, if the marker is physically far away from the behavioral gene, even though on the same chromosome, they will not segregate together because of chromosome exchanges during the reproductive process. Of course, if the gene responsible for behavior and the marker gene are on totally different chromosomes then linkage cannot occur and a different marker must be sought. In the past there were not enough markers to cover adequately all the areas of all the chromosomes in humans. However, with recent developments in molecular genetics an almost limitless number of markers may be developed. These are called "probes" and with them it is possible to examine at present almost the entire range of human chromosomes for genetic linkage (Little, 1986). Already the location of one serious behaviorally manifested illness—Huntington's chorea—has been accomplished with his technique (Guesella, Wexler, Conneally, et al, 1983; Little, 1986). While linkage can establish that a behavior has a genetic factor, the technique cannot determine the influence of environment; other types of studies, such as adoption designs, are needed for this. In the future, however, use of such markers will be invaluable for genetic counseling since it is possible to identify individuals who carry genes that cause behavioral abnormalities and to predict within limits the transmission of these genes to offspring. But, for the present, genetic counseling for many behavioral conditions must be more tentative and much less exact.

It is apparent from a large number of studies of twins and adoptees that behavior ranging from personality traits and intelligence to psychopathology, such as substance abuse and manic-depressive disease, have at their base a genetic factor (Nurnberger, Goldin, & Gershon, 1986). Obviously, many of these genetic factors are important determinants of adoptee behavior and explanations of adoptee adjustment must take these into account. In the past, environmental factors have been studied extensively in adoptee adjustment, almost to the exclusion of genetic factors. For example, a review of adoption research in the United Kingdom, United States, and Canada between 1948 and 1965 comprising 51 abstracts and 302 other references contains no study which relates adoptee psychopathology or adjustment problem to biologic parent characteristics (Pringle, 1967). Instead, environmental factors such as adoptive parent attitudes were closely examined as an exclusive factor in adoptee adjustment. Several studies from this period will illustrate this preoccupation with the environment. Nemovicher (1960) reported that adopted boys were more hostile, tense, dependent, and fearful than nonadopted boys and concluded that the adoptive parents' feelings about sterility, and their overconcern with achievement, contributed importantly to the adoptees' personality (biologic background was not examined). In another study Toussieng (1962) reported that 39 adoptees treated at the Menninger Clinic were more likely to show emotional disturbances than nonadopted children. He hypothesized that the adoptive parents unconscious and unresolved aversion toward parenthood was responsible for the disturbance in the adoptee. Again, genetic factors were not controlled. A third and final example is a study published in 1956 (Wittenborn et al., 1956) which correlated adoptee childhood aggression with the type of childrearing practices experienced by the adoptive mother. This study reported a positive correlation between adoptee aggression and unsympathetic and harsh childrearing experienced by the adoptive mother. Again inheritance from biologic parents was not controlled.

It was not until the mid-1960s, starting with Heston's paper on schizophrenia (1966), that interest swung toward elucidation of genetic factors in adoptee psychopathology (and by extension to adoptee adjustment). In the two decades since 1966, a large number of studies has witnessed the revival of interest in genetic factors. This development will be reviewed in the later sections of this chapter. Most of these studies involve the use of the adoption paradigm described previously, and have covered a wide range of behaviors from personality to a number of psychopathologic conditions—all of which are relevant to the subject of adoptee adjustment. The work of the last two decades with adoptees has also sought evidence for environmental effects as well, and this will be reviewed. All in all, the research record of the past twenty years shows a more balanced approach to the nature–nurture problem and thus offers potentially more valid results and practical suggestions for adoption professionals.

BIOLOGIC FACTORS IN ADOPTEE ADJUSTMENT

There are a large number of characteristics influenced by genetic and environmental causes that affect adoptee adjustment. For many years, agencies placing newborns for adoption have considered physical features as hair and eye color which are known to be genetically determined. The object ostensibly was to match adoptees to adoptive parents so that families would not stand out by having obvious biologically impossible combinations—for example, brown-eyed child with two blue-eyed parents. Body size was another feature sometimes considered since height, as well as being influenced by diet, is genetically determined. Recent work has shown that obesity is also inherited genetically (Stunkard, Thorkild, Harris, et al., 1986) and thus represents another physical characteristic which could enter into matching. One study (Price, Cadoret, Stunkard, et al., 1987) found that obese adoptees were more likely to be found in adoptive homes in a rural environment and where someone in the home other than the adoptee had a behavior problem.

But it is the behavioral characteristics of individuals that are the main determinants of adjustment. These characteristics encompass such areas of behavior as temperament, personality, intellect, the marked deviations from norm in behavior known as personality disorders, and psychopathology, such as major depression, panic disorder, and schizophrenia. The remainder of this chapter will discuss these characteristics and psychopathologic behaviors and their genetic and environmental roots, based for the most part on actual data from studies of adoptees.

Practically all of the adoption studies whose results vis-à-vis nature versus nurture, which will be reported in the following sections, are of two design types. In one, the starting point is selection of a proband adoptee with a behavior of interest (such as drug abuse) and a suitable control adoptee (such as one without the trait or behavior of interest). From this starting point one identifies biologic and adoptive parents and determines the presence of the trait of interest in both sets of parents. If the biologic parents of the adoptee have a higher incidence of the trait or behavior (e.g., drug abuse) than the adoptive parents, then, all other factors being equal, that is considered evidence for a genetic factor. An example of this design is Schulsinger's (1977) report on inheritance of sociopathy.

In the second type of adoption design, the starting point is the biologic parent (e.g., one with a trait or behavior of interest) and a suitable control parent (without the trait). The adopted-away offspring are then identified and studied for evidence of the trait. The adoptive home environment can be studied as well and correlated with adoptee outcome. In the second type of design, the sample of adoptees is not selected for the trait or behavior of interest (as in the first design); hence, correlations of behaviors with each other and with environments within the sample might be expected to be more representative of those occurring in the general population. This is an important consideration in assessing factors relevant to adoptee adjustment. If adoptees are selected on the basis of some adjustment problem (e.g., antisocial behavior) such samples usually come from treated or otherwise identified samples. However, treatment might depend on a host of environmental factors as well as other behaviors in an adoptee proband. These factors for selection of a proband could then lead to spurious identification of environmental factors "important" to the adoptee behavior of interest. Fortunately this error is minimized in the second type of adoption design and most of the adoption studies which have identified environmental factors have used this design (e.g., Cloninger, Bohman, & Sigvardsson, 1981 study of alcohol abuse in men).

While many of these studies demonstrate the importance of genetic and environmental) factors in diverse behaviors, they do not allow us to estimate how many adoptees in the population will be "disturbed." For that estimate we would require more information about the genetic makeup of biologic parents. This type of information about biologic parents is not readily available, though one study of unwed pregnant mothers (the largest source of babies for adoption in North America) showed that they had significant elevations on five of nine clinical MMPI scales when compared to married pregnant women (Horn et al., 1975). This study would suggest that if conditions leading to scale elevations are heritable, then adoptees should show higher levels of mental illness than the general population, other factors being equal. Far better would be a direct estimate of behaviors in adoptees from studies of individuals randomly sampled from the population. Thus the adoption study as defined above can identify both genetic and environmental factors important in a behavior. The following sections will present the evidence for the importance of nature and nurture in a wide variety of behaviors relevant to an individual's adjustment in society.

TEMPERAMENT AND PERSONALITY

Temperament has been recently defined as "those dimensions of personality that are largely genetic or constitutional in origin, exist in most ages and in most societies, show some consistency across situations and are relatively stable, at least within major developmental eras" (Plomin, 1981).

Temperament research has focused extensively on young children. The most well-known research in temperament is the work of Thomas and Chess (1977). They have postulated nine dimensions of temperament such as activity level, rhythmicity, intensity of reaction, quality of mood, to name a few. Combinations of these factors make up clinical types such as the "slow to warm up" or the "difficult" child. The latter is characterized by intense reactions, negative mood, and lack of rhythmicity (an unpredictable daily schedule). Unfortunately there is no direct evidence suggesting the heritability of the Chess-Thomas temperament constructs.

Another more recent theory defines temperament as genetically influenced traits which appear early in life (Buss & Plomin, 1984). These theorists propose emotionality, activity, and sociability as three traits meeting these criteria. These conclusions are almost entirely based on twin studies and should be confirmed in adoption studies. A recent longitudinal study of adopted children (The Colorado Adoption Project) may help settle this question (Plomin & DeFries, 1985). Preliminary results from the first two years of the adoptees' life indicate that adoptive parents' personality has little power to predict infant temperament. However there is some evidence (Plomin & DeFries, 1985, p. 233) that the genotype of the child might react to environmental factors in the adoptee's home, indicating that adoptive parents are likely responding (or reacting) to the genetic makeup of the child. Similarly, little evidence was found for the effect of deviant adoptive parent behaviors, (e.g., depression, sociopathy, "hysteria") on variants of adoptee behaviors such as feeding, diapering, or difficult temperament (Plomin & DeFries, 1985, chapter 11).

With regard to personality manifestations later in life, adoptee studies generally indicate modest positive correlations between biologic parents and adopted-away children but almost no correlation between adoptive parents and their adoptee (Loehlin, Willerman, & Horn, 1985). Extraversion–introversion appears to be one dimension of adult personality for which there is substantial evidence of genetic inheritance (Eysenck, 1982; Loehlin et al., 1985). The major finding in most studies is that shared environment contributes very little to adult personality characteristics. However genetic effects, while demonstrable, do not appear to be all controlling and other factors such as special unique experiences or gene-environment interaction might figure significantly in personality development.

In view of the early state of knowledge about genetics and personality and temperament it would appear to be reasonable to question the applicability of this information to practical questions about adoptive placement. If, for example, it could be shown that children from extraverted biologic parents did poorly when placed with introverted adoptive parents, then personality genetics would be an important consideration in adoptive placement. We must await the outcome of current longitudinal adoption studies such as The Colorado Adoption Project to answer such questions.

INTELLIGENCE

In the nature–nurture arena, no question has generated more polemic and heat than the heritability of IQ (Lewontin et al., 1986). It is ironic that the question is not better settled since the issue has been investigated with adoption studies for two generations. Interest in heritability of human intellectual abilities was one of the main investigations sponsored by the early eugenic movement. From 1922 to the present, there have been a series of published reports using adoptees. These reports are summarized in Munsinger (1975) and support the importance of genetic factors in intelligence. More recent reports are still appearing (Horn, 1983; Plomin & Defries, 1985; Scarr, 1981) which deal with IQ as well as development of cognitive styles. Findings in IQ studies generally support the genetic heritability of IQ but demonstrate less evidence for environmental effects. However, the best known IQ study from the past done by Skodak and Skeels (Skeels, 1936, 1938, 1966; Skodak, 1939; Skodak & Skeels, 1949) showed that in addition to a genetic effect on IQ that in a "proper" environment low IQ scores could be improved over time. Although the effect of the environment was likely to be overestimated by their experimental design (Munsinger, 1975), it did show the ability of adoption studies to pick up environmental as well as genetic factors.

Despite the polemic over IQ it is very likely that a large proportion of variability in human intelligence is affected by genetic factors. This fact is reflected in the widespread adoption practice of placement that is based on expectations of the child's "potential," in that decisions as to what type of adoptive home is suitable were largely based on IQ estimates of the adoptee in addition to consideration of socioeconomic backgrounds of both the child and the eventual adoptive family.

PSYCHOPATHOLOGY

There is no question that adoptee adjustment is reflected in a wide range of psychopathologies. Many very common psychiatric conditions, such as depression, have genetic factors in their etiology. The remaining section of this chapter will deal with important psychiatric problems which are in part genetically determined (and often environmentally as well), and thus might be considered in adoptive placement.

In the sections on psychopathology which follow, psychiatric conditions will be described in accordance with the diagnostic criteria set forth in the *Diagnostic and Statistical Manual of Mental Disorders (DSM-III)* of the American Psychiatric Association.

Antisocial Personality

Antisocial personality is strongly associated with conditions such as delinquency and criminality. Many adolescents and younger children with conduct disorders become antisocial adults. The antisocial personality shows chronic and recurrent disturbances in social behavior prior to age 15. Such individuals demonstrate truancy and other problems such as fighting, running away from home, persistent lying, early use of drugs or alcohol, stealing, vandalism, and chronic violation of school and home rules. Following the age of 18 such individuals also demonstrate an inability to sustain consistent work, are often unable to function as a responsible parent, frequently are involved with the law in the commission of serious crimes such as felonies, continue to be irritable and aggressive leading to physical fights or assault, are often financially irresponsible, impulsive, and frequently "con" others.

Pursuing the kinds of activities noted above frequently leads these individuals to be declared either delinquent as adolescents or criminal as adults. However, it must be recognized that the terms "delinquency" and "criminal" are judgments imposed by the social system and that there are many individuals so adjudged who are not themselves antisocial personalities. Thus the terms antisocial, delinquent, and criminal are not interchangeable although there is an extremely high correlation among them.

Adoption studies have been done with both antisocial personality and criminality as outcome variables. Two groups of investigators have shown significant genetic factors in criminality. Mednick and colleagues (Hutchings & Mednick, 1974; Mednick & Christiansen, 1977; Mednick, Gabrielli, & Hutchings, 1984), working in Denmark, have shown a high correlation between biologic parents who are criminals and criminality in adopted-away children. Bohman and co-workers from Sweden (Bohman, Cloninger, Sigvardsson, et al., 1982; Cloninger, Sigvardsson, Bohman, et al., 1982; Sigvardsson, Cloninger, Bohman, & von Knorring, 1982) have also shown significant genetic effects in criminality. Crowe (1974) working in the United States with the adopted-away offspring of female felons (most of whom were likely antisocial personalities) found a significant increase in incidence of antisocial personality among their offspring when compared to a control sample of adoptees who did not come from an antisocial background. Crowe also found some possible environmental effect in that adoptees who at an early age were exposed to an adverse environment, such as divorce and separation in the adoptive home, were more likely to be antisocial as adults. Another Scandinavian author (Schulsinger, 1977) has shown an increase of personality disorders including the antisocial among the biologic parents of personality disordered adoptees. Cadoret has reported several studies in which offspring of biologic parents with antisocial behaviors were compared to adopted-away offspring of control parents and has found a higher incidence of antisocial personality diagnosis in the offspring of biologic parents who had demonstrated antisocial behavior (Cadoret, 1978; Cadoret, O'Gorman, Troughton, et al., 1985). In one study the author (Cadoret, Troughton, & O'Gorman, 1987) showed that certain environmental factors also increased the chance of an adoptee being antisocial. These factors involved psychiatric disturbance of some type occurring in other members of the adoptive family, especially antisocial behaviors.

While there are no studies describing delinquency as an outcome, Cadoret has investigated antisocial behaviors in adolescents, many of whom had been judged delinquent, and found again, that an antisocial biologic parent predicted significantly higher rates of adolescent antisocial behaviors (Cadoret, 1985; Cadoret & Cain, 1981, 1982). Evidence for gene–environment interaction was also found in that several environmental conditions, which increased the number of antisocial behaviors during adolescence, when discovered in combination with antisocial biologic parents produced much higher rates of adolescent antisocial behavior than expected if each factor acted independently (Cadoret, 1985; Cadoret & Cain, 1982). In general, the environmental effect was the presence in the adoptive home of another family member with some kind of a psychiatric or behavioral problem.

Because of its genetic factor as well as the evidence for environmental effect, antisocial personality is a very important consideration in adoption practice. Its importance arises not only because of the long-term nature of the condition that causes high amounts of social incapacity and disturbance, but also lies in the fact that many parents who give up children for adoption demonstrate considerable antisocial behaviors and many are undoubtedly diagnosable as antisocial personalities. In the author's own work with four different adoption agencies over the past 15 years, the commonest psychopathologic condition found among biologic parents giving up children for adoption has been antisocial behavior or antisocial personality (Cadoret, O'Gorman, Troughton, et al., 1985; Cadoret et al., 1987; Cunningham, Cadoret, Loftus et al., 1975). Knowledge of environmental factors that enter into the equation of adoptee adjustment can lead to selective placement in which homes are picked for adopted-away children from high-risk antisocial backgrounds where there is no evidence of psychiatric or behavioral disturbance in family members. Information that the antisocial condition in genetically transmitted might enable early diagnosis to be made and treatment instituted.

Alcohol and Drug Abuse

Substance abuse has become one of the leading social problems of our time, especially with increasing use of illegal drugs by youth (Alcohol, Drug Abuse, and Mental Health Administration, 1986). Alcohol or drug abuse can be characterized by the following behaviors. There is usually a pattern of pathological alcohol use as evidenced by the daily use of alcohol, and an inability to cut down or stop which leads to binges.Pathological substance use is also evidenced by continuation of drinking or drug use despite serious physical disorders associated with their use. The heavy use of alcohol or drugs generally leads to marked impairment in social or occupational functioning manifested by fighting, legal difficulties such as public intoxication or drunk driving charges, and poor job performance. Should alcohol or drug use reach a certain level, then physical dependence can occur as shown by tolerance—a need for markedly increased amounts of the drug or alcohol to achieve a desired effect. Dependence is also associated with withdrawal symptoms (physical or psychological symptoms which occur in response to abstinence). Obviously these behaviors cause a great deal of social disturbance including perpetration of crimes for the purpose of getting money for drugs or alcohol. Thus many crimes are committed under the influence of drugs and alcohol as well as other self-destructive acts such as suicide.

   In the last decade adoption studies have confirmed that alcohol abuse has a genetic factor. Prior to this, one study done in 1944 failed to show a significant genetic or environmental element in transmission of alcohol abuse (Roe, 1944). Starting in 1973, however, Goodwin and associates (1973) have provided evidence that there is a genetic factor in alcohol abuse in a group of adopted-away Danish sons of alcoholics. By comparing alcoholism rates in adopted-away sons with sibs who were not adopted out, these investigators also looked for an environmental effect but failed to find one (Goodwin, Schulsinger, & Moller, 1974). Bohman and co-workers in Sweden have also described genetic and environmental factors operating in alcohol abuse (Bohman, 1983; Bohman, Sigvardsson, & Cloninger, 1981; Cloninger et al., 1981). These investigators have suggested that there are several types of alcoholism, some with genetic factors more important and others more affected by environmental factors (Cloninger et al., 1981). They also described similar genetic and environmental factors operating in female adoptees as well as in males (Bohman et al., 1981). In the United States Cadoret has also found evidence for genetic factors in the transmission of alcohol abuse (Cadoret & Gath, 1978; Cadoret et al., 1985; Cadoret et al., 1987). Both male and female adoptees seem to follow the same pattern of inheritance. Cadoret also described an environmental factor that increased the rate of alcoholism in adoptees: having some other adoptive family member with an alcohol problem (Cadoret et al., 1985; Cadoret et al., 1987).

Substance abuse is generally highly correlated with antisocial personality. The Bohman study cited above takes this fact into consideration and that author has described types of alcoholism strongly associated with criminality (Bohman et al., 1982). Cadoret has also found significant relationships between antisocial personality and alcohol abuse (Cadoret et al., 1985; Cadoret et al., 1987). However, even controlling for the fact that an individual is antisocial there is still a strong genetic effect with an alcoholic biologic background predicting increased alcohol abuse in adoptees. There is no evidence for significant gene–environment interaction in these studies that found environmental and genetic effects in alcohol abuse.

Drug abuse is also very strongly correlated with antisocial personality. A recent study of adoptees who were drug abusers demonstrated this fact (Cadoret, Troughton, O'Gorman, et al., 1986). This study describes several possible routes to drug abuse, one through antisocial personality and another occurring in individuals who themselves were not antisocial but who came from biologic parents with an alcohol problem. In this same study several environmental factors increased the chance of an adoptee being a drug abuser. One of these was having an adoptive parent who was psychiatrically or behaviorally disturbed including divorce or separation. Interestingly, these environmental factors appeared to be different from the ones leading to increased alcohol abuse which, as noted above, were having a family member with a drinking problem.

Obviously, there is a great deal of human misery associated with substance abuse of any kind and any measures which can be taken to avoid this complication should be taken. Since there is evidence for a genetic element in alcohol abuse and possibly in drug abuse, these are important elements to consider in adoptive placement. Again, as with antisocial personality, alcohol abuse frequently occurs in biologic parents who give up children for adoption and so the risk of these conditions in adoption is quite high. The studies above would indicate that given a biologic background of alcoholism the chance of abuse in offspring is four to six times higher than if the offspring did not have this genetic factor in their background.

Affective Disorders: Depression and Mania

Affective disorders comprised of depression and mania are probably the commonest psychiatric syndromes, with depression being far more common than mania (Winokur, Clayton, & Reich, 1969). Depression is characterized by a cluster (or syndrome) of symptoms consisting of appetite disturbance, sleep disturbance, agitation or retardation in movement and thinking, loss of interest in activities usually enjoyed, decrease in energy, feelings of guilt or self-depreciation, decreased ability to concentrate, and morbid thoughts about death or illness including suicide and death wishes. This syndrome usually lasts for a number of weeks and the illness is an episodic one with a complete remission of symptoms being the more usual course, but with recurrence at some later time being a definite possibility in most cases. If an individual has only depression this is known as "unipolar" illness. As mentioned above, a small number of individuals with depressive illness also have episodes of mania and are said to have "bipolar" illness. Mania is characterized by a syndrome lasting for several weeks of euphoric mood, hyperactivity, speeded-up activity such as a push of speech and a rapid sequence of experienced ideas, a grandiose mood, decreased need for sleep, and an excessive involvement in potentially disastrous social activities.

In view of the ubiquity of depression, it is ironic that there have been relatively few adoption studies of this condition. The most positive correlation was reported by Mendlewicz and Rainer (1977), who followed up the offspring of individuals who had mania and depression (bipolar illness) and found strong evidence for a genetic factor. It is not certain whether these investigators looked for environmental factors as well. Other evidence from family studies and genetic linkage studies also support the genetic element in the transmission of bipolar illness (van Eerdewegh, Gershon, & van Eerdewegh, 1980).

With regard to transmission of depression alone the record is less clear. One adoption study reported by Cadoret (1978) showed a positive correlation between biologic parents with affective disorder and depression in their adopted-away offspring. This finding, however, was in a very small sample, and a later report (Cadoret, O'Gorman, Heywood, et al., 1985) found little evidence for a genetic factor when this same sample was enlarged. But the latter study did report a number of environmental factors for both males and females that increased the chance of depression occurring in adopted-away children. These factors were: for males, placement in a home where an adoptive family member had a drinking problem; and for females, placement in a home where another individual had a behavioral problem or where the home was broken up by death or divorce. Adoptees exposed to these environmental conditions during childhood and adolescence were more likely to have depression as adults. One other adoption study from Sweden (von Knorring, Cloninger, Bohman, et al., 1983) has also looked for genetic factors in depression and has failed to find clear-cut evidence for them. However, this study did report that psychiatric disturbance in an adoptive family member was associated with adoptee depression. Thus the genetic status of transmission of unipolar depression is unclear at the present time, at least from adoption studies. However, the evidence from adoption studies that environmental factors are involved in depression must be taken seriously in considering placement of children for adoption.

Anxiety Disorders

Anxiety disorders, such as panic attacks and phobias, are relatively common in the general population. Anxiety or panic disorder is characterized by discrete panic attacks, in which an individual experiences heart palpitations, chest pain or discomfort, difficulty with breathing including choking or smothering sensations, symptoms of dizziness or unsteadiness, tingling in hands and feet, sweating, and faintness. Individuals sometimes tremble or shake and are consumed with an overwhelming fear of dying, of losing their mind, or of doing something shameful, criminal, or bizarre during an attack. Some individuals have, in addition to panic attacks, a marked fear of going out or of being in certain situations. These individuals are known as agoraphobics.

There are a number of family studies which indicate that panic disorder and agoraphobia are certainly transmitted in families (Crowe, Noyes, Pauls, et al., 1983). Unfortunately, there is no evidence from adoption studies regarding genetic transmission of these conditions, but twin studies indicate a genetic factor (Torgerson, 1983). The importance of environmental factors is not clear.

Schizophrenia and Related Disorders

Schizophrenia is usually a severe chronic psychiatric illness characterized by long-term disability and deterioration of personality, especially in the area of motivation. Individuals with this illness generally have prominent delusions of various types, with the commonest involving persecutory themes. These individuals also have auditory hallucinations and sometimes visual hallucinations. There is also, in many sufferers, marked difficulty with thinking so that concentration is impaired and coherent trains of thought and rational reasoning are difficult if not impossible. Because of the seriousness of the condition and its chronicity, this illness accounts for a high proportion of psychiatric hospitalizations and results in long-term disability.

Three studies have reported evidence for genetic factors in schizophrenia. One of these is Heston's (Heston, 1966), which reported on the adopted-away offspring of hospitalized schizophrenic women. He found that a higher proportion of these adopted-away offspring had schizophrenia than a comparison group of offspring from non-schizophrenic women. Although Heston sought environmental factors, such as social class, none were found (Heston, Denny, & Pauly, 1966). The second study to report positive evidence for a genetic factor in schizophrenia is from Denmark and is an extensive collaborative study (Kety Rosenthal, Wender, et al., 1971; Kety, Rosenthal, Wender, et al., 1978; Rosenthal & Kety, 1968; Rosenthal, Wender, & Kety, 1971; Wender, Rosenthal, Kety, et al., 1974). This study also found an increase in schizophrenic illness among the offspring of separated-away adoptees of schizophrenic parentage. A number of studies have been done with the Danish adoption data in order to elucidate the role of environmental factors, but little evidence of environmental influences, such as psychopathology in adoptive parents, poor child-parent relationships, or abnormal psychometric test results in parents, has been found (Rosenthal et al., 1971; Wender, Rosenthal, Rainer, et al., 1978). In a further analysis of the same data Kinney and Jacobson (1978) reported that postnatal cerebral injury, season of birth, and sociofamilial factors were implicated as environmental effects leading to schizophrenia. Personality traits in adoptive parents such as shyness as an adult or lack of spontaneity during a diagnostic interview were identified as possible social factors. However, the sample size was very small and needs to be replicated. The third adoption study on schizophrenia is currently being conducted in Finland. Recently reported data from this group has found a higher number of psychotic offspring from schizophrenic parents than from control parents (Tienari, Sorri, Lahti, et al., 1985). This group also reports higher psychopathology in adoptees in adoptive families with severe family relationship disturbances than in "healthy" adoptive families.

For a number of years it has been thought that conditions other than schizophrenia occur more frequently in the families of schizophrenics (Rosenthal, 1975). This has been shown to be the case by reanalysis of the Danish adoption data by Kendler, Gruenberg, and Strauss (1981), who report that a personality disorder known as schizotypal personality was found more frequently in the adopted-away offspring of schizophrenics. Schizotypal personality is characterized by certain bizarre beliefs and behaviors but without the full panoply of schizophrenic symptoms mentioned above. In addition to schizotypal personality disorder, paranoid personality disorder has also been found more frequently in families of schizophrenics in Danish adoption studies (Kendler & Gruenberg, 1984). Paranoid personality is a diagnosis characterized by unwarranted suspiciousness and distrust of people including hypersensitivity and hypervigilance against perceived threats, and very restricted affective reactions such as emotional coldness.

These findings that two types of deviating personality disorders are related to schizophrenia suggest that the ''spectrum'' concept of schizophrenia as proposed by Rosenthal (1975) has some merit and certainly some applicability to adoption practices.

Because schizophrenia and other conditions in the schizophrenia ''spectrum,'' such as paranoid personality, result in such a chronic and serious illness in offspring, it is important to detect their presence in biologic families in the adoption process. In spite of the lack of evidence at the present time of significant environmental effects, it is possible that work in progress, as with the Finnish adoption studies of schizophrenia, may uncover significant environmental factors that should also be taken into consideration in adoption.

Somatoform Disorders

Somatization disorder is characterized by a history of physical symptoms generally beginning before the age of 30. These symptoms are often not adequately explained by physical disorder or injury and are not side effects of medication or drug use. Symptoms vary widely and involve almost every organ system in the body. They generally cause a patient to seek help from physicians and other health-care professionals and can lead to a great deal of disability and unnecessary medical tests, medications, and hospitalizations. Individuals with somatization disorder usually have large numbers of different types of symptoms over their lifetime such as: abdominal pain, nausea, vomiting spells, food intolerances, painful menstruation, severe vomiting during pregnancy, sexual indifference, multiple pain complaints in the back, joints and extremities, and many symptoms referrable to the nervous system such as trouble swallowing, loss of voice, deafness, blurred vision, blindness, fainting, loss of consciousness, loss of memory, seizures and convulsions. The incidence of this disorder appears to be somewhat higher in women than in men.

Most evidence for genetic transmission of somatoform disorder comes from Swedish studies by Bohman and his group (Bohman, Cloninger, von Knorring, et al., 1984; Cloninger, Sigvardsson, von Knorring, et al., 1984; Sigvardsson, von Knorring, Bohman, et al., 1984), who describe several types of somatization disorder (Cloninger et al., 1984) but also report that both types of somatization disorder were associated with biologic backgrounds of criminality or alcoholism (Bohman et al., 1984). Cadoret et al. (1976) has found that female adoptees who come from antisocial biologic backgrounds report more somatic symptoms at adolescence. However, whether such individuals become somatizers as adults is unknown at the present time.

Parents adopting from biologic backgrounds of individuals with antisocial behavior might be apprised of the possibility of increased somatic complaints in their adoptees. While these complaints, of course, have to be investigated medically, the possibility that they may be part of a somatoform disorder might help in their management.

Attention Deficit Disorder

Attention deficit disorder has been closely linked with hyperactivity. It is a condition that appears early in life and is characterized by motor overactivity including distractibility, impulsiveness, and inability to concentrate for long periods of time. The condition is important because it appears to be a precursor of later antisocial behavior (Hechtman, Weiss, Perlman, et al., 1984) and is associated in later life with conditions such as low self-esteem and failure to do as well socially as might be expected from the individual's background.

Family studies appear to show relationships between precursors of antisocial and alcoholic behavior in parents and childhood hyperactivity and attention deficit disorder (Cantwell, 1975). One adoption study found an increase in hyperactivity in children who came from a variety of disturbed biologic backgrounds (Cunningham et al., 1975), and a later study found that childhood hyperactivity and attention deficit disorder were associated with alcoholic and antisocial biologic backgrounds (Cadoret & Gath, 1980). In the latter study environmental variables, such as medical problems arising during pregnancy, labor, and delivery, were not found to influence the hyperactivity and attention deficit outcome.

Since hyperactivity and attention deficit appear to have serious consequences in regard to adult adjustment, it would be helpful in adoption placement to consider children from biologic backgrounds of alcohol abuse or antisocial behavior more liable to demonstrate this type of behavior. Parents so appraised might be able to recognize the condition earlier and institute corrective measures.

Miscellaneous Conditions

In view of the fact that a number of personality traits appear to be transmitted genetically (see the section "Temperament and Personality") as well as the fact that antisocial personality, a rather deviant behavior pattern, is also genetically transmitted, it is likely that many other extreme personality deviations could also have genetic factors at their basis. Certainly evidence is present that schizotypal and paranoid personality may stem in part from a schizophrenic genetic background, and there is a definite possibility that other currently recognized personality deviations, such as a borderline personality and obsessive-compulsive personality, might have genetic components as well.

CONCLUSION AND IMPLICATIONS

The consideration of genetic transmission adds an important and practical dimension to explanations of many human behaviors. The older view that children are a "tabula rasa" as far as behavior, socialization, and the like are concerned would appear to be invalid. Not that environment is unimportant. It demonstrably is important and hopefully with the aid of studies of adoptees, the role of environment (as well as genetics) in human behavior will continue to be clarified further.

An example of adoptee psychological disorders, which this newer view of genetics helps clarify, is the repeated observations made over the years of greater than expected numbers of adolescent adoptees appearing in psychiatric facilities with psychiatric problems. In a number of studies reviewed by Simon and Senturia (1966) conduct disorders were the principal reasons for referral. More recent studies have found similar trends (Austad & Simmons, 1978; Fullerton et al., 1986; Senior & Himadi, 1985; Work & Anderson, 1971). Interpretations of these findings, in addition to the usual concerns about sampling, have usually centered on psychodynamic explanations. For example, Simon and Senturia (1966) posited adoptive parent behaviors that ''subtly encouraged all types of aggressive and destructive behavior,'' or again tied the ''acting out'' behavior to adoptee identity problems brought on by adoptees' fantasies of biologic parents as ''bad,'' and abandoning but nevertheless strongly identifying with these ''bad'' parents.

To these interpretations we now add the genetic dimension and ask: in how many cases of adoptees who come to clinics are biologic parents antisocial, depressed, and so on? Perhaps a large part of the variance in adolescent conduct disorder can be ascribed to biologic background. Furthermore, the actual findings with adoptive families suggests that environmental variables, such as behavioral or psychiatric problems in other adoptive family members, play an important role. This role may be very different from many of the psychodynamic models put forth in the past (Austad & Simmons, 1978; Schechter, 1967; Simon & Senturia, 1966). Recent writers on this theme have begun to cite genetics as a factor but unfortunately do not have the data to distinguish between their interpretations (Brodzinsky, Chapter 1; Deutsch et al., 1982; Fullerton et al., 1986; Senior & Himadi, 1985).

The evidence given above for involvement of genetic factors in many significant human behaviors and deviations therefrom raises a very real question for adoption professionals: What biologic family conditions should be screened and what is to be done with the information? Obviously, more information needs to be collected about biologic backgrounds, especially about the biologic father, who is often not very involved in the adoption process. The question also arises how this data should be collected practically. Should biologic parents be administered structured psychiatric interviews to detect conditions which might be important, and should elaborate family histories of biologic backgrounds be obtained, involving gathering information about more distant relatives? Interviews of biologic parents can be misleading since failure to discover the presence of a condition, such as depression, may merely mean that the individual is too young to have developed this illness. Nonascertainment is especially likely to occur with individuals who give up their children for adoption when they are young, before they have had a chance to develop many of the illnesses that might have a potential for genetic transmission. For this reason more information about distant relatives would appear to be a partial antidote for the problem of nonascertainment in biologic parents. Similar caveats arise in determining what investigations should be made regarding IQ and personality and temperament as a variable. Again, since biologic parents are often very young they have not had a chance to develop their full potential for personality-trait development, and it is certainly possible that such traits might change over a person's lifetime. IQ, on the other hand, is more easily determined, although again factors of educational and socioeconomic advantage may play a role in obscuring true value.

One approach to the problem of assessment of risk from genetic factors might be to ascertain conditions which are of considerable importance because of chronicity—the frequency of their occurrence or their severity. Such conditions would certainly include schizophrenia, manic-depressive illness, alcohol abuse, drug abuse, and antisocial personality. Screenings for these conditions are certainly within practical reach at the present time by the use of structured psychiatric interviews and family history inventories mentioned above. The extensive number of conditions in which genetic factors have been found to play a role would appear to require changes in the adoption practice of informing prospective adoptive parents in order for them to make totally informed decisions. It would appear essential that important conditions be screened for and parents advised of their presence in their biologic background. While this practice might lead to concern in some parts that knowledge of a child's biologic background might influence the outcome adversely, it should also be kept in mind that such information might prove of even greater benefit in allowing for earlier intervention and recognition, and of, perhaps, allowing for effective preventative measures when such are or become available. Application of empirically derived figures to assess the risk of transmission from biologic parent to the offspring, as done in genetic counseling, is another practical possibility which could be applied in the adoption process.

Environmental factors and their application to adoptions are not so easily solved. For one thing, there does not appear to be as much clear evidence for the type or quality of environmental factors associated with adoption adjustment that can be applied directly to the adoptive process or to give adoptive families practical advice. We must note the fact that although adoptive families are carefully screened, psychiatric problems as well as other vicissitudes of life occur many times *after* the adoptive process is completed, and to determine the risk of this is almost impossible. However, as more is learned about environmental factors and their interaction with genetic factors, practical application will be more likely. In the future, studies of adoptee adjustment that consider both genetic and environmental factors should add considerable science to the art of adoptee placement as well as the art of raising a child.

3

Adoption from the Inside Out: A Psychoanalytic Perspective

PAUL M. BRINICH

I would like to begin this chapter with a reminder to the reader that, as Freud (1926/ 1959) himself stated, "Psychoanalysis is part of psychology; not of medical psychology in the old sense, not of the psychology of morbid processes, but simply of psychology" (p. 252). Psychoanalysis is just as much concerned with normality as it is with psychopathology; and the inclusion of this chapter on adoption from a psychoanalytic perspective does not suggest that there is any necessary relationship between adoption and psychopathology. It is, rather, an attempt to highlight the conscious and unconscious attitudes that adoptees, adoptive parents, and relinquishing parents have toward themselves, as they have been observed via the technique of psychoanalysis.

I would also like to make clear from the outset that, although it appears that adoptees are somewhat overrepresented in samples of psychiatric patients (Brinich & Brinich, 1982), and although nonclinical samples of adoptees may have more psychological problems than nonadopted children (Brodzinsky et al., 1987), there does not appear to be any one-to-one relationship between adoption and particular psychiatric diagnostic categories. This should not be surprising, as the life circumstances of adoptees and adoptive families vary widely; nor is "adoption" a unitary entity.

Nonetheless, when adoptees are referred for psychological help, their adoptions often seem to have played a significant part in the origin of their difficulties. This has been documented repeatedly in clinical case reports (e.g., Barnes, 1953; Berger & Hodges, 1982; Berlin, 1986; Bernstein, 1983; Brinich, 1980; Brown, 1973; Colarusso, 1987; Davidson, 1985; Harmon, Wagonfeld, & Emde, 1982; Hodges, Bolletti, Salo, & Oldeschulte, 1985; Kaplan, 1982; Kernberg, 1986; Kramer, 1986; Nickman, 1985; Reeves, 1971; Schechter, 1973; Sherick, 1983; Wieder, 1977a, 1977b, 1978a, 1978b). Because of this, some psychoanalytic clinicians have suggested that, if possible, it is best to keep the fact of adoption "secret" from the adopted child until the child has weathered the normal developmental problems of early childhood (e.g., Wieder, 1978a). This suggestion is based on the idea that "telling" a child of his [1] adoption inflicts a psychological injury which cannot be mastered without certain inner emotional and cognitive resources, resources which are not usually available to the child before the developmental period of latency (i.e., approximately 7 years of age).

Other psychoanalytic clinicians recognize the intrapsychic problems posed by ''telling'' the child of his adoption but suggest that the pain, sadness, and mourning which follow this knowledge can and should be contained and mastered within the (adoptive) parent–child relationship (Berger & Hodges, 1982). Blum (1969), writing about the adoptive family dynamics implicit in Albee's play *Who's Afraid of Virginia Woolf?*, notes that

> the secret that is shared and uncovered in the play is often really shared by adoptive parents and then revealed in a dramatic message to their child. This can be likened to a deadly traumatic telegram *unless the revelation is in the context of a lovingly secure parent–child relationship.* (p. 899) [my italics]

My own opinion is that knowledge of adoption, given by loving parents in ways that are ''in step'' with their child's emotional and cognitive development, is not pathogenic per se. The vast majority of adoptees manage to live productive lives without major psychopathology.

However, I do think that adoption imposes certain psychological stresses on each of its participants: the relinquishing parents, the adopting parents, and the child. These stresses are connected inextricably with some of the most basic of human impulses: sexuality and aggression, procreation and rivalry. They also are connected with some of the most elemental of human relationships, those of spouse to spouse, of parent to child, and of child to parent. Indeed, the issues raised by adoption are profound enough that the topic of adoption appears in many of our most venerable myths.

ADOPTION AND MYTH

Adoption is an essential component of myths as old as the story of Moses, as new as that of Superman, and as tragic as that of Oedipus. The topic of the foundling child is prominent in literature: Kipling's Mowgli and Kim, Dickens's Oliver Twist, and J. M. Barrie's Peter Pan are examples that spring to mind. The closely related theme of the step-child is central to such classic fairy tales as Cinderella, Snow White, and Hansel and Gretel.

Why is this theme—of the child abandoned by, separated from, or taken from his parents—such a popular one? What is it about this theme that grips our attention?

Here we can turn to psychoanalysis for an answer to this question. For, as Freud (1909/1959) noted in his paper entitled ''Family Romances,'' it is a commonplace event that, as the latency child begins to separate himself from his parents and become critical of them, he develops the idea that he is a stepchild or an adopted child. That is, he imagines that his parents are *not* his parents, but surrogates or imposters.

The fantasy of being an adoptee often moves one step further, to the idea that the child's *real* parents are nobler than those with whom he feels he has been left. Freud (1909/1959) points out that the characteristics of the noble parents are, generally speaking, nothing more than slightly disguised versions of the child's parents *as they appeared to him in younger years.*

Indeed the whole effort at replacing the real father by a superior one is only an expression of the child's longing for the happy, vanished days when his father seemed to him the noblest and strongest of men and his mother the dearest and loveliest of women. He is turning away from the father he knows today to the father in whom he believed in the earlier days of his childhood; and his phantasy is no more than the expression of a regret that those happy days are gone. (pp. 240–241)

Or, to put this another way, the "family romance" fantasy is an expression of every child's ambivalence toward his parents.

The child's ambivalence is met and matched by the ambivalence of his parents. For children are never unmixed blessings; they are always competitors as well as heirs. (For a contemporary exposition of this theme, consider the relationship between Luke Skywalker and Darth Vader in the *Star Wars* films.)

Our psychoanalytic answer to the question about the popularity of adoption themes in myth, literature, and fairy tales is this: fantasies of adoption allow us to reclaim early images of our parents when we wish to discard the parents we now see. Fantasies of adoption allow us to express both love and hate, at the same time, and to direct these feelings toward different aspects of our parents, these aspects being represented by the two sets of parents included within the "family romance." (See Blum, 1969, for an elegant discussion of this point.)

We turn, now, from myths to some of the elemental issues that led to the creation of the social institution we call adoption. First, we will raise the question: Why do people become parents?

PARENTHOOD AND ADOPTION

Some may consider parenthood as little more than an accident—an unfortunate complication encountered in the satisfaction of human sexual needs. It would be difficult to hold this position for long, however, were one to spend much time talking with infertile couples who want to have children but are unable to do so. While one cannot consider parenthood independently of sexuality, the motivations toward parenthood go beyond the sexual and include parenthood's important defensive, gratifying, reparative and creatively sublimated psychological functions.

Parenthood is, in some ways, a defense against the aggressive impulses and trends in us all which lead, inexorably, to our own deaths. Here I am not referring to conscious suicidal impulses but rather to the aggressive impulses which Freud first described in his essay "Beyond the Pleasure Principle" (1920/1955). While we are usually able to keep these impulses in check, their existence is no secret; all we need to do is to look at the morning newspaper to see how human aggression constantly breaks through into incidents of individual violence, into political repression, into wars, and so on. In becoming parents—that is, in creating children—we ensure that others will be able to carry on after we have been exhausted by the struggle against the destructive side of our nature.

Besides being a very practical defense against our own destructive impulses, children also help us to defend ourselves from the anxiety that is stimulated in us whenever we are reminded of our own mortality. Insofar as we can see ourselves replicated in our children, our children help us to live with the fact of our own mortality.

As Freud (1914/1957) wrote in his essay "On Narcissism," "At the most touchy point in the narcissistic system, the immortality of the ego, which is so hard pressed by reality, security is achieved by taking refuge in the child" (p. 91).

These defensive functions of parenthood are complemented by the narcissistic gratification implicit in parenthood: In creating and loving our children, we re-create and love part of our selves. We give to our children the task of fulfilling the dreams that we were not able to satisfy, and insofar as they are able to achieve what we have wished for them, they gratify our own wishes for ourselves. To quote Freud (1914/1957) again, "Parental love, which is so moving and at bottom so childish, is nothing but the parents' narcissism born again, which, transformed into object-love, unmistakably reveals its former nature" (p. 91).

Parenthood is also an opportunity to creatively "resolve" the losses we have suffered throughout development. Although we have lost the gratifications of our own infancy, we can indulge our earlier needs once again in our own infants. Although we could not gratify our oedipal wishes in childhood, we can now, as adults, possess a modified version of the spouse-to-spouse relationship from which we were excluded as children. And although we had to give up the support of our parents in our adolescent quest for independence, we can resolve some of those losses by becoming parents ourselves, supporters of and guides to our own children.

Finally, parenthood offers many opportunities for the creative and positive expression of both our aggressive and libidinal wishes. Our children's active and loving engagement with the world is a reflection of the transformation (or sublimation) of our own primitive impulses into the ability "to love and to work."

Given the fact that parenthood has such important defensive, gratifying, reparative, and creative functions, and the fact that parenthood does not always come when it is wanted, it is not surprising that we have developed alternative pathways toward (and away from) parenthood. Like Voltaire's God, adoption is an institution that, if it did not already exist, would *have* to be invented.

Adoption exists as a social institution because some parents do not want to or cannot care for their children, while other people wish to care for children but do not want to or cannot conceive or bear children themselves. It is impossible to understand adoption from an intrapsychic point of view without taking into account these two facts: first, that the child was not wanted by his biological parents; and second, that the adoptive parents were unable to conceive.

THE UNWANTED CHILD

It has long been popular in adoption circles to emphasize that the adopted child is a *wanted* child or, as in the title of Wasson's (1939) classic children's book on adoption, a "Chosen Baby." This emphasis is a fairly straightforward piece of denial: Usually a child is available for adoption only because he was *un*wanted. It is no accident that Wasson's story neglects to mention the existence of *biological* parents. The same tendency to deny the unpleasant fact that the adopted child is an unwanted child before he becomes a wanted child appears in many other forms. Consider the name of one well-known adoption agency, "The New England Home for Little Wanderers.'' In reality the children served by such institutions are almost never *lost* children; they are *unwanted* children.

It is not surprising that some mental health and adoption professionals would like to protect adopted children from the harsh reality of having been unwanted by postponing the ''telling'' until the latency years or later. Such a postponement might allow the children to get a bit of a handle on the ambivalence and magical thinking which so strongly influence the first few years of their lives. It might also give them time to develop the cognitive ability to keep two aspects of the meaning of ''adopted'' in mind simultaneously, that is, that they were unwanted but are now wanted children. Such concerns are not without clinical foundation; many reports of psychotherapy with psychologically troubled adopted children mention that some children have come to view themselves as unwanted. These children often provoke their families into treating them as they expect to be treated; that is, to discard them as they feel they have been discarded before.

It is not an easy task to change an unwanted child into a wanted child. This challenge is, however, exactly the task faced by adoptive parents. They must convey to their adopted child that, although he was born to other parents who did not want him, he is now their beloved child and shall always remain so.

Adoptive parents must manage this transformation of their child—from unwanted to wanted—not only in the mind of the child but also within their own thoughts. This process is not easy, for adoptive parents are often also infertile parents, with all that is implied by that adjective.

THE INFERTILE PARENTS

Infertility is not usually something that ''happens.'' Rather, it is a reality that is forced on a couple over a period of months which then stretch on into years. It includes anxieties about sexual performance and about bodily integrity. It includes medical investigations and the possibility of drugs and of surgical interventions. It includes the allocation of responsibility for the infertility—to the man, to the woman, or to both. And it requires mourning.

I use the term ''mourning'' deliberately, as infertility implies some very significant losses. There is the loss of an image of oneself or of one's partner as biologically intact and capable of conceiving a child. There is the loss of the hoped-for status of biological parent (which includes a fantasy of presenting a grandchild to one's own parents). And there is the loss of the hoped-for biological child, a child who carries both one's own genes and one's own dreams. This last loss is, for many people, an especially painful one. Paradoxically (except within a psychoanalytic framework) it is a loss of which they often are not conscious. Fantasies regarding their imagined biological child often remained hidden until they are exposed by a discrepancy between the *real* adopted child and the *imagined* biological child.

Unfortunately the adoptive parents' fantasies regarding their (nonexistent) biological child are not at all inactive. They silently color many aspects of the relationship between the adoptive parents and their adopted child. And, of course, they are not alone in this process; sooner or later the adopted child also develops his own fantasies about his biological parents.

These fantasies—whether they reside within an adoptive parent or within the adopted child—are not necessarily pathogenic. However, the clinical literature contains many examples of families in which such fantasies prevented one person or another from ʒeing the real person in front of them. (The adopted playwright, Edward Albee, uses an especially powerful example of such fantasies as the focal point for his play, *Who's Afraid of Virginia Woolf?* In this play the ''son'' of the two major protagonists, George and Martha, is gradually revealed to be a fantasy—a fantasy who has himself wondered if, perhaps, he was adopted.)

If the adoptive parents are to be able to see their adopted child for whom he is, and if the adopted child is to be able to see his adoptive parents for whom they are, they must mourn the loss of their respective fantasied biological child and fantasied biological parents. The lost (fantasied) relationships must be mourned before the new (real, adoptive) relationships can flourish.

ADOPTION, MOURNING, AND AMBIVALENCE

Mourning is, under the best of circumstances, a painful process. It is, however, seriously compromised whenever the relationship to be mourned is an *ambivalent* one (Freud, 1917/1957). By ambivalent we mean that a relationship is characterized by warring feelings of love and hate, each ascendant at times; this is in contrast to a relationship in which there exists a relatively stable preponderance of either love or hate. Unfortunately, the adoptive ''triad'' (biological parents, adoptive parents, and child) may by its very structure tend to encourage resolutions of internal, psychic conflict that do not bring loving and hating feelings together into useful alloys. Instead, resolutions may tend to be ones which keep these feelings of love and hate apart, with one set of feelings reserved for one point of the triad and another set reserved for the other point.

To return to the ''family romance'': the child who lives with his biological parents may allow himself to imagine that he has other, more noble, parents somewhere. But this is imagination, not reality. This child is forced to live with the fact that the parents whom he loves and the parents whom he hates are the same parents. While this situation is not an easy one, it does tend to encourage the amalgamation of these warring feelings within the context of one set of child–parent relationships.

In a parallel way, the parents who are raising their own biologial child may allow themselves moments (sometimes rather long moments) when they ''disown'' their child. Usually this takes the form of an externalization: father turns to mother and says, ''Do you know what *your* son did today?'' Or one parent says to the other, ''Let's just pretend he's not ours.'' These disavowals are, however, usually temporary. We are forced to acknowledge that our children are *our* children; we have to take the bad with the good.

Within the adoptive family (and hence within the minds of the adopted child and the adoptive parents) this situation is changed. For the child really does have other parents; and however little he knows about them, they are real, not imaginary. This gives his fantasies about these parents extra force. It also makes it relatively easy for the adopted child to direct his loving and hating feelings at different sets of parents. Sometimes love is focused on the adoptive parents while hate is directed outwardly, toward the biological parents. The adoptive parents become all good and the biological parents seem all bad. While this might seem an attractive solution to the problem of warring feelings of love and hate, it generally is a rather unstable solution. It avoids the difficult task of learning to live with people toward whom one has feelings of *both* love and hate.

The same maladaptive solution can occur within the adoptive parents. For while the adopted child is theirs, he was born to other parents and carries the genes of those biological parents. I have seen adoptive parents who quite openly disowned certain aspects of their adopted child—usually messiness, sexual behavior, or aggressive acts. These aspects were bad—they were not "theirs." These parts of the child were not "theirs."

This kind of attitude on the part of the adoptive parents presents the adopted child with a cruel dilemma. He either must disown his own "bad" behavior (i.e., part of his "self") or he must disown his relationship to his adoptive parents (which is also part of his "self"). It is as if he were confronted with the question, "Which eye would you like to pluck out: the right or the left?"

OEDIPUS WAS ADOPTED

I will use this image of cruel choice to return, for a moment, to the topic of myth and its relationship to conscious and unconscious mental life. As both Feder (1974) and Hodges (1983) have pointed out, Oedipus was adopted. In Sophocles's play *Oedipus the King,* adoption was used to attempt to sidestep some of the most powerful currents in human psychology—the sexual and aggressive impulses which develop, are nurtured, find expression within, and eventually destroy the triadic relationship of mother-father-child.

The oracle at Delphi had predicted that the child of Laius and Jocasta (king and queen of Thebes) would kill his father and marry his mother. The royal parents therefore pierced the infant's feet with a thong, tied them together, and left him to die on a mountainside. A shepherd found the boy, released him, and took him to Corinth. There he was adopted by the king and queen of that city, Polybus and Merope; they named the child Oedipus ("swollen foot"). They did *not* tell him that he was adopted.

When Oedipus reached manhood he visited Delphi himself; there he was told that he would kill his father and marry his mother. Thinking that this meant Polybus and Merope, he fled Corinth and traveled to Thebes. Enroute he encountered a group of five men, one of whom struck him. He returned the blow and killed the man—his father, Laius (unknown to him).

When Oedipus reached Thebes he found the city in terror of the Sphinx, who was killing the inhabitants one by one. Oedipus vanquished the Sphinx when he solved her riddle; and in gratitude he was given the throne as the king (Laius) had been killed. Oedipus took the dead king's wife, Jocasta (his mother), as wife. And it was not until many years later—when Oedipus and Jocasta had already had four children of their own (Eteocles, Polyneices, Antigone, and Ismene)—that the story began to unravel into Sophocles's famous tragedy.

Oedipus sought to discover and to punish the murderer of King Laius. He failed to heed the aged, blind Tiresias, who warned him, "You are yourself the murderer you seek." When the truth finally broke upon him, he put out his own eyes, condemned by his own edict and by the gods.

The story of Oedipus revolves around a center of love and hate, of sexuality and aggression. Biological parents attempt to kill their child; the child is spared and then adopted but returns to his original home a paricide. Incestuous union yields sons fated to kill each other. Sophocles reveals, bit by bit, the fateful forces which, to Greek audiences of the time, betrayed the work of the gods. Post-Freudian audiences see the same forces at work, but locate their origins within the individual members of the royal house.

As Sophocles demonstrates, this story of an adopted child draws from deep within the human psyche. And while most of us do not commit the deeds which Oedipus did, we all have had such wishes—and so have wished ourselves adopted.

Thus far this chapter has been an exercise in "applied psychoanalysis." I have tried to demonstrate that fantasies of adoption are part of normal psychological development insofar as they offer some respite from warring feelings of love and hate. I have suggested that both parents and children are faced with the difficult task of creating a workable alloy of these feelings, a "fusion" (Furman, 1985) of libidinal and aggressive drives. And I have pointed out that the existence of two sets of parents in the adoptive triad tends to make it somewhat easier for all the parties in the triad to *avoid* the need to work out relationships with people toward whom they feel both love and hate.

I will now turn to actual clinical psychoanalysis and what it teaches us about the inner, mental worlds of adoptees, of adoptive parents, and of relinquishing (biological) parents.

CLINICAL PSYCHOANALYSIS AND ADOPTION

Psychoanalytic treatment involves patient and analyst in an intensive, long-term dialogue structured in a way that leads to the "return of the repressed" in dreams, free associations, and transference phenomena. Interpretation of unconscious wishes leads to changes in the balance of power among the id, ego, and superego. Psychoanalysis is an invaluable research technique for understanding the complexities of adoption because of its appreciation of the *unconscious* aspects of human psychic functioning that are often neglected by other perspectives.

Adoptees

Much of what appears in the clinical psychoanalytic literature on adoption centers on reports of the treatment of child or adolescent adoptees (Barnes, 1953; Berlin, 1986; Brinich, 1980; Brown, 1973; Colarusso, 1987; Daunton, 1973b; Davidson, 1985; Harmon, Wagonfeld, & Emde, 1982; Hodges, Bolletti, Salo, & Oldeschulte, 1985; Kaplan, 1982; Kernberg, 1986; Kramer, 1986; Krugman, 1968; Nickman, 1985; Reeves, 1971; Schechter, 1973; Sherick, 1983; Wieder, 1977a, 1977b, 1978a, 1978b).

I have found only one report of the psychoanalytic treatment of an adult adoptee (Bernstein, 1983), although Nickman (1985) reports on two adult adoptees seen in psychotherapy. (I feel certain that other reports exist; however, their authors did not highlight the issue of adoption in the titles or abstracts of their papers.) The issue of adoption figures prominently in Volkan's (1984) report of the psychoanalytic treatment of the adult child of an adoptee, suggestively titled "What Do You Get When You Cross a Dandelion with a Rose?" (the two flowers being symbols for the patient's mother's two opposing self-representations, now reflected in her son). Finally, a brief, fascinating report on the treatment of a boy who was told falsely that he was adopted in order to conceal the fact that he was the child of his older sister (Coppolillo, Horton, & Haller, 1981) highlights in reverse some of the psychodynamic issues associated with adoption.

In addition to these case-oriented reports, there are a number of papers which draw on psychoanalytic data in order to address specific theoretical or practical issues (Berger & Hodges, 1982; Bernard, 1953, 1974; Bleiberg, Jackson, & Ross, 1986; Brinich, 1980, 1986; Glenn, 1985–86; Hodges, 1984; Hodges, Bolletti, Salo, & Oldeschulte, 1985; Peller, 1961, 1963; Sants, 1964; Wieder, 1977b, 1978a).

Since adoptive status does not necessarily lead to psychopathology or guarantee psychological health, it is not surprising that adoptees vary a great deal in terms of their adaptation to life. Nonetheless, certain themes do tend to emerge when adoptees are seen in psychoanalytic treatment. Although many of these themes are also encountered in the treatment of nonadoptees, they appear to take on special force in the inner, mental lives of adoptees.

Adoptees often report fantasies of having a lost, invisible, or imaginary twin; of being "secondhand" or of having been bought; of being kidnapped or stolen; of being the object of a battle between warring sets of parents; of having been abused, neglected, or abandoned in infancy; of being a messy, dirty child, a "slut," or a murderer (specifically, a paricide). And adoptees often feel that their therapist is a biological parent in disguise.

These fantasies convey clearly that the self-representations of many adoptees who are patients seem to revolve around the feeling of being *unwanted*. Various "explanations" of this psychological "fact"—that is, of being unwanted—are worked into the fantasies.

This sense of being unwanted plays a part in each of the five "themes" cited by Hodges, Bolletti, Salo, & Oldeschulte (1985): "conflict over dependence, fear of rejection, anger and the wish for revenge, the repetition of earlier experiences of helplessness, and the process of mourning" (p. 169).

This self-representation interdigitates with normal developmental issues. For example, adoptees must, like anyone else, find their way along the path of libidinal phase development (i.e., the oral, anal, phallic, oedipal, latency, preadolescent, and adolescent phases). However, the reality of adoption creates some important *potential* trouble spots in this progression.

The anal phase, with its oscillations between messiness and cleanliness and between hate and love, is a case in point. The anal phase child is confronted with the necessity of "getting rid of" bodily excretions in socially acceptable ways. At the same time he has developed new cognitive, linguistic, and motor abilities. He is able to maintain a mental image of his mother in her absence, at least for a while. He has become, both physically and mentally, more "separate" from mother than was true in infancy. He has a new range of activity, expression, and physical movement. And he must struggle with the problem of simultaneous feelings of love and hate toward the same person.

Several psychoanalytic authors (Barnes, 1953; Bernstein, 1983; Brinich, 1980; Daunton, 1973b: Wieder, 1977a) have noted that some adoptees bring together normal anal phase conflicts with the question: Why was I given up (for adoption)? It seems that they explain the rejection implicit in adoption on the basis of their newly-emerging feelings of disgust (toward bodily excretions) and their inner experience of conflict between love and hate.

Put in everyday language, it appears that these adoptees say (to themselves, at least): we get rid of dirty things; I was gotten rid of; I am sometimes dirty; it follows that I was gotten rid of because of my dirtiness. Or, in the case of the conflict between feelings of love and hate: When I hate or am angry with someone, I want to get rid of him; I was gotten rid of; therefore I must have been hated, perhaps because I harbored angry feelings toward others within myself; it follows that *I* am hateful.

Another example of the interdigitation of normal developmental conflicts with the specifics of adoption can be found in adolescence. Here a major psychological task in that of "object removal" (Katan, 1937)—the intrapsychic separation of the adolescent from his parents—together with its complementary task of identity formation (Erikson, 1950).

The intrapsychic separation of the adopted adolescent from his adoptive parents brings to the surface many old conflicts and anxieties. Some of these are echoes of the ambivalence of the anal phase. The fact that the adopted child has two sets of parents, biological and adoptive, makes it possible for him to think of going away from one set and toward the other set. This is an avoidance of a crucial step in adolescent development. It is similar in some ways to the situation of the adolescent whose parents have divorced and who is caught in a struggle between the two sides of the parental conflict. For the adopted child, however, one side of the conflict usually is hidden in the mists of secrecy.

The adolescent, adopted or not, repudiates parental values and authority as he attempts to define his own independent standards and identity. If, in the midst of this process, an adopted adolescent decides that he does not wish to be like his adoptive parents, he must go one more step as well and decide whether or not he wishes to be like his biological parents (or, rather, like his *fantasies* about his biological parents). This process of separation and identity formation is complicated by the fact that, on an unconscious level, to be like the adoptive parents is to be barren but loving; while to be like the biological parents is to be fertile, promiscuous, and rejecting (in fantasy, irrespective of other realities).

(These adolescent conflicts stimulate complementary conflicts in the adoptive parents. Many of the clinical case reports of adopted adolescents describe quite clearly how adoptive parents were overwhelmed by their fantasies about their adolescent's biological heritage. They unconsciously expected the child to repeat his biological parents' unhappy story and, in trying to prevent this outcome, sometimes succeeded in provoking that which they feared.)

Of course, adoption has implications for both intrapsychic and psychosocial development at phases other than those of anal ambivalence and adolescence. Brodzinsky (1987) has provided a very useful elaboration of how adoption affects the accomplishment of the psychosocial tasks outlined by Erikson (1950).

I would like to close this section on the inner world of the adoptee, as revealed in psychoanalytic treatment, by noting the relative absence of adult adoptees in the clinical psychoanalytic literature. Why is this so?

It may be that the psychological importance of adoption recedes in adulthood, when the adopted child has grown into independence. Or it may be that a scotoma (or blind spot) develops in both patients and their analysts. (While we might hope that the latter possibility is prevented by the personal analyses of the treating analysts, it is sobering to note that when we reviewed psychiatric records of adult patients who identified themselves as adopted, there was no record of the age of adoptive placement in 34 of 67 cases and in 24 of these 67 cases we could not decipher whether the patient was adopted by relatives or by nonrelatives [Brinich & Brinich, 1982, p. 491].) A further possibility is that, for adopted individuals who later become analytic patients, their adoption is only one of many contributors to the conflicts which lead to their seeking analytic assistance, and this accident of personal history (their adoption) takes second place to the biologically founded psychological forces that lie at the center of psychoanalytic treatment.

In any case, however, we see little support in the psychoanalytic literature for Feder's (1974) strongly worded contention that there is "an 'adopted child' pathology, which can flower into narcissistic character disorder, psychotic episodes, delinquency, homosexuality, fantasied or attempted suicide, incest, homicide, fratricide, murder of one or both adoptive parents, and to patricide or matricide" (p. 491). While we have no doubt that there are adoptees who fall into each of Feder's categories, these outcomes are not the result of adoption per se but of a confluence of factors that may or may not include the fact of adoption.

Adoptive Parents

When we turn to what psychoanalysis has to teach us about adoptive parents we find ourselves on much thinner ice than that trodden in the earlier section on adoptees since there are very few case reports available on the psychoanalyses of adoptive parents. Harold Blum (1983) reports on the analyses of two adoptive parents and of three mothers of adoptive parents (i.e., grandmothers by adoption). Schechter (1970) reviews many of the dynamic issues encountered among adoptive parents but without analytic case material to support his observations. Roiphe (1983), writing on self-object differentiation, uses as one of his case examples an adopted child with her adoptive mother and notes that this mother–child dyad showed little evidence of the kind of "merging" that seems to be a normal part of early mother–child relating. Lucille Blum (1959) reports on her treatment of a woman who became pregnant after she had decided to adopt (but before she actually did so). Finally, there are a number of nonanalytic reports on postpartum psychoses in adoptive mothers (e.g., Melges, 1968; Tetlow, 1955; VanPutten & LaWall, 1981) which suggest that the stresses involved in taking on the role of (adoptive) parent can sometimes lead to dramatic decompensations in psychic functioning.

Blum (1983) begins his discussion of the intrapsychic conflicts encountered among adoptive parents (and grandparents) by reminding his readers that "no specific syndrome or disturbance has been associated with adoption. All parents and children have conflicts and problems; all parents and children are ambivalent toward each other; and parenting may be added to the list of the impossible professions" (p. 141).

Blum's psychoanalytic case material illustrates how each of the partners in an adoptive couple (treated by separate analysts) brought to the task of adoptive parenthood internal conflicts from his or her own past history.

The adoptive father was unconsciously gratified by withholding grandchildren from his parents who, he felt, had withheld their love and support from him. At the same time, he very much wanted to be a biological father like his own father; he wanted to continue the family "line" (he himself was an only child born to older parents). He viewed his own body, and especially his genitals, as defective; to adopt a child was to accept and confirm this defect. He felt that adoption was a kind of stealing that would provoke retaliation. His fear of the aggression involved in intercourse led to a phobic withdrawal from the "command sexual performances" demanded by his wife as she tried to become pregnant.

The adoptive mother, for her part, was angry and demanding; she wanted a baby from her husband and when he did not provide it she insisted on adoption. Her anger toward her husband, who had a low sperm count, broke through into actual painful pinching of his scrotum; this led to his retaliatory withdrawal. She wished to leave her husband in favor of a fertile man; adoption of a child was her required price for continuation of the marriage.

Blum sums up: "At the time of adoption, these potential parents were feeling defective, different, depressed, disappointed in themselves and each other. Unconsciously they believed they also were disappointments to their parents and so felt unloved and singled out for special punishment" (1983, p. 154). He goes on to comment that

> the setting in which an adopted child arrives is frequently one of mourning rather than celebration, with the collusive denial concealing the unresolved conflicts over infertility. It is not surprising that many adopted children feel rejection and estrangement. They have been "rejected" by their biological parents, and their adoptive parents and grandparents may have difficulties in attachment to the new baby. (p. 155)

Schechter's (1970) review of dynamic issues encountered among adoptive parents includes the following subset, chosen on the basis of their *intrapsychic* importance:

1. The discovery of one's infertility inflicts a narcissistic wound (analogous to the amputation of a body part).
2. This wound requires both mourning and a painful reworking of one's own mental self-representation.
3. This wound provokes intense anger (at one's partner, parents, self, and others).
4. The sense of defectiveness, the envy of others' fertile sexuality, and the anger consequent to infertility can all find expression in the adoptive parents' relationship to their adopted child and in their fantasies about the child's biological parents.
5. Many of these issues are re-encountered when the adopted child reaches puberty. Envy of and anger about the adopted child's sexuality and fertility,

together with the adoptively reduced incest taboo, create intense intrapsychic conflicts in the adoptive parents which can mesh with those of the adopted adolescent.

While Roiphe's (1983) case report is based on external observations rather than on psychoanalytic data it is, nonetheless, suggestive. Roiphe describes a girl, adopted at two weeks of age, who seemed to differentiate herself from her mother at a precocious age, using anal zone activities as the behavioral mediators of this psychical process. He notes that the adoptive mother, for her part, did not "merge" with her daughter during the early months of their relationship. That is, she did not allow herself to regress to a point at which she might share her infant daughter's experiences (physiological, affective, and cognitive) and then, from the base of this shared experience, begin to build a communicative dialogue with her.

Roiphe's description and understanding of this dyssynchrony is reminiscent of Reeves's (1971) thoughtful analysis of the interactions he observed between three child patients and their surrogate parents. Reeves suggested that the fact that the adopted child and adoptive mother come to each other as "aliens," without having shared the biological unity implicit in pregnancy, "can hinder and affect the genesis of what Winnicott (1956) has termed 'primary maternal preoccupation' in the mother" (p. 169).

Beebe and Sloate (1982) have noted how early problems in mother–infant atunement can lead to far-reaching developmental interferences. Unfortunately, while they illustrate their premise with a case of an adopted infant girl and her mother, they do not examine a number of hints by the mother that the child's adoptive status played an important part in the mother–infant disturbance. For example, "the mother openly complained the infant did not look at her, and the child's gaze at anyone else was 'evidence' to the mother that the other person was 'preferred' over her" (p. 606). The mother complained, "I cannot relate [sic] to this child" (p. 617), and she "openly expressed her fears that the baby would prefer the therapist over herself, that the therapist would prefer the baby to [her], and that the therapist's wish to assess the baby was primarily an attempt to demonstrate [the mother's] own inadequacy" (p. 611).

I would like to bring this section on the psychoanalytic understanding of adoptive parents to a close by referring to two papers which report the development of psychoses in women who had just adopted infants. Although this data is not derived from psychoanalytic treatment, it supports some of what we have seen earlier.

VanPutten & LaWall (1981) report on a 29-year-old professional biologist who was hospitalized three weeks after adopting an infant from an agency.

> She believed she was pregnant with the twin of her adopted child, who she feared losing to the adoption agency. She had slept minimally, worrying that she might not hear her baby crying. . . . She wrote numerous notes to her mother requesting forgiveness. . . . The notes revealed significant confusion about her roles as daughter and mother and her marked identification with her child. (pp. 1087–1088)

Melges (1968) includes in his review of postpartum psychiatric syndromes the case of a 41-year-old social worker who,

> childless for her 5 years of marriage, became giddy and confused upon the arrival of her adopted male infant—an event she had been anticipating for 18 months. Within 2 days

she was insomniac, garrulous, and felt inadequate as a mother, fearing that she might harm the child. She thought her mother-in-law was trying to usurp her role as mother. (p. 102)

While the overt symptomatology of these two adoptive mothers could have very different intrapsychic foundations, it seems safe to say that both were in intense conflict regarding the role of "mother." Both feared that they might do something harmful to their babies and both feared retaliation from mother figures. The reality of adoption precipitated reactions in these women which overwhelmed their normally stable ego functioning and left them prey to anxieties associated with conflicts and impulses that were previously repressed.

This is not to say, of course, that such reactions are peculiar to adoptive mothers. Melges's (1968) paper is a review of 100 mothers who experienced postpartum psychiatric syndromes. Only 3 of these 100 had adopted children; the other 97 had borne the children themselves. We might say, then, that adoptive mothers are not immune to the kinds of psychological stress and occasional disorganization that is seen in many pregnant mothers (Bibring, 1959; Bibring, Dwyer, Huntington, & Valenstein, 1961) and in mothers who have recently delivered their babies.

In summary, our rather meager psychoanalytic evidence regarding adoptive parents suggests that they, like biological parents, must contend with many internal conflicts regarding both sexuality and aggression. In adoptive parents these conflicts tend to cluster and to express themselves around issues of defectiveness (of one's spouse, self, or the adopted child), of dyssynchrony and alienation (in early parent–child interactions), of entitlement and oedipal guilt (both related to the possession of a child born to someone else), and of externalization of impulses (onto the adopted child or onto fantasies about the biological parents).

These intrapsychic conflicts seem to be especially problematic at at least five different points in the evolution of the role of adoptive parent: (1) the discovery of infertility and the resultant decision to adopt; (2) the establishment of the early parent–infant "dialogue"; (3) the negotiation of the separation–individuation phase (with its associated conflicts of anal ambivalence); (4) the parental coping with the child's emotional responses to the understanding of what it means to be adopted (which come with the cognitive developments of latency); and (5) the reworking of the separation–individuation process which appears during the adolescence of the adopted child.

Relinquishing Parents

Reports of psychoanalytic work with parents (invariably mothers) who have relinquished a child for adoption are few and far between. The most detailed case studies available are those of Gedo (1965) and Richards (1987). Fischer (1974) reports his psychoanalytic treatment of a woman who had multiple induced abortions (presumably as an alternative to adoption). There are several reports on the dynamics of unmarried motherhood which, in the past, was often resolved by relinquishment (e.g., Cattell, 1954; Clothier, 1943a; Heiman & Levitt, 1960; and Littner, 1956c). Recently a few reports have appeared on how relinquishing mothers react to the loss of their children (see A. Brodzinsky, Chapter 16; Deykin, Campbell, & Patti, 1984; Millen

& Roll, 1985 and Rynearson, 1982). And most recently we have the first report on the psychological reactions of relinquishing birthfathers (Deykin, Patti, & Ryan, 1988).

Gedo's case report involves a 27-year-old woman who gave up two children for adoption because she found herself unable to marry either of the fathers of these children. It was her inability to marry that brought her to treatment.

Gedo conceptualized his patient's dynamics around three axes: (1) the need for pregnancy; (2) the inability to marry; and (3) the need to give up her child.

The first of these three axes, the need for pregnancy, had several contributors. The patient's father and maternal grandfather had died during her childhood; both of her pregnancies were begun on the anniversary of her father's death. Thus it seemed that the pregnancies—or at least the sexual behavior which led to them—had important links to the patient's experience of object loss. Other contributors to this first axis seemed to be the biologically founded reproductive drive; the need for self-punishment; and an identification with an older sister. (This sister had two illegitimate pregnancies which she terminated by abortions; she then became a nun.)

The second axis of this patient's dynamics, the inability to marry, appeared to be the result of the confluence of two factors. First, she wished to remain independent, denying her dependent wishes and the vulnerability to loss which she carried within her. And second, she wished to avoid the role of wife as she had seen her own mother live it (a masochistic version which involved spousal bereavement, poverty, and suffering).

The third and, for our purposes, most crucial dynamic axis was the patient's need to give up her child. This appeared to be the patient's way of trying to master her own early, traumatic losses. She abandoned her babies as she felt she had been abandoned by her father, her grandfather, and her depressed mother. From the psychoanalytic point of view, this patient's relinquishment of her babies was an intergenerational manifestation of the repetition compulsion.

Richards's (1987) paper reports his analysis of a 22-year-old woman, "Fran," who gave up her first child (a daughter) for adoption when she was 19 years old. The baby's delivery and relinquishment precipitated a three-year psychiatric hospitalization. Psychoanalytic treatment eventually led to the recovery of memories which suggested that the relinquished baby had been fathered by Fran's own father. When she began her analysis Fran was thoroughly caught up in multiple repetitions of oedipal–incestuous conflicts. There was even some case material which suggested that she might have been an incestuous product herself (which, paradoxically, would have changed the nature of her own incestuous relationship with her "father"). Treatment led to marked improvement; Fran was able to marry, have children, and raise them without repeating the self-destructive behaviors that had marked her earlier life.

This seems an appropriate place to refer once again to Feder's (1974) paper "Adoption Trauma." Feder believes that there is "an 'adopted child' pathology" (p. 491) that can be traced backward to serious psychopathology in both the adoptive and the biological parents. As far as the latter are concerned, he hypothesizes a sequence of (1) ambivalent, conflictual sexual intercourse which leads to (2) an unwanted pregnancy, (3) fantasied or real unsuccessful attempts at abortion, and (4) a "traumatic birth, resulting from the attitudes of a rejecting, filicidal, foeticidal mother" (p. 491).

While I think that Feder highlights some profoundly malignant trends which exist in *all* parents (not just in those who relinquish their infants), I take issue with the mechanism of transmission he seems to hypothesize. I believe that the malignant fantasies and impulses Feder describes *can* make themselves felt, even *in utero* (via poor nutrition, e.g.). However, it seems to go beyond the data to suggest that such psychological factors in the biological parents are then reflected in the (rejected) (adopted) infant's own psyche by virtue of his parturition.

Fischer (1974) reports his psychoanalytic treatment of a 28-year-old woman, "Mrs. K," who had five abortions over a 10-year period. Fischer understood Mrs. K's repetitive abortions as an undoing of an incestuous wish—fulfilled in each pregnancy—for her father's penis and his baby. The abortions also expressed her intense rage at her unfaithful oedipal father; in destroying the fetus she destroyed his penis and his baby. Fischer adds, as an aside, that Mrs. K's father was "a product of a mysterious illegitimate union" (p. 398).

It seems possible to argue, on the basis of the cases presented by Gedo, Richards, and Fischer, that the relinquishment for adoption of a baby by its mother is frequently based on unresolved oedipal conflicts. We might add that, in at least one and possibly two of these cases, the incest taboo had been violated in reality (as well as in fantasy).

As we move on from reports of psychoanalytic treatments to psychodynamically oriented studies of groups of unmarried, pregnant women I would like to highlight a point that already must be obvious to the reader. There are at least three steps involved in being a relinquishing mother. First, one must become pregnant; second, one must decide to relinquish the baby; and third, one must learn to live with that decision. Most of the existing studies of relinquishing mothers focus on the first two steps (e.g., Clothier, 1943a; Cattell, 1954; Heimann & Levitt, 1960). It is only recently that some attention has been given to the relinquishing mother's experiences of loss, grief, and bereavement, and to the searching that sometimes grows out of this (Deykin, Campbell, & Patti, 1984; Millen & Roll, 1985; Rynearson, 1982).

Clothier's (1943a) review of the psychodynamics of unmarried parenthood follows classical psychoanalytic lines and gives great weight to oedipal conflicts as they have been observed in unmarried, pregnant women. Clothier emphasizes the part played by fantasies of rape, prostitution, and parthenogenesis in the sexual lives of these women. Her observations, based on her clinical work and collected in an unsystematic way, were made with sensitivity but without control groups. She notes that, for some of these mothers, pregnancy seemed to be an unfortunate accident secondary to their primary interest in sexual intercourse; while for another group the pregnancy seemed central, with sexual activity quite secondary. She warns us that "each case must be regarded individually. Illegitimate motherhood, *like all motherhood,* has as its psychological background an urge to solve conflicts and fulfill deep personality needs" (p. 548) [my italics].

Cattell's (1954) observations of 54 unmarried mothers led to his description of a number of different motivations for becoming pregnant. These included: (1) a wish to achieve a feeling of being loved (by either the sexual partner or by the baby); (2) a magical attempt to achieve maturity and the resolution of problems via intercourse, childbearing, and parenthood; (3) the enactment, in displacement, of incest fantasies; (4) an identification with the sexual behavior of one or both parents; and (5) an act of defiance of family mores. Unfortunately it is easy to imagine some or all of these factors contributing to wanted pregnancies in married couples as well as to unwanted pregnancies in unmarried women.

Cattell noted that 54% of the 17 women diagnosed as "schizophrenic" opted to keep their babies while only 30% of the 37 women diagnosed as "neurotic reactions" and "character disorders" opted to keep their babies. He suggested that some schizophrenic mothers tended to keep their babies "as a supplementary ego to be completely possessed, who would be a dependable and lifelong source of love for the patient" (p. 338). Cattell's implication is that those unmarried mothers who relinquished their babies did so out of health rather than out of weakness.

Heiman and Levitt's (1960) study of unmarried mothers differs from both Clothier's and Cattell's in that they focused on the role of object loss in illegitimate pregnancy. They noted that many of the mothers they studied seemed to be seeking, via their pregnancies, the re-establishment of lost relationships with their own mothers: "Some of the girls look at the baby as a source of succor for themselves since they have recreated the lost love object (i.e., the mother) in the baby" (p. 171). Unfortunately such motivations are not confined to unmarried mothers, though they are perhaps more frequent in that group because of the multiple losses and chaotic family backgrounds that are found so frequently in their histories.

Perhaps the only safe conclusion to be drawn from studies, such as those of Clothier, Cattell, and Heiman & Levitt, is that there is no single motivation for illegitimate pregnancy. Likewise, the decision to keep or to relinquish one's infant represents the summation of *many* different factors which resist simplification.

Generally speaking, the decision to relinquish one's infant is "easy" only when outside forces are brought to bear and the decision is made under duress. And it is "easy" only as long as we choose to ignore what is going on in the mind of the relinquishing mother.

Changes in the social acceptance of and support for single, unmarried mothers has led to a decrease in the proportion of infants relinquished for adoption. These changes have also led many mothers who previously relinquished infants to reassess their decision. Rynearson (1982) reports on a group of 20 mothers who had relinquished infants 15 to 30 years before they were studied. He points out that relinquishment confronts mothers with "a discordant dilemma of separation and loss. First, the separation is permanent and was initiated by the relinquishing mother. Second, the loss is irresoluble because the child continues to exist" (p. 338).

Rynearson notes that, although these mothers seemed to deny their relationship to their infants during pregnancy (most had denied their pregnancy until between the fourth and seventh month) and although they were encouraged to continue this denial at birth (all 20 had general anesthesia and 18 of the 20 were "not allowed" to see their infants), in retrospect these mothers' ties to their infants were very substantial. Nineteen of the 20 mothers

> developed a covert maternal identification with the fetus; this identification became more manifest in the second trimester with quickening. During this time the subjects established an intense private monologue with the fetus, including a rescue fantasy in which they and the newborn infant would somehow be "saved" from the relinquishment. The 19 subjects also decided on names for the developing baby and experienced the common apprehension that they might miscarry or that the baby might be defective.

All of the subjects perceived relinquishment as an externally enforced decision that over-whelmed their internal wish for continued attachment to the baby. (p. 339)

Millen and Roll (1985) studied 22 mothers who had surrendered a child for adop-tion and who later sought psychotherapy. They noted many elements of the patterns of bereavement described by Bowlby (1963, 1980) and by Parkes (1972). Although these mothers had been assured at the time of relinquishment that the experience was then over, this did not turn out to be true.

Instead, after some initial relief, many of these mothers experienced (1) persistent fantasies of their child's presence; (2) a sense of loss of self, along with feelings of mutilation, emptiness, or destruction; (3) anger at themselves for having agreed to the relinquishment; (4) guilt, both for having the child and for relinquishing it; (5) an impulse to search for the child; and (6) an identification with the lost or abandoned child.

It appears, then, that it is not easy to master the experience of relinquishing a child for adoption. Further evidence of this can be found in the explosive growth of groups such as Concerned United Birthparents (CUB), a support group of parents who have relinquished children for adoption (see Deykin, Campbell, & Patti, 1984). The fact that relinquishing fathers experience difficulties as well as relinquishing mothers is just now beginning to be documented (Deykin, Patti, & Ryan, 1988).

I would like to close this section by pointing out the fact that in almost all the literature on this topic, no mention is made of fathers. Clothier (1943a) is one of the few who have reflected on this fact. She suggests that fatherhood, unlike mother-hood, is not achieved in the months of gestation and parturition but in the months and years of "fatherly" activity that follow birth. Since fatherhood is not established, in *most* fathers, prior to delivery, relinquishment means something very different to fathers than it does to mothers.

While I cannot substantiate my disagreement with Clothier on more than rather flimsy clinical grounds, I think that what she presents is a stereotypical view of the development of fatherhood that requires some re-examination. Most helpful would be two or three reports of the psychoanalytic treatment of men who have fathered children who were then relinquished for adoption. I suspect that this kind of investi-gation would yield much more than the vacuum that previous authors have suggested exists.

ADOPTED CHILDREN AS THE PRODUCTS OF INCEST

We have discussed adoptees, adoptive parents, and relinquishing parents from a psy-choanalytic point of view, trying to understand what "adoption" looks like from the inside—that is, in the conscious and unconscious mental lives of these participants in the adoption triangle. I would now like to focus briefly on one specific issue that has surfaced in our consideration of each point of the triangle. This is the fact that *some* children who are given up for adoption are the products of incestuous relation-ships. As I mentioned in the section "Relinquishing Parents," Richards (1987) has reported on his analytic treatment of a woman who gave up her first child, a girl, for adoption; it was only after several years of analytic work that the patient was able to recover repressed memories of a seduction by her father which apparently led to the pregnancy. I have myself treated an adult woman who had two children; the first, a girl, was given up for informal adoption while the second, a boy, she raised herself. It was only after a year into intensive treatment that my patient revealed that both children had been fathered by her own father.

The *reality* that some adopted children are the products of incestuous unions is undeniable. I would even venture to say that many more adoptees are incestuous in origin than we will ever know, as this kind of situation is easily hidden, and hidden with the full weight of our cultural taboo against incest.

The reality that *some* adopted children are the products of incestuous unions has an important psychological consequence, which is: that potential adoptive parents who have not resolved their own oedipal conflicts (including the incestuous wishes that are central to those conflicts) will find it particularly easy to project these unresolved conflicts onto their adopted children.

Let me emphasize that this state of affairs is structurally little different from that of the infant who is conceived, borne, and raised by his biological parents. Such a child can also be the target of unresolved oedipal conflicts in his parents. But the secrecy about the adopted child's parentage and the *reality* that he may have been the product of incest gives extra room for psychopathological developments. And it also makes it just a little bit harder for the adoptive parents to face the adopted child's questions about his origin.

This underlying current of concern about incest may partly "explain" the curious fact that it is often very easy to discover details of the adopted child's origins that are supposed to be confidential. And this confidentiality may produce more anxiety than any of the adult parties (adoptive parents and adoption workers alike) are able to bear. In the past 15 years I have requested copies of agency records on adopted children many times. When these records are sent to me, the names of the biological parents are omitted on the first page of the records. But I have yet to come across a case where I could not find some place where the name(s) had escaped deletion. It might require reading page 4 of a case history, or holding a page up to a light to see through the white-out correction fluid, but *without exception* (to date) the name of at least one biological parent has been included in the records sent to me.

The fact that these "secrets" are so often easily discovered suggests to me that we cannot tolerate *not* knowing the adopted child's parentage. I would suggest that it is our own incestuous, oedipal fantasies that make this ignorance so intolerable. And it is these same fantasies that fuel the fires of controversy and conflict both regarding the issues of "telling" and "open" adoptions. In "telling" and in "open" adoptions we (unconsciously) risk violation of the secrecy which Oedipus disregarded to his great regret.

CONCLUSION

What have we learned in this review of adoption as it appears through the perspective provided by psychoanalysis?

First, adoption is an issue for nonadopted as well as for adopted children. "Family romance" fantasies are widespread (Conklin, 1920) and they frequently appear, in one form or another, in both fairy tales and myths. Not only does the triangular relationship of adoptee-adoptive parents-relinquishing parents mirror the oedipal triangle of child-mother-father, but "adoption" includes elements that are drawn from the very roots of human psychology: fertility and infertility; love and hate; acceptance and rejection.

Second, adoption implies losses and demands mourning of those losses. The adopted child loses the precious fantasy that he is and always has been wanted. The adoptive parents lose their view of themselves as fertile; they also lose the imaginary biological child conceived in their fantasies. The relinquishing parents lose a real child who is replaced by fantasies that cannot be corrected by exposure to the light of reality. These losses need to be recognized for what they are—neither less nor more—and they must be mourned.

Third, adoption and its associated losses confront the participants in the adoption triangle with some special problems in the management of ambivalence. It may appear easier, in the short run, to avoid struggles with questions such as

- Why was I not wanted by my biological parents?
- How and why did my adoptive parents get possession of me?
- Will my adoptive parents keep me, no matter what?

And it may appear easier, in the short run, to emphasize the "sunny" side, to ignore the dark side of adoption.

But these are only short-term gains. Solutions like these convey a message that the other aspects of the story *are* unspeakable, that there really *is* something which cannot be accepted, that the love of the adoptive parents is *not* sufficient to act as a protection and support against the pain of having been given away.

Every life is, in some ways, a Sisyphean struggle to master one loss after another. This is as true for nonadoptees as it is for adoptees. Psychoanalysis provides a way of viewing how individual people struggle both with the forces within them and with the forces from without. It is a psychology of normality as well as of psychopathology. What we have found, in this review, is that adoptees and their families (biological and adoptive) must struggle along with the rest of us.

NOTE

1. For convenience only, the masculine pronoun will be used throughout the chapter.

4

The Meaning of the Search

MARSHALL D. SCHECHTER AND DORIS BERTOCCI

And the end of all our exploring
Will be to arrive where we started
And know the place for the first time.
"Little Gidding"
T. S. Eliot, *Four Quartets*

The winds of change are swaying the structure of adoption. Portions of that structure have been undergoing radical modification, sending its current generation of architects back to examine the original design. The search by the adopted person for birth information or for the birthparents themselves has in some respects shaken the structure to its foundations.[1] For however large or small a subgroup searchers may constitute, the search confronts some of the most fundamental premises, tenets, and values of adoption as an institution of North American and possibly Western culture. The clashing of views on the subject tends to obfuscate a more dispassionate and probing attempt to understand, from the subjective experience of the adopted person, what the need to search really means.

Adopted persons, attempting to search for essential connections to their past, find in much of Western society blockages to acquiring this information because of laws sealing the adoption records which identify the family of their birth.[2] There may be a total absence of any recorded evidence of their birth or of even valid relinquishment papers. The adoptee who wishes to discover any parts of her preadoptive history finds a nearly impenetrable iron curtain between herself and her genealogical background.[3] For the subgroup of adoptees confronting this phenomenon, the thwarting of their attempts to establish a full personal history creates a particular anguish virtually unknown in any other psychosocial context.[4]

Historically, in English-speaking countries laws sealing the adoption record began to be passed in the 1920s and 1930s, partly in response to evolving social attitudes embraced by the fledgling adoption field that the adoptive family should be regarded as "the same as any other family" and protected accordingly. As reflected in adoption laws and in agency policies, focus was on the psychology of the adoptive *parents* and the adopted *infant* or *child*. The rationale for sealing the adoption record was thus based primarily on a *static* concept of the psychology of adoption; that is, the needs of the adoptee and her parents were understood with respect to only the early phases of family life and development.

In the United States the significance of the search as a social phenomenon has been questioned by those convinced of the necessity for maintaining the adoption system as is (Zeilinger, 1979). Despite the development of formal best-interest-of-the-child doctrines (Goldstein, Freud, & Solnit, 1973), the legal status quo with respect to the sealed record, which indicates the family of birth, continues to be defended vigorously. Furthermore, legislative process and courtroom practice have continued to gravitate toward best-interest-of-the-parent solutions (Derdeyn, 1979; Derdeyn & Wadlington, 1977). The "status quo" position has been justified primarily on the bases that: (1) the "rights" of both sets of parents to privacy preempt the adoptee's need to know; (2) parental rights and prerogatives prevail in other matters of childrearing and the search need be no exception (note that in this context the adult adoptee retains child status); (3) future birthmothers would be threatened by the open record and would be less likely to surrender their babies; and (4) the adoption system should not have to accommodate the needs of a small minority. Ambivalence about the search has been expressed by some who believe that unsealed records would change adoption to permanent foster care (Andrews, 1979).

Largely through the activism of searchers, the adoption establishment has slowly come to recognize that, for all personally involved, adoption is a lifelong process. The new generation of adopted children will undoubtedly benefit from certain modifications in adoption practice, including expanded pre- and postadoption counseling services (Auth & Zaret, 1986; Hartman & Laird, Chapter 12; Weidell, 1980; Winkler, Brown, Van Keppel, & Blanchard, 1988). However, earlier generations remain entrapped within the errors of a system that, overall, continues to resist change (Feigelman & Silverman, 1983) and remains rigidly bound by archaic rules of law (Derdeyn, 1979; Kirk & McDaniel, 1984; Levin, 1979; Watson, 1979).

The adoptee is presented with opposing, irreconcilable dilemmas: on the advice traditionally given the parents, she is told early in her life that she comes from a different family of origin. She comes to learn, but not to understand, that the mother of whom she was once a part has been inexplicably lost. When she questions who her original parents were, where they are now, and why she was relinquished, the adoptive parents tell her they have little or no knowledge about them. When as an adolescent or adult she again raises basic questions about her origins, she may discover that what little information the parents were given by the placement source was modified, distorted, or "saccharinized." Also, until recently, adoption personnel tended to give relatively short shrift to genetic contributions generally, and specifically to contributions from or involvement with the birthfather (Deykin, Patti, & Ryan, 1988; Pannor, Massarik, & Evans 1971). This attitude has filtered through to the adoptive family and has contributed to the adoptee's fantasies of parthenogenic birth.

What is it in a certain percentage of adopted individuals that compels them to search for their birth information or for the birthparents themselves? Is it that searchers wish to assuage their frustrations and disappointments, or to undo a sense of rejection? Is it that they are so dissatisfied with their adoptive families that they feel the need to rebel or to replace them? Is the search intended to reassure the birthmother that her decision to place the adoptee was sound, and that the adoptee is thriving? Or is there some yet-unexplained inner force compelling them to find someone who looks like them, feels like them, laughs like them, is artistic like them—a need to fill a void or give them a sense of completeness with a full familial history? Is their sense of past, present, and future any different from the nonadoptee's and, if so, how does this relate to the search? Or are searchers just "naturally curious" and acting in accordance with more generalized propensities for unraveling life's mysteries (Pannor, Sorosky, & Baran, 1974)? In other words, are searchers responding to external factors in their life experience, or are they responding to internal forces, beginning with innate aspects of the human psyche, which then undergo culturally influenced elaborations? Is there any common feeling which runs through most or all searchers, or are there subgroups representing discrete differences in intrapsychic perceptions, aims, and motives? Or is the combination of factors infinite and not subject to generalizations?

The laws sealing records were ostensibly intended to protect the anonymity and confidentiality of all parties to the adoption.[5] However, their reported effect on the adoptee has been to blur boundaries between fantasy and reality (Blum, 1983) and to enhance feelings of secrecy, sordidness, abandonment, artificiality, and differentness (Reynolds, Chiappise, & Danzl, 1975; Triseliotis, 1984). Since the need for cognitive understanding of causal relationships is inherent in the human (Piaget, 1954), limitations and discrepancies in birth information result both in a plethora of fantasies, none or few supported by reality, and in cognitive dissonances that demand reconciliation.[6]

For the adoptee discussed in this chapter, sorting out the heredity–environment riddle has become an integral and automatic part of her cognitive life. It is in the context of continually perceiving a realm of differences between herself and members of her adoptive family, and in being unable to account for the source of many of them, that biological origins become a point of reference in her thinking. Most likely the only aspect of herself, which her environment could not substantially change over time, is her body (e.g., eye coloration, etc.), a major link to the birthparents. And so the adoptee's psychic energy becomes heavily invested in pondering the exquisite details of coloring, features, and shapes, her own and those of all around her including strangers. Her frustrated search (symbolic or intrapsychic) takes the form of seeking likeness somewhere, anywhere, which might confirm her bond with humanity itself.

For the adoptee the missing experience of perceiving likeness-to-self is compounded by the lack of a full and coherent birth story; for many adoptees there is a vacuum of information about their infancy as well. As a consequence of this, and its elaborations throughout the life span, the adoptee may have difficulty acquiring an internal sense of human connectedness—that is, *the subjective experience of the self as fully, literally, and genuinely human with an attending capacity to conceptualize one's own personal evolution from past through the present and into the future, physically, temperamentally, psychologically, and intellectually.* We would emphasize, however, that in no way does the problem of acquiring a sense of human connectedness imply any deficit in the development of either attachments to the adoptive family or interpersonal object ties.

On the basis of what we have learned about the strength of the desire to search and about its intrapsychic sources, we submit that the need to experience human connectedness through one's family of origin has innate (constitutional) origins in complex, interrelated sequences involving perception, cognition, emotion, and active response. In this sense the need for an internal sense of human connectedness meets the criteria of a drive state:

> a genetically determined, psychic constituent that, when operative, produces a state of psychic excitation or . . . of tension. This tension impels the individual to activity, which is also genetically determined in a general way, but which can be considerably altered by individual experience. (Campbell, 1981, p. 193)

For some adopted persons the absence of a sense of human connectedness assumes intolerable proportions at a conscious level. For them, search becomes a rational response to certain irrational circumstances over which they have heretofore had no control and from which they seek finally to extricate themselves.

In this chapter, we explore the meaning, implications, and outcome of the search from the perspective of the adoptee. We begin with a review of the empirical literature on various aspects of search phenomena. Next, we present a conceptual analysis of some of the fundamental issues that we believe underlie the need to search.[7] These include: (1) the adoptee's attempts to repair intrapsychically a basic sense of loss of attachment to her birthfamily; (2) the roles of envy and jealousy in the adoptive situation that contribute to searching behaviors; (3) the presence of developmental blocks in some adoptees which affect aspects of their sexual identity; (4) the impact of perceptual lacunae and cognitive dissonances on body image, in particular, and on locus of control generally; and (5) the innate, driven need in certain adoptees to search for their biological origins as a means of experiencing human connectedness. In support of the validity of the above issues, direct quotations from respondents in our own study (Bertocci & Schechter, 1987) are scattered throughout the text in brackets to illustrate and amplify specific concepts.[8] Finally, we conclude with a position statement regarding social policy on access to birth information for the adopted persons who experience the need to search.

REVIEW OF THE LITERATURE ON THE SEARCH

Historical Review

The adopted person's search for a biological relative is referred to only tangentially, or not at all, in the various "how-they-fared" follow-up studies (Jaffee & Fanshel, 1970; McWhinnie, 1967) and in the clinical literature speculating on pathogenic aspects of the adoption experience (Peller, 1963; Sants, 1964; Schechter, 1960; Schechter, Carlson, Simmons, & Work, 1964). Until the 1980s, the mental health and social service literature tended to accept as a given that the adoptee would never know the true facts or identity of the birthparents (Clothier, 1943a, 1943b; Stone, 1972). Focus was thus on the adoptee's task of integrating on both an intellectual and emotional level two sets of parents, one real (adoptive) and one that would have to remain fantasied. At most the search was usually viewed as fantasied or symbolic rather than literal or *activated* (the term we use in this chapter) with respect to the birthfamily. Also, search ideation was generally presumed to be particularly salient during the developmental phase associated with consolidating identity, that is, adolescence (American Academy of Pediatrics, 1971; Barinbaum, 1974; Frisk, 1964; Goldstein et al., 1973; Kirk, 1964; Simon & Senturia, 1966; Toussieng, 1962; Wieder, 1978a, 1978b). For example, Blos (1978) discusses the search by a male adoptee as an example of adolescent acting out that operates in the service of ego synthesis. It was not until research turned to adoptees engaged in activated search that identity issues in late adolescence and adulthood were addressed (Sorosky et al., 1975).

For two decades the search went virtually unnoticed by the child welfare and mental health professions, while journalistic accounts (Erlich, 1977; Lifton, 1979; Marcus, 1981; Paton, 1954, 1968) and autobiographical accounts (Allen, 1983; Fisher, 1973; Leitch, 1984; Lifton, 1975; Marcus, 1981; Maxtone-Graham, 1983; McKuen, 1976; Paton, 1960) developed momentum in the popular literature. In the mid-1970s the adoption field began to stir, bracing itself against the mounting criticism of certain of its policies and practices, criticism coming from articulate adult adoptees and from professionals within its own ranks (Anderson, 1977; Burgess, 1976; Cominos, 1971; Freedman, 1977; Jones, 1976; Pannor et al., 1974; Smith, 1976; Thompson, Stoneman, Webber, & Harrison, 1978; Triseliotis, 1973). On the one hand, England settled into an uneasy acceptance of the open adoption record for adult adoptees (Day & Leeding, 1980), 45 years after Scotland had established adoption laws stipulating open records. On the other hand, the Canadian provinces have thus far maintained the sealed record, some provinces compromising on a registry or intermediary system instead (Garber, 1988). In the United States, the statutory language in two states (Idaho and South Dakota) appeared to allow access to court adoption records on demand as of 1986, while three states (Alabama, Alaska, and Kansas) will release the original birth certificate on demand. Even in these states, however, the system does not always operate as legislated (Harrington, 1986, 1988). In distinct contrast to Great Britain, "American adoption services have always been fragmented by state legislation and local practice" (Silverman & Weitzman, 1986, p. 2). Canadian adoption services developed similarly (Kirk & McDaniel, 1984). Consequently, in the United States and Canada the adoptee's access to even background information varies greatly depending on the state or province where she was born, the state or province where she was adopted, the individual(s) or agency(ies) which originally handled the adoptive placement, and the attitudes of the person(s) presently representing the placement source.

Demographic Data

Since 1973 there have been sporadic but increasing attempts to study both the demographics of "who searches and why" and the outcome when reunion takes place (Bertocci & Schechter, 1987; Day & Leeding, 1980; Depp, 1982; Kowal & Schilling, 1985; Lion, 1976; Simpson, Timm, & McCubbin, 1981; Slaytor, 1986; Sobol & Cardiff, 1983; Sorosky et al., 1978; Thompson et al., 1978; Triseliotis, 1973; Webber, Thompson, & Stoneman, 1980). The studies generally see searchers as divided into two subgroups—those seeking genealogical or medical background information and those seeking to locate or reunite with the birthfamily.

In all 12 studies the majority of subjects were female. In the two studies from countries with open records (Day & Leeding, 1980; Triseliotis, 1973), with subjects obtained through an official registrar, the female majority was considerably smaller (59% and 58% respectively) than that of the other studies. For the studies from countries with sealed records, the female majority ranged from 63% (Simpson et al., 1981) to 82% (Sorosky et al., 1978). The Sobol and Cardiff study (1983) points out that attempts to study the full spectrum of search behavior, including *disinterest*, yield a disproportionate number of female subjects willing to respond to inquiry.

The age range of respondents in these studies was often wide, from the teens into the 60s and 70s, but peaked in the young-adult group, with most searchers clustering in the 25 to 34 age range Bertocci and Schechter (1987) found that male subjects tended to skew into the older age groups. A slight majority of the subjects in these studies had been placed by 6 months of age.

In the above studies the searchers tended to be married and to have stable positions in middle-income jobs. There was a good deal of variation in the subjects' sibling status; the percentage of adoptees who were only children ranged from 25% (Thompson et al., 1978) to 60% (Sorosky et al., 1978). When there was discussion of factors precipitating the search, reference was usually to *external* life changes in young adulthood such as death of an adoptive parent or concern about having children. Sobol and Cardiff (1983) noted that searchers tended to report a higher number of *chronic* life stressors. Regardless of the extent of significant *external* life events, however, in its growing appreciation of the lifelong impact of adoptive status, empirical inquiry demonstrates that search is an *internal* process that begins in childhood when the child, usually in latency, becomes more fully aware of the meaning of adoption (Brodzinsky, 1987).

Extent of Search Interest and Search Behavior

The question is often raised as to the prevalence in the total adoptee population of search interest and search behavior. (Search *ideation* must be distinguished from *activated* search, which may or may not follow.) However, with reference to the United States, not even remote numerical estimates are possible for either category. This is in part because, according to the Department of Health and Human Services in Washington, D.C., since 1971 no national statistics have been compiled on the numbers of legally adopted persons in any age group (Sambrano, 1987). The studies from Great Britain, where adults have legal access to original birth certificates, indicate that less than 1% of eligible adoptees have availed themselves of the open record *within any given year*. In a recent essay, Triseliotis (1984) suggests that a more meaningful figure would be the proportion of adoptees who search *over the course of their lifetime* which, by his calculations, would raise the figure to about 15%. In any event, one cannot reasonably assume a direct applicability from Scotland to the United States. American adoptees who have joined search organizations number in the tens of thousands (Fisher, 1988; Vilardi, 1988). It is impossible to know the numbers of adoptees searching independently.

In a study of identity formation in 50 adolescent adoptees, Stein and Hoopes (1985) cited 16 (i.e., 32%) adoptees who "actually wished to search for their biological parents" (p. 57). In a Canadian study of 83 adult adoptees solicited through urban newspapers, Sobol and Cardiff (1983) found that 35% were actively searching for their birthfamily. In our own study (Bertocci & Schechter, 1987) involving 94 adult adoptees who were mostly active searchers, there was a consistent and pronounced increment in search ideation from childhood and adolescence into the adult years.

Factors and Psychological Issues Associated with Search

In the 12 studies cited earlier, there was general agreement that one of the primary factors relating to the need to search was the adoptee's dissatisfaction with the parents' communications about adoption issues. These were viewed as ranging from inadequate to traumatic. Anguish in this regard seemed particularly acute for the subjects as reported in the Great Britain studies (Day & Leeding, 1980; Triseliotis, 1973). They emphasized, however, the overriding importance of the quality of the family relationships. Six of the 12 studies made reference to the issue of age when disclosure had been initially made (Bertocci & Schechter, 1987; Kowal & Schilling, 1985; Sobol & Cardiff, 1983; Sorosky et al., 1978; Thompson et al., 1978; Triseliotis, 1973). The only apparent consistency was that, except for the subjects of Sorosky et al. (1978), a majority of the adoptees in the North American studies recalled they were told "early," by age 5.

With regard to searchers' evaluations of the adoption experience, the findings varied greatly: Triseliotis's (1973) study of searchers in Scotland noted primarily unsatisfactory evaluations, while other studies found a majority of searchers satisfied (Day & Leeding, 1980; Lion, 1976; Simpson et al., 1981; Thompson et al., 1978). Four studies (Bertocci & Schechter, 1987; Kowal & Schilling, 1985; Sobol & Cardiff, 1983; Sorosky et al., 1978) found a more or less even distribution of evaluations among those whose search had become activated.

Feigelman and Silverman (1983) noted that the growing group of adoptive parents who are *fertile* tend to be "significantly more approving" (p. 68) of search interest in their children, particularly if the child is foreign-born. However "the families of searchers reported significantly more adjustment problems" (p. 215) than nonsearchers, including "discomfort about their appearance" (p. 216). Stein and Hoopes (1985) similarly noted that the adolescents interested in searching tended to perceive themselves as more markedly different in physical appearance from the adoptive parents. The investigators concluded that "mismatch issues seem to increase the likelihood of search behavior" (p. 64).

Unlike most of the other studies, Bertocci and Schechter (1987) inquired explicitly into the significance of (lack of) physical resemblance to the adoptive family. Sixty percent of the respondents indicated that the lack of perceived similarities had been a significant factor in their sense of frustration, embarrassment, and insecurity as an adoptee. Bertocci and Schechter (1987) also found that 56% of the respondents cited health problems in the adoptive parents, the vast majority of the problems emotional in nature and primarily cited for the mother ["tense," "fearful," "depressed," "neurotic"]. This, along with other descriptions given of the adoptive parents, suggested personality mismatches as well as the physical mismatches referred to above. Sobol and Cardiff (1983) found that "the degree of perceived similarity between adoptive parent and child, based on either physical resemblance or personality, bore no relationship to the adoptee's search activities even though both of these variables were related to the adoption ratings and the rated adoptive family relationships'' (p. 480).

Bertocci and Schechter (1987) inquired additionally into the nature of fantasies over time about the birthparents. Of the respondents who gave information with a clear positive or negative valence, nearly five times as many had formed *positive* images or fantasies of the birthmother as had formed negative images or fantasies.[9] This contrasts with data reported by Triseliotis (1973), who noted that searchers tended to have a negative image of their birthparents.

The social science literature offers little enlightenment with respect to inner motives and intrapsychic meanings of the search. Similar to the debate in the clinical literature over the adoptee's ''vulnerabilities'' to stress and symptom formation (Bernard, 1974; Brinich, 1980; Brodzinsky, 1987, Chapter 1; Schechter, 1964, 1967), intrapsychic meanings have tended to be confused with psychopathology and clinical syndromes. On the one hand, psychiatric observations on the intrapsychic meaning of the search include ''acting out a fantasy of re-attachment'' (Thompson et al., 1978, p. 2); a form of nonconformity, that is, a rebellion against parental standards out of a need for ''autonomous self-definition'' (Nickman, 1985, p. 372); an attempt to find reassurance that she was not given away for being bad and that the birthparents were still alive, that is, not destroyed by her anger over being abandoned (Blum, 1983; Silverman, 1985). On the other hand, the frequent references to ''curiosity,'' typically as a ''natural'' reason for searching, represent attempts to avoid implications of deviance (pathology). They also conceptualize search as a simple cognitive phenomenon.

Pannor et al. (1974) delineated a range and variety of underlying motives and issues for the searcher. They stated that adoptees' ''desire for background information is ubiquitous'' (p. 193) and that the ''break in the continuity of life through the generations . . . [i.e., the] block to the past may create a feeling that there is a block to the future as well'' (p. 193). Social workers have referred to the search as a developmental task having to do with the adoptee's need to reconcile and integrate his likeness and difference to both adoptive and biological families (Auth & Zaret, 1986; Lion, 1976). Restating the ''natural curiosity'' theme, the sociological perspective of Haimes and Timms (1985) emphasized the adoptee's ''social identity'' that had evolved from social attitudes about adoption. They (Haimes & Timms) view searchers as ''seeking to place themselves in a narrative . . . in order to correct that part of their lives which gives them a marginal identity, that is, their ignorance about certain key people and events in their lives'' (p. 50). In a psychoanalytically based study, Hodges (1984) related the child's ''psychological need or wish to know'' (p. 49) to her frustrated attempts to construct a mental representation of the birthparents without having the necessary building materials to do so. In several of the children the ''desire to be able to resemble someone was of great importance'' (p. 51). Earlier, Kornitzer (1971) and Stone (1972) had touched briefly on the adoptee's wish for a physical image of the birthparents. The Australian researchers Winkler and Midford (1986) emphasize the adoptee's threatened sense of ''biological identity,'' the latter defined as the ability to place oneself in biological time.

In the various Anglo-American studies cited earlier that asked adoptees to describe the innermost feelings which prompted a search, virtually the same terms are used by the subjects, for example, references to not feeling ''whole'' or ''connected.'' The Bertocci and Schechter (1987) study found that these same terms were used across the board, regardless of how the adoption experience was evaluated. For instance, consider the statement of one of our respondents who regarded his adoption as satisfactory: [''I want to stop running from life, to feel complete, to stop looking at every stranger wondering if I'm related—to settle my self-image anxiety''].

Characteristics of Nonsearchers

Adopted adults who do *not* search are also a subject of interest and debate although relatively little is known about this group. To our knowledge nonsearchers have been studied, not as a separate group but in the context of investigating a comparative group of searchers (Aumend & Barrett, 1984; Reynolds, Eisnitz, Chiappise, & Walsh, 1976; Sobol & Cardiff, 1983). These studies demonstrate the difficulty of finding a ''pure culture'' of nonsearcher who is not actively (consciously) interested in reflecting on adoption-related issues.

The above three studies seem to agree that the nonsearchers (in contrast to the searchers) tended to be more satisfied with certain aspects of the adoption experience, such as the way adoption issues were handled by the parents. Nonsearchers also tended to score higher on self-esteem–self-concept scales (Aumend & Barrett, 1984; Sobol & Cardiff, 1983) and lower on need for self-abasement (Reynolds et al., 1976). Aumend and Barrett (1984) found a ''greater degree of happiness'' as reported by the nonsearchers (37% of their sample) and concluded that identity conflicts are not an intrinsic aspect of adoptive status.

Thus attempts to draw distinctions between the searcher and the nonsearcher are no more conclusive or generalizable than attempts to substantiate empirically personality differences between adoptees and nonadoptees in the nonclinical population (Brodzinsky, 1987; Brodzinsky, Schechter, Braff, & Singer, 1984, 1987; Lindholm & Touliatos, 1980; Mikawa & Boston, 1968; Norvell & Guy, 1977; Stein & Hoopes, 1985).

Outcome of the Search

In the 12 studies cited earlier, there was variation as to whether the majority of subjects sought reunion and whether reunion had already been achieved. For example, those who achieved reunion ranged from 22% (Kowal & Schilling, 1985) to 66% (Sorosky et al., 1978). This range is not particularly significant because the studies tapped different points in the time span of the search process. Also, four studies (Depp, 1982; Slaytor, 1986; Sorosky et al., 1978; Webber et al., 1980) were exclusively focused on subjects who had already had a reunion. Of the studies reporting reunion data, all emphasized the positive results expressed by the adoptees. References were to their ability to ''come to terms with their condition and circumstances'' (Triseliotis, 1973, p. 160); to ''feel more 'whole' and integrated'' (Pannor et al., 1974; p. 194), and ''free of unknowns'' (Sorosky et al., 1978, p. 171); to be free of a ''feeling of non-existence prior to adoption'' (Thompson et al., 1978, p. 28); and to ''establish a better sense of identity'' and finally experience the adoptive parents as ''real'' (Depp, 1982, p. 117). Mentioned in several places was improvement in the relationship with the adoptive parents (Bertocci & Schechter, 1987; Lion,

1976; Slaytor, 1986; Sorosky et al., 1978). The Webber et al. (1980) study also obtained corroborative information from the adoptive parents themselves. Many of the parents had shifted from a negative attitude toward the search to an accepting attitude after they perceived positive postsearch changes in the adoptee. Few of the studies made much if any mention of the birthfather.

In the Bertocci and Schechter (1987) study, all respondents who had completed some portion of the search for a birth relative indicated that the postsearch changes marked considerable improvement in their lives. The largest group made explicit reference to significant changes in self-esteem, self-confidence, and assertiveness; the next-largest group made explicit references to the importance of looking like, or being like, a birth relative, with important changes in body-image and self-perception ["From seeing people who look like me, I'm much more able to see myself"]; many mentioned feeling "connected," "grounded," or "belonging" in a way they had never experienced before. Another grouping of responses referred to a sense of "validation," feeling "real," and "authentic"; peace of mind and a sense of calmness were mentioned by several, as was a greater ability to handle and express emotions ["Feelings seem like gifts instead of curses now"; "I'm not so afraid anymore"]. Several respondents made extensive references to the effectiveness of the search in breaking an impasse in their development as persons ["I have better ability to work and love adequately—my life has been stabilized"].

Summary

In summary, until recently the adoptee's search for a complete biological history, and sometimes for a literal encounter with a birthparent, was addressed only in the popular literature. The social science literature generally presumed the search to be primarily a symbolic phenomenon occurring most prevalently in mid-to-late adolescence. However, studies of search behavior in the primarily English speaking countries (the United States, Great Britain, Canada, and Australia) demonstrate that, while the activated search appears to be undertaken thus far by a very small proportion of adult adoptees, the extent and significance of search behavior can be understood only when the adoptee's entire life span is taken into account. The studies reach different conclusions as to whether the need to search is predominantly found among adoptees with unsatisfactory adoptive experiences. The studies tend to agree, however, that the majority of searchers are females in young adulthood; and that when a search is completed it usually results in significantly improved psychological changes within the adoptee. It remains that very little has been understood about the complex psychological meaning of search behavior, and even less is known about the nonsearcher. Thus methodologies and sampling deficiencies continue to plague adoption research. And in the absence of sufficient knowledge or understanding, debate and controversy flourish.

FUNDAMENTAL ISSUES UNDERLYING THE NEED TO SEARCH

In this section we discuss some of the major fundamental intrapsychic issues that we believe underlie the need to search (whether fantasied or activated). Unquestionably loss, envy, sexual identity, body image, cognitive dissonance, locus of control, and human connectedness are universal issues in human development. We contend that adoptive status can involve complex variations of universal psychological themes, always subject to the unique genetic or constitutional predispositions, and to the particular vicissitudes of life experience, of the individual person.

Loss and Mourning: Themes of Reparation

In both the popular and the professional literature, virtually all references to the meaning of adoption for the parties directly affected (the adoptee, the birthparent, and the adoptive parents) involve the concept of loss (see Brinich, Chapter 3; A. Brodzinsky, Chapter 16; D. Brodzinsky, 1987, Chapter 1; Nickman, 1985). However, the literature on loss and mourning in human experience focuses almost exclusively on loss by death, although even Freud's classic paper "Mourning and Melancholia" (1917/1957) allows for "the loss of some abstraction which has taken the place" of a loved person (p. 243). Nickman (1985) distinguishes between the "overt loss" the adoptee experiences when originally separated from the birthmother and from other caretakers prior to adoptive placement; and "covert losses," which he considers primary, having to do with the knowledge of having been relinquished, that is, of not having come into the world as a wanted person (p. 376).

Under the best of circumstances many adoptees may still be predisposed (Bowlby, 1980) to a pervasive anxiety that, if loss (of the object, birthmother, and of the object's love) happened once, it can happen again (i.e., with anyone the adoptee values). The adoptee's anxiety in childhood about potentially losing the adoptive parents reemerges with great force if the adoptee in adulthood contemplates an activated search. Related fears and fantasies are almost universally cited as inhibiting any activation of search. ["Fear of losing my adoptive family, for being 'ungrateful' "; "fear of hurting my parents—guilty about how they must think I don't love them."] For some adoptees the anticipation of potential loss becomes an integral aspect of their character structure, hence common variations of tenaciousness ["I can't seem to let go"] and inclinations to "reject first." ["Interpersonal relationships never last. . . . I assume they want me to get lost so I leave."]

In addition to vulnerability to potential losses in the future, we propose that one of the most prevalent losses experienced mutually by adoptee and adoptive parent can be the loss of the biological tie *with each other;* around this there may be a subtle but perpetual mourning process (Hodges, 1984). ["As a child I didn't want to be adopted—I was going to stop eating so I could get smaller and be born over to my adoptive mother—I wished she was my birthmother."]

Under detrimental circumstances within the adoptive family, we find that a profound loss for the adoptee (unrelated to the birthparent) has to do with the absence of a viable, consistent, and enduring empathic response from the adoptive parents— response to her not only as an adoptee but as a person. Under these circumstances, unlike nonadoptees who may be emotionally abandoned too, the adoptee experiences a double abandonment. As a typical concomitant of emotional abandonment by the adoptive parents, adoptees in this subgroup have often come to feel "used" for the narcissistic gratification of other persons, for example, used more or less exclusively as a means for the adoptive parents to repair deficiencies in their own lives. ["I found out my parents only wanted me to save their marriage.'' ''My adoptive mother had a breakdown and the doctor thought a baby would make her better—no one investigated this family.'' ''I feel I was loved for what I could do for them, rather than for who I was or might become.''] For these adoptees the search constitutes in part a means of reparation for profound deficits in their life experience which have come to be organized extensively around adoption-related issues.

How does the concept of loss for adoptees (and especially those who were placed early) relate to the birthparents, and to the search for them, when they (the birthparents) have never been directly experienced as objects in the adoptee's world? Both formal and informal observations have shown that adopted people experience complicated perceptual, cognitive, and affective reactions to learning that there occurred an allegedly permanent separation from a person to whom they were originally connected biologically (Brodzinsky, 1987, Chapter 1; Brodzinsky, Schechter, Braff, & Singer, 1984). It is the issue of the (im)permanence of the object's absence that becomes central to the adoptee–searcher's attempt to address her sense of amputation vis-à-vis her biological relatives. In her protest and striving to recover the lost object, which is part of the sequence of innately determined responses to loss described in Bowlby's classic works (1961, 1980), *the searcher does not consciously accept the permanence of the loss.* The adoptee knows it is entirely possible, even likely, that there was no actual death. The shroud between the adoptee and the lost birthparent is not of death but of sociolegal strictures and injunctions. The searcher is prepared to remove that shroud even though in a sense, like the melancholic (clinically depressed) mourner described by Freud, the adoptee ''cannot consciously perceive what it is he has lost'' (1957, p. 245).

More than a decade ago, Wieder (1977a, 1977b) brought our attention to complications in his adopted patients' fantasy lives, particularly with regard to the family romance which, for nonadoptees, serves to relieve the child of routinely experienced anger and disappointment in the parents. Because of some adoptees' fantasies that they had been ''gotten rid of'' by the biological parents and saved or rescued by the adoptive parents, anger toward the latter was too threatening since it carried the risk of reabandonment. Thus Wieder's patients reversed the traditional family romance fantasy, imagining the birthparents in denigrated forms.

On the basis of our exposure to the adoptee who searches, we suggest that, rather than necessarily reversing the fantasy, many adoptees have a complex mixture of fantasies about the birthparents containing both idealization and denigration (Sherick, 1983). The *balance* will vary from adoptee to adoptee and also *within* the individual adoptee at different times in her development. In our own study (Bertocci & Schechter, 1987) most of our respondents recalled being given fairly typical explanations that they had been placed because the birthmother was unable, because of youth and poor financial circumstances, to take care of a child. The adoptee who searches may very well entertain predominantly a *variation* of the paradigmatic family romance fantasy (Freud, 1909/1959, p. 240), that is, that the birthparents are of a *humble* origin though exceptionally *good* and *caring*.[10] It is the latter aspect of the fantasy that beckons many searchers, eager to confirm their own inherent goodness and to reassure a birthmother fantasied as sharing the adoptee's sense of loss. [''I wondered if she cared or ever thought about me at all''; ''I wondered if my birthmother was still sad without knowing me and where I was.'']

The interface of the sense of loss for both adoptee and adoptive parent, with regard to the search, is apparent in the parents' fantasy that the adoptee inherently prefers the birthparents. The adoptive parents' fear of losing their child (e.g., through search) can be a projection of their own unconscious rejection of the adoptee for not being the preferred biological child they could not have (Blum, 1983).

Observers of search phenomena usually note that the adoptee's decision to begin or continue a search is often precipitated by a loss in the adoptee's life, for example, when an adoptive parent dies ["the death of my adoptive mother released me from the collusion we both had to deny this elephant in the living room"] and by other critical life changes, for example, marriage, contemplated or actual parenthood ["when I gave birth to my first child I realized what a hard thing it is to give up a child—I was no longer afraid of being 'rejected again' "]. Since the unconscious observes no time barriers, losses tend to aggregate. The adoptee's emotional energies return to seeking the birthparent since that loss remains potentially reversible. However, the literal object of the search, the birthparent, is typically a means to another end, an attempt to repair aspects of the self that have to do with the sense of disconnectedness from the human race and with the sense of disadvantage vis-à-vis people who are "born rather than adopted."

Envy and Jealousy: Relieving the Sense of Disadvantage Through Search

As alluded to earlier, even under the best of circumstances the adoptive situation is a ripe breeding ground (irony intended) for hypersensitivity to differences and same-nesses, for attempts to account for "where things come from" in explaining observed differences, for rivalries and comparisons, and for concerns with obtaining and holding on to that which is valued. This brings us to consider the pervasiveness of envy and jealousy as they are experienced and expressed in the adoptive situation, with particular reference to their role in the need to search. It is important to emphasize that within certain bounds envy and jealousy are *normative aspects of the human condition*. The adoptive situation is simply, or not so simply, a context that throws their universal dynamics into relief. Here we are concerned with the search as a means of breaking through developmental impasses which originated from unresolved envy and jealousy.

Anderson (1987) has proposed a psychodynamic theory in which mental life is organized by the interplay of envy and jealousy. He indicates that they are separate but mutually dependent psychological response patterns which have their origins in physiological survival mechanisms. He notes that envy and jealousy are usually confused with one another as to meaning and misconstrued as simply denoting affective states. Envy denotes the painful awareness of *lacking* some advantage (i.e., some essential trait, possession, or experience) in comparison with another person. Envy is presented as a complex human experience involving distortions in perceptual, cognitive, affective, and intentional mental functions. When the envious individual compares himself to others, he does not simply perceive differences, he perceives threats. His sense of self is diminished; he feels shamed, humiliated, frightened, outraged, or depressed. He resents the other for possessing the advantage.

In its departure from traditional psychoanalytic theory, envy psychology understands "loss" in terms of *loss of advantage* (Anderson, 1987). Jealousy denotes the *possession* of an advantage threatened with loss to a rival. A typical cognitive distortion occurring throughout the experience of envy and jealous possessiveness is the presumption that the asset or advantage has only limited quantity, as if one person's gain is necessarily another's loss.

Applied to the experience of adoption in the lives of children and parents, in varying degrees and forms, envy and jealousy are inevitable, pervasive, and sometimes painful aspects of life with which all parties must contend throughout the life cycle. Regardless of when and how the adoptee learns of her adoptive status, disclosure may set in motion a continuing sequence of perceiving her difference from the nonadoptee world and of yearning to be the same as others. The fiction of "special" status, sometimes created in the parents' story of the adoption, is at least in part an attempt to compensate for the adoptee's lacking the advantage of blood-tie and for the adoptive parents' possessing it (with their own biological relatives).

Since the adoptee cannot be the same as those others she perceives in the nonadoptive world, she may find herself (unconsciously and perhaps consciously) in a state of envy, with its price of diminished self-esteem and shame and, for some, paralysis and social alienation. ["The greatest effect my being adopted has had is the constant feelings of not being good enough and not being 'like' the others." "I always envied other families who looked like one another." "I felt different from my friends, rather 'unconnected,' envying people who had biological families." "I want to know all the things which non-adoptees take so infuriatingly for granted. I feel that I have somehow been robbed of something vitally important."]

The psychology of envy interprets the adoptee's anger (resentment) not as retaliatory toward the birthparents for the abandonment per se; but, rather, as resentment toward all objects and systems (adoptive parents, birthparents, society-at-large, and the legal structure it supports) that are perceived as having deprived her of the advantage of blood-tie. The adoptee perceives herself as denied the experience of sameness and of being-part-of-a-family which she has been prevented from knowing in the way that biologically related people do. For a number of our respondents the search represented a hoped-for means of breaking the psychological block or impasse they had come to realize characterized their life. ["It was the things that were *not* changing—the anger, mistrust." "I can't help feeling that knowing more about my origins will somehow make future decisions and choices easier." "I want to stop longing for answers. I hope to get on with my life."]

An internal prerequisite for the conscious decision to search is a shift in the adoptee's perceptual and cognitive understanding of the balance of power between herself and her parents. That is, she ascends from a position of perceiving herself as unentitled and indebted (i.e., paralyzing forms of disadvantage) to a position of acknowledging the validity of her feelings and needs, however confused she may be about articulating them. ["Once I made the decision to search, I found that an overwhelming fear about myself as a person began to disappear."] Despite social ideologies to the contrary, the adoptee cognitively may come to recognize that all "elective" parenthood is undertaken first and foremost in order to meet the needs and aspirations of *adults*. Those needs are for the structure and for the social and personal rewards of a family life, as well *perhaps* as the need and desire to nurture a child. In the adoptive situation, this basic fact of life may take an exaggerated (overdetermined) form in the adoptee's perceptions, particularly if family life was characterized by rigid or closed patterns of communication and by little in the way of empathic dialogue (Nickman, 1985).

The search, then, becomes a means for the adoptee to reinforce at an emotional level fragile cognitive (ideational) systems having to do with the "legitimacy" of her inner needs. In Anderson's theory, one option for resolving envy is by eliminating the difference through effort to acquire the desired advantage. Accordingly, the search constitutes the adoptee's conscious attempt to free herself of her sense of disadvantage, for example, of the corrosive resentment and sense of powerlessness that keep important dimensions of her life immobilized through unproductive and unconsciously perpetuated coping patterns.

The problem of the adoptee's envy becomes enmeshed with the problem of the adoptive parents' envy. For instance, the adoptive parents feel robbed (e.g., of "sameness" vis-à-vis their fertile social environment) if the adoption followed failed attempts at pregnancy. They envy the advantages of fecund couples, which include the potential for physical immortality through generational continuity (Blum, 1983), and feel ashamed and resentful of all that they are subjected to by a society that regards adoption as second-best. Success in acquiring a child is envied by those competing in a depleted "market" of available babies. The acquired child then becomes a valued "possession," jealously guarded (against loss of the advantage). This may sometimes underlie the overprotectiveness seen in some adoptive families (Frisk, 1964; Hoopes, 1982; Sorosky, Baran & Pannor, 1977) and mentioned by a number of our respondents (Bertocci & Schechter, 1987). The problem of the adoptive parents' envy and jealousy may become relevant to the search if they have difficulty in acknowledging and accepting the ways in which the adoptive situation varies from biological parenthood (Brodzinsky, 1987; Kirk, 1964). More pointedly, to the extent that the child has to remain unconsciously viewed as a jealously guarded "possession," the search by the adult adoptee will be perceived as a threat and a betrayal. (See Feigelman & Silverman's [1983] finding that fertile adoptive parents tend to be less threatened by search.) To the extent that adoptive parents imagine emotion to have limited quantity (i.e., if the adoptee has any feeling in regard to a birthparent, there will be "less left over" for the adoptive parents), a potential reunion will be viewed with distrust, anxiety, and even hostility. The adoptee is painfully aware of these circumstances when they prevail in her life. Dutifully wishing to avoid "hurting my parents" (a repetitive theme with our respondents), thoughts of search may be put aside, even if felt to be at her own expense.

At the macrocosmic sociopolitical level, the issue of possession or ownership of children (Derdeyn, 1979), which influences all aspects of child welfare (e.g., foster care, custody), continues to be pervasively reflected in the reluctance society and the law have shown in giving priority to the needs of its children. In our view the issue of possession or ownership of children remains a central dynamic in the maintenance of the sealed adoption record.

Complications in Sexual Development and Their Relation to Search

At the same time that the adoptee experiences herself as disadvantaged, she also possesses certain advantages over the adoptive parents, perhaps the most powerfully experienced being her anticipated fertility. Regardless of the cause of the parents' infertility (where this is relevant), in the literal communications to the child, it is always the *mother* who was "unable to get pregnant." Thus in the development of the adopted female, the most fundamental difference from the parent with whom she will most closely identify will be her presumed capacity to bear a child. Herein lies a central source of the mother's envy and shame and the daughter's jealous possession and guilt as they may repeatedly play off each other via various projections and displacements.

In the only published longitudinal study (birth through latency) of sex differences in the extent and form that normal children express adoption ideas, Farber (1977) reported that girls seemed much more invested and involved with adoption themes than boys; girls were particularly invested in the issues related to pregnancy and birth. The study concluded, in part, that the central issue for female children in latency seemed to be not the fact of adoption but the "problem of working out a feminine identification with a mother who had difficulty or inability in bearing babies" (p. 648). Related to this the girls seemed also concerned over the possible rivalry with mother (i.e., concerns about *being* envied), which their own potential for conceiving might engender.

In addition to the common themes of envy and rivalry in this regard, the question has also been raised whether sexual feelings are suppressed or repressed as easily or as fully as in the biologically related family (Easson, 1973). For instance, adopted adults have reported retrospectively that the lack of blood-tie was used as the rationalization when traumatic incestuous sexual seductions occurred.[11] But even under healthy circumstances, the sexual tensions between the adopted female adolescent and males in the family have a valence of a different intensity than that in the biological family. Memories of these tensions remain vivid years later when, in activating a search, the adoptee decides it is time to know once and for all to whom she is and is not related.

And so, central to the female adoptee's struggle with her sexual identity may be an ambivalent identification with the barren (in fantasy—asexual) or damaged adoptive mother. Fantasizing about pregnancy, and sometimes literally acting it out, can represent the adoptee's attempt to alter that identification, that is, to reassure herself of *not* being (damaged) like her mother. Pregnancy fantasies can also represent an attempt to achieve a closer bond with the adoptive mother through providing her with the baby she could not have herself. Actual pregnancy can represent defiant flaunting of the advantage vis-à-vis the adoptive parents. Also, the adoptee's pregnancy can constitute both an unconscious reunion with the birthmother through reenacting her pregnancy and an unconscious attempt to restitute lost nurturance. For both sexes, the choice of sexual and love partner(s) can be influenced by fantasies of the birthparents, and a symbolic search can be a common unconscious dynamic.

With regard to the relevance of sexual issues to the literal search, to expand on a speculation mentioned in Farber's (1977) investigation, the adopted woman may maintain an inner sense of unreality ("as if") about the integrity and capacity of her own body, particularly to reproduce. In having no internalized sense of having been born herself, the adopted woman may regard the process of pregnancy and giving birth with foreboding or awe, and in any event much confusion. ["I finally feel able to be a mother myself, which I couldn't even consider 'til I found my birthmother."]

Her search for the birthmother could represent her attempt to form a connection (identification) with the only object that can confirm and consolidate her body-image and her internalized self-perception as capable of human reproduction. However, in this aspect, of those respondents to our survey who associated the need to search with the issue of having children, the majority mentioned having already had one or two children. The search was typically conceived as a means of establishing hereditary links, including medical protection, for their children as much as for themselves. ["My children only tie my roots into the future, not the past; what is a person without his past and true identity?" "It's one thing to be a second-class citizen oneself, it's quite another to condemn one's children to no information or heritage."] Hodges (1984) noted that, for the adoptee, producing a child means producing "someone with whom there can be resemblances and in identification with whom, perhaps, one may find a biological parent who is there to resemble" (p. 52). For our respondents described above, having a child was not a solution to the wish to encounter the birthparent but, rather, intensified the need for it.

In pondering the reasons for relinquishment, it is common for adoptees to fix on particular features which they imagine may have been responsible for the birthmother's decision. In addition to unacceptable physical features, adoptees sometimes imagine that the birthmother would have kept them had they been of the other sex (Hodges, 1984). This fantasy can be an underlying dynamic in adopted children's imitation of the opposite sex and in confused sexual identity as seen clinically in older adoptees.

The sexual development of the adopted male most certainly has its own variations and complications (without implying psychopathology), although much less is known about it. Bertocci and Schechter (1987) have noted the paucity of clinical material about the adult adopted male, and in the few empirical studies of adoptees, males are markedly underrepresented. In attempting to understand sexual development in the male adoptee, with particular reference to search behavior, one is forced to speculations, some of which reflect common psychosocial ideas about differences between the sexes. For instance sociologists emphasize the greater importance women place in family relationships, women occupying "a pivotal position in the maintenance of kinship ties" (Feigelman & Silverman, 1983, p. 202). In informal collegial contacts, psychologists have proposed that search-for-mother may stimulate longings for dependency that are stereotypically less acceptable for the male. Adoptees themselves tend to speak of the female's greater psychological (conscious) access to issues bearing on emotions and on the body. For example, since reproduction-related functions (menstruation as well as pregnancy) are not an intimate feature of the male's routine experience as it is for the female, he may not experience adoption-related matters as overtly conflict-ridden as the female does. The above notions may tend to explain why the male adoptee appears to be less likely to activate search fantasies. Bertocci and Schechter (1987) speculate that females more than males are able to form and sustain empathic fantasies regarding the birthmother's conflicts concerning relinquishment. This may account for the apparent predominance of female searchers.

In the interest of beginning more of a dialogue in the clinical literature about the psychology of the adult male adoptee, we offer the following case vignette.[12] Despite some atypical aspects, the report highlights a number of issues referred to in this chapter, but with particular attention to the interrelationships between confused identity about being human, anxiety about women, and ambivalence about the search.

Eric, a single graduate student in his early 30s, came to the university mental health service with a concern that initially sounded familiar enough in a "healthy student population": he could not seem to sustain his relationships with women for very long.Though this had been a pattern for many years, it was now interfering with his concentration on his studies. For reasons he could not understand, he experienced incapacitating panic attacks after the early stage of any relationship. These would seem to occur in a context of his hypersensitivity to nuances in the woman's behavior that led him to suspect that she might "leave him for another man." He would then break off contact with her altogether. Eric acknowledged a similar pattern of abrupt departures in his previous contacts with therapists.

Eric had found himself continually distracted by his mounting conviction that his difficulty in sustaining any relationship with a woman related to his suspicions that he might be adopted. (Meanwhile his therapist had at the outset noted the disparity between his dark, possibility racially mixed features and his Scandinavian surname.) Eric then presented the various reasons for his suspicions which were striking for the fact that he was obviously adopted but had, until now, maintained the family's denial fairly intact. These reasons included hushed references in the family to the mother's having had a hysterectomy some years prior to Eric's birth, and Eric's having overheard his father express doubts about the wisdom of "getting" him when the family's finances had turned out to be unstable. During the middle of his short-term treatment Eric managed to share his confusion with his parents. He had always felt quite attached to them despite a chronic irritation with them. He attributed the latter in part to their vagueness about the facts of his birth. (Eric had been placed at a few weeks of age.)

When finally confronted, his parents admitted his adoption, confessing their fears of hurting him. The confirmation of his suspicions left Eric feeling "disoriented" and preoccupied more than ever with his ethnic background: "I don't know what I am, I even wonder what race I am, maybe I'm an alien from space." Nevertheless now that his adoption was confirmed, "the rock that's been sitting in my stomach as long as I can remember is now gone."

Eric, who all along "knew but didn't know" he was adopted, then discussed at some length his troubles with women which he felt related directly to his adoptive status. In his adolescence and young adulthood he had had a "promiscuous past," but in recent years he had started to date people with whom he sought an emotional involvement. Eric was often confused as to who was more anxious about closeness: his girlfriends typically had troubled histories involving neglect or abuse. Always, he had limited his choices of women to those with very different coloring from his own. "I wouldn't want to get involved with someone I might be related to."

By the latter part of his treatment, Eric was beginning to drift away from his latest girlfriend. He believed that he now needed to find his birthmother, stating that otherwise he would not be able to resolve "subconscious needs" he could not define or explain. He had decided to obtain birth information from the agency that had placed him. He struggled to digest the little he was initially told about his birthparents, still wondering about some details but not inclined to inquire further. Meanwhile his intentions to leave school were firmer than ever as he reflected on the meaning of the field he had chosen, cultural anthropology, a perpetual search for his ethnic and racial identity.

Consolidation of Identity

In any reference to the adoptee's seeking of information about biological relatives, and in reference to the psychology of the adoptee generally, probably no concept is used more frequently and with less definitional clarity than that of "identity" (Brodzinsky, 1987). Adoptees themselves typically comment on "the part of me that's missing" and on their desire to "find out who I really am," to "learn my true identity," and so forth. Such statements may too readily be taken as indicative of significant underlying psychopathology. There is a difference, notes Abend (in press), between true identity problems and a disturbed "sense of identity" as experienced *subjectively*.

There is no consensus on the meaning of identity though it is associated with developmental issues of childhood and adolescence. Writers tend to emphasize different dimensions, both generally (Abend, 1974) and with respect to problems for the adoptee (Brinich, 1980; Frisk, 1964; Haimes, 1987; Kornitzer, 1971; Sorosky et al., 1975). Definitions in general references point to qualities of *sameness* (similarities to other individuals and also qualities that are consistent over time) and of *difference* (aspects of the self that distinguish one person from all others) (Abend, 1974, in press). The present authors find particular merit in Abend's (1974) definition of identity, which is the sense in which we use the concept in this chapter:

> a loosely organized set of conscious and preconscious self-representations that serve to define the individual in a variety of social contexts. These self-representations are formed at a relatively high level of psychic development and are therefore complex products of instinctual drives, defenses, identifications, and sublimations . . . some degree of change over time . . . is to be expected in the various parameters of identity. . . . Ideas . . . may contain some notion of the future . . . which could contribute to a sense of continuity. (p. 620)

Even within the subgroup of adoptees who are searchers, there are differences in the subjective sense of identity as to whether it is experienced in dichotomy (e.g., the fantasy of a "false" self as an adoptee vs. the "real" self pertaining to the biological family) or in unity (Haimes, 1987). Complications for the adoptee are related to their "dual identity" (Sorosky et al., 1975) with respect to self-representations influenced by two sets of parents (Brinich, 1980). The points to be emphasized are that identity does not have closure in adolescence or young adulthood but continues to evolve over the life span and that through the search adoptees are seeking a reconciliation and cohesion of many complex perceptions, cognitive systems, and self-object representations. Consolidation of identity, then, is an all-encompassing theme running through all issues addressed in this chapter and reflected in the comments of our respondents (Bertocci & Schechter, 1987).

Reconciliation of Cognitive Dissonance and Internalization of Locus of Control

In his *A Theory of Cognitive Dissonance,* Festinger (1957) defines consonance and dissonance as the fitting and nonfitting relations between pairs of "elements." These "elements" or "cognitions" are the things a person knows about herself, her behavior, and her environment. "The relation between . . . two elements is dissonant if . . . the one does not, or would not be expected to, follow from the other" (p. 15). When there is tension between consonant and dissonant elements, Festinger states there is a need for dissonance–reduction through activity. He notes, "Dissonance acts in the same way as a state of drive or need or tension" (p. 18). He also indicates, "A fear of dissonance would lead to a reluctance to take action—a reluctance to commit oneself" (p. 31).

There are numerous examples of dissonant elements in the lives of adopted persons. To cite a few:

1. Adoptees have an amended birth certificate which states that they were born to their adoptive parents; however, the adoptee has been told she was born to a different set of parents (whom society calls "real" or "natural").
2. When adoptees are asked as school children to prepare a family tree, or when a physician asks for familial medical history, the adoptee finds herself in a conflicted bind.
3. The adoptee may be told as part of her birth story that she was relinquished for adoption because her birthmother loved her. Does love equate to abandonment (as the child subjectively experiences it)?
4. If the adoptee was "given up" once, might she be given up again, particularly if she offends the presumptively loving adoptive parents by thinking about, talking about, or actually activating the search?
5. Adoptees who note physical and personality dissimilarities to their adoptive parents are often confounded when outsiders remark on similarities which they believe they perceive. The adopted person is increasingly aware with age that there is no genetic connection between herself and the adopters; similarities are experienced as "unreal" rather than coincidental.
6. Adoptees contending with empathic deficits in the parents hear messages from the social environment that they were "lucky to be adopted" and must have been "specially wanted."

The search, therefore, whether early (intrapsychic) or late (activated) in life, is an attempt to reconcile cognitive dissonances, to bring order out of a sense of chaos, and to gain active control over forces to which the adoptee has had to respond passively in the past. ["I decided to actually search because I had heard too many stories that clashed together or just didn't make sense. I want to find out the truth—I need to KNOW."] Having experienced herself as subject to the vicissitudes of a capricious fate, the adoptee, through searching (a unique *rite de passage*) attempts to bring the locus of control (Rotter, 1975) from "out there" to "inside" herself. It is a way the individual can experience the self as capable of actively "acting upon" the environment rather than passively "being acted upon"—a major factor in the establishment of a healthier identity.

Perception of Difference and Body Image

The impact of perceived differences with particular regard to physical appearance, has been referred to by many authors (Feigelman & Silverman, 1983; Frisk, 1964; Hodges, 1984; Kowal & Schilling, 1985; Sherick, 1983; Sobol & Cardiff, 1983;

Sorosky et al., 1978; Triseliotis, 1973), but reference has been only in passing. The importance to the adoptive *parents* of the issue of resemblance is mentioned in the follow-up study by Jaffee and Fanshel (1970) and in Blum's (1983) reference to "the narcissism of self-perpetuation" (p. 151). The British follow-up study by Raynor (1980) found that both adoptees and adoptive parents "were much more often satisfied (with the adoptive experience) when they "were able to perceive or even imagine likenesses between them" (p. 59). The importance of the issue of (lack of) resemblance for the adoptee, and its meaning, has not yet been adequately addressed.

Similarly, researchers in the area of body image have not considered the significance of perceived physical similarities in the development of the young child's body image. This is particularly interesting given the omnipresent social references in ordinary experience to how a child resembles its parents. Indeed, people often cannot restrain themselves from commenting on it, even when there may be striking dissimilarities. ["Each time someone remarked on a resemblance I felt confused and tongue-tied." "I hated the way people made a big deal of figuring out who I resembled because I desperately wanted to *really* look like someone in my family—I was constantly searching for someone whom I looked like in any way."]

For the adoptee, however, note that inherent in the perception of differences is, consciously or unconsciously, an awareness of those "other parents" whom she resembles more ("a stranger who looks like me"), but whose recall stimulates again an awareness of having been relinquished. Sants (1964) and Hodges (1984) come the closest to recognizing that there is missing in the adoptee's life the reciprocal perception of body similarities between child and parent, which occurs subliminally in the biological family (where dissimilarities are typically overlooked). In struggling to construct mental representations of the birthparents, the adoptee has only her own body to go by; however, some adoptees reportedly experience lacunae in their own body image since they could not find the biological mirror. ["I had no concept of what I would look like and I had no one to share concerns unique to my physical self."] Further, since the adoptee's body, in infancy, was all that the birthmother knew of her, the body itself can become associated with relinquishment, for example, defectiveness (Hodges, 1984). ["Certainly I felt inadequate simply because my differences were pointed out."] Body image, then, becomes inevitably linked with larger aspects of self-esteem. ["I've had ridiculous expectations for myself which made it difficult to enjoy life. . . . There has been a need always to prove to a faceless parent that I was good."]

The sense of impoverishment that our respondents (Bertocci & Schechter, 1987) expressed the most passionately and with the most frequency had to do with their craving to see physical similarities, if only through photographs, between themselves and biological relatives. ["Sometimes I think 'There is someone out there that I look like' and I can't believe it."] This need to see themselves as part of a family *in some concrete form* was unavailable to them in the adoptive family regardless of whether some coincidental similarities could be perceived. ["Once I know who I look like, I will be a complete person."]

Particularly if this sense of impoverishment is coupled with the adoptive parents' own narcissistic injuries or empathic deficits, the adoptee is left to feel especially alone in the world. The theme of "why me?" is part of the experience of envy and self-diminishment that comes to pervade such an adoptee's daily life. The association between the perception of differences, envy, self-diminishment, and a sense of emptiness and amputation or castration is illustrated by a young man in our survey who commented on the small size of his feet which were so unlike his adoptive father's: ["Even today, I still cannot fill my father's shoes"].

(As important as perceived similarities appear to be for many adopted people, we would strongly add the caveat that in no way should their significance be taken as support for arguments that would override other considerations in the placement of children, such as emotional attachments [Goldstein et al., 1973]).

The sense of incompleteness, then, is often expressed in the concrete context of the issue of physical (dis)similarities but is experienced in many different forms and variations. In our clinical work we find it commonplace to hear adoptees making references, often associated with body-image issues, to spaces within themselves ["a sense of emptiness," "a hole in myself," "a large gap that needs to be filled"] as well as spaces outside themselves ["I hoped the search would lift me out of the hole I had dug myself into"; "I don't yet feel there is a place for me in this world"; "I wondered if I was extraterrestrial"] as representing a painful sense of inadequacy, deficiency, and detachment from humanity. The activated search becomes a last-resort attempt to alter these feelings and self-perceptions.

Attachment

Bonding between child and adult is an intimate, continuous, and consistent interplay of communication. The adult gives evidence of recognizing the expressions and intuiting the child's emotions at every level of function and need. The adult responds to these feelings with actions based on an empathic sense of the child's inner state. If the parents are unable spontaneously to reflect (in infancy and throughout their child's life) and then respond appropriately to the child's needs as they evolve, the bonding or attachment may be strained (Bowlby, 1980). Shared features, behavioral and physical, are part of what permit continuation and strengthening of feelings of connectedness—a feeling of belonging and of permanence.

In order to fully separate and individuate (Mahler, Pine, & Bergman 1975), one must first be firmly attached. The introjection of the parents—their values, goals, morality, ethics, and so forth—is a basic element of a stable self-image. However, the other set of "real parents" may introduce a certain tenuousness with reference to the parental (adoptive) introjects. Where the adoptive parents are struggling with their own insecurities around attachment, the dilemma for the adoptee may be how to feel a sense of belonging without being possessed. As an extreme expression of this: ["Since I was little I had a feeling of not being where I belonged. . . . My mother never wanted me to be a separate person. I was an extension of herself."]. Whereas it appears that mother–infant attachment is the same in adoptive and nonadoptive families (Singer et al., 1985), the subsequent awareness of difference and the evolving meanings of being adopted occur first in latency and then become increasingly defined through the life cycle (Brodzinsky, 1987).

The adolescent, adopted or nonadopted, psychologically separates and disengages from her parents by being different and distinct through alternate actions, dress, mimicking heroines and heroes, and experimenting with value systems; she disjoins herself from the internalized image of the parents and all they stood for in the past.

Here the dilemma for some adoptees, however, is both how to separate from their adoptive parents without losing them, and also how to separate (individuate) from internalized images (albeit entirely fantasy) of their biological parents whose physical attributes, values, vocations, personalities, and so forth are at best vaguely known and therefore exert a magnetic pull. How, in other words, is it possible to disattach from someone with whom you have not in reality attached and toward whom the vacuum of information draws you? ["I always wondered what my parents (biological) did. . . . I would be driven to all kinds of things to study or activities to do, wondering did my family do this? Should I have an aptitude for it?"] The attachment to the birthparents has been forcibly maintained in fantasy. These issues are illustrated by the following case.

> Jody was a 13-year-old who matured early. With physical maturation, her academic performance plummeted. Her friendships with children of similar socioeconomic and educational backgrounds deteriorated and she persistently began running away from her home. Her adoptive parents were puzzled and angered by her behaviors which were totally unexplained by Jody. Periodically, from ages 13 to 15, Jody raised questions about her birthparents, and she repeated "the facts" of her relinquishment as told to her originally at age 5. These "facts" were that Jody's birthmother was unmarried and too poor to care for her. The birthmother, out of her love and concern for Jody, decided on adoptive placement. Jody's wandering away from home continued increasingly, and for longer periods of time. The adoptive parents noted she was always found together with families, not just a single male companion, who were of much lower socioeconomic, vocational, and intellectual levels than the adoptive family or Jody herself. When this was specifically inquired about, Jody's response was that she was *more comfortable* with people of the *same class* as she imagined her birthmother to be from. Disadvantage had more meaning for her than the material and cultural advantages of her adoptive family. At age 16, Jody married a young man from one of these families, a family with many relatives and in which there were a number of out-of-wedlock pregnancies.

The Innate Need to Experience Human Connectedness

The human being has the capacity in adulthood to remember the past, savor the present, and conceptualize the future. The capacity to anticipate the future serves in part as a survival mechanism; it fortifies the individual's sense of potential control over forthcoming events in life experience and, in so doing, maintains anxiety at manageable levels. The ability to perceive oneself in the present and the capacity to anticipate the future is highly influenced by the past and present developments within one's own birthfamily (e.g., the course of one's physical maturation and body changes over the life span; one's vulnerabilities to genetically related diseases). From the perspective of the adoptee, all genetically related diseases are possible since none can be ruled out. When the individual is disconnected from her biological family of origin, important aspects of the past and the future are obscured. ["I seem so different from my family—I need to know that I was a person before I was six months old." "My preoccupations with my birthparents prevented me from fantasizing a lot about my future. There was no concept of the possible span of my lifetime, just a past and an eternal present globbed together."] A respondent who had completed her search: ["I no longer feel that I was 'happened'—I now know that I was 'born' just like everyone else. I am less afraid of aging and I have a better sense of myself."]

It appears that adoptees may attach to their adoptive families but not necessarily *assimilate*, particularly if dissonances and differences (as described above) are sufficiently marked so as to cause intrapsychic tension. With the psychological need to separate pushed by the biological changes of adolescence, the dissonances and differences for the adoptee are highlighted and eventually create, in our view, *a driven need to experience human connectedness*. This craving grows with time, experienced subjectively by some adoptees as equivalent to starvation. We believe this concept more accurately identifies the adoptee's fundamental anguish than the concepts of "genealogical bewilderment" (Sants, 1964), "need for human continuity" (Pannor et al., 1974), or threatened sense of "biological identity" (Winkler & Midford, 1986). The latter concepts strike us as emphasizing cognitive aspects of the experience without engaging the profundity of the affective experience. As we tried to suggest above, we draw a clear distinction between the seeking of human connectedness and the seeking of object attachment. The latter concept refers to a normal propensity of human beings throughout the life cycle to form and maintain "strong affectional bonds to particular others" (Bowlby, 1980, p. 39). Adopted people are generally as capable of healthy object attachments as nonadoptees; still, some harbor deep within a sense of being "like human" without being "really human." A male respondent to our survey who evaluated his adoptive experience as satisfactory indicated: ["I might feel more real, more valid, if my origins were confirmed for me. This may sound crazy, but how can I know that I exist if I don't know how I came into existence or from whence, where, and when?"] Also from a woman satisfied with her adoption: ["People said my daughter resembled my husband more than me. This made me feel very isolated, as though I were not even human."] Another adoptee described her postsearch experience: ["I felt at peace inside—I finally knew she (birthmother) was okay, and that I wasn't hatched as I'd sometimes thought as a child."]

Apparently innate aspects of the human capacity for attachment and for intersubjective relatedness have come to be understood only through extensive research in early childhood development (Stern, 1985). Similarly, the innate need for human connectedness, which evolves along with the development of cognition and abstract thinking, continuing its elaboration throughout the life span, may come to be understood only through study of those whose deprivation of it has made us aware of its existence.

Conclusion

The need to search has to do with a craving, much of it having innate sources, for particular psychological experiences missing in the lives of certain adopted people. In an attempt to integrate and illustrate the issues that bear on those psychological experiences, we offer the case vignette of Amy.

> Amy, an exquisite university student in her early 20s, came to the mental health service to discuss her confusion and anxiety about her career plans now that completion of her degree was within reach. As she shared her earlier history she described an event in her early childhood, about age 5, when she was informed of her status and thereafter "something within me forever changed." She experienced "a feeling of not belonging, of being acknowledged as not looking like somebody—a feeling of alienation. Maybe until that

point it wasn't important that I didn't look like someone in order to belong, because I never noticed. Now I didn't fit in any more. For the first time, the difference made a difference."

The "status" which Amy had suddenly come to learn about herself had nothing to do with adoption. She was not adopted. Amy was born within an interracial marriage, mother a White European, father a Black American serviceman. No one had ever before commented on any lack of physical resemblance between herself and either of her parents. The event occurred on a European sidewalk as Amy and her mother passed another woman and child. The other child pointed to Amy and said, "Look at that little Negro child." Amy recalls feeling hurt as, for the first time, she noted that her own skin tone was significantly darker than her mother's. Amy had never before thought of her mother as "white," only as "Mother"; she had thought of herself as "colorless." Suddenly Amy was confronted with a world of contrasts and differences. These began with perceptions of variations in skin coloration and eventually extended in an overdetermined way to features, race, socioeconomic status, and power inequities between males and females.

Amy's father died unexpectedly when she was 11. Years later, as Amy's body fully matured, relatives began to comment on her physical resemblance to her father. On learning about the similar eyes, high cheekbones, and sturdy frame, Amy said she felt enormously reassured: "It's nice to know what features you share with your parents. It makes you feel you belong." As she emerged from a turbulent adolescence, Amy had developed sympathies with the "underprivileged" of all varieties; intellectually she had found a "unified system" in the ideologies of Black feminism. Amy herself represented her interest in Black issues generally as "a search for my father and his culture." Idiosyncratically dressed, accented by combat boots, Amy now felt drawn socially to a counterculture area of the city where, having found a "home of those who are different," she could "blend in."

The case of Amy presented us with some irresistible features that offer both similarities and contrasts with the adoptees we have been discussing. Perception of difference, lowered self-esteem, healthy adaptation, and symbolic search for the lost object through identification with it—all these are shared experiences for adoptees and nonadoptees alike. Amy illustrates the cognitive change that begins with the oedipal period and leads to radical reorganization perceptually and affectively. She, in fact, uses some of the same language as some adoptee–searchers, for example, her intense feelings as a child of alienation and not belonging. The contrast with adoptees, however, is equally striking, for Amy never questions whether she is fully and authentically a member of the human race. Though she mourned the lost father, she never alludes to a pervasive inner sense of amputation or disconnection. And though she struggled to find a group of people with whom she could identify and "blend," she had no enduring sense of emptiness or incompleteness about herself as a person. Information about her past, when needed for integrative purposes, was available to her. She was anxious about her career choices for reasons other than an incapacity to envision her future.

In asserting that activated search is primarily a phenomenon of adulthood, we propose that the intrapsychic stage for the adoptee's need to seek a literal encounter with the birthparent is usually set by a combination of factors, including (1) the gradual emancipation from the internalized representations of the adoptive parents, which can take well into the 20s and 30s; (2) establishment of social ties and supports outside the family; (3) the more active contemplation of parenthood or the actual transition to parenthood (i.e., the awesome encounter with a biological relative—one's own child—for the first time); (4) the acquisition of life experience, with reflection on already-established patterns of functioning and relating; and (5) attempts at more realistic or concrete conceptualizations of one's own personal future, physically and psychologically, which potentially draw much of their validation from knowledge of genetic antecedents.

SOME COMMENTS ON SOCIAL POLICY
ON ACCESS TO BIRTH INFORMATION

["Connectedness to an adopted person is like water to a person in the desert. You spend your whole life having it hidden, denied, and desecrated."]

From our understanding of the biopsychosocial complexities of the adopted person's need to search, and of the internal resolutions which evidently come from the completed search, it obviously follows that we support the adoptee's access to full birth information. From the few states (United States) and countries permitting the adoptee's access to birth information, no substantive evidence has emerged to support the fears and claims used to defend the sealing of the adoption record. We are not surprised by investigators' discoveries that adoption personnel have a priori tended to question the normality and stability of the adoptee–searcher (Haimes & Timms, 1985). Our own view is that pervasive irrational anxieties about relinquishment exist in the social unconscious and are manifest in the prevailing atmosphere of distrust of the adoptee–searcher (Small, 1979). Attending hostilities toward the adoptee, however subtle, become projected onto the adoptee in the form of prejudging her as potentially intrusive, retributive, and so on.

The treatment of the child as a commodity for the adoption market is no more evident than in the area of independent placements in states where little or no professional regulation is mandated. But even with agency placements, particularly public agencies, the protection of the adoptee through maintenance of records, in our experience, has tended to be haphazard and at the pleasure of the individual administrator. In recognition that adoption is a lifelong process for all parties to it, a multiplicity of services is required before and after the child's placement. The need for these services beyond the placement should compel the provision of adequate legislation, funding, and staffing, with expansion of research efforts at all levels (Baran & Pannor, Chapter 17).

In addition to increasing services and research, formal curricula should be developed in order to train more adequately all whose employment bears even indirectly on adoption; in particular, training is essential for social workers, lawyers, physicians, educators, and mental health professionals (Winkler et al., 1988).

It is important to note that in the United States, adoption—which involves some of the most sensitive, fragile, and complicated aspects of all human services—has historically been "more completely in the hands of lay persons than any other area of social welfare" (Silverman & Weitzman, 1986, p. 2). This has particularly been the tendency in public welfare agencies handling placements (Cole & Donley, Chapter 15). There is, further, the problem of persisting lay attitudes among professionally trained adoption workers, for example, the assumption that the need to search implies either a criticism of the adoptive family or a wish to have remained with the birth-parent.

With regard to the adopted person's access to birth information, we believe that no effort should be spared in assuring the preservation and provision of all records pertaining to the adoptee's birth and birthparentage, including hospital and updated health records. The adoptee should have the protection of a professional adoptee advocacy team charged with representing the child at placement (if independent) and, for all adoptees, available on request at any other subsequent point in the adoptee's development. Such a team should include a jurist, a specialist in child development, and any other advocate or specialist who can make a contribution relevant to the particular adoptee's needs. Ideally the adoptee would have access to needed information within the context of an encounter with an adoptee–advocate rather than in the context of "counseling," which too easily risks a patronizing undercurrent (Smith, 1976). With regard to the psychological needs of the adoptee, the various attempts to circumvent the open record—for example, state registries (which, for complicated reasons, relatively few birthmothers utilize) and compulsory intermediary systems—abrogate one of the most fundamental principles of social work practice, self-determination. Under such systems the locus of control, which the search serves to remedy, remains outside the adoptee, thereby keeping her in a position of passivity and dependence. There is also the unsupportable assumption that reunions mediated by adoption workers have better outcomes than reunions worked out solely by the adoptee and birthparent themselves.

It is undoubtedly evident that throughout our consideration of the theoretical, clinical, and human issues involved in the search, we take a firm and unequivocal stand that the needs of children—those who are the most vulnerable and in no way responsible for the events affecting them (in this case the adoptee)—should take precedence over the presumed needs and alleged rights of adults. From this most fundamental principle follow certain conclusions as to how adoption practice must be altered if it is to serve rationally, responsibly, and compassionately. In adoption as in other contexts of child welfare, failure to accord children priority assures the perpetuation of needless emotional suffering from generation to generation.

We would finally note the bizarre paradox that the foster care system determinedly maintains the biological tie at all costs, even at risk of continued neglect or even abuse for the child. The system of adoption with legal transfer of the child's ownership, however, determinedly severs the biological tie at all costs, even at risk of potential lifelong complications for the adoptee (Triseliotis, 1984).

SUMMARY

The need to search, which for some adoptees comes to have compelling and driven components, has multiple, interrelated sources in: (1) genetically predisposed aspects of personality organization, including innate response patterns to loss, to attachment, and to cognitive dissonances which become intrinsic to adoptive status; (2) psychodynamically influenced response patterns to the perception of difference and to the sense of disadvantage. Perception of difference, particularly the missing experience of likeness-to-self, is associated with the cognitive awareness of having been relinquished. All of the above issues are profoundly impacted by the adoptive parents' own particular personality constellations, defenses, and attitudes; (3) pervasive social attitudes toward adoption as second-best and toward the adoptee as "different" (mysterious origins ≅ not to be trusted). These attitudes have originated in, and been reinforced by, legal systems and constructions (e.g., the sealed record) which, under the guise of protecting all parties to adoption, serve in fact to "protect" the adoptee as a "possession" of the adoptive parents and to "protect" society from the adoptee.

The search therefore constitutes the adoptee's attempt to repair a sense of loss, relieve the sense of disadvantage, consolidate identity issues including body image and sexual identity, resolve cognitive dissonances, internalize the locus of control, and satisfy the most fundamental need to experience human connectedness.

If we could finally "know for the first time" the place where the adoptee-searcher has been trying to lead us, in her striving to feel fully human, we might make some discoveries, too, about many aspects of our own humanity. ["I really love my adoptive parents but I was so different from them. . . . I hope to find a person that looks like me and who looks at life the way I do. I want to close the circle of my life."]

ACKNOWLEDGMENTS

We wish to thank the Adoption Forum of Philadelphia, the New York Chapter of the Alma Society, and the Adoption Circle (New York) for their cooperation in distributing our questionnaire. Most of all we want to thank the adopted people who responded so earnestly to our survey. We hope that we have made some contribution toward their need to search being better understood.

NOTES

1. While search phenomena may pertain to persons adopted by relatives, reference in this chapter is to persons adopted by nonrelatives.

2. As of this writing, the adoption record remains sealed in nearly all states in the U.S. and provinces in Canada and Australia. We have been unable to ascertain the legal status of adoption records in countries other than England, Finland, Israel, Scotland, and Sweden, where adult adoptees have access to original birth information.

3. Throughout this chapter the pronoun she or her is used but is representative of either gender. We elected this pronominal form since it appears, from a perusal of the membership of adoptee search organizations and of all published studies, that a majority of searchers are female.

4. The full psychological repercussions in children and adults are yet to be studied for those born of the revolution in reproductive technologies. Included in this cohort would be those conceived through artificial insemination, in vitro fertilization, the use of surrogates, and embryo transfer. These serve as examples where knowledge of the genealogical background is often unknown in at least one of the donors (e.g., ovum or sperm) or entirely irretrievable because of the use of pooled samples, frozen zygotes, etc. More to the point, they serve as examples wherein a product-oriented society sacrifices vital aspects of human psychology, many of which are directly relevant to the adopted person as discussed in this chapter (Learner, 1986).

5. Requests to open the record for "due cause" are usually denied by the court.

6. We use this concept as developed by Festinger (1957); we discuss its particular relevance to search later in this chapter.

7. This chapter does not address other defense-related issues and dynamics that may pertain in individual circumstances—that is, search as a partially maladaptive solution.

8. Three adoptee search support organizations offered to distribute our seven-page questionnaire that included both fixed-answer and open-ended questions. Though the organizations were locally based, our responses came from 14 different states from across the United States. The total number of usable returns was 94. Of these, 76 of the respondents (81%) were female and 18 (19%) were male.

9. Most of our respondents had little information about the birthparents (and reference was usually only to the birthmother), and what little they possessed had neither a positive nor a negative valence overtly, for example, ["young, unmarried, and unable to care for a baby"]. A smaller group had no information at all or did not answer the question. Of the 17 respondents whose descriptions of the birthparent carried a definite valence, 14 were positive—for example, variations of "she was unable to care for me but loved me so much that she wanted a better life for me."

10. "Many children, in their Oedipus daydreams, develop fantastic ideas of not really being the child of their parents; they dream of being some kind of foundling, an offspring of some family of very different social standing; this may be either a high and especially privileged family or a very poor and low one *[sic!]*" (Fenichel, 1945, p. 96). It is noteworthy that the paradigm has elected exclusively the former.

11. The definition of incest may be as confused within the adoptive family as it is within the law: aside from the nearly universal slight of sexual behaviors other than intercourse, penal codes for two-thirds of the states (U.S.) use "consanguinity" as the criteria for incest (Herman, 1981), with no mention of other forms of familial relationships, for example, adoption. We subscribe to a definition which comprehends that the essential connection between parent and child is *psychological,* not biological (similarly between any parent–surrogate, such as stepparent, or other relative, and the child). Accordingly, we would define incest as the corruption and abandonment of necessary parental–familial functions (e.g., nurturing, protection, containment of impulses), usually together with exploitation of the child's trust (i.e., the abuse of power), through any form of sexual activity with a family member regardless of whether blood tie exists. Sexual activity between consenting adults who are related by either law (as in adoption) or biology still constitutes, in our view, violation of appropriate familial psychological boundaries, and thus remains a form of incest.

12. All case material in this chapter has been modified in whatever way was required to maintain full confidentiality.

II

RESEARCH ON ADOPTION

5
Outcome in Adoption: Lessons from Longitudinal Studies

MICHAEL BOHMAN AND SÖREN SIGVARDSSON

As a legal measure to protect abandoned and socially deprived children, adoption has rather recent traditions in Europe and Great Britain. While legislation on adoption for the benefit of the child was first introduced in the United States in the mid-nineteenth century, such laws were not enacted on the European continent or in Great Britain until some hundred years later. For instance, the first Swedish Adoption Act came into force in 1917, but not until 1959 did adopted children become full legal members of their new families. In the German Federal Republic modern adoption laws were not implemented until 1977. This reluctance to recognize the legal rights of the adopted child may reflect the fundamental importance of biological family relationships in Roman–European legal tradition, which still prevails in most European countries.

ADOPTION AND FOSTERING

Despite the traditions noted above, adoption has now become a respectable and socially sanctioned way of caring for children who for some reason cannot grow up with their biological parents. Since World War II, adoption has also been used as a way of dealing with the problems of deprived and displaced children from underdeveloped countries. In this chapter, however, we will restrict ourselves to children born and adopted in their own country—in this case, Sweden.

Adoption and fostering are often wrongly treated as synonymous concepts. In Sweden, as well as in other Western countries, abandoned, neglected, or abused children who were placed in foster care often lived under deplorable conditions and with no legal rights. Taking in a foster child was a means for some people to improve their economy and to get a cheap labor force in the household. Although times and practices have changed, fostering is, contrary to adoption, still regarded as a more or less temporary solution to an emergency situation and not always entirely in the best interests of the child (Triseliotis, 1973).

93

RESEARCH ON ADOPTION AND FOSTERING

In his now classic World Health Organization monograph, *Maternal Care and Mental Health,* John Bowlby recommended early adoption as an important preventive measure for children deprived of their biological parents (Bowlby, 1951). This book was written under the influence of the deplorable conditions which at that time were common in many institutions for children. It also reflected the prevailing opinion about the disastrous consequences of institutional care and parental deprivation for the individual's long-term social development. Although many of Bowlby's original conclusions about the effects of adverse early experiences in childhood turned out to be overstated (Clarke & Clarke, 1976), his ideas have proved to be basically sound. Moreover, these ideas have inspired much research about the social and psychological consequences of adoption and fostering.

Concern for the social and psychological well-being of adopted and foster children stems, in part, from the fact that many of these children have spent part of their infancy in institutions with frequent changes of attendants, thereby deprived of a consistent maternal contact. Furthermore, these children are often born out of wedlock after unwanted pregnancies. In addition, the biological parents of these children often have social or psychiatric problems, including alcohol or drug abuse (Bohman et al., 1981; Cadoret, Chapter 2; Cloninger et al., 1981). These facts have led researchers and clinicians to question whether adopted or foster children are more vulnerable to symptoms of nervous disturbances or social maladjustment during childhood, adolescence, or as grown-ups.

In their social and psychological context, adoption and fostering also tend to give children and their new parents a minority status. As a consequence, these individuals have to cope with a special existential situation. This may constitute a considerable stress on both parents and children. David Kirk (1964), in his now classic book *Shared Fate,* refers to the incongruent role obligations of the adoptive family and its character as a minority group lacking the support of social and historical traditions common to biological kinship in relations.

Thus, there are many factors that may interfere with the successful development of adopted and foster children. In fact, several studies have shown that adopted and foster children are overrepresented in clinical populations (Borgatta & Fanshel, 1965; Brinich & Brinich, 1982; Deutsch et al., 1982; Schechter, 1960; Simon & Senturia, 1966), from which has been concluded that they are more prone to social maladjustment and mental disorders than the general population. Such studies, however, may be biased because they do not take into consideration subject selection factors, thereby giving a misleading picture of the adjustment among adopted and foster children *in general.* Conversely, beginning with a large, representative study of "independent" adoptions by Witmer and her colleagues (Witmer, Herzog, Weinstein, & Sullivan, 1963), a number of well-designed, representative studies were subsequently published in the United States, Great Britain, and Sweden (Bohman, 1970; Brodzinsky, Schechter, Braff, & Singer, 1984; Brodzinsky, et al., 1987; Hoopes, 1982; Hoopes, Sherman, Lawder, Andrews, & Lower, 1969; Seglow et al., 1972). These studies, which did take into account selection factors, generally suggested that, as a group, adopted children do show less satisfactory adjustment compared to matched controls, or to children from the general population. Moreover, as grown-ups, adoptees also tend to display more psychiatric, psychosomatic, and other nervous disorders than nonadoptees (Bohman & von Knorring, 1979; Sigvardsson et al., 1984). Despite these conclusions, the studies also have suggested that adoption is a better alternative for children who lack parents than long-term fostering or institutional care (see Triseliotis, Chapter 6).

SOME METHODOLOGICAL CONSIDERATIONS IN ADOPTION RESEARCH

In interpreting the results of adoption research, the ambiguous meaning of the term "adopted children" must be taken into account. It is obvious that it represents a very heterogenous group. Thus it is necessary to control for different preplacement experiences as well as for differences in social or biological background in the evaluation of the outcome in adoption. Moreover, adoption and fostering are also sometimes treated as equal social measures, which may lead to false conclusions concerning the outcome of adoption per se.

If the aim of a study is to evaluate the outcome or adjustment of adopted children, the most appropriate research strategy is a prospective, longitudinal investigation carried out over many years with a representative, well-defined population. By studying a whole cohort of prospective adoptees, from birth to maturity, it may be possible to avoid the methodological problems associated with retrospective, cross-sectional, and clinical studies. Such an approach also allows the investigator to control for the influences of pregnancy or birth complications, institutional care, and other preplacement experiences. In addition, the prospective design permits repeated assessments of adjustment over time, and the evaluation of the influence of home environment and school at different ages. Finally, different kinds of adoption, de facto adoptions versus long-term foster care, and the impact of institutional life can also be evaluated separately.

In keeping with the objective of evaluating the long-term impact of adoption on children and families, this chapter presents an overview of a prospective, longitudinal study that was carried out in Sweden. The specific goal of the study was to determine which factors in the child, the adoptive family, or in the placement procedures are of importance for the prognosis and outcome of the adopted child. In addition, it was the hope of the investigators that the data may be useful for improving placement procedures in adoption and fostering.

A SWEDISH PROSPECTIVE AND LONGITUDINAL STUDY OF ADOPTIONS

In a prospective, longitudinal study of children who were registered for adoption at a social service agency in Stockholm, Sweden, in the mid-1950s, we were able to control for several prognostic and selective factors: biological background, perinatal conditions, hospital or institutional care before final placement, and so on (Bohman, 1970, 1972; Bohman & Sigvardsson, 1978, 1979, 1980). A total of 624 children

Table 5.1   Longitudinal Study Design

Age	Data
11 years	Adjustment and school achievement; School marks; Interviews with teachers and parents
15 years	Adjustment and school achievement; School marks; Teachers' questionnaires
18 years	Records for military enlistment; procedure: (boys only) Mental and intellectual capacity
23 years	Records from the Criminal Register and Excise Board; Register (for offenses against the Temperance Act): alcohol abuse and criminality

Note: Original cohort = 624. Group I (adoptive homes), 28%; Group II (biological homes), Group III (foster homes), 35%.

were registered by their mothers with the adoption agency of the Social Child Welfare Board of the City of Stockholm. The application was filed just before or shortly after the birth of the child, but for various reasons only about one quarter were, in fact, placed in adoptive homes (N = 168). Roughly equal numbers of the other children were brought up by the biological mothers, who had changed their decisions about giving up the child (N = 208), or were placed in permanent foster homes (N = 203).

Most of the children were born out of wedlock and after unwanted pregnancies, and subsequently were given very different social and rearing opportunities. This made it possible to study, in a longitudinal perspective, the future consequence of the decisions made by parents and social workers during the first months of their lives.

Material and Methods

Methods and procedures have been detailed elsewhere (Bohman, 1970, 1971) and are only summarized here. The study was planned as a longitudinal study, starting at the time of pregnancy with retrospective data from records from maternity hospitals and the adoption agency. Based on information about school marks and interviews with the class teachers, studies have been carried out at age 11 and 15 years concerning school achievement and adjustment. For boys, information was also obtained from the medical and psychological investigations that were carried out in connection with their enlistment for military service at age 18. Finally, we obtained information about the boys and girls at about 23 years of age from the Criminal Register and from the Excise Board Register for alcohol abuse (a nationwide register concerning offenses against the Temperance Act). Controls, matched for sex and age, have been selected from school or population registers. Table 5.1 summarizes the various stages of the investigation.

The aim here is to give a brief presentation of the outcome of adoption and long-term fostering among children with a negative social heritage and to discuss the implications of our results for preventive work and social policies. The specific questions we want to elucidate here may be formulated as follows:

1. Does early placement of children of antisocial, or otherwise socially handicapped parents, in an adoptive or fostering home protect them from future social maladjustment?
2. Are outcomes different for adoption and long-term fostering?
3. What is the prognosis for disadvantaged children, born after unwanted pregnancies and registered for adoption, but later restored to their biological parents?

The adopted children (henceforth referred to as "Group I") were placed with families who had been thoroughly prepared for their role as new parents through a series of interviews before placement. Most of the families lived in larger towns. The adoption agency took care to ensure that the children were not placed in homes where there might be marital problems or where the husband or wife had a serious illness or was registered for alcohol abuse or illicit behavior. Most adoptive parents had a fairly good and stable social and economic standing. There was an overrepresentation of parents with professional and intermediate occupations in this group.

Children in the two other groups had less favorable placement conditions. Most *biological mothers,* who took care of their child themselves (Group II), were young, unmarried, and worked in unskilled or semiskilled occupations. In general, their economic and social opportunities were very limited at the time when the child was born. The majority lived in Greater Stockholm. Very little systematic information has been available about the subsequent development of these families.

The *foster parents* (Group III) mostly lived in smaller communities or in rural areas. They were stable families but did not have the higher status of the adoptive parents in Group I in terms of financial means, education, or occupations. Their mean age was higher than that of the adoptive parents and later on many appeared to have somatic health problems. These parents were not specially prepared for their task, as nonbiological parents, in the way that the parents in Group I were prepared. For this type of placement in foster homes, there was no clear contract or agreement from the beginning of the placement about a future legal adoption. In most cases, however, there seems to have been a tacit understanding that the goal was a legal adoption in the future. As a rule, the foster parents were paid by the child welfare organization as long as the children were not legally adopted. By age 7, though, most children (70%) had been legally adopted. There was very little, if any, contact between the biological relatives and the child in the foster home.

It is important to consider that the children in Group III de facto became adopted. With few exceptions, all children grew up in the foster home where they first had been placed. Nevertheless, it is obvious that this kind of placement implied an atmosphere of insecurity, for both children and foster parents, especially during the preschool years. This may have had negative consequences for the child's development. The situation, with no definite borderline between adoption and fostering, is representative of the somewhat haphazard adoption placements that earlier was more common both in Sweden and other countries.

Biological parents in all three groups mostly worked in unskilled or semiskilled occupations at the time of the child's birth and they seldom had higher education or professional training. Both fathers and mothers were heavily overrepresented in the public records for criminality and alcohol abuse. Thus about 40% of the biological fathers were found in public records on criminality or alcohol abuse.

Selection Bias

When comparing the outcome of the three different groups, it is obvious that the process of placement involved a certain amount of selection. Thus foster children in Group III, significantly more often than those in Group I or II, had biological parents with criminal records or alcohol problems. Also their mothers more frequently suffered complications during pregnancy or delivery. Children in group III stayed on the average longer in institutions before placement than children in Groups I and II. In addition, the few children who had biological parents with higher education were preferentially placed in adoptive homes or reared by their biological mothers. Children of unskilled parents were more often placed in foster homes.

In summary, foster children in Group III represent a negative selection compared to Groups I and II.

The Investigation at Age 11

At the age of 10 to 11 years, the children were followed up for an assessment including a semistructured interview of their school teachers (Bohman, 1971). There was some attrition from the original cohort of 624 children: 14 had died and 31 were emigrated or otherwise not available. In 75 cases the biological father was unknown, but these children were still included in the study. However, only 492 interviews were carried out due to limited resources at that time. Foster children both in one year-group, 1957, had to be excluded. The children studied here include 164 adoptees (Group I), 213 reared by their biological mothers (Group II), and 124 children reared in foster homes (Group III), all of them registered once for adoption. For each of the probands a classmate of the same sex was randomly chosen as a control.

A detailed behavioral assessment was made based on a semistructured interview with the teacher, usually during the end of the fourth school year (when children in Sweden are about 11-years-old). This evaluation was supplemented by copies of the children's school grade reports and school health cards. The children were all in different classrooms distributed throughout Sweden. The class teacher was interviewed by telephone using a questionnaire described elsewhere (Bohman, 1970) and adapted from the Berkeley Growth Study (MacFarlane, Allen, & Honzik, 1954). Adoptive parents living in Greater Stockholm were also interviewed, which has been reported elsewhere (Bohman, 1970).

Finally, a narrative summary with descriptive examples of each child's behavior was prepared by the interviewer. The adjustment of the child was then classified on the basis of the interviews, using a 5-point scale of adjustment scores; manifest problems at school, "problem children," having a score of 4 or 5 (Bohman, 1971). The ratings and narrative summaries were also later used to rate childhood personality dimensions independent of any knowledge of adolescent or adult behavior, in order to analyze the structure and stability of the children's personality and to predict later social adjustment. (Sigvardsson, Bohman, & Cloninger, in press).

Table 5.2   Adjustment in School at 11 Years

	Boys		Girls	
	Probands (%)	Classmate controls (%)	Probands (%)	Classmate controls (%)
Adopted (Group I)				
Few or no symptoms	44	70	77	84
Moderate symptoms	34	18	12	11
Problem children	22	12	11	5
With biological mother (Group II)				
Few or no symptoms	54	70	65	76
Moderate symptoms	26	18	26	18
Problem children	20	12	9	6
Foster children (Group III)				
Few or no symptoms	55	69	71	79
Moderate symptoms	23	23	9	17
Problem children	22	8	20	4

Source: Bohman, M. (1971). *Acta Ped. Scand.* suppl. 221, 1–38.

Outcome at Age 11

Our results of the outcome study at age 11 showed that adopted boys in Group I had a high rate of nervous and behavioral disturbances compared to their classmates. Thus 22% were classified as ''problem children,'' compared with 12% among class controls. There were, however, very few among both subjects and controls who could be classified as antisocial or having conduct disorders at this age. The two other groups also showed a significant increase in behavior disturbances and maladjustment among boys, with 20% in Group II and 22% in Group III (compared with 12% and 8%, respectively, among class controls). Adopted girls likewise had a higher rate, although not significantly higher, of maladjustment than controls (11% vs 5%). Similarly, girls in Groups II and III were more often classified as ''problem children'': Group II, 9% versus 6%, Group III, 20% versus 4%. Results are summarized in Table 5.2.

Comparisons between the subjects and their classmates with respect to certain behaviors in school (e.g., psychomotor activity, proness to conflicts, intelligence) also showed that the teachers experienced the subjects as deviating and in a negative direction. Intergroup comparisons showed that the foster children in Group III were seen as most deviating by their teacher. The subjects in all three groups had somewhat lower average marks in Swedish than controls, but this difference was not significant except in Group III. Also, marks in mathematics were somewhat lower than for classmates (differences significant for girls in Group I and for both sexes in Group III).

These results were somewhat surprising to us, since we had expected a better general adjustment among the adoptees in Group I (due to their more favorable social conditions), at least in comparison with the other two groups. Looking more closely at our cases, however, it was obvious that disturbances among children in Groups II and III were qualitatively often more serious than among adoptees in Group I. It is of some interest in this context that adjustment of children in Group I appeared to be largely independent of various background variables, such as perinatal complications, age at placement, socioeconomic status of the adoptive parents, or registered criminality or alcohol abuse among the biological parents. This observation was also true for children in the other two groups, with the exception that in these cases we had only limited information about the children's rearing situation.

Discussion

At this stage of our study, we drew the conclusion that children of unwanted pregnancies, irrespective of the three alternative options of placement, were at a substantial risk of maladjustment during the early school years. Although adopted children in Group I seemed to be somewhat better off than the children in the other two groups, they still had an increased risk, despite more favorable social conditions. Thus our result was largely in line with other investigations, which also have found that adopted children are more at risk of developing maladjustment at school.

The Investigation at Age 15

Four years later, when the children were attending the eighth class of the nine-year Swedish comprehensive school, they were reevaluated in a similar way. The schools provided copies of the children's grade reports and the class teachers were asked to rate the adjustment of the subjects and of two controls from the current class on a 7-point scale. Again, the teachers who made the ratings did not know anything about the aim of the study or prior ratings; they also did not know that some of the children were probands and others were controls. The questionnaire included nine variables: tension, withdrawal, aggressiveness, psychomotor activity, ability to concentrate, contact with peers, social maturity, intelligence, and school motivation. (Bohman & Sigvardsson, 1980; see Magnusson, Duner, & Zetterblom, 1975).

Briefly, to give an example, the extremes of the rating scale for *social maturity* were defined as follows:

Scale point 1: Social adjustment pervasively poor; frequently plays truant; runs away; abuse of alcohol or drugs; repeated thefts or other illicit behavior; behavior which has led to intervention by the child welfare authorities or the police.

Scale point 7: Functions well for his or her age in different social contexts; mature, has further studies or an occupation in mind; reliable, trustworthy, takes responsibility for him or herself and others. Children with scores of 1 to 2 have arbitrarily been classified socially maladjusted.

The teachers completed 577 questionnaires, each concerning one proband and two controls. There were only a few drop-outs in this part of the investigation.

Results at Age 15

The relatively high rate of maladjustment found in Group I at age 11 now seemed to have been compensated. There was still, admittedly, a slight tendency for this group

Table 5.3 Social Maladjustment (scores 1 and 2) at 15 Years

	Boys		Girls	
	Probands (%)	Controls (%)	Probands (%)	Controls (%)
Group I	(*n* = 89)	(*n* = 173)	(*n* = 71)	(*n* = 140)
(Adopted)	4.5	5.8	1.4	2.9
Group II	(*n* = 108)	(*n* = 209)	(*n* = 105)	(*n* = 194)
(With biological mother)	13.9	5.3	15.2	6.7
Group III	(*n* = 112)	(*n* = 222)	(*n* = 92)	(*n* = 180)
(Fostered)	12.2	4.1	7.6	2.8

Source: Bohman & Sigvardsson. (1980). *Acta Psychiat. Scand., 61,* 339–335.

to have lower mean adjustment scores and lower mean grades compared to their class controls, but the differences were only occasionally significant.

In contrast, a considerable proportion of subjects in the two other groups now displayed more signs of maladjustment and school failure than was found at age 11. Among *boys* in Groups II and III social maladjustment was 2 to 3 times more frequent than among controls: in Group II, 13.9% versus 5.3%; in Group III, 12.2% versus 4.1%. Similarly *girls* in these groups had a higher frequency of maladjustment: in Group II, 15.2% versus 6.7%; in Group III, 7.6% versus 2.8%. For probands in Group I, the corresponding figures were for boys 4.5% and for girls 1.4%. The results are summarized in Table 5.3

The results were reanalyzed in view of intergroup differences concerning biological background, perinatal complications, and early preplacement experiences. Such background factors, however, only weakly explained some of the differences between the adoptees in Group I and the other two groups. In Group I, maladjustment at 11 years only weakly predicted social maladjustment at 15 years, but was a somewhat better predictor in the other two groups. (Bohman & Sigvardsson, 1980).

Although the design of this study was not originally directed toward specific genetic questions, some tentative conclusions may be drawn. As in the 11-year study, we found no association between registered criminality or alcohol abuse among the biological *fathers* and the adjustment of children in nonbiological homes. In contrast, such an association was found between registered biological *mothers* and their children in adoptive or foster homes. This association may indicate a genetic link between the social maladjustment of both mothers and their children. It may also indicate that registrations for criminality or alcohol abuse among females reflect more severe personality disorders than the same registrations do among males, a conclusion supported by other investigations (Cloninger, Reich, & Guze, 1975; Sigvardsson et al., 1982).

In summary, the adopted children in Group I, who were placed by a public adoption agency, had largely compensated for their handicaps seen at age 11. On the one hand, the risk for maladjustment in their mid-teens was in no way greater than for children in the general population. On the other hand, our study indicated a considerable risk of maladjustment and school failure among children reared by their mothers, who once had expressed a wish to have their children adopted. The same risk is true for children who, due to indecision on the part of the mothers or the adoption agency, were placed by the Social Welfare Board and reared in foster homes.

Discussion

In Group I, the differences between probands and controls at age 11 had almost disappeared at age 15, but not so in the other two groups. The question is whether this intergroup difference is due to environmental factors in the rearing situation, a reflection of selective placement, or both.

Unfortunately, we had no possibility to make personal interviews or assessments of the children's rearing conditions at age 15, which means that we have to rely on data from earlier follow-ups. Regarding environmental factors in the children's home situation, we know from the 11-year study that probands in Group I grew up under better and more stable circumstances than probands in Groups II and III. The interviews with the adoptive parents showed that their children by this time were well integrated within these middle-class families. In contrast, we found in interviews with foster parents that these children were not so well integrated within their current families. Both parents and children often displayed signs of insecurity about their situation.

We know already that in infancy the three groups were handled and selected in a way that may explain some of the differences among them. For instance, perinatal complications were less common among children in Group I than among the other children. Social and occupational status among the biological parents was highest and frequency of criminality and alcohol abuse was lowest for biological parents of children in Group I. This reflects a bias in the placement. However, the analyses of these background variables did not offer a reasonable explanation for the differences among the three groups.

The 18-Year Study

In Sweden, there is general conscription and military training for men from the age of 18 years. Before entering military training, conscripts undergo a series of medical and psychological tests. Since 1968, about 90% of all male youths have been required to attend this enlistment procedure. Exemptions are generally due to emigrations, religious or sociomedical reasons. The results of these examinations were made available to us and were used as one of the steps in our longitudinal evaluation.

From an original cohort of 329 boys, 263 completed a two-day intensive medical, psychological, and social examination as part of the general military conscription (Bohman & Sigvardsson, 1978). For each subject a control, born on the same day, was selected from the public population register. The attrition rate was about the same for adopted boys in Group I and their controls, but was significantly higher for probands in Groups II and III. The higher attrition rate in these groups was due to exemption for sociomedical, mostly psychiatric, reasons.

The investigation includes standardized evaluations of intellectual capacity, psychosocial capacity, and medical–anthropometric assessments. The intelligence tests include four standardized tests: logic-inductive, linguistic, spatial, and mechanical abilities. The assessment of "psychological function capacity" involves a semistructured interview by a clinical psychologist, which thoroughly evaluates the boy's education, occupational experiences, social background, interests, personality, and social adjustment. This is summarized by a 9-point scale. Leadership capacity is also assessed based on intelligence performance, adjustment in school and work, use of leisure time, home situation, and emotional stability. The medical examination includes measures of height, chest and waist circumference, weight, and muscular strength.

Results of Military Enlistment Investigation

In all four IQ subtests there was no difference in performance between the adopted boys in Group I and their controls. In contrast, boys who had grown up with their biological mothers or in foster homes scored significantly lower in most subtests compared with their controls (Table 5.4). Note also, as we mentioned earlier, that more subjects were exempted from the enlistment procedure in Groups II and III than in Group I, due to sociomedical reasons. Similarly, there is a good agreement between adopted boys (Group I) and controls for the psychologist's assessment of "physical function capacity," while boys in Groups II and III scored much lower than their controls.

In summary, the interviews, tests, and investigations during the military enlistment procedure confirmed our observations at 15 years in all three groups. The adopted boys showed much the same achievements as did their age-matched controls. By contrast, boys in the other two groups scored significantly lower than their controls in intelligence and psychological tests. They were also more often exempted from military service for social or psychiatric reasons than the adoptees in Group I.

Registrations for Alcohol Abuse and Criminality

As a last and tentative step in our longitudinal study, we made a search for entries in the Criminal Register and the Excise Board Register for offenses under the Temperance Act. The latter contains information about fines imposed for drunkenness, records of supervision by the Temperance Board, and time spent in institutions for alcoholics. The records cover the period from the subjects' sixteenth birthdays up to 1979, when they were about 23 years of age. A search for entries was made for all subjects and for age-matched controls.

It is obvious that these types of registers are rather inaccurate instruments for evaluation of social maladjustment. It is well known that registrations for criminal offenses only cover a minor part of crimes committed. Likewise, records kept by the Temperance Board do not give a true picture of alcohol abuse in the general population, not even in Sweden, where there has been for a long time a fairly efficient and comprehensive system of temperance control and supervision. Still, registrations of this kind may be seen as indicators of social maladjustment, especially when occurring repeatedly.

Results

Among the adopted *males*, 18% were registered for either criminality, alcohol abuse, or both, compared with 15.5% among the controls, a nonsignificant difference. Sub-

Table 5.4   Tests at 18 Years at Military Enlistment Procedure
(intelligence, means for subtests)

	Subjects	Controls	p
Group I (Adopted)			
Subtest	$(n = 79)$	$(n = 74)$	
Logic–inductive	5.24	5.46	NS
Linguistic	5.18	5.15	NS
Spatial	5.53	5.30	NS
Technical	4.96	4.91	NS
Group II (Biological Mother)			
Subtest	$(n = 90)$	$(n = 102)$	
Logic–inductive	4.87	5.62	0.005
Linguistic	4.86	5.58	0.005
Spatial	5.34	5.98	0.01
Technical	4.40	5.13	0.005
Group III (Fostered)			
Subtest	$(n = 87)$	$(n = 99)$	
Logic–inductive	4.44	5.28	0.005
Linguistic	4.52	5.35	0.005
Spatial	4.77	5.61	0.005
Technical	4.22	4.77	0.05

Source: Bohman & Sigvardsson (1978).

jects in Group II appeared about as often (16.5%) in the two registers. In contrast, 29.2% of the males who had grown up in foster homes appeared in the registers, a highly significant difference compared with the other two groups and with the controls.

None of the adopted *females* appeared in any of the registers. In Group II, two females were registered for alcohol abuse, both probably seriously addicted. Three females were known for occasional abuse in Group III. There was no registration for criminality in females in any of the three groups or among controls. Thus five female probands (all in Groups II and III) were known as alcohol abusers, compared with two controls in all three groups. The results of this part of the investigation seem to give further evidence that children who have been brought up in foster homes are at greater risk of social maladjustment than is true for the general population.

GENERAL DISCUSSION AND CONCLUSIONS

The results of our longitudinal studies indicate that the long-term prognosis for adopted children is in no way worse than for children in the general population, provided that the adoptive home is psychologically well prepared for the task of rearing a nonbiological child. The study at 11 years admittedly indicated an increased frequency of nervous disturbances and maladjustment. This was, however, largely overcome in the subsequent follow-up studies.

In regard to the very high frequency of social maladjustment, that is, criminality and alcohol abuse among the biological parents, the conclusion is warranted that adoption largely reduced the risk of social incompetence and maladjustment. This conclusion is supported by the comparison with the children who were taken back by their biological mothers or who had grown up in foster homes. Among these children, maladjustment and school failure were common and persistent features over the years. Regarding the fact that adopted children had grown up in families with higher education and occupation than average, one could have expected a somewhat better school achievement than among their classmates. There may be various reasons for this not occurring. The adoptive situation itself is sometimes fraught with complications and stresses (Brodzinsky, 1987; McWhinnie, 1967, Triseliotis, 1973), which may have impaired the general level of achievement. However, our interviews with the adoptive parents at the 11-year study indicated few such complications.

An unexpected finding was the poor outcome at different ages among the foster children in Group III. These children were mostly placed at an early age (mean age 9 months) in socially stable foster families for a permanent stay. In other words, these placements may be seen as de facto adoptions. About 70% had been legally adopted before age seven. It is important to take this into consideration when evaluating the outcome of ''adoption.'' Both children in Group I and in Group III are long-term placements by the Child Welfare Board and may be regarded as adopted, although under somewhat different circumstances.

As mentioned, most studies have shown that adopted children are overrepresented in clinical populations; also in epidemiological investigations these children are more often maladjusted. As we have shown in our large epidemiological study of adult adoptees (Bohman & von Knorring, 1979), there is also a substantial overrepresentation of nervous or psychiatric disorders among adoptees of both sexes as grown-ups. The present longitudinal study illustrates the importance of taking into account differences in biological background, early experiences, and placement procedures in the evaluation of adoptive placements.

Children in Group III did represent a negative selection. For instance, criminality and alcohol abuse were significantly more common among their biological parents than among parents in the other groups. Also socioeconomic status and education was lower among these biological parents.

Finally, it is conceivable that the strongly negative outcome among the foster children may be connected with placement procedures. Foster parents were seldom prepared before the placement of the child when compared with the adoptive parents in Group I. But more important, there was no guarantee that the child might not some day be returned to the biological mother or father. In interviews the foster parents often expressed their concern about this insecure situation, which could last for many years after the placement of the child. It is conceivable that this insecurity has influenced the relationship between foster parents and children. It may have impaired the normal, healthy psychological development of the child and made them more vulnerable to stress. This suggestion is supported by findings in other reports on the situation of adopted and foster children (Raynor, 1980).

Our study also indicates a considerable risk of social maladjustment and school failure among subjects who were registered for adoption but reared by their biological mothers. As in our analyses of the other groups, the various background factors known to us explained very little of the variance. It is conceivable that the high rate of maladjustment among these children may be seen as a result of insecure family and rearing conditions. This is, of course, a tentative conclusion, as we had very little first-hand information about these families.

The general implication of our study for the policy of the care of children from disadvantaged families concerns the importance of early prevention. Preparation and support should be given to everybody in charge of a child at risk. The implementation of this often repeated recommendation is basically a political question—a question of social justice. We certainly do not believe that adoption is always the best solution for children and parents with social handicaps. But our studies clearly indicate that decisions about the child's legal status should be made as early as possible. Any unnecessary prolongation of the socially, legally, and psychologically insecure limbo-situation of foster care should be avoided, in the best interest of the child (Goldstein, et al., 1973).

Finally, our studies have demonstrated the advantages of a longitudinal, prospective design. If, for instance, the investigation had been restricted to the first, cross-sectional follow-up at age 11, then conclusions concerning adoption would have been quite different from those we have now reached. Taken as a cross-sectional study, the results at 11 years would have indicated that the subjects, who were born of socially disadvantaged parents, had a less favorable prognosis than children in general, irrespective of whether they had grown up with a biological parent or had been placed in foster or adoptive homes. It is reasonable to infer that the much better situation of Group I at 15 and 18 years, compared with the assessments at 11 years, was an effect of the stable situation in the adoptive homes.

6

Contrasting Adoption, Foster Care, and Residential Rearing

JOHN TRISELIOTIS AND MALCOLM HILL

In this chapter, we aim to contrast three different types of rearing or caring by comparing the current personal and social circumstances of adults and older children who, as children, were separated from their biological parents and subsequently adopted, fostered with a family, or cared for in residential institutions. Our central claim is that those growing up adopted, even if placed when older, appear in adulthood to have a stronger sense of self and to function more adequately at the personal, social, and economic level compared with those who were formerly fostered and, particularly, those who grew up for a large part of their lives in institutions. Furthermore, adoption, as a substitute form of care, has a greater potential for reversing earlier adverse experiences, than foster and residential care.

Evidence to support these claims will come mainly from two studies carried out in Britain. The first, a comparative or contrast study, involving 124 people in their twenties, split about equally among those who were adopted, fostered with families, or grew up in residential care. To meet the main criterion of long exposure to a particular way of rearing, samples had to be drawn from many social service agencies across Scotland. Individuals adopted under the age of three years were deliberately excluded from the sample as the aim was to concentrate on older, hard to place children. Those adopted individuals in our study were placed in their adoptive family between the ages of three and nine years; those fostered had spent an average of 11 years in family foster care by the age of 16 years; and the residential group had been cared for in institutions for an average of 11 years. (For a more detailed description of the sample, see Triseliotis & Russell, 1984.) The theoretical basis for the research was mainly derived from the field of child development studies and particularly that part which involves separated children. The research design was largely influenced by the interpretive approach which places the emphasis on how the participants themselves "describe and explain" their past experiences and current circumstances. Information of this type was obtained through a semistructured questionnaire and the interviews were tape-recorded. Other data was obtained from agency records referring to the children's baselines at the point of entering care and at different points during their in-care careers, as well as information about the circumstances on the family of origin.

Outcome judgments were based on a range of concrete criteria such as educational attainment, occupation, income, housing, marriage and divorce, health record (physical and emotional), behavior problems, criminal convictions and alcohol consumption. Less tangible outcome criteria used included: social and personal relationships, quality of life, identity, attachments, parenting, well-being, and coping with life situations. Apart from the subjects' accounts describing the nature and quality of their experiences, a number of self-rating scales were also administered to elicit additional quantitative measures of the subjects' more subjective experiences and states. Statistical comparisons were made where appropriate with regard to the frequency of different factors. Some of the methodology used to measure states of ''well-being'' and ''quality of life'' were also used by the Social Survey Unit in their quality of life surveys in 1975 and earlier. (For a more detailed account of our methodology, see Triseliotis & Russell, 1984.)

The second study providing evidence for the claims made in the opening paragraph involved 52 children between 9 and 18 years of age who recently experienced a transition from family foster care to adoption with the same families. The adoption was made possible through the payment of an adoption allowance (subsidy). This was a subsample of a much larger study to evaluate the impact of adoption allowance schemes on families and children. One question we wanted to pursue with the children and which is the subject of discussion here, was whether it mattered to those in long-term foster care to be adopted and if so, why. We decided from the outset not to interview children with substantial mental handicaps or those who were below eight years old. It was felt that they were unlikely to have the understanding and expressive ability required to communicate effectively about foster care and adoption. Previous studies have used similar age thresholds for their interviews with children in care (Fanshel & Shinn, 1978; Rowe, Cain, Hundleby, & Keane, 1984; Thoburn, Murdoch, & O'Brien, 1986). We were fortunate in that the parents seemed to trust us enough to allow us access for separate interviews with most of the children that fell within the sample population. As a result, we had very few refusals. Some of the children had met us before so we were not total strangers to them. We tried to resolve some of the methodological problems of how to develop effective communication with children and teenagers by developing a range of techniques. Some followed accepted practice but others involved breaking some new ground. Eventually the interviews were based on both oral and written approaches. The oral part of the interviews was based on a range of themes about foster care and adoption while the written part included ecograms, listing of important people, word choice, sentence completion, and happiness scales. There was a core of topics and elements used for all the children, plus others which could be adapted selectively according to the age and nature of the child in order to encourage interest and rapport. Similarly, we felt free to adapt the order and wording of schedules and questions to fit the child. This was done in the knowledge that data analysis would be primarily qualitative. All the interviews were tape-recorded to avoid taking notes which could result in the loss of rapport. (A paper detailing the methods used to collect information will appear in a subsequent publication.)

CONCEPTS OF IDENTITY AND SECURITY

The study *In Search of Origins* (Triseliotis, 1973), which was based on the accounts and circumstances of adoptees seeking access to information about their origins or seeking contact or reunions with a biological parent, provided some insights linking the search with issues of personal and social identity and possibly social adjustment that were to influence our subsequent studies. In the context of this paper, identity and a sense of security are seen as being the outcomes of multiple personal, social, and cultural influences, which includes the influences of the adopted person's relationship with his adoptive parents. The possibility of genetic factors is not excluded and receives some attention. The concept of identity as such is used here to denote the kind of consciousness that we all carry within us about ''who'' we are, how secure and worthy we feel in what we are, and the kind of self-image we carry about ourselves. A sense of security contributes to the overall sense of identity while also being its artifact. Depending on its quality and strength, a sense of identity conveys feelings of self-esteem and relative confidence in performing a number of life roles. It also encompasses a positive body image and a feeling of uniqueness and separateness from others while, at the same time, being able to enter into daily social interactions and relationships with a degree of confidence.

Erikson (1968) remarked that an ''optimal'' sense of identity is experienced as a ''sense of psychological well-being, a feeling of being at home in one's body, of knowing where one is going, an inner assuredness of anticipated recognition from those who count'' (p. 165). While he puts the emphasis of identity building mainly on personal and internal experiences, Mead (1934) elaborates on the part played by social influences, particularly family and community ones. Our studies suggest that the two types of experience outlined by Erikson and Mead are not separate but part of the same developmental continuum.

Outcome Studies: Methodological Considerations

The use of outcome studies to contrast issues of identity, current adjustment, and quality of life of people, who experienced different types of rearing, disguises many methodological problems surrounding such evaluation. For a start, a major difficulty is comparability in baselines between the different samples at the time the children entered their contrasting forms of rearing. All the respondents in our contrast study shared, before being placed, a background of social deprivation, separations from parents, and several moves between different types of placements. In addition, they had parents with a history of social disadvantage, social and emotional instability, including alcohol abuse and criminality. Although the biological parents of the adopted group had experienced somewhat fewer social adversities compared with the other two groups, a higher percentage of them were described by social workers as having serious learning difficulties and there were fears that the children might turn out to be like their mothers. Because of this, they were held back initially from being placed for adoption. As children, the adopted group presented at the time of placement more physical and emotional problems compared with the other two groups, which contributed also to their being held back from adoption. They equally had an average of four moves between coming into public care and their adoption placement. The characteristics of the adopted group would qualify them to be classified as "high risk" in the way described by Kadushin (1971). It is recognized that the ethical constraints that rightly operate in this kind of research make it almost impossible to compare "like with like" in all aspects. Some "trade-offs" between groups are, therefore, inevitable.

Questions of definition and measurement can legitimately be raised about all outcome studies that purport to establish levels of "security," "identity," "self-esteem," or "a sense of well-being." Not only are these concepts elusive and difficult to define but also difficult to measure. All the methodological approaches used by different researchers, such as standardized tests, self-rating questionnaires, and self-reporting, have their pluses and minuses, not to mention the possible influence on them of prevailing psychological or sociological theories. As already pointed out, our own studies have largely relied on an analysis of extensive qualitative and quantitative data which included self-reporting accounts and self-rating questionnaires asking respondents to rate, besides reporting, a range of affective states relating to themselves. The drawbacks and advantages of self-reporting in retrospective studies of this kind will not be recounted here except to acknowledge that a certain amount of detail is bound to be lost. There are equally dangers in ascribing differences relating to a single factor, that is, the different rearing experiences, when other external circumstances may have been responsible. To counteract these possibilities, states of "well-being," "security," and "self-esteem" were approached in multiple ways, but one can never be certain.

Who sets outcome criteria is another salient point. Should this be done, for example, by the respondents themselves, by practitioners, by those around the respondents, the researchers, or a combination of these. Each and everyone of these agents may have their own views about outcomes. In the end, our contrast study relied on the accounts of the participants and on recorded information. When we had the opportunity to interview separately a small group of adoptive parents and their adopted offspring, no significant differences emerged between the two accounts.

It is also recognized that preestablished long-term criteria for separated children in the areas examined do not exist. To some, the whole notion of long-term criteria appears theoretical and impractical, because the intervening variables increase with the length of time since separation and subsequent placement in their rearing environment. It may also be viewed as unrealistic to expect similar outcomes from adoption and residential or foster care rearing when possibly no other options existed at the time, either because of parental or child opposition or because of difficulties in securing families. What was somewhat reassuring for us was the early finding that once a child could not return home, it was largely accidental whether it subsequently went into adoption, long-term foster care or residential care. (We have to be reminded though, that somewhat better outcomes should be expected from adoption compared to other forms of substitute care because a small number of children placed for adoption are removed before the adoption order is granted [see Festinger, 1986, Chapter 11]. Even though adoption agencies try to place many of these children in new adoptive homes, some will not be successfully integrated into new families and consequently will not appear in a sample of adoptees.) We were also aware that although the main study succeeded in identifying three contrasting groups, it still lacked a comparable group of people who were reared in their own homes. Finally, as far as the idea of outcomes is concerned, Whitaker (1984) reminds us that there is no neat package. "Rather than talking in terms of 'success,' " she writes, "it is ,etter and nearer to the realities to think in terms of a pattern of gains and losses of costs and benefits" (p. 43).

Bearing in mind the limitations and constraints outlined above, our studies suggest that the achievement of a clear sense of identity and a sense of security for separated children growing up in "substitute" forms of care, is linked to several factors, including (1) the quality of caring and attachments experienced in childhood; (2) the knowledge and awareness about their heritage, genealogy, and personal history; and (3) their experience of how other people perceive them and behave toward them and how they see themselves in relation to the rest of society. Depending on how others see us, we may come to view ourselves as "good," "bad," or "second class." Barring new major upsets in an individual's life, a positive outcome in these three areas should enable them to perform satisfactorily a wide range of life tasks and roles covering personal and social relationships and sexual and parenting roles. In the discussion that follows, the personal and social performance of each group of respondents is contrasted with the three qualities identified above.

The Quality of Caring and Attachments Experienced in Childhood

Those who were adopted and, to a somewhat lesser extent, those formerly fostered experienced more intimate, consistent, caring, and closer attachments to their caregivers compared with those who grew up in residential establishments. Significant qualitative differences emerged between the three groups but particularly between those adopted or fostered and the residential group. Children who grew up in residential homes seemed to experience few opportunities for closeness, individual caring, and continuity of care.

Adopted people mostly referred to "being brought up as their (adoptive) parents' own," "being made to feel secure through their parents' love," "enjoyed the love, care and kindness of my parents," "they (parents) were a real mum and dad," "wanted and loved for myself," and so on. Overall they felt "entitled" to their parents. With very few exceptions, the adoptive placement provided a strong sense of belonging and a strong identification with the adoptive family. Only about 15% of adoptees expressed misgivings and dissatisfaction with their growing up experience mainly for what they considered to be unreasonable expectations by their adoptive parents in terms of educational achievements and behavior.

Among those who grew up in residential homes, only one in every eight expressed any real enthusiasm for the quality of care and attachments they experienced with houseparents. The rest expressed either qualified satisfaction, mixed feelings, or outright dissatisfaction. The former residential people said they missed "closeness and intimacy to carers," "no-one to get attached to," "no-one taking a personal interest in you," and "no opportunities for attachment because of the frequent changes of staff." Some said with obvious bitterness mingled with regret: "I have never been mothered or fathered," "you wanted an awful lot of love but there wasn't any. Not like parents give their children," "there was always different people looking after you."

Overall most of those who grew up in institutions felt they missed a great part of their childhood and attributed many of the problems they were currently facing to the kind of rearing they had. Almost nine out of ten said they missed the experience of growing up in a family. Many of them found the impersonality of the institution, the lack of continuity in caregivers, the rigidity of the rules, the lack of privacy, the severity of punishment, and the stigma associated with living in an institution as soul destroying. Berry (1975) maintains, on the basis of her study, that children living in residential establishments require "benign daily experience" over a long period of time to counteract previous harmful experiences. The residential group's experiences in our study may account for the significantly higher levels of psychiatric referrals and current problems of personal and social adjustment found among them compared with the other two groups and especially with those who were adopted. Their accounts and self-rating of certain current affective states indicated a low level of self-esteem and emotional well-being and few life satisfactions, compared again and especially with those who had been adopted.

In contrast to those adopted, and somewhat less to those fostered, the residential group expressed less confidence in their ability to form relationships, cope with life's demands, and carry out parenting roles. Almost every individual in the residential group who was a parent referred to difficulties in coping with their young children, which they blamed on their institutional upbringing. Those adopted and who were married and had young children shared few uncertainties or difficulties in carrying out parental roles. Our findings are supported by a follow-up study reported by Rutter, Quinton, and Liddle (1983), which indicated that children who experienced prolonged periods of institutional care were more likely to encounter considerable social problems as adults and frequently went on to make poor parents.

Over half of those formerly fostered expressed real enthusiasm for the quality of care they received and the close bonding that developed between them and their foster families. The rest expressed either qualified satisfaction, mixed feelings, or dissatisfaction. Feelings of satisfaction were reflected in comments such as "they (foster parents) are a real mum and dad," "loved me and my sister as their own," "we were one family," "my world would have been shattered if I were taken away," "they did everything for you." Though many of their comments indicated considerable identification and attachment to their foster families, nevertheless there were some qualitative differences between their experiences and those of the adopted group. These differences had to do with an element of anxiety about the impermanency of their position as foster children. They were more conscious of their fostering status than adoptees of their adoptive status. While adoptees perceived themselves as growing up "like any other child in a family," many of those fostered were aware of differences in their situation in spite of most foster parents' efforts to make them feel secure and one with the rest of the family. A separate surname, welfare visits, very sporadic appearances by a natural parent or sibling, the comings and goings of short-stay foster children all contributed to a sense of "unusualness" which stressed their difference from, rather than oneness with, the family.

It needs to be recognized that the psychological implications of long-term fostering are very different from those of temporary foster care. In the latter children are usually expected to rejoin their families, but in long-term foster care they frequently lack contact and psychological bonds with natural parents. What we have found is that they are largely left in limbo searching for ways to cement their attachments to those who care for them. Discontinuity in their lives could have resulted from the action of the care authority, or of foster parents, or as a result of their own behavior. Fears and desires of being reclaimed by a natural parent added to their sense of insecurity. Similar fears were also found among foster parents who sometimes either openly or unintentionally conveyed these feelings to the children.

It was perhaps to be expected that this type of anxiety was not present in the adoptive home. The insecurity present in long-term fostering generated various degrees of anxiety in both the children and their caregivers. Caught between foster parents, the majority of whom wished to offer security and continuity of care, and the possibility of disruption, children were left in an ambiguous position which inevitably affected their sense of identity (see also Triseliotis, 1983).

The Transition from Foster Care to Adoption

We pursued the issue concerning the relative insecurity felt by those who are fostered in a study whose details are still to be published. In this investigation, we had the opportunity to speak to 52 children between the ages of 9 and 18 who, after a number of years as foster children, were adopted by their foster parents. The interviews were aimed, among other things, to obtain the children's views about the meaning of adoption to them after a long period in foster care. One of the key themes explored was perceived similarities and differences between foster care and adoption and the symbolism of the adoption order.

Most of the children were clear about their former fostering status and of their recent transition to adoption. Most, but not all, had been given some explanation about being fostered but further understanding about the meaning of this emerged only gradually. A very small number were brought up to think of themselves as adopted and it was only recently with the adoption proceedings that it dawned on them that they were only fostered. Many of them said they knew at least one other child who had been fostered but it was not usual for them to have known other adopted persons. Therefore, they had little chance to learn about adoption through someone who had experienced what it meant.

At the time of the interview most of the children and young people had a good idea about the main differences, as they saw them, between fostering and adoption. The image of fostering they carried with them was of "temporariness," "moving on" to other families and possibly a return to one's own family. It conveyed the feelings of anxiety and uncertainty and of having no control over one's life, the control resting mostly with outside authority. In the eyes of many youngsters, outside people could decide "to move you on" without even asking the foster parents or the child. Somewhat similar apprehensions and anxieties were expressed by the foster parents, in spite of the fact that some of the children had been with them for years.

In contrast, in the words of the same children and adolescents, adoption meant "permanence" (their word), "being there for ever" and "being part of the family"; also that "no one can remove you" and "no more social workers visiting." Other comments offered by the children included: "In fostering you are there for two or three years. Adoption is for life and you cannot be taken away"; "Adoption is a permanence, fostering is for a wee while"; and "Adoption means you are a proper part of the family."

Still other comments indicated that adoption conveyed a sense of "belonging" which emerged with the adoption order going through. It was not as if suddenly these children and young people felt different or transformed or things changed for them. Rather, they gradually became aware of a change in status that conveyed intangible feelings of "belonging" and being the family's "real child" which was unlike fostering: "You being really their child"; "you are part of the family and not feeling left out"; "having a family for life."

When asked to elaborate on some of these comments, most of the children and young people used phrases that conveyed a sense of security, permanence, and continuity of care that was secured through adoption. Some examples include: "will be more secure"; "no more moves and changes"; "it is up to the parents what we do and not up to others"; "adoption means to me, to mum, and to the rest of the family that I belong now." One teenager remarked on the paradox that in one way adoption made no difference, yet it was an important and desired change because it demonstrated to other people that she was now a member of the family.

In spite of being fostered by the same family over a lengthy period of time, the children still felt some lack of security and full belonging which was eventually provided by adoption. Although the children felt confident of their foster parents' love, they were conscious that their full family membership was brought into question in the eyes of outsiders by their different names and by experiences they had to undergo which other children did not. Therefore, they saw adoption as bringing about some immediate tangible gains such as not having to undergo medicals or receive social work visits. The main benefit though was the relief of not having to explain to friends and teachers why they had a different surname from that of their adoptive parents.

Goffman (1963) argues that whenever a change in name occurs "an important breach is involved between the individual and his old world" (p. 76). This theme was taken up by others to suggest that whenever a change of name takes place this has a negative impact on the person's identity. While this may be so in some instances, no account is being taken, as in this case, of the feelings of being "different" or of "not belonging" generated in a child whose surname differs from that of the substitute family. Many writers on the subject attribute moves for a change in surname as solely related to expressed or unspoken pressures on the part of the family. Yet another explanation for such a step is to satisfy a child's long felt wish to erase tangible signs of difference.

The Symbolism of the Law. As interviewers we were struck by what the law symbolized to these children, something that we had not anticipated. The children seemed to attach a lot of importance to their family membership becoming "legal," even to those who were approaching adulthood (see Brodzinsky, Singer, & Braff, 1984, for a discussion of developmental changes in children's understanding of adoption). There was awareness about the legal transfer of powers that adoption brought with it, and that control was being transferred from an outside authority to the family. Typical comments included: "It is something permanent and by law" or simply "it is legal." One young person described graphically the internal meaning of this transition: "I was wanting to be adopted but it was just really the same, I mean it didn't change anything—yet if I had not been adopted, I would have been quite disappointed because by law I wouldn't be here."

For these children and young people, the adoption order was a symbolic act creating a deep, satisfying psychological feeling for them. Even for those who would soon become adults, the change from fostering to adoption was a very important one. It conveyed to them a sense of security and belonging, the right to feel as part of the family and to call the foster parents, "parents." These findings also confirm Triseliotis's (1983) earlier observations about the insecure and "ambiguous" status of children in long-term foster care compared with those in adoption. In this respect concern can be expressed at some recent judicial decisions which, by opting for custodianship instead of granting an adoption order to foster parents, may be depriving the child of long-term security. For example, in re M (minor), whose case was heard in 1984 in the British Court of Appeal following an application by the foster parents to adopt the child, Justice Ormond stated that in his opinion adoption was not designed to cater to children in long-term foster care and custodianship was better. (Under British legislation, custodianship provides considerable security to foster parents in that the child cannot be returned to its birthparents without the consent of the court, but it obviously fails to provide the full security of adoption.)

Another argument proposed by the courts in subsequent cases for refusing an adoption order to foster parents and granting instead a custodianship one, was the need to safeguard access by natural parents to their offspring. As we have found from this study, children's links with meaningful people from the past need to be preserved but when the natural parents do not even plan or wish to provide a home for the child, then adoption with access safeguards security and continuity of care for the child without breaking important family links. Certainly the very few children in our sample who were grieving for the loss of meaningful links from the past, did not necessarily wish to go back to their original parents or relatives but simply to preserve that link through occasional contacts. There was no doubt though from the comments of these children that they did not feel as well integrated within their adoptive families as most of the rest of the sample. As the numbers involved were small (3), the findings should be seen as suggestive rather than conclusive.

Reversibility of Early Adverse Experiences and Intergenerational Continuities

Both the adoption and foster care sample, but particularly the former, demonstrated that the impact of early adverse experiences can "fade away" with the opportunity to form new positive attachments. Similar observations were also made by Kadushin (1970), Clarke and Clarke (1976), and Tizard (1977). The view that children are held hostages to adverse early childhood experiences seems too deterministic. Our study also showed that emotional difficulties displayed during childhood are not necessarily predictive of similar behavior in adult life. We arrived at this conclusion after having tracked the children's behavior, and particularly the seeking of psychiatric help, before placement during childhood and in the last 12 months before the interview took place. The age also at which the adopted and foster care groups were placed with their substitute families or the number of moves within the public care system were unrelated to outcome. (A reminder though that all the children were placed with their respective families under the age of 10. Our study, therefore, makes no statement about children placed in substitute forms of care when aged 10 and over). In addition, on a range of personal and social functioning variables, those adopted were not any different from the rest of the population. Stein and Hoopes (1985), who contrasted adopted with nonadopted adolescents, also noted that there were no significant differences between the two groups, and that adoptees displayed no deficiencies in functioning on measures of overall identity when compared with their nonadopted counterparts.

No evidence was also found to support a theory of intergenerational continuities in matters of social and personal behavior and circumstances among children separated from their birthfamily, although in the case of the residential group, there appeared to be more continuities compared to the other two. If such a pattern exists, or if genetic influences operate, then adoption, and to some extent long-term foster care, but not residential rearing, seem to have the capacity to intercept and offset it (see Bohman & Sigvardsson, Chapter 5, for a similar pattern of findings). Caution though is required in seeing such continuities, especially in social functioning, as "inevitable." Some of the evidence suggests that, although past experiences can influence, more important than continuities and predestinations are opportunities in life. For example, there was nothing different in the background characteristics and experiences of those in the residential group who coped better than the rest. The main distinguishing factors that appeared to contribute to more successful coping appeared mainly to do with more recent events. This included a more stable marriage, continuity of work, and a somewhat wider circle of relatives, some acquired through marriage, which provided a fairly supportive environment. (See also Brown & Madge, 1982).

Genealogical Information and Identity Formation

The study *In Search of Origins* (Triseliotis, 1973), which looked at the search behavior of adopted people in Scotland, where access has been possible for over 50 years, provided a number of insights that linked identity formation in adopted people with, among other things, knowledge about origins and the past. This study came to the conclusion that a vital part in the jigsaw of identity formation is knowledge about one's background and forebearers, including the history of one's family and by extension of one's race and ethnic group. Other studies have also confirmed the importance of background genealogical information to the development of a personal and social identity (see Haimes & Timms, 1985; Picton, 1980; Schechter & Bertocci, Chapter 4). The sharing of such information in a positive and open way, which takes account of the adopted person's age and understanding, is now seen as a step that helps to promote identity and general personality development. Openness about backgrounds far from undermining relationships with adoptive parents, on the contrary, seems to strengthen them. This issue is assuming greater importance now than in the past because with the increasing diversity of lifestyles and different methods of conception, an increasing number of children are now being brought up in circumstances where one or both people are not their biological parents. (For a fuller discussion of the issues involved in open adoption and the open records controversy, see Baran & Pannor, Chapter 17.)

Triseliotis's 1973 study, referred to earlier, could justifiably be criticized for being based solely on a select sample because it was limited to people who set out on a "search" quest and consequently did not include a representative sample of adopted people. Such a broad-based sample would have made it possible, among other things, to test propositions arising from the 1973 study, such as (1) the wish for access to birth information is not universal among adoptees but rather is confined primarily to those for whom genealogical information and the truth about their origins was withheld by adoptive parents, or those who perceived their growing-up experiences as less than satisfactory; (2) the quality of family relationships and "open" styles of communication about adoption and related issues correlate with the development of a positive sense of identity in adopted people and with general adjustment; and (3) among a high percentage of those searching, particularly those seeking contact rather than information, there is a high level of stress and personal difficulties.

The conclusions of our contrast study were based, as already stated, on a broader sample, which included searchers and nonsearchers to modify the earlier findings in one important respect. Although searching for origins is still a minority interest, it has to be recognized that the wide publicity focused on the subject of "origins" and "roots" in the last 15 to 20 years and the emphasis on minority rights has helped to generate a much greater consciousness among all people, including adoptees, about genealogy. In this respect, more adoptees are now likely to be searching for their origins out of curiosity than before. Public opinion and, in some countries, the law have come to sanction the search for information or contact without generating a sense of guilt, betrayal, or shame. As a result, the motives and intentions of those individuals seeking access now is not necessarily the same as those doing so 15 or 20 years ago. (For a fuller discussion of the motives and dynamics of searchers, see Schecter & Bertocci, Chapter 4.)

In this contrast study, about a quarter of the adopted samples and over a third of the fostered samples were not told or did not find out their true status until they were 12 years or older. Knowing about their real status did not always mean that there was also discussion around it or information about their first family. Altogether about three quarters of those adopted, half of those who grew up fostered, and 85% of those reared in residential establishments said that there was never, or hardly ever, any discussion of these issues. While some adoptees maintained that they would not have desired more discussion anyway, others still felt uncomfortable about the big gaps in their knowledge about their background. There was considerable ignorance and confusion among many of those who had been fostered or reared in residential centers concerning the names and circumstances of their parents and siblings. Ignorance of many basic genealogical facts was proving problematic and embarrassing to them, especially in their interactions with peers and friends.

Among a number of adopted people there was the feeling that their parents did not enjoy talking about the subject. Some parents would discuss it only if the child asked questions. Examples of comments about this aspect of family life include: "I can't remember when my adoption was ever discussed with me and I never brought it up"; "I couldn't talk to my parents about my adoption. It was one of the things you didn't talk about"; "It was up to them to take the initiative."

About 9% of the adoptees had obtained access to their birth records by the time of the interview and half of these were still hoping to establish contact with a birth-parent. In addition, about a quarter of the total sample said they would have liked to have had more information about their background, circumstances of adoption, and reasons for being given up for adoption. A few added that they would like at some future date contact with a birthparent or the opportunity to see them from a distance. It is a matter of speculation as to how far the latter is linked to issues of body image, the assumption being that some adopted people may find it difficult to develop a complete sense of body image without a visual picture of their birthparents (see Schecter & Bertocci, Chapter 4).

As hinted earlier, the large majority of adoptees said that they had no intention to set out on a quest. Their main explanation was that they had parents, their adoptive ones, they were leading a "happy" life, and they saw no point in a search, contact, or reunion. These findings confirm those of Raynor (1980), who also found from her study of adopted people that at the time of interview, 75% were unconcerned about their birthparents. Similarly, Stein and Hoopes (1985) found that only a small proportion of adoptees in their sample expressed an interest to search for their biological parents. They also found that searchers were somewhat less well adjusted than non-searchers and perceived their adoptive family relationships to be less satisfactory. Obviously, attitudes to access are not static and intentions can change. Motivation for a search may change as a result of a variety of factors including a personal crisis, increased curiosity fostered by publicity or those around the adopted person, or the need for an accurate medical history.

Since the opening of the English birth records to adopted people in 1977, those applying for access each year represent approximately 0.3% of all adopted adults. Taking this annual rate over the whole period of the average life span (i.e., from age 18 when access is possible to age 70), it would yield about 15% of all adoptees searching at some stage in their lives (see Triseliotis, 1984). The numbers are about evenly split between those seeking information and those hoping to establish contact with a birthparent. Obviously, the percentages quoted above may change in response to social changes in personal circumstances.

Looking at the propositions posed earlier and their relationship to current search behavior among adopted people, our study found no direct association between the disclosure and timing of adoption and the sharing of background and genealogical information and a number of variables concerning satisfaction or dissatisfaction with the adoption experience. However, a small group of adopted people who had psychiatric help in childhood or in their adult life were more likely to be among those who felt that their adoption was not openly discussed. This same group was also featured among those who expressed reservations about the quality of their growing up experience within the adoptive home. Our analysis of the data, however, led us to conclude that in a hierarchy of needs, the quality of the adoption experience seems to take priority over issues of disclosure, its timing, and the sharing of background information, a point also made by Jaffee and Fanshel (1970). These findings do not minimize the importance of open communication within the family about adoption. Far from it, open communication and positive relationships are part of the same continuum and were frequently found to go together. Our findings concerning the value of "open communication" lend support to Kirk's (1964) theoretical assumption that "acknowledgment of difference" enhances the adoptive parents' relationship with the adopted child and that, in contrast, "rejection of difference" would tend to disturb that relationship since it would probably inhibit the adoptive parents' "capacity for empathy with the special problems that only the adoptee experiences" (Kirk, 1981, p. 9).

Many of those fostered shared similar experiences of secrecy and evasiveness with those adopted, especially those fostered very young. The fact that social workers visited at certain intervals made little difference as they tended to collude with the foster parents not to raise the subject: "I was 12 or 13 before I realized I was fostered . . . this made me become mixed up . . . there was no talk or explanation about it." "I never knew much about my own family . . . I still don't." Those who had been fostered appeared more inhibited and uncertain, compared with adoptees, as to whether and what kind of additional information they wanted. Their inhibition was possibly not unconnected with the ambiguity of their position referred to earlier vis-à-vis their foster parents. Like the adopted group, no direct association was found between the disclosure of the fostering situation (where this was relevant) and the sharing of genealogical information and a number of variables concerning satisfaction or dissatisfaction with the fostering experience. Those whose fostering arrangements broke down were more likely than the other groups to be seeking members of their original family.

Individuals who grew up in residential institutions were aware of their status but they too were given little or no information about their parents and their own circumstances. They were more uncertain and unclear about the past compared with either adoptees or those formerly fostered. They wanted to know "why they were in care," "why in a Home," "who were my parents," "what happened to them," and "what the future holds for me." "Neither housemothers nor housefathers nor social workers nor anyone else attempted to discuss my circumstances with me whilst in the Home." "I would like to have discussed many things with the staff, but they didn't seem to have the time. They were there to do a job only." Overall it seems to matter a great deal that children may grow up uncertain and confused about themselves, their circumstances, and their personal and social history. Such awareness seems a necessary ingredient to the formation of a whole self.

The Attitudes and Behavior of Other People

The pioneer work of writers such as Goffman (1963) has helped us to understand how the way others see us can affect the image we develop about ourselves. Our identity depends, at least in part, on our perception of our place in society and on how others view us. Goffman developed the concept of "spoiled identity" to signify the impact of stigma and labeling on individuals and minority groups who are seen to depart from or defy the norm. Minority groups such as blacks, the handicapped, or those fostered or adopted may be effectively perceived as "inferior," "bad," or "second class" simply because they are different and do not conform to traditional expectations. Goffman points out that "failure or success at maintaining norms has a very direct effect on the psychological integrity of the individual" (pp. 152–153).

In our contrast study, adoptees experienced few open negative community attitudes because of their adoptive status. There were a few exceptions, mainly at school, but the predominant climate was one of acceptance. However, these people were still not keen on telling others that they were adopted and disliked being introduced by their parents as "my adopted son or daughter." They believed it should be left to them to share such personal information with people who were meaningful to them and trustful. Those fostered seemed to experience more negative encounters, particularly at school. The different surname from that of the foster family seemed to attract attention. Others factors that stressed the difference of their position included the "welfare visits," the perceived failure of the family of origin, the very sporadic appearance of a parent or sibling, and the ambiguous nature of their relationship with the foster parents. Fanshel and Shinn (1978) postulated the view that a child who is neither living with his own family nor adopted "may come to think of himself as being less than first rate, or an unwanted human being" (p. 479). The traditional perception of fostering as "low status" vis-à-vis adoption seems to add to feelings of low self-esteem among those in long-term fostering.

Of all the three groups, those who grew up in institutions appeared most stigmatized and most troubled about their position. The image of themselves, based on how they thought the community perceived them, was of being "bad," "abnormal," "inferior," and "different." "People think if you are in a Home it is because you are bad." "What stuck at school was being called a 'Homey child.' " "If anything happened in the village the police would come to the Home." What was even sadder was that some individuals came to see themselves as "not normal" or "different." "When you said you lived in . . . there was instant dislike by other kids because you were different. . . . I knew I was different from them." Some of the residential-reared individuals would refer to other children as "normal" implying that they themselves were abnormal because of the circumstances under which they grew up.

CONCLUSIONS

Our studies identified three important factors that contribute to the development of a personal and social identity, including a sense of security, in individuals growing up in "substitute care." These factors are: the quality of care experienced; knowledge about origins and the past; and being part of the wider community with no stigma attached. The evidence points to the relative security provided by a family-type rearing and its positive influence on the developing self compared with the impact of long-term residential care. While long-term foster care provides considerable satisfactions, its ambiguous status gives rise to an element of insecurity not found in adoption. The adoption of "high risk" children provided evidence about the reversibility of early psychological trauma and further evidence showing that emotional or behavioral difficulties in childhood are not necessarily indicative of similar behavior in adult life. These findings held fairly well with those in long-term foster care but not with those who experienced long-term institutional care.

Evasiveness and secrecy employed by "substitute" parents and caregivers tended to foster feelings of shame, guilt, and abnormality. Such feelings were frequently reinforced by community attitudes, particularly in the case of the former residential-reared individuals, many of whom came to perceive themselves as peripheral to society. There was no evidence to suggest that "identity" problems are inevitable with children growing up in "substitute care," particularly in adoption. The vast majority of adopted people, many of those fostered, and some of those who grew up in residential care were well settled in the community.

7

Acknowledgment or Rejection of Differences?

KENNETH KAYE

In our family, adoption was a joke. We older cousins would tease the younger ones by pretending to let slip the fact that they were adopted. In reality, no one was; it was simply a way of saying, "You're different; you'll never fit in." We inherited the joke from our mothers, who have been recycling it on their baby sister for nearly 60 years. Since I have come to know adoptive families, the humor has been lost on me.

For the past quarter-century, an untested hypothesis has pervaded the clinical literature about adoption. The hypothesis concerns parents' (and, as a consequence, children's) "acknowledgment versus rejection" of the differences between adoptive and biological parenthood, and of the fact that being adopted colors a child's life and identity. There are indications that some parents impose on themselves and their children an implicit eleventh commandment, "Thou shalt insist that adoption is no different from the biological parent–child relationship." Many social workers, child psychologists, and family therapists regard such a rule as tantamount to denial. If obeyed, it forces children to repress their normal curiosity about roots, leading to "genealogical bewilderment" (Brinich, 1980; Sants, 1964; Stone, 1972). Virtually all authors—clinicians (e.g., Kent & Richie, 1976; Sorosky et al., 1978) as well as researchers and personal chroniclers (e.g., Kirk, 1964; Lifton, 1975)—agree that honoring such a prohibition leaves adoptees no room to express grief, anger, and fears about loss, abandonment, or rejection; nor to work through their doubts about the adequacy of their bonds with the adoptive family. In effect, the literature sees some adoptive parents, left to their own denial mechanisms, as unreceptive to their children's tentative expressions of feeling "different" (or worse) about being adopted. This deprives the children of opportunities to resolve inevitable questions about their bonds, thus impairing their sense of security and self-esteem. At least, that has been the hypothesis; but there have been no empirical data as to whether such repression of negative feelings actually occurs to an extent that is detrimental to adopted children's healthy emotional growth.

Kirk (1964), on the basis of questionnaires completed by a widespread sample of adoptive parents, distinguished two alternative "coping strategies," which he called "acknowledgment of differences" and "rejection of differences." He saw a dilemma for adoptive parents: on the one hand, the former strategy could be used to relabel positively their family's and their children's uniqueness, but would sacrifice the comfort of fitting society's norms; on the other hand, the alternative strategy would force them to act and pretend to feel like all other parents, thereby sacrificing the benefits of truth and openness in their family relationships. Kirk saw the latter as the worse sacrifice. His title *Shared Fate* suggested a way out of the dilemma: that infertile parents need to acknowledge and work through their own fate as frustrated nonchildbearers, while helping their children resolve the loss of biological roots and build on the special nature of their family bond.

Parents' coping strategy may indeed be important in adopted children's development. Prospective studies have generally found either few or no differences between groups of early-adopted children and demographically matched controls but have concluded that the adoptive family environment is a crucial factor in adoptees' adjustment (Bohman & Sigvardsson, 1985; Stein & Hoopes, 1985; Witmer et al., 1963). Although school and behavior problems have been found more prevalent in adopted children during the elementary years (Bohman & Sigvardsson, 1980; Brodzinsky, Schechter et al., 1984), such differences seem to disappear by adolescence. For example, Stein and Hoopes interviewed 50 adopted adolescents and a matched sample of 41 nonadopted adolescents. On standard measures of self-image and of ego identity, they found no differences between the groups. Both adopted and nonadopted adolescents' positive perceptions of their family relationships were the best predictor of identity formation and social adjustment. Within the adopted group, however, there was an additional significant predictor of overall adjustment, especially concerning school and self-esteem factors: self-reported "openness of family communication about adoption issues."

We recently explored the dimension of acknowledgment versus rejection or (to avoid attributing honesty to one end of the continuum and denial to the other) *high versus low distinguishing*. We hoped (1) to investigate Kirk's coping strategies a generation later and (2) to observe, in action, how parents and children "process" the emotional content of their experiences as an adoptive family. Does the fact of being an adoptive family have inevitable implications for parents' and children's feelings about themselves and each other? How much room is there for disparity of feelings? Do relatively trouble-free adoptive families differ from more problematic ones in their manner of discussing adoption issues? Is the freedom to express different, perhaps ambivalent, feelings an important aspect of identity formation in the adoptee?

The theoretical significance of these questions goes beyond adoption. The study of family processes and their impact on children's development requires a complexity of analysis that has been most productive when applied to particular developmental issues rather than to the general, sometimes vague notion of family systems (Kantor & Lehr, 1975; Kaye, 1982, 1985). Adoptive families present a natural paradigm for the study of adaptation to deeply meaningful events, on the part of the whole family system as well as its individual members. By combining a microanalysis of family discussions with a multivariate analysis of individual interviews with adopted teenagers and their parents, we were able to see the phenomenon of high versus low distinguishing in more intricate and potentially more useful ways. Methods and statistical analysis of this study are reported in more detail by Kaye and Warren (1988). This chapter adds a few additional results, proposes directions future researchers might take, and elaborates on the implications of "acknowledgment versus rejection of differences" for clinical work with adoptive families.

ACKNOWLEDGMENT OR REJECTION AS A DISCOURSE PROCESS

The contrast between a low-distinguishing family discussion and a high-distinguishing one is readily apparent in transcripts from our study. The following excerpt comes from one of the families scoring *lowest* on the "distinguishing" variables to be discussed later in this chapter. (Codes on the left pertain to the categories listed in Tables 7.2 and 7.3.)

In this family, the father and mother are 53, and the daughter, 18; the following question was asked:

Would your family life have been different over the years if you had all been one another's biological parents and children?

	Mother: I can
XR5	*Father:* The answer is no.
XR5	*Mother:* That's right. (laughs).
	Interviewer: Okay, but I'm going to leave the room anyway, so you can talk about why you feel that way.
P	*Mother:* Okay, read that question again.
PM	*Daughter:* Family life—
PM	*Father:* "Has your family life been different from how it would have been if you had all been biologically related to one another?"
R5	*Daughter:* I don't think it changes it much.
	Father: No, except for—
R5	*Mother:* Not for us, no.
A3	*Father:* Except for the trip to The Cradle that we made once or twice.
R3	*Daughter:* It just changes little things, you know, like when I was little, most little kids just threaten to run away, I'd threaten to go to The Cradle and get readopted (laughs).
	Mother: (laughs).
R3	*Father:* Well, yes, most other little ones wouldn't think of such things.
	Mother: (laughs).
R3R5	*Daughter:* Well, they (i.e., the adoption agency) knew about it, so what the heck. I can't think of anything else different, you know\
R5	*Mother:* I can't think of any.
R5	*Daughter:* \specific things that would change. You know, other families do things together, you know, they have their ups and downs. We're certainly not exempt.
R5	*Mother:* That's right.
	Daughter: You know. I can't see\
	Father: I still say\
R5	*Daughter:* \any major difference.
R5	*Father:* \the answer is a simple no.

R5	*Mother:* Simple no.
R3	*Daughter:* I don't think you can just go ahead and say no, I mean I'm sure there have been, I can't really say, but
R5	*Mother:* I cannot think of any.
R5	*Father:* Well, I cannot recall any that we could\
R3	*Daughter:* Uh-huh. I know, but it's just, little things like that, that would be different\
	Father: \identify to this question.
R5	*Mother:* Yeah.
R5	*Daughter:* \but, nothing major at all. That I'll agree with, but I'm sure there are little differences that don't make that much difference (laughs).
X	*Father:* Next question.
	[Discussion continues]

The same family, two questions later:

Do you think any of your feelings about yourselves or about one another are different in any way from what they might be if you had all been one another's biological parents and children?

R5	*Daughter:* I don't think so.
R5	*Mother:* (laughs) I don't think so either. Same feelings
P	*Father:* "Do you think your feelings about one another are different in any way from what they would be if you were all biologically related?"
R5	*Mother:* You seem like our biological daughter (laughs).
R5	*Daughter:* I don't think twice about it.
P	*Father:* Do you think your feelings are at all different\
	Daughter: Maybe sometimes\
	Father: \had you been biologically
S6R5	*Daughter:* \when you're little you think to yourself, "Gee, they picked me, only a baby," you know. I know perfectly well that's not true. I mean, you know, you can use that to make yourself feel special and that kind of thing but other than that, no. Perfectly normal.
R5	*Father:* Then\the answer to the question is no.
R5	*Mother:* That's right.
R5Q	*Daughter:* Coming right down to it, yes, the answer is no. I mean, am I supposed to treat you differently, is there something they didn't tell me (laughs)?
R5	*Mother:* Not to my knowledge (laughs). I think it has all been very natural.
R5	*Father:* Yes.
R5	*Mother:* Yes.
	Father: Next question.
	Daughter: Shot that one down quick.

The following excerpt comes from one of the family discussions scoring *highest* in distinguishing. In this family, the father is 50, the mother 38, and the son 13.

Have other people ever treated you differently because of their attitudes about adoption?

	Son: This one is good.
PT	*Mother:* Okay, why don't you start then.
O1	*Son:* A lot of kids at school, like Chris, he's made fun of me, when he's mad at me he uses that against me. Big deal. And

OQT	*Father:* How has he used that against you?
O1	*Son:* Said at least he knows who his father is, stuff like that.
	Father: Hm. Well you
O4	*Son:* I forgot what it was.
	Father: Yeah.
O3	*Son:* My teacher, Mrs. N. treats me a little bit differently.
OQT	*Mother:* Do you think that's because you're adopted?
O3	*Son:* Yeah, I mean in a way.
OQT	*Father:* Better or worse?
O1	*Son:* Worse.
OQT	*Mother:* How?
O1	*Son:* She'll say stuff like "You think because you've gone through one experience in your life you've paid all your dues," and stuff like that.
O3	*Father:* Oh, that was that suffering bit, whether you've suffered enough.
O3	*Son:* Yeah, long time ago.
O4O6	*Father:* I don't know that it enters into my relationships with anybody, the fact that we've adopted children. I've never thought about it before, but it seems that people sometimes say it's wonderful that we've adopted children, but I don't know if they act any differently toward us because of that.
O1	*Mother:* What first came to my mind is an incident that happened in the grocery store. Somebody came up to me and said about *(10-year-old, not present),* when he was two or three, "He's not your child, he must be adopted." But that's never happened in relation to you *(Son)* because people have always said\
OQM	*Son:* Well what did you say then?
O4O1R5	*Mother:* I don't remember. My main concern was protecting you and him, I think all three of you were there, from hurt feelings. I just wanted to get away from that person. I'm sure what I said was "He is my son, these are my children." Whether or not you were adopted or looked like me, my main concern was for you, this person was obviously a jackass.
O1R2	*Father:* Those feelings are around, different people have them. I guess to some extent we ourselves might, even. It's not the usual way to have children
O3	*Mother:* I remember once taking *(9-year-old, not present)* to the Irish festival at Ridge Park, these 10 musicians looked alike and she said, "Mommy, why do they all look alike?" and I realized that for her, brothers and sisters don't automatically look alike.
	Son: (inaudible).
XT	*Father:* (Starts to call interviewer).
PM	*Son:* Well, does Dad think we were done?
PF	*Mother:* Yeah, (to Father) I don't think *(Son)* is finished.
PT	*Father:* What more do you have to say, *(Son)*? I'm sorry.
O3	*Son:* I told earlier about Granny.
OQT	*Father:* Oh yeah Granny. Maybe you should talk about that more.
O4	*Son:* Well, I don't have to, it's already in there (on the tape), I've said basically what I thought I meant.
O1	*Father:* Well you picked up some real problems in grandmother and grandfather's feelings.
	[Discussion continues]

One reason some family discussions have a predominant tone of "rejection of differences" and others a predominant tone of "acknowledgment" is that the system exerts pressure on each member to confirm the consensus being formed by the others.

In the first family above, the daughter was talked out of her initial assertion of some fairly mild differences, not by direct argument, but merely by her parents' ignoring her point and reasserting that they "can't think of any" differences. In the second family, the son began by indicating he had something to say, Mother encouraged him and then confirmed his position with supporting anecdotes, and Father eventually acknowledged that they had a point.

METHOD

Besides exemplifying two poles of the continuum, the foregoing transcripts illustrate our method of observing "acknowledgment versus rejection of differences" as a process of family discourse (Kaye & Warren, 1988). We asked many of the same questions Kirk (1964) did. Unlike Kirk, however, we (1) interviewed our informants individually, in person; (2) interviewed their adolescent adoptees; and (3) also recorded them in family discussions to see whether manifestations of those coping strategies might be found in the ways different parents communicate with their children.

Sample

The population sampled was a restricted subset of all adoptive families: only maritally intact, racially homogeneous families with at least one teenage child who was adopted before age 2. In addition, all lived within a 90 minutes' drive from downtown Chicago. Through two large adoption agencies' mailing lists, we distributed flyers describing a study of "communication in adoptive families." This recruitment method dictated that all children had been told about their adoption, parents had remained on their agency's mailing list, and all members of the family were willing to be interviewed. As with any sample of volunteers, the possibility exists that their feelings and opinions may be unrepresentative of the population from which they selected themselves. Our interest, however, was in comparing these 40 families with one another. We shall refer to each family's oldest adopted child between the ages of 13 and 19 as the "target" child.[1]

Procedure

A pair of investigators made a single visit to each family's home, lasting 2 to 3 hours. They began by assembling the family around the kitchen or dining-room table, obtaining informed consent from each child and both parents, and then charting a genogram, which mainly served to establish rapport and bring the relevant chronology to the forefront of everyone's attention. A semistructured family discussion followed (similar to the dialogues quoted above), and then the members were interviewed individually.

The family discussions consisted of seven parts (Table 7.1). An interviewer presented each question to the family, made sure it was understood (e.g., did the youngest child know what "biological" meant as opposed to "adopted"?), and left the

Table 7.1 Questions Asked as Separate Parts of Family Discussion

1. What are the three things you like best, that you do together as a family? What does each person like to do alone, or some of you without the others? What are some things you all do together that you don't like?
2. Tell the story of how Mom and Dad adopted *(Target).*
3. Would your family life have been different over the years if you had all been one another's biological parents and children?
4. Have other people ever treated you differently because of their attitudes about adoption?
5. Do you think any of your feelings about yourselves or about one another are different in any way from what they might be if you had all been one another's biological parents and children?
6. Besides what you have already said, are there any other ways life has been *harder* for any of you because of being a member of an adoptive family?
7. Besides what you have already said, are there any other ways life has been *easier* for any of you because of being a member of an adoptive family?

Note: Each question, typed on a card, was left with the family when the interviewer left the room.

family alone to discuss it. The family was to decide whether they agreed on one answer or preferred to say that some members felt one way and others another way. In either case, they were to talk about *why* they felt as they did, and only then call the interviewer back for the next question.

Afterward, each parent and each child aged 13 or over was interviewed privately and confidentially. Subjects filled out a standard 10-item self-esteem instrument (Rosenberg, 1979). Then the interviewer administered a questionnaire similar to Kirk's. This questionnaire included a few items of factual information, such as annual income, and questions like "Has anyone in the family been involved in professional counseling or therapy?" Most of the items, however, garnered subjective responses. These the interviewer rated on the spot, using a 5-point scale (e.g., "Do you ever feel uncomfortable talking about adoption?").

One question of particular importance to this chapter fell somewhere between factual and subjective matters: "Can you think of any problems such as these in the family over the years?" The interviewer probed specifically for "school problems," "behavior problems," "problems with other children," "marriage problems," "health problems," "emotional problems," and "other kinds of problems." In each case, she checked "yes" if any such problems were recalled, not necessarily involving the target child. Then she went back through the items that had been answered affirmatively, asking whether the informant thought those problems had any relationship to their being an adoptive family. The replies to the latter question were rated on a 5-point scale from "definitely unrelated" to "primarily related to adoption" in that family member's opinion. Thus we obtained two distinct variables from each individual, the number of "yes" items and the mean rating (referred to below as Problems due to Adoption) across those items.

"OPEN" DISTINGUISHING IN FAMILY DISCUSSIONS

Tables 7.2 and 7.3 list our coding categories, illustrated by actual examples. As Table 7.4 shows, the levels of distinguishing in the family discussions varied with

Table 7.2   Brief Definitions and Exemplars of Coding Categories

Process codes
P   Comments or injunctions about the *process* of discussion ("Read the question again.")
Q   *Queries* more specific than the interviewer's ("Why?")
X   *Terminating* discussion when others appear to have more to say ("We're getting long-winded.")

Topic codes
A   *Adoption* decision, application, waiting, getting baby, etc. ("We waited exactly 9 months."—**A5**)
B   *Biological* parents, background, possible search, etc. ("I can fantasize that John Lennon was my father."—**B6**)
D   *Developmental* tasks ("You kids have had a lot more trouble in the area of self-confidence."—**D1**)
H   *Heredity* vs. environment ("We would all have had blue eyes."—**H3**)
 I   *Inability* to give birth ("I was 32 by then, and they said it might take several years."—**I2**)
O   *Others* ("It upset you that time your friend teased you."—**O1**)
R   *Relational* feelings —"You three are that much more special to us."—**R6**)
S   Child's *self-concept* and sense of roots ("This is who I am, right here."—**S5**)

the question asked and with the issues raised in response to each question. Talking about the process of adoption, including infertility, applications, and interviews (Question 2 and Topics **A** and **I**), brought out acknowledged differences and disadvantages, as did other people's reactions (Question 4 and Topic **O**) and the child's curiosity about roots (Topic **B**). Conversely, with regard to feelings about the family or about the children's development, distinguishing was low (Questions 3, 5, 6, and 7; Topics **D**, **R**, and **S**).

The microanalysis does not concern us here, but its results can be summarized briefly. All three family members could be seen influencing one another toward consensus, in that the likelihood of each person's high- or low-distinguishing remarks depended on what the other speakers had most recently said; however, the moment-to-moment influence of parents on adolescents was no greater than that of adolescents on parents. Thus we found no evidence, at this age, that parents repress acknowledgment of differences or elicit rejection of differences any more than adolescents and fathers constrain mothers' expression of feelings in the family discussion, or adolescents and mothers constrain fathers' expression of feelings. The mutual influences were characteristic of a commonly observed group process: it becomes increasingly difficult to express and maintain a deviant opinion, as other participants in the conversation confirm one another's consensus.

Table 7.3   Levels of Distinguishing

1. Unqualified high distinguishing of *disadvantages* or *costs* of adoptive relationship ("I would feel closer to you, and we might not fight as much."—**R1**)
2. Mild or qualified distinguishing of disadvantages or costs ("It's just this little teeny question in the back of my mind, I don't know where I come from."—**S2**)
3. Mentions difference without clear advantage or disadvantage ("Our relatives wanted to know what kind of family the baby would come from."—**O3B3**)
4. Denies remembering, or ever thinking about it; or explicitly refuses to answer ("How would I know, I wasn't born."—**A4**)
5. Asserts *no difference* ("Isn't it how you're raised that determines who you are?"—**H5Q**)
6. Asserts *advantages* of adoptive relationship ("You didn't have to go through labor."—**I6**)

Table 7.4   Levels of Distinguishing by Question and Topic Codes

	Percentage at Each Level[a]					
	1 Unqualified Disad- vantage	2 Mild Disad- vantage	3 Neutral Differ- ence	4 Can't Say	5 No Differ- ence	6 Adoption Advantage
Question[b]						
2 Story	12.6	30.1	29.1	17.5	9.7	1.0
3 Family life	2.8	2.6	19.1	8.4	62.6	4.5
4 Others	12.8	7.9	33.7	3.4	38.8	3.5
5 Feelings	6.0	3.3	17.0	8.7	59.0	6.1
6 Harder?	14.9	8.5	10.2	6.0	55.3	5.1
7 Easier?	4.1	6.0	8.7	7.7	48.5	25.0
Topic[c]						
Adoption	20.9	4.9	41.5	28.0	3.5	1.2
Background	15.0	9.8	42.3	15.3	11.0	6.6
Development	3.8	2.0	4.2	9.2	68.3	12.6
Heredity	6.6	4.6	34.4	2.0	37.5	14.9
Infertility	2.2	50.5	12.0	1.6	12.9	20.8
Other people	14.1	8.5	36.6	2.8	35.0	3.0
Relationship	3.0	1.7	12.6	9.8	66.7	6.2
Self-concept	9.2	6.5	17.2	3.7	38.4	25.0

[a] See Table 7.3 for Levels of distinguishing.
[b] See Table 7.1 for Question list.
[c] See Table 7.2 for Coding categories.

Although the microanalysis involved each of the six levels as distinct events in the discourse (Kaye & Warren, 1988), we also derived a single score, Open Distinguishing, as a reflection of how each person's level codes were distributed.[2] This index enabled us to relate what mothers, fathers, and adolescents said in the family discussion with what they told us privately.

"PRIVATE" DISTINGUISHING

In addition to Open Distinguishing, six of the variables from our individual interviews had been hypothesized as possibly related to an underlying dimension of acknowledgment versus rejection of differences: Discomfort in talking about adoption; Life Was Harder due to the adoption (including Kirk's questions about recollected frustration and sadness); Problems due to Adoption (given that any of the seven types of family problems were reported, to what extent were they considered adoption-related?); how much the person Knows About Birthparents; Thinks About Birthparents; and Feels About Search (difference-rejecting parents would be less comfortable with their children's searching, and difference-rejecting children less likely to do so).[3] These variables did constitute a unitary dimension among the adolescents, as indicated in Table 7.5. All 21 linear coefficients in the triangular matrix are positive, and 17 of the 21 are significantly so.

Among the parents (with whom Kirk originally postulated the dimension of "ac-

Table 7.5   Predicted "Acknowledgment" Variables

	Open Distinguishing	Think Birthparents	Know Birthparents	Problems Due	Life Harder	Discomfort
Adolescent						
Will Search		.62***			.39**	.48***
Discomfort	.52***	.56***	.28*	.54***	.69***	
Life Was Harder	.48***	.53***		.79***		
Problems due to Adoption	.34*	.51***	.30*			
Knows About Birthparents	.31*	.44**				
Thinks About Birthparents	.43**					
Mother						
Feels if Child Searches	.29*		.28*			
Discomfort						
Life Was Harder						
Problems due to Adoption		.35**	.27*			
Knows About Birthparents		.40**				
Thinks About Birthparents						
Father						
Feels if Child Searches	.32*					
Discomfort	.31*	.47***		.48***		
Life Was Harder						
Problems due to Adoption		.27*				
Knows About Birthparents						
Thinks About Birthparents						

*$.01 < p < .05$; ** $.001 < p < .01$; *** $p < .001$ (39 d.f., one-tailed)

knowledgment versus rejection of differences''), the cluster of variables was far from unidimensional. Only 10 of 42 coefficients were significantly correlated, and 11 of the nonsignificant ones were in the negative (theoretically wrong) direction. We conclude that these seven variables essentially measure different things, and may even have a somewhat different meaning to mothers than to fathers. There is no underlying dimension of ''acknowledgment'' in general, among parents, though there definitely appears to be such a dimension among adolescent adoptees.

INTRAFAMILY AGREEMENT AND DIFFERENCES

Family members tended to agree with one another on five of the six forms of distinguishing we tapped privately (Table 7.6, rows 2 through 6). The highest parent–child correlations (row 7) were between the single question ''How much does your child want to know about his or her biological parents?'' and a composite of 16 items asking the children how much they did, in fact, think, wonder, and talk about those biological parents. So the children's degree of interest in the lost parents was no secret from their adoptive parents; and, in fact, the families seemed to share a common degree of knowledge and curiosity about the birthparents (rows 5 and 6). Nonetheless, in answer to the question ''How do you think your parents will feel if you some day search for your birthparents?'', the adolescents' answers bore no re-

Table 7.6   Concordance Among Family Members

	Father ↕ Mother	Father ↕ Target	Mother ↕ Target
Open Distinguishing	.57***	.10	.08
Discomfort	.29*	.47***	.01
Life Was Harder	.29*	.42**	.26*
Problems due to Adoption	.57***	.36*	.22
Know About Birthparents	.58***	.55***	.61***
Think About Birthparents	.29*	.33*	.50***
Child Wonders About Birthparents	.54***	.66***	.58***
Parents Feel About Search	.37**	.21	.15
Parents Feel x Child will Search		.02	.09
Child Thinks Parents Feel x Will Search		.01	.01
Self-Esteem	.18	.20	.29*

*.01 < p < .05; **.001 < p < .01; ***p < .001 (39 d.f., one-tailed)

lationship to how their parents actually felt about the prospect of their searching. We have reason to suppose that the parents' reported feelings were reliable, since the two parents tended to say the same thing. Yet the children's answers to "What is your best guess: that you some day will or won't want to search?" bore no relation to how the children thought the parents felt, as well as no relation to what the parents actually felt.

There was a moderate degree of family concordance on whether life had been any harder or easier than it would have been had they all been biologically related, and on their comfort in discussing the topic. The two parents' overall levels of Open Distinguishing were highly correlated; yet adolescents managed to express a weight of opinion *un*correlated with their parents (top row of Table 7.6). This is not inconsistent with everyone's influence on what the others were saying (revealed in the microanalysis mentioned above). It simply means that individual differences among the adolescents contributed much more variance to what they said over the course of the whole family discussion than did the moment-to-moment influences of their parents.

Matched pairs can be significantly correlated, as the variables are in Table 7.6, yet significantly different. For example, although the parents' reply to Know About Birthparents was highly correlated, mothers claimed to know slightly more about their children's biological parents than fathers did (paired t = 2.3, p < .05). Mothers also acknowledged thinking, wondering, and talking about the original parents more than fathers did (t = 2.1, p < .05). And their Open Distinguishing was much greater than their husbands' and adolescents' (t = 5.1 and 5.2, p < .001).

UPDATING KIRK'S COPING STRATEGIES

We drew several conclusions from the foregoing results. First, the various questions that Kirk (1964) found reflecting a continuum for adoptive parents, which he called acknowledgment versus rejection of differences, remain relevant dimensions, even in a generation far less secretive about adoption. The family concordance on those variables suggests that they are meaningful characterizations of how the subject of adoption has been handled by different families.

Second, an observer can easily discern (by discourse analysis or merely by reading transcripts such as those quoted above) the process of consensus-building in a family discussion of adoption. Although the baseline question about favorite activities usually led to a split decision (as allowed by our instructions), that virtually never happened with the adoption questions; dissenting views were expressed, then suppressed.

Conversely, the various questions asked of the parents—predicted to be components of a common factor—failed to correlate with one another. There appear to be *several*, relatively independent, dimensions along which they might distinguish their own experiences and feelings, as adoptive parents, from those they attribute to biological parents. (Among the adolescents, as Table 7.5 shows, high versus low distinguishing *is* a single strong factor.)

A minor discrepancy between our results and Kirk's (1964) was that Discomfort with the topic of adoption positively correlated with the other six types of distinguishing. (Kirk had suggested the opposite, that *rejection* of differences would lead to discomfort in discussing adoption issues.) All six correlations were significant among the adolescents, three out of six among the fathers (and the fathers and target adolescents agreed on Discomfort). Discomfort was simply not operative among the mothers, perhaps due to self-selection; they probably had been the ones who took the lead in the family's consent to participate.

However, our study does not constitute a failure to replicate Kirk's (1964). In fact, he actually developed separate indices of acknowledgment, empathy, communication, and trust; the idea of a single continuum comes more out of his discussion, and others' oversimplification of it, than out of his data. Furthermore, our methods were different, and we focused only on the adolescent stage of the family life cycle. (The fact that one-third of our sample had biological as well as adopted children may partially explain the multidimensionality of their answers to our questions; but Kirk's sample also was mixed.)

The fact that we did not find a unidimensional continuum of high versus low distinguishing among these parents does not mean we failed to see much "rejection of differences." It means that what we saw was more subtle and multifaceted than the literature suggests. For example, one mother reminisced, in the family discussion, about how she had handled a crisis brought on by another child's remark to her daughter:

R5   *Mother:* You came home and said, "Mother, do I have two mothers?" And we went through "what is a mother?" We went through all the things a mother does—helping her children, making their clothes, shopping, and so on—and I said, "Okay, how many mothers do you have that do those things for you?" And that was the end of that.
R4   *Daughter:* I don't even remember.
R5   *Mother:* You don't remember, so that *was* the end of that!

Handling the child's question in that way was a rejection of differences; the first thing most mothers do for their children is to bear them, which this mother seems to have omitted from consideration. Yet over the course of the discussion her low levels of distinguishing (codes 4, 5, and 6) were counterbalanced by an equal number of high distinguishings (codes 1, 2, and 3). She told the interviewer, "When they were babies and I was changing them I would say, 'Oh you darling adopted child.' I wanted them to know from Day 1 that they were adopted, so they would grow up knowing what their situation was, I didn't want it to be a shock." This family frequently watched 8mm movies of their early birthday parties and other important occasions, including the days they went to court for their adoption decrees. So there was a mixture of low distinguishing with respect to family roles and bonds, high distinguishing with respect to origins. Perhaps the mother was giving lip service to acknowledgment of differences, keeping her options open: if problems developed, the children would "know what their situation was, it would not be a shock"; but if appreciation was to be had for maternal services, she could fall back on the "one mother" reasoning.

The fact that most parents and children expressed a mixture of distinguishing and nondistinguishing sentiments would not in itself require us to revise the "acknowledgment versus rejection of differences" idea. What does argue against this idea is that there is no evidence low distinguishing should be equated with "rejection" or "denial." The latter terms imply that all adoptive families really experience important differences and, deep down, feel them; with some acknowledging those differences while others resist doing so. The data to be reviewed next indicate quite the contrary, that when people say their adoption has or has not been a major distinguishing factor, they are probably telling the truth.

FAMILY PROBLEMS

All but eight families in our nonclinical sample (80%) had at least one experience with professional counseling or therapy of some kind in the years since the target child's adoption. In one family, both parents and the target child had been psychoanalyzed, a sibling had received psychoeducational tutoring for learning disabilities, the father had been treated for alcoholism, and the parents were currently in marital counseling; another family had been in six different therapies totaling 19 years (some concurrently), individually and as a family, for reasons including a son's violent aggression and learning problems in elementary school and drug problems in high school, the father's alcoholism, the mother's depression, and marital problems. Those two cases were extremes, however. More typical would be one parent's brief treatment for depression or anxiety, or one course of family therapy initiated because of a child's school problems. The proportion of target children who had ever seen a psychologist or psychiatrist was 21% (about 50% higher than a national sample of adolescents adopted in infancy, and four times the rate among nonadopted adolescents; Zill, 1985). Out of seven types of problems queried, mothers' numbers of *yes*es ranged from zero to seven, and fathers' and children's from zero to six.

Kaye and Warren (1988) derived a concatenated measure from all three individuals' answers to probes for school, behavioral, social, emotional, marital, health, and "other" problems, as well as engagement in professional counseling or therapy. Variables predicted by this index of Problems are listed in Table 7.7, the target's age having been partialed out of the correlations. The more adopted children in a family,

Table 7.7   Correlates of Problems and Self-Esteem

	Family Problems[a]	Adolescent's Self-Esteem
Number Adopted	.34*	
Counseling with Child	.74***	− .41**
Adolescent		
Open Distinguishing	.35*	− .37*
Discomfort	.32*	− .28~
Life Was Harder	.44**	− .58***
Problems due to Adoption	.62***	− .45**
Knows About Birthparents		
Thinks About Birthparents	.45**	− .42**
Probably Will Search		− .39*
Talks with Mother	− .31*	.50***
Talks with Father		.26~
Self-Esteem	− .47***	(1.0)
Mother		
Open Distinguishing		
Discomfort	.40**	− .33*
Life Was Harder		
Problems due to Adoption	.31*	
Knows About Birthparents		
Thinks About Birthparents	.41**	− .31*
Child Talks with Me		.27~
Father		
Open Distinguishing		
Discomfort	.29~	
Life Was Harder		
Problems due to Adoption	.25~	− .28~
Knows About Birthparents		
Thinks About Birthparents	.29~	− .45**
Child Talks with Me	− .38*	.31*

[a]After partialing out target adolescent's age, because Problems increased with age.
*.01$<p<$.05; **.001$<p<$.01; ***$p<$.001 (39 d.f., two-tailed)
~.05$<p<$.10 (included to show consistency among family members)

the more problems. (Whether a sibship was all adopted or mixed biological and adopted made no difference.) As problems increased in number, they were more likely to involve counseling that centered on or included the children; and the problems were more likely to be regarded, especially by the children, as having been due to adoption. Target children in "problem" families expressed discomfort in talking about adoption, thought their own and their parents' lives had been more difficult than if they had been biologically related, and more frequently thought about their birthparents. They also expressed such feelings in the family discussion, reflected in the variable Open Distinguishing. However, they rated themselves as less likely to talk with their mothers about things that worried them. And they scored extremely low on Rosenberg's (1979) self-esteem instrument.

In addition to considering their family's problems as being adoption-related, both fathers and mothers in these "problem" families thought and talked about the child's biological parents more, yet felt less comfortable talking about adoption. Fathers (but not mothers) thought their children were less likely to come to them with worries (Child Talks with Me), than did fathers in families with a smoother history.

There are inherent weaknesses in retroactive self-report data, regardless of reliability. It cannot be proven that our subjects' reports of problems in their families were objective; what if "rejection of differences" led people to deny problems they actually experienced? However, we presume our Problems variable is valid for several reasons. First, the large number of problems our subjects reported; they hardly seem to have been denying them. Second, the fact that we originally assessed Problem Types, Therapy, and Counseling with Child as separate variables; they were highly correlated, which implies validity. Third, the reliability among family members gives credibility to those variables.

PROBLEMS *CAUSE* "ACKNOWLEDGMENT"

Clearly this cluster of "acknowledgment" variables is no manifestation of a problem-*preventing* strategy, since five of them as measured in the children, and three as measured in both parents, were positively associated with a history of family problems. To explore this further, we split the sample into a low-Problems group and a high-Problems group (using the median, $n = 20$ in each group) and ran the correlation matrix in Table 7.5 separately for each group. Of the original 21 predicted correlations, 15 were significant among the targets from high-Problems families, whereas only 5 of the 21 were significant among targets from low-Problems families. Most important, the same five "distinguishing" variables still correlated significantly with Problems in Table 7.7, even within the high-Problems group.

We conclude that the intercorrelations shown in Table 7.5 were due primarily to children who had experienced more than the median degree of problems over the years. A set of at least six variables—Discomfort, Life Was Harder, Problems due to Adoption, Think About Birthparents, Probably Will Search, and Open Distinguishing—appear to have represented children's reactions to actual family and developmental difficulties over the years. There was no evidence of variability in openness versus denial, such as might have been inferred either if the "distinguishing" dimension had emerged regardless of Problems or if it had been uncorrelated with Problems within the high-Problems subsample.

The direction of effects we infer is the most parsimonious account of these admittedly nonlongitudinal data, since the problems reported were supposed to be historical facts, whereas most of the other variables in Table 7.7 involved present opinions or retrospective feelings about the past.

SELF-ESTEEM

The adolescents' Self-Esteem (as measured immediately after the family discussions) was significantly related to most of the variables measuring feelings or opinions in the subsequent individual child interviews (Table 7.7). In addition to family Problems, other indications of difficulties in the family—attribution of problems to the fact of being adopted, lack of communication, a sense that life had been harder due to the adoption—predicted low Self-Esteem in the adopted adolescent. The amount of factual information known about the birthparents was unrelated to Self-Esteem (and unrelated to Problems). Each person's frequency of thinking about the biological parents was associated with low Self-Esteem in the target child. Surprisingly, children with low Self-Esteem were those with higher Open Distinguishing; that is, those who had acknowledged more differences and disadvantages in the family discussion. One might have predicted the opposite—that a child would need good self-esteem to acknowledge differences—had the various measures of distinguishing not been so closely associated with Problems.

Inspection of the data revealed that all types of family problems predicted low Self-Esteem in the target child—not only school, peer, or behavior problems (on the part of any child in the family), but also marital, health, "emotional," and "other."

There is reason to consider the Rosenberg Self-Esteem Scales a valid instrument when administered in an emotionally neutral setting (Rosenberg, 1979). In the present study, however, these scores may have been affected by the immediately preceding family discussions. The self-esteem we measured may have been a state rather than a trait: differences between children whose families had experienced problems (attributing many of those problems to adoption) and those whose families had been more peaceful, may be less salient and not necessarily important when the children are in other situations. This remains a question for study.

In a situation where the subject of adoption has been brought up, there are clearly big differences among adopted adolescents in manifesting self-esteem as well as in related feelings about life satisfaction and relationships with parents. The target children ranking in the top half on Self-Esteem had mean scores roughly the same as the *whole* sample of fathers and mothers. Such a score would be obtained by someone who answered positively on about half, and *strongly* positively on the other half, of items like "At times I think I am no good at all" (agree = negative) or "I take a positive attitude toward myself." The target children ranking in the bottom half on Self-Esteem agreed, on the average, almost as frequently or as strongly with the negative items as with the positive ones.

In short, at least half of our sample of adolescents showed extremely low self-esteem at the time we tested them, and that fact was strongly associated with a history of family problems.

THE ADOPTIVE FAMILY LIFE CYCLE

Clearly, one would like to draw developmental conclusions from this study: that high distinguishing (i.e., a strong identification with the circumstances or consequences of having been adopted or of being an adoptive parent), far from preventing problems over the course of the adopted child's development, results from them; and that a tendency to feel "no different," far from causing problems, is a natural, straightforward outcome of good family functioning. It seems sensible to theorize that feeling "my adoption has made our family's life difficult" impairs children's self-esteem. Unfortunately, the opposite direction of effects is equally plausible: that some children's low self-esteem both creates problems for them and leads them to attribute those problems to the fact of being adopted. All such conclusions demand longitudinal research.

In hopes that other investigators will undertake such research, let me propose a theory quite the opposite of Kirk's (1964). The more problems they had had, the *more* the parents and children attributed those problems to adoption and the *more* they thought about the birthparents. Such behavior would appear therefore to be a strategy for coping with developmental problems in adoptive families; but probably not an adaptive strategy.

On the basis of clinical experience, Brodzinsky (1987) interprets high distinguishing, as I do, as a coping strategy. He suggests reserving the term "acknowledgment" for moderate distinguishing, and proposes that the opposite extreme from "rejection of differences" is "insistence on differences," which is no better for the child. Our study provides empirical support for such a curvilinear model. However, when we look at the results of our study as a whole, they indicate that adolescents whose adoptive families have had developmental difficulties use the coping strategy on their own, not merely (if at all) in response to their parents' emphasizing differences. The general point (on which Brodzinsky and I agree) and the specific question of whether the coping originates in parents, in children, in the family system, or at all three levels demand longitudinal research. Our theories can be tested only by assessing distinguishing, problems, and recovery from those problems, throughout the years from adoption to launching.

Although systems exert pressure on each member to confirm the consensus being formed by the others, the children wound up fairly independent of their parents' consensus. This is not so surprising at this period of their lives. It is in the nature of adolescents to call into question their parents' attitudes. Furthermore, the fact that parents affirmed their adolescents' opinions, at least as much as the other way around, also seems age-appropriate. Parents have a motive to agree with the adolescent rather than to dispute every independent thought—the more so if they fear the child may break ranks radically, and adoptive parents have special fears of that kind (Sorosky et al., 1978). Thus by this age, reasonably self-assured children are somewhat buffered against the parental "party line," especially if it happens to refute their own experience. Less self-assured adolescents may err in the direction of exaggerating the causal significance of their adoption in every family problem that arises, even when their parents overtly deny that connection.

We know what powerful socialization tools parental frames are in early childhood (Kaye, 1982), yet we did not find the hypothesized parental frames in this domain and at this stage of parent–child interaction. In a similar study with families whose children are younger, we would expect more asymmetry than was found in our data. The moment-to-moment influences of parents' assertions on 6-, 9-, or even 12-year-old children would be more apparent, we predict, than the influences of children's assertions on parents'.

Ideally, investigators sensitive to how discourse processes shape children's development would record and analyze parent–child conversations at vital points in the adoptive family's life cycle: for example, at the various stages of telling, when parents disclose more information to their children and (hopefully) adjust their explanations to the children's cognitive levels of understanding (Brodzinsky, Singer, & Braff,

1984); or at the time when a search for birthparents is contemplated. But it is hard to envision how such moments could be captured on tape systematically.

SUBCULTURES

The number of adopted children in the family, the number of biological children, the target child's age and position in the sibship, the age at which he or she was told about being adopted, and the importance attributed to God in their daily lives all failed to correlate with father's, mother's, or target's "distinguishing" scores. (Furthermore, analysis of variance showed no interaction among any of these independent variables.)

Three effects of demographic variables within our sample point to the role of culture in how adoption is conceptualized and discussed in families. They also point to unanswered questions.

Sex Difference

Girls did more Open Distinguishing than their male counterparts ($t = 2.4$, 38 d.f., $p < .02$, two-tailed), echoing the difference between mothers and fathers reported above. But no sex differences were found in the various measures of *private* distinguishing: the individual interviews elicited no consistent differences between girls and boys, between mothers and fathers, or between what the parents said about target girls and target boys. We found no sex differences in Problems.

The fact that girls did significantly more distinguishing than boys in the context of family discussions, yet scored no higher on any of the six forms of distinguishing manifested in the private interviews, raises the question whether boys simply speak with less candor in family discussions. If that were the case, the boys' Open Distinguishing should correlate less well with Problems and with the "private distinguishing" variables from their interviews than the girls' Open Distinguishing did. This was not the case. The pattern for boys alone, or for girls alone, was not substantially different from what appears in Table 7.5 for both sexes combined. Therefore, although the sex difference indicates *elevated levels* of Open Distinguishing by the girls, *variability* among the boys was related to family problems and to private acknowledgment of differences in the same way as among girls.

Farber (1977) reported, in a small sample of latency age girls, markedly more interest in the topics of adoption, infertility, and birth than among boys. The creation of babies is inherently important to females; and girls may more closely identify with their biological mothers. (Farber also found more conflicts with their adoptive mothers among girls than among boys.) Our data suggest that girls may also identify with their adoptive mothers' greater readiness than fathers to discuss the topic. The latter explanation would account for our finding this disparity only in the area of *open* distinguishing, not in our private interviews; it has something to do with the perceived appropriateness of such statements in the family context. The fathers and boys were no less candid, as measured by the correlation between their public and private assertions; but their levels of *open* distinguishing have to be interpreted in relation to the norm for their gender.

Socioeconomic Status

The better educated the parents, the more they and their children tended to mention differences or the less they tended to deny them ($r = .35, .31, .36$ for fathers, mothers, and targets respectively; $p < .05$, two-tailed). But Problems were unrelated to education (or to income). Assuming that defense mechanisms are distributed without regard to socioeconomic status, this finding further disconfirms the idea that low distinguishing is a matter of denial.

Religious Differences

One-third of the parents said they were Protestant; one-half, Catholic; the rest, except for one Jewish father, were agnostics of Christian upbringing. Faith, the importance attributed to religious faith, was included as a question in our individual interviews because some adoptive parents reject differences in the following way: "He meant us to be a family, even if we may not know what His reasons were for bringing us together through adoption."

We frequently heard God invoked by parents when insisting on the predestination of their familial bonds. God's will was used as an explanation. Not surprisingly, in answer to another question we borrowed from Kirk (1964), religious parents rated heredity much less important than the environment: biology is held in ill repute today by many deeply Christian parents. This suggests that the variable Faith might have predicted low distinguishing. But it did not; faith in God turned out to be just as strong among high-distinguishing parents.

Although unrelated to any of the family members' open distinguishing, Faith did correlate with the children's answers to Probably Will Search—positively, which means the children did not think God would frown on an adult reunion with their biological parents. Did the belief that God brought their families together assure them that the adoptive bond was strong enough to survive meeting their birthparents? Religious beliefs and values warrant further study by investigators of the adoptee's motives to search.

CLINICAL IMPLICATIONS

Our data point toward three principal conclusions. First, feelings about "differences" are largely independent of "openness of communication about adoption issues." There is plenty of evidence to support the need for the latter—both in the literature on adoptees' development and in what we know about family processes in general. Lifton (1975) writes eloquently from the adoptee's perspective: "The child swears to the secret and because children take such promises seriously, she never discusses with her adoptive father the one subject that, had it been aired, might have made them close." Reiss (1981) and many others describe the communication loops by which family members define their own and one another's identities. Students of parental behavior find that when parents' belief systems are organized rigidly, with insufficient accommodation to the reality of their children's lives, social adjustment problems and school problems result (Elias & Ubriaco, 1986; Emmerich, 1969;

McGillicuddy-DeLisi, Sigel, & Johnson, 1979). So "openness" is certainly important. But there is no evidence that asserting "I don't feel that I myself or my relationships with my family are different in any important way because I'm (or he's or she's) adopted" has anything to do with a lack of open family communication.

This conclusion runs counter to some clinicians' beliefs about denial and suppression of ambivalent feelings, implied by the phrase "rejection of differences" (Kirk, 1964). Adopted adolescents' frankly telling their parents that they believe their lives have been harder in some ways, or that their feelings about self and parents might be different from those of biological children, turned out to be consistent with what the children said privately, and more strongly predicted by a reliable checklist of problems over the years than by the contextual pressure to agree. This suggests that when adolescent adoptees deny feeling very different or being disadvantaged by adoption, they may be telling the truth. For at least some adolescents, and probably for their parents as well, "denial of differences" is simply a manifestation of actually not having experienced many negative experiences, rather than of having repressed them.

The form that "acknowledgment" takes in some adolescents, extending so far as to blame most of their family's problems on this one aspect of themselves—being adopted—is surely excessive, as is the association we found between a history of problems and an interest in the birthparents. In principle, knowledge of their biological ancestry and parentage ought to be of equal importance to all adopted children, regardless of how happy their adoptive situation is. If an interest in searching increases in response to family problems, it would seem more reasonable to describe such an interest as a strategy for coping with the personal meaning of these problems than to assume that the child who expresses no interest in searching is either denying or, as the proponents of searching would say, "not yet ready."

It might be the case that adopted children can suffer from too much distinguishing as well as from too little. Defense mechanisms come into play more evidently in acknowledging differences than in rejecting them. Adoptees surely do face fundamental "differences" in that some significant people in their lives have vanished. There are also hurts and embarrassments caused by a social stigma and by people's cruelty. But it seems that many adoptees cope with such difficulties, acknowledge feelings about them, and can discuss them with their parents, without attaching central importance to them. Perhaps they, the *moderately* acknowledging, are the best-adapted adoptees (Brodzinsky, 1987).

Support Rather Than Selection

A second conclusion from our study is likely to be echoed by other contributors to this volume: we should be providing better preparation and long-term support to adoptive families. Both adoption policy and adoption research have been far too concerned with how to *select* adoptive parents who will be so free of neurosis that they just naturally create a happy environment full of open, age-appropriate communication about any issues that arise. By focusing on the problem of selection and then disappearing from adoptive families' lives (reappearing, here and there, in order to assess outcome), adoption agencies, laws, and customs have, in fact, modeled "rejection of differences" and a norm of minimal communication (Kirk & McDaniel, 1984).

Despite the increased numbers of late, transracial, foreign, special-needs, stepparent, and single-parent adoptions, the adoption of a newborn by an infertile couple of the same race remains the most common situation, and the one in which the issue of emphasizing or downplaying the adoption most directly arises. (The other situations all intrinsically present reminders that the child's biological roots are different.) Those who work with adoptive families over the course of time need to beware of stereotypes and oversimplifications. The idea that adoptive parents can be categorized into two piles, plucky candor versus defensive denial, is one such myth.

In the population we studied (closed adoptions of healthy white newborns by parents who remained married at least into the children's teens), the "low distinguishing" parents almost completely denied being or feeling different; their adolescent children also almost completely denied such differences. But even in the relatively "high distinguishing" or "acknowledging" families, our questions elicited mostly replies of "no difference" or "no important differences." Acknowledgments of differences and disadvantages, though freely expressed, were outnumbered by assurances about nondifferences. It is important for professionals serving adoptive families to recognize that a sprinkling of distinguishings amid many assurances of normalcy is probably healthy and accurate, rather than label all such assurances as "rejection of differences" in a pathological sense.

Parents' "acknowledgment versus rejection of differences" is simply not a unidimensional, pervasive tension between alternative coping strategies. To a far greater extent than adolescents, parents were able to isolate particular problems or disadvantages without generalizing to their lives as a whole or to their self-worth. For example, some parents managed to attribute family problems largely to the adoption while at the same time denying that their lives or their children's had been harder in any way when compared with a biological family. Perhaps the ability to make such qualifications may be the best coping strategy. If so, it is one the adolescents we studied did not have available to them, either because they had not yet learned it or because they were the persons most centrally involved.

It may well be true that what is implied by the phrase "rejection of differences"—proscribing all expression of doubts and ambivalence—leads to problems. But family members' failure to report many differences or much interest in the birthparents should not, in itself, be interpreted as evidence of such a proscription. It certainly can no longer be held that denial of differences leads to problems. Without longitudinal research, we have no way of knowing whether the various forms of acknowledgment or rejection of differences had been characteristic of different parents over the years. But if "acknowledgers" were engaged in an effective long-term problem–preventing strategy of working through their grief over infertility, they should have experienced fewer problems, not more than the "deniers" did. In fact, a history of family problems was *acknowledged* in various ways, rather than being associated with any of the hypothesized forms of denial.

The Search for Roots

Although the relation between family or developmental problems and low self-esteem is hardly surprising, the relation between low self-esteem and thinking about one's biological parents is less obvious. We know that searchers overcome powerful fears of their own as well as strong external resistance to their efforts (B. J. Lifton, 1979; Sorosky et al., 1978). Had two other recent studies not found the same relationship between poor self-concepts and searching for birthparents (Aumend & Barrett, 1984; Sobol & Cardiff, 1983), we might have predicted that only adoptees with good feelings about themselves would have the courage to confront the fears of some of their parents, the norms and constraints of society, and the Pandora's box their search may unlock.

Our findings suggest that parents don't necessarily share their child's interest in searching, but they don't especially oppose it, and they do share in being more curious about their child's biological origins, if they have had more problems in their relationship.

The terribly low self-esteem we found among adolescents whose adoptive families had experienced problems vividly demonstrates our third conclusion and what too few developmental theorists have acknowledged: a strong sense of self is inseparable from a sense of belonging. We see support in these data for Kaye's (1982) Vygotskyan theory of the self's origins, for Winnicott's (1965) concept of the holding environment, and Kohut's (1971) concepts of mirroring and the parental self-object. Adopted adolescents whose schooling or family lives have been problematic, and who consequently feel doubts about their self-worth, seem to be highly interested in learning about, possibly reuniting with, a lost set of parents. When something is missing in their sense of self, they experience themselves as missing persons in two senses: persons who are themselves missing and who miss particular significant others. Adolescents with self-esteem problems in biological families may have somewhat similar feelings. But the adopted child has a real historical loss of ties to which to attribute the problem or in which to see hope of rectifying it. Self-esteem and attachment are functionally inseparable.

The movement toward more possibilities for information exchange between the bearing and rearing parents ("open adoption") suggests an entirely different kind of experience from that of the families in our sample. It is encouraging that the issue of "acknowledgment versus rejection of differences," as formulated by Kirk (1964) in an era of embarrassment and frequent secrecy about adoption, requires revision a couple of decades later. Perhaps it will change even more, if wondering about the birthparents is replaced by knowing more about them.

ACKNOWLEDGMENT

The author is grateful to a private donor to the Center for Family Studies, Northwestern University Medical School, for financially supporting this project; and to the two agencies, Catholic Charities of Chicago and The Cradle, which helped us recruit the adoptive families. Special appreciation goes to Sarah Warren for interviewing and coding, and to Susan Blake and Judith Heyhoe for transcribing the interviews.

NOTES

1. All target children had been placed with the parents before the age of five months; all but eight when less than two months old. In all cases, the parents (like Kirk's subjects) had experienced prolonged difficulty in conceiving or in carrying a baby to term. In most cases, the application process had then taken another year or two.

2. The index of distinguishing was defined as a weighted sum $3a + 2b + c - d - 2e - 3f$, where a through f are levels 1 through 6 as proportions of all the level codes an individual's utterances received. Thus each instance of level 1 counted 3 points, each instance of level 6 counted -3, and so on.

3. These variables are defined more fully in Kaye and Warren (1988); complete questionnaire and formulas for reducing separate items to these summary variables are available from the author.

8

Adoption and Identity Formation

JANET L. HOOPES

The title of this chapter links two very complex constructs: identity and adoption. Identity is a personality construct that has been defined and discussed in much theoretical writing as well as in research, while adoption presents an equally complex social and family phenomenon with a clinical and research literature of its own. The interrelationship of these two complex phenomena has rarely been specifically addressed in adoption outcome research, although speculation has appeared in the literature and data presented in clinical studies, with inferences drawn concerning this interrelationship. The goal of this chapter is to summarize the theory on identity formation, examine some of the complexities of adoption, and then to look at the research and clinical literature on adoptive families and children. From this research and literature it is hoped that conclusions can be drawn regarding identity development in the adoptee.

IDENTITY

The concept of identity, widely used in developmental literature, is highlighted in Erikson's (1950, 1959) psychosocial concept of the "eight stages of man." Identity formation or development is seen by Erikson as a continuing process that has roots in earlier stages of growth. Erikson spoke of the meshing of all life stages, with the earlier stages preparing for and leading into the next sequential stages. However, it is the period of adolescence which is identified by many writers as the time when the primary task is that of identity formation (Blos, 1970; Douvan & Adelson, 1966; Erikson, 1950; Marcia, 1967). During adolescence an individual faces the crises of discovering and establishing a mature personal identity; of evaluating the attitudes, beliefs, and goals acquired from his or her parents, and of ascertaining, "Who am I?", "Where have I been?", and "Where am I going?" Also during this period, the adolescent is characterized as one seeking individuality and autonomy, both of which are considered essential to the construction of a coherent, well-delineated identity.

Erikson (1950, 1959) views the process of personality development as extending through the whole life span which he divides into eight stages. Each stage represents an encounter between the individual and the environment that must be resolved in order for the individual to achieve continued growth. Each of the stages is also marked by a specific conflict, with the solution to the encounter resulting in one of two directions—one being adaptive and the other maladaptive. According to Erikson's theory of personality development, the foundations for identity formation are established in the successful resolution of earlier psychosocial crises of childhood, that is, "trust versus mistrust," "autonomy versus doubt," "initiative versus guilt," "industry versus inferiority"—all of which precede adolescence and thus contribute to an accruing sense of ego strength in the adolescent. A lasting ego identity cannot begin to exist nor can one achieve a healthy sense of self-esteem without a successful traversal of all four stages.

Erikson's fifth stage of psychosocial development is characterized by the crisis of "identity versus role diffusion," in which the individual, confronted with fundamental physiological changes, becomes concerned with self-concept and social role. Erikson (1959) postulates that every adolescent is apt to go through some serious struggle at one time or another before he or she reaches a mature identity. Mature identity implies an acceptance of and comfort with one's physical self, a sense of direction, and consequently an ability to make decisions. Failure to resolve the adolescent crisis may contribute to "identity diffusion," a maladaptive outcome implying doubts about one's physical and sexual self, an inability to make decisions and commitments, and the lack of a sense of continuity of the self over time.

The integration taking place in the form of an evolving identity is more than the sum of childhood identifications. Rather, Erikson (1968) sees identity formation as the developmental consequence of multiple life experiences. Although resolution of a perceived crisis through personal exploration is proposed as an essential condition to healthy identity formation, Erikson also recognizes that the identity formation process includes the integration of early childhood identitication with psychological aspects of one's childrearing history as well as other important social–psychological events. Although Erikson points to the "uniqueness" and "independence" that accompany the adolescent's new found sense of identity, he nonetheless stresses the importance of a solid anchoring within the family, in which the adolescent's history of positive identification with the same sex parent and a stable, growth-productive relationship with the parent of the opposite sex conjointly contribute to the establishment of a good sense of sexual identity in adolescence.

For Erikson (1959), an optimal "sense of identity" is experienced as a sense of psychosocial well-being, "a feeling of being at home in one's body, a sense of knowing where one is going, and an inner assuredness of anticipated recognition from those who count" (p. 165). This latter aspect attributes a sense of psychosocial mutuality to identity, implying a reciprocal or mutual relationship with one's immediate community or peer group. In the development of a "social self-definition," the adolescent attempts a meaningful consolidation of social roles through peer interaction and the commitment to a peer group.

While Erikson's psychological theory of development in general and his construct "identity versus identity diffusion" in particular have had a large influence on psychological thought, empirical studies to validate these theoretical formulations are limited. Attempts at operationalizing and measuring ego identity have utilized self-descriptive Q sorts (Block, 1961; Gruen, 1960; Heilbrun, 1964), self-report questionnaires (Dignan, 1965; Hershenson, 1967; Rasmussen, 1964; Simmons, 1970), and sentence completion methods (Loevinger, 1970). The most widely used methodology, however, has been the semistructured interview devised by Marcia (1966) and his followers and refined by others (Marcia & Friedman, 1970; Schenkel & Marcia, 1972; Waterman & Waterman, 1971). The Identity Status Interview was administered to college students and adults and the results of Marcia's research led him to describe four ego-identity statuses: Role Diffusion, Foreclosure, Moratorium, and Identity Achieved. While each of these four typologies could be viewed as following a continuous growth process toward mature identity, Marcia believed that not every individual experiences every status, and either role diffusion or foreclosure could become terminal if further search for identity is abandoned.

Marcia was concerned about defining the psychosocial criteria for determining the degree or level of ego identity. He maintained that there were two criteria: the presence of crisis and commitment. If an adolescent has experienced a *crisis* or period of experimenting with alternative roles, and has subsequently made relatively enduring *commitments* to a system of values and an ideology, thus completing his or her self-definition and finding a place in the community, then that adolescent has an achieved identity.

For Marcia, the identity diffusion adolescent is characterized by a lack of commitment to a system of values or beliefs; the foreclosed adolescent by avoidance of crises and commitment to a system of values accepted unquestioningly from others (frequently his or her family); the moratorium adolescent by confrontation with crises, search for solutions, and reluctance to accept explanation and values from others; and the identity-achieved adolescent by personal commitment as an outgrowth of resolved crises.

Marcia (1980) views identity as an evolving, dynamic entity involving numerous reorganizations of contents throughout one's life. He diverges from Erikson in his emphasis on the meaning one attributes to life in the form of basic life commitments and in his focus on the changeability of identity contents throughout a person's life. For Marcia (1980), "identity involves commitment to a sexual orientation, an ideological stance, and a vocational direction" (p. 160) in contrast to Erikson's more fundamental definition. Thus, according to Marcia, the individual's commitments are what provide him with a definition of self.

Much research has followed from Marcia's creative work. The Identity Status Interview has been expanded to include sexual attitudes (Marcia & Friedman, 1970) and attitudes of women toward family and career (Archer, 1985; Freedman, 1987). Not only have college populations been studied, but also high school samples (Archer, 1985; Meilman, 1977). Changes in identity status through the college years and into adult years have been studied by Waterman and Waterman (1971); Waterman, Geary, and Waterman (1974); Waterman and Goldman (1976), and Whitbourne and Waterman (1979). While few sex differences have been noted in the process of identity development (Frieze, Parsons, Johnson, Ruble, & Zellman, 1978; Marcia, 1980), Archer's (1985) work and that of Freedman (1987) suggest that the content of identity concerns may differ for males and females.

Differences in family relationships and parenting styles associated with various identity statuses have been explored, although as Waterman (1982) has pointed out, methodological difficulties prevent positive conclusions regarding antecedent variables relating to identity development. Most studies have been cross-sectional rather than longitudinal and have depended on verbal reports of the subjects rather than direct observation.

A somewhat different treatment of the concept of ego or "self," particularly the adolescent self-image, is found in the empirical work of Offer and his colleagues (Offer, 1969; Offer, Ostrov, & Howard, 1981). Offer has maintained that the normal adolescent is usually willing and able to report on self-feelings and that these consciously expressed self-feelings provide valid data for measuring adolescent self-image.

A major goal of Offer's research on adolescent self-image has been to elucidate the nature of the "self" in general. With the use of a self-image questionnaire approach, Offer identified five separate aspects of the adolescent's self-system amenable to evaluation: the psychological self, the social self, the family self, the sexual self, and the coping self. To the extent that the adolescent may feel differently about himself or herself in different contexts, he or she can be thought of as having many selves or self-dimensions (Offer et al., 1981).

For Offer et al. (1981), the adolescent's desire to know the self is tied up with learning how to relate to others while also acquiring a sense of separateness and autonomy, the quest to achieve what Erikson calls "identity." Thus while Offer avoids direct reference to the term "identity" in his own writings, his theoretical overlap with Erikson and Marcia is apparent.

ADOPTION

Before examining identity formation in the adoptee, let us look first at the social phenomenon of adoption, since an understanding of the complexity of the adoption process may help in interpretation of the clinical and research literature.

Adoption is not a homogeneous phenomenon and can occur in several ways. Hence simple comparisons should not be made between adopted and nonadopted (or biological) families, but between specific kinds of adoptive and biological families. The results of the comparisons we make depend on what kind of adoption we are talking about.

The most common form of adoption is *within-family* adoption where a child is legally adopted by a relative. Grandparents, aunts, uncles, and cousins or other family members may adopt a child whose parent or parents are deceased or unable to care for the child in some way. Step-parent adoption is also common in the case of either divorce or death and remarriage of a parent. There is literature on children of divorce and some beginning research on "blended" families. That literature will not be discussed further in this chapter. Rather this chapter will focus on *nonfamily* or *nonrelative* adoption. That is not to say that identity formation may not take some unique routes in within–family adoption or in blended families. Yet the continuity of genealogy probably introduces fewer complications into child and adolescent development in such families.

Nonfamily or nonrelative adoption, which is most frequently researched and discussed in the literature, is also accomplished in a variety of ways and for a variety of reasons. Most families adopt when biological parenthood is not possible. Some families adopt for altruistic reasons to provide homes for either the racially, physically, or intellectually different child who needs permanency and a loving family. Such altruistic reasons may be confounded with personal reasons too, such as infertility or the desire to expand the family beyond the one-child family.

Some children are placed through social agencies while others are placed through private arrangement. The agency-sponsored adoption may entail greater study of the family and child, a longer period of preparation (i.e., waiting), and greater opportunity for postadoption services, such as family counseling, than the privately arranged adoption which sometimes allows no chance for adequate preparation, often provides minimal information about the biological parents, and rarely offers ongoing support to the family.

Most children come to adoption as infants and hence have little or no memory of their biological parents. Others, however, have lived for varying periods of time with biological parents and siblings and hence have bonded to this family of origin. Children placed as infants or toddlers come to adoption at a very different stage and with very different experiences than children placed at older ages.

Some children enter homes where there are already biological children, and some parents bear a biological child after adoption placement. Other children have been foster children for a period of time and then are adopted by the foster parents. Another group of children may have suffered physical or emotional abuse at the hands of the biological family or a foster family. Others have received good care and emotional bonding in either foster or biological families. Children may have lived in institutions or shelters for many months, or children may have moved from one culture to another.

The pool of potential adoptive families and children available for adoption often determines the nature of an adoption. For example, Reid (1957) states:

> Twenty or thirty years ago, agencies had to go out and recruit adoptive parents for white infants; they had to ''sell'' the country on adoption. Attitudes toward illegitimacy, toward bringing children of different ''blood'' into the family set up strong barriers to adoption. So it was only natural for many social workers to believe (consciously or unconsciously) that the adoptive parents were doing the child and the agency a favor by adopting him. (p. 23)

In the 1950s and 1960s, however, the volume of couples applying to adopt increased to the point that limitations were placed on the numbers of adoption applicants. However, as the number of infants available for adoption also increased, families often were able to adopt two and sometimes three or four children. Today, due to changes in abortion laws and differences in attitudes toward illegitimacy and single parenthood, there are many more families wishing to adopt than there are infants available. This demand has led to larger numbers of adoptions from foreign countries, of adoptions of special needs children or of older children who have been without families for a number of years. A study of identity development of children placed in these very different time periods might lead to a variety of outcomes.

It has been assumed that there are some identifiable qualities in both families and children, and factors in their interactions, that will predict success or forecast problems for their lives together. If such qualities could be defined, then adoption placements would be made with families and children possessing these same qualities. Unfortunately discovering these qualities through clinical practice and both cross-sectional and longitudinal research has been slow and difficult. The myths have been exploded about some of the superficial factors which make for a "successful" adoption—for example, the age of the parents, the financial security of the family, the age of the child at placement, and so on. These are not necessarily as important as more intangible qualities, such as love, affection, positive discipline, or a well-functioning marriage. Such factors lead to normal growth and development in any family. But there are some special factors that enter into positive outcome with adoptive families: openness of communication about adoption, acceptance of infertility (if this is the reason for adoption), and acceptance of racial, intellectual, cultural, or other differences. These are some of the factors unique to adoption. (Kirk, 1964; Lawder, Lower, Andrews, Sherman, & Hill 1969)

What combination of factors or qualities contribute to the child's growth and development and, more particularly, to his or her identity development? The answers are not easy ones. Does identity development in the adopted child proceed along relatively normal versus deviant paths, is identity development different for the adopted child compared with the biological child, and just what is the nature and sequence of identity development in the adopted child?

The child himself or herself brings a genetic-based temperament with intellectual and physical differences which influence the family interaction and may confound the most stable of parental predictive variables. The extended family and the broader community present certain biases, either positive or negative, which in turn influence the development of a particular child. Studies of children and families, who adopted in different decades and who came to adoption with differing backgrounds, motivations, genetics, and family interaction patterns, will undoubtedly produce enormous variability of outcome. Identity development may indeed vary along a wide spectrum depending on the experiences of both child and family when they are united in adoption.

IDENTITY FORMATION IN ADOPTEES

Though identity problems may reach a crisis stage for any adolescent, there is no consensus as to whether these problems are more severe for adopted individuals who are perhaps preoccupied with the fact that they are adopted (Tec & Gordon, 1967; Toussieng, 1962). It is commonly speculated that the resolution of the identity crisis is a more complex task for adopted adolescents. Goebel and Lott (1986) write:

> As they attempt to integrate past with future, they are hindered by the existence of two sets of parents; they experience an absence of generational sequence (Josselson, 1980) as a consequence of unrootedness. . . . Adoptees not only must form a synthesis of past and future, but must also integrate the now with those parts of self that have been left in the past. (p. 6)

A convincing and testable model for researching the questions regarding identity formation in the adoptee has been presented by Brodzinsky (1987). He bases his model on Erikson's psychosocial theory which might predict greater risk for the adoptee at all developmental stages, including the ego identity stage. Brodzinsky mentions the adopted adolescents' difficulty in coping with questions about their origins—who their birthparents were, why they were relinquished. The sense of loss and grief, experienced even earlier in the school age years, extends into adolescence and includes a sense of loss not only of the birthparents, but also a loss of part of themselves. Incorporating the extensions of Erikson's theory by Marcia (1980), Bourne (1978a, 1978b), and Waterman (1982), Brodzinsky proposes that adopted adolescents, like their nonadopted peers, will confront differential resolutions of identity conflicts. Some may struggle with the meaning of adoption for themselves and remain in moratorium. Others emerge as foreclosed or identity diffused, while some become identity achieved. What is important is the identification of those factors in the adopted family, in the broader social system, or even within the adoptee, which lead to these various identity outcomes. How can the adopted adolescent be helped by the family and society to cope with the identity issues unique to adoption?

A review of the literature on identity formation in adoptees seems to indicate that adolescent identity struggles are adversely affected by the adoptive experience. Statements relating to the intensification of typical adolescent conflicts abound. Frisk (1964), for example, states:

> We must realize that the chances of developing disturbances during adolescence are great in the adopted child. Ego development, identification, and the forming of identity, together with the social environment, are inclined to become complicated. In the course of my studies of the adopted child, it has become apparent that a special problem in the formation of identity has been present. (p. 7)

Similarly, Schoenberg (1974), writing on adoption and identity, asserts that "the creation of families based on psychological, not blood, ties contains inherent identity problems that practice and law seek to mitigate, but can never eliminate" (p. 549).

Psychological Difficulties in the Identity Process

In a well-synthesized discussion of the subject, Sorosky and associates (1975) conclude that "adoptees are more vulnerable than the population at large because of the greater likelihood of encountering difficulties in the working through of the psychosexual, psychosocial and psychohistorical aspects of personality development" (p. 24). Four categories of psychological difficulties related to identity conflicts in adoptees have been delineated: (1) disturbances in early object relations; (2) complications in the resolution of the oedipal complex; (3) prolongation of the "family romance" fantasy; and (4) "genealogical bewilderment."

Early Object Relations

Regarding disturbances in the infant's earliest development, Clothier (1943b) comments on the loss of fundamental security that distinguishes the adoptee who is deprived of a primitive, nurturant relationship with the biological mother, asserting that "it is to be doubted whether the relationship of the child to its postpartum mother . . . can be replaced by even the best of substitute mothers" (p. 223). Despite more recent theoretical statements to the contrary (Bowlby, 1969), Clothier's comment typifies the unscientific formulations found in the literature on which conceptions of adoptees are still based. Although Bowlby's (1969) extensive work on attachment, for example, has led him to conclude that "what is . . . essential for mental health

is that the infant and young child experience a warm, intimate and continuous relationship with his mother or *permanent mother substitute* (author's emphasis) in which
both find satisfaction and enjoyment'' (pp. xi–xii), his formulations have often been
ignored by many adoption theoreticians.

Schechter (1960) and Simon and Senturia (1966) support Clothier's rather negative view of the potential for greater difficulty in establishing secure and stable early
attachments. They point out that adoptees find it difficult to synthesize ambivalent
feelings for the adoptive parent into a workable, realistic identification.

A more positive note is found in the research of Singer et al. (1985) in which
adoptive and nonadoptive mother–infant pairs were compared on the quality of attachment relationships. Using the Stranger Situation paradigm of Ainsworth, Blehar,
Waters, and Wall (1978), Singer et al. (1985) conclude:

> Like nonadoptive mother–infant pairs, most adoptive mothers and their infants develop
> warm and secure attachment relationships. The initial postdelivery bonding, as described
> by Klaus & Kennell (1976) and others, which is obviously not part of the adoption ex-
> perience, does not appear to be necessary for the formation of a healthy family relation-
> ship. What seems to be more important is the emergence of caretaking confidence and
> competence on the part of the parents, and a general caretaking atmosphere that is warm,
> consistent and contingent on the needs of the infant. To the extent that adoptive parents
> develop these characteristics and provide this type of environment, there is little reason
> to believe their attachment relationships with their young infants will differ markedly from
> nonadoptive parents. (p. 1550)

Oedipal or Sexual Complications

The issue of oedipal complications and sexual conflicts has been addressed in part
by Easson (1973), who refers to difficulties experienced in three related areas of
emotional growth that can affect the development of a stable sexual identity in the
adopted adolescent: (1) the adolescent's process of emancipation from adoptive parents; (2) the resolution of incestuous strivings in the adoptive relationship; and (3)
the final identification with the parent of the same sex and the concomitant development of mutuality with the opposite sex parent.

Regarding the emancipation process, Easson suggests that the longer the youngster delays accepting the adoptive parents with their normal human qualities, the
more he or she slows down the necessary preadolescent identification with them and
they with him or her, precluding the possibility of the comfortable relationship that
is so essential to emancipation. Easson's views are supported by Sokoloff (1977) and
Sorosky and associates (1977), who similarly describe exacerbations of the normal
dependency–independency conflicts in adopted adolescents, who appear to be more
vulnerable to experiences of loss, rejection, and abandonment.

Commenting on the possibility of enhanced incestuous strivings in the families of
adopted adolescents where the incest barrier between parent and child or between
siblings is ''not nearly as strong'' as in a blood-related family, Easson (1973) writes:
''This unresolved incestous bond slows down the sexual emancipation of the adopted
adolescent and makes it more difficult to develop appropriate peer sexual relationships outside the family (p. 102).

Easson also points to the difficulties inherent in the achievement of a satisfactory
identification with the same sex parent. Adopted adolescents may still want to hold

on to glamorous or not-so-glamorous fantasies about biological parents, which delay acceptance of the adoptive parents and impede a final identification with them. Schechter (1960) concurs, viewing the resolution of the oedipal complex to be so fraught with difficulty that he advises postponing the revelation of the child's adoptive status until after the resolution of the oedipal conflict to avoid complicating this stage of psychosexual development.

The Family Romance

Several theorists (Clothier, 1943b; Glatzer, 1955; Schechter, 1960; Simon & Senturia, 1966) have postulated a prolongation and reinforcement of the family romance fantasy in adopted children that impedes the adolescent's identification with the adoptive parent. The family romance fantasy refers to that brief state in normal child development in which children experience doubt about their natural-born status, often believing they are adopted. The fantasy develops as a result of children's inability to tolerate ambivalent feelings toward parental figures and leads them to ameliorate real or imagined disappointments within the parental relationship by imagining something better. For the adopted child, the fantasy appears more attainable and interferes with its intended function of mastery, thus impeding the identification process as a whole (Clothier, 1943b; Wieder, 1977b). Lawton and Gross (1964), however, caution those who attribute a universality to the family romance as a source of specific problems for the adopted child. They believe that the prolongation of the family romance and its fixation in the adopted child results when certain adoptive parents drive their children to open rejection and stimulate comparisons with the biological parents.

Genealogical Problems

The issue of genealogical bewilderment has been discussed at great length by many writers who echo Clothier's (1943b) sentiments that the lack of racial antecedents lies at the core of what is unique to the psychology of the adopted child. The term itself was coined by Sants (1964), who described a state of confusion and uncertainty in a child who either has no knowledge of his biological parents or only uncertain knowledge of them. Sants thought that this state of uncertainty could fundamentally undermine the child's security and result in the development of an insecure self-image and confused sense of identity in adolescence. Sants discusses the problems engendered by different heredities in adoptive families, explaining how differences in appearance or intellectual skills can severely hamper an adoptive child's capacity to identify with the adoptive parents, impeding a sense of belonging and the security that accompanies it.

Others (Frisk, 1964; Wieder, 1978b) also have concluded that the adopted adolescent's identity formation is impaired because an essential part of himself or herself has been cut off and remains unknown. All these writers are obviously echoing Erikson's belief in the importance of having an unbroken genetic and historical attachment to the past, present, and future in the process of identity consolidation. Wieder (1978b), like Sants (1964), discusses how the lack of a "blood line" complicates the process of identity consolidation by the absence of "biological mutuality" in adoptive families.

Frisk (1964), in dealing with the genealogical problems from a slightly different perspective, has described how the lack of family background knowledge in the adolescent adoptee prevents the development of a healthy "genetic ego," which is then replaced by a "hereditary ghost." Since the genetic ego is obscure, the adolescent has no way of knowing what might be passed on to the next generation. Furthermore, the adolescent's knowledge that the biological parents were unable to look after him or her is interpreted as proof of the biological parents' inferiority, giving rise to fears of hereditary psychic abnormalities that can lower self-esteem.

This literature presents a rather compelling view of the stresses that adoptive status brings to the ongoing attempts at identity resolution in adolescence. Much of the foregoing discussion is theoretically based, with the preponderance of conclusions drawn from the clinical data of writers who have attempted to account for the existence of pathology in their clinical patients. Let us turn at this point to some of the empirical research.

EMPIRICAL RESEARCH ON ADOPTION

Adoption Outcome Research

As noted in the theoretical discussion of identity development, Erikson has stressed that identity formation is a continuous process that has roots in earlier stages of growth (Erikson, 1959). Hence studies dealing with adoption outcome at all stages seem relevant to looking at identity formation in the adoptee. What do both clinical studies and more controlled research tell us about development in the adoptee?

Many studies of adoption have reported on the "success" or "failure" of adoption outcome rather than on specific personality or developmental variables. While the definition of success has varied from study to study, a great deal of research on adoption outcome has indicated about a 70% succes rate, in general, by whatever definition the authors have chosen to use (Addis, Salzburger, & Rabel, 1954; Amatruda & Baldwin, 1951; Bohman, 1972; Fairweather, 1952; Grow & Shapiro, 1974; Hoopes, 1982; Hoopes, Sherman, Lawder, Andrews, & Lower, 1970; Jaffee & Fanshel, 1970; Kadushin, 1970; Lawder et al., 1969; Morrison, 1950; Nieden, 1951; Nordlie & Reed, 1962; Ripple, 1968; Stein & Hoopes, 1985; Witmer et al., 1963).

What does a successful adoption outcome mean? In some of the research, the adopted families and children have been studied without comparison groups, and in other studies, comparisons have been made between adoptive and biological children. For the most part, successful outcome must be interpreted to mean that these children, in both cognitive and emotional areas, demonstrate functioning within the normal range and show no significant differences from biological children. In these studies, the children are meeting parental expectations, are achieving in school (although not always up to capacity), are accepted by peers, have good self-esteem, and are free from behavior disorders or neurotic symptoms. In ego identity terms, it appears that the children are satisfactorily negotiating the earlier Eriksonian stages of trust, autonomy, initiative, and industry, and are also resolving the identity crisis of adolescence. Is this in fact the case?

Studies of *clinical* populations of adopted children and adolescents have noted the overrepresentation of adoptees in psychiatric clinics (Deutsch et al., 1982; Goodman, Silberstein, & Mandel, 1963; Kenney et al., 1967; Mech, 1973; Schechter, 1960; Simon & Senturia, 1966) and a symptom pattern of aggressive, acting out behavior (Eiduson & Livermore, 1953; Menlove, 1965; Offord et al., 1969; Reece & Levin, 1968; Schechter et al.,1964; Silver, 1970; Triseliotis, 1973).

Empirical research with *nonclinical* samples, comparing adopted and nonadopted populations on specific personality characteristics, and social and academic adjustment, has yielded mixed results. In some studies few differences are found between the two groups (Carey, Lipton, & Myers, 1974; Elonen & Schwartz, 1969; Hoopes et al., 1970; Mikawa & Boston, 1968). Other studies have reported significant differences between the two groups in emotional adjustment and, particularly, in school adjustment (Bohman, 1970; Hoopes, 1982; Lindholm & Touliatos, 1980; Witmer et al., 1963). Teachers rate adopted compared with nonadopted children as higher in conduct disorders, in personality problems, in hostility with peers and with teachers, and in anxiety with peers and teachers.

Brodzinsky, Schechter, Braff, and Singer (1984) evaluated psychological and academic adjustment in a sample of 260 adopted and nonadopted children ranging in age from 6–11 years. Maternal ratings on the Achenbach Child Behavior Profiles and teacher ratings on the Hahneman Elementary School Behavior Rating Scale revealed that adopted children were rated higher in psychological and school-related behavior problems and lower in social competence and school achievement than nonadopted children.

The authors of these studies do point out, however, that although the two groups may differ, the adopted children usually measure within normal ranges on personality and behavioral measures. One study, which contradicts this finding, was done by Brodzinsky et al., (1987) in which the adopted children manifested not only more symptomatology than nonadopted children, but also more extreme or more maladaptive symptomatology.

These findings suggest that in fact adoptees may be at higher risk for negotiating successfully the early psychosocial stages which lead eventually to successful identity formation. Brodzinsky (1987) has argued just this point. He hypothesizes, for example, that developing a basic sense of trust for the adopted infant is complicated by the adoptive parents' need to resolve the issues of infertility and to accept adoption as an alternate route to parenthood even when the infant is placed at an early age. For infants placed at older ages, there is even more difficulty presented by separation from other caregivers and rebonding to the adoptive parents. During the preschool years, a child's striving for autonomy moves that child away from the parents. That differentiation of child from parent may create anxiety for both the adoptive parent and child as the parents begin to tell a child that he or she is adopted. Mastering the tasks of middle childhood, namely, learning the skills necessary for academic achievement may be difficult for the child who is struggling to understand what it means to be adopted.

Family Interaction Studies with Young Adoptees

In Hoopes (1982) we find an interesting approach to this question of the early foundations of identify by looking at family interaction. The family in which the individual lives is of utmost importance in influencing the process of identity development.

The family in its development and interaction must maintain a balance between the establishment of an autonomous identity and the achievement of intimate relations with others. One of the core family tasks, then, can be defined as an ongoing effort to resolve a continuous and inherent developmental dilemma—that of achieving autonomous separation while maintaining interrelated dependency. Underlying this effort will be conscious negotiation among all family members, with each other as well as with the interrelated units and with the social milieu. The family system, at its best, will support a constant urge toward individuation, providing the necessary emotional resources to withstand traumatic schism and loss, and sustaining continuity without rigidity.

One can discern here two results of healthy family interaction—results that develop in the individual family member certain personality dimensions. One is the sense of individuation, signifying that each family member is an individual within that unit, functioning within the limits of his or her capacities, as an autonomous person. Rather than a symbiotic tie between mother and child, father and child, or child and child, each member is an individual with a realistic recognition of self in relation to uniqueness and differentiation from others. To be individuated is to possess the ability to express perceptions of one's differences from mothers, specifically in relation to the family group as well as other significant groups, such as friends, school, community, and church.

A second result of healthy family interaction is the achievement of a sense of self-worth or self-esteem, defined as a basically realistic acceptance of the self in regard to strengths and weaknesses. A person with realistically high self-esteem is able to assert opinions and feelings and project a clear image of one who feels worthwhile. Such a person would behave as though she or he has a place that matters in the family and the world.

The processes of individuation and building of self-esteem are closely related to identity. One must define oneself as different from others in crucial ways, as possessing unique strengths and weaknesses, if one is to achieve the "style of individuality" to which Erikson refers. The building of self-esteem is viewed as a continuing aspect of the individuation process.

Within the family context, the fact of adoption interjects an additional reality difference into family functioning—that of biological origin. This difference may affect the family's efforts to accept and integrate its members. The psychological effects of the biological differences poses additional problems for the adoptive family. Kirk (1964) proposes a theory of adoptive relations which suggests that the ability of parents to "acknowledge difference," as a mechanism in coping with their adoptive parenthood, is important to a positive outcome for children raised in the family. He says that coping activities that "reject difference" of adopted children would result in poorer communication within the family and be subsequently disruptive to growth and maturation. Kirk states:

> Problems of identity tend to arise when we have conflicting loyalties to persons, groups, or associations. Identity problems arise for adopted children not simply because they have been told there are adopted, but because they are conflicting cultural values around them, those concerned with nurturing parenthood held by their adoptors, and the values concerning biological bases of kinship that are still very much alive in the culture generally. (p. 20)

Table 8.1   Dimensions for Rating Interviews

Realistic	Defensive
1. Recognition of difference in characteristics of self and other family members.	1. Denial or vagueness about different characteristics of self and other individual family members.
2. Recognition of family values and individualized family rules.	2. Inability to designate differentiated family rules or to acknowledge family values.
3. Recognition of sexuality—own and others.	3. Denial of sexuality—own and others.
4. Expression of acknowledgment of self in relation to outer system (societal values, community norms, etc.).	4. Lack of expression of or acknowledgment of self in relation to outer systems.
5. Ability to acknowledge limits and set rules.	5. Inability to acknowledge limits and set rules.
Self-esteem	
1. Open recognition of feelings of positive parental accomplishment.	1. Failure to express feelings regarding parental self—inability to see positive and negative in parenting adequacy.
2. Open recognition of doubts and anxieties regarding parental accomplishments of adequacy.	2. Sensitivity about critical attitudes of spouse, parent, etc.
3. Acknowledgment of coping capacities and dilemmas and problems in family living.	3. Denial of conflicts or dilemmas regarding family living.
4. Ability to express expectations of self.	4. Inability to express expectations of self.
5. Expression of feelings of entitlement—i.e., self-worth.	5. Expression of "hurt feelings" in response to expression of hostility.
6. Open confrontation allowed.	6. Open confrontation not allowed.

In our research (Hoopes, 1982), it was hypothesized that if family members were able to develop a sense of self-esteem and also appear well individuated, then they had clearly acknowledged differences and been open in communication, as Kirk has defined. Such families would have realistic attitudes about adoption (and its differences) and would be judged realistic in attitudes about parenting.

Our study evaluated a sample of adopted and biological families ($N = 54$) through an interview which included both parents and children. An assessment was made as to whether the family was comfortably "individuated," had a healthy sense of self-esteem, was functioning well as a family unit, and expressed realistic, rather than defensive, attitudes about adoption. Specifically, operationalization of individuation, self-esteem, family functioning, and attitudes about adoption were conceptualized as seen in Table 8.1.

The interviews were taped and separate raters listened to the interviews and rated the families on a 1 to 5 scale on each of these four dimensions: individuation, self-esteem, parental functioning, and attitudes about adoption. As a whole, all families scored very well: they clearly recognized and acknowledged differences so that individual family members were seen as individuals with their own roles within the families (Mn = 1.8); possessed a sense of self-esteem and feelings of self-worth (Mn = 3.0); and demonstrated clear satisfaction in the parental role and a sense of

Realistic	Defensive
Parental Functioning	
1. Recognition of feelings of both satisfaction and difficulties of parenting.	1. Denial of either satisfaction or difficulties.
2. Acknowledgment of capacities and shortcomings as a parent.	2. Expression of either great shortcomings and inadequacies or no recognition of any shortcomings.
3. Recognition of need for both parents to be involved in decisions regarding family activities and child discipline, although may not always agree.	3. Expectation that one parent is responsible for decisions and discipline. Overlook disagreements.
4. Recognition that children are both like and different from parents.	4. Perception of the children as exceedingly different from or very much the same as parents.
Attitudes About Adoption	
1. Acknowledgment of difference.	1. Rejection of difference.
2. Relatively comfortable communication about adoption.	2. Absence of communication about adoption.
3. Some ability to perceive special problems of adoptive families.	3. Denial of special problems of adoptive families or overidealization of adoption.
4. Some experiential illustrations, either of actual occurrences or feelings about adoption.	4. Denial of experiential illustrations, either concrete or ideational.
5. Acknowledgment that there were biological parents who are unknown, and that this fact may be a subject of questioning and some source of confusion and discomfort.	5. Rejection of discussion or questioning around historical cultural background or genetic endowment—denial that there is some validity in thought and feeling regarding this.

mutuality in decision making (Mn = 1.5). All families appeared to possess realistic attitudes about adoption (Mn = 1.8). This sample does represent a highly homogeneous and selective group of middle-class families who adopted from a private adoption agency. Generalization with other samples of adoptive families should be viewed with caution.

When adoptive and biological families were compared, few significant differences occurred. Adoptive families did appear less individuated, less able to perceive and acknowledge differences and similarities among family members. Whether this signifies a glossing over of differences regarding adoption in Kirk's terms, is difficult to determine from these results.

Another interesting aspect of the Delaware Family Study (Hoopes, 1982) is the family role study (carried out by Coche) where a family systems approach was taken in collecting the data. Here the family was studied in action as the members participated in a gamelike task. The purpose was to examine directly the interaction patterns within a group of adoptive, mixed (both adoptive and biological children), and biological families, concentrating especially on which members filled the expressive and instrumental leadership roles (Parson, 1955). What differences would be noted between the three groups on patterns of role behavior, what relationship would there be between the pattern of leadership and the family's ability to function well as a unit?

Forty-nine two-child families were studied for a total of 98 children, 73 of whom were adopted, and 25 of whom were biological. There were three types of families: 9 had 2 natural children; 32 had 2 adopted children, and 8 had mixed birth status. The family was asked to construct from velcro-backed mosaic blocks, which could be placed on a felt board, a "person or persons doing something." Families were observed and rated on expressive and instrumental role behaviors, as well as on the "goodness" of the product created, and the type of family they appeared to be. The types of families were defined as follows: *integrative*, where communication channels for expression of feelings were relatively open and there was no struggle for relatedness even though conflict in the family was observed: *struggling*, where the family seemed to be stretching and straining its energies and capacities to keep open communication channels that would otherwise close off, and *isolating* families where there was an observable failure in present or past attempts to bind the family unit. Communication lines were closed off within the system as a whole and between individual members. Families were also rated as child dominated or adult dominated.

The data showed that sex-linked role functioning was not crucial for families to function well, for example mother expressive and father instrumental. Rather it was of vital importance that the families worked toward achieving an observable form of cohesiveness as a unit, in which feelings are not blocked from expression, and difficult issues, such as those inherent in the adoption process, can be dealt with forthrightly. There was only one dimension in which the adoptive, mixed, and biological families differed in this study. Adoptive children were more able, for the most part, to successfully influence members of their family. Adopted children did not *attempt* to influence family members more often than biological children, but when they did attempt to influence family members, their attempts were proportionately more successful.

Families in which children dominated, were families that functioned less well together than those in which leadership was shared or held by the parents. It seems apparent that when children are enabled to lead, that is, become parentified, the parents are not comfortable with their identity as parents and cannot fill the parental roles adequately. These conflicts about parenting may be magnified in adoptions where issues relating to the choice to adopt are unresolved. It follows naturally that, in such families, the seeds for difficulty in handling adoption may well be traceable to personal issues of self-respect and individuation in the parents that become observable in the relinquishment of parenting duties and in the tension and communication difficulties as seen in certain families in this study. In other words, important family interaction variables rather than the fact of adoption per se influence how the adoptee negotiates various developmental stages.

Research on Identity Comparing Adopted and Nonadopted Adolescents

Few empirical studies have been made comparing adopted with nonadopted adolescents. Those that are reported have often studied groups of varying ages, for example, young adults (Ijams, 1976) versus adolescents (Norvell and Guy, 1977), defined identity achievement in differing terms, for example, self-concept (Norvell & Guy, 1977) or nondeviant personality patterns (Reynolds, Levey, & Eisnitz, 1977), and utilized differing methodologies, for example, self-report (Goebel & Lott, 1986) versus interview (Stein & Hoopes, 1985). For the most part, the more recent studies have utilized nonclinical populations, a significant improvement over earlier clinical studies which reported on the maladjustments of adoptees referred for therapy.

In a comparison of self-concept in 18- to 25-year old nonclinical adoptees and nonadoptees, Norvell and Guy (1977) found no significant difference between the two groups, using the Berger Self-Concept Scale. In fact, the adoptive group obtained slightly higher mean scores. On the basis of these results, they concluded that adoptive status alone does not produce a negative identity and suggested that other factors, such as the quality of parent–child interaction, are perhaps more pertinent to successful adjustment in adoption cases.

Simmons (1980) studied identity formation in 18- to 30-year-old adopted and nonadopted subjects, using a nonclinical population from each group. Various scales, including the California Psychological Inventory, the Tennessee Self-Concept Scale, and the Adjective Check List, were used to measure dimensions of identity. Simmons found significant differences between the two groups, indicating that adoptees were less well socialized, tended to be more impulsive and demanding, and had lower self-esteem. His results were interpreted as supporting the hypothesis that adoptees have more difficulty forming a sense of identity than nonadoptees, thus contradicting the findings of Norvell and Guy (1977)

Stein and Hoopes (1985) studied adopted adolescents who were part of the longitudinal Delaware Family Study. A sample of 91 adolescents (50 adopted and 41 nonadopted) between the ages of 15 and 18 were studied. The comparison group of nonadopted adolescents was matched as closely as possible for age, sex, social class, intelligence, and family constellation. The two groups were compared on three separate measures which assessed dimensions of identity as defined in this study: (1) the Tan Ego Identity Scale (Tan, Kendis, Fine, & Porac, 1977); (2) the Offer Self-Image Questionnaire (Offer, 1973) for adolescents; and (3) an interview developed by the authors. In this semistructured interview, questions were designed to tap aspects of the adolescent's functioning relevant to identity formation. Four sections included questions on family relatedness, peer relations, school performance, and self-esteem. An additional section dealt with questions relating solely to adoption, such as knowledge about why they were adopted, how satisfied they were with the information provided by adoptive parents, at what age did they believe children should be told about adoption, ease of communication about adoption in the family, and questions on searching for biological parents. The interview was intended to enrich the self-report measures of Offer and Tan by providing a phenomenological account of how adolescents view themselves in different contexts without the constraint of forced-choice answers.

When these two groups of adolescent adoptees and nonadoptees were compared along the dimensions of identity formation, no significant differences emerged. The findings suggest that, as a group, the adolescent adoptees interviewed were doing quite well. One must remember that this is a somewhat selective population, in that families who remained with this longitudinal study were probably the more stable ones, and the adolescents who chose to participate may have been better adjusted. This sample of adoptees were all adopted by the age of two and were predominantly middle-class children. Other samples of adoptees might not appear as well functioning. What the results do demonstrate, it seems, is that not all adopted adolescents have greater or more sustained difficulty with the tasks of adolescence. Adoptive status, in and of itself, need not be predictive of heightened stress among adolescents.

Goebel and Lott (1986) likewise found no difference between adopted and non-adopted groups in measures of identity. Their sample was also comprised of individuals who had been adopted before they were 18-months-old. The variance in developmental characteristics in their study of 18-to 35-year-olds appeared to be accounted for by age, family and personality variables, rather than adoptive versus nonadoptive status.

SEARCH BEHAVIOR AND IDENTITY FORMATION
IN THE ADOPTED ADOLESCENT

As the adopted child enters adolescence, he or she becomes more acutely aware of the biological link of the generations (Blum, 1976). One need only recall Erikson's (1959) definition of identity to know how essential to the process of identity formation is the presence of unbroken historical connections to the past, present, and future. As both Sants (1964) and Frisk (1964) have indicated, the identity conflicts of many adolescent adoptees are intensified by the knowledge of having genetic links to hereditary "unknowns." The adoptees' "dual identity" problem may prompt them to search out their past and pursue information about this unknown self in an effort to resolve the break in the continuity of their lives.

Controversy as to the extent of curiosity that adoptees manifest about their genealogical background has continued, although all theorists tend to agree that the adolescent's identity concerns intensify his or her interest in this area (Sorosky et al., 1975). Some authors contend that the adolescent's concern about genealogy is common to all adoptees and is not a sign of emotional disturbance or family conflict (Sorosky, Baran, & Pannor, 1975; Blum, 1976; Kirk, Jonassohn & Fisch, 1966; McWhinnie, 1969; Schechter et al., 1964). Nospitz (1979), for example, claims that the adopted adolescent's increased interest in his or her biological parents occurs in the normal process of separating from one's parents and seeking the roots on which to build an identity.

Many different theories have been proposed to explain the intensification of "search behavior" in some adolescents, although actual search behavior has not been consistently differentiated in the literature from "intense curiosity." Some theorists have suggested that curiosity and search behavior are greatest in adoptive homes in which there has been a strained relationship and difficulty in communicating openly about the adoption situation (Clothier, 1943b; McWhinnie, 1969; Triseliotis, 1973). Clothier (1943b), for example, suggests that the need of the child to know about the biological parents may vary with the lack of positive identification with the adoptive parents. McWhinnie (1969) similarly concluded, from her retrospective study, that the more secure and happily accepted the adopted child feels within the adoptive family, the less will be the need to search out origins. In a retrospective study of 70 adult adoptees, Triseliotis (1973) found that the greater the dissatisfaction with the adoptive family relationship and with themselves, the greater the possibility that adoptees would seek a reunion with the biological parents, whereas the better the image of themselves and of their adoptive parents, the greater the likelihood that they would merely seek background information. Other studies by Sorosky et al. (1975) have proposed that an adolescent adoptee's genealogical concerns and search efforts are more reflective of innate personality traits, such as inquisitiveness and curiosity, and are less dependent on the nature of the adoptive family relationship.

In their study, Stein and Hoopes (1985) defined searchers as those adolescents who described themselves as actively seeking information with or without the intention of meeting their biological parents. Intention to meet was not considered a mandatory attribute because of the legal restriction on actually pursuing records imposed by the age of these adolescents (15 to 18 years). Only a small number of adolescents in this study actually expressed an interest in searching for their biological parents—16 out of 50, although all of the 50 adoptees studied, expressed an interest in general background information, with health history heading the list.

What differentiated adolescent searchers from nonsearchers? Searchers as a group were found to score somewhat lower on 10 of the 12 dimensions of identity considered in this study. The data showed only slight differences and reached significance in only one area—the family factor in the interview (p<.05). Their lower scores approached significance on the Offer Self-Image family subscale (p = .12). There is thus the suggestion that adopted adolescents with greater difficulties in identity may be the ones more prone to initiate a search for biological parents. When family relationships of searchers and nonsearchers were compared, significant differences emerged in that the greater number of searchers (75%) reported unsatisfactory family relationships in contrast to nonsearchers who seemed significantly (62%) more satisfied with the quality of their family ties.

Another interesting finding in this study (Stein & Hoopes, 1985) relates to the issue of perceived mismatch between the adopted adolescent and the adoptive family. The adoptees were asked how similar in physical appearance to their adopted parents they perceived themselves to be. Searchers as a group perceived themselves as more strikingly mismatched physically (44%) than nonsearchers (17%) did. In view of the importance of genetic links to identity formation, this result suggests that issues of mismatch in adoption, both physically and perhaps also intellectually, do promote identity concerns that accelerate search behavior in some adoptees (see Schechter & Bertocci, Chapter 4).

Goebel and Lott (1986) also found differences between searchers and nonsearchers in some personality traits and in perceptions of family factors. Searchers perceived their families as more isolated and higher in conflict, while nonsearchers perceived their families as higher in cohesion, expressiveness, and encouragement of independence. The fact that the differences between searchers and nonsearchers, when they did occur in both these recent studies, were in the area of family relationships seems to corroborate the findings of earlier studies cited above.

It is possible that adolescents at both ends of the identity continuum would be prone to search. On the one hand, those adolescents, with a strongly consolidated identity and with a greater security in their definition of self, may be less vulnerable to information about their origins and, therefore, more curious, and would search. On the other hand, adolescents with little sense of "who they are," might likewise attempt to search to consolidate their fragmented or poorly defined sense of identity. An examination of the distribution of scores on the identity measures employed by

Stein and Hoopes (1985) showed no tendency for searcher's identity scores to cluster at either the high or low end of the distribution. Despite the lower identity scores found in the search group, a polarized phenomenon could not be confirmed.

Not all adoptees want to search. According to the American Academy of Pediatrics (1971), ambivalence about searching is apparently common. Even Frisk (1964) noted that although some adoptees experienced the need to investigate their genetic background, they were at the same time afraid of not being able to integrate the information intrapsychically. Blum (1976) has indicated that "sometimes adequate information is all the adoptee is seeking and this, openly shared, can make the search for the actual parent unnecessary" (p. 247). Wieder (1978b) corroborated Blum's findings with clinical data that analyzed the wish to search and showed it to be a wish to know about, not to rejoin, the biological parents. McWhinnie (1969) similarly found that although many adoptees retrospectively spoke of wanting to meet their biological parents out of curiosity, they were emphatic about not wishing these parents to know who they were—that is, they would have liked to observe their biological parents without being observed in return.

In the Stein and Hoopes (1985) study, when the adolescents were given an opportunity to place significant persons in an imagined life space, none of the adoptees included their biological parents either spontaneously nor on suggestion from the researcher. This held for searchers and nonsearchers alike. An interest in searching for their biological parents is undoubtedly compelling for some adoptees and may be particularly important in the late adolescent and young adult years as the young person consolidates the identity stage and moves into intimacy. In this selective sample, all under 18 years of age, the findings suggest that it is with their adoptive parents that these adolescents primarily identify. Although biological parents may exist in the fantasy lives of the adoptees, they appear to have no significant place in the adopted adolescent's relational system.

FACTORS INFLUENCING IDENTITY RESOLUTION IN ADOPTEES

Does the literature and the research yield identifiable factors that enhance or impede identity resolution in adopted adolescents? If so, can families be aware of these factors and thus be helped in family interrelationships so as to promote healthy identity formation? Several such factors have been noted in (1) family relationships; (2) communication about adoption; and (3) parental attitudes about adoption.

Family Relationships

Quality of parenting, whether it be an adoptive or biological family, is obviously important in identity formation. Erikson certainly emphasizes that the roots of identity formation are in the earlier stages of trust, autonomy, initiative, and mastery. The family plays the major role in assisting the developing child through these various life stages. Much of the literature on poorly adjusted adoptees, such as those coming to the attention of mental health practitioners or the courts, concludes that it is the quality of parenting rather than adoption per se that plays the significant role in causing these adjustment problems (Barinbaum, 1974; Goodman & Magno-Nora, 1975; Rickarby & Egan, 1980; Sabalis & Burch, 1980). McWhinnie (1969) likewise attributed an adolescent's positive attitude toward adoption to a solid relationship with the adoptive parents.

When the adoptees in the Stein and Hoopes (1985) study were asked their perceptions of their relationships with parents, those adoptees who described a compatible relationship with mother, father, and siblings did reveal higher scores on measures of ego identity (Tan Ego Identity Scale, Offer Average Self-Score). These adolescents felt that they were comfortably esteemed and had a definite sense of belonging in the family; they also thought that their opinions counted and that differences could be negotiated. Family communication was described as open and easy most of the time. As Offer and associates (1981) have stated: "If everything else is kept constant, the family will contribute relatively more to the positive development of adolescents than any other psychosocial variable" (p. 65). It appears that satisfactory family relationships could perhaps effectively mitigate or even eliminate the "intensification" of identity concerns that many authors (Frisk, 1964; Schoenberg, 1974) attribute to the inherent stresses of the adoptive situation.

The child development literature in general has indicated the importance of childrearing attitudes and parenting behavior in subsequent behavior in the child (Baumrind, 1967, 1971; Becker, 1964; Sears, Maccoby, & Levine, 1957). Becker notes that power–assertive techniques of discipline tend to be used by hostile parents and in this context tend to promote aggression in young children, resistance to authority, power assertion to other children, and externalized reactions to transgressions. Love-oriented techniques of discipline tend to be used by warm parents and in this context tend to promote acceptance of self-responsibility, guilt, and related, internalized reactions to transgressions. Restrictive childrearing techniques, while fostering well-controlled, socialized behavior, tend also to lead to fearful, dependent, and submissive behaviors. Permissiveness fosters outgoing, sociable, assertive behaviors and intellectual striving, and is often associated with lack of persistence and with increased aggressiveness.

In a recently completed study by Schwartz (1986), early parental childrearing attitudes were correlated with the adolescent identity measures in the same sample studied by Stein and Hoopes (1985). Parental attitudes were analyzed during three time periods. The results revealed that, in this sample of adoptive parents, attitudes remained quite stable across time. Correlations between parental attitudes and identity measures, while not strong, were consistent and showed that higher self-image and higher self-appraisal in relation to family, peers, and school were associated with a parenting style that encourages autonomy, communication, and independence of behavior. Authoritarian control correlated negatively with self-esteem and identity measures.

Communication About Adoption

How communication about adoption is handled may influence an adolescent's progress toward identity resolution. Stein and Hoopes (1985) hypothesized that adopted adolescents who perceived an open communication style about adoption within their family would obtain higher scores on measures of ego identity than adolescents from families in which the issue of adoption was perceived to be closed. Style of communication about adoption was determined by asking the adolescents whether adoption was openly discussed, only occasionally discussed, or never mentioned. Categorizing the responses into an "open" versus "closed" style, the results indicated that an open style resulted in higher identity scores on the Interview measure, while a trend in this direction was noted on other measures of identity (Tan Ego Identity Scale and Offer Self-Image). Since all adoptees in this sample had been exposed from birth to at least a minimum of ongoing discussion about adoption (because agency practice encouraged it and they had participated in this longitudinal study), the findings were not as strong as they might be in a random sample of adoptees who had not participated in such a study. The results nevertheless tend to provide empirical evidence for the theoretical ideas of Blum (1976), Schoenberg (1974), and Sorosky and associates (1977), who strongly advocate a climate of openness in discussions of adoptive status. One would have to agree that families who encourage open discussion of the facts tend to produce more secure, identity–solid adolescents. McWhinnie (1969) cautions, however, that too much talk about adoption can be detrimental, especially if parental discussions do not coincide with the childrens' feelings and needs.

Parental Attitudes About Adoption

Parental attitudes about adoption have been shown to influence the adolescent's achievement of a healthy sense of identity. McWhinnie (1969) found that the comfort level of adoptive parents in discussing adoption played a role in the adjustment of the adolescent. She suggests that parental discomfort in discussion of adoption "relates to doubts about their adequacy as parents, their fear that their children will love them less if they know they are not biologically their own children and concern that they may seek out their 'other mother' " (p. 134). Blum (1976) also noted that for the insecure adoptive parent, conversations about genealogy were fraught with feelings of rejection and guilt that could only intensify the adolescent's struggle with identity-related issues. She concluded that parental attitudes reinforced by feelings of inadequacy could do much to influence the child's negative self-image. Schechter (1960) observed that adoptive mothers in his clinical caseload often presented intense feelings of inadequacy regarding their childbearing functions, an attitude that contributed to their tendency toward overprotectiveness and difficulties with issues of independence.

A finding by Lawder et al. (1969), while somewhat tangential to this discussion, is interesting. These authors found that when either mother or father were critical of the baby during the supervisory period (i.e., before legal adoption) that adoption outcome of the child at àge 10 to 15 was not as good as when there was little or no criticism. Likewise, Hoopes et al. (1970) found fathers' inability to discuss infertility (when this was a factor) had a small but significant relationship to the child's functioning in school and other areas. These findings—criticism of the baby or inability to discuss infertility—imply a reluctance to accept adoptive parenthood and perhaps a negative attitude toward adoption.

Critical attitudes of adoptive parents toward the biological parents can also interfere with the adolescent's identity process. Frisk (1964) indicated that unfavorable reports about biological parents gave rise to identity problems in adolescent adoptees, who interpreted these reports as proof of their own genetic inferiority. Rickarby and Egan (1980) found that notions of "genetic inferiority" arose in response to parents' attempts to mitigate their own feelings of guilt and inadequacy in relationship struggles with their adopted adolescents. According to Blum (1976) and Nospitz (1979), the criticism adoptive parents sometimes level at biological parents tends to impede a positive identification with the fantasied biological parent.

Blum (1976) suggests that the need of the adoptive parent to downgrade the biological parent tends to reflect feelings of insecurity or the lack of feelings of entitlement as a parent. The "negative identity" that results in the child or adolescent often leads to social deviation or delinquency, according to McWhinnie (1969), who noted that "where adoptive mothers feared that their adolescent daughters would inherit instability or immoral behavioral patterns from their biological mothers, their mistrusting behavior toward these adolescents drove them into behaving in just the way that their mothers feared" (p. 135). McWhinnie (1969) concludes that "the aim must be to help the inquiring adolescent . . . to learn of his biological parentage in a positive, acceptable and undamaging way, emphasizing what is known of the positive attributes of his natural parents and encouraging consideration of what may have been the difficulties in their human condition" (p. 141).

Both Frisk (1964) and Sorosky et al. (1977) comment on the oversensitivity of adoptive parents to their adolescents' strivings for independence. Frisk believes that the parents' overreaction to insignificant relational phenomena is attributable to feelings of inferiority originating from their incapacity to bear children. Sorosky et al. (1975) similarly suggest that adoptive parents tend to "view any disengagement from themselves as an abandonment and a return to the lonely, insecure feelings associated with the preadoption childless period" (p. 55). They point out that this may result in infantilization of the adolescent and thus prevent an emerging individuation. In these cases, Sorosky et al. (1975) note that the adolescent is often pushed into a state of rebellion to preserve his or her sense of integrity.

As mentioned earlier in this chapter, Kirk (1964) described a tendency on the part of some adoptive parents to deny the basic differences (inability to conceive biologically) that originally created the need for adoption. He felt that the coping mechanism of "rejecting difference" could result in poorer communication within the family and prevent a healthy adaptation for all family members. Sorosky et al. (1977) concur with Kirk's statement, concluding that the "healthiest adaptation occurs when the adoptive parents have been reasonably successful in resolving their feelings about infertility and are willing to acknowledge that their role is different— than that of biological parents" (p. 65).

SUMMARY

Identity formation and adoption are two complex experiences with multiple interlocking family and social inputs. The answer to the question as to whether identity development is more difficult for adoptive adolescents than for comparable samples of biological adolescents is not a simple one. Research has identified some of the variables that influence identity formation in the adopted child; many of the same variables are important to the biological child also. It is clear that it is totally possible for the adopted adolescent to achieve a mature identity if the factors outlined above are present in the family, and many adopted adolescents have successfully navigated this stage of development. As Goebel and Lott (1986) point out, perhaps adoptees work harder at the task of achieving an identity and hence master it better than the nonadoptee. It is also clear, however, that there are some stresses for the adoptive family which are not present in the biological family, thus leading to crisis and difficulty for the adopted adolescent in completing this stage of development and emerging with a strong ego identity.

ACKNOWLEDGMENT

The author would like to acknowledge the help of Leslie M. Stein, Ph.D. and Anne D. Schwartz, M.A. in preparing this chapter.

9

Adopted Adolescents
in Residential Treatment:
The Role of the Family

HAROLD D. GROTEVANT AND RUTH G. McROY

Adoption is a social and legal process in which a parent–child relationship is established between persons unrelated by birth. Through this process a child born to one set of parents becomes the child of other parents, a member of another family, and thereby assumes the rights and duties of children in birthfamilies (Costin, 1972).

Researchers have paid close attention to the demographic and social–psychological factors associated with parents' decisions to adopt (Chambers, 1970; Fellner, 1968; Kadushin, 1962; Maas, 1960) or to make adoption plans for their children (Bachrach, 1986). However, much less attention has been given to adoptive family relationships and to the long-term adjustment issues in adoptive families (Brinich & Brinich, 1982; Fanshel, 1972; McRoy, Grotevant, & Zurcher, (1988); McRoy & Zurcher, 1983).

A major concern of adoption workers and adoptive families is whether adopted children are more ''at risk'' for emotional disturbance than nonadopted children. Research data suggest that adopted children are referred for psychological treatment two to five times as frequently as their nonadopted peers. This finding has been replicated in countries as widely dispersed as Great Britain, Israel, Poland, Sweden, and the United States (Bohman, 1971; Brinich, 1980; Eiduson & Livermore, 1953; Humphrey & Ounsted, 1963; Kadushin, 1967; Lifshitz et al., 1975; McWhinnie, 1969; Reece & Levin, 1968; Schechter, 1960; Senior & Himadi, 1985; Simon & Senturia, 1966; Sweeney, Gasbarro, & Gluck, 1963; Toussieng, 1962; Work & Anderson, 1971; Ziatek, 1974).

According to the literature, adopted children referred for treatment generally were adopted as infants and placed with childless couples. They typically exhibited behavior characterized as impulsive, provocative, aggressive, and antisocial (Brinich, 1980; Eiduson & Livermore, 1953; Goodman & Magno-Nora, 1975; Jackson, 1968; Menlove, 1965; Offord et al., 1969; Schechter et al., 1964; Simon & Senturia, 1966). Diagnoses have ranged widely from personality trait disorders to adolescent adjustment reaction (Weiss, 1985).

167

When the high incidence of adopted children referred to mental health clinics was first reported (Goodman et al., 1963; Schechter, 1960; Sweeney et al., 1963), several psychodynamic hypotheses were proposed to explain their problematic behavior. These hypotheses were provocative, but typically incorporated variables that were difficult or impossible to operationalize. Clinicians have also noted several factors that could more often predispose adoptive families than non-adoptive families to seek help for their children. For example, compared to the general population, adoptive parents tend to be socioeconomically advantaged and may be more likely to provide mental health services for their children. The adoptive parents can feel unduly vulnerable to rejection by the adopted child, leading to maladaptive reactive defenses by parents and child. Furthermore, adoptive parents might be anxious about unknown hereditary factors influencing the child's development (Wilson, 1985).

Adolescence is a developmental period during which children and their families can be at particular risk for the manifestation of problem behavior. Significant changes during this period include the physical development brought about by puberty and adolescents' psychological reactions to their emerging sexuality. Cognitive changes enable adolescents to think beyond the here and now to the world of possibilities and abstractions. Significant others in adolescents' social environments encourage them to take on more responsible roles and act in a mature manner. As a result of these internal and external events and changes, adolescents are challenged to form a mature sense of identity in order to answer the adult question: "Who am I?"

For the adopted adolescent, questions about birthparents and origins play an important role in the identity formation process. How these issues are handled within the adoptive family can have an important bearing on the adolescent's feelings and behaviors. In addition, behavioral problems that had been manageable during childhood can become intolerable in the family setting when the child becomes an adolescent.

Although there has been speculation about the situational factors that place the adopted child at risk for developing emotional problems, most of the research has been inadequately controlled or designed. With the exception of Kirk's (1964, 1981) work, limited theoretical attention has been given to adoptive family relationships. Thus, due to theoretical and empirical limitations, many important questions concerning the etiology of emotional disturbance in adopted adolescents remain unanswered.

The purpose of this chapter is to describe a program of research designed to identify familial and other contextual factors associated with the placement of adopted children in residential treatment for emotional disorders during the adolescent years. In this study adopted and nonadopted adolescents in treatment have been compared in order to separate issues specific to adoptive families from issues that may lead to emotional disturbance in all types of families. Questions of particular interest include the following: What are the specific factors or clusters of factors that appear to be related to the adolescents' emotional disturbance? Once these general areas have been identified, what are the specific family processes and dynamics that initiate and maintain the problem?

THEORETICAL FRAMEWORKS

This research project has been guided by several theories, each of which has generated substantive predictions about the consequences of adoption for the child and the family. In this section, pertinent aspects of these theories will be summarized.

Genetic Theory

A genetic account of the etiology of disturbance among adopted children would begin with the assumption that the backgrounds of adopted and nonadopted children are different on both genetic and environmental grounds. Parents who make adoption plans for their children are likely to be younger than married parents at time of birth (thus placing the child at higher risk during gestation), be more ambivalent about the pregnancy (thus creating the possibility that they will take health risks during the pregnancy), and be less likely to obtain adequate prenatal care. It is also likely that some birthmothers relinquish their children for adoption because they are unable to care for them due to their own emotional disturbance. There is clear evidence that genetic factors contribute to psychiatric disorders, such as schizophrenia and depression (Scarr & Kidd, 1983), thus placing children of these birthmothers at higher risk for future psychopathology than their nonadopted peers.

Few studies have documented differences between birthparents who place children for adoption and parents who keep their children. However, using the National Survey of Family Growth, Cycle III, conducted by the National Center for Health Statistics in 1982, Bachrach (1986) found that women who placed their babies for adoption were similar with respect to income, welfare dependency, and educational attainment at the time of the survey in contrast to women who married before giving birth or women who had abortions. Compared with unmarried women who chose to raise their babies, the women who placed their children for adoption were less likely to be poor, less likely to have received some form of public assistance in the past year, and more likely to have finished high school. These indicators, however, do not adequately address the emotional or intellectual status of these birthmothers.

In other studies comparing personalities of unwed birthmothers who keep their babies with those who place them for adoption (e.g., Horn & Turner, 1976; Vincent, 1961), the birthmothers who place are usually considered "healthier" than unwed birthmothers who choose to keep and raise their infants. Horn and Turner (1976), however, found substantial variability within both groups, suggesting that blanket generalizations are not warranted. Further research is needed in order to determine definitively if birthmothers who relinquish their babies for adoption constitute a significantly different gene pool either from married women who give birth to their own children or from adoptive mothers.

Genetic theory would also acknowledge the contribution of heredity to individual differences in both intellectual ability and personality. Because adoptive parents are typically of middle to upper-middle class, they tend to have high expectations for their children in terms of educational attainment and achievement. If their adopted children fail to meet those expectations, issues of "goodness-of-fit" between the children and their respective adoptive families may arise. Similar issues may emerge concerning personality differences. In biologically related families, inheritance acts in such a way as to maximize the possibility that there will be some similarity between parents and their children. In adoptive families, there is no guarantee of similarity. It is possible that a lower degree of perceived similarity (Scarr, Scarf, & Weinberg, 1980) or actual similarity may be associated with distancing between adoptive parents and their children when behavioral problems begin to occur.

Psychoanalytic Theory

Psychoanalytic theory suggests that the circumstances surrounding the child's birth, including adoptive parents' unresolved concerns about infertility and the adoptees' concerns about having two sets of parents, can set the stage for emotional disorders in adopted children (Brodzinsky, Schechter et al. 1984). Several psychoanalytic hypotheses have been advanced, including the following: emotional disorders among adopted children may result from the unconscious and unresolved aversion toward parenthood in one or more of the adoptive parents, particularly the mother (Toussieng, 1962). The child's efforts to determine the reasons for being relinquished for adoption may generate an identity problem, especially in adolescence as he or she might come to identify with perceived ''bad'' birthparents (Simon & Senturia, 1966). Emotional problems can result from adoptive mothers' guilt about taking children that did not belong to them, a guilt that presumably arises from unresolved anger and rivalry toward their own mothers (Dukette, 1962; Walsh & Lewis, 1969). Relationships between adopted children and their parents may be vulnerable to ''splitting,'' in which adopted children attribute all the bad qualities to their adoptive parents and all the good qualities to their unknown but idealized birthparents (Freud, 1986).

Attachment Theory

Attachment theory has its roots in ethological theory (Ainsworth, 1973, 1979; Bowlby, 1969) and holds that the primary function of the attachment relationship is to insure the proximity of the immature infant to its caregiver for provision of safety and food. Recent versions of attachment theory emphasize not only the goal of proximity maintenance, but also the goal of achieving ''felt security'' through the relationship (Sroufe & Waters, 1977).

Focused attachment relationships develop gradually over the first six to eight months of life. According to Ainsworth and colleagues, the roots of secure attachment lie in the caregiver's responsiveness to the needs of the infant. In a feeding situation, mothers of securely attached infants have been found to be more sensitive, accepting, and psychologically accessible than mothers of anxiously attached infants (Ainsworth et al., 1978). Mothers of avoidant infants seemed to be especially rejecting and had an aversion to physical contact. Recent evidence (Egeland & Farber, 1984) suggests that some resistant babies are more difficult to care for early in life (e.g., are less alert or active than other babies). When coupled with caregivers who were not unusually sensitive, the attachment relationships have taken this distinctive turn.

A sizable body of evidence has accrued to indicate that attachment relationships in infancy have long-term consequences for the psychological and relational functioning of the individual child. For example, toddlers who were more securely attached as infants have been shown to be more willing to explore a novel physical environment than do toddlers who were anxiously attached infants (Hazen & Durrett, 1982). In addition, securely attached infants showed better problem-solving ability and sociability at age 2 (Matas, Arend, & Sroufe, 1978; Pastor, 1981); and more curiosity and flexibility during preschool years (Arend, Gove, & Sroufe, 1979). These and other studies suggest a great deal of continuity in behavior from infancy through early childhood in terms of the legacy of attachment.

The implications of attachment theory for the study of adoption are profound, especially for infants who were adopted when they were "older." Since the attachment relationship develops gradually over the first six to eight months, it seems plausible that any child placed after that age would be "at risk" for developmental difficulties to the extent that disruptions or variations in parental responsiveness occurred. Similarly, to the degree that early placements are associated with continuous and responsive caregiving, it seems reasonable that the earlier the placement, the better the outcome. An important mediating variable in the situation for "later" adopted children would be the quality of the foster home or preadoption placement(s). Because children can develop multiple attachments, attachment to a birthmother or foster mother should not preclude later relationships with adoptive parents. However, abuse or neglect during the first year could have strongly negative consequences in terms of the child's ability to establish a sense of "basic trust" (Erikson, 1950).

A recent study of attachment in adopted children placed as young infants found no differences between the frequencies of adopted and nonadopted children in the "strange situation" attachment classifications (Singer et al., 1985). The authors concluded that "lack of early contact per se does not place middle-class adoptive families at risk for the development of anxious mother–infant attachment relationships" (p. 1547), and therefore "it is unlikely that the higher incidence of psychological and academic problems among adoptees in middle childhood and adolescence . . . can be explained in terms of insecure family attachment patterns in the infancy years" (p. 1547). However, most of these infants were placed quite early. Furthermore, the insecurely attached adopted infants had experienced an average of 0.63 foster placements prior to adoption in contrast to the 0.16 foster placements experienced by securely attached infants. These data do not preclude the possible impact of adoption history on attachment. Further research with a more heterogeneous sample will be necessary in order to test these predictions adequately.

Family Systems Theory

In family systems theory, family *structure* is viewed as a network of interdependent individuals and relationships (e.g., Beavers, 1977; Hill, 1971, Minuchin, 1974; Walsh, 1982). The child is seen as one element in this network of developing individuals in which the behaviors of each member mutually regulate those of others. Thus systems theory constructs allow one to consider complex directions of effects in socialization. Family systems are organized into subsystems (e.g., marital, parent–child, and sibling subsystems) which may emerge because goals are shared by certain parts of the system but not by others. The functioning of key family subsystems is predictive of family effectiveness. For example, clinicians (Haley, 1980; Napier & Whitaker, 1978) have documented the way in which a weak spousal subsystem can negatively affect the development of autonomy in adolescents. In the family systems view of *process,* individual developmental changes as well as the addition or departure of family members represent continuing sources of new information to which a family must adapt.

Family systems theory contributes to an understanding of adoption in terms of considering the couple's adaptation to the new adopted child entering the family and the mutual adaptation that occurs between parent and child over time. Clinically, it also facilitates understanding of the emergence and maintenance of dysfunctional behavior patterns within the family that ultimately result in the child's placement outside the family. In addition, it permits consideration of what happens to the family's boundaries when the adolescent leaves home for the treatment center and how possible it will be for the adolescent to return home.

Goodness-of-Fit Theory

Goodness-of-fit theories hold that an individual's development is optimized in those situations in which compatibility exists between characteristics of the individual and characteristics or demands of the salient environment. Examples of this model include Hunt's (1961) "notion of the match" in intellectual development; Holland's (1973, 1985) concept of person–environment congruency in the occupational world; and Lerner's (1985) goodness-of-fit model of infant temperament and environmental responsiveness. Consistent with attachment theory, goodness-of-fit theory states that when infants are raised by parents who understand them and are sensitive to their needs, development will be optimized. When parents are not able to accommodate to the needs of their children, mismatch problems can occur. Although parental sensitivity is a key determinant, compatibility is viewed as a joint product of the characteristics of the child, the characteristics of the parents, and the family's social situation (Lamb & Gilbride, 1985). The characteristics of parents or children are not static; both change in dynamic responsiveness to one another. Goodness-of-fit, then, involves both the family members' ability to attain this state and to retain it through dynamic interaction over time (Lamb & Gilbride, 1985).

Compatibility problems can occur with greater frequency in adoptive than in biological families, since adoptive parents usually are less similar to their children. For example, the correlations for both the personality and IQ scores of biologically related parent–child pairs are higher than the correlations for parents and their adopted children, even though the children were adopted in early infancy (Horn, 1983; Scarr & Weinberg, 1983). In addition, adoptive parents typically are more highly educated, more often in middle-to upper-middle socioeconomic status, and are married longer when they first become parents (through adoption) than are biological parents and children living together (e.g., Zill, 1985).

From results such as these, it could be predicted that the degree of actual and perceived similarity would be less in adoptive than in biological families. Mismatches can occur between intellectual levels or personalities of parents and children, between characteristics of adopted siblings, or between adopted children and biological children within the same family. When major mismatches occur, there is a potential for conflict or for parental disappointment. The impact of such mismatches can be profound when adoptive parents attempt to diminish the importance of the child's biological heritage and behave as if he or she were just like their own birth-child (see discussion of Kirk's adoptive kinship theory below).

Other factors that can reduce adoptive parents' ability to be optimally responsive to their infant and potentially lead to a perception of mismatch include: unresolved parental ambivalence concerning infertility; parental tentativeness in interacting fully with the infant in order to protect against loss, should the agency or birthparents not permit the adoption to be finalized; lack of support typically available to biological parents, such as childbirth preparation classes and hospital-based programs; and attributions that the child is "different" and therefore "not ours."

Attribution Theory

Attribution theory refers to a family of theories (e.g., Heider, 1958; Jones & Davis, 1965; Kelley, 1971, 1972) that are concerned with how individuals ascribe meaning to their observations about responsibility for the behavior of others and themselves. The attribution process includes three steps: observation of an action (either of another person or of oneself); judgment of presence or absence of intention; and formation of a causal attribution of responsibility (Shaver, 1975). The goal of the attribution process is to be able to explain current and past behavior and to predict future behavior. The focus of the theory, then, is on the processes impinging on perceivers that affect their explanation and prediction of events. Most theories are concerned with such phenomena as attributions about success or failure, intentionality, and how people cope with uncontrollable situations.

In a recent application of attribution theory to the study of parent–child relations, Dix (1984; Dix & Grusec, 1986) has outlined sources of potential bias in attributions parents make about their children. Attribution theorists note that behaviors perceived to harm or benefit the perceiver in an impactful way (i.e., are *hedonically relevant* to the observer) are likely to motivate the perceiver to search for a cause of the behavior. In the case of the aversive behavior demonstrated by the adopted children in this study, the principle of hedonic relevance implies that parents will attempt to assign responsibility for the behavior.

Several attributional errors can influence the process of inferring responsibility. First, the parent may make the *fundamental attribution error,* preferring to attribute the behavior to a disposition of the child (because he's adopted) rather than to situational factors influencing behavior (e.g., the family dynamics). This error may be further reinforced by the attributions made by friends and relatives. Second, parents may be affected by the *self-serving bias* (Heider, 1958) which holds that, in an intimate relationship, members have an investment in one another and parents are motivated to perceive their children's behavior in ways that make both the parents and the child feel and look good. Parents can make themselves feel good by disclaiming responsibility for the child's behavior. ("I know I'm a good parent—the adoption agency approved me, didn't it? Therefore, it must be my child's fault.") They might also make themselves feel good about their children by taking away the child's responsibility for his or her behavior ("He can't help it—it's in his genes.") Once this line of reasoning has begun, subsequent attributions can be affected by the *confirmation bias,* in which incoming data are fit into well-entrenched views. Attributions of these adolescents can be accentuated because of the *feature-positive bias,* which holds that attributions are more strongly influenced by the commission of behaviors (e.g., negative acting out behaviors) than by their omission.

Complex motivational and affective factors are involved in adoptive parents' attributions about their children, as illustrated by Heider (1958): "Since one's idea includes what ought to be as well as what is, attributions and cognitions are influenced by the mere subjective forces of needs and wishes as well as by the more objective evidence presented in the raw material" (pp. 120–121).

Cognitive-Developmental Theory

In recent research, Brodzinsky, Singer, and Braff (1984) documented developmental changes in children's understanding of the meaning of adoption. In keeping with the cognitive-developmental tradition, they suggested that the child's understanding of adoption is a constructive process that does not reach a mature level until adolescence.

Although adoptive parents might begin talking with their child about adoption at an early age, it is necessary for ongoing discussion to take place in order to help the child develop a mature concept of the meaning of adoption. In terms of cognitive-developmental theory, then, the timing and content of adoption revelation has a major impact on the child's emerging concept of adoption as well as on the child's concept of self-as-adopted-child.

Brodzinsky, Singer, and Braff (1984) suggested that many adoptive parents overestimate their child's understanding of adoption and might stop talking about it before the child has a mature concept. Their results imply that information about adoption must be developmentally matched to the child's ability to understand it, and that repeated discussions of the meaning of adoption must take place over time, especially into early adolescence.

Kirk's Adoptive Kinship Theory

Kirk (1964, 1981) has applied social role theory to adoptive family relationships, noting that biological and adoptive parenthood are inherently different experiences in a number of ways. For example, adoptive parents must deal with the feelings associated with their infertility. They have no other adoptive family experiences to serve as models, and they have no physical pregnancy to serve as emotional preparation. They are subjected to intensive screening and must endure a probationary period following placement that creates insecurity. Their parents or family members may not be supportive, and they must undertake the difficult task of revealing the adoption to their child. Kirk believes that these situational discrepancies create stressful experience for adoptive parents and result in their being handicapped in their role performance.

Kirk contends that the adoptive family situation is different from biological parenthood at the interpersonal level. To ensure family cohesiveness, this difference must be acknowledged. Adoptive parents suffering from role handicap might cope by rejecting rather than acknowledging the differences between adoptive and biological parenting. This rejection-of-difference coping mechanism can lead to poor communication between parent and child and can adversely affect adoptive family relationships. The acknowledgement-of-difference coping mechanism is considered by Kirk to be conducive to good communication between parent and child and can contribute to the dynamic stability of adoptive families.

A FRAMEWORK FOR UNDERSTANDING ADOPTIVE FAMILY RELATIONSHIPS

We have drawn on the pertinent theories summarized above to develop a framework for understanding the familial and contextual factors associated with the placement of emotionally troubled adopted adolescents in residential treatment. The framework is divided into three major sections representing (1) parent and child background factors, (2) the child and family's developmental history, and (3) the outcome for the child (see Figure 9.1). Factors pertaining to parents in both the adoptive and control groups are enclosed by solid lines; additional factors that apply to adoptive parents and children are enclosed by broken lines.

The framework reflects our belief that behavior is multiply determined and that no single causal factor leads directly to emotional disturbance. The framework is *developmental*, taking the perspective that emotional disturbance evolves over a lengthy period of time. It is *transactional*, taking into account the interactions over time between the developing individual and his or her changing environment. It also examines the *interaction of factors across multiple levels of analysis*, as it takes into account more distal factors such as genetic background and societal norms, as well as more proximal factors such as the social ecology of the family, the family environment experienced by the child, and the child's psychological treatment history.

Parent and Child Background Factors

This component of the framework concerns the attitudes and characteristics that predate the adoption or birth of a child. For parents in both the adoptive and control groups, it includes their attitudes toward becoming a parent, their expectations for the child, their individual personality characteristics, and the quality of their marital relationship before the child's birth or adoption. Additional factors concerning adoptive parents include their motivation for adopting, their willingness to submit to the screening process involved in adoption, and their attitudes toward adoptive parenthood.

Child background factors include both genetic risk factors, such as a family history of schizophrenia or alcoholism, and the quality of the child's prenatal environment. For adopted children, other pertinent background factors include the quality of care the child received with birthparents, foster parents, or other adoptive parents before final placement.

Developmental History

In this component of the framework, we consider the development of the child within the family and the family within a broader social context over time. The adaptation of the family during the child's early years is given special attention because of the

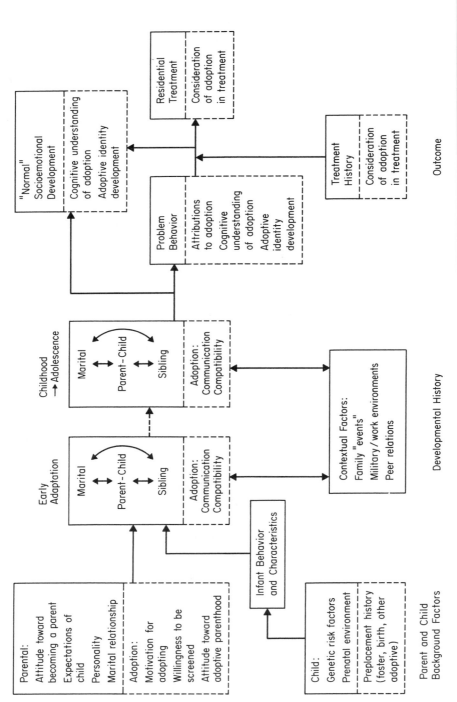

Figure 9.1 A framework for understanding adoptive family relationships.

foundational role that early attitudes and expectations play in later relationships (e.g., Sroufe & Fleeson, 1986). The birth or adoption of a first child creates major changes in the family, modifying it from a two-person relationship to a more complex triadic system (Belsky, 1981). Not only must the child be considered as an individual, but the family must also be considered in terms of the reciprocal impact of the new child on the marital relationship (and vice versa) and the creation of two new parent–child subsytems. If siblings are already present in the family, the picture becomes more complex. Specific patterns of child behavior, such as hyperactivity, physical disabilities of children, and avoidant attachment relationships with parents, are considered in this component of the model.

In addition to the significant changes experienced in biological families, adoptive families must also develop a method for communicating with one another and with outsiders about the adoption. As mentioned earlier, Kirk (1964, 1981) has discussed the impact of acknowledgment or rejection of the differences between adoptive and biological parenthood on the family's adjustment. Adopted children may be different from their adoptive parents in appearance, temperament, or talents. The assessment of the perceived compatibility of the child with the family is considered in terms of its role in the child's development.

As indicated in Figure 9.1, development within the family is considered with respect to the ongoing, reciprocal relations between marital, parent–child, and sibling interaction. Marital relationships are considered for their quality as well as for disruptions involving death, divorce, and remarriage. Parent–child relationships are examined, with a dual focus on parenting skills and parental mental health or pathology. Sibling relationships are examined for potential contributions to the child's difficulties.

Development of the child within the family takes place within a broader social context. Important contextual factors that are considered in this framework include traumatic family "events," such as a severe physical injury or an untimely family move. Other contextual factors under consideration include military or work environments that involve prolonged parental separation, frequent moves, and discontinuities in school and peer experiences. Finally, peer relations are examined in terms of their contribution to emotional disturbance as well as the consequences of the disturbance for the quality of subsequent peer and family relationships.

Outcome

For the adopted and nonadopted children in this study, the common outcome is placement outside the family into residential treatment. Our framework considers the child's pathway to residential treatment in terms of the child's early expression of problematic behavior and the response of the family and helping professionals to it.

As indicated in the framework, adoption may play a key role in the family's interpretation of the child's problem behavior and the action they take concerning it. For example, parents might assign responsibility for the problem behavior by attributing it to the child's poor genetic heritage or difficult preplacement experiences. The child's cognitive understanding of adoption in general (Brodzinsky, Singer, & Braff, 1984) as well as the child's identity as an adopted child (Stein & Hoopes, 1985) can motivate the child to behave in provocative ways toward his or her parents.

The child's treatment history and the degree to which adoption was considered in the child's treatment are also considered. Attempted interventions have the potential to determine whether the behavior can be rerouted into more normal developmental paths, or whether the behavior will become progressively so unacceptable that treatment outside the family becomes necessary.

The framework described above was used to guide the design of our study of adopted and nonadopted adolescents. The purpose of this exploratory study was to examine emotional disturbance in adopted adolescents within a broad framework of familial and contextual factors in order to identify important factors and the interactions among them.

A STUDY OF ADOPTED AND NONADOPTED ADOLESCENTS IN TREATMENT

Subjects

All residential treatment centers located in Texas and Minnesota were contacted about participating in the study in the fall of 1983. Staff from each of these facilities were asked to identify institutionalized adopted and nonadopted children (if adopted, before the age of two) who were currently between the ages of 11 and 18 as potential participants in the study. Criteria for participation were as follows:

1. At least one parent must provide written consent for participation of self and child.
2. The child's caseworker or therapist must agree that the interview would not be psychologically harmful to the child at his or her stage of treatment.
3. The child must provide written consent for his or her participation and for the audiotaping of the interview.
4. A professional staff member of each of the centers who was familiar with the child must be present during the interview.

Fourteen treatment centers, diverse in treatment approach and philosophy, ultimately participated.

Two availability samples of families with adolescents in residential treatment participated in this study. The first sample consisted of 50 adopted adolescents in residential treatment and their families. Every effort was made to interview the adoptive father, adoptive mother, adopted adolescent, and the caseworker or therapist for each family. Interviews in this sample of 50 families were ultimately completed with 36 adoptive fathers, 44 adoptive mothers, 47 adopted adolescents, and 49 caseworkers. Some individuals did not participate because they could not be located, refused, or were deceased.

The adopted adolescents included 26 males and 24 females ranging in age from 11 to 17 (mean age = 14.96). The majority of the children (72%) had been placed in their adoptive homes by the age of 6 months; 86% had been placed by the age of one year. The median age of placement was 3 months. The adoptive parents mostly were middle class, with a median annual income approximating $45,000. Mothers had an average of 14.3 years of education; fathers, 15.7 years. Mothers averaged 43.6 years of age at the time of the study; fathers, 46.8 years.

The second availability sample (the "control sample") consisted of 50 non-adopted adolescents in residential treatment and their families. Again, every effort was made to interview the father, mother, adolescent, and caseworker for each family. Interviews were ultimately completed with 22 fathers (4 of whom were stepfathers) and 26 mothers (including 1 stepmother); 49 adolescents; and 48 caseworkers. Some individuals did not participate because parental rights had been terminated, they could not be contacted, they refused, or were deceased.

The control adolescents included 31 males and 19 females, ranging in age from 11 to 18 (mean age = 14.90). The parents of these adolescents had a median family income of approximately $35,000 per year. Mothers had an average of 13.5 years of education; fathers, 15.4 years. Mothers averaged 39.5 years of age at the time of the study; fathers, 42.5 years. The demographic data on the control families must be considered with caution because of the large amounts of missing data from parents.

Adopted and control adolescents' problems were most frequently diagnosed as conduct disorders. Specific behaviors included running away, stealing outside of home, antisocial or delinquent behavior, drug or alcohol abuse, disobedient or rebellious behavior at home, truancy, disobedience at work, and fighting with peers and siblings. The majority of adolescents in both groups had been in multiple residential settings and had moved to the current setting because previous treatment approaches had not worked.

Procedure

After receiving written parental consent for participation in the study, separate interviews were scheduled with the child, the father, the mother, and the caseworker for each family. All of the children and their caseworkers were interviewed at the treatment facility. Although the majority of interviews with the parents were held during their regular visits to the residential treatment facility, a few families were interviewed by telephone because they lived out of the state and infrequently visited the center. All interviews were tape-recorded and were later transcribed verbatim. Interviews with parents lasted from 1 to 2 hours; interviews with children and caseworkers lasted approximately 30 minutes to 1 hour.

Instruments administered to parents included the interview; the Quality of Marriage Index (Norton, 1983); the Acknowledgment of Differences, Empathy, and Communication scales concerning adoption (Kirk, 1981) (for adoptive parents only); and a demographic questionnaire. Instruments administered to the children included the interview and the Kirk adoption scales (for adopted children only). The caseworkers were administered an interview. This chapter focuses only on the interview data. Information on the other measures may be found in McRoy et al. (1988).

Instruments
Parent Interview

The semistructured interview, administered separately to mothers and fathers, consisted of questions designed to evaluate the issues identified in our conceptual framework, including the parents' marital history and relationship (including any divorces or remarriages), the family's history, the child's social adjustment in the family with peers, circumstances leading to the child's institutionalization, parental perceptions of the problems leading to treatment, and recommendations to other parents. In addition, adoptive parents were asked questions concerning the child's birthparents, previous adoptive or foster placements, and how the family has dealt with adoption.

Child Interview

The child interview included items concerning the child's perception of the family history, the circumstances leading to the child's institutionalization, the child's school performance, and the child's relationships with parents, siblings, and peers. In addition, adopted children were asked questions concerning their understanding of adoption, their knowledge of their birthparents, and their reflections about being an adopted child.

Caseworker Interview

The caseworker interview included questions about the adolescent's presenting problems, course of treatment, diagnosis, and prognosis. In addition, caseworkers were asked to discuss the adolescent's relationships with his or her parents and peers and how they would assess the factor of adoption in the adolescent's disturbance (if applicable).

Data Analysis Approach

Four complementary approaches were used in the analysis of the interview data. First, content analysis of the interviews was undertaken, using the family as the unit of analysis. The research team examined interview transcripts in order to develop a pattern code through strategies involving frequency counts of cases, clustering of cases in which similar effects appeared or failed to appear, and consideration of further reduction of variables (e.g., Miles & Huberman, 1984). The application of the code to succeeding cases and the cross-validation of conclusions with other analytic methods were used to test the importance and validity of the proposed patterns. Second, codebooks were developed for the parent, child, and caseworker interviews. Quantitative scales (usually at the ordinal or quasi-interval levels) were developed for most questions on each interview schedule, and interviews were coded independently. Average percentage agreement across items ranged from 74.4% to 96.0%. Reliability checks and discussions were held throughout the coding process. Third, a computer program designed for qualitative analysis was used to search interview protocols for key words, phrases, and combinations of words. This approach was used as an adjunct to the two approaches discussed above, to explore new hypotheses, and to search for specific cases in which certain issues were present. Finally, since up to four interviews were conducted with each family, the perceptions of the different family members were compared in order to examine the degree to which they viewed the family's issues in a similar way.

Limitations

The data from these samples are limited in that they rely on the retrospective recall of children and their parents. Therefore, the account of the child's developing emotional disturbance is subject to the parents' recall and interpretation of what actually happened. In addition, since many of these parents and children have received mental health services of various kinds over an extended period of time, their accounts are subject to the additional filtering and interpretations of the various professionals with whom they have interacted. In order to counteract this bias, the four participants for each family were individually interviewed. Differences in perceptions of mothers, fathers, adolescents, and caseworkers are noted and discussed.

The data in this study are also limited in that they are all self-reporting in nature, relying on interviews and questionnaires. No systematic observations of interaction were made; however, all four participants in each family discussed interactions that had occurred within the family. Very little information was available about the birthparents and the biological backgrounds of the adopted children in the study. The only information available was filtered through what the adoptive parents were willing to share and how well they remembered information obtained at the time of the child's placement. Finally, the study is correlational, and no claims can be made for one particular direction of effect over another.

Results

The purpose of this investigation has been to identify familial and other contextual factors associated with the placement of adopted adolescents in residential treatment. We have attempted to understand our families at multiple levels of analysis and through multiple theoretical lenses. Since there is currently no single theory that adequately accounts for relationships and outcomes in adoptive families, a major objective of this study has been to use existing theories and data in an interactive manner in order to sharpen our own framework of adoptive family relationships. Although inferences about causality are difficult to draw from this retrospective and correlational study, the data suggest possible causal explanations that await validation in future studies.

In the following section, the results will be briefly outlined and discussed in terms of the framework developed for this study (Figure 9.1). A fuller treatment of the data may be found in McRoy et al. 1988.

Parent Background Factors

Most of the parents in the adoptive families appeared to be fairly mentally healthy, especially in comparison with the parents of the control adolescents. Over half of the control parents exhibited some sort of pathological behavior. For example, either child or spouse abuse was noted in over half (26) of the control families in contrast to 16 of the adoptive families ($\chi^2 = 4.11$, $p < .05$). The incidence of substance abuse by parents was also higher in the control families than in the adoptive families (19 v. 6, respectively; $\chi^2 = 9.01$, $p < .001$). Similarly, there was a marked difference in the quality of marriages in the two groups: the marriages of adoptive parents appeared to be healthier and longer-lasting with fewer multiple marriages and cohabiting relationships. In the adoptive group, the children had been adopted by couples who had spent many years hoping to become parents; in the control group, many of the children were the products of unplanned pregnancies and unstable marriages.

Child Background Factors

Birthparent disorders that may have a genetic basis, such as schizophrenia and alcoholism, appear to have placed some children in the study at risk for later problems. For example, 3 of the adopted children and 1 control child were believed to have had schizophrenic biological parents. In addition, 1 adopted child was known to have had an alcoholic birthparent and 6 adopted children had alcoholic adoptive parents; 19 control children had alcoholic parents. Genetic contributions to intelligence and personality may have also set the stage for disharmony between adoptive parents and children. Multiple poor foster placements, as well as abuse and neglect prior to the adoptive placement, appear to have disrupted the development of trust in at least 12 of the 50 adopted children's family relationships.

Early Adaptation in the Family System

Several interactional patterns present from infancy appear to have lead to problems in establishing harmonious early adaptation of the child within the family in both the adoptive and control families (Grotevant, McRoy, & Jenkins, 1988). Without effective intervention, these problems presumably escalated over a period of years. For example, there were almost equal numbers of hyperactive children in the adoptive (16) and control (15) families, and all parents of such children noted the difficulties involved in coping with the hyperactivity.

A second problematic pattern that emerged clearly in eight of the adoptive families but in only one of the control families concerned the compatibility of the child within the family. As predicted by goodness-of-fit theory, development should be optimized when there is a good match between the child's temperament and his or her environment. In these families, parents noted major discrepancies between their children's personalities and what was acceptable within the context of their family. Incompatibility problems were most likely to occur in adoptive families in which the parents either discounted or accentuated the importance of the adopted child's heredity. When the importance of heredity was discounted,parents appeared to deny the difference between adoptive and biological parenting, which may have led to problematic communication about adoption (Kirk, 1981). When the importance of heredity was accentuated, parents attributed the problems to biology and abdicated responsibility for their role in creating or ameliorating the problem; "It's not our fault, it must be because he is adopted." Abdication of responsibility for the problem by the parents often signaled an early stage in the emotional distancing of the adoptive parents from their child. Over time, this distancing served to reinforce the child's feelings of rejection not only by birthparents, but now by adoptive parents as well.

A third pattern, present in 10 of the adopted and none of the control children, involved the parent's perception that the child was not sufficiently affectionate from early infancy. In five of these cases, the infant's behavior may have simply been a reflection of generally based temperament styles. In the other five, the child was placed in the adoptive home between 2.5 and 22 months of age; in four of these cases, the child had been abused or neglected before placement. Therefore, these preplacement experiences may have influenced their ability to display affection toward their adoptive parents.

Developmental History Within the Family

Parenting was problematic for almost all families in both samples. Almost invariably, parents' initial attempts to control problematic behavior became increasingly unsuccessful over time. Some families appeared to lack credible sources of accurate childrearing advice, others were given conflicting advice that exacerbated their difficulties, yet others appeared to have problems implementing the advice they were given.

Some of the main parenting problems encountered by the children in the adoptive and control families are outlined in Table 9.1. (The frequencies of problems total more than 50 in each column because many families experienced multiple problems.) As the table indicates, the most common parenting problems included the use of ineffective, overly punitive, or inconsistent discipline; abuse or neglect by the parent(s); and drug or alcohol abuse by the parent(s). Stress associated with troubled marital relationships, divorce, and maladaptive postdivorce family relationships may have influenced some of the emotional and behavioral problems experienced by the institutionalized children in this sample. Frequent father absence, relocations, abuse, and distant parent–child interactions might have also contributed to some of the children's adjustment difficulties.

The Role of Adoption

In the sample of adopted adolescents, adoption appeared to play a major role in the emotional disturbance of 33 of the 50 adolescents. Adoption issues appeared to play a minor role in 9 more of the cases and no role at all in 8 cases. The adoption-related problems experienced by some children in this study included the following: feelings of being rejected by their birthmother, anger toward birth and adoptive parents, self-hatred, rootlessness, exaggerated feelings of differentness (especially in transracially adopted cases), and resentment about being adopted.

The adoption revelation was problematic for some of the children in the study. In several cases, their parents claimed that the children "always knew" about their

Table 9.1 Frequency of Parenting Problems in Adoptive and Control Families

Problem	Adoptive	Control	Chi-Square
Ineffective discipline	31	23	2.58
Punitive discipline	11	9	0.25
Inconsistent discipline	17	10	2.49
Marital problems inflicted on child	7	6	0.09
Not willing to let child grow up/overprotective	4	3	0.15
Abuse/neglect by parent	15	25	4.17*
Drug dependence or alcohol abuse of parent	6	19	9.01**
Parents insecure about parenting adolescent	6	6	0.00
No discipline/overly permissive	5	7	0.38
Child expected to fill adult role	0	5	0.54
Natural parent never present	N/A	12	N/A

$*p < .05$; $**p < .001$

adoption, whereas the children said that they found out when they were about 7 to 8 years of age. This problem is consistent with Brodzinsky's work on children's understanding of adoption (Brodzinsky, Singer, & Braff, 1984). Although the parents may have actually told their children of the adoption when they were young, the children did not understand its real meaning until they were into middle childhood. This pattern is illustrated poignantly by one 14-year-old adopted child in the study:

> When I was 8 years old I was looking through my baby book and asked my parents about it [my adoption]. I couldn't handle it. I went out on my own. I got real rebellious because I wanted nothing to do with my family. I was real different from everybody—I started hanging out in the streets. I didn't like it because all my parents had to do was sign a couple of forms and I was theirs.

Outcomes

The majority of all the institutionalized children had problematic peer relationships which were characterized as being superficial, cold and distant, or nonexistent. Peer problems seemed to be symptoms rather than causes of behavioral difficulties. Overall, the samples of adopted and nonadopted adolescents in treatment did not differ dramatically in terms of symptoms, syndromes (internalizing and externalizing), diagnoses, or treatment goals. The prognosis for the control group was considered slightly better, on the average, probably because some of the nonadopted adolescents were in treatment centers, since their parents were unable to care for them and not necessarily because their behavior was intolerably out of control. Similarities in the two samples probably stem from the fact that admissions to treatment centers are more strongly based on symptoms, diagnoses, and treatment goals than on etiology of disturbance. Even though the clinical pictures were not substantially different for the two samples, other evidence summarized above suggests that the dynamics of emotional disturbance are not identical for adopted and nonadopted adolescents.

General Conclusions

There appears to be no common denominator underlying the disturbance of all the adolescents in the study. Multiple factors, in different combinations and with different weights, contributed to the disturbance experienced by each adolescent. This study makes a number of contributions to the literature. First, the model developed in this investigation will facilitate future research and provide a framework through which the findings of existing studies may be interpreted. Second, through the broad-scale interview procedure used in this project, a number of risk factors for adoptive families have been identified. Some of them have been mentioned extensively in previous literature; others are new. However, they have not been previously brought together as a coherent group in the analysis of adoptive family relationships.

IMPLICATIONS FOR RESEARCH

A number of interesting research questions and approaches are suggested by the results of this study. A prospective longitudinal approach, following a large sample of adoptive families from placement through adolescence, would clarify many questions about developmental patterns. In addition, further work is needed on the dynamics of "successful" adoptive families to understand the processes of coping and adaptation in adoptive families, as well as studies on identity formation in adopted adolescents (see Hoopes, Chapter 8). In addition, further research on varying degrees of openness in adoption (e.g., McRoy & Grotevant, 1988) is needed in order to examine the consequences to the members of the adoptive triad of contact among adopted children, adoptive parents, and birthparents. Further information is necessary to understand more fully the contribution of genetic background factors in relation to adopted children. Attention should particularly be paid to the role of hyperactivity and learning disabilities in the child's school and family adjustments.

Since most of the adopted children had been in multiple treatment settings before the current institutionalization, it is evident that research is important to evaluate assessment and treatment approaches currently used with such youth. More effective early intervention strategies may eliminate the need for some of the long-term, costly, out-of-home placements with the children in this study experienced.

Additional research on such issues as the impact of multiple parental figures on children's adjustment, treatment approaches which have been successfully used to offset the effects of early maltreatment or multiple placements, fear of displacement in the family at the birth of a sibling, and parental attachment issues with rejecting infants are all needed. We anticipate that research on each of these topics will increase knowledge about adoptive family dynamics and mental health issues in adoption and improve agency practices in the selection and preparation of families for adoptive parenthood.

IMPLICATIONS FOR CLINICAL INTERVENTION

Although infant adoptions are generally considered "low risk," the findings of our study suggest that problems may arise. Adoption agency staff as well as mental health practitioners need to consider these issues in the selection, preparation, and counseling of adoptive families. Agency workers must be aware of the potential influence of genetic risk factors, the quality of the child's prenatal environment, and the quality of care the child received in preadoptive placements on how the child will adjust in the adoptive family. Moreover, parent background factors, such as their reasons for adoption, expectations for children, their individual personalities as well as their marital and family interactional dynamics, are all influential in developing a relationship with an adopted child and should be thoroughly assessed prior to the adoptive placement. Social workers must dispel the belief of many adoptive families that love and a positive environment will resolve all problems and must provide counseling services to help families deal with the problems that may arise when mismatches occur.

The findings of this study suggest that there is a need to provide on-going parenting education and support to adoptive parents. Some adoptive parents may be too permissive in their behavior toward their adopted children because of their desire to be loved and appreciated by their adopted children. Some children will test the limits set by adoptive parents and use their adoptive status as a weapon and reason for not complying with their parents' wishes. For example, they might boast that their adoptive parents have no right to discipline them since they are not their "real parents."

Parents should be trained to handle these specific manipulative comparisons and problematic behaviors effectively and consistently as they occur.

The impact of family stressors, such as divorce, multiple moves, troubled marital relationships, and parental absence, should also be addressed in clinical work with adopted and nonadopted children and their families. Our findings indicated that often parents and children exhibit different perceptions of the influence of such significant family events. For example, parents, who may not have felt that the absence of a consistent father figure in the home had a significant impact on the children, often had children who sometimes thought that this may have been very detrimental to their adjustment.

Since the majority of the adopted children in the sample were having some problems related to the adoption, it is clear that adoptive status must be viewed as an essential component in assessing their psychosocial history and functioning and the interactional family dynamics. Adoptive parents should receive information about the children's cognitive understanding of adoption so that they can be prepared to answer their own child's questions at the appropriate developmental levels. Parents must also be sensitized to the child's feelings of loss and separation relating to his or her adoption. Counseling may be especially appropriate when adopted children reach adolescence and need to deal with identity concerns and questions.

Finally, the findings suggest that each adoptive family is unique and should be treated individually. Adoption is an issue for some children and not for others. Also, clinicians should note that some parents may attribute problems to the adoption which may really be caused by other factors. A thorough assessment based on the developmental model presented in this chapter is a useful tool for identifying contributing factors which lead to the development of emotional disturbances among adopted children.

ACKNOWLEDGMENTS

Funding for the project described in this chapter was provided by the Hogg Foundation for Mental Health, the University Research Institute of the University of Texas at Austin, and Project QUEST, a joint venture of IBM and the University of Texas at Austin. We especially thank Kerry White and Bernabe Marrero for their assistance with data collection an analysis, and the late Louis A. Zurcher for his support and collaboration on this project. Other staff members who made significant contributions include William Affeldt, Susan Ayers-Lopez, Kim Gibbens, Vivian Jenkins, and Kathryn Kramer. We especially thank Dale Erdmann of the Oaks Treatment Center and Marietta Spencer of Children's Home Society of Minnesota for facilitating our data collection. We also thank the administration and staff of the 14 participating treatment centers and the families themselves, without whose cooperation this study would not have been possible.

10

Adjustment in Interracial Adoptees: An Overview

ARNOLD R. SILVERMAN AND WILLIAM FEIGELMAN

This chapter is divided into four parts. In the first part we offer a historical overview of transracial adoption; the second part examines how laws and social agencies presently encourage or impede this practice. Next, we summarize the social science research on the outcomes associated with transracial adoption. Last, we speculate on the future of this new pattern of adoptive relationships.

HISTORICAL OVERVIEW OF TRANSRACIAL ADOPTION

Adoption is a relatively enduring phenomenon in American life. Although much of American law was inspired by their English forebears, it was in Massachusetts in 1851 where the first adoption statutes were enacted (Kirk, 1981). Great Britain, Scotland, and Wales developed comparable adoption laws much later, at least 75 years afterward. Of course, throughout most of its long history in this country, adoptions were usually made between relatives. Nonrelative adoptions expanded steadily during the late nineteenth century and into the 1920s, a period when massive immigration and industrialization caused extensive disruptions in American family life (Silverman & Weitzman, 1986). During this formative period, after the turn of the century, adoption agencies were created and social work began to professionalize itself (see Chapter 15 for a fuller discussion of the history of adoption in America). Nevertheless, throughout this time, and up to World War II, transracial adoptions were extremely rare.

Transracial adoption—the joining of racially different parents and children together in adoptive families—is a recent event. After World War II, the first large numbers of transracial placements occurred as American soldiers and their families adopted children from the war-ravaged countries of Asia. Richard Weil (1984) reported that nearly 3,000 Japanese children were adopted by Americans between 1948 and 1962; he also noted that 840 Chinese children were adopted by mostly white American families during this same time. With the assistance of international relief efforts and indigenous economic and social developments, such adoptions gradually fell off to a trickle by the 1960s.

The Korean War (1950–53) created the next stage of renewed interest in transracial placements. The American farmer Harry Holt took initiatives to find homes for the children dislocated by the Korean War. Owing to his efforts, eventually the largest international adoption program was created. Today the Holt program places children not only in the United States, but throughout the developed world. The Holt organization was largely responsible for professionalizing social services in Korea. Weil reported over 38,000 adoptions of Korean children in America during the period from 1953 to 1981. Nowadays, in any given recent year, there are usually between a thousand and two thousand such adoptions taking place in the United States; of course, these adoptions usually involve Korean children being adopted by white Americans. The Vietnam War added to the numbers of Asian transracial adoptions, as American involvement in the war and in relief efforts hastened the placements of many refugee children into white American homes. As American military involvement in Vietnam concluded, the adoptions of Vietnamese children by U.S. citizens ceased.

Hispanic children from parts of Central and South America have been slowly and steadily contributing to the numbers of foreign born nonwhite children adopted by white Americans. Rising from a mere handful in the 1950s and 1960s, these adoptions now number nearly a thousand annually, and principally come from Colombia, El Salvador, and Mexico (Feigelman & Silverman, 1983; Weil, 1984).

In the late 1950s Native American children became the recipients of professional social services. A joint program (The Indian Adoption Project) sponsored by the Bureau of Indian Affairs and the Child Welfare League of America—neither of whom were adoption agencies—supported efforts to find conventional and transracial homes for displaced Indian children (Simon & Altstein, 1977). Close to 700 children were placed, most transracially, before Indian opposition finally led to the abandonment of these endeavors.

Another important resource of transracial placements comes from black children placed in white homes. With the movement of blacks from the rural South to northern, midwestern, and western cities, the need for expanded social services for this population became more readily apparent. Evidence suggests that there were few such adoptions during the 1940s and 1950s (Day, 1979). The early 1960s marked the starting point of a spiraling rise of black–white transracial placements that was to continue until the early 1970s. Sparked by interests in such placements by citizen advocacy groups in Montreal, Canada (The Open Door Society), and in rural Minnesota (Parents to Adopt Minority Youngsters) transracial placements began to expand throughout the country (Simon & Altstein, 1977). Social service agencies soon became increasingly involved in making such placements as they offered aid to their needy black urban clients.

The number of black–white placements rose steadily through the 1960s and peaked in 1971 with over 2,500 such adoptions (Boys and Girls Aid Society of Oregon, 1975). During the time span from 1960 to 1976, in what might be regarded as the expansionary period of transracial black–white placements, over 12,000 such adoptions were recorded (Silverman & Weitzman, 1986).

When the interest in transracial placements began to widen, adoption policy makers felt obliged to reevaluate earlier adoption standards which discouraged such practices. Well aware of the social and psychological deficits linked with persisting child-hood institutionalization and foster care, agency leaders saw transracial placement as an antidote to such problems. The Child Welfare League of America, the primary establishment body for child serving agencies, explicitly stated in their 1968 edition of adoption standards that "racial background in itself should not determine the selection of a home for a child." At that time policy makers showed unequivocal support for transracial adoption as a measure to foster permanency for children with disrupted family lives.

Yet, as the number of transracial placements rose sharply, black social workers began to ponder whether sufficient efforts were being made to find homes for black children within the black community. Many wondered whether this new enterprise was aimed at diminishing and destroying the integrity of the black community. In 1972, at its first annual convention, the National Association of Black Social Workers (NABSW) expressed "vehement opposition to the practice of placing black children with white families." Attempting to reconcile the accusations of cultural genocide made by the NABSW, the social service establishment began to reevaluate the utility of transracial placements. The Child Welfare League of America revised its adoption standards in 1973. At that time it was acknowledged, "In today's climate, children placed in adoptive families with similar racial characteristics can become more easily integrated into the average family and community."

Thereafter, there was declining activity invested in promoting black–white transracial placements. By 1976, it was noted that black–white placements dropped to 1,076 (Boys and Girls Aid Society of Oregon, 1976).

PRESENT POLICIES AND PRACTICES CONCERNING TRANSRACIAL ADOPTION

At the present time one cannot ascertain the total numbers of adoptions nor of transracial placements in particular. With increased governmental budget cutting, child welfare issues have assumed a position of diminished importance. The federal government agency that collected adoption statistics in the past—The National Center for Social Statistics—no longer functions. Private, voluntary tabulating efforts have also been discontinued. In the past, The Boys and Girls Aid Society of Oregon collected data from most of the nation's adoption agencies on the numbers of transracial and inracial placements. As criticism of transracial adoptions mounted, the incentive to do this tabulating work apparently waned. Now, one can only guess at the numbers of transracial placements.

The only firm statistical base for speculation on today's transracial adoptions is in the numbers of immigrant orphans known to have entered the United States. (This, of course, would exclude counting the adoptions of domestically born minority children to white parents.) Such figures are regularly collected by the Immigration and Naturalization Service. This data suggests that there may be 3,000 to 5,000 transracial placements yearly, primarily of Korean, Indian, and Hispanic children, adopted by white Americans. A modest guess at the number of black–white domestic placements would be between 1,000 and 2,000 of such adoptions yearly. Today's black–

white transracial placements are likely to involve older, physically and emotionally disabled children, and sibling groups. Such "hard-to-place" children may have spent years in ever changing numbers of foster and group homes and institutional settings. In most instances, the likelihood of ever finding inracial placements for these children would have been extremely unlikely.

For now, transracial adoption still remains controversial. On the supporting side, one finds groups like the North American Council on Adoptable Children (NACAC) representing over 400 child advocacy organizations in the United States and Canada, who have long expressed their commitment to transracial placements. As their president testified at a White House conference on families.

> We believe every child has the right to a loving, "forever" family of his or her own. For a great many children now in foster or institutional care, permanency and love can only be found through adoption. . . .
>
> We are not talking here about the adoption of racially matched infants by white middle-class couples. That is not adoption today. . . . "Adoptable children" today include many who are older, who are of school age, who are emotionally troubled, physically handicapped, of mixed or minority race, or members of sibling groups. These are "special needs" adoptable children. They need special families. . . . We know such families exist. . . .
>
> However, built into the very system that exists to serve children, there are specific barriers which make permanence difficult or impossible for great numbers of children. . . .
>
> Criteria and methods for recruiting and approving applicants . . . eliminate, the very people most able to meet the needs of waiting children. (Simon & Altstein, 1981)

Adoption agencies have also shown support for transracial placements. The National Committee on Adoption, a lobbying organization representing 145 nonprofit private adoption agencies from all over the country endorses transracial placements. As William Pierce (1988), its executive director stated, "We wholeheartedly favor transracial placements; whenever all parties to the adoption willingly agree to it, we would have no quarrel with those kinds of adoptions."

The Child Welfare League of America, the premier moral authority among social services professionals, assumes a position of qualified support for transracial placement. Their position remains the same as it was expressed during the mid-1970s. In their current *Standards for Adoption Service* it is stated: "Children in need of adoption have a right to be placed into a family that reflects their ethnic or cultural heritage. Children should not have their adoptions denied or significantly delayed, however, when adoptive parents or other ethnic or cultural groups are available." (Child Welfare League of America, 1988).

Consistent with the League's stand a Presidential Task Force, comprised of government officials selected from a variety of social agencies, took a similar position when they recommended to President Reagan that, "while it is preferable to place a child in a family with a similar racial background, transracial adoption should be permissible method of providing a loving permanent home" (*Los Angeles Times,* 1987).

At the other end of the attitude spectrum one also finds sharp rebuke of this practice. The National Association of Black Social Workers hasn't changed its position of "vehement opposition" to transracial placements, first announced in 1972.

They, and other Native American tribal councils, see this practice as a form of cultural genocide aimed at destroying their groups.

But the minority community is by no means uniformly opposed to transracial adoption. One study, conducted in a midwestern black community, found nearly three-fifths (57%) generally receptive to the idea, while only 7% were totally opposed (Howard, Royse, & Skerl, 1977). Another study of black child care professionals found a similar division of opinion on transracial adoption between workers with varying exposure to the practice. Those with direct experience of it tended to have favorable evaluations, while those with no contact were much more critical (Herzog, Sudia, & Harwood, 1971).

Simon and Altstein (1987) report that as of 1985 transracial adoption was a legal form of adoption in every state. Yet, the various state courts have sometimes been known to deny adoption petitions, if for no other reason than racial difference. In other cases, courts have denied racial arguments against transracial adoption, holding that denial would be contrary to the Fourteenth Amendment which assures different racial groups equal protection under the law. In most court controversies race has become one factor among a variety of others weighed by judges in determining the "best interests of the child."

How judges decide these cases is often based strictly on value positions, with little use of information from social science research on transracial adoptions. Public opinion on this subject, too, is often not well informed about what is known concerning how minority children do in their transracially adopted families. What does the cumulative record of the research data show about the outcomes of transracially adopted children? Let us now turn to this important question.

RESEARCH EVIDENCE ON THE OUTCOMES OF TRANSRACIAL ADOPTIONS

Research on transracial adoption reflects the needs of adoptive parents, child care professionals and placement agencies, on the one hand, and the changing dynamics of race relations on the other hand. The interests of Afro-American, Native American, and Asian communities—whose children are most frequently adopted across racial lines in the United States—have also had an important influence on this area of research. The concerns of transracial adoptees and birthparents have been much less consequential in setting research agenda.

The term transracial adoption is sometimes reserved for the adoption of black children by white families. This represents a change from earlier usage and reflects the relative strength of the racial barrier between white and black communities. The social distance between white and Asian or Hispanic communities is far less than that between whites and blacks in the United States, but it is by no means unimportant and unrecognized. Here, the term transracial adoption will be used to include the adoption of Asian, Native American, Hispanic, and black minors by white families.

Perhaps the earliest piece of research on postwar transracial adoptions was conducted by H. David Kirk in his 1953 doctoral dissertation in sociology at Cornell University. Kirk was concerned about the response of white Americans to transracially adopting families. His dissertation studied the attitudes of a sample of white Americans in a small rural community. Kirk posed questions about transracially adopting families to his sample and recorded their responses. He found that his respondents were far more receptive to racially integrated families than he or most of those concerned with the placement of nonwhite children in American families would have expected (Kirk, 1953).

Kirk's informative study of attitudes toward transracial adoption is interesting for the responses it did not evoke when it first appeared. Although Kirk moved from his initial dissertation research to become one of the more prolific and influential North American social analysts of adoption, his doctoral research remained unpublished at a time when it might have spoken directly to questions that many child care professionals had about the responses to transracial placement. Unfortunately, this valuable early piece of research has been neglected. Both popular imagination and placement policies continued to exaggerate the hostility toward transracial adoptees and their families.

One of the most thorough studies of transracial adoption is David Fanshel's *Far From The Reservation,* a study of Native American children placed in white families between 1958 and 1967. These children were placed with white families as a result of the inability of placement agencies to find suitable placements with Native American families. Difficulties in finding inracial placements is frequently a motive for initiating transracial placements. Certainly, much of the initial impetus for the transracial placement of Afro-American children in the United States came from the inability of agencies to find inracial homes. Nearly 700 Native American–white placements were made through the coordinated efforts of the Bureau of Indian Affairs and the Child Welfare League of America. Fanshel's study followed these children through the first five years of placement. Most of the children were less than 21 months at placement. The study, then, was confined to the adjustment and adaptation of very young children and their families.

The study followed 98 families. There was no control group. Fanshel felt this was a weakness of the study, a problem of design engendered by cost considerations. Both fathers and mothers were interviewed during the five years of the study. Their responses were the primary data, not only for their own adaptations to adoption, but also for assessing their children's adjustments. No systematic observations were made of the young adoptees by independent clinicians or researchers. The use of parental reports by students of transracial adoption is quite common. It is an almost universal mode of data collection. Although there are clearly limits on the usefulness of parental reports of children's behavior, alternatives have often been too intrusive and expensive. Fanshel addressed these problems by noting the strong correlation of adjustment ratings made by parents, interviewers, and clinicians who reviewed interview materials.

Fanshel did not find the 98 adopting families to be particularly distinctive in their social characteristics. They seemed drawn from a wide range of the American population. Fanshel drew no particular inferences from this material, but it reinforces the implication from Kirk's earlier research showing support for transracial adoption to be widespread.

Fanshel found the children to be adjusting well to their adoptive environments. He commented in his conclusion:

My overall impression is that the children are doing remarkably well as a group. From a physical growth and developmental standpoint, they appear to be thriving. . . . In the realm of personality and behavior patterns there are more incipient signs of difficulty than in other areas, but this is true of only thirty percent of the children and most of these are seen to have moderate rather than serious problems. (pp. 322–323)

Although Fanshel regarded the level of problems encountered through the fifth year of adoptive placement as modest, he was very much aware that problems are likely to increase as children grow older. Nonetheless, his expectations were optimistic. In many ways Fanshel's findings were typical of those reported by many studies of young transracially adopted children (Fricke, 1965; Keltie, 1969; Kim & Reid, 1970; Nutt & Snyder, 1973). No study reports widespread problems and few report serious problems with any frequency at this age. Findings such as these raise serious questions for those who suggest that transracial placements inevitably, or even frequently, produce serious adjustment problems.

One of the most interesting features of Fanshel's work was his finding that the problems afflicting the birthmother, such as alcoholism and physical or mental illness, had a demonstrable impact on the child's adjustment long after placement. Fanshel found an overall correlation of .26 between his Index of Biological Mothers' Disability and his Child Overall Adjustment Rating, a summary measure of the child's adjustment over the 5-year period of the study. This data suggested that many of the problematic features of adoption may have their source in the child's preplacement experience. Fanshel was cautious about the implications of his findings because the data provided by the agencies was far from complete. The consequences of the adoptive relationship need to be clearly distinguished from the impact of preplacement surroundings. Despite his reservations, Fanshel's data on the preplacement environment of adoptees was more complete than in most other studies of transracial adoption.

One of the persistent concerns in transracial adoption is the response of family, friends, and neighbors to the presence of a nonwhite adoptee. Fanshel's respondents indicated that reaction to their Native American children was largely positive. Most parents reported few if any incidents of hostility. Ten percent reported hostility from neighboring children; more than two-thirds of the families reported that their relatives were either initially supportive of the adoption or had come to be enthusiastic about it. Friends were, if anything, even more supportive of the adoptions (pp. 132–135). Despite this relatively benign experience in early childhood, a sizeable minority of mothers, 27%, expected their children to experience some future discomfort because of their Native American origins. What is perhaps most interesting is the fact that the virulent opposition frequently projected for transracial adoptees did not materialize.

Although most parents in the study did not initially intend to adopt a Native American child, a majority took a positive view of the child's racial and cultural heritage. About half of the parents planned to make a special effort to acquaint their children with their cultural background. Another 20% planned to respond to the child's interest in their background. One mother acknowledged her son's connection to another culture in these terms:

Our child will have to seek out an identity for himself besides being a member of our family. He is different in two ways: he has experienced being adopted and he is an Indian.

In a sense, that makes him a different person and he and we have to be comfortable with that difference. (p. 133)

Not all parents were as comfortable and positive about their child's background as this mother; 20% of the parents indicated they might minimize the child's Native American heritage. None of the parents, however, sought to deny the child's ties to his or her Native American background.

Much of what Fanshel found is interesting and has important implications for issues regarding placement policy, but it leaves several important questions unanswered: How does the experience of Afro-American, Asian, and other transracial adoptees compare with that of the Native American adoptees; how does the experience of the adoptees and their families change as they grow older; and how does the experience of transracial adoptions differ from that of inrace adoptions?

Lucille Grow and Deborah Shapiro's study (1974) of Afro-American children adopted by white parents provides at least some of the answers to the questions posed above. Grow and Shapiro studied 125 Afro-American children adopted by white families in seven American and Canadian metropolitan areas. All of the children were at least 6-years-old when the study was initiated in 1972 and had been in their adoptive homes for at least three years. The adoptees were placed earlier than the Native American children discussed above. In Grow and Shapiro's study the average age at placement was 14 months while in Fanshel's study it was 21 months. The Afro-American adoptees, however, were older than those in Fanshel's study; 77 were 8 or older at the time of the first interview and 20 were 12 or older. This difference enabled Grow and Shapiro to ask questions about adjustment to the school environment and to receive ratings of the adoptees' behavior from their teachers.

The methodology of both studies was quite similar. Grow and Shapiro relied principally on interviews with the adoptive parents. The parents were interviewed twice in the course of a year. Unlike the parents of the Native American adoptees, the adoptive parents of the Afro-American children were distinctly drawn from middle-class professional backgrounds and had decidedly liberal political leanings. Fifty-six percent of the fathers in Grow and Shapiro's study were professionals as against 37% in the Fanshel study.

In terms of overall adjustment, most of the adoptees in the Grow and Shapiro study appeared to be faring reasonably well. Grow and Shapiro combined scores on personality tests administered to the children with data supplied by parents', teachers', and interviewers' evaluations to create an overall measure of success. By this measure 77% of the adoptions were "successful" (p. 224). This figure compared similarly with 75% of the adoptees in the Fanshel study who were performing "extremely well in all spheres of life" or "in a way that makes the outlook for their future adjustment very hopeful" (p. 323). In contrast to Fanshel's study, adjustment appeared unrelated to age at placement. This factor may be related to the earlier age at placement of the Afro-American adoptees.

Grow and Shapiro found that the attitudes of the adopting parents had an impact on both their children's adjustments and identifications as Afro-Americans. Parents who regarded their adopted children as Afro-American in appearance were found to have adopted children with higher (more positive) adjustment scores (pp. 224–233).

The transracially adopting parents in Grow and Shapiro's study were, for the most part, strongly supportive of their child's identification with the Afro-American community. Ninety-three percent of the mothers (and 86% of the fathers) agreed that it was very important for their black child to develop pride in their black heritage. Responses to similar questions on fostering links with the Afro-American community and culture also received high levels of support from the adopting parents.

These responses seemed to produce positive attitudes on the part of the adoptees toward their Afro-American identity and heritage. The third of the parents having the strongest "pro-black" attitudes reported 49% of their children had positive attitudes toward their Afro-American background; the third of the parents having the weakest "pro-black" attitudes reported 26% of their children had positive attitudes toward being Afro-American (p. 192).

Unfortunately, Grow and Shapiro's study did not permit comparisons with non-adopted Afro-American children or with Afro-American children adopted by black parents. Making these kinds of comparisons would permit a more definitive evaluation of the impact of adoptive parental attitudes on adoptees' racial self-consciousness and pride.

Fortunately, subsequent studies have provided us with more complete comparisons. A study by Simon and Altstein (1977) examined the racial attitudes of transracially adopted black children and their white siblings. In this study the authors used the classic doll preference test pioneered by Kenneth and Mamie Clark. Simon and Altstein gave the children who were interviewed several minutes to play with three dolls. One doll was black, one white, and one Asian or Native American. Children were asked to point to the doll they liked to play with best, looked bad, looked nice, had a nice color, and so on. Although the study was confined to children between ages three and eight, the findings were, nonetheless, startling:

> It appears that black children reared in the special setting of multiracial families do not acquire the ambivalence toward their own race reported in all other studies involving young black children. Our results also show that white children do not consistently prefer white to other groups, and that there are no significant differences in the racial attitudes of any category of children. Our findings do not offer any evidence that black children reared by white parents acquire a preference for black over white. They show only that black children perceive themselves as black as accurately as white children perceive themselves as white.

These findings take on special significance against the background of earlier studies that report prowhite attitudes among white and black children, and children of other racial backgrounds. Simon and Altstein's (1977) study indicates that young black children see themselves as black and do not attach any negative evaluation to that assessment.

Simon and Altstein gathered their data from a sample of 206 transracially adopting families who were contacted through their membership in the Open Door Society and the Council on Adoptable Children. The study was initiated in 1972 and the authors were able to requestion parents and children in 1979 and 1983. The study involved interviewing both parents and children and the use of projective testing with the transracial adoptees and their siblings. Most of the transracial adoptees had at least one black birthparent, but a minority had one birthparent of Native American or Asian ancestry (Simon & Altstein, 1987).

The adopting families were similar to those selected in the Grow and Shapiro study: sharing liberal ideas, college and postgraduate educations, and professional occupations. As had been noted elsewhere, the social characteristics of white families who adopt black children are remarkably similar from study to study despite dramatic differences in sampling methods (Silverman, 1980, pp. 52–74).

The longitudinal nature of the study makes it particularly useful for evaluating transracial adoption. This facet of the study enabled the authors to examine the degree to which the initially favorable evaluations made by the adopting parents held up. The authors concluded that their initial impressions were largely borne out by subsequent findings at a time when many of the adoptees had completed college, married, and were raising families of their own. Despite family relationships that were sometimes troubled, most parents expressed considerable satisfaction with their experience as transracial adopters and recommended it to others.

One of the most interesting findings reported by Simon and Altstein (1987) is that, if anything, the adoptees—now adults or older adolescents—seemed firmly committed to their adopted parents. As they stated:

> For the children . . . their adoptive parents are the only family they have and the only set of parents they want. Some of the family relationships have been rocky, accusative and angry—and some remain so—yet they are a family and they are fully committed to one another. (p. 140)

The judgments of parents and children on the quality of their lives seemed supported by less subjective measures of adjustment. The adoptees and their siblings were asked to respond to a 10-item questionnaire measuring self-esteem. There were no significant differences in the self-esteem scores of black transracial adoptees, transracial adoptees of other nonwhite backgrounds, and their nonadopted siblings (p. 77). Comparable data is reported by McRoy and Zurcher (1983), who administered similar tests to a sample of black transracially adopted children. These investigators also found no difference between the self-esteem scores of their transracial adoptees and a sample of nonadopted white children.

Simon and Altstein (1987) reported that 63% of the transracially adopting parents described their children as identifying with both the racial backgrounds of their birthparents as well as with their adoptive parents (p. 47). Only 27% of the sample reported that their transracially adopted children identified themselves exclusively as white. These responses seemed to correspond closely with the choices made by the adoptees themselves. When asked what kind of community they themselves would choose to live in, 64% of the transracial adoptees preferred integrated communities and 27% favored communities that were mostly white. Only 2% opted for communities that were predominantly black (p. 81). These choices seemed to reflect the realities of the everyday lives of the transracially adopted young adults and adolescents. Most of them attended integrated schools in communities that were predominantly, but not exclusively, white. Their friendships and dating patterns included young men and women from both the white and black communities (pp. 61–63).

The study conducted by McRoy, Zurcher, and their associates provides an opportunity to test out some of the assumptions that underlie the continuing criticism of transracial adoption. This study selected 30 white families who had transracially adopted black children and 30 black families who had adopted similar children. This permitted a comparison of adaptations by black children in white and black families. (McRoy, Zurcher, Lauderdale, & Anderson, 1982, pp. 522–524). As in the Simon and Altstein study (1987), parents and children were interviewed and the children took a series of pencil and paper psychological tests.

It is frequently argued that in the absence of a black home, a black family, and a black community, a transracially adopted black child will be unable to develop either a satisfactory sense of self or a positive assessment of his or her black heritage. A 1972 position paper developed by the National Association of Black Social Workers presented their argument in these terms:

> Black children should be placed only with Black families whether in foster care or for adoption. Black children belong, physically, psychologically and culturally in Black families in order that they receive the total sense of themselves and develop a sound projection of their future. . . . Black children in white homes are cut off from the healthy development of themselves as Black people. (Simon & Altstein, 1977, p. 50)

The most clear cut data presented by McRoy and Zurcher (1983) was their finding that black inracial and transracial adoptees had similar self-esteem scores as measured by the Tennessee Self-Concept Scale; and both groups had average scores remarkably close to the mean response given by nonadopted white children in the same age range. This would seem to be yet another indication that positive self-esteem is not necessarily related to inracial placement.

Perhaps their most interesting quantitative finding on racial identification was the absence of any relationship between measures of racial identification and self-esteem. This data suggests that self-esteem and racial identity are not as inextricably bound as is sometimes asserted. They appear, in fact, to be independent dimensions. It implies that a transracially adopted black child might develop a positive sense of self without an exclusive identification with the black community.

McRoy et al. (1982), in fact, reported that most of the transracially adopting parents were reluctant to see their children entirely in terms of their own black heritage. Eighty-six percent of the white parents who adopted a child with one white and one black parent regarded their children as biracial (p. 525). This perception seemed to have been communicated to some degree to their children. Of the 18 transracially adopted children who spontaneously used racial terms to describe themselves on the Twenty Statements Test, eight chose to describe themselves in terms of a mixed racial background.

The behavior of the adopting parents was as important as their attitudes in shaping the racial perspectives of their adopted children. As McRoy, Zurcher, and their colleagues put it: "Transracially adopted black children who attended racially integrated schools and whose families resided in racially integrated communities and accepted their child's black racial identity tended to feel positive about themselves as black persons."

On the one hand, children whose parents deemphasized their racial identification and who isolated themselves and their families from the black community, often raised children who accepted, at least in part, some of the negative stereotypes about black people in American society. These findings were also supported by the data collected by Simon and Altstein (1981). These studies suggest that simply providing a child with a good home will not, by itself, lead to the child's identification and acceptance of their racial heritage. These data clearly raise questions about the desirability of placing black children with parents who are not prepared to accept part of their child's racial heritage.

On the other hand, it does seem abundantly clear that white parents who accept a child's racial identification with the black community can and do raise children who are emotionally whole and who have a positive relationship to their Afro-American heritage. Perhaps because of the controversy surrounding their placement, there has been considerably more research on the fate of transracially adopted black children than on the far larger number of transracially adopted Asian children and the growing number of transracially adopted children born in South and Central America.

A study by Feigelman and Silverman (1983), the authors of this chapter, attempted to link the research on transracially adopted black children with the study of Asian and Latin American transracial adoptees. Feigelman and Silverman initiated their research on transracial placement in 1975 with a sample of 713 families who had adopted black, Korean, Vietnamese, Colombian as well as white children. Data was gathered for this study primarily by mail questionnaires to the adopting parents in 1975 and 1981. As other studies of white parents who adopted black children found, these families were disproportionately upper-middle class and liberal. Parents of Asian and Latin American children, however, were drawn from a much more broad-based population.

Feigelman and Silverman's findings are congruent with the research already presented. Their results suggested that most black adoptees adapt reasonably well to their white homes and that most of their emotional and developmental problems can be traced to their preadoptive experiences (Feigelman & Silverman, 1983; Silverman, 1980). This also seemed true of Asian and Latin American transracial adoptees.

Compared with the other groups of transracially adopting parents, white parents of black children did encounter more racial and ethnic hostility. The research suggested that racial hostility did create problems for both the transracial adoptees and their families. However, multivariate analysis clearly showed that delays in placement were considerably a more important factor than racial hostility in accounting for the difficulties in the adjustments of black transracial adoptees (Feigelman & Silverman, 1983).

The patterns described for black transracial adoptees seemed to apply as well to Korean, Vietnamese, and Colombian transracial adoptees and their families. Delays in placement and problems in the preadoptive environment seemed most closely linked to later adjustment problems. Most of the adoptees and their families were the targets of some ethnic hostility, but for the vast majority of these families this was not a harmful or continuing problem (Feigelman & Silverman, 1983).

If black transracial adoptees face more hostility than other transracial adoptees, they are also more clearly tied to their Afro-American identities than the other groups. This may, in part, be a result of the hostility itself. It is probably also a part of the greater commitment that the white parents of black transracial adoptees have toward their children's Afro-American background.

Such commitments are ultimately transmitted to their transracially adopted children. Feigelman and Silverman reported that 70% of their sample of black transracial adoptees sometimes or often expressed pride in their Afro-American heritage, while only 57% of the Korean transracial adoptees and 50% of the Colombian adoptees demonstrated similar feelings (Feigelman & Silverman, 1983).

Families who adopted black children were generally open to their childrens' interest in their birthparents. This attitude was true of all families who adopted transracially, but the support given to black transracial adoptees was most pronounced, Silverman and Feigelman also found that 75% of the white fathers of black adopted children opposed the sealing of adoption records, while 51 and 53% of the fathers of Korean and Colombian adoptees had similar feelings. In contrast, only 28% of the fathers of white inracial adoptees had similar feelings. Again, family attitudes were reflected in the behavior of their adoptees with 63% of the Afro-American, 39% of the Korean, and 43% of the Colombian adoptees expressing interest in knowing more about their birthparents. Thirty-nine percent of the black adoptees, but only 21% of white inrace adoptees were considered likely to search for their birthparents. The data in the Feigelman and Silverstein study was very similar to that reported by Simon and Altstein (1987). The latter reported that 38% of the predominantly black transracial adoptees in their study tried or definitely intend to try to locate their birthparents.

Transracial adoption, of course, is not confined to the United States. There are research efforts, some available in English, on transracial adoption in western Europe. The work by Gill and Jackson (1983) in their monograph *Adoption and Race: Black, Asian and Mixed Race Children in White Families,* dealing with transracial adoption in Great Britain, is a useful comparative work for American or other English language readers. This research presents little challenge to the picture presented above of transracial adoption as a generally successful enterprise from the perspective of the adopting parents, adoptees, and the investigators completing this study.

CONCLUSION

The present investigation of transracial adoptions suggests that the interest and desire to foster these adoptions is likely to continue for some time to come. Even if the numbers of adoptions of black children by white families does not return to the levels of the late 1960s and early 1970s, the continuing adoptions of foreign-born children from Asia and Latin America is likely to remain, if not expand beyond its present levels. Given the scarcity of adoptable domestic infants and the increasing interest in adoption due to delayed marriage and rising infertility, strong demand forces prevail. Our survey of the transracial adoption literature has shown that cross-racial adoptive parents come from a wide variety of social backgrounds. The response of family, friends, and neighbors also tends to be an encouraging one.

The research that has been done to date suggests that transracial adoption is a viable means of providing stable homes for waiting children. The process of transracial adoption seems to produce children whose self-esteem is at least as high as that of nonadopted children and whose adjustment appears more than satisfactory.

Transracial adoption is a product of American race relations. Barriers between what is white and nonwhite have diminished to the point where transracial adoption, interracial marriage, and other forms of intimate contact across racial boundaries is increasingly possible. These changes have by no means eliminated racial hostility in the lives of transracially adopting families. The research reviewed here, however, strongly suggests that such prejudice is sporadic. It is a problem, but by no means the most serious issue that transracial adoptees face. Studies reviewed here suggest that problems in the preadoptive history and delays in permanent placement account for a much more substantial portion of the adoptee's postplacement difficulties compared with those created by racial antagonism.

Nonwhite children raised in white homes, for the most part, identify with both white and nonwhite communities. This is true of black, Korean, and other nonwhite transracial adoptees. Though they are afflicted with some degree of doubt and discomfort, there is every evidence that most transracial adoptees have a positive evaluation of their nonwhite backgrounds and appearance. Transracial adoptees do not deny their racial identification. Neither, for the most part, do their adoptive parents.

Perhaps the most disturbing part of our review of the transracial adoption literature is the extent to which it is ignored in formulating adoption policy. We are not recommending transracial placements as a panacea for the problems of family disintegration among nonwhite minorities in the United States. But their success suggests that they may at least be a useful resource. The effort to expand intraracial placement for minority children, however, does not require the cessation of transracial placements. At a time when few black leaders are sanguine about the deplorably low-income and employment levels found among minority underclasses, as the rates of adolescent out-of-wedlock pregnancies continue to mount, transracial placement is a resource that cannot easily be ignored.

11

Adoption Disruption: Rates and Correlates

TRUDY FESTINGER

Adoption disruption commonly refers to the removal of a child from an adoptive placement before the adoption has been legalized. The term came into use some years ago (Donley, 1978; Unger, Dwarshuis, & Johnson, 1977) as a substitute for such harsh words as ''breakdown'' or ''failure,'' reflecting a viewpoint that a child's removal from a particular adoptive placement signified an interruption in the path to a goal, rather than a final outcome. A distinction has also been made between adoption disruption and dissolution, the latter referring to situations where a legalized adoption has been annulled.

Over the years there has been a growing concern about disruption (Cole, 1979), fueled by the belief that its occurrence was apt to increase dramatically as caseworkers sought adoptive homes for children who in the past were considered unadoptable. Misgivings arose that accountability mechanisms might increase the likelihood of disruption if time pressures resulted in premature decisions about placements. Concern has also been kindled by guesses and rumors about high rates of disruption. Such concerns are not surprising, since disruptions are painful for all involved—the children, the adoptive parents, and the caseworkers.

In order to provide a perspective, it is important to ask: What is known about how frequently disruptions occur? One purpose of this chapter is to answer that question. A second purpose is to identify the correlates of disruption. Here I will address the question: What is known about the circumstances that distinguish placements that are maintained from those that are not? Throughout I will rely heavily on a recently completed study (Festinger, 1986) that dealt with both questions.

A REVIEW OF LITERATURE

Past reports on rates of disruption are quite scattered. Until the early 1970s adoption disruption was rarely mentioned. No doubt this was so because the phenomenon occurred so infrequently. For instance, Kadushin (1980) cites nine studies, including one of his own (Kadushin & Seidl, 1971), covering the period up to 1970. These studies were mainly concerned with children who were white, very young, and without known handicaps at placement. Although there were minor variations among the studies, of the more than 34,000 placements of children that were monitored, only 1.9% disrupted.

More recent studies have increasingly focused on, or included, children who were older, from minority groups, or handicapped. These studies have reported higher rates of disruption. For example, Kadushin cites figures from a North Carolina agency that showed a disruption rate of 8% among 410 placements of children with special needs who were placed between 1967 and 1974 (U.S. Congress, 1975). Statistics from California public agencies noted a disruption rate of 7.6% in 1973, a considerable increase over the 2.7% reported by the same agencies in 1970, apparently reflecting "the increasing number of older children being placed" (Bass, 1975). A Michigan agency that specializes in the placement of children with special needs reported that of 199 children placed from 1968 through 1976 the rate of disruption was 10.6% (Unger et al., 1977). A Canadian report cited an increase in annual adoption disruptions in the province of Ontario from 4% to 7% between 1971 and 1978 (Cohen, 1981), but noted that disruptions occurred with greater frequency among private and kin placements than in agency placements. Disruption figures were also reported by the evaluators of an effort to place 115 children with special needs from a number of New York State counties. Of the 41 adoptive placements between 1975 and 1977, 15% had disrupted by the time data collection stopped in 1977 (W.R.I., 1978). The authors observe that this may have been a conservative figure because additional disruptions may have occurred when they were no longer collecting information.

Developmentally disabled children placed for adoption during a 12-month period between 1978 and 1979 are the subject of a recent report of a mail survey of agencies in the United States and Canada (Coyne & Brown, 1985). The authors report descriptive data on 693 children placed in adoptive homes by 292 agencies. A majority of the responding agencies were located in smaller cities and towns, and over half of the children were of preschool age. Placement workers were asked to provide information about disruptions during the study year, regardless of whether the child had been placed for adoption during the 12-month period or earlier. On this basis the authors report an overall rate of 8.7%. They point out that this was not a comprehensive picture of disruptions during 1978 and 1979, since they did not include disrupted placements of children whose placement workers were no longer with an agency. Soon thereafter, a report from Connecticut of a program serving emotionally disturbed children of "latency age" noted disruptions of placements for 4 of the 13 children placed in adoptive homes (Fein, Davies, & Knight, 1979). At roughly the same time in Ohio, a report of a demonstration project designed to expand adoption services to children with special needs noted a 13.6% rate of disruption for the 59 children placed (Roberts, 1980), and a small study of children from a group care setting in North Carolina reported that 9 out of 19 initial adoptive placements did not hold (Borgman, 1981).

In 1982 the results of a follow-up of cases from a demonstration project in Oregon were reported (Lahti, 1982). At the time of the original project all children were under the age of 12 and had been in foster care a year or more. A sample of cases was tracked for 15 months after the project's conclusion in order to determine placement stability. The report shows that of 107 children in adoptive placements with new or foster parents, that placements of 5.6% had disrupted. No differences in rates of disruption were noted between children selectively assigned to workers, who had been specially trained to work intensively to find permanent homes for foster children, and a comparison group receiving regular casework services. Furthermore, no differences in disruptions were apparent between adoptive placements with new and with foster families.

Another agency study (Kagan & Reid 1986) of adoptive placements, between 1974 and 1982, of 78 older youths with severe emotional and learning problems, noted that roughly 53% had earlier been in at least one adoptive placement that disrupted. Unfortunately such calculations, based on prior disruptions, are not comparable to other reports on rates. At about the same time, Tremitiere (1984) distributed questionnaires to 116 agencies in Pennsylvania and 40 agencies located outside of that state. The latter were all known to serve children with special needs. Usable responses were received from 45 agencies. These were divided into four groups, according to their location and whether they were public or voluntary. For each group, yearly totals of placements and yearly totals of disruptions from 1979 through 1983 are reported. Despite the problem that in any one year these might not refer to the same children, Tremitiere reports on the range of disruption proportions within various age groupings of children. My calculations from her tables show that disruptions of placements among the youngest children (those under 6) were fairly level between 1979 (1.4%) and 1982 to 1983 (1.6%). For older children (those who were 6 to 18), however, the proportion of disruptions rose from 7.2% in 1979 to roughly 12% in 1982 to 1983. Furthermore, a report from a New Jersey agency that specialized in adoptive placements of children with special needs showed that of 309 children, the adoptive placements of 21.4% had disrupted by the end of the data collection period in 1981 (Boyne, Denby, Kettenring, & Wheeler, 1984).

Roughly at the same time Argent (1984) reported on the work of Parents for Children, a British agency dedicated to the adoptive placement of children with special needs. Between late 1976 and early 1983, the agency placed 75 children into 56 families. By May 1983, the placements of 14 children (18.7%) had disrupted. The subject of disruption was also touched on in a study by Macaskill (1985), who examined the same agency's "most complex placements" of children, all with a variety of handicaps. Although the focus of this study was on adoptive parents' perceptions of difficulties encountered at various stages of placement over time, the author notes that of 37 placements, 21 adoption orders had been granted at the time of the study. It is not clear what proportion of the rest had disrupted, and what proportion still remained with their adoptive families.

More recently, Partridge, Hornby, and McDonald (1986) present data on 235 placements of 212 children from six agencies in four northeastern states. Most of the children were white, nearly 8-years-old on the average at the time of adoptive placement, and almost all were considered to have special needs. The six agencies provided information on all disruptions (a small number of dissolutions were included also) that had occurred in a two and a half-year period from 1982 to 1984, and on one of four nondisrupted placements made during that time. All together, 64 placements disrupted. Thus, after appropriate adjustments were made for oversampling of disruptions, the investigators arrived at a disruption rate of 8.6%.

The problem of estimating rates of disruption are highlighted in another recent report that presented figures from five state agencies (Benton, Kaye, & Tipton, 1985). In some instances disruption rates were based on the ratio of disruptions (of placements that could have begun in prior years) to new placements in a given year, whereas in others they were based on a cross-sectional sample of cases in adoptive home placements. In three state agencies, current disruptions were counted, whereas in two agencies, the children in current adoptive home placements were examined to determine their prior histories of disruptions. Data obtained from this mixture of approaches showed a range of disruption rates for 1984 to 1985 from 6.9% to 20%. In only one of the states, Virginia, was a sample tracked over time. This consisted of 53 children who were placed in adoptive homes in 1983. It was reported 18 to 24 months later (by June 1985) that 19% of these had one or more disruptions.

The variety of approaches used in all of these reports and studies attests to the difficulty faced when attempting to arrive at an accurate estimate of the rate of disruption. Ideally one would single out a group of children at the start of their adoptive placement, follow them longitudinally over time, and calculate the proportion of disruptions in that group. So as to have a large enough sample, and to include placements at different points during a year, it would be important to select new adoptive placements over a span of many months. Of course, such tracking takes considerable effort and time since one has to wait until the outcome of each new placement is known. If instead one focuses on prior disruptions among adoptively placed children, as some have done, the rate is based on those who have again been adoptively placed. Figures based on such a select group are apt to be inaccurate because they omit all cases of children whose placements disrupted earlier but who were not subsequently in another adoptive placement. Alternatively, if one uses all children in adoptive placements at a particular point in time and follows these until an outcome is known, there are also inaccuracies in a description of rates. The problem in such a cross-section arises because placements at any one moment in time not only include new adoptive placements but also children who have been in their placements for some time. The latter started out with others who no longer remain in their adoptive placements because of disruptions or adoptions. That is, one has lost their history. In other words, a cross-section deals with a residual group, who up until that time were not adopted and whose placements did not disrupt. It is risky to use such a group for an accurate assessment of rates of disruption.

The New York City Study

My study of adoptive placements sought to overcome these difficulties of arriving at an accurate estimate of the rate of disruption. It did so by starting with a computerized listing (prepared by the Child Welfare Information Service) of children in adoptive placements, then using longitudinal methods to follow this cross-section of children forward in time, and collecting the histories of new placements over time as a substitute for lost history information. The details of this nontraditional strategy, which I called a ''wrap-around'' approach, have been described elsewhere (Festinger, 1986). The sample consisted of all children who in March 1983 were on adoptive status and who were 6-years-old or older when that designation occurred. They were in adoptive placements supervised by 36 voluntary agencies as well as the public services of New York City. All together, the outcomes of the first 12 months of adoptive placement were established for 482 children who were placed alone, without siblings, and 415 children who were in sibling groups of two to five children placed together. Roughly 63% of the latter were groups of two and another 23% consisted of three siblings placed together.

Outcomes were of four sorts: (1) placement disruption; (2) ongoing foster care in the same home; (3) adoption; and (4) an unresolved outcome category, the remainders. The latter group consisted of children who continued to be on adoptive status 12 months after families signed agreements to adopt. The second outcome, ongoing foster care, consisted of cases in which children were removed from adoptive status but remained in their adoptive homes on a continuing foster care basis. Virtually all of these youths were in their teens at the time adoption agreements were signed. All wished to remain with their placement families, with typically signed affidavits stating that they did not want to be adopted, and in most instances the families provided no hint that these youths would ever be asked to leave. Such cases seemed conceptually different from situations in which children were removed from their adoptive homes. Nevertheless, these older children did not achieve premanency, in the usual sense of that term. They remained, by mutual choice, with the same families. To call these cases disruptions seemed misleading; consequently, they are treated as a separate group in the discussion on rates.

Approximately 53% of the children were males. Most (63%) were black, 21.2% were Hispanic, 12.4% were white, and the remaining 3.4% were Oriental or had interracial backgrounds. A large majority were Protestant (59.7%) or Catholic (38.4%), and only a small fraction were Jewish (1.5%) or listed as having no religious affiliation. At the time of their most recent placement into foster care they were on the average four-years-old and ranged in age from less than 1 month to 16 years. About 41% were under age three and an additional 35% were between 3- and 6-years-old at that time. They were, on the average, 9-years-old when they were free to be adopted. They were yet older by the time families formally committed themselves to adopt, usually by signing agreements to do so. At that time the youths ranged in age from 6 to 19 years and were on the average 10.2-years-old.

Over the 12 months that followed the signing of adoption agreements, an estimated 8.2% of all the adoptive placements disrupted, 1.3% of the placements changed from adoptive status to ongoing foster care in the same home, 46.2% of the children were adopted, and the outcome of the remaining 44.3% was not yet known. This last group continued to remain on adoptive status in the same homes that had signed adoption agreements 12 months earlier. Following the first 12 months of adoptive placement, estimates were used to examine trends in rates over time. These estimates were based on information that was available for those who remained on adoptive status past the initial 12 months. The trends over time revealed a relatively steady trickle of disruptions during the second and third years of adoptive placement. Thus in the long run, the overall rate of disruption can be estimated to fall somewhere between 12% and 14%. The estimated rate of disruption was therefore highest during the first 12 months following the point when adoption agreements were signed, and it did not vary substantially over those 12 months. In contrast, the rate of adoption increased steadily over the first 18 months and continued, but at a slower pace, for the remaining time. Let us look at all of this in a slightly different way. During the first 12 months after adoption agreements were signed, there were roughly five to six legalized adoptions for each disruption. The rate of adoptions over disruptions then increased. For instance, during the fifteenth and sixteenth month, there were about eight adoptions for each disruption, and in the months that followed this increased to nine or ten adoptions for each disruption.

Differences in rates of disruption were also examined. This was quite limited because of the paucity of pertinent or usable information that was available from the computerized listing of children. In sum, disruption rates were quite similar regardless of the sex or race of the child, and did not differ substantially among diverse groupings of agencies. However, the ages of children at the time the adoption agreements were signed unmistakably made a difference in rates of disruption. Thus during the 12 months after these agreements were signed, the placements of 13.1% of children age 11 or older did not hold, in contrast to 4.5% for children ages 6 to 10. These differences existed regardless of sex, race, or religious affiliation. There were also considerable age differences between those whose placement disrupted (mean = 11.2 years) and those who were adopted (mean = 9.8 years). Since the age of the children was such an important indicator of the risk of disruption, the rates for the second and third year of adoptive placement were estimated for the two age groupings, those who were ages 6 to 10, and those who were age 11 or older at the time the adoption agreements were signed. For the former age group, in the long run, the overall estimated rate of disruption fell somewhere between 8% and 11%, whereas for the older group it fell somewhere between 16% and 19%. Among older children the rate of disruption was highest during the first 12 months after agreements were signed; for the younger ones, it was fairly level over time. It is quite possible that younger ones, who were not adopted during the first year of adoptive placement, were with families who were ambivalent about adopting, perhaps because of these children's problems.

Finally, disruption rates differed between children who were placed by themselves and those who were placed as part of a sibling group. Perhaps surprisingly, children placed alone had a significantly higher rate of disruption (10.7%) during the 12 months following their adoptive placement, in contrast to a 5.6% rate among siblings. This difference held regardless of sex, religion, and ethnic origin, with the single exception of whites, where no difference existed. The difference also held among those who were age 11 or older or age 10 or less when the adoption agreements were signed, as well as when various agency groupings were examined. The difference could not be explained on the basis of the children's ages at the time the agreements were signed, as those who were placed alone and as sibling groups were roughly the same age, on the average, at the time. I will return to this issue later on, in the discussion on correlates of disruption, and will then also discuss some other studies that have yielded different results.

Summary

What can one say about all of this? For one thing, available figures show that the proportion of disruptions has risen over the years. This fact appears to be the case in spite of problems of methodology and precision and in spite of probable variations in the definitions used. The general rise in disruption rates is not terribly surprising, in view of the fact that adoptive homes were increasingly sought for older children and for those with other special needs, for instance, sibling groups, children from minority groups, or children with physical, educational, or emotional handicaps. It is also clear that disruption rates are not uniform. This must be kept in mind as one thinks about rates; a global rate is really a composite of many rates that may differ depending on which group is examined. Furthermore, the focus on disruption, while dramatic, distorts the picture. When evaluating levels of disruption, it is best not to think of such rates in isolation, but to view them in conjunction with adoptions. Worries and rumors about disruption rates appear to have exaggerated the extent of the problem. It is indeed impressive that the rates reported in so many recent studies, despite some variations here and there, do not differ substantially. In my study (1986), the estimate for disruptions hovered around 13% for the group as a whole. Since the children in that study were, on the average, over age 10 at adoptive placement, had been in foster care for some time, and, as we shall see, had a high incidence of problems, such a rate hardly needs to arouse astonishment or be viewed in a negative light. One must not lose sight of the fact that in the long run the vast majority will have been adopted. Risks had to be taken or else this might never have occurred.

CORRELATES OF DISRUPTION

Figures on overall rates of disruption tell us little about the characteristics of the children whose placements do not hold. For this information one has to turn to those efforts that have systematically compared disruptions with adoptions. A number of studies have done just that in an attempt to tease out those elements that may be important to consider when efforts are made to find permanent homes for children with special needs. Some of these studies have already been mentioned because they also reported on rates (Benton et al., 1985; Boyne et al., 1984; Coyne & Brown, 1985; Festinger, 1986; Kadushin & Seidl, 1971; Partridge et al., 1986), whereas others have not (Boneh, 1979; Schmidt, 1986; Zwimpfer, 1983).[1] Most frequently in all these studies the data were gathered from some combination of case records, questionnaires, and interviews with various levels of agency staff. Here and there, although rarely, a small group of adoptive parents were also interviewed. No study, to my knowledge, has presented data from the children themselves.

There is a problem in almost all of these studies, namely, that the children who were placed together in sibling units were individually counted and were not separately assessed in the comparisons of outcomes. The problem hinges on the fact that their inclusion, rather than separating them for purpose of analysis, creates serious difficulties for the interpretation of the statistical results on which the conclusions are based. This problem has been elsewhere discussed in some detail (Festinger, 1986). In addition, when one reviews all of these studies, it quickly becomes clear that there are differences in such things as the method of sampling, the nature and wording of questions that were asked, the depth of analyses, and even in what was called a disruption. Nevertheless, I will take the liberty of presenting a rough picture of some of the findings.

The Children and Their Placement History

Demographic characteristics of the children have essentially no bearing on the outcome of adoptive placements. As can be seen in Table 11.1, in most studies the sex of the children made no difference. There were just two studies that showed sex to be a factor. In each of these, among placements that disrupted, males were overrepresented. The race of children also did not distinguish among those whose placements disrupted, when compared with children whose placements held. Only one study that focused on very young children in New Zealand reported that the placements of children from minority groups were more apt to disrupt than was the case among nonminority children. The religion of children also had no bearing on outcome (Boneh, 1979; Festinger, 1986).

Age has been a consistent predictor of outcome. Whether one examines age at entry into foster care (see Table 11.1), age when the children became legally free for adoption (Boneh, 1979; Festinger, 1986; Partridge et al., 1986), or age at the time of the adoptive placement (see Table 11.1), children whose placements disrupted were older than those who were adopted. In addition, some have reported that the disruption group took longer to become legally free than those whose placements held (Boneh, 1979; Partridge et al., 1986), whereas others reported no time lag differential whatever (Boyne et al., 1984; Festinger, 1986). The total length of time in foster care prior to the adoptive placement has also yielded mixed results. Some data

Table 11.1 The Relationship of Selected Child Factors to Disruption[a]

Study	Sex	Race	Age at Entry into Foster Care	Placements	Age at Adoptive Placement	With/ Without Siblings	Number of Problems
Benton et al. (1985)	No	No	—	—	Older	With	More
Boneh (1979)	Male	No	Older	More	Older	With	More
Boyne et al. (1984)	No	No	—	—	Older	No	More
Coyne & Brown (1985)	No	No	—	—	Older	—	—
Festinger (1986)	No	No	Older	More	Older	Without	More
Kadushin & Seidl (1971)	No	—	—	—	Older	With	—
Partridge et al. (1986)	No	No	Older	More	Older	—	More
Schmidt (1986)	Male	—	—	More	Older	Without	More
Zwimpfer (1983)	No	Minority	—	—	Older	—	—

[a] "No" indicates that the factor was not related to disruption. —indicates that data are not presented for this factor. Other entries give the direction of the relationship to disruption.

show that this time was longer for those whose placements eventually disrupted than for the adoptees (Boneh, 1979; Partridge et al., 1986), whereas other data show no such connection (Festinger, 1986) or report that the time was shorter (Zwimpfer, 1983).

The children initially entered foster care for many reasons. One study showed the reasons to be quite similar for children with disruption or adoption outcomes (Festinger, 1986), whereas another study noted that death of the primary caretaker or neglect of the child was more common among those whose placements disrupted (Boneh, 1979). The latter finding was primarily a function of the children's older age at entry, since a major reason for placement among adoptees was that they had been given up at birth. Several other investigators have focused on the histories of the children prior to the adoptive placements, rather than on the reasons for entry into care. They have noted that the histories of those whose placements disrupted showed a higher incidence of various kinds of abuse or neglect when compared with children whose placements held (Partridge et al., 1986; Schmidt, 1986). Also, a prior removal from a foster home due to inadequate parenting has been cited as a factor in disruption (Boneh, 1979).

The average number of placements in foster homes and group settings has been a consistent predictor of disruption. After their entry into foster care, these averages have been considerably higher for disruption than for adoption outcomes (see Table 11.1). If one only counts foster family placements, the outcomes also differ (Festinger, 1986). Previous disruptions of adoptive placements have also been cited (Boyne et al., 1984; Festinger, 1986; Partridge et al., 1986). The nature of the previous placements also differed for the two outcomes. More of those whose placements eventually disrupted, when compared with the adoptees, had at some point resided in a group facility (Boneh, 1979; Festinger, 1986). A difference also stood out on examining the length of time children had resided in an earlier foster home. This period was longer for children whose placements later disrupted than for the adoptees (Boneh, 1979; Festinger, 1986). Finally, assessments of the adjustment of children in a previous foster home showed that among those with a disruption outcome a larger proportion received poorer ratings (Partridge et al., 1986; Schmidt, 1986). Although based on information in case records, such findings must be treated with caution in view of the retrospective nature of these assessments. After all, case reviewers knew the outcome at the time of their ratings.

Some of the children were placed together with their siblings, whereas others were placed by themselves. The data on whether this was a factor connected to the outcome are exceedingly mixed, as can be seen in Table 11.1. Three studies show that placements with siblings were overrepresented among disruption outcomes, two studies indicate that such placements were less likely to disrupt, and one study showed no difference in the outcome. Two of the studies yielded further data to shed light on their findings. For instance, in the Kadushin and Seidl (1971) report, siblings were older, which probably was a factor in their higher disruption rate. In the Festinger (1986) report, siblings who were living together were less apt to have problems of various sorts, which very likely was a factor in their lower rate of disruption. Furthermore, in that study, children who were separated from siblings (who were in other adoptive homes) were overrepresented among disruptions. Perhaps the separation was problematic for these children and influenced their adaptation in the adoptive home; or perhaps they had more serious problems to begin with, which may have influenced their having been separately placed.

To summarize, when compared with children who were adopted, those whose placements disrupted were older all along. They had more placements of all sorts, had been placed in more families, and their longest stay there was more protracted. Furthermore, they were more apt to have had an earlier adoptive placement or a placement in a group setting. Their prior histories of care were more problematic. Their more checkered placement history suggests that these children exhibited more problems early on or developed them during their stay in care. They entered into an adoptive relationship on the heels of a more varied placement history. Since that history included a longer family placement, one can imagine past disappointments when these relationships ended and perhaps more wariness about subsequent placements. In addition, they were older. Thus they brought with them a history of past experiences. It is plausible to assume that they were therefore less malleable and had more difficulty adapting to new situations in foster care. In short, they were more difficult to manage. One can speculate that the older ones may have been faced with a conflict between their growing need for independence, in conjunction with a non-idealization of parents, and the attachment tasks inherent in adoption. These difficulties could have been exacerbated if adoptive parents lacked sufficient skills and the flexibility needed to bend with, and be responsive to, the ebb and flow of emotions of older children. It is also quite possible that because of their older age more had developed firmer psychological links to their families of origin and may even have viewed adoption as an act of disloyalty. All of these elements combined are apt to have interfered with these children's assimilation into their adoptive families.

The Adoptive Parents

The demographic characteristics of the adoptive parents—their age, race, education, and income—have essentially no bearing on the outcome of adoptive placements, although some unexplained variation does exist among findings (Table 11.2). Transracial placements also were not connected to outcome (Boneh, 1979; Festinger, 1986; Partridge et al., 1986), with the exception of one report that showed such placements to be overrepresented among disruptions (Zwimpfer, 1983). Finally, the fact of employment of either or both adoptive parents has had no bearing on the outcome (Benton et al. 1985; Festinger, 1986).

The couple or single status of the adoptive parents is unrelated to the outcome, with the exception of one study finding single parents overrepresented among disruptions (see Table 11.2). Among couples, two reports showed the length of their marriage to be unrelated to outcome (Boneh, 1979; Festinger, 1986), in contrast to a third that found a connection between shorter marriages and disruption (Zwimpfer, 1983). A previous divorce had no bearing on outcome in two reports (Boyne et al., 1984; Festinger, 1986), but was a factor in disruption in another (Boneh, 1979). Finally, Schmidt (1986) reported that ratings of such factors as the quality of the marital relationship were less positive among placements that disrupted than among those that did not. Once again caution must be used here, since the raters knew the outcome at the time the ratings were made.

Aside from such things as previous divorces, the background of adoptive parents

Table 11.2   The Relationship of Selected Adoptive Parent Factors to Disruption[a]

Study	Couple/ Single Parent	New/ Foster Parent	Age	Race	Education	Income	Biological Children in the Home
Benton et al. (1985)	No	No	No	White	No	No	—
Boneh (1979)	—	—	Older[b]	No	No	—	Present
Boyne et al. (1984)	No	—	No	No	No	No	No
Coyne & Brown (1985)	—	New	—	—	—	—	—
Festinger (1986)	No	New	No	No	No	—	No
Kadushin & Seidl (1971)	—	—	Older	—	—	—	Present
Partridge et al. (1986)	Single	—	—	Minority	No	No	—
Schmidt (1986)	—	New	—	—	No	No	—
Zwimpfer (1983)	—	—	Younger	Minority	—	Lower	No

[a] "No" indicates that the factor was not related to disruption. — indicates that data are not presented for this factor. Other entries give the direction of the relationship to disruption.
[b] Among couples with no biological children.

has received little attention. One study that dealt with this issue (Schmidt, 1986) found that the "number of children in the adoptive parents' family of origin i.e., some rather than none," was moderately related to an adoption outcome. Although the reference to children is somewhat ambiguous, this finding suggests that if adoptive parents, during their youth, lived with siblings, the placements of children were somewhat less likely to disrupt.

Four studies have examined whether the adoptive families were foster parents with whom the children had been living for some time or were new families. It is hardly surprising that most of these studies report that among placements that disrupted a larger proportion of the children were with new families rather than with foster families (see Table 11.2). This result is explained in one study that showed that children placed with new families had been in more previous placements and were more apt to have problems and more severe ones than was the case for those placed with foster families (Festinger, 1986). There has been very limited investigation of adoptive placements with relatives. One study that included a moderate number of such homes found that these placements were less likely to disrupt (Festinger, 1986).

Parental preferences about the characteristics of children they want to adopt has also been examined by a few investigators. Among placements that disrupted when compared with those that did not, a larger proportion of adoptive parents were less flexible in their preferences (Boneh, 1979). Numerous preferences were also a danger signal (Festinger, 1986). Clearly, such pickiness at the start did not augur well in the long run. Furthermore, disruptions were more likely where stated requests, for instance, concerning age, were not met (Boneh, 1979; Schmidt, 1986).

The Composition of the Home

Questions concerning a possible effect of the presence of biological children have generated considerable interest, hence a number of studies have examined this issue. As can be seen in Table 11.2, three studies found no connection to outcome, whereas two showed that disruption was more likely when biological children resided in the adoptive home. The authors of one of these two studies suggested, however, that this result was probably confounded; that is, adoptive parents with biological children were older and were in turn offered older children for adoption, and it was the older age of the placed children that was linked to disruption (Kadushin & Seidl, 1971). The presence of adopted children in the home has also been examined. Two studies reported no bearing on outcome (Boyne et al., 1984; Festinger, 1986), yet a third noted that among placements that disrupted, when compared with those that did not, a smaller proportion of the adoptive families had previously adopted a child (Partridge et al., 1986). Finally, the number of other children in the home, not biological siblings of the sample child, did no distinguish among placements that disrupted, when compared with adoptions (Festinger, 1986).

A number of other factors, such as the ages of the other children, their sex, and the racial composition of the home, have also been examined. On the one hand, in one study the difference in age between the children in the sample and the oldest or youngest children in the home was not related to outcome, but the age distribution was. Sample children who were in the middle position, flanked by both older and younger children who were not biological siblings of the sample children, were more vulnerable to disruption than those who occupied the oldest or youngest position (Festinger, 1986). On the other hand, another study noted that in homes were biological children resided, a larger proportion of the placements resulted in disruption, rather than adoption, where the adoptive child assumed the position of the eldest (Boneh, 1979). As for the sex of the other children in the adoptive home, one study showed this to be unrelated to outcome, but noted that among children placed alone, rather than with siblings, the proportion of disruptions was considerably higher than that of adoptions if they lived with biological children who were all of the opposite sex (Festinger, 1986). Perhaps the presence of offspring who were all of the opposite sex meant that the motivation to adopt stemmed mainly from a desire for a child of the opposite sex rather than for a child. Alternatively, perhaps the existence of offspring all of the opposite sex produced a special situation for the child placed without siblings, one where the parents were especially leery about sexual encounters that might ensue. Another element, the racial composition of the adoptive home, has been examined in one study that showed this to be totally unconnected to the outcome (Festinger, 1986). Finally and not surprisingly, one study reported that those whose placements disrupted were more likely to be in conflict with the other children in the family, when compared with nondisruptions (Partridge et al., 1986).

In sum, most aspects of these households—the number of other children, their ages, sex, and race—were not linked to outcome. Here and there, some elements distinguished between disruptions and adoptions. These are isolated findings, warranting replication. Overall, one is impressed by the limited significance of household composition in the outcome of adoptive placements.

The Children's Problems

The presence of problems at the time of the adoptive placement has been a consistent predictor of disruption, as can be seen in Table 11.1. Usually this has referred to one or a combination of problems whether emotional, cognitive, or physical. But some studies have noted that while other problems were linked to disruption, mental retardation (Boyne et al., 1984) and physical or intellectual handicaps (Benton et al., 1985) were not. Prior school performance and the receipt of special education services before the adoptive placement also have not been factors, but those who received "tutoring" at the time of the adoptive placement were less likely to disrupt (Partridge et al., 1986). In view of the overall connection of problems to disruption, it is not surprising that the granting of a medical subsidy (Boyne et al., 1984) or frequent medical appointments at the time of the adoptive placement (Partridge et al., 1986) were also predictors of disruption. Outcomes have also differed according to the ratings of problem severity. Among children whose placements disrupted, a much larger proportion were judged to have one or more moderate or severe problems than was the case with those who were adopted (Festinger, 1986), although the retrospective timing of caseworkers' ratings no doubt exaggerated the magnitude of the difference. The existence of specific problem behaviors prior to the adoptive placement has also been examined. Thus, in contrast to nondisruptions, a larger proportion of those whose placements disrupted exhibited behaviors, such as serious eating problems, sexual promiscuity, stealing, suicidal behavior, fire setting, wetting or soiling, vandalism, or had physically injured others (Partridge et al., 1986). Finally, adoptive parents' capacity to deal or cope with the problems presented by the children has been studied. It is no surprise that disruption outcomes were linked to lower ratings of the parents' ability to cope than was the case among adoptions (Festinger, 1986; Schmidt, 1986).

Contact with Biological Parents and Others

That a child may have unresolved feelings about separation from past biological figures has been suggested as an important element in his or her ability to accept and attach to an adoptive family. One study approached this issue by collecting information about the timing of each child's last contact with biological parents. The recency of their contacts was immaterial to the outcome. However, children whose placements disrupted were older at the last contact than those who were adopted (Festinger, 1986). This was in line with their older age all along and suggested that more of those whose placements disrupted had developed firmer psychological links to their families of origin than the youngsters who were adopted.

Furthermore, children who maintained contact with someone who was thought to be opposed to their adoption were more apt to be in a placement that disrupted than one in which they were adopted. This was the case whether that person was someone from their biological family (Festinger, 1986) or a previous foster parent (Boneh, 1979).

Motivation and Placement Risk

It should come as no surprise that the ratings of the strength of motivation to adopt are reflected in the outcome. Whether one examines the adoptive parents or the placed children, lower ratings were linked to disruption (Festinger, 1986). Furthermore, couples who share an equal commitment to the adoption were less likely to experience a disruption (Partridge et al., 1986).

Information has also been sought on how risky these placements were regarded at the time of the adoptive placement (Festinger, 1986) or when the adoptive parents were evaluated (Zwimpfer, 1983). Although most placements were not regarded as particularly risky, there were large differences among outcomes—a larger proportion of disruptions were thought to be risky situations when compared with adoptions.

The ratings of motivation and risk, like other ratings reported earlier, were undoubtedly influenced by the fact that they relied to some extent on inferences made after the outcome was known. Therefore the differences just reported are probably exaggerated. In view of this likely distortion, it is noteworthy that in one study roughly 42% of the children with disruption outcomes (Festinger, 1986) and in another study over 60% with that outcome (Zwimpfer, 1983) were in placements that were not considered particularly risky. Apparently there were some surprises when trouble arose. In fact, one study reported that for nearly one-half of the children whose placements disrupted, signals of trouble were never given or recognized, or were first noted only four or more months after the adoptive placement (Festinger, 1986). Another study indicated that in 58% of cases of disruption the social worker did not learn of the problems in these placements until two months or less before the actual disruption (Partridge et al., 1986). A third study attempted, through a review of the records, to provide evidence of a "suspected tendency by social workers to ignore warning signals" and noted that less than 20% of cases of disruption "attracted any negative observations at all by the social workers during the supervision period" (Zwimpfer, 1983). The tendency not to recognize signs of trouble in adoptive placements has been discussed by others as well (Brown, 1963; Gochros, 1967).

What was going on? Perhaps home visits were cursory because staff had too many other responsibilities (Goodacre, 1966). Perhaps signs of problems were overlooked because the implications of such recognition, that perhaps one made a mistake, are anxiety producing (Brown, 1963). My own speculation leads me to suggest an alternative interpretation. Let us look at the larger picture. Generally, the children whose placements disrupted were older, had been in foster care for some time, and most were thought to exhibit problems of one sort or another. Finding new families who would adopt them or encouraging foster families to convert to an adoptive status often could take considerable effort. As has been stated by others (Meezan & Shireman, 1982), this no doubt sometimes involved persuading people who were reluctant to take such a serious step and at times led social workers to oversell a child (Kadushin, 1980). In recent years, pressures for the timely achievement of adoption goals possibly prompted workers to induce people to avoid delays in making decisions. In the process, workers probably also persuaded themselves about the strengths of these placements. Thus it is plausible to imagine that once the goal of an adoptive placement was achieved workers overvalued the families and exaggerated their desires and abilities to cope. Risks may have been inadequately assessed and signals of trouble not spotted or belatedly recognized. This is no to say that all disruptions could have been avoided, but to suggest that a more open and conscious recognition of practices, which include persuasion and the attendant effects on workers themselves, could be salutary. Such recognition would help social workers to anticipate and therefore increase their accuracy in assessing the weaknesses or potential areas of risk in many situations at an early stage. This in turn could lead workers to explore ways to counteract forces that contribute to the deterioration of placements.

Service Characteristics

Sometimes children were adoptively placed with families whose homes had been studied and approved by a different agency. This occurred more often among placements that disrupted than among adoptions (Boneh, 1979; Festinger, 1986; Partridge et al., 1986). One study examined this conclusion in some depth and cautioned that it would be wrong to conclude that reliance on studies completed by others were risky because in most instances the children were placed with new families rather than with foster families, and placements with new families were more apt to disrupt for other reasons than who had studied and approved the home (Festinger, 1986).

Another study found the time spent in preparing the child for the adoptive placement to be unrelated to the eventual outcome (Boneh, 1979). Others have found that preplacement meetings between the child or foster family and the adoptive parents were unrelated to the outcome (Boyne et al., 1984; Festinger, 1986). Yet others have reported that group sessions with the current caretaker, referred to as "the goodbye blessing," prior to the adoptive placement reduced the likelihood of disruption (Partridge et al., 1986) or had no bearing on outcome (Schmidt, 1986).

Staff discontinuities of a particular sort have been linked to disruption (Festinger, 1986). That is, staffing patterns in which the same social workers did not simultaneously prepare both a child and an adoptive family were disproportionately in evidence among placements that disrupted than among those that resulted in adoption. In other words, where somewhere along the way different workers had responsibility for preparing children and their families, the risk of disruption increased. Furthermore, situations, where the last worker who prepared the child did not continue to supervise the adoptive home, were also more frequently seen among disruption than adoption outcomes. Perhaps when the responsibilites for preparing a child and the family were not clearly lodged with the same worker, disparate things may have been communicated to a child and the family. When preparation and supervision were carried out by different staff members the child was not only faced by a new family but also by a new worker. It is also possible that the relationship between foster care and adoption staff members may sometimes have been strained (Donley, 1978) and played a role in the clarity of what was communicated. All these things could have hindered a smooth transition into an adoptive placement.

During the period of supervision that followed the adoptive placement, worker contacts with adoptive families and children were, on the whole, more frequent when placements disrupted than among those who were adopted (Festinger, 1986; Partridge et al., 1986). Worker time with the families and children clearly increased somewhat in response to serious problems in these placements. In addition, Partridge et al. (1986) reported that nearly half of these cases were referred for counseling or psychotherapy, about a quarter were provided with respite care, 20% were referred to parent support groups, but in only 15% of the cases was a trial separation attempted.

Disruption Circumstances

Studies have reported on the large rosters of reasons given by workers for disruption, reflecting the complex nature of family–child interactions as well as numerous, sometimes idiosyncratic, situational elements that were at play (Benton et al., 1985; Festinger, 1986; Kadushin & Seidl, 1971; Partridge et al., 1986). In view of the variations in the categories used to classify these reasons and the variations across studies in the meaning of each category, one can only attempt a very crude summary. Nevertheless, there is general agreement that the largest group of reasons for disruption concerned the families' inabilities or unwillingness to cope with the children's problems, demands, and behaviors, combined with unrealistic parental expectations. Reasons concerning the marital relationship or situational factors, such as illness of parents or financial stress, are much less frequently cited. It is important to note that when adoptive parents were interviewed (Benton et al., 1985; Partridge et al., 1986), although such interviews were few in number, many differences between their perceptions of adoption and those of workers emerged. For instance, with respect to the reasons for disruption, Benton et al. (1985) note that whereas workers emphasized a child's behavior, parents cited their lack of preparation for or knowledge of a child's problems or felt they were misinformed about a child's prognosis. Furthermore, whereas workers spoke of a child's not meeting parental expectations or of a failure to bond to the parent, parents emphasized a child's not wishing to be adopted or spoke of deficits in "bonding with other siblings."

After Disruption

What happened to these children after their adoptive placements disrupted? This is a key question, since the answer to it is of utmost importance when one thinks about adoption disruption. The focus here is not on the kinds of placements that immediately followed the disruption, nor on how many of the children experienced another disruption, but rather on a more important question: How many were ultimately adopted or were, at a minimum, in another adoptive placement awaiting legalization? Unfortunately, accurate figures are not available because the percentages reported are totally a function of when, after placements disrupted, the investigators asked the question. Therefore the figures underestimate the final outcome. Nevertheless, a review is important. For example, Kadushin and Seidl (1971) indicated that about 50% were adopted by other families and that adoptive placements were planned for yet more. Unger et al. (1977) reported that roughly 90% of the children were replaced in other adoptive families. Donley (1978), based on accumulated information from a number of specialized adoption programs, noted that more than 75% were successfully replaced. Boneh (1979) stated that nearly 40% of those whose placement disrupted had been legalized in another placement by the end of the study period. Boyne et al. (1984) reported that "many of those who disrupted" went on to a legalized adoption with other families. Benton et al. (1985) indicated that, in one state where information was usable, 41% were subsequently residing in another adoptive home and that others possibly would be so placed. Partridge et al. (1986) noted that 58% were placed again for adoption but that of the replaced cases 24% had again disrupted when case records were reviewed. Finally, Festinger (1986) found that within 6 to 18 months after a placement had disrupted, 42% had either been adopted or were in adoptive homes awaiting legalization, and adoption remained the plan for another 21%.

It is evident that disruptions, where they occur, are not the final blow and cannot be so regarded; nor can one say that these children could not make an adequate adjustment to an adoptive placement. The figures just cited show otherwise. In view of the emotional baggage that children bring to a placement, the multiplicity of factors in the home environment, and the flaws in our ability to predict their interaction, it is inevitable that some disruption will occur. The point is that disruptions do not end the hope for, nor likelihood of, a later successful adoption. In the process, children, families, and workers can learn how to improve the chances that the next placement will hold.

The figures on replacement suggest that for many there was a kind of mismatch, in the sense that the "chemistry" appeared to be wrong or soured after a time. This pattern is akin to what has been called a problem in the "goodness of fit" (Thomas & Chess, 1984), when the properties of the environment, its expectations and demands, are not in accord with the child's "own capacities, motivations, and style of behaving." It is also possible that some of these families misjudged their own abilities or were encouraged to adopt children who were really more than they could handle. Whatever the reason, it is apparent that at this particular point in time "these specific children and these specific parents were a failing combination" (Kadushin & Seidl, 1971).

This is not to say that adoption services for children like these need not be strengthened. The findings from studies suggest otherwise. They have shown that some configuration of factors are more risky and require more concentrated service efforts, and that staff training needs and the problems posed by staff discontinuities require review. Agencies need to consider ways to assist workers to recognize any tendency to ignore warning signals, and such mechanisms as self-persuasion, in order to help them to anticipate and assess vulnerability and areas of risk so that early intervention is possible before a crisis occurs.

The wonder is that in the long run most of these children do get adopted. That happy news is fast forgotten when disruptions occur. It is a jarring experience for all involved. Moves in foster care are handled with much more equanimity. The expectation that moves will not occur in adoptive placements all too often leads adoption workers to feel they have failed. This thinking needs to be addressed. More can be done by agencies to provide an open forum for discussion of these situations (Fitzgerald, 1979, 1983) and to foster an environment that avoids recrimination, blame, and defensiveness, an environment that moves "away from a model of practice based on success or failure" (Aldgate & Hawley, 1986). Adoptive placements of older children and of children with special problems oblige agencies to take risks. To do so implies that goals may not be reached. But not to do so also entails taking risks vis-à-vis children.

All children are not so vulnerable as they are often assumed to be. More faith in their strength and resilience is warranted (Festinger, 1983; Garmezy, 1974; Rutter,

1979). Ultimately the challenge we face does not concern the risk of disruption. Rather, the challenge is to do all that is necessary to identify and to free all children who do not have families that care or homes to which they can return, and to risk their adoptive placement so that all children are given the opportunity to grow up in families they can call their own.

NOTE

1. Since this chapter was written, another study on adoption disruption has been reported (Barth, Berry, Yoshikami, Goodfield, & Carson, 1988). In brief, the authors report on 926 children in adoptive placements between 1980 and mid-1984 in California. All data came from adoption placement forms filed with the state, supplemented by information about case outcomes. Most children were white, placed with foster parents, and at the time of the adoptive placement ranged in age from 3 to 17.9 years. By 1986, the overall rate of disruptions before or after legalization was 10.2%, a rate that was expected to rise to an estimated 11% with additional time. In comparison with stable placements, the children whose placements disrupted were more likely to be older, to be male, to have more problems, to have had a previous adoptive placement, and, if they were white, to be placed with nonfoster parents. Although higher rates of disruption were associated with higher education of the adoptive mothers, this was not the case for foster parent placements. Using a combination of five of these variables, the authors correctly predicted 70% of adoption placements. Other variables individually examined, such as sibling placements and single parent placements, were unrelated to outcome.

III
CLINICAL ISSUES IN ADOPTION

12

Family Treatment After Adoption: Common Themes

ANN HARTMAN AND JOAN LAIRD

Adoption is a social arrangement constructed in some human societies to respond to children in need of parents and parents in need of children. Adoption is defined and shaped through political and social processes and expresses the world views and values of its social context (Benet, 1976). This value-laden social arrangement varies from society to society and will change over time in relation to changes in the surrounding sociocultural contexts.

For example, among some groups in Polynesia, there is no adoption because children do not "belong" to their parents. They "belong" to the whole society and move at various points and for various reasons to different homes. Among some ethnic groups in the United States, where the extended family form is strong and viable, formal adoption is rare since children "belong" to the total extended family that shares and replaces parenting when necessary. In traditional Japan, as an expression of the importance of intergenerational continuity through the male line, it was not uncommon for a man to give his second son to his brother if that brother were without a male heir.

What are the values that have shaped adoption in this country? In our society, the legal foundations and ancestral definitions of adoption rest in English common law (Cole, 1985). Children "belong" to their parents. Children's rights have been sharply limited by the conception of the parent–child relationship. For example, translated into adoption, this not only means that parents may "give their children away" but may also deprive children of the right to know their families of origin. In another value and legal system, it might be possible to take the position that a mother cannot deprive her child of the right to know her own mother. This, of course, is the issue around which the search movement and open adoption revolve.

A second characteristic of North American culture that has a profound effect on adoptees and adoptive families is the strong value placed on the traditional nuclear biological family. This perspective has led all other families, including adoptive families, to be defined at best as substitute and at worst as deviant or deficient. Until very recently, adoption policy and practice largely were shaped by this value; the effort has been to model adoption as much as possible on biological parenting. In traditional adoption practice, only healthy infants were considered "adoptable" and every effort was made to "match" the baby to the parents in terms of biological characteristics. The presence of the agency was a concrete reminder that the family was different and, therefore, removed itself from the situation as soon as possible. Furthermore, since adoption was to mirror the process of building a family biologically, there was no need for postadoptive services. If parents or children had difficulties, questions, or concerns, they risked being labeled as "troubled."

The existence of the biological family was the most dramatic reminder that the adoptive family was indeed different from the biological family; thus there was collusion among those involved in adoption to remove this troublesome force in every way from the life of the child. Closed adoption, secrecy around the identity of the family, and the transmission to the child and adoptive parents of very limited and selected information about a biological family was the order of the day.

The effort to model adoption after biological parenting and even to deny the differences between these ways of building a family led to several outcomes. First, research on adoption and on how different members of the adoptive triangle experienced adoption was limited until relatively recently. David Kirk's (1964) early study was one exception. Kirk discovered, interestingly enough, that the family's and the adoptee's readiness to recognize, understand, and deal with the reality of adoption and the differences between the adoptive and the biological family was a crucial factor in the success of the adoption. (For a different point of view, see Chapter 7 by Kenneth Kay).

Second, not only did adoption agencies fail to recognize the need for or to offer postadoption services, but mental health and counseling professionals working with adoptees, adoptive families, or birthparents in the ordinary course of practice failed to recognize the central importance of adoption in the lives of their clients. Small (1987) has compared the collusive and protective processes, which go on in a family denying the importance of adoption and the existence of the biological family, with the dynamics of codependence in families organized around and protecting an alcoholic member. She suggests that professionals working in adoption have also exhibited codependent behaviors, colluding with the family and denying the difference between adoptive and biological parenting.

The past decade has witnessed a revolution in the construction of adoption. A social context has evolved in which adoption has been redefined and many of the beliefs and values that for many decades shaped the practice have been challenged. Many factors have contributed to these changes and although some agencies, professionals, and members of the adoptive triangle continue to cling to the traditional model, others are experimenting with new ways of responding to the needs of children in need of parents, parents in need of children, and parents unable to provide a permanent home for a child.

Key to the changes have been the "rights" movements, which were born in the 1960s and spread to many oppressed and disenfranchised groups in the 1970s. The children's rights and child advocacy movements contributed to the demand that every child has a right to a permanent family and home. The conviction that "every child is adoptable" began to shape a new kind of adoption practice, a practice that emphasized the adoption of older children and of children with special needs and a range of physical or psychological difficulties. Such adoptions could not mirror the biological model, as children came to families with histories, with memories, with lives that began before the day they joined the family (Borgman, 1982).

The adoptee's rights and search movements, supported by a family therapy movement with a body of theory that stressed the importance of connection with the family of origin and the destructive effects of secrets in the family, questioned the basic structure of traditional adoption. Some agencies, responding to this challenge, began to experiment with various forms of open adoption. At the same time, the availability of adequate birth control measures, legalized abortion, and changing norms that made it possible for an unmarried woman to keep and raise her child sharply diminished the supply of white infants available to white childless couples. Such couples began turning to interracial and international adoption or to special needs adoption to build their families.

Finally, the growing interest in the family and in adoption has led to increased attention to this fascinating human arrangement and to the gathering and sharing of knowledge and theory about adoption, which is found in this volume. Some clinicians have identified themselves as specialists in adoption practice, working with adult adoptees, adoptive families, and birthparents. However, it would appear that many clinicians continue to be unaware of and unresponsive to adoption when it emerges in their caseloads. Issues surrounding adoption are rarely explored in the clinical journals or at the major professional conferences. Instead, conferences and workshops focused on adoption, even if aimed at the therapeutic community, are primarily attended by adoption workers.

The practitioner, working in a mental health facility, a hospital, a family agency, in private practice, in fact in any clinical setting, will encounter some connection with adoption in many of his or her cases; the client whose mother was adopted, the adult adoptee, the man or woman who relinquished a child, the adoptive family seeking help for an adopted child or for some kind of family stress. Furthermore, because of the many changes in the institution of adoption, therapists will see adults and young people in conflict over search issues, they will see families that adopted an infant through the traditional model and families that have had quite a different experience, perhaps having adopted an older child or a child with special needs. In each of these situations, the relevance of adoption must be explored, losses surfaced and dealt with, mysteries demystified, and connections made.

Adoptive families may come to the attention of mental health professionals or enter into counseling situations for the same reasons or concerns that lead any family to seek or be referred for help. They may identify the adoption as an issue of concern, but often do not. Many therapeutic approaches may be used, as with any family, depending on the nature of the problem or the orientation of the therapist.

A comprehensive approach to the treatment of adoptive families will not be presented here, since much of the work is generic, requiring knowledge and skill in family treatment. A family-centered treatment approach to adoptive families receiving postplacement services primarily around the adjustment period and the integration of the child into the family has been presented elsewhere (Hartman, 1984). The focus of this chapter will be on the common themes that arise with some frequency in the course of therapeutic work with adoptive families. Our wish is to sensitize practitioners to these themes so that when they encounter adoptive families, no matter what the presenting problem, they may listen more carefully for adoption issues and may be more alert to the possibility that adoption-related experiences are interacting with or complicating other issues of concern to the family and the therapist. The themes explored here include:

1. Assessment issues with adoptive families
2. Powerlessness and empowerment
3. The salience of adoption
4. The "bad seed" myth
5. The adoption story
6. Kidnapping guilt
7. The "perfect parent" requirement
8. Cutoffs and connections
9. Leaving home

As the various themes are explored, they will be illustrated with examples drawn from a family-centered practice center. Work with two families, each of which sought help for an adopted teenage child, will be drawn on most heavily. In one family, the child was an older "special needs" adoptee, and in the other, the child came to the family when she was 5-days-old via a traditional adoptive agency placement.

ASSESSMENT ISSUES WITH ADOPTIVE FAMILIES

In most families with children, the child has been a part of the family system since birth; both nature and nurture have been provided by the family system. The adoptive family has had a different experience, however, and thus the adoption situation provides a different context for assessment. The adopted child of today, for example, has frequently had several years of life experiences before placement, experiences that may have been, at least in part, painful and destructive. Most adopted children have suffered major and multiple losses and disruptions; many have experienced severe neglect, physical abuse, or sexual abuse.

It is, of course, crucial to complete a family assessment and to listen for and explore very carefully the adoption story and related myths, and the influences of the adoption experiences in this family. Each family will have had its unique experiences and will have organized around the adoption in particular ways. There are some commonalities of experience, however. In the following pages, we present some of the different kinds of postadoptive family situations encountered. These clearly are very general and overlapping descriptions, but suggest ways families typically present; the postadoption clinician must be alert both to general themes and to the particularities of each situation.

The Average Family with a Troubled Child

In this situation, a family that probably would not have experienced too much difficulty with an average child is struggling to manage a child that came to them after a damaging infancy or early childhood. The child may have behavioral or other difficulties that would strain the patience and the resources of the most competent of families. Such a family may need affirmation and support as well as help in enhancing their management skills. Therapy may involve linking the family with extrafamilial resources, structural interventions, help in setting limits and boundaries, or clarifying roles, rules, and communication. An important task in family work is to discover in what ways the family's responses to the child's difficulties inadvertently may be exacerbating them and to help the family alter or even reverse their responses.

For example, the Wagners, who had adopted a 4-year-old girl, Kerry, about 18 months before coming to the agency, were concerned that they were failing as adoptive parents. (All case materials are carefully disguised to maintain confidentiality and to protect the identities of families and children.) Kerry had been badly neglected in a foster home and had many symptoms of emotional disturbance when she arrived at the home of the Wagners. An extremely bright, active, verbal child who had quickly made many gains in the Wagner home, Kerry, a month into kindergarten, stole some materials from another child's desk. Mr. and Mrs. Wagner, mental health professionals themselves, were extremely distressed and had overreacted to the incident. In this situation, in spite of their knowledge of child development and the fact that healing might take a long time, the adoptive parents began to worry that Kerry was simply "too disturbed" and that they were not adequate to "make the difference" in her life. Kerry's incident was positively reframed as her wish to make a connection with another child, while the Wagners were reassured that they were doing a heroic job of parenting. Together we worked to further understand the meaning of the stealing.

The Troubled Family with a Troubled Child

In this kind of situation, either the family has organized and is maintaining itself around the child's troubles or is using the troubled child as an object on which to project the family's or the marital pair's difficulties. Adoptees, particularly since they tend to be located closer to the outer boundary of the family, make very convenient scapegoats. Not only may all of the family's troubles be heaped on the adopted child's back, but also, when such a scapegoated child develops symptoms, the troubles may be blamed on his or her preadoption experience or heredity. Finally, to complete the scapegoating process, it is sometimes easier for the family to drive such a child out than to face their own unresolved conflicts.

A failure to recognize this kind of situation can lead to painful outcomes for all involved, as in the following example.

Donna and Jack McDonnell sought help with their 15-year-old son, Steven, whom they had adopted at age 7. Steven was described as aggressive and hostile with the family, although he seemed to be doing fairly well in school in terms of achievement and did have a small circle of friends. At the time of the referral by an adoption agency, the family was in the midst of finalizing the adoption of David, an 8-year-old boy whom they had been fostering for some months. The family believed that Steven was very threatened by the change and claimed that his behavior had deteriorated markedly since David's placement.

The parents, clearly worried that the second adoption might be in jeopardy, presented themselves as concerned, "perfect" parents who had done their best to cope with Steven, whom they saw as a very damaged, violent child who had come to them that way at age 7. Their view was that they had done their best, had made many sacrifices, but that Steven was hopelessly disturbed and in need of placement in an institution. It quickly became clear to the therapists that the family's hope was to expel Steven and to replace him with David, a seemingly docile young boy. The parents were extremely guarded about family history as well as about their marriage. They preferred to blame Steven for the family difficulties and resisted attempts to broaden the discussion.

After several weeks, the parents and David came in without Steven, whom the mother reported had been kept after school for a makeup exam. In this session, the family's guard was somewhat lowered and, while David became involved in an elaborate building game, the couple talked more freely. This discussion surfaced some indications of serious marital tension as well as intergenerational patterns of alcohol abuse and violence. It became clear, from the description of an incident over the previous weekend, which involved excessive drinking and irresponsible behavior on the part of Jack, that Donna's rage toward her husband was being channeled through Steven. Jack, on the other hand, seemed relieved to have a substitute. It also became evident through some oblique references that Jack's drinking problem, which had been carefully hidden, was long-standing. The therapists believed that they were finally making some progress in understanding the family dynamics and that the family was beginning to be engaged in the process of change.

The parents arrived for the next session without Steven. Donna immediately announced, with a somewhat triumphant expression, that Steven had been hospitalized in the adolescent unit in the state hospital over the weekend, after "attacking" his father with an axe. Although presented as an unprovoked attack, careful and detailed tracking of the actions and interactions around the event revealed that there had been enormous provocation and escalation by both parents and that, in actuality, Steven, chased and cornered by Jack in the garage, had picked up an axe, saying "Don't come near me!" at which point the police were called.

The family terminated treatment, indicating that their problem was solved. Steven seemed headed for long-term hospitalization; the scapegoat had been extruded from the family system. It is quite likely that, in the previous session, the family's survival strategy had been threatened and they had had to reestablish a balance and a definition of themselves as a healthy and long-suffering couple, struggling with a seriously disturbed child.

The Troubled Family with an Average Child

This type of family typically will not come to the attention of the helping professions unless neglect or abuse of the child is suspected, or unless the child begins to demonstrate symptoms which call the attention of school personnel or others to the family. A serious example of this kind of situation was referred to one of the authors some years ago. A 3-year-old girl from Southeast Asia, adopted through an international group that did not conduct a home study, was badly scalded by her adoptive mother. The mother had dipped the child's hands in boiling water, seeing the child as sexually evil, after she found the child scratching a vaginal rash. Subsequent exploration exposed other incidents of abuse. The child was removed from this very dysfunctional family after the father finally admitted he was concerned for his daughter's safety, indeed her life. A home study might have surfaced the mother's paranoid ideation, the serious marital difficulties in this family, the father's need to keep his wife occupied, and the mother's need to have a perfect child.

The Average Family with an Average Child

This type of family may also experience some difficulty because of the special demands, stresses, and vulnerabilities inherent in the adoption situation. In this chapter, we will focus primarily on such families. Although the special characteristics of the adoptive situation may exacerbate problems in families which already had the potential for serious dysfunction, they increase the vulnerability in the average family as well.

POWERLESSNESS AND EMPOWERMENT

One theme that echoes and reechoes in the adoption experience is that of powerlessness. Aspects of the adoptive situation may serve to disempower every member of the adoption triangle. The fact that the parents in an adoptive family have been unable to have a biological child likely has been experienced both as a loss and as disempowering (Blum, 1983; Brinich, Chapter 3; Kirk, 1964; Schechter, 1970). They probably planned to have children, wanted to have children, and found themselves helpless, unable to carry out the socially expected roles and functions that accompany marriage. The couple may also experience a sense of powerlessness in their relationship with the adoption agency. No matter how skillfully the adoptive home study and decision-making process is conducted, no matter how much the adoptive couple is encouraged to participate, the couple is still placing themselves in a position where others—the workers, the agency, the court—will decide whether or not they may become parents. The couple is very likely to feel helpless and anxious in this situation.

When a family seeks help, it is important that the therapist explore and be sensitive to the previous experiences the family has had with helping professionals and to understand that some of the residue of that experience may affect the current process. The family may, initially, seem very compliant, giving considerable power to the therapist, or they may be guarded and wary, expecting to be evaluated or judged. It is important early in the contact to learn about the experience with the adoption agency, to surface the connection the family may be making between the therapy and the home study experience and, appropriately, to separate the two.

The adoptive family may also feel powerless to alter what they interpret as the powerful forces of heredity and the lasting damaging effects of early trauma. Families feel particularly powerless when they have been deprived of information about children's backgrounds, information that might provide them with clues to understanding and helping. They also suffer from feelings of helplessness and incompetence when they find they are unable to experience themselves as successful parents.

Birthparents also feel powerless in that they often regretfully relinquish a child, forced to do so by social or family pressures, lack of resources, or court action growing out of their inability to provide care. In most cases, although the situation may be partly, at least, "of their own making," it is rarely of their own choosing (Brodzinsky, Chapter 16).

Finally, adoptees are the most disempowered of all, having generally had no opportunity to participate in the decisions that have so powerfully shaped their lives and their identities. Their fates have literally been in the hands of others. They are further disempowered as adults when they are deprived of the right to know their birthfamilies or to learn firsthand of their heritages (Schechter & Bertocci, Chapter 4). Even adult adoptees who seek professional help in conducting a search may experience further disempowerment. Many progressive agencies and professionals who work with adoptees in the search process insist that they play a mediating role, thus to a large extent controlling the process. Leaders of the adoptee search movement, however, object to this division of responsibility on the basis that it replicates the disempowering adoption situation, once again putting the destiny of the adoptee in the hands of others.

The empowerment theme should also help to inform the child's experience in treatment. Adopted children become empowered as they are given permission to be interested in or curious about their backgrounds and as the fact of their existence prior to placement is validated.

An important practice principle, then, is to work in such a way that helps to empower adoptive families, a way that increases their ability to shape their own situations. This principle implies an egalitarian, collaborative, consultative model in which all concerned contribute their own special resources and skills to the problem-solving situation.

THE SALIENCE OF ADOPTION⁻

The salience of adoption should always be explored and evaluated in any situation where it exists, even though it may seem remote to the issue at hand or the family is denying its importance or relevance. For example, intergenerational adoption themes may surface during the construction of a genogram. In one family, a very strict, rigid, religious family, all three of the daughters had become pregnant out-of-wedlock at around the age of 17. We learned that their unknown maternal grandmother had given birth to their mother when she was 17, then relinquished her for adoption. Their mother had died without learning anything of her birth heritage.

Another family, the Cartwrights, whom we will follow throughout this chapter, sought help for their daughter Sharon, age 15. In not atypical fashion, in the first few moments of the first session, the parents volunteered that Sharon was adopted and then quickly added that they were sure that had nothing to do with the current problem.

This is the family's invitation to the worker to join them in ignoring and denying the importance of the adoption. It is often useful at this point for the worker to take a different position, commenting that often adoption is an extremely relevant issue in any family where one has taken place. The worker reframes the adoption as central and important and does not join the family's denial. Such a stance is often a surprise to the family, but also a relief, since it denotes a beginning of open communication about the adoption. We are likely to move more slowly than did Carl Whitaker, whom we observed opening an interview with an adoptive family by turning to the teenage adoptee and asking "Where are your real parents?" However, by the end of the first session with the Cartwrights, it was apparent to all how crucial the adoption was to Sharon and to her adoptive parents.

THE "BAD SEED" MYTH

Although our culture is generally thought to subscribe to the view that nurture is more powerful than nature, the theme of the power of biology and heredity is frequently encountered among adoptive parents. Such parents come to feel that no matter what they do, the "taint" of heredity will shape the character or personality of their child. This dread of the influence of heredity is often suppressed or denied, only to emerge in an overreactive response to what in other families might be defined as a minor infraction of the rules.

An extension of the "bad seed" theme is found in the fear in parents that have adopted older children that the child will never recover from early, preadoptive experiences, no matter how much care and love they invest. This dread of the shadow of the past, whether it be biological or experiential, emerges and is dealt with in different ways in different families.

Frequently, such fear is dealt with by attempting to totally cut off the past, to pretend that the biological family never existed and the early years never took place. Such an emotional cutoff, of course, makes the past even more powerful, as it severs the family from the knowledge and understanding of the past that can lead to mastery and the consolidation of the adoptee's identity.

Furthermore, both psychodynamic and family systems theorists suggest that the lost or cut off figures can assume great importance. These ghosts from the past are incorporated; they become strong sources of identification, even though their images may be misty or distorted (Bowen, 1978; Hartman & Laird, 1983; Littner, 1956d). In fact, many theorists suggest that cut off, denied, and lost figures, the so-called family "ghosts" who become part of family mythology or family secrecy, can become as powerful a force in individual and family dynamics as familiar family members or available information that can be dealt with and mastered. When the fear of the influence of the past is handled through a cut off, the very thing the adoptive family is most afraid of becomes more likely. For example, Sharon's family sought help when their adopted daughter, who had always been a loving and rather conforming child, suddenly began acting out sexually. Sharon had been placed at the age of 5 days through a very traditional agency that supported totally closed adoption. All Sharon knew of her biological parents was that they were college students and unmarried.

This was the family that announced in the first minutes of the session that they knew Sharon's troubles had *nothing* to do with her adoption. After an exploration of the presenting concern, the family therapist asked Sharon, "How old was your birth mother when you were born?" Sharon shrugged and looked anxiously at her mother who responded that she had been 20. The therapist turned to Sharon and said, "I don't see why you are in such a hurry, you still have five years!" At first the family looked shocked and then the parents began to laugh and even Sharon smiled. The tension was broken, the sexual behavior reframed, and the salience of the adoption was suggested. This laid the groundwork for the family to begin to deal with the adoption issue together in the following sessions. Of course, the potential power of the family's expectations in shaping a child's self-image, the power of a self-fulfililng prophecy is obvious. The family's fears tend to contribute to the creation of the very thing it dreads most.

The theme of the "bad seed," the dread of the power of the past, was a central and recurring theme in the Higgins family. Jeff and Mary had adopted Tom, a hearing–impaired child, at the age of seven. They sought help when Tom was 15, after he was caught stealing a box of condoms from a drug store. It was clear that the parents, a socially conservative working-class couple, were intensely overreacting to the incident and were interpreting this behavior as the beginning of a downward cycle that could only end in antisocial or criminal behavior. They arrived at the first session carrying an inch-thick case record which contained extensive and rather grave psychological, social, and psychiatric reports on Tom. The case record seemed to be a metaphor for their "bad seed" fears.

The resolution of their fears about the power of the past was a major focus of therapy with both the adoptive parents and Tom. First, the unspoken fears were explored; simply bringing their anxieties to light was relieving. Second, in the course of our exploration, it was discovered that the placement agency, in its wish to be as fully sharing as possible with the family, had turned over all of Tom's records. These included frightening and confusing psychological terms that convinced the couple that something was very wrong with Tom, although they were not sure what it was.

One of the members of the therapy team was a psychologist, and as most of the frightening reports were written by a psychologist, the team agreed that she should review the reports and clarify the materials with the family and the therapy team. She used this opportunity to demystify the reports and challenge their power as predictors of the future or as very relevant to Tom, to the young man he had become in this family.

As the theme was further explored, it became apparent that the parents, out of their fears, had been overcontrolling and overintrusive. Tom had responded by being secretive and self-protective. The family framed Tom's efforts to keep some territory private as sneakiness and dishonesty. Furthermore, Tom's silence fueled the family's fears and exacerbated their need to control. Tom's mother said over and over that the only thing she couldn't stand was "not knowing." This turned out to be a very important theme in the family as not only Tom but his father also kept his own counsel, which drove Mary to distraction. Both Tom and his father handled Mary's anxious and sometimes explosive reactivity by falsely reassuring her or by the strategy that "what she doesn't know won't hurt her."

In more troubled families, the bad seed theme creates a fertile soil for scapegoating, as the family can totally repudiate any connection with the child's problems, attributing all of the family's difficulties to what they have decided are the child's character defects.

THE ADOPTION STORY

Human beings story their worlds. Through story and narrative they endow experience with meaning, transmitting those meanings in various altered forms throughout the family life cycle and down through the generations. Stories and other narratives are used to explain ourselves to ourselves and to others and to consolidate a sense of self (Byng-Hall, 1988; Laird, 1989, Schafer, 1980; Whan, 1979). Family stories are shared narratives that encapsulate and transmit values and prescriptions for living, shaping and ordering the family's history. Stories are particularly likely to develop around major events in the individual's or family's life as explanations, as cautionary tales, as crucial aspects of the family's narrative. The family "story" explains and recreates its origin and its identity, its proclamation of "this is who we are, this is how we got here, this is what it means to be part of this family." Events that are somewhat ambiguous or contradictory particularly invite storying, perhaps as a means through which the ambiguity may be clarified or resolved.

Recently, we have become interested in the importance of story in the individual's or the family's life and the meaning of story in therapy. Therapy, for individuals and families, can be a process through which stories are told and retold, shared and understood, the meanings examined and reconsidered, the endings confirmed or refashioned (Draeger, 1983; Laird, 1989).

Central in the life of the adoptive family, of course, is the adoption story. The importance and uniqueness of the event, the lack of definition, and the ambiguity seem to stimulate storytelling. The adoption story is so important that stories have been published for adoptive families to read to their children, universal adoption stories, such as *The Chosen Baby* (1950). In fact, the notion of the "chosen baby" serves to mythologize adoption, presenting a stereotyping explanatory image with which the family and child may identify. One adult adoptee, who remembers being read *The Chosen Baby* and making it, for a time, a part of her adoption story, recalls thinking that women made babies for people who wanted them; then adoptive parents would go to a place, rather like a furniture store, where there were many babies, selecting one that they thought would fit into their home (Hartman, 1984).

Families, aware of the importance of the adoption story, frequently seek help from adoption agencies concerning what and when they should tell their child about the adoption. In working with adoptive families and adult adoptees over the years, it became apparent that the construction and transmission of the adoption story is a great deal more complicated than reading *The Chosen Baby*. What becomes obvious is that there is a public and official adoption story, often brief and without detail; furthermore, each member of the family has shaped his or her own version, often unshared. The adoption story tends to be an explanatory tale that includes some kind of answer to the following questions. Where did the child come from? Why was he or she available for adoption? Who were the biological parents? What were the circumstances of the adoptee's birth? Why did the parents relinquish the child? Why did the adoptive parents choose to adopt? How did it happen that this particular child and this particular family got together?

Adopted children piece their stories together from many sources, a little factual information, a chance remark, stories they have heard from others, and their own fantasies. The less information the child has and the less the adoption story is told and retold, the more the child creates his or her own explanatory tale. The more secrecy there is about the adoption and the more anxiety generated around the story, the more the child is likely to become convinced that the adoption story is dangerous, bad, or hurtful.

For example, one adult adoptee of 45 had lived all her life with the adoption story that her mother did not want her and thus gave her away in infancy to friends who then gave her to her adoptive parents. The image of an unwanted infant passed around until a generous adoptive family takes her in was an important part of her sense of herself. Another part of her story was that she was characterized by her adoptive family as having been a serious, sober child who never smiled from the day she came to their home. This corroborated the picture of the unloved and unlovable baby.

The client's detective work around her own adoption story revealed to her that she had remained with her birthmother, a single working woman, until she was 18-months-old. She learned that her mother, long before social or economic supports were available, had made every effort to keep her. Finally, with great pain, she had given up her daughter for adoption. Not only does the mother become redefined as the adoption story is reconstructed, but the unlovable, unsmiling infant becomes a depressed toddler who has inexplicably lost her mother.

We have found that frequently the core of work with an adoptive family or with an adopted individual is the telling, the retelling, the sharing, and the reconstruction of the adoption story. Some writers have termed this therapeutic narrativizing process a "self-constructive" process (Gergen & Gergen, 1983).

The major portion of the work with the Cartwright family, previously mentioned, might be described as a reshaping, a reconstructing of the adoption story. The telling of the story began in the first session when the worker asked Sharon how old her birthmother had been when she was born. Sharon's lack of information and anxious glance at her parents signaled the need for adoption story work. As Sharon was asked more about her adoption and was vague and uncertain, the parents expressed their amazement, saying they had told Sharon all about her adoption. The worker responded supportively, saying she was sure that they had, but that it had been discovered in working with adoptive families that the story must be told over and over again.

The next three sessions were devoted to the telling of the adoption story in all of the detail appropriate for a young person of Sharon's age. In the next session, the family brought their photo albums and with great feeling went through the day by day process of the adoption. They had obtained Sharon from a traditional adoption agency that offered a residential program for primarily middle-class pregnant women. Sharon's birthparents had been college students.

Sharon's version of the adoption story had been that her mother had given birth to her but had never seen her. The Cartwrights were stunned by this news, indicating they had no idea where Sharon had gotten that idea. The fact was that Sharon's biological mother had insisted not only on seeing Sharon, but on taking care of her for the few days before she was placed with her adoptive family, even though the agency was somewhat disapproving. This information was enormously meaningful for Sharon. Fantasies of maternal rejection have many levels and for Sharon the story had been that her birthmother had not even wanted to touch her, to look into her face! When she learned about her birthmother's caring, she beamed, her eyes filling with tears, and she asked, "You mean she really held me? She really knew me?"

A second major theme in this adoption story was the joy and fulfillment experienced by the adoptive parents through the adoption. As they reminisced about seeing Sharon for the first time, about bringing her home, about their first days and weeks together, Sharon reexperienced their happiness and pleasure in her.

The part of the narrative that had not been shared with Sharon was the full story on why the family had adopted, of their infertility. Mrs. Cartwright had clearly not wanted to share her pain about her infertility, partly through shame about her sense of failure as a woman and partly because it might communicate to Sharon a feeling that they were disappointed that they had to turn to adoption. As Mrs. Cartwright told this part of the adoption story, she wept again about the loss but also spoke of how adopting Sharon had healed the pain. Sharon was clearly very involved.

Different life stages and different individual concerns make different parts of the adoption story more salient. For this young woman, at this time in her life, issues of mothers and babies, of fertility and infertility, of female sexuality are central, and when these issues are rich with special significance but clouded with secrecy, their salience can be intensified. Young women can wonder, "Will I be fertile like my birthmother (often negatively framed as "too fertile"), or infertile like my adoptive mother?" An early pregnancy can provide an answer to that question. In most adoption stories, the birthfather is strangely absent—an even more mysterious figure than the birthmother. The fantasy is often that the birthfather impregnated the birthmother and then abandoned her. In all the detective work the older adoptee mentioned above did to reconstruct her adoption story, she was able to obtain no information about her birthfather. Often, the only access to information about the birthfather is through the mother and, even if-she is available, she may be reluctant to discuss the father. In the past, agencies serving unwed mothers often joined in the exclusion of the putative fathers, as if males had little to do with the process and no real connection with the child, an assumption now more actively questioned in the adoption literature (Deykin, Patti, & Ryan, 1988).

For the young woman, who as a child thought that women made babies for people who wanted them, it was many years before she was able to write her father into her story. When she finally found her mother, who had been abandoned by her father, a married serviceman stationed far from home, her birthmother was reluctant to identify him. When the adoptee finally did learn enough about him to be able to search for him, she discovered that he had died some years earlier; however, she was able to locate an older half brother. Her father had told his son, as an adult, about the existence of this child, had expressed guilt and sadness, and had continued to wonder and worry about her.

Agency policy and case law regarding putative fathers and protecting their rights will make it more difficult in the future for the father to be excluded from the adoption story (*Stanley* v. *Illinois,* 1972). In working with families around the adoption story, even if there is no information, it is important that therapists not fall into the trap of excluding him or fantasies and assumptions about him from the story.

The adoption stories in the Higgins family surfaced in bits and pieces over the several months of family therapy. Tom spontaneously brought his life book to the second session, guiding the therapists through the album as he reconstructed his life. Since Tom had not been placed for adoption until he was 7-years-old, the adoption story was much entangled: a complex situation in the birthfamily; two extended stays in foster homes; and much information, misinformation, memory, and fantasy about the adoption story to be shared, sorted out, and clarified. The long process cannot be detailed here, but some stories and reminiscences that were shared are particularly germane to this discussion.

The generally accepted adoption story was that Tom's mother, Marge, had been unable or unwilling to care for Tom and had abandoned him. Tom's version was that she had been unable to manage him because his hearing impairment made him so difficult to handle, because he was "bad," a version that was to some extent shared and promoted by his adoptive parents. For the parents, this version supported a contrasting parental image of themselves as burdened but dedicated "good" parents. At one point, however, Tom told of his mother's several visits to his foster home. He remembered these visits clearly and described them in some detail. Mr. and Mrs. Higgins were amazed to learn that Tom had continued to have contact with his birthmother until shortly before his adoption, a fragment of historical information that conflicted sharply with the abandoning mother assumption.

Another important moment occurred when everyone was telling his or her version of the actual placement and Tom was able to tell his parents that he hadn't wanted to leave his foster home. While this contribution restimulated Mrs. Higgins' feelings of insecurity about her status as primary mother, both parents were able to listen, to hear of Tom's losses, to empathize with his pain and to understand and accept his attachment to the Andersons, his last foster family. The issues of "impaired" hearing became a metaphor for everyone's issues in this family.

We have discovered that not only does each adoptive family and each member in the family have their adoption story, but also that most people working in the field of adoption and, for that matter, most therapists, also have their own adoption stories. In workshops on adoption practice and in working with therapists around adoption issues, it became quite apparent that counselors, as well as the members of the adoption triangle, feel passionately about adoption, about whether adoption should be open or closed, about the search process, and about other issues which emerge from their own "adoption" experiences. We began to encourage professionals we were working with in training sessions to share, in small groups, their own "adoption story." Most of us have such stories, a narrative of an adoption, a placement, some kind of adoption-like situation which has had significance in our lives. The almost universal fantasy of having been adopted and the many fairy tales with adoption or confused parenthood themes give further evidence of the importance of the adoption theme and frequently provide a context for people's adoption stories. In the course of doing this exercise, adoption professionals come face to face with their own adoption stories for the first time, heightening awareness of their own special images of adoption, images which often have great relevance for their approaches to practice.

KIDNAPPING GUILT

Recently one of the authors received a Christmas letter from an adoptive family she had studied for an out-of-state adoption. The mother wrote, "Not a day goes by that I don't think about Brian's birthmother and what she is missing." Many adoptive families experience strong feelings of empathy, pity, or even what might be called "kidnapping guilt" in relation to the birthparents, particularly the birthmother. In other words, they experience sadness for the birthmother around the loss of the child and they feel grateful and sometimes even guilty that they have benefited through another's misfortunes. (For more discussion of this point, see Chapter 3 by Paul Brinich.) In order to deal with these painful feelings, in order to justify having the child, they may characterize the birthparents very negatively. If they can see the birthparents as unworthy they can separate themselves from them and feel that the child is far better off in the adoptive home. Empathy with the birthparents may be supportive of the adoptive child but can be difficult for the adoptive family.

The "kidnapping" issue came up in a particularly dramatic way with the Higgins. The therapists, wanting to surface some of the depression evident in the family asked, "Tom, who do you think is the saddest person in the family?" "Marge," he said, referring to his birthmother. Everyone, including the therapists, was surprised. Mary Higgins, with considerable anxiety and pressure, said "I don't think Tom understood the question." "Yes, I did," said Tom quietly, and then began to look anxious himself.

The image of Marge as a sad figure who had lost her child, as a person who had maintained contact, who had tried and failed to make a home for Tom, began to emerge, a picture quite different from the neglectful, abandoning image expressed in the first version. In time, Mary, who had defended herself from kidnapping guilt by being extremely critical of the birthmother, began to feel sorry for her, to identify with her, and to see her, at least in part, as a victim of overwhelming circumstances. The pain in this shift was evident when, during one session, Mary cried for Marge and her difficult life. This shift was extremely helpful for Tom and culminated in his writing Marge a letter, with the support of his adoptive parents, to tell her how well he was doing so that she would not feel so sad.

THE "PERFECT PARENT" REQUIREMENT

Very much connected with kidnapping guilt is the tendency on the part of adoptive parents to feel that they must be perfect parents. This tendency often has several sources. The obvious one is the special pressure to do well with a child brought into the world by others. This is exaggerated by the home study process, no matter how carefully and respectfully accomplished, which tends to set up expectations that adoptive parents somehow must be better than parents who create families biologically. They, unlike biological parents, must demonstrate before the fact that they will be good parents. It may also be that infertile couples experience a sense of failure in their inability to have a child, have a need to undo that failure, and thus have a greater need to prove that they can be successful parents (Kirk, 1964).

Mary Higgins, who tended to demand a great deal of herself in every area of her life, also demanded perfection of herself as a mother. This perfectionism became a major focus of our work with her. She could not forgive herself when she became angry with Tom and alternated between a "bad seed" explanation of Tom's difficulties to feeling each problem was evidence of her failure as a mother.

After a particularly painful conflict between Mary and Tom, Mary was so ashamed that she cancelled two family sessions. The turning point came when the family returned to therapy and Mary was able to talk about her own reactivity to Tom and how badly she felt when she was unfairly and inappropriately angry at and critical of him. She was also able to ask her husband for help with her overreactivity. Jeff, more calm and less concerned than his wife about some of Tom's behavior, nevertheless felt helpless and uncertain during the conflicts. If he could be more active in dealing with Tom, if he could give her more emotional support and more feedback, she felt that she would not have to carry the complete burden and could "let up" a little. She invited Jeff, who was never critical of her and was somewhat fearful of her emotionality, to give her more feedback, to let her know when she was overreacting. He agreed he would give it a try.

At the end of the session, the therapy team congratulated Mary for having the courage to acknowledge that she could not be a perfect mother. They pointed out that this confession had been very helpful to Tom who could not be a perfect son and to Jeff, who could not be a perfect father. Her ability to accept and own her imperfection was reframed as a way to help the whole family.

The issue of Mary's perfectionism, self-condemnation, and depression continued to be a focus in working with this family. The contributions of intergenerational and marital issues to the maintenance of Mary in this position were further explicated and shifts were made. It was clear that the theme in which the adoptive parent must be a perfect parent fell on fertile soil in this family.

CUTOFFS AND CONNECTIONS

Cutoffs and connections are important themes in all families and frequently become central in therapeutic process with any family in treatment. In adoptive families, the issue of cutoff, of severed connections, is almost always of major concern, although it may well be cloaked in secrecy. The adoptive parent tends to be threatened by the shadowy figures from the child's past and the child, sensing the parents' anxiety and fear, protects the family by denying and burying his or her curiosity, concern, or longing. In any adoptive family, the connection, or the severed connection with the past, must be surfaced, discussed, and dealt with. How it is dealt with will differ in relation to the specific circumstances in each situation.

The telling and retelling of the adoption story begins the process of making connections. In situations where there has been a sharp cutoff at the point of adoption and the past is forbidden territory, the child's sense of the continuity of person, of identity, is ruptured. Robert Jay Lifton (1986) and Betty Jean Lifton (1975) have written meaningfully about the importance of continuity with the past and with the future for our sense of humanness, and about adoption and the possibility of nuclear war as two very different threats to continuity.

Sharon and her family moved quite quickly to address the issues of cutoff and making connections. The sharing of the adoption story healed one rupture in Sharon's sense of continuity when she learned that her birthmother did not abandon her at birth, but chose to care for her until her placement. Subsequently, the family spoke together about the possibility of undertaking a search for Sharon's birthparents, a possibility that was very much complicated by the philosophy of the agency through which they had adopted. Sharon said, as adoptees typically do at this age, that she did not want to search for her birthparents, but her parents told her that if she ever did want to embark on a search, they would help her in any way they could. This permission and possibility for the future symbolically helped heal the cutoff. In the fifth and final session the family announced their intention to return to their home state for a visit in the summer and to go to the agency and meet with Sharon's social worker who, they had learned, was still on the staff. Sharon wanted to see where she had come from and to talk with someone who had actually known her birthmother. The family supported the plan and felt it would be helpful for them all to have more information about Sharon's birthparents.

Tom had experienced several cutoffs in his life, the most important of which were the one from his birthfamily and the one from the Anderson foster family, where he had lived for several years. Tom had been particularly protective of his adoptive family, especially Mary, and had expressed no interest in any kind of connection with either his birth or foster family until well into our work. Finally, after he had been able to tell his family of his reluctance to leave the Andersons, and they were able to hear that, Tom began to express more interest, in a very guarded way, in the Andersons. His parents initially discouraged that interest, and the therapists' first assumption was that they were feeling insecure and threatened. However, when it was learned that they had supported Tom's ongoing connection with the foster family in earlier years, even to the extent of taking him to another state to visit them the year after the adoption, it became apparent something else was going on. When this was explored, the Higgins, with anxious looks at Tom and lowering their voices so that he could not hear, expressed protectiveness of Tom and their anger at the Andersons who had not answered the last two letters Tom had sent three years earlier.

As this information was brought into the session, Tom expressed his hurt and anger that they had not written and then the fact came out that the Andersons, a farm family with several children, had adopted two foster children placed with them, but of course not Tom. This was a new part of the adoption story. After considerable discussion of this, with opportunity for all to express their interpretations of that experience, the therapy team felt that Tom and his adoptive family were ready to try to recontact the Andersons and to deal with the disappointments and hurt, should they not respond.

Since it was shortly before Christmas, the therapy team gave the family the assignment of sending a Christmas card to the Andersons, enclosing a picture of Tom. Before long, an apologetic, enthusiastic, and newsy letter arrived, giving information about all of the family and inviting Tom and his parents to attend the wedding of one of the older boys, which was to take place in a few months. Correspondence continued back and forth through the winter and early spring and at the time treatment ended, the Higgins were planning to attend the wedding.

The search for and the building of connections was, for Tom, similar to the work of an archeologist on a dig who first explores a more recent civilization and then digs deeper to the older city on which the newer one was built. After considerable talk and reminiscence about the Andersons, conversation shifted to a focus on Tom's birthfamily, culminating in Tom's letter to his mother, which was written around the time of his birthday, a time that often stimulates feelings of longing, loss, anger, and curiosity for birthparents and adoptees.

Tom was able to tell the Higgins that he would like to see his birthmother again sometime, but not right away. Mary, out of her own insecurity, thought Tom had said that he wanted to *live* with his mother one day, and she became quite upset. Her mishearing of what Tom said, pointed out by Jeff, in his new role of helping her with her reactivity and of giving her feedback, provided an opportunity to explore her fantasies about losing Tom to his birthmother. Tom, in turn, was amazed that she was worried and frightened, a meaningful validation of her caring for him. Jeff, when asked, indicated that he did not feel competitive with Tom's birthparents, that he knew they were important to Tom, but that he also knew that Tom loved them and that they were his "real" family. Clearing up the misunderstanding allowed all three to reaffirm the meaning of their family to each of them. The session ended with Mary and Jeff supporting Tom's wish to one day see his birthmother, offering a promise of their support when he is ready.

LEAVING HOME

Finally, a major task, perhaps *the* major task facing every family, is the successful completion of the launching phase. The "leaving home" transition entails some loss in any family as children establish themselves separately from their parents. New ways of relating and staying connected must be established as parents relinquish both control and daily involvement with their children. Families are vulnerable to conflict and the development of problems in this developmental stage (McCullough & Rutenberg, 1988). And, since loss is one of the core issues in the launching phase and since loss and the threat of loss is often a particularly sensitive area for adoptive families, adoptive families are particularly vulnerable. A major concern is that once the caretaking task is complete, they will lose the child because the biological tie is lacking. It was probably significant that both the Higgins and the Cartwrights sought help following evidence of developing sexual interests on the parts of their children, presaging growing up and leaving home.

The Higgins were evidently having a very difficult time thinking about letting Tom go and tended to envision him and treat him considerably younger than his chronological age. They worried about "preparing him for adult life," concerned that he wouldn't be ready.

When they were so responsive to a comment by one of the therapists that they hadn't had as much time with him as they would have had they been able to adopt him when he was younger, it became apparent that they felt they didn't have enough time, that their opportunity to parent had been foreshortened. The family, including Tom, was very relieved when the therapy team slowed down the time schedule, suggesting that since Tom didn't join the family until he was seven, they all may want to postpone his leaving home for a few years, perhaps until he was 21 or 22.

CONCLUSION

Adoptive families seek treatment from mental health and social agencies with the same range of problems and concerns that trouble other families. However, several themes relating to the dynamics of the adoption situation frequently emerge to color and shape the family's intrapersonal and interpersonal issues. If the adoption themes are ignored by therapists, therapists may be colluding in empowering their mysterious qualities and thus their potential to exert subtle and potentially destructive influences on other family processes and transitions. In this chapter, we have described and illustrated some of the themes that so frequently appear in adoptive families. Our hope is that therapists working with such families may be sensitized to listen for these themes and to respond to them in helpful ways when they are hindering the family's healthy functioning.

13

Brief Solution-Focused Therapy with Adoptive Families

JUDITH SCHAFFER AND CHRISTINA LINDSTROM

How can you choose the right therapy when problems arise with an adoptee? If you turn to the psychiatric, psychological, or social work literature, you'll find that most accounts of therapeutic interventions with adoptees, largely theoretical in nature, focus on the intrapsychic life of the adoptee. These accounts fail, however, to distinguish between those difficulties that may be normal complications of adoption not requiring treatment, those that may be adoption related and require adoption-specific treatment, and those that are not adoption related, but require generic treatment.

Primary clinical issues described in the literature focus on identity and self-concept in the adoptee. The traditional view is that since the adoptee was removed from her or his birthmother at an early age, and because the adoptee must come to terms with having two sets of parents, the probability that identity and self-concept problems will arise is high. Adoptees are thought to lack an ability to trust (Stone, 1972), to be more insecure (Barinbaum, 1974), and to have major identity conflicts, especially during the adolescent years (Sants, 1964; Schechter, 1967; Tec & Gordon, 1967; Wieder, 1977b).

These assumptions, influenced by psychoanalytic theory, have influenced the type of treatment available to families of adoptees over the past several decades. Thus the treatment emphasis has been based on a psychopathological view that demands that intrapsychic issues be addressed. As early experience may be either partially or completely unknown, uncovering the original causes for the current problems may be impossible. Thus using such a model can cause some interesting complications, which are worth considering.

Adoptive family life is more complicated by its very nature (Kirk, 1981; Schaffer & Lindstrom, 1989). In addition to the developmental tasks involved in the maturation of a nonadoptee, the adoptee and the adoptive family must come to terms with the facts of separation from the birthfamily and of being a part of a family whose members are not related by blood. Adoptees, who are by societal definition set apart from others in that they are not living in the family to whom they are genetically related, risk being set apart even further if they alone are singled out to participate in therapy. This risk may be especially true given that relationships in adoptive families are more dependent on commitment for reasons other than blood tie compared with those in nonadoptive families where such a connection is assumed (Bohman & Sigvardsson, 1982; Brodzinsky, Schechter, et al., 1984; Lindstrom, 1986).

It was with the notion that adoption is an issue that necessarily affects the whole adoptive family that we began our work in 1983 at the Center for Adoptive Families (CAF).[1] Over the past five years, the Center has been investigating the elements of effective psychotherapy with adoptive families. It follows that since adoption is a factor which affects all members of an adoptive family to a greater or lesser degree, the family unit itself should become the focus of the intervention. The view of the problems of adoption, then, naturally shifts from an intrapsychic to an interactional perspective. The therapist with this perspective attempts to discover how the interactions between adoptive family members can be improved so that the family can function more effectively and with fewer difficulties (for more on family therapy see also Hoffman, 1982).

This chapter is a report of our findings in treating adoptees within the context of their family units. An important factor in comprehending these findings is to understand the way adoptive families are viewed as systems. This view takes into account that numerous people are involved, either actually or psychically in the adoptive family system, that is, birthfamilies, social workers, former foster families, and child caring personnel. Looking at the system in this way is key in employing the fluidity and flexibility necessary to involve other significant people in the adoptee's life in order to maximize the potential for a successful outcome. Using this model, any or all of the above-named people are included in treatment along with the family if such inclusion seems useful and is possible.

DEMOGRAPHICS

Of the 278 families seen at the Center in the past five years, 41% are adoptive families. Adoptive families are defined as one- or two-parent families who have at least one adopted child who is not related by marriage or blood. The remaining 59% of families treated at CAF are birthfamilies, foster families, or families who had an adopted child placed with them but who had not legally finalized the adoption of that child at the time of treatment. Only families who had finalized the adoption of their child(ren) will be discussed here.

Families in this sample either choose the agency or are referred by an outside source, usually a child welfare agency, for specialized treatment relating to adoption. Since the vast majority of adoptees and their families do not seek mental health services (Schaffer & Kral, 1988), this group cannot be considered representative of the population at large. However, it is interesting to note that in each case, the family considered itself to be having a problem that somehow related to the fact that one or more of their children is adopted. Additionally, many of these families have had some prior experience with therapy either as individuals or as a family.

Approximately one-third of the families who come to the Center adopted their child(ren) as infants. The remaining two-thirds adopted children who were at least 2-years-old at placement. The mean age of the children at the time of placement in this second group is 8.3 years. Interestingly, in both sets of families, most of the children who were the Identified Patients (IPs) were 13- or 14-years-old at the time treatment began. In the infant-adopting group, boys and girls were equally identified as being the IP. In the older child-adopting group, however, boys were somewhat more likely (56%) to be the ones with the presenting problem. Nearly 70% of the IPs were either only or oldest children.

Over one-half of the adoptive families (59%) seen are two-parent families. Most of the single-parent families had been two-parent families at the time of adoption but had become single-parent families through death or divorce. In every case, these single-parent families are headed by women. In older children adoptions, a much larger percentage were adopted by single parents, 17% of whom are men.

Although a sizeable number of these families adopted children of another race, racial problems are not cited as a reason for being in therapy by any of the families.

In the infant-adopting families, nearly one-half seek treatment for their teenage daughters. Problems in this group, which occur both at home and at school, are often described by the parents as suddenly appearing in their formerly well-behaved girls. Truancy, refusal to do school work, rudeness, and abusiveness are the complaints most often cited. It is possible that these parents may be lacking in experience with adolescents and the difficulties involved with their efforts to achieve independence. This idea, suggested by Talen and Lehr (1984), further proposes that crises in adoptive families often coincide with stages in the family life cycle as the adoptive family fails to successfully manage the transition into the next stage of development (see Brodzinsky, 1987).

Overall, a vast majority of complaints are related to conduct and externalized behavior. Problems such as school difficulties, lying, stealing, aggressive behavior, noncompliance, sexual acting out, running away, and drug abuse are common. Parents of the older adopting group report more school-based problems than parents who adopted infants. This conduct appears to be especially frustrating to them as they are barraged by irate calls from the school and yet cannot oversee their children's behavior while they are not at home. Generally, these findings support the work of Brodzinsky, Schechter, Braff, and Singer (1984), Bohman and Sivgardsson (1982), and Hoopes (1970), which suggests that, as a group, adopted boys, at certain ages, tend to act out somewhat more than their nonadopted peers. However, adopteesare seen as being somewhat more likely to externalize rather than internalize behaviors.

Using a Brief Therapy Model, the average number of sessions at CAF for families who adopted infants is 6.0 and for families who adopted older children is 7.3. Single-parent families average 8.0 sessions whether or not they had adopted infants. Early information, based on the follow-up of 20% of the families, suggests that three-fourths of the clients report that they are doing better than they were before treatment, their goals for therapy were largely met, and the problem has not reoccurred. Although many families enter therapy suggesting that adoption dissolution is the solution of choice, only one family actually chose this as a final solution. In three cases, there was a temporary out-of-home placement with continuing parental involvement.

THE BRIEF THERAPY MODEL

The therapy team at the Center for Adoptive Families has been greatly influenced by the treatment approach of Milton H. Erickson. O'Hanlon (1987) discusses the basic treatment assumptions that guide Ericksonian psychotherapists.

1. People have within them the abilities to overcome difficulties and maintain health. The role of the therapist is to create a context that allows people to identify and utilize their own resources to resolve problems.
2. The purpose of therapy should be to orient the client to the present and future, rather than to try and change an unchangeable past.
3. The cause of a problem does not need to be known in order to resolve it.
4. Insight and awareness are not necessary for change. Most psychological functioning occurs outside conscious awareness.
5. People can change their behaviors, a visable expression of personality. Alternative aspects of a client's personality can be elicited for the client's benefit.
6. Symptoms may not serve a function. Perhaps problems arose for functional reasons, but they usually become habits that are no longer related to the original symptoms. These habits can be changed without discussion or resolution of an underlying problem.

The team at CAF is further influenced by the model of Brief Solution-Focused Therapy, based on Ericksonian practice, as developed in Milwaukee by the team at the Brief Family Therapy Center (deShazer, 1982, 1985; deShazer & Molnar, 1984; deShazer et al., 1986). Most of the adoptive family cases are treated using this model, so while it is more fully described elsewhere, a short overview is useful.

Principles of Brief Therapy

An overriding principle of Brief Therapy is its adherence to a nonpathological view of families and individuals. Problems are seen as a result of ineffective patterns of interactions between members or elements of a system. The "task" of Brief Therapy is to help clients do something different by changing their interactive behavior or their interpretation of behavior and situations so that the solution (the resolution of their complaint) can be achieved (deShazer, 1985).

This changing of the interpretation of the behavior is key in treating adoptive families. As long as the family "blames" the problem on the issue of adoption, they can feel guilty and stay stuck, as there is nothing anyone can do to change what is fact. However, if they can see the problem as having other causes or explanations, the chances of finding a solution are greatly increased.

CASE 1

After a high school guidance counselor noticed changes in Ann's behavior, she and her mother were referred to the Center. Ann told the counselor that she was adopted and that her problems stemmed from this fact. The counselor, who was herself an adoptee, felt that adoption-specific treatment was indicated. As a result of a recent divorce, Mrs. C. had recently returned to work. Around the same time, Ann began to refuse to go to school, though school attendance had never before been a problem.

Ann, who is an only child, was adopted as an infant, but was never told about her adoption. A year earlier, during her parents' separation, Mr. and Mrs. C. argued often over the telephone. During one of these arguments, while Ann was listening on an extension phone, Mr. C. mentioned the fact that Ann had been adopted. Ann subsequently confronted her mother, who first denied that it was true and then, seeing the futility of her position, finally admitted the truth. Mrs. C. explained that she feared hurting Ann by telling her that she had been given up by her first mother. She also expressed her fear that Ann might stop loving her and might even try to return to her birthmother. Realizing her mistake, she promised to "make up for it" even if it meant helping Ann locate her birthmother.

Ann, at this point, was confused about a number of issues: her adoptive status; her parents' lies; her mother's return to work; her reduced economic situation; and her parents' separation. As a result, Ann withdrew. She refused to go to school or to leave the house. She faced possible expulsion from her high school for truancy.

As a result of her guilt for having lied, Mrs. C. was limited in her effectiveness in handling the situation of Ann's truancy. A pattern of interaction between mother and daughter had developed. The daughter would misbehave; the mother would anxiously speculate about the reason for the misbehavior. Mother would therefore act indecisively, and the daughter would continue to misbehave. Therapy was focused on interrupting this pattern. The therapy team assumed that nothing could be done to change an unchangeable past. However, Ann and her mother clearly had developed a more honest relationship but were, as yet, not fully aware of this fact. The team further assumed that Ann needed some "time off" from school initially to sort things out. This perfectly understandable need for time alone had developed, however, into truancy, a habit which would cause serious consequences if it was not broken. Mrs. C.'s behavior was characterized by the team as protective of Ann when she was younger but as a bad habit when Ann became old enough to know the truth.

Thus redefining the problems as a series of bad habits which had to be broken in order for a better relationship to continue, the team and the family worked together to build a new future for Ann and her mother.

Families often come into therapy with some idea about solutions. However, because they are feeling so hopeless and helpless, they fail to recognize that there are times when the problem does not occur. Concrete examples of viable solutions are elicited by the therapist during the session to establish "exceptions." An exception is defined as a time when the problem could have or would have typically happened but did not. Therapy focuses on the specifics of what the client(s) did and thought at those times and establishes what will have to happen to repeat the exception (solve the problem). In cases where clients are unable to find exceptions to the problem, the therapist assigns a task designed to assist the client(s) in discovering exceptions outside the session.

CASE 2

Mrs. L. and her 16-year-old daughter, Kate, came to the Center complaining of Kate's chronic bedwetting. Mrs. L. told the therapist that Kate did not have a single night without an accident and, in fact, occasionally wet her bed more than once per night. Mrs. L. feared that this problem was related to the fact that her daughter, who was adopted at age 7, had been sexually abused by her birthfather. Over the years, Kate was examined by several physicians and psychiatrists but nothing had helped. Both mother and daughter felt that it was an impossible situation and that there was no possible solution.

The team decided that since there had been so much focus on the problem through previous treatment, it was not useful to focus on the complaint. Instead, the team focused on the times when Kate was able to control her bladder (the exception). Questioning revolved around the times when Kate was able to control her bladder and revealed that Kate was, indeed, an expert in controlling her bladder during the day. As it turned out, because she was shy and disliked calling attention to herself by using the toilets at school, Kate did not urinate for up to 9 hours during the school day and managed to control her bladder normally during her waking hours away from school, accounting for 16 hours per day.

The team expressed their amazement that Kate could control her bladder so well during the day and asked her to observe and make notes about how she did this for the next session. At the next meeting, Kate revealed that she had had three dry nights during the previous week. The team continued to focus on the issue of bladder control, and therapy ended after two more sessions.

Using a Brief Therapy model means accepting the client's view of the problem and the goals which they wish to set. Clients are not expected to see things the team's way, nor are they expected to learn a new language of psychotherapy. They are merely encouraged to do more of what they are doing that is effective.

CASE 3

The R. Family came to therapy complaining about their 9-year-old recently adopted son, James. They were concerned that he had not "bonded" to the family, which also included a 6-year-old birth daughter.

The family complained that James would ask his father to cook special things for him and then refuse to eat. He asked his father to do projects with him and then lost interest. This behavior left Mr. R. frustrated and angry. As James had been in many foster homes before he came to live with the R.'s, the family was concerned about the issue of attachment.

Since Mr. R. is a teacher, the team suggested that James, because of his history, had little experience in being a part of a family or a son to his new father. The team suggested that Mr. R., having been a son himself, take on the task of teaching James how to be a son. Challenged by this interpretation and confident in his abilities as a teacher, Mr. R. was able to attribute James's misbehavior to a lack of knowledge and understanding rather than pathology. Freed from this interpretation, James's behavior lost much of its potency for Mr. R. and he found himself able to respond to it more constructively, sometimes, to even ignore it. James, on the other hand, no longer found it useful to manipulate his father in this manner and began to give up this behavior. After the fourth session, the family and the team agreed that the goal was accomplished and that therapy should be terminated.

Another basic principle, which applies in working with families using the Brief Therapy Model, relates to making small changes that have a ripple effect. Borrowing from systems theory, the problem is seen as existing within a context of the family as a system. Therefore, a small change in any part of the system can be sufficient to bring about a significant and lasting solution. This simple principle can actually free the therapist from feeling he or she has to do so much. Rather, therapy is a process that advances in small steps with an open expectation that the solution may be reached at any point—it simply needs to be recognized and firmly established over time.

Consequently, the therapy is brief in the sense of a limited number of sessions. The total time in treatment, though, may last a number of months as clients take the necessary time to test solutions and adapt to changes which occur.

CASE 4

Mr. and Mrs. G. came to therapy with their 16-year-old daughter, Sue, who had been recently discharged from a psychiatric in-patient hospital. Sue, who was adopted at age 5, ran away from home at age 13, thus initiating a series of events which eventually led to psychiatric hospitalization. This behavior took her parents by surprise as they reported as having no problems with her before that time.

During Sue's stay at the hospital, her parents had felt isolated from her. They subsequently discovered that Sue had made two suicide attempts during that period about which they had not been informed. The staff of the hospital considered Sue to be psychotic.

While hospitalized, Sue accused her father, grandfather, and brother of having sexually abused her. The investigation which followed cleared all three, but greatly increased the family's concerns for her.

When Sue returned home, these worries took the form of constant watching and questioning. As Sue grew less and less responsive, her family became more fearful that she would have to be rehospitalized. They began to doubt that they were up to the task of parenting Sue. During the first session at the Center, Sue refused to speak and stared at the carpet, seemingly confirming her parent's fears.

As this was a critical situation, the team decided to try to secure one small change which would give the family some hope. First, the team sent a message that let the family know that they understood how traumatic the past three years had been and how the family had suffered. The parents were reassured that any parents in their situation would be worried. Sue was told that the team understood how, after being hospitalized, it's easy to feel as though one is living in a goldfish bowl. Further, they told Sue that they knew how hard it was to be a normal teenager when everyone was worried and watching.

Next, the team asked the family to do two tasks before the next session. The first task, known as the "first session task" (see below) is for each person to observe what is happening in the family that he or she would like to have continue. The second task asked the parents to refrain from all obvious worrying and all questioning for one week and to let us know what they observed.

The change in the second session was remarkable. Sue was lively and involved in the session. Mr. and Mrs. G. reported that Sue had socialized with her brothers and their friends several times over the past week. The therapy continued for four more sessions as the team encouraged small steps to help Mr. and Mrs. G. feel more competent and to encourage the perception of Sue as a teenager rather than a patient.

FORMAT OF BRIEF THERAPY SESSIONS

The concepts and procedures involved in Brief Solution-Focused Therapy have been fully described by deShazer and his colleagues and interested readers should refer to these writings for a more complete description (deShazer, 1985; deShazer et al., 1986). For the purposes of this chapter, these ideas are summarized below.

Most families and individuals are seen by a treatment team. The members of the teams vary but the team always consists of a therapist, who sits in the room with the family, and a treatment team who sit behind a one-way mirror. The therapy suite consists of two rooms with a one-way mirror between them, an intercom, and video-taping equipment. The following steps are the elements of the first session:

1. Introduction to the set-up
2. Statement of the complaint

3. Exploration of the exceptions to the complaint
4. Establishment of the goals for therapy
5. Definitions of potential solutions
6. Consultation break
7. Delivery of the team's message

Introduction

The therapist explains about the mirror and the team. After she explains the general procedures, she asks the family to give permission to be videotaped. In our experience, families seldom refuse to give their permission.

Statement of the Complaint

A few minutes are spent developing rapport by asking questions of each family member, such as "Where do you live?", "Who is in school and where?", "Who is adopted?"

The therapist then asks, "What can we help you with?" Following the answer(s), the therapist elicits as many concrete details about the pattern of the complaint as possible. In this process, the therapist wants to establish several things:

1. Who is involved in the problem? Are both parents involved? Does it happen only when Dad (or Mom) is around? What other family members are present? Are others outside the family involved?
2. Where does the problem take place? At home (in the kitchen, living room, bedroom)? At school? Somewhere else?
3. When does the problem happen? Once a day? Once a week? Mornings? Evenings?

Here, the therapist has the opportunity to "normalize" certain behaviors that the family may consider pathological. For example, most adopted children test what their parents will do when they break a family rule or misbehave in some way with statements like, "You're not my REAL mother!" The therapist can also "reframe" or alter the meaning which the family applies to a set of observable events, giving a positive rather than negative flavor to them. One example of this would be to refer to misbehavior of a recently placed older adopted child as "testing behavior to see if they will keep her." This slightly alters the clients' perceptions by offering a somewhat different interpretation of the same behavior and may help set the stage for subsequent interventions.

Exceptions

The therapist then tries to establish what happens when the problem could have occurred but did not, in fact, happen. The therapist asks questions about what family members did to prevent the problem from happening. At this stage, it is important for the family and the therapist to know what the client(s) are doing that is already effective. This information is then used to develop a model for intervention design and solution.

Goals

By deciding on concrete goals with the family, the therapist establishes a way to measure effectiveness. When these goals are met, therapy ends unless the therapist and the family negotiate new goals and decide to continue treatment.

Solutions

The therapist asks specific questions of family members about how they will know when the problem is solved. The therapist also asks family members to speculate on what life will be like when the problem is solved. Asking the family these kinds of questions is particularly useful in that it encourages them to focus on the future and gives them a sense that a solution is possible.

Consultation Break

After about 40 minutes, the therapist leaves the family and meets with the team behind the mirror. During this meeting, the group decides what to do and how to do it. Most of the discussion centers around the exceptions to the complaint pattern and how they can be expanded. The team then develops a message for the family consisting of two parts (1) the compliment and (2) the clue.

Compliments focus on what the clients are doing that is useful. These are usually simple but true statements like: "It is clear to us that you are both very caring parents who have great concern for your daughter." Or, "We can see that you are trying hard to find activities that you and your dad can share together." Or, "The team understands that, though times have been difficult, you have established a more honest relationship together."

Clues are therapeutic suggestions or tasks that will encourage the family to come closer to a lasting solution to the problem. In the case of Sue and her parents above, the task was for the parents to stop worrying and watching their daughter for one week. The time frame in this type of task is crucial since, undoubtedly, others had told the parents to stop worrying but they could not. However, expressed as an experiment with a definite end, most people can alter their behavior temporarily and in the process discover that this new behavior has benefits.

For families who present vague problems or complaints during the first session or cannot list any exception to their complaint, there is a "formula first session task." This task or clue asks the family to observe, between sessions, what happens in the family that they would like to have continue and be prepared to describe those things at the next session.

By focusing on the things that are going right, families often find exceptions to problematic situations and refocus on their strengths instead of solely on their weaknesses. Often, on completion of this simple task, families report that things are somewhat improved and seem increasingly able to solve the complaints at hand.

Delivering the Message

The therapist returns to the family and reads the message from the team, a new appointment is scheduled, and the session is ended.

Second and subsequent sessions take the same form as described above, with the exception of steps 1 and 2, which are eliminated. The focus of these subsequent sessions is on the exceptions and their solutions, *not the complaint*. As the complaint has been clearly established in the first session, further rehashing would serve no purpose and could make the family feel more hopeless. The focus, then, is on building a new future in which family members will adjust to and in which the complaint no longer exists.

CASE 5

The following case, as reported in Kral, Schaffer, and deShazer (1989), is a dramatic yet not atypical illustration of cases referred for adoption-specific treatment.

The W. Family was referred to the Center for Adoptive Families by an adoption agency social worker. They had sought advice from a psychiatrist and their pediatrician who had both recommended that they terminate the adoption of their 7-year-old daughter Missy. Missy had been the victim of repeated sexual abuse suffered while she was in foster care. This information was apparently unknown to her foster care worker and, therefore, was not a part of her agency records.

The W.'s were not aware of Missy's history of sexual abuse when she was placed with them. Gradually, however, as Missy grew to trust them, she told her new parents about her experiences. Upset, they contacted the agency. The agency suggested that, since there was no way to confirm Missy's story and since she was adjusting well to the family, there was nothing that they could recommend.

Two years following her adoption, Missy and her adoptive brother were discovered having sexual intercourse. Both physicians contacted by the family indicated that not only was Missy at fault but that she was likely to repeat the pattern over and over again. Their opinion was that Missy was so damaged by her former experience that she would be compelled to seek out inappropriate sexual contacts throughout her childhood. The family was warned that this was inevitable and no treatment could be expected to "cure" Missy.

Despite the dire predictions the family had received, the therapist and team proceeded by ignoring the assumptions the family had been encouraged to make. The first session was conducted as if there was a solution to be found for the complaint presented, sexual activity between siblings. The therapist asked the W.'s how they had responded to the incident and what had occurred since.

The parents detailed their response and discussed measures taken since to prevent a reoccurrence. While it is true that the parents were terrified that "it" might happen again, they also had arrived at an alternative meaning for the behavior. Mrs. W. put it most clearly when she said, "We have to teach Missy to be a sister to her brothers, since she has never had a chance to learn that." Mr. W. stated his belief that Missy needed to learn that she had a right to expect others to respect her body and she had to learn that respect herself. He suggested that such respect could be taught along with learning about what it means to be in a relationship with a boy that is age-appropriate.

Clearly, the W.'s are an exceptional family. The family members are well connected to each other and the placement, with the exception of the sexual incident and the events which followed, was progressing very well. The W.'s were committed to their daughter and retained this commitment even when they were discouraged from doing so by the "experts." Missy clearly trusted her new family, as she indicated by confiding so fully in them.

The team decided not only to accept and encourage the W.'s definition of why the problem occurred but further stated that it was an attempt to demonstrate caring, not pathology, though it was inappropriate between siblings and for children of Missy's age.

The team also noted that Missy was far less damaged than a child who had her background but did not have the opportunity to live with a loving and concerned adoptive family where she could feel safe and learn to trust adults.

Obviously, Missy's past was unalterable. However, her future behavior could be changed. Mr. and Mrs. W. are competent parents who had already solved the problem but were not fully aware of the solution, so it became the task of the team to give this information to the family. By combining these ideas and assumptions, the team developed the following intervention during the consultation break and the therapist read this message to the family:

"The team is very impressed with the way in which this family has responded to a major crisis. Mr. and Mrs. W., the team sees that you have set limits and given support to your children which assures that such an incident will not happen again. Missy, we are very impressed with how much you care for your new family and how willing you are to learn to be a real part of that family in the ways that your parents can feel comfortable with. George, the team also feels that you have learned and are learning many new ways about what it really means to be a brother to a new sister and how to show your caring.

"The team feels that the problem has been solved. However, we would like you to do one more thing about this situation. Next Sunday, we would like the whole family to gather in the backyard for a little while. Before this gathering, Dad will dig a small hole with a shovel. When the family gathers, each family member will put their painful memories into that hole and cover them up with a shovelful of dirt. When the hole is covered up, the family will have a cake and punch to celebrate its new future together."

Such a message was intended to free the family member from dwelling on the past. This is not to say, of course, that at some future date Missy might not want to deal with her abusive past in some other way. Rather, this clue gave family members permission to bury the unchangeable past and proceed toward a more positive future.

At regular intervals over the two years since that session, the family has been contacted. They report that things are going well and that there has been no indication that inappropriate sexual behavior is a problem. Missy has made excellent progress at home, at school, and with peers in her neighborhood. This one session helped the family focus on the solutions they had already developed. It empowered them to have confidence in their ability to be parents to a child with a history like Missy's and offered them an alternative "expert" explanation for the same series of events which had brought the family into treatment.

USING A BRIEF THERAPY MODEL WITHOUT A TEAM

While it is certainly an advantage to have access to a team when working with adoptive families, it is not necessary in achieving the kinds of results described here. Many therapists who work with adoptive families and were trained at the Center for Adoptive Families use the techniques as individual practitioners.

The key elements in adapting this model for use by an individual clinician are taking notes during the session and taking a consultation break.

As there is no team to observe details of the session, therapists working individually often find it useful to make a few notes about the complaint and the solutions (exceptions). This notetaking is not to suggest making a verbatim record but to suggest a guide that will help the therapist remember some important elements which will be useful in planning the intervention (compliment and clue).

By leaving the room and taking a consultation break, the therapist working without a team gives herself a few minutes to reflect on the information and plan a message. Away from the family, ideas and strategies can flow more easily and she can return with a consise, well thought-out compliment and clue.

Although working with a team is stimulating and useful for research purposes, the Brief Solution-Focused Therapy Model seems to be equally effective whether or not a team is present.

The Brief Solution-Focused Model is effective with those individuals who come to treatment with a clearly defined difficulty and the expressed motivation to resolve it. Such individuals are referred to, in this model, as "customers" and this (and most) model(s) of therapy are likely to be effective in such problem resolution.

This model is also useful with individuals who we refer to as "clients." "Clients" know that they have a problem but aren't especially clear about the nature of the problem or whether it can be resolved. Interventions such as the first session task are designed to create "customers" from "clients" by helping to define a solution (goals or treatment) which will be acceptable to the "client."

The model is only occasionally useful with "visitors," those who only reluctantly enter therapy because they were referred by outside agencies, such as the court, or were forced to come by their parents, spouse, or another agency.

Most families, however, are composed of a combination of actors. The acting out youngster is rarely a customer. Interventions, therefore, are focused on the "customer," who is often the parent, in an effort to break a dysfunctional pattern or create a small change that begins the ripple effect.

CONCLUSION

Although adoptees and their families have been characterized as suffering from inherent difficulties which put them "at risk" for psychopathology, our clinical experience and preliminary investigations suggest that as a group those who enter treatment at CAF are unusually responsive to Brief Solution-Focused Therapy. The complicated nature of these families, especially those who have adopted older children, requires that the therapist carefully make distinctions about what to focus on during treatment and what not to focus on (Kral et al., in press). The therapist can be tempted to "do too much," more than the family is in fact requesting. As clinicians, the team has been satisfied that the methods which we have presented are useful in helping clients meet or exceed the goals that were set at the start of therapy. To meet the standards of scientific rigor, additional and more objective follow-up needs to be reported in the future.

This chapter does not seek to deny the very real difficulties for adoptees that are a natural result of the secrecy that surrounds their birth backgrounds and has been supported by law and public policy. Family therapists are uniquely aware of the negative histories of many former foster children now being placed for adoption, and how these early experiences color their current family interactions. We are consciously made to acknowledge the very real difficulties which may face adoptive families and adoptees in the process of providing useful assistance for their change. Here we have confined ourselves to reporting on a treatment approach that we have found effective in helping families with children resolve the problems that they brought into therapy in a brief and respectful manner.

NOTE

1. At various times over the past five years, the therapy team at CAF has consisted of Debbie Castaldo, Patti Feuereissen, Arnold Frucht, Helen Hazan, Anne Hoerning, Christina Lindstrom, Judith Schaffer, Mary Walker, Jeanne Warnock, Maryanne Yanulis, and Trish Welsh.

14

The Residential Treatment of Severely Disturbed Adolescent Adoptees

WELLS GOODRICH, CAROL S. FULLERTON, BRIAN T. YATES,
AND LINDA BETH BERMAN

INTRODUCTION

Adolescents require hospitalization (Miller, 1980) when their disturbed behavior becomes dangerous to themselves or to others, and when their affective states, cognitive dysfunctions, or personal suffering are so extreme as to make outpatient treatment infeasible. Hospitalization also may be indicated when age-appropriate behavior and adaptation are no longer possible in relation to peers, to school, or to the patient's family. Finally, disturbed adolescents may require hospitalization when the family psychopathology exacerbates the patients' difficulties so that the patient becomes unmanageable as an outpatient. Approximately 3% of the United States' adolescent population will enter a psychiatric hospital and 0.5% may require repeated or long-term psychiatric hospitalization (Almqvist, 1986).

The type of treatment for adoptees described in this chapter is referred to as "tertiary care," since most adolescents admitted to Chestnut Lodge had been previously hospitalized without improvement and had attempted outpatient treatments which in turn had failed. Chestnut Lodge's treatment approach (Goodrich, 1987) is similar to other psychodynamically oriented programs (Redl, 1972; Redl & Wineman, 1952) in that it relies on four related therapeutic settings: a residential nursing milieu, a special school, family therapy, and four times per week individual therapy. Besides these primary therapeutic programs, group therapy is applied with all patients; and medication may be used with the more severe affective or schizophrenic disorders.

Since 1975, when Chestnut Lodge opened a 28-bed, long-term hospital treatment unit for chronically and severely disturbed adolescents, we have admitted 148 patients aged 9 to 21 years (55% male), of whom 28 (19%) have been adoptees. Over the past 8 years, using research interviews, observations by hospital staff, and analyses of hospital records, we have documented that a significant proportion of the adoptees do not complete the recommended course of treatment. This chapter reports clinical case material and research data that clarify the special resistances of the adoptees to this form of treatment. The situation of adoption, when it occurs within

253

severely disturbed families, tends toward a well-defined pattern of adolescent psycho-pathology. The adoptee's conflicts and defenses, which have emerged in relationship to severely disturbed parents, move toward a particular kind of partial therapeutic impasse.

The most common *DSM-III* (APA, 1980) diagnoses for our entire patient popu-lation on Axis I are conduct disorder, dysthymic disorder, or schizophrenia, and on Axis II are borderline, schizoid, or schizotypal personality disorders. Common symp-tomatic behaviors accompanying these diagnoses include substance abuse, running away from home, promiscuity, self-cutting, and other self-destructive or violent be-haviors.

We conclude our chapter with a number of technical recommendations for mod-ifying the usual residential treatment program to better address the special needs of adoptees.

PSYCHOPATHOLOGY IN THE ADOPTEE

Our experience with adoptees follows that found in the literature (Menlove, 1965; Offord et al., Schechter et al., Simon & Senturia, 1966), which reports that most emotionally disturbed adoptees exhibit oppositional or antisocial behavior. At Chest-nut Lodge, adoptees often receive a diagnosis of narcissistic personality disorder, borderline personality disorder, conduct disorder, dysthmic disorder, or substance abuse. Attention deficit disorder is also common among adoptees (Deutsch el al., 1982). Relatively few of our adoptees have presented with schizophrenia or schizo-typal personality disorder. On the one hand, our clinical observations have been consistent with the literature that suggests that among adoptees (1) there may be a genetic predisposition (Cadoret, Cain, & Crowe 1983; Crowe, 1974) to antisocial or oppositional behavior, and (2) that the fact of adoption often acts as a specially disruptive developmental stress (Brinich, 1980; Stone, 1972; Wieder, 1977a, b) when infants are placed with adoptive parents who themselves suffer from borderline or psychotic disorders. On the other hand, it is important to keep in mind that the adoptees in this report are quite different from the "average adoptee." By virtue of our hospital's admission criteria, our sample is drawn from among the most seriously and chronically disturbed adoptees. Researchers (Bohman, 1981; Bohman & Sigvardsson, 1980) that have studied adoptees from a broader, more inclusive sample suggest that the majority of adoptees are not emotionally disturbed, although their development may tend to be marked by special conflicts and defenses that are similar to those exhibited by patients in our hospital in a more extreme form (see Brodzin-sky, Schechter, Braff, & Singer, 1984; Brodzinsky, Radice, Huffman, & Merkler, 1987).

Regardless of the *DSM-III* (APA, 1980) diagnosis or the symptomatic behavior, our patients uniformly exhibit forms of severe separation anxiety and dependency conflicts, guilt, rage, or the projection of rage onto feared authority figures. Most of our patients employ denial, splitting, and projective identification as defenses against dependency and separation conflicts. That is to say, these adolescents will misper-ceive socially imposed, expectable constraints on their behavior as malevolently mo-tivated when in fact such constraints are appropriate. These adolescents will tend to respond oppositionally or ragefully, not because their real needs have been deprived, but because they, themselves, are more comfortable in a state of opposition or ragefulness than they are when experiencing themselves as dependent, uncertain, passive, or internally conflicted. In these ways our adoptees are similar to our nonadopted patients who have been diagnosed as personality disordered. The exception is that our adopted patients tend to have stronger needs to control the treatment, to have stronger distrust of the nurturing authority, and to persist in the use of projective identification even after many months of insight–oriented psychotherapy.

Clinical observers (Brinich, 1980; Brodzinsky, 1987; Brodzinsky, Schechter, Braff & Singer, 1984; Fullerton et. al., 1986; Kernberg, 1985–86; Schechter et al., 1964; Stone, 1972; Wieder, 1977a) as well as psychotherapists at this hospital have described the self-concept of severely disturbed adoptees and the relationships to their families as having become conflicted from specific experiences. Positive acceptance of their adoptive parents often has been severely damaged by the child's awareness of unresolved parental depression, of marital alienation between the parents, or of other serious parental psychopathology. The adoptee's sense of having been "an outsider" in the family or the adoptee's fantasies, involving symbiotic or incestuous parent–child relationships shared with the parent, may interfere with trusting and normally dependent parent–child bonding. These conflicts tend to increase the disturbed adoptee's self-doubt, identity confusion, depression, and anxiety, which in turn tend to be defended against by denial, rageful rebellion, or by an attitude of stubborn entitlement.

It appears that our adopted patients have come to see a position of vigilant opposition to authority as tantamount to adaptation and personal survival. This position is also in some sense gratifying since adoptees tend to trust in their own pseudomature judgments and aspirations and to feel entitled to challenge the adult world. For our adopted patients it would appear that the family reality itself has been interpreted as supporting the adoptees' needs for premature autonomy and to avoid trusting dependent relationships

RESIDENTIAL TREATMENT AND THE ADOPTEE

Prior to admission to Chestnut Lodge, as well as immediately following hospitalization, extensive evaluations are made of the patient's current state, the family, and the developmental history of both the patient and the family, and a psychological test battery is administered. Ratings of the patient's behavior from the nursing unit are obtained. The patient's responses to the unit's support and limit–setting are evaluated particularly as they regard the patient's capacity for change and more appropriate adaptation.

In successful long-term residential treatment, it is useful to define the treatment processes as occurring in three approximate phases (Goodrich 1984, 1987; Masterson & Costello, 1980; Rinsley, 1980). The first phase, which may last 4 to 12 months or more, is the *containment–support phase* in which the staff attempts to resocialize the disturbed adolescent by means of an empathically regulated balance between staff support and staff limit-setting. The school program also provides a structured environment (Hirschberg, 1972) wherein the patient's cognitive and adaptive difficulties can be observed, defined, and gradually modified. When the patient's internalized conflicts are masked by resistances, defensive rage, or antisocial behavior, school or nursing staff confront the patient (Redl, 1972; Redl & Wineman, 1952) and encourage the patient's introspection and communication (Goodrich & Boomer, 1958). The patient is then urged to discuss the preconscious or unconscious transference conflicts, which may thereby be uncovered, with his individual psychotherapist for ongoing exploration. During this first phase every effort is made by all hospital staff to build a comfortable working alliance with the patient. At the same time, in a parallel fashion, the social worker works to develop a formulation of the family's strengths and conflicts and to foster a treatment alliance with the parents in family therapy.

Phase 2 gradually emerges toward the end of the first year or in the second year, marked by (1) the patient's most maladaptive behaviors subsiding, and (2) the patient's achieving some tolerance of and comfort in a more dependent attachment to the therapist and to other hospital staff. During this second phase, in the successfully treated patient, both *insight and identification processes* may lead to significantly more integrated experience of self and others (Simenauer, 1985). As a result of such insight and new identifications, inner conflicts may become significantly resolved (Kernberg, 1984; Laufer & Laufer, 1984). In cases with a successful outcome, it is not uncommon to observe for a period of time the adolescent experiencing increased anxiety and depression as he or she gives up persecutory or alienated perceptions of others. Dependent needs then tend to intensify, and transferential separation experiences become painful or even intolerable. Adolescents in this second phase at some times may require an especially strong attachment and support, and at other times require the staff to give them space and freedom to try out their newly internalized positive identifications. Judgments on the part of the staff as to how to assist such patients through these transferentially regressive periods, without losing the alliance, are difficult and require much intuitive capacity and clinical experience.

Toward the end of the second year, or in the third year of treatment, new self-esteem and the capacity to invest in work and educational activities may appear, along with greater interpersonal sensitivity and appropriateness. These traits herald the emergence of phase 3. During this phase, very gradually, the staff will begin to encourage the patient's moving back into the community and separating from the hospital. This *separation–individuation phase,* begins as the terminal 6 to 18 months of the hospitalization and ends with the first years of the patient's testing out his or her capacity for effective self-dependence in the community as an outpatient.

This model for treatment (Goodrich, 1987), a sequencing of processes from containment and support through dependency, insight, and hopefully new positive identifications toward a new identity and a greater capacity for healthy autonomy, seems to "fit with" or "take" more easily with certain diagnostic groups of adolescents than with others. It is also interesting to observe that some severely disturbed adolescents seem to accept certain of these therapeutic processes while rejecting or failing to utilize other processes. Presumably these differences between adolescents in the acceptability of various aspects of the treatment may reflect differences in their development, in the nature and rigidity of their defenses, and in the nature and intensity of their conflicts. Impressionistically, it has appeared that chronically schizoid–depressed adolescents accept the first and second phases of the hospital's treatment processes but have great difficulty in responding in a useful manner to the third separation phase. In cases where the admission to the hospital of an adolescent with a less severe borderline personality disorder has been precipitated by family neglect and by a prolonged family stress situation, such a patient tends to accept all phases of treatment with relief and with the least resistance. These patients whose pathology has been stimulated by an unusually noxious environment during the years immediately preceding hospitalization generally show the most rapid improvement. Psychotic patients may or may not show improvement very slowly in all three phases; psychotic adolescents may show some degree of amelioration of severe symptoms while not relinquishing core conflicts nor completely resolving ego deficits.

Adoptees at this hospital often are diagnosed as having conduct disorder, dysthymic disorder, or some combination of these two diagnoses. During the first phase, these patients form intense peer attachments (Goodrich, 1984) and tend to "settle down" and accept the staff's containment and support. Many of them, however, become much more anxious and resistant in relation to the second-phase efforts the staff makes toward insight and toward helping the adolescent to accept responsibility for his or her own history of conflict, anxiety, and frustration. After the patient has resided in the hospital a number of months, the expectation that he or she will learn self-observation, will learn to reflect and to reevaluate cherished fantasies, feelings, and relatedness-patterns seems especially threatening to the adoptees. In this way, adoptees resemble nonadopted patients who are also diagnosed with conduct disorders or narcissistic personality disorders. Our observations, which will be presented subsequently in this chapter, support the conclusion that the severely and chronically disturbed adolescent adoptees' special difficulties during the second phase of residential treatment are so predictable and so much more intense than the qualitatively similar conflicts within the nonadopted, personality-disordered patients, that different therapeutic interventions often are required if a successful treatment outcome is to be achieved.

OBSERVATIONS: DIFFERENCES BETWEEN ADOPTEES AND OTHER HOSPITALIZED ADOLESCENTS

Here we report on quantitative observations made over the past 10 years on the hospital behavior of adopted patients as compared with nonadopted patients. This population of adolescents ($N = 148$) has been selected for admission due to the chronicity and severity of their psychopathology. They are of average or above average intelligence and in the preadmission interview have shown some availability for positive therapeutic relatedness. Adolescents who are brain damaged or retarded, as well as those judged to be extremely violent, are not admitted to the program. Differences and similarities between adoptees ($n = 28$, 19% of the sample) and nonadoptees ($n = 120$, 81% of the sample) were examined for admission characteristics, aspects of the patients' adaptation to the hospital after one month, the patients' subsequent responses to the treatment, and their manner of terminating inpatient hospitalization.

These young people were admitted between the ages of 9- and 21-years old, with most being between 14- and 16-years old at admission. The adopted patients tend to have been admitted at a significantly earlier mean age than the nonadopted patients—

there were significantly more adoptees under the age of 14 on admission (15.2 years for adoptees; 16.0 years for the nonadoptees; $p < .05$). The gender distribution of the adopted patients at admission was similar to that of the nonadopted patients: 45% female, 55% male. The duration of hospitalization for adoptees tends to be the same as for nonadoptees with similar diagnoses (mean $= 19$ months, sd $= 14$ months), except for those adoptees who had a terminal elopement from the hospital, then the duration of hospitalization tends to be about 6 months shorter.

As regards patients' severity of illness at admission, symptomatic improvement over time, ways of relating to other patients, and relating to many aspects of the treatment program, the adoptees resemble the other personality-disordered and conduct-disordered adolescents. For our total population on *DSM-III* Axis I, the most common diagnoses are dysthymic disorder alone, conduct disorder alone, or these two diagnoses combined. Among the nonadopted patients, 33% are diagnosed with dysthymic disorder only, 12% conduct disorder only, and 31% combined dysthymic disorder with conduct disorder. While the percentage of adoptees who are diagnosed with dysthymic disorder is not different, the likelihood that our adoptees have a diagnosis of conduct disorder is significantly greater than for nonadopted patients ($\chi^2(1) = 3.83$, $p = .05$).

After one month in the hospital, the nursing staff, who live with the patients are asked to rate each patient on 80 items of adaptive and nonadaptive behaviors using the Chestnut Lodge Adolescent Interaction Report (CLAIR, unpublished). The 80 ratings arrange themselves into 6 factors or clusters of items. Three of these factors can be described as ''hostile, unmanageable behavior,'' ''peer attachment,'' and ''cooperativeness with staff.'' Nonadopted adolescents diagnosed with personality disorders or conduct disorders after 1 month in the hospital tend to display a rather high level of *hostile unmanageable behavior* and an intense *peer attachment* as well as varying degrees of *cooperativeness with staff.* As regards the adoptees' level of positive attachment to peers or their intensity of hostile unmanageable behavior, most of their scores ($n = 25$) on the CLAIR are similar to the personality-disordered, nonadopted patients. The adopted patients, however, are rated significantly less cooperative with adults and more oppositional to rules and unit policies than are the nonadopted patients. This difference is significant ($n = 90$, $p < .05$ $t(102.5) = 2.02$, $p = .046$) using separate variance estimates due to the presence of highly unequal numbers of adopted versus nonadopted patients.

After 3 months in the hospital, we evaluate all patients to assess their severity of illness. Two experienced clinicians, who have administrative responsibility for the program and equal contact with all patients, are asked to rate each patient on Endicott, Spitzer, Fleiss, and Cohen's (1976) Global Assessment Scale (GAS). Generally, we have found that while the patients' basic conflicts and defenses have not changed after 3 months, their severity of symptomatic behavior and poor social adaptation has improved since admission. Doubtless this behavioral improvement is partly a reflection of the change in the patient's environment from a conflict-ridden home to a more neutral and clearly defined social milieu. Presumably, this improvement is due to the staff's work of support and containment—characteristic of the first phase of the program. Indeed, about one-half of the average 20-point symptomatic improvement on the GAS (Endicott et al., 1976) seems to occur between admission and 3 months. The GAS ratings for adoptees as a group do not differ in this respect from the other patients. The scores on the GAS change for both adoptees and nonadoptees from an average admission score of 40 to 45, to 50 to 55 after 3 months in the hospital, and to 60 to 65 at the time of hospital discharge.

At 3 months, we evaluate the intensity of the patients affective attachment to the treatment situation by means of our modified Summers Scales (Summers & Walsh, 1977) which measure possessiveness, separation anxiety, loss of ego boundaries, and two forms of dependency. These scales are rated from a semistructured research interview administered individually to the patient and to a nursing staff member who is best acquainted with the patient. We also rate the patient's sense of individual autonomy by means of the Nowicki–Strickland (1973) version of the Locus of Control questionnaire administered to the patient. Here again the adoptees appear to form as intense an attachment as the nonadoptees and also appear to gain the beginnings of a sense of autonomy at a level similar to other personality-disordered adolescents.

The average Summers Score at 3 months is 12 for nonadopted patients and 13 for the adopted patients; the range is from 6 to 20. Fifty percent of all patients score 10 to 15. The average Locus of Control score for both groups was 12 (range 1 to 25, 50% of all patients score between 9 and 15 points).

More dramatic differences between adopted and nonadopted patients appear in relation to runaway behavior and in relation to the adoptees' mode of terminating their hospital treatment. Interestingly enough, these differences emerge with particular clarity toward the end of the first year and early in the second year of treatment, leading us to interpret these observations as indicating the adoptees' special sensitivity to transference conflicts involving trust, dependency, and separation issues. Like the nonadopted patients with similar diagnoses (on Axis I) of conduct disorder and dysthymic disorder, or (on Axis II) the spectrum of borderline–narcissistic–oppositional disorders, our adopted patients are made anxious by the expectation that they tolerate and examine their dependent experiences and not seek defensive relief in premature autonomy and distance from both the treatment situation and from their families. The adopted patients appear to find avoidant, pseudoautonomous behaviors more ego-syntonic than do nonadopted patients with similar psychopathology. These conclusions have been derived in part from individual case reviews of the adoptees' treatment and in part from the quantitative data (Berman, Fullerton, Goodrich, & Yates, 1986; Fullerton et al., 1986).

Sixty-two percent of our overall sample of 118 discharged patients exhibited runaway behavior at some time during hospitalization; 25% of the total sample used an occasion of "absent without leave" to terminate treatment. Adoptees were significantly more likely to terminate treatment by running away than were nonadoptees (48% compared with 20%, a statistically significant difference $p < .01$). Interestingly, the behavior of running away from the hospital also distinguished adopted patients from nonadopted patients. Ninety percent of adoptees run away from the hospital at least once while only slightly over one-half of the nonadoptees exhibited this behavior (this difference is significant, $p < .01$) The age of the patient at the time of first runaway episode, however, does not distinguish the adoptees from the nonadoptees, nor does the number of months residence in the hospital at the time of first runaway. The duration of the first runaway episode (mean $= 3.5$ days) also does not distinguish adoptees from nonadoptees (Berman et al., 1986).

Table 14.1 summarizes these observations. In addition, adopted patients are more

Table 14.1   Adoptees vs. Nonadoptees and Running Away

	Adoptees	Nonadoptees	Male	Female
Patients discharged	21	97	65	53
(N = 118)	(18%)	(82%)	(55%)	(45%)
Patients who never ran away	2	43	25	20
(N = 45)	(10%)	(44%)	(56%)	(44%)
Patients who ran away	19	54	40	33
(N = 73)	(90%)	(56%)	(55%)	(45%)
Patients who terminated hospitalization by running away	10	19	13	16
(N = 29)	(48%)	(20%)	(44%)	(56%)

liable to participate in multiple runaway episodes over their course of hospitalization (prior to termination) than nonadopted patients ($p < .0004$). If one considers simply the total number of runaway episodes ($N = 250$) observed for the 73 patients who exhibited such behavior, 95 of these episodes (38%) were exhibited by the adoptees, despite the fact that these adoptees made up only 20% of the patients who ran away at least once. What characterizes the adoptees is their proneness to running away, their tendency for repeated runaway episodes, group runaways, and their tendency to use a nonnegotiated process to terminate treatment (Berman, 1987; Berman et al., 1986). This pattern is consistent with the nursing staff's ratings for the adoptees— made after one month in the hospital—of more distrustful, noncooperative behavior with staff, as reported above. It indicates that although our residential treatment approach achieved a working alliance with the adoptees during the early containment– support phase of treatment, this alliance was not strong enough to withstand the intensified transference of abandonment issues that tends to occur during the second phase of psychoanalytic hospital treatment. An early treatment predictor of this second-phase runaway behavior appears to be the nursing staff's postadmission ratings of high oppositionality.

COURSE OF TREATMENT: THREE CASES

We hope that an examination of the following three cases in some detail will serve to make the general trends reported above more comprehensible.

For all three of these adopted adolescents, a severe, chronic depression coupled with both self-destructive and hostile-aggressive behavior was dramatically evident on admission. From studying the family dynamics it was clear that much of the adolescents' pathology derived from the family rather than from the situation of adoption, as such. In all three cases, the mother was rigidly intrusive and controlling. Two of the patients' mothers had established a confusing, demanding, and guilt-inducing attachment without boundaries, which in a real sense blocked the patient's potential for healthy adolescent identity formation. In all three cases the father was not available to the patient, serving as a positive but at times distant parent, one often preoccupied with his own concerns rather than with his adopted child. Having internalized their parent's unresolved conflicts over intimacy, dependency, and separation, these adolescents also developed special difficulties in maintaining appropriate peer relationships or in coping with the loss of friendship.

For all three patients, parental alarm about the adolescent's self-destructive behavior and violence mobilized the parents to insist on hospitalization. All three patients were admitted just before or just following their sixteenth birthday.

CASE 1

Ann was accompanied to Chestnut Lodge by attendants from her second hospital because her stay there had been marked by repeated runaway episodes and violent destruction of furniture and seclusion room walls. She had received a preadmission diagnosis of schizoaffective psychosis and had been medicated daily with 900 mg lithium carbonate and 20 mg Navane. Her developmental and family history was as follows.

At age 3 weeks, Ann had been adopted into a strict Catholic family by her scientist father and her homemaker mother. Her only sibling, a brother four years older, also had been adopted. She was described as a "good baby," only giving concern because of psychosomatic skin difficulties. As a latency child she did well in school and became extremely attached to two female schoolmates and their families. In the years preceding Ann's adolescence, family life was overshadowed by parental concern for her older brother's chronic hyperaggressive behavior and his need for outpatient psychotherapy. Ann's father traveled about one-third of the time in connection with his scientific work. When he was at home, he often took Ann to baseball games or to the zoo, occasions Ann treasured for her father's warmth, support, and private comfort in the absence of her mother. At home the mother kept the family in a constant turmoil and looked to Ann for reality-testing and dependent gratification.

As with many of the parents of psychiatrically hospitalized adoptees (Weiss, 1984), Ann's mother suffered from an untreated and moderately severe personality disorder, specifically one with schizotypal, histrionic, and borderline features. Under stress the mother evidenced confusion and a definite thought disorder. Ann's mother needed to keep a constant, intrusive check on all of Ann's activities, inner thoughts, and feelings. To gain some separateness in late childhood, Ann began spending more and more free time at her two chums' houses, becoming intensely attached to their mothers. Both of these women seemed to sense Ann's need for appropriate support, mirroring, and freedom of action. When Ann was 11-years-old, both her chums' fathers changed jobs; these families on whom Ann had depended so much, especially when her father was absent, moved out of town.

Almost immediately Ann started joining the "drug crowd" at school. The first year she would meet her new friends before and after school to share beer. The second year they shared marijuana as well. Secretly Ann cultivated the friendship of an older girl, Marie, from an antisocial family of whom Ann's parents disapproved. Marie's parents welcomed open drug use and drug trade in their household. During her thirteenth and fourteenth year Ann was absent from home more and more, began truancy from school, and solidified her secret dependence on her new drug-using friends. When Ann turned fifteen she fell in love with a 19-year-old motorcycle gang member and began disappearing from home for a week at a time to live with him. Her school grades, always excellent in the past, plummeted. As a by-product of her ambivalence toward her mother and their escalating power struggle, Ann began to suffer suicidal thoughts. She was trapped between the wish to disown her mother and the wish to sacrifice her own autonomy for her mother. When her often-absent father and confused mother attempted to set limits on Ann's behavior (with the help of outpatient professionals), Ann easily outmaneuvered them. This led to her first hospitalization.

The staff at that hospital found Ann depressed and suspicious. When they insisted that she conform with ward life policies, she became violent, and required seclusion and medication. Her boyfriend then engineered her escape from that hospital. Several weeks later, with the help of police, Ann was located and forcibly hospitalized at a second hospital. She again regressed and the staff reached an impasse in attempting to deal with her violent behavior. After several months she was transferred to Chestnut Lodge.

From the beginning here, Ann almost completely eschewed violence. She presented initially as a shy, emotionally infantile but physically tall and attractive 16-year-old girl. At first she avoided fitting into the nursing unit. Several times she retreated, weeping, to her bed that was covered with 20 comforting, stuffed animals. Perhaps this more dependent and more cooperative style of relating to Chestnut Lodge, as compared with her adaptation within the previous hospital, was related to the family's greater acceptance of Ann's need for major psychosocial treatment. At the previous hospital, the early discontinuance of Ann's medication (which appears in her case to have had a negative effect), may also have supported her cognitive controls and acquisition of more adaptive behavior.

During the early weeks in this hospital, Ann gradually opened herself to the emotional support offered by fellow patients and staff. Very slowly she also was able to accept the staff's limits on her behavior. After an anxious testing period (with regard to unit policies, chores, and duties) in which she expressed her fears by a brief runaway episode, and by chronic avoidance and passive–aggressive behaviors, Ann slowly relaxed and began to contribute to the milieu as a constructive community member. After several months she fully accepted the program's support and containment. She had become deeply attached to several patients, including a young male patient and an adopted, female patient, who had a similar history and family pattern.

In individual psychotherapy Ann exhibited the distrustful, controlling, inhibited communication that she had learned in coping with her mother's intrusiveness. At other times she would demonstrate in therapy her own positive, dependent yearnings. She spent a number of interviews attractively dressed in the chair across from her male therapist, fixing him with a silent, yearning, "hungry infant" stare. She was determinedly passive and for weeks would not talk about her feelings or observations. Using the defense of splitting, she deposited her deprived, depressive, and angry self with the therapist while her creative, positive responses emerged in other settings. Schools, which, from the ages of 6- to 10-years-old, had been a source of dependable gratification and achievement, quickly became again a setting for Ann's healthy ego growth. Six months after hospitalization at Chestnut Lodge, she had redressed the one year's school deficit she showed on admission.

About halfway through her fourteen-month hospital stay, her therapist announced his plans to take a three week vacation. While withholding from him any acknowledgment of separation feelings, Ann did confide to the nursing staff how upset she was by expressing to them her angry feelings toward the therapist and her guilt over these feelings. Ann couldn't stop worrying that in the therapist's absence she might impulsively cut her wrists or run away from the hospital. The staff responded by requiring that she be escorted at all times that she was outside of the unit, until the therapist's return. In reaction to this supportive limit-setting, she responded ambivalently. Sometimes she complained angrily; at other times she was grateful.

After the therapist's return from vacation, the transference split moved into the therapeutic situation. On "good days," Ann seemed at ease and openly conversational. She reviewed her anger at her distancing father and controlling mother. This review had the character of a cautious admission rather than a spontaneous catharsis or free association. She also was able to evaluate and review with the therapist her ambivalent feelings toward Marie and her rescuing 19-year-old boyfriend at home. But even during Ann's phases of greatest comfort with, and trust in, the therapist, she could not discuss the transference experience directly. Instead she would become proudly secretive and withholding. On her "bad days" in therapy, she would indicate angry or petulant distrust of the therapist and often march out of the session if he pushed her into some meaningful exchange. Direct interpretation of this behavior, as a pattern that derived from her battles with her mother, was experienced by Ann as overly intrusive.

Both the negative and the positive side of her transference ambivalence to the therapist intensified. As before, while Ann localized her symbiotic rage and positive merging into the psychotherapy situation, she adapted well elsewhere in the program. School and nursing staff members came to respect and appreciate her and to feel that plans for Ann's hospital discharge soon might be appropriate. During her final weeks in the hospital the "good therapy days" predominated and she finally seemed to be accepting a psychotherapeutic alliance. Unbeknownst to the hospital staff, however, the split was still being expressed by means of Ann's carefully crafted plan to run away from the hospital with her chum, the female adoptee who had similar problems.

Ten days after running away from the hospital, Ann called her family, offering to return home, and to cooperate at home providing her family agreed to have her discharged from Chestnut Lodge. Her mother, who had become totally disheartened by this second experience of not knowing Ann's whereabouts, agreed to her daughter's demand. According to a later follow-up inquiry, Ann's parents have seen her subsequent development as relatively trouble-free.

One might evaluate this patient's total course of residential therapy as relatively successful. Unlike her two previous hospitalizations, Ann was able to accept the support and containment of phase 1 at Chestnut Lodge. In phase 2 she was able to reincorporate her previous positive work and social identities, which had emerged during latency but subsequently were destroyed by the early adolescent regression. Yet in relation to her core, preoedipal, separation anxiety and her conflict between the need to both murder and merge lovingly with the maternal object, Ann progressed in psychotherapy to the point of revealing and expressing the conflict but not in resolving it. The conflict was too anxiety-producing in the transference. Her manipulative splitting defenses were too attractive and polished. Her entire life history taught her not to permit this degree of vulnerable dependency and intimacy, not to give up her vigilant autonomy and distancing defense.

Ann's final *DSM-III* diagnoses were Axis I Dysthymic Disorder, Chronic and Axis II Borderline Personality Disorder. Our impression, based in part on clinical experience with other similar nonadopted patients and in part derived from the quantitative observations reported above, is that had Ann not been adopted she would have been able to tolerate the transference anxiety focused in the psychotherapy relationship. She therefore would have been able to relinquish the splitting defense. If not adopted, she might have been able to give up the need to distance herself from therapeutic intimacy and dependency (Dreyfus, 1967).

CASE 2

The intrapsychic and familial processes leading to hospitalization, as well as the unfolding of the treatment processes as observed in the hospital, in the case of Brenda bear many similarities to Ann's. Brenda's defensive style showed more active and violent protest and less distancing and passive-aggressive behaviors than Ann. This difference may reflect identification with the adoptive mother, who in Brenda's case was more vengeful and retaliatory than Ann's more helpless and responsive adoptive mother. Brenda, who also terminated hospitalization by running away, stayed in the program 8 months longer than Ann. Apparently this was because of Brenda's greater intrapsychic disorganization, impulsivity, and greater tendency to regress under stress into self-destructive and ineffective rageful behaviors.

Brenda's admission to Chestnut Lodge was her fifth hospitalization. Her "chief complaints" were 4 years of severe depression and gradually escalating assaultiveness, self-mutilation, sexual promiscuity, running away from home, alcoholism, and substance abuse. The conflicts generating these symptoms appear to have derived from three major sources: the closeness between her mother and brother, which appeared to Brenda to exclude her from a satisfying attachment to her mother; her father's disabling physical condition, which when she was 10-years-old, removed her father as a supportive person; and her early preadolescent maturation at ages 11 and 12. During her early months here she tested the limits more than Ann did with more assaultiveness and more unpredictable oscillations between satisfied dependency on the nursing unit and sudden rejections of the unit's support. Eventually, however, Brenda did form intense peer attachments and ambivalent but intense attachments to both her female psychotherapist and to several other staff members. Over time she had less need to test the containment of the program.

Unlike Ann's stable splitting between psychotherapy and other therapeutic settings (a passively controlling defense presented to the therapist and a more relaxed acceptance of the unit and school), Brenda's splitting defense varied dramatically over time within all her relationships. At any one time, Brenda might divide her world into the "good guys" and the "bad guys." This enabled her to express intensely her rage and distrust with one set of staff members while concurrently experiencing nurturance and safety with others. This splitting pattern defensively prevented Brenda from confronting her own internal ambivalence toward "parental" figures as they were represented by the staff. During the early weeks of treatment she remained distrustful and aloof with her psychotherapist while slowly accommodating on the unit and steadily doing better in school. After 4 months at Chestnut Lodge, Brenda began to feel comfortable with her therapist, until she announced a forthcoming vacation. Thereupon Brenda became preoccupied, both with getting a change of therapist and with planning to run away from the hospital. When she was provided with a male interim therapist, during her therapist's vacation, Brenda soon decided that he was too aloof (like her mother) and uncaring; so she refused to attend therapy meetings.

Toward the end of her first year in the hospital, however, Brenda began to tolerate more intimate, dependent, and trustful experiences with her female therapist. As the anxiety accompanying Brenda's intensified dependency increased, her behavior on the unit and in school deteriorated. After 1½ years here, Brenda's transference anxiety over confronting her own core depression and her history of unmet dependency needs again intensified, finally leading her to refuse further psychotherapy. The hospital then assigned a new therapist to her case. Brenda's early attempt to form an alliance with the new therapist was accompanied by the appearance of a psychosomatic skin rash. When, after 2 months with the new therapist, the therapist left for a 4-day holiday, Brenda angrily began to plan her final and termination elopement, which occurred shortly before her eighteenth birthday. Her discharge diagnoses were Axis I Dysthymic Disorder, Chronic and Axis II Borderline and Oppositional Personality Disorders. Subsequently we learned from Brenda's family that she obtained work in another part of the country and never returned home. Later she married a member of the Armed Services and moved to an assignment in Asia.

Similar to our evaluation of Ann, our impression is that had Brenda not been adopted, she would have been less rigidly oppositional over a less prolonged period of residential treatment. No amount of corrective experience or interpretive work with her obvious tranference conflicts reassured her. She continued to feel, in an almost persecutory manner, that even minimal interruptions of therapeutic support (due to the therapists' vacation) were intolerable and indicative of the staff's lack of dependability.

Like Ann, Brenda accepted the program's support and containment except during phases of intensified transference anxiety. She became attached and made some useful new identifications. She used her 22 months at Chestnut Lodge to attain considerable new social skills and to give up most of the symptomatic behavior she exhibited on admission. Brenda never mastered her deep-seated, preoedipal, dependency conflicts nor became able to negotiate a shared therapeutic responsibility for separation from the program. Ironically, as with Ann, Brenda's own manipulatively executed departure occurred only a matter of months before a planned therapeutic termination probably would have occurred. Brenda's insight process foundered on her inability to tolerate, even with the support of four-times per week psychotherapy, the therapeutic shame of examining her dependent yearnings. How unrealistic yet inevitable, given her earlier experience, were her angry demands for an omnipotently devoted parent in the person of the therapist. Like Ann, when overwhelmed by anxiety, Brenda turned to self-assertion and autonomy (at all costs) to help assuage her inner suffering. Yet this final elopement from the hospital—while it did serve to maintain Brenda's sense of self-control and self-direction—also robbed her of an opportunity to understand more fully her own dependent needs and separation fears.

CASE 3

Sam's treatment shows many of the same characteristics as the first 2 cases. Sam was admitted to Chestnut Lodge shortly after his sixteenth birthday and was hospitalized for 20 months. He had had one previous brief hospitalization. For 3 years prior to that hospitalization, Sam had become increasingly depressed, lost in fantasy, avoided school, and suffered both sleeping and eating disorders. He had engaged in impulsive sexual approaches to his mother and grandmother; prior to his first hospitalization, he set several fires while involved in fantasy. He suffered intense guilt and made a suicidal gesture 6 months before his first hospitalization. Sam's admission diagnoses were Axis I, Dysthymic Disorder and Conduct Disorder; and Axis II, Avoidant Personality Disorder.

Unlike Ann and Brenda, Sam had not been adopted in infancy. After birth he had experienced a few months living with his biological family, then lived in several foster homes before being adopted at 4-years-old. He also suffered abuse at the hands of his older, adopted brother who repeatedly sexually and physically abused him throughout childhood. This older brother had to be removed from the home and hospitalized several years before Sam was hospitalized. Sam had a history of encopresis until age 6 and enuresis to age 12. He also had asthma until age 3. The adopted parents had a highly disturbed marriage. The parental behavior had included neglect by the father; from the mother highly anxious and controlling behavior predominated.

Over the first 6 months of hospitalization here, Sam gradually learned greater sensitivity to the needs of others, greater age-appropriate responses, and greater self-control. Early in the hospital stay he formed an intense symbiotic dependency with a female patient. It was interesting that in relation to his psychotherapist, Sam showed a mixture of the transference behaviors exhibited by both Ann and Brenda. Soon after admission, he took a defiant, withholding, suspicious, avoidant stance toward his therapist. Two months after hospitalization, for a short time, he refused to come to the therapist's office. The therapist was seen as an intrusive, controlling mother from whom Sam had to withhold any thoughts or feelings. If the therapist pushed for more communication, there would be a brief, incendiary outburst. In the transference he would try to evoke a power struggle around therapeutic communication. Like Ann and Brenda, Sam found the therapist's summer vacation extremely difficult. When the hospital provided an interim therapist for this 3-week period, he idealized the interim therapist so that he avoided attending the first two or three meetings after this assigned therapist returned from vacation.

During his second 6 months in the hospital, with a great deal of psychotherapeutic work with Sam around these deep-seated transference fears of depending on the therapist, Sam opened up in a more trusting fashion. He verbalized many themes of separation anxiety and reviewed the many experiences of repeated abandonments throughout his life, although when anxious, he would again retreat into noncommunication.

Sam gradually gained a new sense of identity and confidence in dealing with the hospital and the unit during his second year in the hospital. He took responsibility well and began a part-time job off hospital grounds. He also formed close bonds with several other patients who were in the process of being discharged from the hospital into an outpatient phase. Concomitantly he began to show appropriate adolescent independence from his parents at the age of 17. His father had remarried and failed to provide financial or emotional support. His mother, who up until this time had been supportive, could not tolerate Sam's new found self-assurance and informed the hospital that she could no longer communicate with him and therefore would no longer provide support for his treatment.

For several months efforts were made by both hospital staff and by the patient to reestablish an alliance with the patient's mother. The staff believed that Sam was not yet ready to leave the hospital and feared that premature discharge might bring on a return of Sam's symptoms. In the end, in order to continue the support of Sam's individuation, the decision was made to support him in his wish to attempt to leave the hospital for a while, at the same time, not returning to live with his family. He moved out to join a group of former patients. In Sam's case, the unresolved impasse, which led to a somewhat premature discharge, arose within his relationship to his mother. By enacting the final impasse in this manner, he was able to maintain some therapeutic contact with his therapist and with the nursing unit after his termination from the hospital program.

DISCUSSION

Many of the adopted patients, although not all, show the same characteristics as described in the 3 cases above. In regard to their transference conflicts, the treatment team is split off in such a way as to permit the release of rage, hurt, and disappointment against those who, at the moment, the patient has decided not to be dependent on. These controlling behaviors and distancing maneuvers support the patient's perceptual distortions of reality at a behavioral level. These include denial of the patient's own legitimate dependency needs and denial of the fact that these needs in fact can be met. Those staff members who are the recipients of the negative side of this splitting defense, then also become invested with the patient's projective identification defense in which the patient transfers onto the staff the feared parental images. These negative transference figures are seen by the adoptee as narcissistic and abandoning, rather than as simply having needs of their own, and some limits as to what they can provide.

In the cases that we have reviewed, there is another element that undermines the treatment. This happens when the therapist becomes the recipient of the negative side of the patient's splitting defense, and when the therapist is seen by the patient as abandoning and narcissistic, the treatment program as a whole then loses its principal interpretive resource on which a psychoanalytically oriented, residential treatment depends.

As we have just described, there is a repetitive pattern of transference conflicts and defenses. This pattern is particularly liable to occur in the mid-phase of treatment with an adoptee and consists of five elements: (1) easy regression within a nurturing environment; (2) exaggerated sensitivity to separation issues in the transference; (3) anxious need to use transferentially motivated distancing and controlling behaviors in dealing with negatively viewed adults in the treatment environment; (4) presence of particularly rigid forms of denial, splitting, and projective identification as transference defenses that undermine the earlier, established treatment alliance; and (5) undermining of the interpretive power of the treatment program through these defensive maneuvers so that the therapist is no longer credible to the patient. In discussing the similarity of this pattern among a group of such patients, and in noting that it is a transferential "bind" frequently encountered in nonadopted borderline patients, David Feinsilver (1986) has labeled the pattern "the malignant abandonment syndrome."

Before discussing several specific alterations of the usual format for long-term residential treatment for adoptees (and perhaps for others who show this malignant separation syndrome), it must be pointed out that to date there have been few studies in which admission characteristics of adolescents have been shown to predict later treatment processes or technical psychotherapeutic issues. Admission diagnoses and other admission assessments, of course, do indicate the general nature of the patient's defenses and may predict in general the nature and difficulty of trying to provide treatment. But with the exception of projective test data, admission characteristics have relatively little predictive power with respect to the specifics of the patient's later transference resistances and course of treatment. Therefore what has happened as a matter of practice is that—from the point of view of psychodynamic issues in the hospital—each patient is viewed as a unique and original problem. Psychoanalytically oriented clinicians working in these settings are not accustomed to using simple admission data such as "adoptee" as relevant to psychotherapeutic technique, although most would anticipate the content of the patient's fantasies to be around issues of abandonment or loss.

A review of cases demonstrating this malignant separation syndrome suggests several technical therapeutic innovations. First and simplest to implement is the suggestion that when an adoptee is admitted to long-term, psychoanalytically oriented, residential treatment, more effort needs to be made to educate the newly admitted patient concerning the difficulties of the malignant separation syndrome which lie ahead. This education ideally would occur at the time of the initial treatment planning conference with the patient and the family, and continue during the early weeks of family and individual therapy when the patient is still relatively comfortable within the hospital. Such an educational approach may serve to "immunize" the patient and take some of the strangeness and "out-of-control" unreality away from this special transference. For, in fact, what seems to have happened in many of our previous cases is that the patient loses the ability to perceive the difference between current reality and his or her early infantile reality. While this experience borders on a transference psychosis, on careful scrutiny the reaction is more accurately described as a willful retreat from reality.

It also may be useful to use antidepressants or psychostimulants, as has been suggested by Hans Huessy (1987). A number of clinical investigators have found that such medication is useful in adolescents who suffer from this form of depressive overactivity and impulsivity. Adolescent patients have been observed to gain considerable self-control from the use of these medications, particularly when they show the kind of genetic history that may be present with conduct disorders or borderline personality disorders.

It can be observed with many of our adolescents, and also in the first phase of hospital treatment with adoptees, that having several competing loci for treatment (namely, the school, the nursing unit, the family therapy, and the individual therapy) provides a security-giving therapeutic split. Many adolescent patients, early in the hospital stay, find it natural and comforting to experience different affective and defensive modes in the different settings and in relation to the different staff members with whom they are emotionally involved. It is only during the second phase, toward the end of the first year in the hospital, that this fit between the patient's need to use a splitting defense and the program becomes problematic. As regards the overall treatment process, the effort becomes one to assist integration of both sides of the patient's ambivalence. The fact that there is more than one adult therapeutic resource in the environment may invite the patient *not* to resolve his ambivalence but to continue acting out both negative and positive feelings in an unintegrated manner, unless the component staff of the various programs keep in close communication. With adoptees it appears that, especially in phase 2, a vigilant, supportive, and intimate containment should be reinstituted for 4 to 6 months, or until the patient can learn to avoid self-destructive action and to obtain insight into his or her needs to control and to distance when anxious.

In addition to the special reinstitution of the hospital containment process, the therapist's interpretive function could be taken over temporarily by the unit or by the family therapist (or by some other part of the program), at those times when the therapist is immobilized as a useful therapeutic figure because of the adoptee's negative projective identifications in the transference. At such times, whichever staff is invested with the trust and dependent yearnings is in a position to confront the patient with the fact that he or she is projecting onto the therapist a real experience which did happen early in life, but is not in fact being recreated now in reality by the therapist. This role-sharing process, in which the nonpsychotherapist is invested with the responsibility to make focused interpretations, may support the patient's ego and may help the patient gain self-control.

To summarize, our treatment recommendations for the malignant separation syndrome in the transference are (1) advanced preparatory education of patient and family; (2) medication; (3) tighter communication among staff and reinstitution of containment in the second phase of treatment; and (4) assigning an interpretive role to other, more positively invested staff when the psychotherapist temporarily becomes the negative object of the patient's misperceptions.

We are currently in the process of carrying out a follow-up study of the adaptation and symptom status of all of our patients 5 years after discharge from Chestnut Lodge. It will be interesting to see how those adoptees, who left during the second phase of treatment and avoided the work of the final separation–individuation phase, have adapted at the time of such a follow-up study. If one were to ask our adopted patients, doubtless they would say that they did not require as prolonged a hospital stay as we believed they did. This opinion, of course, flies in the face of recommendations by a number of clinicians, including comments by Gossett, Lewis, and Barnhart (1983), in which they state that the patient's condition at the 5-year follow-up study very much appears to be correlated with whether or not the adolescent continued outpatient psychotherapy following hospitalization.

ACKNOWLEDGMENTS

Gratefully we wish to acknolwdge the support of our investigations from Dexter M. Bullard, Jr. (Medical Director), John P. Fort (Clinical Director), Jaime Buenaventura (Director of Adolescent and Child Division), Teresita DiPinto (Assistant Director, Adolescent and Child Division), and from the nursing service, Mary-Louise Schmidt, R.N., M.A. (Director of Nursing) and Phyllis Stang, R.N., M.A. (Coordinator of Nursing, Adolescent and Child Division). Other colleagues whose collaboration has been significant include Robert A. Cohen, David B. Feinsilver, Roger S. Friedman, Cheryl Shea Gelernter, Robert K. Heinssen, Pat Inana, Herbert Landis, Thomas H. McGlashan, Rebecca E. Rieger, and Carol Thompson.

IV

SOCIAL POLICY AND CASEWORK ISSUES IN ADOPTION

15

History, Values, and Placement Policy Issues in Adoption

ELIZABETH S. COLE AND KATHRYN S. DONLEY

"Adoption" is a term used to describe a personal and legal act as well as a social service. Because adoption is a social construction, it is value laden and shaped by cultural forces. The Child Welfare League of America defines legal adoption as "the method provided by law to establish the legal relationship of parent and child between persons who are not so related by birth" (Child Welfare League of America, 1978, p. 11). Adoption services, in contrast, are the necessary array of professional assistance offered and coordinated by an agency, first, to assist birthparents whose children are placed for adoption, second, to place a child in an adoptive home, and third, to preserve and strengthen the adoptive family.

It is important to understand the difference between adoption and foster care. After an adoption, parents are invested with the same legal rights and responsibilities as biological parents. Foster parents, on the other hand, do not have these legal rights. These rights are either retained by the biological parents while the child is in temporary care or are transferred by the courts to a social agency.

Not all adoptions are arranged by social agencies. Independent or private adoptions are those in which legal adoption is planned and implemented without the participation of a licensed social agency. Stepparent adoptions account for about 75% of all independent adoptions (National Center for Social Statistics, 1975).

To gain a better understanding of adoption, the present chapter identifies and examines 10 basic values that shape the practice of adoption. We also discuss various policy recommendations associated with each phase of the adoption practice. Before entering into an examination of these issues, however, we begin with an overview of the history of adoption.

HISTORY OF ADOPTION

Adoption is an old institution in fact and in myth. References to it abound in the Bible. Perhaps the most popular of these is the adoption of a child found in the bull rushes by Pharaoh's daughter. In many ways, Moses' adoption was atypical of these early ones. Most early adoption was meant to serve a religious or political purpose (Hastings, 1908). For example, in India adoption often was used to provide a male heir in order to meet the demands of religious ceremonies. The Hindus and Chinese also used adoption in the context of ancestor worship and to insure their own passage to heaven. One function of adoption in Rome was to insure that candidates met the qualifications for political office. In addition, many of these ancient cultures used adoption to provide an heir to perpetuate the family or to manage the family's property.

Adoption was also a peacekeeping device in many early societies. It was used to build alliances between families and clans. In addition, by adopting the children of your enemy, you reduced the chances of invasion. Adoption also was a legitimized form of hostage taking.

The oldest set of written adoption law is found in the Code of Hammurabi (2800 B.C.). It reveals that members of that culture struggled with issues of risk in adoption which have a contemporary ring; for example, the unsuitability of adoptor and child for each other; treating biological children differently from those who are adopted; the traumatic impact on the child created by separation from a previous caretaker. Even the topic of adoptees searching for their birthparents is mentioned. In these cases, the adopted person was to be returned to the birthparents. Birthparents, on the one hand, did not have the right to demand the return of their child after the adoption. On the other hand, transgressions against the adoptive parents by the adopted person were grounds to return the child to its birthfamily (Clothier, 1939).

The Roman Empire, with its emphasis on the power of the father over the family, added the concept of complete termination of birthparents' legal rights in the process of adoption. Thus the adoption was absolute and could not be undone. These two concepts were to be central to modern American adoption law (Benet, 1976).

Two conclusions can be drawn from the early history of adoption. First, legal adoption was not a common but rather an exceptional experience. Second, the primary purpose of adoption was to serve adult interests rather than child interests. If a child benefited it was a secondary gain. Certainly the concept of the "best interests of the child" was not paramount, if indeed it was given any weight at all.

Most European countries, with the exception of England, built their law on the Roman and later Napoleonic codes. Napoleon retained the notions of the finality of adoption and the severing of parental rights but added to the exceptional nature of adoption by making it quite difficult to achieve. Napoleonic codes added an eligibility requirement for adoption. In order to adopt, a person had to be: over 50, sterile, at least 15 years older than the person to be adopted, and have reared the person for at least 6 years.

But the law of the United States was not derived from either Roman or Napoleonic codes. Its roots are in English common law, which does not provide for adoption. The major barrier to the introduction of adoption into common law is its conflict with the principles of inheritance. Land could only be transmitted from one person to another based on blood lineage. Land could not be given away in life nor after death by will. It had to go to the sons and relatives in stipulated order (Presser, 1972). Because of the commitment to common law principles in England, it was not until 1926 that adoption was created in the English legal system by statute. Moreover, it was not until 1969, again by statute, that all strictures against adopted persons inheriting were removed.

Adoption in the United States also had to be created by statute. Before this occurred, in the mid-nineteenth century, adoptions were done either informally or by indenturing the child to the new parents. With the advent of the industrial revolution, indenturing was discontinued as a major employment practice. The burgeoning population was larger than any apprenticeship system could accommodate. In response to these factors, adoption laws were created.

Initially, there was no consensus on what role the court should play in adoption. Several states merely provided that parents who had adopted a child be able to legally record the act. The procedure entailed the filing of a deed similar to the one used when acquiring real estate. In other states, the courts were bypassed completely and adoptions were achieved by individual acts of the legislature.

The first of the adoption statutes, as we know them, was passed by Massachusetts in 1851. It provided for court inquiry into and control over adoption. These statutes for the first time articulated that the purpose of adoption law was to promote the welfare of the child who was to be adopted (Presser, 1972).

Efforts to use adoption as a solution for the needs of homeless children began to grow in response to the emerging dissatisfaction with the congregate care arrangements of many charitable organizations. Prior to this time, homeless children who could not be indentured generally were kept in almshouses with the poor, infirm, and mentally ill. Charles Loring Brace, the founder of the New York Children's Aid Society, however, believed that family life was a far better solution for these children than institutional rearing. He stated that the "best of all asylums for the outcast child is the farmer's home" and that farmers were "our most solid and intelligent class" (Brace, 1872, p. 255). He believed that they would make the best foster and adoptive parents because it was in their interest to train children to aid them in their work. Consequently, he began the "orphan train movement" in which thousands of dependent children from eastern cities, who were an economic drain on the public coffers, were transported by railroad to "western" states (e.g., Nebraska, Michigan) where they would be an economic asset.

Although Brace and many others thought this scheme was ingenious, there was major opposition to it from the "asylum interests" and biological parents. The asylum directors felt that Brace was "scattering poison over the country" and that a few years in an asylum or house of detention "rendered these children of poverty much more fit for practical life, and purified them to be good members of society" (Brace, 1872, p. 235).

Biological parents, particularly Roman Catholics, felt that the whole scheme of western emigration was proselytizing since most of the farm families were Protestant. Indeed, many of the reports, sermons, and papers of the Children's Aid Society's board and staff had a strong anti-Catholic bias. It is not surprising then that later, as more complete adoption statutes were drafted, they had clauses requiring religious matching.

Despite the opposition, large scale fostering and adoption began to take hold. In 1859, 4,000 to 5,000 children had been placed in the West and between 20,000 and 24,000 nationwide (Brace, 1872). Children placed generally were between 2 and 14 years of age and were poor. Most children were considered adoptable except for some few who were "so perverse, and inheriting such bad tendencies and so stamped with the traits of vagabond life that a Reformatory is the best for them" (Brace, 1872, pp. 243–244).

Adoptive parents selected the children they wanted. Orphan trains or boats would move from town to town. The children sang or told stories about themselves at special public gatherings. The adults present would select a child for themselves, a relative, or a friend. There was little or no investigation, study, or preparation of these first adoptive parents. Later applicants wrote letters to the agency requesting children to be sent out to them.

Few birthparents were involved in these adoptions. The New York Children's Aid Society found that the poor living in their own homes "seldom wished to send out their children this way." Most children were described as "waifs" or "strays." In fact, children were placed on their own representation that they were parentless. Searches for biological parents, siblings, or extended family were rare (Brace, 1872, p. 266).

During this time, infants were seldom placed for adoption for several reasons. First, those placed in foundling homes seldom survived infancy. In some institutions, the death rate was reported to be as high as 95% (Thurston, 1930). Second, it was not feasible to separate newborn infants from their mothers until the advent of formula nutrition in the 1920s. Between 1900 and 1930, many states passed laws prohibiting the separation of mother and child during a 6-month nursing period (McConnell & Dore, 1983).

Until the 1920s, adoption of infants was not a widely accepted social practice in this country. Fear of the child's heredity was widespread, since children available were from poor or immigrant families against whom prejudice was high. In one request to the Chicago Child Care Society, adoptive parents requested that the agency assure them that the child did not have "one drop of Irish Blood" (McCausland, 1976).

Many professionals serving unmarried mothers did not believe in adoption. A prime example of this stance was the position taken by Kate Waller Barrett, the first director of the nationwide network of Florence Crittenton maternity homes. Mrs. Barrett was against adoption because of the high infant mortality in foundling homes and because she thought it was not good for the unmarried mother. By caring for her child, a mother could "atone for the behavior that led to her unmarried motherhood." In addition, mothering gave her a focus and a goal and would aid in "the reformation of her character" (McConnell & Dore, 1983, p. 10). The national Florence Crittenton Association maintained this stance until 1943.

Because of the written accounts of adoption practice found in agency reports and records, it is easy to lose sight of the fact that most nonrelated adoption placement occurred without the assistance of an organization. "Private" or "independent" (of an agency) adoptions have existed from colonial times to the present. It was the expansion of private adoption after World War I which led to a corresponding growth of adoption agencies both in this country and abroad.

World War I and the influenza outbreak that followed it resulted in a low birth rate that spurred an interest in adoption. Private brokers arranging adoptions made huge profits. Largely unregulated, the brokers were accused of defrauding or coercing unmarried mothers to give up their children as well as placing children with unfit parents (Witmer et al., 1963). These were referred to as "bootleg" or "black market" adoptions. Adoption agencies increased in number to compete with brokers and gave unmarried women an alternative in their placement decision making. Over time, adoption laws were amended to regulate private adoption by requiring that, prior to legal finalization, the circumstances of the placement and the fitness of the adoptive parents had to be submitted to and approved by the court (Witmer et al., 1963). These laws are in effect today in 45 states and in the District of Columbia. Five states only allow agency-approved adoption placements. These states include Delaware, Connecticut, Massachusetts, Minnesota, and Michigan.

After World War II, the renewed public interest in adoption was limited largely to infants. Agencies reported public objections to "illegitimacy and to bringing children of 'bad blood' into the family" (Reid, 1963, p. 24). Professionals themselves, armed with current psychological theories of inherited intelligence and the irreversible effects of poor early childrearing, began to limit their practice of adoption to healthy infants of known background. According to Reid (1963), "agencies were convinced and attempted to convince the public that they could guarantee them a perfect child; that by coming to an agency, adoptive parents could be sure that the child was without physical, emotional or mental defect, that his heredity was sound and adopting a child was a far less risky procedure than having one normally" (p. 30).

It was common practice until the 1960s to keep infants in "study homes" for 6 to 12 months following birth to observe their health and to have psychological testing done regarding their development. This was particularly true in the case of infants of unknown or questionable parentage. Children with known pathology in their background were considered unadoptable (Cole, 1985).

The postwar demand for adoption soon began to exceed the numbers of infants available for placement. In order to select among numerous applications, agencies developed restrictive eligibility requirements based on strictly applied and dubious psychological and social criteria. Prospective adoptive parents, who were put off or eliminated by these criteria, sought independent and black market adoptions and began to complain publicly. They were joined by some professionals who criticized the dubious labeling of infants and adoptive parents resulting from the use of psychological tests (Costin, 1963).

Over time, Senate investigations of the burgeoning black market in adoption and media attention to the rigidity of adoption agency policies and practices gave rise to cries for reform in the field of adoption (and foster care). These cries led in 1955 to a National Conference on Adoption sponsored by the Child Welfare League of America (Shapiro, 1956). Out of this conference grew a momentum that has gradually led to significant changes in social service casework policy and practice, not the least of which has been a reorientation of the field toward a "best interests of the child" philosophy. Many of these changes took place during the 1960s and 1970s and were due to massive political, social and moral changes of that period. The following are just a few of the societal changes that have affected adoption and foster care (see also Cole, 1985):

The *civil rights movement* gave rise to a corresponding child rights movement which focused on child welfare reforms. These reforms included the placement and adoption of children from institutions and foster care. Advocates for integration also became advocates for transracial adoption, while "Black power" advocates decried transracial placements and called for increased efforts to place children within their own race.

Consumerism led to the creation of militant adoptive parent groups such as the Council on Adoptive Parents (COAC) and the North American Council on Adoptable Children (NACAC). These groups urged the repeal of unreliable eligibility requirements; removal of the "unadoptable label" from children in foster homes; creation of adoption subsidies; more parent participation in agency assessment and selection decisions; and court reviews of children in foster care and institutional care. Consumerism also gave impetus to the growth of groups for adopted adults and birthparents. These groups also urged more participation and control over critical adoption decisions.

The *Freedom of Information Act* added more authority to demands by all adoption triad members (birthparents, adoptive parents, and adopted persons) for more open and honest communication and information.

The *growth of public interest law firms* gave birthparents a more powerful legal voice in the adoption process. Termination of parental rights became more difficult. Cases for putative father rights were established. Law suits were brought against agencies for arbitrary eligibility requirements and failure to promptly place children.

Changes in family structure, such as the dramatic increase in divorce, made single parenthood a normal occurrence. Singles became more acceptable as adoptors. Less stigma on single parenting contributed to more unmarried parents keeping and rearing children, thereby resulting in a shortage of infants for adoption. Remarriages resulted in more stepparent adoptions—currently the largest group of adoptions in the United States.

Changes in sexual mores led to a reduction in the stigma attached to out-of-wedlock pregnancy, thereby increasing the number of unmarried parents who are keeping and rearing their children.

The Child Welfare Reform and Adoption Assistance Act of 1980 (Public Law 296–272) marked strong Federal intervention into foster care and adoption reforms and urged agencies to become involved in *permanency planning.* The concept of permanency planning refers to efforts to maintain a child's birthfamily whenever possible, to return a child to his birthfamily as soon as possible, and failing either, to establish for him legally permanent nurturant relationships with caring adults preferably through adoption. As a result of the reforms coming out of this legislation, children who wait for adoption in the late 1980s (and presumably in the near future as well) are those who are 10 years and older; have serious physical, intellectual, or emotional problems; are from minority groups; and are members of large sibling groups. Taken together, these children constitute what is known as "special needs" adopted children.

In summary, adoption has undergone a number of radical changes in this century and, especially, in the past few decades. These changes present the caseworker, the mental health clinician, and the policy planner with many challenges. In order to meet these challenges effectively, the professional community must be aware of the values that currently underlie adoption and their implication for clinical intervention and policy development.

VALUES UNDERLYING ADOPTION PRACTICE

These are particular values that shape current adoption practice. Some of these values derive from the earliest social work principles; others derive from more recent practice developments and center around the rights of children and the conviction that families constitute the most appropriate setting for rearing children.

1. *Children are entitled to grow up within families. They need a safe, nurturing environment with at least one stable adult figure* (see Goldstein et al., 1973).

Our culture offers general agreement that families are where children belong. When parents are unable to rear their children or the children evidence serious behavioral difficulties because of parental action or inaction, professional advice often results in placement outside the family. The difficulty is to find the children an appropriate placement and activate a suitable plan of action to help the family function better or come to terms with the decision that someone else must become the parent to the child.

Traditional values about the need for a child to grow up with both a mother and a father are under heavy assault presently. Societal circumstances have begun to challenge the validity of the customary view of what constitutes a "suitable" family. When we consider the dramatic increase in the U.S. divorce rate, the frequency of single persons heading households, and the reality that many Americans grow up well in single-parent families, the old viewpoint seems open to doubt. Among experienced adoption workers, there is a growing perception that for school-age children single-parent candidates may offer equally appropriate or even superior parenting potential.

2. *If the family of origin is unable or unwilling to provide this experience, the child will need an alternative family* (see Goldstein, Freud, & Solnit, 1979).

The dilemma is how to determine if the birthfamily is truly unable or unwilling. Child welfare workers are often confused about how best to approach this decision. Adoption workers tend to focus on the child in care as the client and view families (birthparents, foster parents, and adoptive parents) as resources. Protective service workers tend to focus on the family as the client and view the children of the family as the prime motivators in the parents' rehabilitative effort.

The recent trend of court opinions in disputed cases is toward demanding that placing agencies produce evidence of their concerted efforts to help birthfamilies ameliorate the conditions which created the need for the child's placement.

3. *For children who need alternative families, adoption is the preferred means of substitute parenting once it is determined the birthparents are unable or unwilling to provide care* (see Child Welfare League of America, 1978).

Another fact which will impact on this particular value is that most often children who have been "in care" while legal issues are resolved or efforts at family reunion have been under way have now formed new parent–child attachments to their caretaking family. If that family has not considered adopting the child or only meets minimal qualifications of the agency, because foster parents and adoptive parents are perceived as distinctly different candidates, the options are not appealing. The agency can honor the attachment and struggle to retroactively prepare the caretaker as adopters or breech the attachment and hope to successfully move the child to a new, adoptive family. The reality is that there will be difficulties in pursuing either option. In the first instance, the foster parent may not be willing to commit to adoption or may resist the preparation for adoption. In the second instance, the child may be so committed to the foster parents that establishing new attachments may prove overwhelming and the adoptive family may face endless behavioral problems.

4. *The adoption decision must be made early in a child's placement and with minimal delay and uncertainty* (see Child Welfare League of America, 1978).

Although this approach seems logical, it is difficult to achieve. Children have lingered in foster care because of court and agency delays in determining whether parents are willing and able to assume their responsibilities. Agency staff turnover and high caseloads frequently result in little rehabilitative effort with birthparents. Courts do not wish to involuntarily terminate parental rights in cases where help was promised families but not delivered. Both agencies and courts have difficulty in deciding whether separation from dysfunctional parents is more helpful or harmful.

5. *Adoption constitutes a lifelong experience for all parties (child, birthparents, and adoptive parents)* (see Nelson, 1985).

The traditional view held that adoption emulated the genetic birth experience. The adopted child was indistinguishable from children born to a family; the parents, once the adoption adjustment was complete, would regard the child as their own; the birthparents would forget the pain and go on with their lives; the child, successfully integrated into the new family, would claim the adoptive parents as his or her true parents; agency involvement would cease on completion of the legal process with only gentle reminders that the agency was available to help if the family requested help.

The emerging views holds that adoption is a unique, life long experience, not to be confused with genetic experience. Many birthparents grieve the loss of the child throughout the rest of their lives (see Brodzinsky, Chapter 16). Even those birthparents who freely choose adoption as the best plan for their child may need help in validating the feelings that surround the adoption experience. Adopted children will need to cope throughout their lives with the reality that they have two families (see Brodzinsky, Chapter 1). Adoptive parents are encouraged to join their children in dealing with this fact and to use the process to increase their attachment to the children they have adopted. The agency anticipates that the adopted person, the birthfamily, and the adoptive family will experience periods of particular vulnerability to stress. Supportive services of a sporadic or on-going nature are developed and offered by the placing agency as a matter of course.

6. *Birthparents and adoptive parents should choose the degree and type of contact and information shared between them before and after adoption* (see Sorosky et al., 1978).

It has been customary for the biological parents to have little or no contact with the agency and child after legal rights have been terminated, either voluntarily or involuntarily. This practice is no longer true; we should expect a different and continuing role for parents. First, more adopted persons, children as well as adults, are seeking out biological parents who are unknown to them. It means that biological parents should know this is a possibility at the time they surrender a child. Second, more older children are being placed for adoption with foster parents or others; they know who and where their biological parents are. In many cases the parents continue contact with the child. Third, the concept of "openness" in adoption is being explored (see Baran & Pannor, Chapter 17). Biological parents may select adoptive parents from agency studies. They may sometimes meet one another (with true identities hidden or, in some cases, revealed). They may agree to exchange information either through the agency or directly. At the very least, there is an acceptance of the need for biological parents to keep the agency informed of medical conditions which may affect the child. Fourth, in the future, agencies may be asked to recontact biological parents to determine if they are willing to take back their child after a reasonable time, if the agency has been unable to find an adoptive family. This provision was recently made into law in Great Britain. Fifth, biological parents will grieve and mourn the loss of their children, even infants they have known only briefly (Brodzinsky, Chapter 16). Some will need professional help with this for some time after termination.

7. *Adopted children are entitled to information about their birth, their birthfamily, significant genetic and social history, their placements, and the circumstances of their adoption* (see Child Welfare League of America, 1978).

This value reflects a basic shift in perspective. In former times, it was believed that background information on the child should be provided adoptive parents in case the child eventually became curious. A newer view holds that children who grow up apart from their family of origin will require explanation and clarification as the realization of their family status grows. Without this type of information, they are likely to experience increased difficulty in resolving the inexplicable losses associated with being adopted (see Brodzinsky, 1987, Chapter 1; Schechter & Bertocci, Chapter 4).

8. *Information should be freely provided the adoptive parents so it can be communicated to the youngster during the early childhood years in an age-appropriate manner* (see Child Welfare League of America, 1978).

Disclosure of information on the child to the adoptive parents remains a controversial issue in that the statutory and regulatory prohibitions were made when infant placement was the prevalent pattern. Most states severely restrict the information that can be communicated once adoption is underway. In most jurisdictions, agencies are permitted to share nonidentifying information but specifically are prohibited from sharing "identifying" information. For older children this prohibition is pointless and confidentiality becomes confused with secrecy.

Some agencies give the new parents full disclosure before the adoption occurs. Some agencies carefully limit the disclosure to nonidentifying information. Most report difficulty in obtaining complete information for adoptive parents. In part, this gap reflects the reality that birthfamilies who lose custody of their children and even some parents who voluntarily relinquish children for adoption fail to provide comprehensive information. In part, it also indicates how recent is the practice which holds that background information is so important.

9. *If the adoptive parents refuse to give the child the information, the adopted person should have access to disclosure at legal majority* (see Sorosky et al., 1978).

While there is still controversy about disclosure to adopted persons, consensus in the field is moving in the direction of disclosure at legal majority to the adoptee despite the adoptive parents' objections. Most professionals seem to want mutual agreement between the adopted person and the birthparent before fully identifying information is made available to the parties.

10. *Preparation of adoptive parents should emphasize enhancing their parenting potential rather than investigating or rejecting them* (see Hartman, 1979).

All adoptions can be divided into two types—those accomplished through agency intervention and those accomplished without agency intervention. While agency and nonagency results may be similar (Meezan et al., 1978), the work with the child placed for adoption and the services afforded the adoptive family may be dramatically different.

Most nonagency adoptions involve very young children, often babies, placed through private sources or intermediaries. Children involved in agency adoptions range from the very young through teenagers. There is much more focus on preparation for placement and support services after the placement, if an agency is involved in the adoption. There is also much more interest in using an educative approach to adoption rather than the more traditional "investigative" approach in an agency placement.

CRITICAL ISSUES IN ADOPTION POLICY
AND PRACTICE

Aside from the values to be considered while gaining a better understanding of adoption, we also need to examine various policy issues at each step in the adoption process. Whether the adoption is accomplished through a child-placing agency or as an independent adoption (without agency assistance), the steps in the process are potentially the same (Cole, 1985):

1. Identifying children needing adoption
2. Legally freeing children for adoption
3. Preparing children for adoption
4. Finding, preparing, and selecting adopters
5. Placement
6. Postplacement services
7. Legal finalization
8. Postadoption services

At each of these steps there are clusters of policy, practice, and legal issues that need to be resolved. None of these tasks are performed as they were 10 to 15 years ago.

Identifying Children Needing Adoption

The first step in the adoption process is to ensure that every child who needs an adoptive family is identified. One's idea of who is or is not adoptable determines which children are selected or eliminated for consideration. On what basis is the critical decision made? Few children other than problem-free white infants or toddlers were classified as adoptable until the 1960s (Kadushin, 1980). Public attitude toward adoption has never been entirely positive (Kirk, 1964). Illegitimacy and a fear of bringing "bad blood" into the family caused doubt about the benefits of adoption. Early findings from psychological testing fed into the belief that defective parents bred defective children. Agencies developed a "blue ribbon" certification of the adoptable child in order to sell adoption (Reid, 1963).

The adoptive parent and children's rights movement of the late 1960s and 1970s began to challenge agencies. They contended that no child was unadoptable. Their advocacy efforts resulted in changing the professional norm to accepting all manner of children as adoptable rather than seeing other than infants as an exception to the norm (Cole, 1985). But this norm, while clearly articulated, is not everywhere accepted and practiced. Identifying negative attitudes about which children are or are not adoptable and correcting them through training and education is a significant practice issue. Meanwhile, advocates have encouraged several strategies to press agencies to consider all children for adoption. The most significant strategies include:

1. Internal case audits and reviews by third parties to examine individual case goals
2. Publication of a comparison of agency performance in the adoptive placement of children by the children's characteristics (age, race, handicaps, etc.)
3. Withholding funding of foster care programs unless the agency has a proactive adoption program for all children or linkage with a proactive program
4. Tightening of licensing requirements for agencies insuring that all types of children are served
5. Legal suits against agencies for failure to place all kinds of children in adoptive families

All these activities add up to an affirmation of the principle that adoption is a service for all children. It is a positive outcome of the changes of the 1980s. The challenge of the coming years is to keep the focus on this group of children with special needs for attention and action. Communities wanting adequate adoption services need to provide resources equally to those groups serving children with special needs and those serving infants.

Legally Freeing Children for Adoption

In the second step of the process, biological parents of children placed for adoption are categorized into two groups: those who freely consent to the adoption (voluntary surrender or termination) and those who do not wish to consent but are overruled by a court of law (involuntary surrender or termination). Until recently, more attention has been given the first group of parents.

Voluntary Surrender of Children

Until the 1960s, adoption was represented by society as the ideal solution for an illegitimate pregnancy, especially when the option of marriage of the parents was not possible. The term "illegitimate" was value laden. It meant unlawful, both in the legal and moral sense. Children were considered "bastards," a word of unquestionable opprobrium. In many jurisdictions their birth certificates were of a different color. Their mothers were considered sexually promiscuous—tainted. Their future career and marriage prospects were dim if the fact of the birth were to be made public. Abortion was a legally limited option and had minimal public acceptance. Paradoxically, although all these factors were present in our society, the majority of single parents never placed their children for adoption. It has never been the parents' preferred option (Kadushin, 1980).

The legal, social, and economic upheavals of the sixties and the resulting shifts in sexual mores, women's rights, and consumerism have further affected the choice of adoption. Access to contraceptives and abortion have come with expanding women's rights; so too have mobility and access to the job market.

It is now easier for a young woman to leave home and find a job. This, plus the availability of welfare benefits, gives today's mother more options. The stigma of being an unmarried parent has lessened as more and more children are being reared by divorced parents. The single unmarried parent does not stand out in today's community as he or she once did.

While it is easy to recognize that there have always been pressures for unmarried parents to place their children, there are corresponding values which mitigate against it. Our society holds that mothers who carry and bear children must want to rear them. A "mystical" bond exists between mother and child. While we recognize the major sacrifice made by many mothers who place their children, it is still seen as an act that goes against nature. What this construct fails to recognize is that there are parents who choose to give birth to a child rather than abort, but do not wish to parent. In the past they could mask this decision with the unselfish, socially acceptable motive of providing the child with a better family. This may no longer be true.

Pregnancy counselors know that many teenagers are under pressure from their peers not to give up their child, since the giving up is viewed as "unnatural." This viewpoint is particularly true in those cultural groups where there is a tradition of kinship networks helping rear and support the nuclear family (blacks, Native Americans, and some Hispanics). This trend will increase as minority groups continue to reaffirm their cultural values.

Teenage parents are caught in the maelstrom of this cross-current of values. It is a perplexing problem as the evidence supports the fact that the teenage mother and her child will be, in all likelihood, at high risk and become medically, educationally, and emotionally disadvantaged (Moore, Hofferth, & Worthheimer, 1979).

Another impact on the voluntary freeing of children for adoption has been the changing perception of the role of fathers. Our society believes it is unnatural for an unmarried father to want to parent his child. In an era of rising entitlements and equal rights, the putative father's situation remains an anachronism. Courts and agencies have viewed putative father as peripheral. Until 1972, it was generally held he had no rights at all. Attempts to accord rights to putative fathers have been met with a variety of responses. Some feel we should not reward the unmarried father with rights—he is not worthy. Others believe it is due acknowledgment of his civil rights and a way to make him responsible for his sexual activity. Recent American court decisions have held that under certain circumstances putative fathers have some right to be notified of an adoptive plan.[1] Which putative fathers and under what circumstances remains unclear and muddled.

Professional social workers express some of the strongest negative opinions about putative fathers. One of the most unpopular provisions of a recent model adoption law, proposed by the Department of Health and Human Services, was one which would have reinforced putative father's potential rights to custody. Many agency respondents objected to this move and described putative fathers as unworthy of consideration as parents, sometimes characterizing them as "rapist," "involved in incestuous relationships," "being rewarded for one-night flings," "callous and uncaring."

Available research on the unmarried father is summarized by Kadushin (1980) and indicates that these negative attitudes are not borne out by the facts. Most pregnancies are not the result of rape or incest. Researchers have found that the father is not unlike the mother in age and socioeconomic background. Their relationship has generally been of some duration preceding the pregnancy. Those few agencies serving fathers have described them as concerned and wanting to be of help.

Many agencies have avoided working with fathers because of the inconvenience of identifying and locating them. Once involved, some fathers may choose another plan for the child in opposition to the plan of the mother or the agency (Barber, 1975). Whether the policy to avoid dealing with fathers stems from negative attitudes toward them or the desire to expedite the adoptive placement of a child, the result may legally deprive fathers of their rights and encourage them to avoid responsibility for sexual activity.

All these questions, it seems, rise out of the equal rights movements and the evolution of an enhanced fathering role of men. Has the responsibility fallen unfairly on the woman in the past? Is it possible for a man who has fathered a child in the most casual of sexual encounters to want to rear that child if the mother does not wish to? Is it unnatural for a single male to want to nurture a child? Should the presumption in law and in fact be that he is unfit until he proves otherwise, or that he is fit until proven otherwise? Are there two classes of putative fathers: those deserving consideration as fathers and those who do not? If so, how do they differ? The law does not judge the fitness of the mother by the circumstances of the conception but rather by her capacity to parent. Should the standard be the same for the father?

At the base of these questions is the acknowledgement that our values about the responsibility for sexual activity and the role of fathers, especially single fathers, are changing. It seems clear that the direction of the expansion is toward according or recognizing the father's rights and responsibilities. It also seems that because of the sharp difference of opinions more legal clashes between unmarried parents and between agencies and fathers are inevitable.

Involuntary Surrender of Children

Among children who become legally free for adoption, a significant number come from families where the biological parents did not consent to the adoption.

As the supply of readily adoptable infants decreased, attention was turned to other children in foster care to determine whether adoption would be the best plan. Most children had not come into care for purposes of adoption. In their study, Jenkins and Norman (1974) characterized the biological parents of children in care as having the problem that led to the child's being placed. In few cases did the child's behavior precipitate the move. They point out that the parents tend to be single women, a high proportion from minority groups, with a problem (mental illness, alcoholism, drug abuse, or lack of employment), and without a strong support group of extended family or friends. She is generally poor. Her needs are both intrapsychic and socio-economic.

The issue with parents of children in foster care is that they have not resumed parenting and have left their children too long in care, raising the need for a planned, permanent family through adoption. The consumer and civil rights movement of the 1960s has led to more and better legal representation for biological parents. Courts now agree that parents have a right to treatment for their socioeconomic and intra-psychic problems. Furthermore, child welfare agencies have been criticized because they represent themselves as offering services to parents, and hold forth to the community that foster care is only temporary while the biological family is being rebuilt. When no services are given to the parents, agencies are guilty of misrepresentation at the very least.

The political question raised regarding the parents of children in care is whether they are being treated fairly. Should they, the holders of the presenting problem, receive casework time at least equal to that given the child and the child's foster parents? Should they be able to receive the same financial and medical benefits received by the foster parents for the child's upkeep? Are they being discriminated against because they are women and of a minority race? Parents' advocates argue that society does not value these parents equally with the middle-class adopters and foster parents.

It seems clear that in the future more time, energy, and attention will be focused on the parents, with an aim toward preventing the family crises which create the initial separation, or in supporting the family in crisis.

Children who are legally freed for adoption then must either become available through voluntary means (the biological parent or parents consents to the adoption) or through involuntary means (a court action terminates parental rights). Voluntary termination of parental rights was once viewed as a relatively simple process. It is now a thicket of issues and problems. Increased focus on insuring parents' rights have created changes. Courts require evidence that parents knew what they were doing and gave informed consent, free of fraud or duress. Written records detailing what was said are becoming increasingly important and thus need to be carefully drawn. There is some support for having all consents or surrenders of custody either taken in court or having a court subsequently approve them.

Debate centers over whether the surrender or release for adoption should be irre-vocable once signed or if there should be a period where parents may change their minds. If there is a grace period, how long should it be in order to be consistent with parents' rights and yet allow early and secure placement of the child?

As we have mentioned, the question of which putative fathers have what rights adds to the muddle. Agencies now generally feel that the putative father must be notified of the adoption plan. He may either acknowledge or deny paternity. If he acknowledges, he may consent to the adoption or bring forward his own plan, which must be considered. These notification procedures take a great deal of time.

Here then is a head-on collision between conflicting values of two professions, law and social work. Social workers believe it is in a baby's best interest to effect a speedy adoption placement and to spare the child as many moves as possible. Courts believe a person is entitled to due process regardless of how much time it takes to satisfy it.

The resolution of this conflict appears to be emerging in favor of speedier due process. In recommending that courts consider termination proceedings like other emergency cases, Goldstein et al. (1979) state that procedural and substantive decisions should never exceed the time the child-to-be-placed can endure loss and uncertainty.

When parental rights are involuntarily terminated by court action, cases are divided into two types: contested and uncontested. Uncontested cases are those in which an agency or individual brings a termination or guardianship transfer action where parents have consented or are incapable of consent (those who are grossly retarded, psychotic, or in a comatose state). The latter cases generally turn on a determination of parental fitness based on expert witness testimony. Parents are not always represented by counsel or a guardian ad litem, who would protect their interest. There is a growing concern about this lack of counsel and appointment of a guardian ad litem seems to be gaining support. This development should emerge over the next several years as common practice.

Most termination cases are contested and commonly involve charges against the parent of abuse, neglect, desertion, abandonment, or a combination of these. Although actions may be brought against parents whose children are residing with them, they are more frequently brought by agencies on behalf of children in foster care.

Several key issues will have to be resolved over the next decade. The first legal question deals with the right to counsel. Parents have been and are being brought to court without legal representation, which is then sometimes ordered by the judge. Not infrequently, parents represent themselves and are disadvantaged from the outset. Agencies should urge the courts to see that all parents are adequately represented, both on principle and to protect against later reversal of rulings.

The second major legal issue has to do with the vagueness of the present termination statutes. Questions have been raised as to their constitutionality. Specific problems have to do with the definition of such conditions as "neglect" or "deprivation," which are often the basis of charges brought against parents. If definitions are too vague, the charges are subjectively assessed and difficult to prove.

Parents' rights to treatment will become a sharper issue over the next several years. Judges are reluctant to terminate parental rights in cases where the parents have sought but not received help from an agency. They are deferring decisions and ordering agencies to provide the needed help for a stated time to see if this makes a difference.

What becomes clear is that although the relationship between biological parents and the agency is really a contract, the terms are not defined so that each party fully understands and agrees to them. In the absence of a written and understood contract, both parties may misunderstand the other's role. It also becomes impossible for third parties (in these cases, the courts) to sort out who promised to do what, to or for whom, and if there was a breach of the treatment agreement.

Preparing Children for Adoption

In the third step of the adoption process, the work with the child depends on several factors. Two are paramount—the age and circumstances of the child and the philosophy and techniques of those adults doing the preplacement work. The first has to do with the child's ability to understand what is happening, the second with the agency's approach to the work to be done.

In general, the younger the child, the more the preparation for adoption will concentrate on collecting information on the medical and social history of the birthfamily. There is a presumption that this information will be useful to the adoptive family as the child grows older. Some effort may be made to prepare the infant or toddler for the impending change by having the adoptive parents visit the child. Visits may occur in the child's current placement family (usually a foster home) to familiarize child and new parents with one another.

If the child is older, able to understand and use language, there is more effort to help the child grasp the meaning of what is happening. Adoption workers use life books—written and pictorial description of the important events, people, and experiences of the child—and other similar techniques to clarify the child's situation by addressing a number of major issues ("Who am I?"; "How did I get separated from my family?"; "What will happen to me?"). Their interest is in helping the child develop the capacity to form attachments to a new family (Backhaus, 1984).

As special needs adoption has emerged, there is a concentration of effort to demystify the child's background, explain current and future behaviors, and prepare the child and the new parents for a longer period of adjustment. This work focuses on the common trauma experienced by all children who are adopted—separation, the sense of loss, and the grief which follows it (Brodzinsky, 1987, Chapter 1; Nickman, 1985).

Many experienced adoption workers now believe that the adjustment to adoption will be largely determined by the child's understanding of the reasons for adoption, the developmental mastery of these reasons, and the adoptive parents' ability to help their child cope with the reality of having two sets of parents (see Brodzinsky, 1987, Chapter 1; Brodzinsky, Schechter, & Brodzinsky, 1986; Brodzinsky, Singer, & Braff, 1984).

Finding, Preparing, and Selecting Adopters

In this fourth step of the adoption process, there is a presumption that the adoption is an agency adoption. If the adoption is an independent or private one, the family is self-selected. Their dilemma is that they are not afforded the "preparation" which parents using an agency will experience. They may consider themselves fortunate if they have heard terrible tales about social workers who are critical and demanding. They may not be so fortunate if their child begins to display serious difficulties or if they later encounter particular problems which stem from some aspect of the adoption process.

Agencies seek out adopters for waiting children. Recruitment of families for special needs children in particular is considered a minor art form in the profession. Two basic approaches are used. General recruitment is designed to reach the public with the board story of children who need families. Telephone responses, letters, brochures, and media stories are useful. These techniques focus on a group of children needing adoptive parents. Specific recruitment is used on behalf of individual children and involves the use of publicity to find interested potential adopters.

Most agency preparation is carried out through a combination of individual and group processes. It often involves the use of experienced adoptive parents to help in the preparation of new families. In former times the preparation tended to be investigative in nature, concentrating more exclusively on the qualifications of the candidates. *Preparation now tends to be more educative in nature, familiarizing adopters with common behaviors among children needing adoption, the intricacies of the child welfare system, the techniques used by experienced parents, and the resources they will need to make adoption work.* This focus is largely due to the emergence of special needs adoption, the reality that adoptive candidates are in short supply for older and handicapped children, and the experience that veteran parents are the best sources of information and help.

Formerly, the selection of adoptive parents was largely the choice of the professional staff. With the developments that special needs adoption has brought to the field, this is no longer true. Often parents actively participate in the selection process, identifying waiting children from media publicity, newsletters, flyers, and exchange books. Final choices of which children should be placed with which families are still determined by agencies but the selection process is more open than previously.

Placement

The fifth step of the adoption process is the placement of the child with the new parents. Once the selection of a potential family is made, the worker moves the parents through a series of activities which will culminate in placement. The activities begin with providing the potential parents more detailed information on the specific child. This effort, often called "presenting," is a crucial step in a planned placement. The parents considering adoption are given enough information to help them take the next step toward placement. Some families report there is still too little detail provided by agencies. Some agencies operate on a "full disclosure" philosophy; many stop short of giving any information that might lead to the identification of the child's birthfamily or any previous caretakers.

The next activity may be "showing." This plan is to bring child and parents together in a situation designed to offer the parents an opportunity to observe the child's appearance or behavior without risk of rejection to the child. This technique is most often used with children who are atypical in appearance or behavior (i.e., with a severely scarred child or an emotionally disturbed youngster) and is largely an effort to verify the responses of the potential parents. "Showing" is not done in all planned adoption.

Once the adoption worker is reasonably sure the parents are genuinely interested in proceeding toward the adoption of this particular child, the next logical activity is introducing child and family. Here the child and the prospective parents, often the entire family, meet for the first time. Whether the child is very young or of school age, the "chemistry" evidence between child and parents is important and introducing the parties is crucial in proceeding toward adoption.

After meeting one another, a series of visits is usually planned between child and parents with the adoption worker assisting. This activity, "visiting," should be organized to offer child and family an opportunity to learn as much as possible about one another, sort out old attachments, and begin to form new ones. Usually there are more visits for school-age children as there is so much information to be exchanged and so many adjustments to begin. Visits tend to be fewer in number for babies and toddlers, to be held in the home of the child's current caretaker, and to concentrate on familiarizing the child and the new parents with the details of the daily routine. In large part, this reflects the limited ability of the younger child to comprehend the changes under way as well as the commitment of the concerned adults to make the transition as positive as possible.

It is well to remember that no matter how the new parents view placement, to a child of any age, this too is another separation experience. The efforts of all concerned must be dedicated to making the gains ahead worth the losses suffered by the child.

Postplacement Services

Once the placement begins and until the legal finalization of the adoption occurs in court, the sixth step of the adoption process is underway. Usually at least 6 months and as much as a year or more may pass after the child is placed with the new parents and until the legal process of adoption is completed. The precise time depends on state law, agency policy, completion of the legal documentation needed, the parents' readiness, and the worker's ability to proceed with completion of the legal process.

While the adjustment between parent and child continues, the agency "supervises" the placement (a term which has passed into agency policy and state statutes). During this time, the alert worker makes regular visits to the family, observing the emerging relationship, providing interpretations, advice, and suggesting resources to the family moving through the adjustment. This support is "postplacement" in nature since it follows the physical placement of the child with the new family. It is a crucial time. The capacity of the parent and child to make a final legal commitment to one another is at stake.

The experience of special needs adoption is that services will be of three general types: remedial work, crisis intervention, and on-going supportive services. The remedial work is continuation work, the preparatory efforts with child and parent which should have been accomplished (but rarely is) before the placement began. Crisis intervention is just that, concentrated efforts to help the adoptive family who has encountered unanticipated difficulties. On-going supportive services are those sporadic or continuous efforts to help the adoptive family in need of long-term assistance.

Legal Finalization

The seventh step of the adoption process is legal finalization. For adoption to become a legal fact, the appropriate court must approve the child's placement with the family. The name of the court varies from state to state (Family or Juvenile Court, Surrogate Court, are typical examples), but the ability of the court to permit or deny an adoption action is common to all. The agency or the family retains an attorney, a variety of documents are produced and delivered to the court, a court date is set, the judge reviews the materials and, based on the validity of the documents and the judge's evaluation in the matter, a legal completion of the adoption is accomplished. (In some states, this is known as "finalization"; other common terms are "confirmation" or "consummation.")

Most state statutes recommend a time frame of about one year from the child's placement with the family until finalization is possible. There are variations. Some statutes are intentionally vague and invite experimentation with the time frame.

Some agencies recommend finalization soon after placement so as to solidify the parent–child relationship and put any remaining anxieties to rest before beginning the postadoption phase of support work. Other agencies extend their supervision by delaying the legal completion of the adoption because of uncertainties about the adoptive adjustment or because of high staff turnover. In either case, the families may perceive the agency as doubting their abilities.

Some families request a delay in finalization of their adoption because of the child's misbehavior or because of their own doubts. If the adoptive relationship is contingent on the good behavior of the child, there will be serious trouble ahead. The youngster is in charge and becomes even more vulnerable. Both courses seem dubious at best and probably damaging at worst. To be effective, finalization should be sought in a timely fashion, as a planned affirmation of the parent–child relationship, and not as a recognition of the good conduct of child or parent.

Postadoption Services

The eighth and final step of the adoption process was virtually unrecognized until recently. It includes those support services afforded the family following the finalization or legal completion of the adoption.

Before the 1960s, agencies fully expected to curtail their involvement with adoptive families after the legal process was completed. This was viewed as a logical step in "normalizing" the family. We now recognize that many children being placed will need continued professional help. Some families will need only an occasional counseling session, others will need more traditional, ongoing therapy. In still other families, the child may need a brief or extended stay in a residential treatment setting. Children and their families often need help with information about the child's background or with becoming comfortable with the whole notion of adoption. To be sure, after the adoption has been legally completed, the family is free to accept or reject further overtures of assistance.

Adoption services no longer stop at the steps of the courthouse but extend on a continuum as long as they are needed. This extension leads to the single most controversial adoption issue today: What should be the nature of service to adult adoptees?

The central question regarding services to adult adoptees is whether, or under what circumstances, to allow them access to information about their birthfamilies, including the identity of their birthparents and siblings. In Western society, adoption, particularly infant adoption, has taken on secrecy as one of its aspects. An English jurist said that the legal process draws "a veil between the past and present lives of adopted persons and makes it as opaque and impenetrable as possible; like the veil which God has placed between the living and the dead" (*Lawson* v. *Registrar General,* 106 L. J. 204, 1956). Agencies and courts have been quite variable in the amounts of nonidentifying background information provided to adult adoptees. Until recently, facilitation of direct contact between adult adoptee and birthparent was rare. This is clearly not true in the case of the adoption of older children, who often know names, addresses, and telephone numbers of bioparents and relatives. In the case of foster parent adoption, bioparents may have visited the home. Contact has also been known to continue after the adoption.

Several of the trends of the 1960s have joined to create a climate where challenge to the secrecy structure is now possible (Baran & Pannor, Chapter 17; Schechter & Bertocci, Chapter 4; Sorosky et al., 1978). First, the stigma against out-of-wedlock pregnancy has relaxed; second, there is a general societal move to see openness as better than secrecy. "Sunshine" statutes and open records laws have increased an individual's access to all kinds of records kept about him or her by organizations. Third, the rise of consumerism has fostered adult adoptee organizations which articulate their point of view as recipients of service. Fourth, there is skepticism that it is appropriate for the state to intervene in private issues regarding adults.

Courts and agencies are being asked to decide whether adults adopted as infants have the right to identifying information about their biological parents contained in the original birth certificate, the sealed court records, and the agency adoption records. The issue is complex. Most statutes give the court power to open these records for "good cause." Generally, that has been interpreted to be a reason connected with a serious threat to the physical or emotional well-being of the adoptee. The following are some of the stated justifications for keeping records sealed.

1. "Sealed records protect adopted children from the stigma of their adopted status; they also protect adopted children who were born to unmarried parents from the stigma of illegitimacy."
2. "Sealed records protect the adoptive family from future intrusion into their lives by the birthparents; they help insulate the adoptive parents from fears that the child they have raised as their own might transfer this affection and loyalty to his birthparents at a later date."
3. "Sealed records protect the birthparents from future intrusion into their lives by the adopted child. Many children adopted years ago were children of unwed teenage mothers who later married without telling their husbands of their secret past. Since these women relied on the promises of sealed records, to be

suddenly confronted with the appearance of an adopted child would be severely disruptive.''

4. ''If birthparents know that the records will not be confidential, they will be discouraged from placing a child for adoption that they would otherwise do with the assurance that records will be sealed forever'' (American Civil Liberties Union, 1975, p. 7).

Recently, each one of these assumptions has come under attack by birthparents and adult adoptees. They hold that while these assumptions have some merit, they can no longer be held to be universally true. Israel and Great Britain have laws that do give adult adoptees access to their original birth certificate, as do the states of Kansas and Alabama. Their experience shows that the dire consequences predicted as a result of giving information have not occurred.

Adult adoptees acknowledge that their request for identifying information poses a conflict of rights with the biological parents who may explicitly or implicitly have been offered confidentiality from agencies and courts. They believe that their right to the information is paramount for the following reasons:

1. Adoption laws have traditionally held that where there are issues of conflicting rights in adoption, they should be settled based on what is in the child's best interests. This principle establishes the adopted person's rights as superior and carries into the adopted person's adulthood.
2. Every human being has the moral right to know their genetic relatives. While circumstances may conspire to prevent many nonadopted people from having this information, it does not abrogate their right to seek and find what exists, should they choose to. Adoptees, by extension, should have the same right.
3. Depriving adult adoptees of birth records and information which other adult citizens may have as a matter of right raises a serious issue of equal protection under the law.

Other arguments are also advanced; for example, the continuation of sealed records perpetuates the stigma associated with adoption. Some hold that closing records connotes something sordid to be hidden and breeds distrust.

Can one violate the birthparents' right to privacy? Is the adoptees' wish for information superior, equal, or inferior to the birthparents' right to privacy? While the issue can be seen as a struggle for rights and human needs, it is also a struggle to shift or at least equalize power. In the past, almost all court conflicts over information have been settled in favor of the adoptive parents or birthparents (Harrington, 1980).

Having a registry where birthparents can signify consent to the information has been seen as an attempt to put parents and adoptees at parity. Some insist that adoptive parents must also consent regardless of the adoptee's age. But all adoptees do not agree and see this consent as acknowledgment of the superiority of birthparents' and adoptive parents' rights because they are given veto power. They argue that if the adopted child's best interests are paramount during childhood, why are they not paramount when he or she is an adult?

How we choose to answer these questions will fundamentally alter the way adoption will be practiced in the coming years.

NOTE

1. *Stanley* v. *Illinois,* 405 U.S. 645, 92 J.Ct. 1208 (1972); *Quilloin* v. *Walcott,* 434 U.S. 246, 98 J.Ct. 549 (1978); and *Caban* v. *Mohammed,* 441 U.S. 380, 99 J.Ct. 2560 (1979).

16

Surrendering an Infant for Adoption: The Birthmother Experience

ANNE B. BRODZINSKY

In modern Western societies, adoption is currently regarded as an acceptable and sensible solution to a critical problem in the lives of three groups of people—infertile couples, unmarried women facing unexpected pregnancy, and children without families. Since the early 1900s, a variety of human service agencies have been the facilitators and guardians of most adoption proceedings. Implied in the designation of this solemn responsibility is the assumption that these agencies will work to meet the needs of all three groups assigned to their care. However, in an agency-supervised adoption, where three clients are seeking relief from a single service and only one of them is paying a fee, the potential for a conflict of interest has been noted (Benet, 1976; Deykin, Campbell, & Patti, 1984; Vincent, 1961). Specifically, until the recent past, it has been fairly common knowledge that, despite some efforts to the contrary (Child Welfare League of America, 1988; Moore & Burt, 1982; O'Leary, Shore, & Wilder, 1984), a greater commitment of both professional energy and financial resources has been made in the service of a relationship between a child and prospective adoptive parents than in support of a relationship between the same child and his or her biological mother (Bernstein, 1963; Child Welfare League of America, 1960; Kadushin, 1974; Riben, 1988; Sorich & Siebert, 1982).[1]

Adoption agency personnel have long fostered the notion that women who surrender an infant for adoption are acting in the best interests of the child and themselves. These professionals have also assumed that, having made a decision to relinquish a child, these women will ''put the experience behind them'' and resume their lives with little difficulty. But is this the case? Is it reasonable to expect that a woman can so easily forget the birth of her child? And if not, what implications does the surrender of a child have for the long-term psychological adjustment of the mother?

This chapter has several specific goals. First, a brief history of the birthmother experience in the United States since 1900 will be presented. Second, a small body of research, which has explored the long-term psychological adjustment of women who have surrendered a child for adoption, will be reviewed. Finally, given that existing research suggests that for some women the surrender of a child for adoption is experienced as a profound loss, the last section of the chapter will discuss infant relinquishment in the context of existing theories of separation and loss. This section will focus directly on the experience of the loss of an infant to adoption in order to illustrate some of the unique aspects of grief and bereavement in the birthmother. Particular attention will be given to aspects of the grieving process which are often unavailable to birthmothers. With this in mind, a set of criteria for adaptive grieving will be presented as a potential context for developing clinical interventions for this group of individuals.

HISTORICAL PERSPECTIVES ON THE BIRTHMOTHER EXPERIENCE

Historically, the literature focusing on unplanned pregnancy has revealed a tendency for professionals to offer simplistic explanations for this highly complex problem. Over the years changes occurring in these explanations have corresponded to shifts in social attitudes and mores regarding "illegitimacy." In colonial America, children born out of wedlock were provided for by the community as long as they could be apprenticed to masters in the trades at a very early age. To this extent, they were accorded the same rights as other children considered to be "in need." Prior to the apprenticing, the child lived with the biological mother. She was expected to remain with and care for the child as a consequence for her immoral and deviant behavior. The proximity of the "bastard child" and the mother were felt to be a graphic reminder to the community of the "depraved" state of the mother. It was not uncommon for the two to be forced to sit in the town square to endure episodes of public humiliation. This type of punishment continued for as long as the memory of the mother's "crime" could be maintained (Kadushin, 1974).

From colonial times until approximately 1930, society's view of unplanned pregnancy and childbirth continued to reflect Puritan, Victorian, and religious influences. In the early decades of this century, perspectives on unplanned pregnancy were also influenced by the growing impact of the theory of evolution. Thus mental retardation and genetic inheritance became customary ways of explaining "illegitimacy" (Kronick, 1966). In this context, the mother was frequently labeled (even in the professional literature) as "feebleminded, and inherently depraved" (Lowe, 1927) or possessed of a variety of other "abhorrent, inborn characteristics" (McClure & Goldberg, 1929; Schumacher, 1927). The wide acceptance of these genetically based designations by professionals and nonprofessionals alike served to insure that the "unwed mother" and her child were clearly understood to be deviant members of the community (Vincent, 1961). After 1930, in keeping with established social reforms in the treatment of the mentally ill and others considered to be "defective," attitudes about unsanctioned pregnancy began to reflect a growing awareness of the impact of broken homes, poverty, and disorganized neighborhoods (Kronick, 1966; Nottingham, 1937; Reed, 1934; Vincent, 1961). In reality, however, this tendency to consider sociological influences as precursors of out-of-wedlock pregnancy was just a more circumscribed way of expressing what were still strong negative attitudes about those individuals who were unfortunate enough to conceive a child before they had married. It also perpetuated a popular myth of the time which held that "illegitimate" babies and their mothers were almost exclusively members of the lower classes (Vincent, 1961).

The 1940s witnessed a natural outgrowth of earlier cultural attitudes and sociological views. During this period, "illegitimacy" was frequently described as an accepted pattern of life in certain subcultures. The latter were primarily defined as either southern rural or inner-city minority groups (Vincent, 1961). However, this position, which was an interpretation of several important studies of black community life (Frazier, 1939; Powdermaker, 1968), failed to acknowledge the growing incidence of unsanctioned pregnancy in the white middle class.

In the 1940s and 1950s psychological theories of behavior began to influence social and professional attitudes about unplanned pregnancy. Most of the relevant articles published during this period were based on psychoanalytic theory. In this context, the unplanned pregnancy was understood to be a form of sexual acting out of unconscious needs and as such was seen as an expression of unresolved parent–child conflicts. Furthermore, it was assumed that the pregnancy represented significant psychopathology in the mother (Cattell, 1954; Clothier, 1943a; Deutsch, 1945; Heiman & Levitt, 1960).

Psychoanalytic theory has fostered the view that unplanned and out-of-wedlock pregnancy is the outcome of both historical and contemporary personality vulnerabilities. Several main ideas have dominated this thinking. First, as noted above, out-of-wedlock pregnancy has been viewed psychoanalytically as an unconscious, acting out of fundamental, unmet needs within the mother. From this perspective, it is thought that historically the birthmother's own mother has been unable to provide sufficient nurturance for her daughter; in turn, the pregnancy and, ultimately, the baby are seen as unconsciously representing a felt need for nurturance and love. Deutsch (1945), for example, has suggested that the daughter, presumably in a state of "longing for tenderness," becomes pregnant prematurely in order to incorporate the "lost mother." She has also linked "precocious motherhood" with a personality structure labeled "infantilism" (Deutsch, 1967). The latter is said to represent an arrest in an infantile developmental stage which has been revived regressively in adolescence. It is characterized by intolerance of frustration, impatience for pleasure goals, and a profound need to be loved. Still other psychodynamic formulations regarding out-of-wedlock pregnancy have emphasized its relationship to ambivalent feelings about dependency and powerlessness in the family (Deutsch, 1945; Young, 1954).

The late 1950s and 1960s marked the beginning of a large increase in the percentage of births occurring to unmarried women in the United States. Zachler and Brandstadt (1975) reported that, in 1960, 5% of all reported live births in the United States were infants born to unmarried teenagers between the ages of 15 and 19. By 1965, that percentage had increased to 8.75%; by 1970, it was 10%; and by 1976, it had reached 24% (Washington, 1982). During those years, however, the social climate in the United States underwent a period of tremendous upheaval. One of the outcomes of the new "freedoms," embraced by the youth of the sixties and the proponents of the women's movement of the seventies, was an increase in the numbers of unmarried mothers who chose to keep their babies as opposed to placing them for adoption (Washington, 1982). In 1970, approximately 80% of the infants born to single mothers were placed for adoption, whereas by 1983 that figure had dropped to only 4% (Deykin et al., 1984; Resnick, 1984).

It is interesting to note that during the late 1970s the birth rate among nonwhite, unmarried adolescents was between two and six times the birth rate for white, unmarried adolescents (Washington, 1982), however, the likelihood of placing the out-of-wedlock baby for adoption was and continues to be substantially greater among whites (Dryfoos & Lincoln, 1981; Resnick, 1984). A variety of explanations have been offered for the racial differences in out-of-wedlock pregnancy as well as the decision-making process surrounding this event. Traditional explanations have been based on the assumption that out-of-wedlock pregnancy in the black community has no stigma associated with it and is, in fact, an accepted way of life rooted in the cultural and economic legacies of slavery (Frazier, 1939; Kadushin, 1974; Vincent, 1961). Some authors have suggested that the shame attached to "illegitimacy," and even the concept that a birth could be "illegitimate," is a "white attitude." Moreover, these authors have indicated that the extent to which blacks feel shamed by an out-of-wedlock birth can be understood as a measure of their assimilation into the white middle class (Pope, 1967; Powdermaker, 1968; Vincent, 1961; Washington, 1982). A particularly poignant view, incorporating several of the latter assumptions, is that of Washington (1982). She notes that the "cultural ethos" explanation is often interpreted by whites as a propensity for blacks to violate social norms. In this oversimplified and superficial form, the idea of a cultural tradition emerges as a rationale for racially biased attitudes toward blacks. In contrast, Washington (1982) suggests that the origin of an "ethos" which regards the birth of any infant as having a fundamental importance for the community, rather than having a negative, "slave"-related history, may be rooted in highly valued African cultural mores. In this context, procreative activities which insured the survival of the group were held in high regard and those couples who conceived offspring as a result of the valued sexual liaisons were able to claim increased status and prestige in the community. Washington suggests that the retention of these norms by some groups of American blacks may be due to an unconscious awareness of their racial heritage, something akin to Jung's notion of a "collective unconscious."

Other authors have noted that illegitimacy rates frequently increase during large-scale migrations. The increase under these circumstances is thought to be associated with family disorganization in general and long separations imposed on husbands and wives in particular. In the case of American blacks, increased illegitimacy rates may correspond to the relatively recent migration from the South to the North as well as to the more widespread migration of this group from rural to urban settings (Kadushin, 1974).

Over the past 20 years, restrictive and moralistic social attitudes about unplanned pregnancy have been in a steady decline (Child Welfare League of America, 1969, 1984; Hartley, 1975; Resnick, 1984). As noted earlier, the origins of this transformation appear to be rooted in what has been called "the sexual revolution" of the 1960s, as well as in some of the fundamental influences of the women's movement. Of specific importance has been increasing social regard for women in general, increased financial benefits for single mothers, a rising divorce rate (making single-parent families very common), and the options afforded women through legalized abortion (Deykin et al., 1984).

In this more accepting and understanding environment, many women, who have relinquished children for adoption in past years, have begun to emerge from long years of silence to express sorrow, anger, and regret which they associate with their decision (Deykin et al., 1984; B. J. Lifton, 1975, 1979; Riben, 1988; Rynearson, 1981; Silverman, 1981; Sorosky et al., 1978). They explain their previous reluctance to come forward as the outcome of both spoken and unspoken prohibitions coming from adoption caseworkers, family members, mental health workers, the religious community, and society in general.

It is estimated that there are currently in excess of one million women in the United States who have surrendered an infant for adoption (Silverman, 1981). Bachrach (1986) reported that, in 1982, women between the ages of 15 and 44 (88% of whom were unmarried) made adoption arrangements for 549,000 children. She notes, however, that this figure must be considered on the conservative side, given problems associated with "failure to report," as well as exclusion of women over 44.

In recent years, a growing number of women, who regret having surrendered their children for adoption, have banded together to form several national support organizations, the largest of which is Concerned United Birthparents (CUB). The organization consists of individuals (primarily women) who refer to themselves as "birthparents" or "birthmothers." Most of them insist that were it not for coercive and insensitive adoption practices, coupled with a lack of family support, they would have been able to parent the children to whom they gave birth. Currently, CUB has branches in eight states and a goal of beginning a branch in 14 others. The organization is committed to educating professionals and lay persons in ways which will increase sensitivity to the complex dilemma faced by every birthmother. Their fundamental goal is to avoid unnecessary adoptions—to "keep families together."

Organizations such as CUB have had a significant impact on the practice of adoption, in general, and specifically on the adoption policies and practices which have direct impact on relinquishing mothers and their families. CUB members have become political advocates for adoption reform. They also have provided a supportive, therapeutic network for women who are having difficulty coping with the experience of child relinquishment. Finally, CUB and related organizations have been instrumental in calling attention to the emotional plight of birthmothers and, in so doing, stimulating increased concern for the mental health needs of this group among both clinicians and researchers.

Another important outgrowth of the birthmothers' self-help movement has been the emergence of what is generally referred to as "open adoption" (Lindsay, 1987) or "cooperative adoption" (Rillera & Kaplan, 1984). The terms "open" and "cooperative" both refer to adoptions involving some degree of ongoing contact between the birthparents (usually the birthmother) and the adoptive parents and, in many cases, the birthmother's participation in the choice of parents for her child (see Baran & Pannor, Chapter 17). According to Rillera and Kaplan (1984), the most compelling rationale for choosing cooperative adoption is a fundamental regard for the child's human rights; that is, in the case of an adoption, the child will retain access to both sets of parents. Lindsay (1987) acknowledges the potential benefits of openness for the child but focuses more directly on the advantages that open adoption appears to have for the birthparents. The trend toward increased openness in adoption is fast becoming the hallmark of adoption policy change of the 1980s. Although some empirical research in this area has recently begun (Grotevant, 1987, personal communication), it is important to recognize that the practice of open adoption raises many important questions for professionals and lay persons alike. In what ways will contact among birthmothers, adoptive parents, and the children so important to both, impact on and influence the adjustment of all of these individuals?

RESEARCH ON THE ADJUSTMENT OF THE BIRTHMOTHER FOLLOWING SURRENDER

Over the many years that women have been relinquishing children for adoption, the professional community has often made assumptions about the impact this experience may have had on their lives. Chief among these assumptions has been the notion (and perhaps the hope) that these women would forget about their children and go on with their lives. However, existing research suggests that this assumption is simplistic and extremely unrealistic. Furthermore, it is clear that, for many of these women, the process of adjustment has been constrained and complicated by these insensitive and self-serving assumptions. In the following sections, recent research in the area of postsurrender adjustment will be reviewed and implications for future research will be discussed.

Sorosky and colleagues (1978) interviewed 38 birthparents (36 of whom were female) regarding their experience during and following relinquishment of their child. The research participants were part of a group of ''hundreds'' from across the United States who had responded by mail to newspaper advertisements announcing the authors' interest in doing research with women who had surrendered infants for adoption. The 38 interviewees were a self-selected group who expressed willingness to meet with the researchers and discuss their feelings in person. These individuals ranged in age from 20 to 62. Age of the birthparent at the time of relinquishment ranged from 14 to 40 years, with 82% between the ages of 14 and 18. The number of years since the relinquishment varied from less than 1 to 33 with the proportions being approximately in thirds: 1 to 10, 11 to 17, and 18 to 33 years respectively. Only one participant had relinquished less than a year prior to the study. In the course of the interviews, 50% of the birthparents expressed continuing feelings of loss, pain, and grief associated with their decision to surrender the child. Typical expressions of these feelings included: ''I never got over the feelings of loss''; ''I still have feelings of guilt and pain when I think about it''; and ''Whenever I see a child, I wonder if its my daughter.'' Eighty-two percent of those interviewed expressed a desire for a reunion with their child, with most adding that they did not feel this would be appropriate until the child was of age.

Burnell and Norfleet (1979) mailed questionnaires to 300 women (members of the Kaiser–Permanente prepaid medical plan) who in the previous three years had placed a child for adoption. Based on a 26% response rate (78 respondents), the authors reported that gynecological, medical, and psychiatric problems were reported by about 60% of those responding. Depression was the most common complaint, with 40% of the women citing it as a problem.

Rynearson (1982) studied a group of 20 women drawn from a population of psychiatric outpatients who did not have either a history or current diagnosis of psychosis. Relinquishment of the infant was not the presenting problem in any of the cases. Those interviewed ranged in age form 30 to 46 and had surrendered their first child between the ages of 15 and 19. In this study, the women reported that in the

2-year period following the relinquishment, they had recurring dreams concerning the loss of the baby. In addition, all the women recalled what was termed "involuntary curiosity" directed toward children "of just about the right age" who were seen in the street. Many reported instances when they actually followed a mother and child, imagining that they might visually retrieve their own child for a moment. In the years beyond the 2-year mark, all the participants continued to experience intense emotional reactions to the anniversary of the relinquishment, with fantasies of the lost baby becoming particularly well-formulated during those periods.

Deykin et al. (1984) conducted a survey of members of CUB by publishing a questionnaire in their nationally distributed newsletter. The purpose of the study was outlined in an accompanying article which encouraged members to participate. The questions were focused on the circumstances surrounding the relinquishment of the child and the participant's assessment of their current life circumstances and adjustment.

Three hundred and sixty four of the birthparents completed the questionnaire. Of these, 339 were CUB members and 321 were women. Among the more interesting findings in this study was the significant correlation between what was identified as the "primary reason" for the adoption and the participant's decision to engage in a search for the child she had surrendered years before. Specifically, these investigators found that individuals who reported that the relinquishment of their child was due to external pressure (family, social workers, or lack of money) were significantly more likely to have instituted an active search for their child in later years than individuals who reported more internal reasons for their decision (age, unpreparedness for parenthood, or desire to complete schooling). This finding suggests that questions of perceived control and helplessness may be an important factor in planning future research with this group. The time that had elapsed since the surrender was also significantly related to the activation of a search for the child. Individuals who had surrendered a child more than 12 years prior to the study were more likely to have searched than those who had made the decision to surrender more recently.

Although no specific measures of psychological adjustment were made in this study, participants were asked to assess who the surrender had impacted on their subsequent marriages and parenting practices. Of the 280 respondents who had been married, 71% stated that their earlier birth experience had negatively impacted on their marital relationship. Furthermore, 81% of the 219 participants reporting on parenting practices indicated that the earlier relinquishment of a child had exerted a powerful influence on subsequent parenting practices. Almost all reported positive as well as negative consequences. Among the negatives reported, overprotectiveness, compulsive worry about the child, and difficulty in accepting the growing child's need for independence were those mentioned most often. Postsurrender consequences designated by these research participants as having "positive influence on parenting practices" led the authors to comment: "It was clear that for many of these research participants, their children constituted their most important source of emotional gratification." The results of the Deykin et al. (1984) study are compromised by the fact that the research participants were all members of a support group known to attract birthparents who were dissatisfied with their decision to place a child for adoption.

In the most complete and comprehensive study to date, Winkler and van Keppel (1984) investigated 213 women who had relinquished their first child for adoption while between the ages of 15 and 25. The surrenders had occurred between 4 and 20 years prior to the study. A control group of community women was included and data were collected on subsequent, possibly confounding, stressful life events. Two particularly important contributions of this study were the success of the researchers in recruiting participants with a wide range of self-perceived adjustment to the relinquishment of their child, as well as their success in recruiting participants who were not members of a birthparent's support group (55.2% of the participants did not belong to such a group). Research measures included a questionnaire developed for the study which focused on specific aspects of the birth and surrender experience, an abridged version of the Holmes and Rahe (1967) Social Readjustment Rating Questionnaire, and the Goldbert (1972) General Health Questionnaire.

A number of hypotheses were examined in this research, including:

1. Birthmothers would manifest more psychological impairment than controls.
2. Birthmothers who reported more available social support would rate the surrender experience as more satisfactory than those who reported less social support.
3. Birthmothers who reported that they were given opportunities to express their feelings about the loss of the baby would rate their adjustment as better than those who reported less opportunity to express their feelings.
4. Birthmothers who had experienced more stressful life events in the 6 months prior to the surrender would rate their adjustment to the loss as less satisfactory than those who had experienced fewer stressful life events.

Adjustment for two separate periods subsequent to the surrender were studied. The first period was the year immediately following the decision, and the second period was the time elapsed since the 1-year mark and May 1981. For the first year following the surrender, participants' perceptions of their adjustment to the decision were normally distributed across dimensions defined as being "not at all adjusted" to "extremely well adjusted." Thirty-two percent of the respondents reported below average adjustment in the first year period. In the years subsequent to the 1-year point, there was a gradual improvement in the group's perceptions of their adjustment to the loss. However, it is interesting to note that although the percentage of women reporting improvement in adjustment increased over the years, 28% of the group reported below average adjustment at the time they were questioned by the researchers.

Overall, other results of the study indicated that the effects of relinquishment on the mother were negative and long-lasting. Approximately 50% of the participants reported an increasing sense of loss, which for many women, extended over 30 years' time. This "sense of loss" tended to be more acute on occasions such as the child's birthday and Mother's Day. When compared with a matched sample, the relinquishing mothers also had significantly more psychological impairment. Three major factors were found to be related to the decreases in psychological well-being: absence of opportunities to talk through feelings about the relinquishment; lack of social supports; and an ongoing "sense of loss" about the child.

Although the use of a control group in this study is a positive step in the development of appropriate research methodologies for the study of birthmothers, the choice of a single control group was probably insufficient because the two groups were not matched for birth experiences of any kind. In addition, there are also some questions that arise when considering what these researchers have labeled "sense of loss." The concept of a sense of loss is somewhat questionable as a construct especially when it. theorectically grounded or operationally defined. Furthermore, the three questions used to assess the phenomena of perceived loss appear to have limited validity and reliability. Finally, the relatively high correlations between "sense of loss" and adjustment outcome leads one to question whether the two are measuring essentially the same thing.

The Winkler and van Keppel research, although not without methodological problems, suggests that it may be inappropriate and, indeed, irresponsible to expect that mothers who surrender their infants for adoption should aspire to a goal of "putting it all behind them." A further implication is that professionals who provide counseling to single, pregnant teenagers need to consider, and to help their clients consider, the possible long-term costs (as well as the benefits) to the mother of relinquishing the child.

Finally, Condon (1986) studied a group of 20 women who were associated with a birthmother's support group in Australia. The participants ranged in age from 25 to 59 years, with a mean age of 40. Most had relinquished children in the mid-1960s. The group was well distributed with regard to socioeconomic status. Participants were asked to complete a questionnaire which focused on the circumstances of their relinquishment and currently, together with their perceptions of any long-term effects. In addition, the participants completed the Middlesex Hospital Questionnaire, a short diagnostic, self-rating scale for assessing neurotic symptomatology (Crown & Crisp, 1966).

Feelings of sadness or depression at the time of relinquishment were, on the average, rated as between "intense" and "the most intense ever experienced." Sixty-seven percent reported either "no change" or "intensification" of these feelings over the intervening years. Anger at the time of the relinquishment was, on the average, reported as between "a great deal" and "intense," with only 33% reporting a decrease over time and over half of the group reporting that their anger had increased. Guilt at the time of relinquishment was rated generally as "intense," with only 17% reporting a decrease over the intervening years. Almost all reported that they had dealt with their distress primarily by withdrawing and "bottling up" their feelings and that this was due primarily to the absence of social and professional support. One-third had subsequently sought professional help but it is not clear that the relinquishment was the primary reason for the latter decision. The results of the psychological assessment indicated that the relinquishing mothers had significantly higher scores on depression, psychosomatic symptoms, and general, chronic psychological disability than did age-matched controls from the same geographical area. As in the case of the Winkler and van Keppel (1984) study, although there is value to the presence of this control group, a more specific matching and set of contrasting groups would be desirable in future research.

Conclusions and Implications for Future Research

Research focused on the psychological adjustment of relinquishing mothers generally is flawed with methodological problems that raise serious questions about the robustness of the findings as well as their generalizability. Of particular note are many examples of sampling bias, the questionable validity and reliability of measures, and the absence of a theoretical context for the research.

Despite these problems, the studies are not without heuristic value. Moreover, the considerable anecdotal data gathered by each of these investigators is consistent with previous professional documentation of profound and protracted grief reactions, depression, and an enduring preoccupation with and worry about the welfare of the child among these women (Condon, 1986; Deykin et al. 1984; Phipps-Yonas, 1980; Rynearson, 1982; Silverman, 1981; Sorosky et al., 1978; Swigar, Bowers, & Fleck, 1976; Winkler & van Keppel, 1984). These findings strongly suggest that, for many women, the experience of surrendering an infant for adoption is a nearly intolerable loss. But what of those women who experience the relinquishment differently? It is clear that not all women who relinquish a child experience the profound reactions noted above. This raises the question as to what factors mediate more favorable psychological outcomes. There are a number of areas of research which appear to have potential for shedding some light on this question.

Social Support

First, although a number of individuals have suggested that the availability of social support is a critical factor in determining the psychological well-being of a surrendering mother (Lindsay, 1987; Riben, 1988; Sorich & Siebert, 1982; Winkler & van Keppel, 1984), there is actually little empirical support for this assumption; nor is there evidence of what type of support is most beneficial for these women. Furthermore, none of these authors have considered the concomitant importance of differences in the individual's capacity to *accept and use* available social supports. Theoretical correlates of individual differences in a person's ability to avail themselves of social support can be found in psychoanalytic theory, Bowlby's (1980) ethological theory of attachment and separation, as well as the psychosocial-developmental theory of Erikson (1950). There is also a large body of literature addressing specific issues in the area of social support (Brown & Harris, 1978; Caplan, 1974; Cobb, 1976; Cohen & Wills, 1985; Olson, 1980) which suggests that this factor *should* be a significant mediator of postsurrender adjustment in this group of women. Thus researchers are well advised to explore the role of social support in future research.

Stress and Coping

Given that the relinquishment of a baby must be considered an extremely stressful experience, another area that would seem to be potentially fruitful for future research is the study of infant surrender for adoption in the context of current theories of stress and coping. Lazarus and Folkman (1984), for example, have suggested that individual differences in the experience of stress are determined both by the person's cognitive style of appraising the stressor and the means that he or she employs to cope with the situation. These researchers suggest that adaptational outcomes in response to a stressful situation are the result of an interaction between the individual's perceptions of the event, their repertoire of coping behaviors, personality characteristics, and the social realities which surround the situation. The structure of the Lazarus model has been objectified for research purposes and would appear to lend itself well to the study of decision making and psychological outcomes in relinquishing mothers. For example, future researchers might examine individual differences in the appraisal of the surrender and the specific coping behaviors used by these women to handle the stress of relinquishment.

Learned Helplessness and Attribution Theory

Another theoretical model that has implications for understanding individual differences in the adjustment of birthmothers is the learned helplessness model of depression developed by Seligman (1975) and reformulated by Abramson, Seligman, and Teasdale (1978). According to these researchers, depression is linked to the experience of helplessness, that is, the feeling that one has little, if any, control over the events (especially negative events) in one's life. Furthermore, the attributions that a person makes regarding their role in the events, as well as the nature of the events themselves, are seen as critical in determining whether a sense of helplessness, and ultimately depression, is likely to emerge. For example, Abramson et al. (1978) suggest that when confronted with a stressful situation, people are more likely to feel helpless and develop depression under the following conditions: (1) when they perceive the problem to be caused by something within themselves; (2) when they view the situation as stable and unlikely to change; and (3) when they believe that the problem affects many areas of their lives as opposed to some limited area.

Research by Resnick and Blum (1986) found that women who had aborted their unwanted pregnancies scored high on measures of helplessness. Although this study did not include research participants who were considering adoption for their babies, the implication of this finding for the latter population is clear. In other words, it is quite likely that women who relinquish their child for adoption, particularly under coercive conditions, and who view their actions as having far-reaching and long-lasting consequences may well be at increased risk for feelings of helplessness and depression. Certainly, this view is supported by those authors who have provided detailed descriptions of the adoption experience from the birthmother's perspective (Riben, 1988; Silverman, 1981). Given the lack of support offered to these women, as well as the subtle, and at times, rather blatant pressure to surrender their child, the assumption of a positive association between a heightened sense of helplessness and postsurrender adjustment problems does not appear to be unreasonable. This relationship needs to be examined in future research.

Adolescent Cognitive Development

The decision to surrender an infant for adoption is frequently made by young women who are still in their adolescent years—a time during which many important cognitive changes are still occurring. However, no researchers have considered the possible impact of cognitive development on the birthmother's decision making regarding her unwanted pregnancy as well as her ability to evaluate her (and the baby's) circumstances in the postsurrender period.

On the one hand, research on adolescent sexual decision making has generally focused on issues surrounding pregnancy resolution as determined by sociodemographic and personality variables (Phipps-Yonas, 1980; Resnick, 1984). On the other hand, Blum and Resnick (1982) have suggested that adolescent sexual decision making may be more completely understood in the context of the normal developmental changes that these youngsters undergo in such areas as relativistic thinking, future time perspective, means-end thinking, moral reasoning, locus of control, and other cognitive and social-cognitive domains. The birthmother's cognitive development is a variable which has, for the most part, been ignored in the literature focusing on pre- and postsurrender adjustment. Given the role of cognition in mediating life circumstances, it is imperative that this factor be incorporated into future research and models of birthmother adjustment.

SEPARATION AND LOSS: THEORETICAL PERSPECTIVES AND CLINICAL IMPLICATIONS

In the following section, some of the experiences commonly reported by women surrendering an infant for adoption will be discussed in the context of theories of separation and loss as well as established models of grief and bereavement. Pertinent aspects of the discussion will then be presented in terms of both the clinical implications and the research questions they suggest.

Psychoanalytic Theory

Psychoanalytic theories of human response to loss have suggested that an individual's adjustment to that loss is dependent on their early experiences with separation and change (Freud & Burlingham, 1944; Goldfarb, 1943; Mahler, Pine, & Bergman, 1975; Spitz, 1945). Moreover, individuals appear to experience loss in ways which suggest that fundamental aspects of their personality have been accessed (Bloom-Feshbach & Bloom-Feshbach, 1987). For example, an individual's unique sensitivity to separation may be expressed in the difficulty or ease with which they are able to change jobs, move to a new home, deal with disappointment, or surrender an old way of understanding. A person who is particularly sensitive to change brought about by the vicissitudes of everyday life is very likely to have increased sensitivity to the inevitable occurrence of more serious losses.

Although Freud laid the foundation for understanding the development of human personality in terms of the individual's early experiences, he did not focus on the importance of the early infant–parent relationship but rather on the later oedipal struggle. The emphasis that he did place on the infant–mother bond was based on the notion of the mother as a satisfier of needs as opposed to a person with whom the infant has begun a relationship (Bloom-Feshbach & Bloom-Feshbach, 1987). The work of Spitz (1945) and others, who studied the effects of institutional life and maternal separation on infants, offered the first impetus to psychoanalytic theorists to focus their attention on the preoedipal period of the child's life. Major contributions were also made during this period by theorists from the British object relations school who suggested that the infant's capacity for relatedness to objects outside himself was a critical development issue with significant implications for the individual's later adjustment to both the development and loss of significant relationships (Fairbairn, 1952; Klein, 1932, 1961; Winnicott, 1953).

Contemporary psychoanalysis is committed to the notion that varying degrees of disturbance in the mother–infant relationship places the individual at risk for a corresponding continuum of adult adjustment problems, including considerable vulnerability to pathological personality formation (Masterson, 1976). The seminal work of Mahler (1967) forms the foundation that underlies some of the current thinking in this area. Briefly, Mahler posits that the newborn infant moves from a completely self-absorbed state to a merger (symbiosis) with the mother and proceeds from that merged state through a series of phases which are characterized by increasing psychological and physical separateness. The achievement of "psychological separateness" (around the age of 3) is felt to be the sine qua non of the development of a healthy capacity for interpersonal relatedness. One aspect of Mahler's theory has particular importance for the individual's ability to adjust to loss. The achievement of psychological separateness is facilitated by the emergence of the infant's ability to form an internal representation of her mother. The capacity for internal representation is an important link between theories of separation and loss and the development of models of grief and bereavement (Bloom-Feshbach & Bloom-Feshbach, 1987). In "Mourning and Melancholia," Freud (1917/1957) emphasized the potential mitigating effects of internalizing or identifying with some aspect of the longed-for person. Although several authors have pointed out that identification in mourning needs to be differentiated from the usual identification with attachment figures (Lachman, Beebe, & Stolorow, 1987; Lerner & Lerner, 1987; Siggins, 1966), it is clear that some form of internal representation is a fundamental component of how human beings adapt to the multitude of separations and losses they are destined to endure.

Bowlby's Ethological Theory of Attachment, Separation, and Loss

In a departure from traditional psychoanalytic theory, Bowlby (1969, 1973, 1980) described children's grief reactions to the loss of their caregiver in an ethological context that emphasized the instinctive propensity for humans to form bonds with attachment figures which diminish feelings of strangeness, isolation, or fear. Bowlby found that when these "attachment relationships" were threatened by separation, acute physiological and emotional distress could be observed in the child. Bowlby noted that when the loss was perceived by the child to be permanent, he or she would go through a process of mourning which was characterized by three phases—protest, despair, and detachment. Bowlby (1980) proposed that healthy personality development, in general, and an individual's capacity to adjust to significant losses, in particular, could be seriously compromised when a child was forced to endure a significant loss and had no opportunity to form a new and comparable attachment.

In summary, the basic tenets of psychoanalytic thinking, as well as the significant contributions of Bowlby, support the notion that an individual's adaptation to loss is dependent on how well or how poorly they have been able to negotiate changes and deal with loss in the past.

Grief and Bereavement: Theoretical and Clinical Perspectives

Experiencing a significant loss is normally followed by a bereavement or grief reaction. These reactions have long been of interest to professionals with Freud (1917/1957) making one of the first important contributions to the formal literature in his classic paper "Mourning and Melancholia." Adaptation to loss is often experienced subjectively and has been described clinically as consisting of a series of phases.

However, it has been noted by many writers that these are not necessarily epigenetic stages per se. Furthermore, individuals report great variability in how long they remain in any one stage as well as the order in which these stages are experienced (Raphael, 1983). In the following section a description of the stages of grieving will be presented along with a discussion of some of the related literature. This section will be followed by the presentation of a model for adaptive grieving that will suggest specific ways in which the normal grieving process is compromised in women who have surrendered infants for adoption.

The first stage of grieving is often characterized by a tendency to retreat from the painful reality of what has occurred. This retreat is frequently manifested psychologically in a state of disbelief and denial. Individuals describing their feelings during this early period often report that they are "stunned, knocked out, paralyzed and/or numb" (R. J. Lifton, 1979; Parkes, 1972; Zisook, & DeVaul, 1985). A sense of "unreality," diminished affect, loss of appetite, confusion, and an increased latency to respond to the environment are common. Zisook and DeVaul (1985) have observed that if the grief process is arrested in the first stage of denial and numbness, the result is often either a psychotic denial of the loss or, more commonly, the development of a chronic feeling of "hoping" that the loved one will return.

The next stage of the grieving process is often more acutely painful than the earlier stage because it includes the development of the full realization of what has been lost. Typically, this period involves protest, anger, crying, and expressions of outrage, guilt, and shame (Lindemann, 1944; Parkes, 1972). Interwoven with these complex feelings are periods of extreme lethargy, cognitive confusion, and disorganization. In addition, grieving people often describe an experience of profound "yearning" or "pining" (R. J. Lifton, 1979; Parkes, 1972; Raphael, 1983; Volkan, 1984–1985). This yearning is often translated into and inseparable from a feeling of sadness and emptiness. Searching behavior may ensue and often includes returning to places where the lost person previously could be found, looking at their belongings while experiencing an acute feeling of expectation of their return, repeated and prolonged reviews of the circumstances surrounding the loss, and scanning of gatherings of people in the hope of finding the loved one (Alexy, 1982; Bowlby, 1980; Parkes, 1972). This period is also associated with feelings of despair, powerlessness, and diminished self-esteem (Bowlby, 1980).

As noted earlier, Freud (1917/1957) was the first to suggest that the mourning process commonly included an identification with the lost person. This phenomenon of identification, or assuming some of the characteristics of the loved one, during the grieving process has since been noted by many observers (Lindemann, 1944; Volkan, 1984–1985; Zisook & DeVaul, 1977). In adaptive or normal grieving, identification is usually a transient phase but, if not permitted or facilitated, it may become an excessively prolonged preoccupation with what are perceived by the bereaved to be some of the more negative or painful feelings of the lost person (Lerner & Lerner, 1987).

In normal or adaptive grieving, the end of the acute phase of the grieving process is marked by a characteristic and critical turning point. This turning point is often described as the reorganization phase and can be recognized by a gradual shift in the cognitive and behavioral focus of the bereaved person from aimless, confused, somewhat arbitrary thoughts and behaviors toward a reordering of life in ways that do not include the lost person (Lindemann, 1944; Parkes, 1972; Raphael, 1983; Schneider, 1984). This new capacity to think about one's life in a somewhat orderly manner seems to represent a renewed sense of personal control and carries with it a partial restoration of self-esteem. It is often the precursor of a return to purposeful and productive activities which may include a new capacity to perceive and desire to alleviate the suffering of others who have experienced similar losses (Lifton, 1973; Rochlin, 1965).

Although professionals writing about the grieving process have used somewhat different terminology, they are generally in agreement with the idea that when given an opportunity to grieve openly and fully in a supportive environment, human beings will experience a reasonably satisfactory resolution of their feelings about a loss (Alexy, 1982; Bowlby, 1980; Freud, 1917/1957; Lindemann, 1944; Pollock, 1978; Shackleton, 1984). However, although most professionals acknowledge various aspects of the social and emotional supports necessary to the grieving process (Bowlby, 1969; Brown & Harris, 1978), and a number of writers have discussed personalities at risk for pathological mourning (Bowlby, 1980; Parks, 1972), there has been, to date, no systematic assessment of what it means to have an *opportunity to grieve*. That is, what kind of emotional and social environment is both necessary and sufficient for adaptive grieving in humans?

In talking with birthmothers and reading accounts of their experiences, a nearly universal story is told. Typically these women have been advised by caseworkers, family members, and lawyers that their baby would be better off with people who can take "proper" care of a child and that the best thing for them to do would be to place their child for adoption and go on with their lives with the comforting knowledge that they have made the best possible plan for their baby. These assumptions and imposed solutions represent variations on a common theme which supports abnegation of personal ideals and suppression of feelings in these young mothers. In this process, psychic numbness and denial, frequently associated with the earliest stages of grieving, are presented as permanent goals to be achieved. As a result, movement through the subsequent stages of grieving, considered necessary for human adaptation to loss (Alexy, 1982, Bowlby, 1980; R. J. Lifton, 1979; Parkes, 1972; Pollock, 1978; Siggins, 1966); are not made available to the birthmother.

There is considerable evidence to suggest that routine and *ongoing* bereavement counseling with women who have surrendered an infant for adoption is rare. When counseling does occur, it is often compromised by conflicts of interest, limited understanding, and lingering social stigmata associated with out-of-wedlock pregnancy (Alexy, 1982). In addition, the absence of a complete psychosocial history (which in these cases should include a detailed outline of the individual's previous experience with separations and losses) often results in superficial and less effective interventions.

Although the research in this area is inadequate, there is reason to suspect that a substantial percentage of mothers who relinquish an infant for adoption experience pathological grief reactions which interfere with their overall functioning for a good portion, and possibly the remainder, of their lives (Alexy, 1982; Pope, 1967; Sorosky et al., 1978; Winkler & van Keppell, 1984). If one accepts the premise that a person must have an opportunity to grieve in order to achieve an adequate adjustment to a significant loss, it seems to follow that there may be unique aspects of the birthmother's experience which make it difficult for her to gain access to a normal grieving process. In the following section a bereavement model will be presented in the context of what are suggested to be five criteria for adaptive grieving. Each of the criteria will be described in terms of social or environmental and emotional norms which appear to influence the behavior of those who typically provide empathy and support to grieving persons. In addition, each of the criteria for adaptive grieving will be considered in terms of existing psychological theories and bereavement models. Some of the experiences most commonly described by birthmothers will be presented in the context of the criteria for adaptive grieving and implications for bereavement counseling with birthmothers as well as adoption practice also will be discussed.

A MODEL FOR ADAPTIVE GRIEVING

Criterion 1: Safety

Societal norms for mourning following a death suggest that family members will make efforts to move toward each other, sometimes from great emotional and geographical distances, in order to provide the unique support they believe that they alone can give to one another. In the absence of family or often as an accompaniment to it, extended family and friends will move in similar ways to be near the bereaved and to express their own grief (Zisook & DeVaul, 1985). The resulting group, although extremely variable in structure and emotional intensity, appears to provide a kind of temporary holding environment—a safe haven for the bereaved. The gathering of family and close friends following a death appears to support several psychological assumptions:

1. Bereaved persons need temporary relief from their usual occupational, academic, domestic, and social responsibilities (Zisook & DeVaul, 1985).
2. Individuals who are grieving experience an increase in their emotional vulnerability (Bowlby, 1980; Lindemann, 1944; Parkes, 1972; Raphael, 1983).
3. Some comfort can be derived from the realization of mutual loss—that is, there is a kind of interdependence which forms between persons who comprehend the meaning and magnitude of a particular loss (Raphael, 1983).

The characteristics of these assumptions suggest a regressive tendency in the newly bereaved individual which is supported by the psychoanalytic literature and is particularly well explained by Volkan (1984–1985).

Most women who have relinquished a baby for adoption have not been provided with a "safe" place to be following the event. In part because there has been no death, and in part because the placement of a baby for adoption is laden with secrecy and shame, there is often no sense in her family or among her friends of understanding and mutuality of loss. Typically, a birthmother is not relieved of many of her responsibilities and, in fact, propped up with assurances that she "has done the right thing" and with platitudes focused on the now insured "well-being of the baby," she is often urged to go on with her life "as though this never happened" (Silverman, 1981). Supported by these poorly conceived assurances, most birthmothers have been directed away from their grief before they have fully encountered it. Of particular importance is the absence of a caring and supportive network of people who, because they comprehend the meaning of the loss, gather around the mother to temporarily protect her from those who do not. It is this author's contention that the need for safety, the first criterion for adaptive grieving, is significantly compromised under these circumstances.

Criterion 2: Freedom to Express Feelings and to Behave Differently

The degree to which individuals are free to express grief openly is to a large extent culturally determined. In many American cultural groups individuals are reluctant to support any outcry of despair and rage. We are embarrassed by open expressions of profoundly felt emotions in most situations, even those in which a person has had a significant loss. "How is she doing?" we ask. A response of "not good" is usually an indication that outward expressions of grief have been witnessed by the observer. In contrast, a response of "He's great—incredible under the circumstances" implies the approval we reserve for those who spare us (and unfortunately themselves) their grief.

Despite these restrictions, the second criterion for adaptive grieving, freedom to express grief openly, does exist in varying degrees in our society. To the extent that it is present in a particular situation, there appears to be a concomitant social acceptance of the loss as a legitimate one. When this recognition prevails, the grieving person is temporarily forgiven a variety of inadequacies assumed to be present as a result of the loss. Related of course to the criterion of safety described above, this "moratorium," as it were, creates an atmosphere in which the bereaved person is temporarily free to be less competent—less "like her old self" than before. The assumption seems to be that given the freedom to be a grieving person for a while, a return to one's "old self" and usual competency is insured.

Psychological assumptions associated with the importance of expressing grief as opposed to withholding those feelings are rooted in psychoanalytic theory. Freud and Breuer's (1895/1955) original description of the "talking cure" introduced the notion of the potential value of expressing long-withheld feelings and emotions. Subsequently, the development of nearly all theories of psychological intervention are supported by the fundamental assumption that there is significant therapeutic value in creating an environment in which a person is free to express their thoughts and deeply felt emotions.

There is a certain "common sense" to these social norms and psychological foundations. They have come to make sense because they are correct according to society's innate and proven capacity to adjust itself to the needs of its members. In this context of "membership," society's reprieve for the bereaved is a privilege. With this understanding in mind, the absence of the freedom to express grief—that is, the withholding of that privilege, is a strong indication of social rejection.

When a young woman surrenders an infant for adoption we set her apart from us. Sworn to secrecy and admonished to return to school or work as though she had been on a holiday or helping with an unfortunate relative, the privilege of grief is denied. The underlying social message here appears to be "you are not one of us." These women often recall feeling that the lack of empathy or concern expressed by family members was just punishment for the shame they had brought to their parents (Silverman, 1981).

The importance of being able to express feelings about the loss of the child necessitates a close look at the nature of the professional counseling available for birthmothers following the relinquishment. Although in recent years there have been improvements in therapeutic work with birthmothers, with many agencies making a particular effort to provide ongoing availability of counseling, there still are serious impediments both within society in general and within the helping professions, in particular, for developing the type of support environment and counseling services that these individuals need (Resnick, 1984; Riben, 1988).

Criterion 3: Proximity, Empathy, and Warmth

The despair of another person is not easy to witness. We feel ourselves starting to move away—to avoid the specter of their disbelief and sorrow. There is often a feeling of embarrassment and helplessness associated with our tendency to retreat. The second criterion for adaptive grieving—freedom to express grief—has a complimentary component, the need to be understood. The process of expressing feelings and having them understood cannot occur in a vacuum. The grieving person needs the *presence* of familiar and loved ones who can express, often simply through eye contact, touching and being available, some measure of "knowing" what has occurred (Raphael, 1983).

Certainly most grieving people experience some isolation. For the birthmother, however, the usual isolation is complicated and exacerbated by a number of unavoidable realities. Her baby is gone but has not died. We cannot recognize this baby in terms of immediate and ordinary social definitions. Family and friends cannot tell fond stories of times spent with the baby. The baby has not been sick, stolen, or lost. The community cannot don work clothes and flashlights and with a team of German shepherds scour the nearby parks and woods. No posters will be printed with the child's picture asking, "Have you seen this child?". Forced to reject outrage and conventional expressions of sympathy, we remember that *this* lost baby is different. Although the traditional labels of shame, which have stigmatized "bastard" children for centuries have virtually disappeared, the woman who relinquishes a baby for adoption is still at a loss as to how to express to her family and the community the dimensions of her sorrow. Others may be physically present but often they cannot comprehend her grief in a familiar context. Without the emotional proximity of empathy of others, the risk to the birthmother's psychological well-being and long-term adjustment to this loss is correspondingly increased.

Criterion 4: Rituals of Passing

As noted above, individuals who are mourning need others to witness their loss. Beyond needing people to be present, there is a widely acknowledged need for ceremonies to mark the time of beginnings and endings. In nearly all cultures, socially proscribed rituals are performed to accomplish this goal (R. J. Lifton, 1979; Raphael, 1983, Schneider, 1984). Such ceremonies insure public recognition of the importance and magnitude of the event. When a person in our society dies, we move into an elaborate series of rituals which provide safety for the bereaved, diminish their sense of isolation, modify their powerlessness, and communicate to all that something very grave and yet familiar has occurred.

Relinquishing an infant for adoption has not been recognized by society as a loss of a magnitude sufficient to warrant rituals of passing or farewell. The absence of rituals in the process of an infant surrender may be the outcome of past social and religious stigmata directed toward unwed mothers and their offspring. If so, it is another clear message of disapproval and rejection. The absence of rituals to mark the passing of her child from herself to another mother contributes to the birthmother's sense of helplessness and is a powerful reminder that she is alone. The absence of a "public" ritual also leaves her without social confirmation of the finality of the event.

Both professionals and family members working with women who are in the process of relinquishing a child can make significant contributions to the adjustment of the mother by helping her to create rituals of passing which are meaningful to her. If the adoption is in any way "open," she may wish to invite the adoptive parents to participate. These ceremonies can include meaningful readings, the exchange of letters, candlelighting, the planting of trees, or virtually anything that seems to represent the event for the mother of the baby. A component approximating social sanction may be introduced by inviting a member of the clergy to be present. There are also ways in which rituals can be used to help birthmothers who surrendered many years ago and yet remain focused on the loss of their child. In these cases, anniversary reactions are common and these are particularly appropriate times for the introduction of a ritual which can become a tradition if the mother finds this to be helpful and comforting. Professionals assessing the need for rituals in women whose grief appears to be "arrested" will enhance the quality of their work by becoming aware of the birthmother's history of experience with separation and loss. Furthermore, understanding that the intensity and persistence of her feelings may be related, in part, to her adjustment to these earlier experiences is crucial in planning effective interventions for these women.

Criterion 5: Opportunity for Reorganization

In describing the "reorganization" stage of grief both Parkes (1972) and R. J. Lifton (1979) discuss a critical turning point during which the aimless searching and yearning for the lost person, which is often evident in the earlier stages of grieving, takes on a purposefulness and order. In the beginning of this phase, the individual may begin a detailed review of the circumstances surrounding the loss. This effort differs from the anxious, often frantic review that may occur soon after full realization occurs. The conduct of this "search" is more organized and controlled. In the process the bereaved person may try to define the roles of all the "players" and may attempt to find a philosophical or religious meaning in the events surrounding the loss. This period often marks the beginning of a bereaved person's attempt to redefine their identity in a world which does not include the lost loved one (Raphael, 1983). In addition, reorganizing the experience is often the first step toward developing ways of making restitution for the loss. Rochlin (1965) suggests that one of the primary ways that human beings adapt to loss is to engage in thoughts and behaviors which symbolically fill the gap left by the loss. Rochlin's ideas are consistent with psycho-analytic theories of psychological restoration, but go a step further by suggesting that the energy created by the need for restoration is a major source of human creativity and productivity.

In a traditional adoption, the agencies, responsible for the placement and the laws that control recordkeeping in adoption, do not provide an environment in which a birthmother can adequately reorganize the experience of relinquishing her child. Once she leaves the child in the care of the agency or hospital and signs the surrender agreement, her access to information about the baby usually ends. In addition, in a typical adoption, any counseling that the birthmother was receiving during her preg-nancy and period of decision making is likely to end rather precipitously. Moreover, to the extent that she attempts to secure such information, she is judged to be making a correspondingly "poor adjustment" (Resnick, 1984).

Professionals working with grieving women who have surrendered a child for adoption need to be aware of the importance of helping those individuals to begin a process of reorganization. In grief counseling, reorganization work can be understood as finding one's way back to what happened, taking a hard look at everything that occurred, and coming to some understanding about the roles of everyone involved—including one's self. Most important, it means helping the birthmother to talk about her experience and ending once and for all the idea that things will be better if the baby is forgotten. For some birthmothers this process may also involve an active search for information about, and possibly contact with, the child they relinquished some time ago.

CONCLUSION

Historically the practice of adoption has been viewed as a means of meeting the needs of infertile couples and homeless children as well as the needs of unmarried women facing unwanted pregnancies. In the process of providing these services (as well as justifying them), we have come to believe a myth—that adoption, by defini-tion, relieves an "unwilling" mother of the burden of raising her child. In the 1980s, we are beginning to hear from that mother and she is telling us that however heavy and cumbersome her burden may have been, relieving her of it may have been too simple a solution. Today the birthmother is asking how we could believe that a sober person could part with a child and "simply go on with their life" without profound consequences. She is asking us why, when we saw that she was carrying a heavy load, we pressured her to part with it instead of helping her to find a way to carry it herself. She is asking us why, having relieved her of her burden, we left her behind. These are difficult problems. They require society, in general, and the professional community, in particular, to address a number of questions with profound ethical implications. And yet this process is both necessary and inevitable. It is necessary because there is compelling clinical and research data which strongly suggests that many of these women are not making the kind of postsurrender adjustment we had hoped for (and promised). It is inevitable because the newly found voice of the silent member of the adoption triangle will not rest until some reevaluation of adoption policy is undertaken. Having offered false hopes and promises in the past, we must now take up the challenge of providing more realistic and more effective modes of intervening with birthparents.

NOTE

1. Historically, the biological father of an adopted child, the "birthfather," has played little role in the decision making surrounding the child's birth and subsequent placement in an adoptive home. However, since the 1972 Supreme Court decision in *Stanley* v. *Illinois,* where a birthfather's legal claim to his child was recognized as protected by the Constitution, considerable interest has been generated in the feelings and legal rights of these individuals. Research with birthfathers has begun (Deykin, Patti, & Ryan, 1988) and subsequent Supreme Court decisions (*Quilloin* v. *Walcott,* 1978; *Caban* v. *Mohammed,* 1979; *Lehr* v. *Robertson,* 1983) have expanded the support available to some single fathers seeking parental rights. Despite the current move toward increased sensitivity to the rights and interests of the biological fathers of adopted children, it is this author's view that interested, committed birthfathers remain in the minority, with most individuals who father a child outside the protection of marriage, continuing in the centuries-old tradition of abdication of responsibility. Perhaps increased legal protection and psychological sensitivity will provide the support necessary for birthfathers to come forward in greater numbers, but until such time as that occurs, it is clear that the major burden of this enormous responsibility remains with the mother of the child.

17

Open Adoption

ANNETTE BARAN AND REUBEN PANNOR

Adoption practice in the United States is still basically closed, secretive, and involved with the protection of everyone's anonymity. However, there is a growing movement toward reform from secrecy to openness. Change is coming about very slowly but steadily as more and more agencies throughout the United States become involved in open adoptive placements.

We were asked to write this chapter because we have advocated open adoption for over a decade. In the early 1970s, there was a sudden shift toward keeping babies instead of relinquishing them for adoption. Without sufficient support systems, many young birthmothers found themselves in great difficulty within a few years. Unable to continue parenting, they came to the agency to explore the possibility of adoptive placement. Essentially, they felt trapped. They could neither relinquish in the traditional manner nor could they continue to care for their children. Despite their problems in parenting, they had developed an emotional relationship with their children which would not permit them to sign a document giving the agency full control of the child's future and severing their own connection completely. Rather than see those children enter the foster home system, we offered these parents the option of open placement. They would help select the family and be part of the child's move and initial adjustment to the new home. Initially, our open placements were very few, and we were cautious, selective, and equivocal in our approach. We theorized that with professional counseling and education some birthparents and some adoptive parents might be able to participate in open adoption placements. We wrote (Baran, Pannor, & Sorosky, 1976) and lectured about the positive effects of open adoptive placement but found that acceptance by the professional social work community was long in coming. We did not perceive how threatening change was to the institution of adoption.

A decade later, agency personnel and those people practicing independent adoption are voicing some agreement and acceptance of open adoption. They argue that it is necessary to move slowly in the progression from a closed to an open adoption system. They insist that birthparents and adoptive parents must be offered a choice of an open or closed process. In reality, they are still more closed than open in philosophy and practice. Moreover, there is controversy over the definition of terms and how open is open.

316

Older children are the first group for whom open adoptive placement has become acceptable. Since the older child clearly remembers his foster parents, birthfamily and earlier worlds, erasing these feelings and images is accepted as an impossibility. Elizabeth Cole (1984) has written about the strong ties binding children to their birthparents, despite being neglected, mistreated, or abandoned. She concluded that social workers must not protect a child from knowledge of his or her family situation but should help the child deal with that reality. We do not believe that older children should be an isolated group. In our own growth and development, equivocation is no longer acceptable. The secrecy, anonymity, and mystique surrounding traditional adoption placement creates numerous psychological problems for adoptees, birthparents, and adoptive parents.

PSYCHOLOGICAL PROBLEMS: ADOPTIVE PARENTS

Relationships within adoptive families are subject to conflicts not found in the typical nuclear family. These conflicts create a particular stress on the adoptive parents with problems similar to those of having a handicapped child (Pringle, 1967) or raising a minority child (Lewin, 1940). The parental conflict is best epitomized by Seglow and colleagues (1972), who described the adopter as caught in a double bind: implored to "make the child your own, but tell him he isn't." Kirk (1964) has emphasized that if adoptive parents can accept themselves as different from biological parents, rather than denying the difference, they will be able to communicate better with the child regarding his adoptive status and have the possibility of handling any problems that might arise throughout his or her development with loving support, understanding, and empathy (Lewis, Balla, Lewis, & Gore, 1975; Mikawa & Boston, 1968; Smith, 1963).

PSYCHOLOGICAL PROBLEMS: BIRTHPARENTS

Parents who cannot keep their infants have a sense of worthlessness and considerable feelings of guilt (Lewis, 1971). Smith (1963) emphasized that the mother who relinquishes her baby is trying to give her child what she knows he needs and what she wants him to have—love, care, and security from two parents in a normal home situation that she cannot provide. Once the adoption proceedings have been completed, the birthparents seem to become the forgotten or hidden parents (Rogers, 1969) around whom the adoptee and adoptive parents have been able to weave fantasies of a positive or negative nature. Our own studies (Sorosky, Baran, & Pannor, 1978) demonstrated that for most birthmothers, relinquishment and adoptive placement was a traumatic experience that remained with them throughout their life (see Brodzinsky, Chapter 16).

PSYCHOLOGICAL PROBLEMS: ADOPTEES

A number of authors have described a vulnerability of the adopted child to stress and the development of emotional problems requiring psychotherapy (Brodzinsky, 1987;

Goodman, Silberstein, & Mandel, 1963; Jameson, 1967; Reece & Levin, 1968; Schechter, 1960; Simon & Senturia, 1966; Sweeney, Gasbarro, & Gluck, 1963). Adopted children and adolescents are subject to greater identity conflicts than the nonadopted population. Erikson (1968) wrote that the development of identity is partially established through identification with the parents, especially the same sex parent. In the case of an adoptee, the process is complicated because he or she has the knowledge that an essential part of the self has been cut off and remains on the other side of the adoption barrier (Kornitzer, 1971), thereby confusing the psychological identity of the adoptee (American Academy of Pediatrics, 1971, 1973; Barinbaum, 1974; Livermore, 1961; Mech, 1973; Schoenberg, 1974). Sorosky et al. (1975) described these adoption-related conflicts as resulting in "identity lacunae" that can lead to a sense of shame, embarrassment, and lowered self-esteem (Schwartz, 1975).

From our experience, we have learned that many of these psychological problems are directly related to the secrecy or anonymity of the closed, traditional system of adoption. We are convinced, therefore, that the closed system must be replaced with a new philosophy and practice of adoption that provides openness and honesty. This means that all adoptions—independent, agency, infant, or older child—would be conceived as part of an open policy involving all of the concerned parties.

DEFINITION OF OPEN ADOPTION

The practice of open adoption begins with the first contact of both the prospective adoptive parents and the birthparents. It is discussed as an integral part of agency procedure in the adoption of all children. Open adoption is a process in which the birthparents and the adoptive parents meet and exchange identifying information. The birthparents relinquish legal and basic childrearing rights to the adoptive parents. Both sets of parents retain the right to continuing contact and access to knowledge on behalf of the child. Within this definition, there is room for greater and lesser degrees of contact between the parties. The frequency and meaning of the communication will vary during different times in the lives of the individuals involved, depending on their needs and desires and the quality of the established relationship.

The American Adoption Congress, meeting for its annual national conference in Boston, Massachusetts, May 1987, adopted the following policy statement. "The Board of Directors of the American Adoption Congress unanimously supports the policy of open adoption as standard practice." Their full statement basically followed our definition (Pannor & Baran, 1984) and concluded with the following: "Open Adoption will permit adoptees, birth parents and adoptive parents to make decisions about the kind and extent of relationships they desire."

The Child Welfare League, at its Biennial Meeting in San Francisco, November 1986, endorsed the practice of open adoption with the following resolution: "All members of the adoption triad are affected by the adoption and as such should be consulted as to their desires, needs and capacities in determining the level of openness in their particular adoption plan. Selection and utilization of the level of openness is based on the consensus of the birthparents, the prospective adoptive parents, and the child if he or she is of age or ability to make such a decision."

Adoption social workers must accept the responsibility of educating themselves and the clients whom they serve. As open adoption becomes standard practice, the sealing of original birth records will no longer serve any purpose. However, for all of the adoptees living with sealed records, the need to open those birth records remains an important issue. There cannot be acceptance of open adoption placement in the future without acceptance of opening the records of the past.

AXIOMS GOVERNING THE PRACTICE OF TRADITIONAL ADOPTION

To fully understand open adoption, we must contrast it with the traditional closed system in adoption. Twenty-five years ago a legal journal article stated that "the adopted child is brought into the family of his adoptive parents as completely as by the process of birth. The purpose of (the adoption statutes) is to effectuate a complete substitution of the adoptive family for the natural in every respect except the biological" (Lee, 1963, p. 223). This definition is still defended by a large segment of the adoption community.

Closed traditional adoption is also buttressed by the sealed adoption record that serves as a barrier to contact between children and their biological families. Adoption practice has continued to function within the same basic system of beliefs for the past 50 years without any real evaluation or change. Unmarried pregnant women are told that they have freedom of choice; yet they are made to feel that the best answer for every child born out-of-wedlock is adoption. Birthparents are assured that relinquishment of their child will be a resolution to their problem and the experience will be forgotten; yet their continued pain and mourning tells them otherwise (Baran, Pannor, & Sorosky, 1977; Brodzinsky, Chapter 16). Adoptive parents have to promise to be honest and tell their children about their adoption and their birthparents; yet adoptive parents typically are told only the positive facts because they aren't trusted to know the whole truth. Agencies accept the fact that adopting is different from giving birth to a child; yet they try to match babies to families as if it is the same. Adoptive families are counseled that adoptees need a positive identification with their origins; yet parents are rarely helped to work through their feelings about infertility and their negative attitudes toward the birthparents. Families are encouraged to bring their children back to adoption agencies for information; yet the agencies assure parents they will divulge nothing to the children. When adopted adults seeking background information return to agencies, it is viewed as evidence of family failure or personal pathology. No one assumes they have a right to know. They are made to feel emotionally unstable for having the need to ask questions.

HISTORICAL OVERVIEW

To better understand the philosophy of open adoption, a brief historical overview of the closing of adoptions over the past century might be helpful. Adoption was not always closed and secret. Adoption was not always focused on the needs of childless couples eager to overcome their infertility through adoption.

Adoption came to the New World with a multifaceted overlay of the cultural mores of many different countries. This merged with the social and economic needs of our developing new society. There were many orphaned, homeless children in the old country and a shortage of labor in the new country. Half-grown children were exported to the colonies to become informal members of families and to provide extra farm labor sorely needed (Presser, 1972).

Adoption in the old world was limited because of the importance of bloodlines and property inheritance. In the American colonies such considerations became relatively unimportant. Most of the new colonists were nonaristocrats who believed in the meaning of what you accomplished rather than who your father was. Here in the United States upward mobility and unlimited opportunity was possible. In this climate adoption became increasingly acceptable and, as a consequence, increased and flourished.

There was no thought of secrecy or anonymity during the first two centuries of adoption in the United States. In fact, secrecy and anonymity were viewed as morally wrong and, therefore, totally unthinkable (Foster, 1973).

Although largely informal and noninstitutionalized, adoption, nevertheless, took on many different forms. As has been noted previously, many orphans were imported into the colonies to meet the need for farm labor. As our population grew, so did our own orphan census. Orphan children of all ages were adopted. Either caring neighbors raised them or relatives included them in their extended families. When neither of those kinds of homes were available, orphans were apprenticed out into the larger community. Childless couples had no problem locating children to parent.

Unwed pregnant women often found families who sheltered them and offered their unborn children a potential home. If the birthmother chose to relinquish her child, she was comfortable with her decision, knowing that she trusted the family, who had nurtured her, to nurture her child. The family was also comfortable with the birthmother and, as a result, accepted her child more totally. The birthmother, a known entity, was not perceived as intrusive or potentially harmful to the adoptive family. More often, the extended family took in the pregnant woman and decided which relative would adopt the child. In fact, it was uncommon to exclude the birthmother from knowing and maintaining contact with her child. The primary parenting role was clearly with the adopting parents but, emotionally, there was room for the birthparent (Paton, 1968).

During this century, adoptions in the United States have undergone many changes. By 1929, every state provided for adoption within their legal system. It is interesting to note that these early laws did not specify secrecy as part of the adoption process. Adoption was not always humane and in the best interests of children. To prevent abuses, institutions came into existence, setting up codes and standards and introducing legislation. Many child welfare laws were enacted, including adoption laws. The country's first sealed record laws were passed in Minnesota in 1917 (Lindsay, 1987). Initially, these laws appeared to be in the best interests of children. In fact, however, we believe that they brought a climate of fear and confusion to members of the adoption triangle and created numerous psychological and emotional problems for all concerned. The sealed record was synonymous with secrecy and anonymity and totally changed the practice of adoption.

What began as an effort to free innocent children from the stigma of illegitimacy evolved into something drastically more rigidified and far reaching in its implications. Until the twentieth century, children had been considered to be miniature adults.

Reform to protect children was sought in every area from birth through adulthood. How did these reforms apply to the institution of adoption?

Adoption experts were intent on erasing the stigmata of the past and insuring equal status and treatment of adopted children with nonadopted legitimate offspring. Their attitudes and goals were commendable. Why should any person carry the life-long burden of a birth certificate, stamped in large indelible letters, "illegitimate"? Why should anyone have to accept the fact that their father is listed as "unknown"? Why should one human being be made to feel different and less acceptable by being labeled "adopted"?

The clear focus was the adoptee who, the reformers argued, should not be held responsible for the sins of the birthparents. Throughout the United States, groups of volunteers and professionals banded together to change the system. They were dedicated and successful in their efforts. By the end of the 1930s, they felt many of these ills were eradicated in most of the states. The adopted child was "reborn" as a child of the new family with a new identity and a new identification in the form of a birth certificate, exactly the same as if the child was born to them.

Sealing the original birth certificate was a natural step in the continuing process of reform. It has been assumed that the original reason for sealing the records was to protect the adoptee and adoptive parents from a disruption by the birthparents and, in turn, to allow the birthparents to make a new life for themselves free of the responsibility of the child and safe from the disgrace resulting from errors of the past. It should be noted, however, that the sealed record was also a means of protecting the adoptive family from intrusion by uninvolved persons. This was clearly stated in a 1940 book on adoptions: "Reporters, nosing around for news, might come upon something really juicy and publish it, causing untold suffering and permanent damage. Unscrupulous relatives could trace a child if they wished and use their knowledge to upset a well established relationship, if they did not do worse, and use it for actual blackmail" (Prentice, 1940). Whatever the original reason, the sealed record and total anonymity of the birthparents assumed enormous importance as a primary safeguard for adoptive families.

Institutionalizing Secrecy and Anonymity in Adoption

Adoption, as part of the larger socioeconomic climate, has always been sensitive to changes within the system. The United States, as a young, ever adjusting and readjusting society in flux, underwent radical changes beginning early in the 1930s. The huge waves of immigration were over. There was mass unemployment rather than a need for more employees. The United States was becoming a largely urban industrial society rather than a rural agricultural one. Families, looking for opportunity were moving further West, leaving the security of the extended family behind. Moral structures were breaking down. The small nuclear family was becoming the norm and with it a new definition and need for adoption arose.

Adoption was largely redefined as a method by which babies born to unwed mothers could find permanent homes with infertile couples desiring to become parents. Older children available for adoption were virtually ignored, for many years, because couples wanted babies who would feel as if they were born to them. By the late 1940s there was a substantial increase in the number of babies available. For about two decades, this situation continued (Gallagher, 1972).

The practice of adoption became both more professional and at the same time oversimplified. From a professional point of view, adoption developed standards, legal safeguards, and minimum requirements for applicants. Conversely, very little thought was given to the emotional and psychological implications for all the parties involved. Adoption was seen as a brief process to meet an immediate need, without recognition of lifelong implications. As soon as the adoption was legally consummated, contact was discontinued between the agency and both the birthparents and adoptive families, since any further involvement was considered unhealthy and intrusive.

Adoption agencies developed a highly sophisticated method of accepting a relinquishment from the birthmother. After the document was filed with the appropriate governmental agency, the birthmother's rights were permanently terminated and the adoption agency assumed legal guardianship of the child for the purpose of adoptive placement. The birthmother had to trust the agency to select a proper home. She renounced all possibility for future information or contact regarding the child. Agencies were proud of this process and contrasted it with the independent method.

Agencies painted dire pictures of independent adoption tragedies. In independent placements, the birthmother was supposed to select the family to raise her child; she retained her legal rights until the adoption was finalized. This meant that she could regain custody of the child during the interim period between placement and court action. Prospective couples were told that, in independent placements, they would live in continuous fear of having to give the baby back before the court hearing, and in lifelong fear of intrusion by the birthmother who knew who they were. However, in agency adoptions, all this was solved. Those adopting were told that the birthmother could never find out where her baby had been placed, could not reclaim the child before the court hearing, and would never be able to locate them or intrude on their lives.

In order to retain this superiority, agencies became more and more closed as the years passed. Whenever a still "not closed enough" item was brought to their attention, immediate steps were taken to close the gap. A few examples might clarify this process for the reader. The adoption petition and decree initially made reference to the original birthname of the child. Adoptive parents were adamant that a legal way to remove this information had to be found. This was accomplished. The amended birth certificate, which replaced the original birth certificate, offers still another example of further closing. Adoptive parents' fears also brought about the deletion of the name of the hospital and the attending physician.

From a psychological point of view, however, it must be recognized that no matter how reassuring adoption agencies attempted to be, it was not enough. Adoption agencies guaranteed secrecy and anonymity but this did not quell the adoptive parents' fears. We now know that it was always possible to gain information and break the secrecy barriers, and agencies, in fact, could not offer such safeguards.

In any retrospective evaluation of past adoption practice, an understanding of the inherent dilemmas of maintaining secrecy and anonymity in a closed system must be explored. It is not accidental that adoption developed along different lines than other areas of social work practice. In child welfare agencies, family service organizations, child clinics, and so on, there was continuous evaluation and reevaluation of policy and practice and, consequently, resulting change. Finding weak or obsolete areas of practice was considered helpful, healthy, appropriate. Adoption agencies could not afford this luxury because their practice was based on rationalizations that would not hold up under scrutiny. This dilemma caused adoption practice to become stagnant. Instead of changing, the institution just added additional layers to justify the same practice. These layers and layers of rationalizations and inherent contradictions finally became so weighty and unwieldy that they threatened the entire institution of adoption.

CONTEMPORARY SOCIETAL CHANGES: IMPACT ON ADOPTION PRACTICE

Adoption is a part of the fabric of our society and reflects social, political, economic, and moral changes. At the same time as adoption agencies were struggling to survive, the world outside was undergoing a revolution in ideas and values. The external forces had an enormous effect on the practice of adoption, and eventually resulted in making agencies reconsider their guarantees of secrecy and anonymity.

The civil rights movement and the resulting freedom of information acts were immensely important. Adoptees' secret feelings and desires for knowledge of their origins found validation through the militant actions of other people who had also felt like second-class citizens (Feigelman & Silverman, 1983). Adoptees organized their own groups, such as the Adoptee Liberty Movement of America (ALMA), founded by Florence Fisher. Provided with a forum and leading to militant action, adoptees demanded the right to their original birth certificates. They filed suits, introduced legislation, and sought access to agency records. Since legal openness of birth records is still largely denied to adoptees, underground activities developed resulting in thousands of reunions throughout the United States and Canada. This movement was one of the steps that advanced open adoptive placements.

The change in sexual mores and the legalization of adoption was equally important in opening the adoption process. The definition of a problem pregnancy was irrevocably altered. Unmarried, pregnant women expressed the feeling that if they completed the pregnancy, it was because they planned to keep the baby. Otherwise, they would terminate the pregnancy. They began to express the thought that having a baby and giving it up left lifelong scars (Sorosky et al., 1978). There was no way, they said, that a woman could truly resolve relinquishing her child. Keeping a baby and raising a child as a single parent had become much more acceptable.

Marriage as an institution was undergoing great change. There was a vast increase in the divorce rate and it was impossible to differentiate the unmarried single mother from the previously married single mother. These single unwed mothers who spoke openly of their status had an electrifying effect on women who, in the past, had relinquished children for adoption. Just as adoptees felt empowered by the civil rights movement, so did birthmothers derive courage and entitlement from this new generation of unwed mothers who kept their babies. The birthmothers also founded their own organization, Concerned United Birthmothers (CUB), as well as joined adoptee groups. Here they finally were able to speak out and express hidden unresolved feelings. This was yet another step in the path toward openness.

The United States, long the melting pot, was suddenly beset with interest in genealogy, ethnicity, and generational connections. Knowledge of bloodlines was not only acceptable but eminently fashionable. This interest gave adoptees an added incentive to solve their own dual identity and to feel entitled to know their own birth heritage.

While these changes were taking place in the outside world, inside the institution of adoption, the future was suddenly uncertain. The source of babies had diminished drastically. Some birthmothers who chose relinquishment and adoption began to request a role in choosing a family for their child. Birthmothers expressed the feeling that agencies were biased in favor of relinquishment and did not give women a fair chance to decide to keep their children. Birthmothers trusted themselves more than they trusted agencies. They began the movement toward open adoptive placement by forcing agencies to rethink their practice. If agencies wanted to continue to serve birthmothers, they would have to include them as real participants in the placement process.

During this period of change, the existence and importance of the birthfather began to emerge. Prior to this time, the birthfather, who had no legal rights, was not accorded any emotional role in the conception, pregnancy, delivery, and relinquishment process. Professionals failed to consider the birthfather as having any needs whatsoever. In fact, the birthfather was seen as an intruder who would complicate the relinquishment process. With the Supreme Court ruling *Stanley* v. *Illinois* (Pannor & Evans, 1975), the birthfather, for the first time, was granted legal rights with regard to the future of the child. Adoption agencies, rather than making the birthfather a part of the counseling and decision making process, sought ways to circumvent the legal ruling. In increasing numbers, birthfathers began to express their feelings—another step toward further opening the adoption practice.

These new movements affected adoption agencies in other ways as well. Without babies to place, agencies began to reconsider adoption for the older and special needs children who were in foster home placement. Adoption agencies had to face the reality that there would be no need for their continued existence unless they offered a broader spectrum of adoption services. The placement of older children was one more step toward openness, since the older child brought connections and memories of the past to the new family that were unerasable.

Adopted adolescents and adults returned to agencies in increasing numbers, demanding more and more background information. Denied this data, they circumvented agencies and turned to search groups for help. The fact that adoptees effected reunions through underground means convinced agencies that they realistically were unable to guarantee secrecy and anonymity.

INADVERTENT OPEN ADOPTION EXPERIENCES

It is not unusual to encounter adoption workers who have admitted that they were aware of or responsible for inadvertent breaches of secrecy and anonymity. It is reassuring to note that no great calamities resulted. Adoptions were not compromised or disrupted. In fact, the present authors recall from their own years of practice that there was real value in the accidental openness. The following three case vignettes illustrate this point.

An Adoptive Mother Accidentally Finds the Birthmother

Jenny and Fred adopted a newborn little girl to join two older sons born to them. They came to the agency because they were fearful of independent adoptions and wanted all of the safeguards possible. However, they also wanted as much background information as possible because they wanted a perfect, superior child. At the same time, they did not want the birthmother to be given very much information about them.

Danielle was a delightful child who fit into the family well. The adoption was openly discussed because the boys had been an integral part of the process, and the family prided itself on the honesty of their relationships. Danielle went to the best preschool in the community and adjusted well to social situations. When she was 5-years-old, her mother applied to a summer day camp of excellent reputation. At the parents meeting, the director, Sandra, introduced herself with a charming biographical description. The adoptive mother listened with a growing sense of déjà vu. There was something, initially, about Sandra's features and mannerisms that seemed familiar. With background data, this feeling intensified, and Jenny decided, without a shadow of a doubt, that she was listening to Danielle's birthmother. She felt frightened, threatened but at the same time relieved that a burden had been lifted and that a fantasy had been replaced by a real human being. The following morning Jenny called her adoption worker in a state of intense excitement. The adoption worker thought fleetingly of denying the truth. After all, she had promised everyone anonymity. However, she was a poor liar, and Jenny was too smart and sensitive to accept false denials. The adoption worker was silent for a few moments and then reached into herself to say, ''Aren't you glad that Danielle has such a nice birthmother, and that you have had an opportunity of seeing her? If you knew her personally, you probably would like her.''

During the following years, Jenny and Fred did meet Danielle's birthmother and gradually included her in what in reality ended up being an open adoption.

This adoption worker became a convert to open adoption placement as a result of this experience. It took her a long time, however, to develop the strength to speak out openly for change.

A Birthmother Accidentally Discovers the Adoptive Family

Marylou was 17 when she relinquished her newborn daughter to the adoption agency. She was in a state of shock and remembered little about the experience. She married George when she was in her early 20s. He knew about the baby. After Marylou had another baby, she began to be plagued with nagging feelings about the first child. She came back to the adoption agency, asking for information about her child and the family. Her adoption worker was still on the staff. The adoptive family lived in an adjacent county and had adopted a second child from the agency. The agency's information was, therefore, fairly current, and the adoption worker shared a great deal of descriptive data. She even called the children by their first names because she wanted to help Marylou feel comfortable about her child's life.

Within the next few years, George was transferred by his large engineering firm to their adjacent county's office. The family, now consisting of two children, settled into the new neighborhood with hopes of becoming active in the community. Toward this goal, Marylou called a few Protestant churches, asking for their newsletter and membership roster. She explained that she wanted to join a church with a large young couple membership so that she could meet other couples and find children for her children to play with. The churches were very cooperative and Marylou received all kinds of literature.

In reading one of the newsletters, she stumbled on a list of the families involved in a community support group. It sounded interesting and she studied the families to see whether they were in her general age category. Among them was a family with two children with the same first names that her adoption worker had used. The father's occupation also matched the information she had been given. She knew immediately this was her daughter's adoptive family, and she was overwhelmed with doubt about what to do with the information.

Marylou went over several options in her mind: she could call the family and identify herself; she could call the minister and ask for his advice; she could call the adoption worker and check it out with her. After ruminating all night, she called the adoption agency and asked for an immediate appointment. The adoption worker listened quietly to the unfolding story. Feeling very guilty, she silently chastised herself for being so open and divulging so much identifying information to the birthmother. She had breached the agency's guarantee of anonymity and who knew where all this would now lead: since the adoption worker did not know what to do, she stalled for time, hoping that some miraculous solution would suddenly occur to her. In the ensuing discussion, she found herself becoming more comfortable with the truth and less frightened at consequences. Together she and Marylou discussed different scenarios. None seemed that terrible and, in fact, Marylou and the adoption worker both agreed that maybe all of them knowing each other some day could turn out to be a good idea.

Marylou saw her daughter and observed her daughter's family in a variety of social and church situations. She decided to postpone formally meeting the family and disclosing the truth until after the child's high school graduation. The two families have developed a friendship that seems to work for them.

This adoption worker and this birthmother faced together a situation previously considered impossible. In the light of rational and nonjudgmental thinking, an open adoptive placement experience became possible and even positive.

An Adoptee Converts a Traditional Adoption into an Open Adoption

Lisa, a divorcee with a 4-year-old son, Eric, married Ted, a man who was infertile. As soon as they met the minimum requirements, they applied to a traditional adoption agency to adopt an infant girl. Within the family group that now included Joanna, the adopted child, there were parents, step-parents, adoptive parents, and a biological child, as well as aunts, uncles, cousins, and grandparents from the varied combinations. They had become one of those, ever more prevalent, blended families with many different kinship patterns.

Joanna was a rather remarkable little girl, precocious and strong-minded, far beyond her chronological age. She may have been the brightest member of the family. Certainly, she confounded all of them with her thought processes. Joanna always knew she was adopted and enjoyed feeling special. She had been told the usual story of being born to a woman who did not have a husband or home and who relinquished her so that she could have a family to grow up with. The birthmother, Joanna was assured, loved her but couldn't take care of her.

Eric's father was a regular visitor to the home, picking up his son, casually chatting with the other members of the family. Eric, Joanna knew, had a father and stepmother and half- and stepbrothers and -sisters who lived in another house, where Eric stayed on weekends and holidays. Eric loved both families and sometimes made Joanna jealous because he had more relatives than she did. Joanna insisted, when Eric teased her, that her other mother loved her and that she probably had a stepfather and half-sisters and -brothers also. The problem was that they never came to visit her, nor did she ever hear from them.

For some time these discussions were private between the children but, eventually, Eric used his weapon of superiority too strongly, and Joanna came crying to her adoptive parents. Initially, the whole thing seemed a "tempest in a teapot" to Lisa and Ted and they treated Joanna's pleas casually with a loving repetition of the adoption story. Joanna was not only not satisfied, she became more and more enraged, agitated, and difficult.

Joanna could not understand why Eric's other family was always available and hers wasn't. If, indeed, her birthmother loved her, as she had been told repeatedly, then why didn't she visit or write or telephone or send a birthday card or a Christmas present or anything? Nothing the parents said sounded true. Finally, they used the adoption agency and the adoption worker Miss T. as the authorities who had decided who visited and who didn't. After all neither Lisa not Ted had ever met the birthmother. Only the adoption worker knew her. The parents promised Joanna they would appeal to the adoption agency and arrange for Joanna to ask for answers.

Although the parents had hoped the agency would dissuade Joanna and satisfy her curiosity, it did not work. Joanna became increasingly obsessed with the need to meet her birthmother. In desperation Lisa and Ted appealed to the adoption worker. It was a strange situation. Lisa and Ted had never thought they would ever be pleading for their 6-year-old daughter to meet her birthmother. They had wanted the secrecy and anonymity. The adoption worker had never thought she would go against the agency's policy. Miss T. knew, however, that agency policy did not allow disclosure. Since she now found herself on Joanna's side, she made a decision based on her own professional judgment and secretly went against agency policy.

The birthmother was contacted by the adoption worker and asked to consider changing the rules of the game on behalf of her daughter. It took some thought and consideration, but with all the parties in agreement, Joanna had her wish met. In the 4 years since the reunion, Joanna has been able to feel equal to her brother Eric. They both have two families, whom they are free to love.

In this situation, a traditional adoptive placement was converted into an open placement because one little girl, clear and direct in her thinking, forced the adults around her to see the contradictions inherent in the closed system.

These three brief case histories, true and accurate except for identifying information, illustrate the dilemmas met by adoption workers in traditional agencies throughout the country. These and other similar experiences have helped prepare adoption workers to move into open adoptive placements. They are no longer so insistent on maintaining tightly separated boxes within the adoption triangle. They have learned that openness is in the best interests of everyone involved.

DISPELLING MYTHS ASSOCIATED WITH OPEN ADOPTION PRACTICE

The field of adoption is still struggling with deeply ingrained attitudes that prevent agencies and their staffs from moving toward a practice where all adoptive placements will be open. What are the arguments against open adoption and how valid are they?

Two mothers competing for the child's love, attention, and loyalty is the fearful spectre raised by those opposed to open adoptions. Permitting the birthmother to know the adoptive family and participate in the placement, according to the opponents, inevitably must lead to interference, intrusive behavior, and rivalry. Within this framework, bonding between the adoptive mother and child are impossible. If the two parents have different values and childrearing approaches, confusion and chaos will result, according to the advocates of continuing the closed system.

How real are these fears? We recognize that it is important to pursue empirical research into the effects of cooperative parenting in open adoptive placements. However, our experience suggests that many adoptive parents and adoption workers believe wrongly that adoption can only work when the birthmother disappears. This is an unrealistic premise, since, in fact, whether in open or closed adoptive placements, the birthmother remains a real person and never disappears. She remains the always present ghost in the closed adoption. We are convinced that the fear of her potential disruptive behavior is a far greater threat than any reality within the open adoptive placement. The fear that parenting an adopted child will not offer the same bonded closeness has always been an issue for adoptive parents (Hoopes, 1982). Adoptive parents would rather have been able to biologically produce their children. Being denied this, turning to a second choice (adoption), adoptive parents wanted to make this parenting as close as possible to "the real thing."

Within this closed system, there has been a great deal of confusion. At the same time that the birthmother was presented to the adoptive parents and subsequently to the child in the image of a loving and caring fantasy object, she was also a nonexistent and nonavailable person. She was seen both as a woman full of admirable attributes and as a "rejector and dumper" of her child. Under this system no member of the adoptive family could ever perceive the birthmother as a real person.

Adoption workers set the tone and climate of adoptive placements. In the years when adoption workers decided that only white, healthy, newborn infants could be placed, that is the only group that adoptive parents asked for. When adoption professionals decided that all children, regardless of color, handicaps, or age could find homes, adoptive parents became available. Now, when adoption workers in selective agencies throughout the country are expecting adoptive applicants to meet and maintain contact with birthparents, adoptive parents are becoming agreeable and available for this new approach.

Adoptive parents are not baby snatchers, leaving behind tragic, assaulted birthmothers. In reality, some birthparents need adoptive parents to help them, to take over and nurture when they are incapable. Birthparents are willing to relinquish their legal and nurturing rights, and they are willing to trust another family to raise the child without interference. However, that does not make them nonexistent; nor does it take away from their original being. They remain what they were, birthparents, and by virtue of that sustain a function within the world of the adoptive family. This function must not be denied because denial brings with it the seeds of dysfunction and emotional problems for all concerned.

Birthparents cannot receive anonymity. Giving birth to a child and being that child's birthmother is a fact of life that cannot be wiped out. Relinquishing a child is an act of commission, not omission. For a birthparents to blame an adoption agency, a family, a community, a system for taking a child away is unreal. When a birthmother helps choose the adoptive family and participates in the placement of her child, she knows that she is giving up her child and that it is not being snatched from her. She is part of the decision process, not a victim of a powerful institution. Her availability to the adoptive family and her existence to the child is of immeasurable value to all of them, including herself. The selection of the adoptive parents relieves her of legal obligations. However, we believe that part of pregnancy counseling should include helping the birthparents recognize a moral responsibility to the child throughout his or her life. On behalf of the child, birthparents must be available to the adoptive family.

Birthmothers are not adopted by the adoptive family. Only their child is adopted. Birthmothers have separate and different lives to lead. After the placement has been accomplished, the role of the birthmother undergoes change in a continuing and unfolding manner throughout the ensuing years. Birthmothers, who are comfortable with their decision and able to know how that child is progressing, are better able to move forward. For the birthmother in an open adoption, there need not be any fantasy families because the adopting family is a known entity and becomes the rearing and psychological family.

CURRENT MOVEMENT TOWARD OPEN ADOPTION

The number of traditional adoption agencies throughout the United States practicing open adoptive placements continues to grow, although slowly. In fact, in order to remain competitive and up-to-date within the field, more and more adoption agencies are offering the option of open placement to birthparents and adoptive parents, even though they may not be totally in favor of the practice. Additionally, agencies are offering an orientation program that includes discussion of open adoption. It may be said that the teachers are also the learners at this time. The option of open adoptive placement is exercized on occasion rather than as standard practice. Nevertheless, significant gains are continuously seen in the growing appreciation of open placement as a healthy practice. As agencies become more comfortable, they will be able to help adoptive parents accept open placement and end anonymity and secrecy. The degree of openness varies within the agency from staff member to staff member, and within the field from agency to agency. There is no single standard of openness currently being accepted by adoption agencies. Instead, adoption workers' ambivalence is reflected by an approach that defines openness in terms of what is acceptable to both birthparents and adoptive parents. Until umbrella organizations, such as state adoption organizations, church adoption consortiums, or the Child Welfare League of America which sets standards for adoption, enunciate a clear policy, the practice of open adoption cannot become standard practice in the field.

Currently, there is little research evaluating the practice of open adoptive placements. Yet the growth of open adoption must not wait for the results of long-term empirical studies. Such studies would clearly help us refine our practice and offer better services. However, there is no question that we are moving continuously in the direction of more openness which should not be reversed.

Despite this, it must be cautioned that open adoption can be used to institute negative, regressive practices. Increasingly, attorneys, independent placement services, and professional adoption workers are aggressively recruiting pregnant women through media advertising campaigns. Promising openness as an inducement for relinquishment, some teenagers and married couples, especially from poverty belts, are being offered financial incentives for surrendering their child, as well as the notion that all they are giving up is responsibility; furthermore, they are assured that they can remain active in their child's life in the postplacement period. Once the adoption is finalized, however, past promises too often disappear. In addition, couples desperate for a child, and only too willing to pay large sums of money, are being manipulated by baby brokers who are using sophisticated marketing procedures in their efforts to recruit vulnerable pregnant women. Clearly, such methods are not part of the reform movement toward openness nor are they sound professional practice. Instead, they have the potential for destroying the hard won gains of the open adoption movement and replacing them with marketing techniques that represent the commercialization of children.

THE REALITIES OF OPEN ADOPTION

Within the triangle, the benefit of open adoption to the child is probably the most significant. It has long been accepted that adoptees live with a dual identity. The adoptive family exists in the child's real world. In the fantasy world are the birthparents, seen alternately as good and terrible. They are illusive and distorted phantoms of the imagination who are supposed to have been loving but were often seen as rejecting. We believe that adopted children, on some level and to some degree, however minimal, feel there is something bad or wrong with them, which is why they were "given up for adoption" (see Brodzinsky, 1987, Chapter 1). No story, regardless of how deftly constructed, is believable to the child. Understanding this leads to the inescapable conclusion that adopted persons not only have two families but that they need contact with both families. The adoptee who is able to see, touch, and feel the birthparent can believe the fact that that person does care, but could not, at the time of the child's birth, take care of him or her.

Today, the adoptive family is one of many different kinds of families in which children are raised. In the middle of this century, the adoptive family, on the one hand, was held up as a happily and permanently married couple who would raise a child perfectly. The birthmother, on the other hand, was alone and her child was stigmatized. Times have changed. Just as we cannot guarantee secrecy or anonymity to the adoptive family, we also cannot guarantee, to the birthmother marital permanence and an idyllic life for the child. Adoptive families are as vulnerable to the myriad of problems as any other family group. Adopted children now live in as many different families as do biological children. Adoptees see around them a variety of family constellations. This change in family patterns helps them overcome the feeling that they are different from everyone else. Within this framework, adoptees who know their birth relatives are the same as their friends who know their step, half, and foster relatives.

It is clearly impossible to set any boundaries for the relationships within an open adoption. The extent and kind of relationship that the birthparents will maintain with the members of the adoptive family, the extent and kind of relationship that the adoptee will continue with the birthparents, and the extent and kind of relationship that the adoptive parents will desire with the birthparents are all dependent on the interaction of the individuals involved as well as the changing situation over the years.

It is not important that the relationship be close, strong, and constant, or the reverse, that the relationship be distant, detached, and casual. What is important is that an open adoption permits, within its framework, whatever is necessary and meaningful for the individuals involved.

Certainly open adoptions will encounter difficulties in the same way that complicated family relationships do. Some of these relationships may be so enmeshed or difficult that the people involved sever the connections, but even when that occurs, the possibility for reconnection always exists. Some birthparents may be too needy and adoptive parents may need to set strict limits. Some adoptees may want too much connection with birthparents and they may feel rejected when the response is minimal. Some adoptive parents may wish for more or less involvement with their child and be upset.

In the best of all worlds, all couples would be happily and permanently married, able to have children, and competent to meet their emotional and physical needs. But we do not live in that idyllic garden of Eden. We live in an imperfect world where we must try to cope with problems in the best possible ways available to us. Unfortunately, we are also all imperfect specimens, scarred and flawed, but trying to find the most advantageous ways of surviving. Adoption is certainly part of that imperfect world.

No claim should be made that all adoption problems will be solved under the open adoption plan. However, open adoption addresses some very basic dilemmas and offers a psychologically healthier way to handle the needs of the individuals involved.

18

Foster Parent Adoption:
The Legal Framework

ANDRE P. DERDEYN

In the United States today the basic purpose of adoption of minors is to benefit children in need of parents who will nurture them. The emphasis is on benefiting children rather than on gratifying the wishes of would-be adopters. Despite the acceptance of child-oriented goals in adoption, current adoption practice is strongly influenced by legal vestiges of the past that seem inconsistent with this approach. Most important, there remains important judicial unwillingness to break with the concept that parents have something approaching a legal property right in their children.

This chapter is concerned with the common situation in which the biological parent, on the one hand, has little or no relationship with a child while on the other hand, the foster parents have an established, committed, long-term role as psychological parents of the child. Therefore, the healthy development of these children is served by protecting the stability and longevity of placement with the foster parent, ideally in adoption. Here some legal issues will be explored affecting the ability of such parents to adopt children in their care.

The book *Beyond the Best Interests of the Child* (Goldstein, Freud, & Solnit, 1973), probably has done more to call attention to the needs of children in foster care and to point to the directions that change should take than any other factor that has influenced this field. Authors Goldstein, Freud, and Solnit emphasized the importance of the psychological parent-child relationship, whether it be with a biological parent or with a third party with whom a parent–child type of relationship has developed, and made a strong case that the court's mandate should be to maintain the stability and continuity of that relationship. In *Beyond the Best Interests of the Child*, the psychological parent is defined as ''one who, on a continuing, day-to-day basis through interaction, companionship, interplay and mutuality, fulfills the child's psychological needs for a parent, as well as the child's physical needs. The psychological parent may be a biological . . . parent . . . or any other person'' (Goldstein, Freud, & Solnit, 1973, p. 98). Because so many children spend such a long time in foster care, many foster parent–child relationships evolve into relationships emotionally indistinguishable from biological parent–child relationships, and the foster parent becomes a psychological parent in Goldstein, Freud, and Solnit's terminology.

For the great majority of children in foster care, the resistances to terminating parental rights will insure that they remain in foster care. It is relatively easy to remove children from their homes, but extremely difficult to take the final step of making them free for adoption. To set the stage for an understanding of the problems besetting adoption of foster children, legal issues pertaining to parent–child relationships will be presented first.

PARENTAL RIGHTS IN THE LAW

Fourteenth Amendment Rights of Parents

In 1922, the U.S. Supreme Court stated that the liberty protected by the Fourteenth Amendment includes the right "to marry, establish a home, and bring up children" (*Meyer* v. *Nebraska*, 1922, p. 399). An Oregon law requiring all children to be sent to public primary schools was overturned in 1925 because it "unreasonably interferes with the liberty of parents and guardians to direct the upbringing and education of children under their control" (*Pierce* v. *Society of Sisters*, 1925, pp. 534–535). In 1943, the court wrote, "It is cardinal with us that the custody, care, and nurture of the child reside in the parents" (*Price* v. *Massachusetts*, 1943, p. 166). A 1953 opinion referred to parental custody of a child as "rights more precious . . . than property rights," and held that Fourteenth Amendment liberties included the "immediate right to the care, custody, management, and companionship of . . . minor children" (*May* v. *Anderson*, 1953, p. 533). In a 1968 case, the court wrote that "constitutional interpretation has consistently recognized that the parents' claim to authority in their own household to direct the rearing of their children is basic in the structure of our society" (*Ginsberg* v. *New York*, 1968, p. 639). In 1974, an opinion held that "freedom of personal choice in matters of . . . family life is one of the liberties protected by the due process clause" (*Cleveland Board of Education* v. *LaFleur*, 1974, p. 639).

The 1977 decision *Moore* v. *East Cleveland* extended the protection of relationships beyond those of the strictly nuclear family. The court found that a housing ordinance limiting occupancy of a dwelling unit to members of a single family was too restrictive in its definition of "family." The case involved a household consisting of a grandmother and her two grandsons who were each other's cousin. The opinion states:

> Ours is by no means a tradition limited to respect for the bonds uniting the members of the nuclear family. The tradition of uncles, aunts, cousins, and especially grandparents sharing a household along with parents and children has roots equally venerable and equally deserving of constitutional recognition. . . . Even if conditions of modern society have brought about a decline in extended family households, they have not erased the accumulated wisdom of civilization . . . that supports a larger conception of the family. (*Moore* v. *East Cleveland*, 1977, pp. 504–505)

The opinion concludes with, "the Constitution prevents East Cleveland from standardizing its children—and its adults—by forcing all to live in certain narrowly defined family patterns" (*Moore* v. *East Cleveland*, 1977, pp. 504–505). This widening of the view of families, however, does not readily include foster families. It will be instructive to bring up to date developments in the rights of biological parents and to discuss the issues comprising the "foster care compromise."

Recent Developments in the Rights of Biological Parents
A Heightened Evidentiary Standard for Terminating Parental Rights: Santosky v. Kramer

In 1982, the U.S. Supreme Court in *Santosky* v. *Kramer* struck down the New York child neglect statute that permitted termination of parental rights on proof by "fair preponderance" of the evidence that a child is permanently neglected. The "fair preponderance" standard had been the rule in many other states as well. It was found, however, to violate the due process clause. Due process in this instance was found to require that allegations supporting termination of parental rights be proved by at least "clear and convincing evidence." The rationale for the protection of parental rights in *Santosky* v. *Kramer* (1982) goes as follows:

> The fundamental liberty interest of natural parents in the care, custody, and management of their child does not evaporate simply because they have not been model parents or have lost temporary custody of their child to the state. Even when blood relationships are strained, parents retain a vital interest preventing the irretrievable destruction of their family life. If anything, persons faced with forced dissolution of their parental rights have a more critical need for procedural protections than do those resisting state intervention into ongoing family matters. When the state moves to destroy weakened family bonds, it must provide the parents with fundamentally fair procedures. (pp. 753–754)

The opinion went on that

> the parents and the child share an interest in avoiding erroneous termination. . . . For the child the likely consequence of an erroneous termination is the preservation of an uneasy status quo. For the natural parents, however, the consequence of an erroneous termination is the unnecessary destruction of their natural family. (*Santosky* v. *Kramer*, 1982, pp. 755–756)

Psychologically, however, that natural family as a parent–child unit had not existed for several years. In the dissenting opinion written by Justice Rehnquist, it was pointed out that for 4 1/2 years, the children had continuously been in the care of persons other than their parents, great effort and expense on the part of the state had been devoted to preparing the parents for the children's return, and the decision to terminate parental rights had been made after more than seven complete legal hearings. The dissenting justices felt that New York State's procedures were quite adequate and that a requirement of a higher standard of evidence was superflous. The majority was constituted by four judges and the dissent by three, a close decision.

After discussing the constitutional rights of parents, the dissenting opinion in *Santosky* v. *Kramer* (1982) contains the following paragraph, remarkable for the clearly thought-out implications for children:

> On the other side of the termination proceedings are the often counterveiling interests of the child. A stable, loving home life is essential to a child's physical, emotional, and spiritual well-being. It requires no citation of authority to assert that children who are

abused in their youth generally face extraordinary problems developing into responsible, productive citizens. The same can be said of children who, though not physically or emotionally abused, are passed from one foster home to another with no constancy of love, trust, or discipline. If the family court makes an incorrect factual determination resulting in a failure to terminate the parent–child relationship which rightfully should be ended, the child involved must return either to an abusive home or to the often unstable world of foster care. The reality of these risks is magnified by the fact that the only families faced with termination actions are those who have voluntarily surrendered custody of their child to the state, or, as is in this case, those from which the child has been removed by judicial action because of threatened irreparable injury through abuse or neglect. Permanent neglect findings also occur only in families where the child has been in foster care for at least one year. (pp. 788–790)

The effect of *Santosky* v. *Kramer* can easily be seen to increase the difficulty of children's passage through foster care to eventual adoption. For many children in need of permanent homes, this decision is an unfortunate one because of the increased impediment to terminating parental rights.

The Rights of Putative Fathers

In the area of the rights for putative fathers, the Supreme Court's decisions have evolved to a position that is uniquely psychologically sound for the children involved. Historically, adoption statutes in virtually all states treated the mother as the sole parent with regard to consent to adoption (DeMoss, 1984). In recent years, the challenges of unwed fathers have presented the Supreme Court on four occasions with fundamental questions concerning the legal nature of the parent–child relationship (Buchanan, 1984). A view of what has happened to the rights of putative fathers regarding adoption of their children provides an interesting perspective on the U.S. Supreme Court's consideration of parent–child relationships.

In 1972, the rights of the putative father were considered by the U.S. Supreme Court for the first time in *Stanley* v. *Illinois* (1972). Stanley's children were made wards of the state on the death of their mother, in spite of the fact that Stanley had lived with and supported his family intermittently for 18 years. Under Illinois law, children of unmarried fathers could be declared wards of the state without a hearing on the natural father's fitness. The U.S. Supreme Court declared that "[illegitimate] children cannot be denied the rights of other children because familial bonds in such cases [are] often as warm, enduring, and important as those arising within a more formally organized family unit," and decided that Stanley was entitled to a hearing on his fitness as a parent (*Stanley* v. *Illinois*, 1972, p. 652). Here, as in *Moore* v. *East Cleveland,* discussed previously, the court expanded its view of family units which warrant Fourteenth Amendment protection.

In the series of cases involving fathers and their illegitimate children, the Supreme Court has developed a concept that the putative father's rights generally correspond to the responsibilities he carries for the child (*Quilloin* v. *Walcott,* 1978; *Caban* v. *Mohammed,* 1979). In these cases, the Supreme Court has made important distinctions between the mere fact of biological parenthood and actual parent–child relationships. When the father of an illegitimate child demonstrates commitment to the responsibilities of parenthood, "his interest in personal contact with his child acquires substantial protection under the due process clause. . . . But the mere existence of a biological link does not merit constitutional protection'' (*Lehr* v. *Robertson*, 1983, p. 2994). ''Parental rights do not spring full-blown from the biological connection between parents and child. They require relationships more enduring'' (*Caban* v. *Mohammed*, 1979, p. 397).

The Oklahoma Supreme Court recently found Oklahoma's adoption statute to be constitutionally sound. The court found no due process or equal protection defects in the statutory scheme that requires only the consent of mothers for adoption of their out-of-wedlock children and does not require an opportunity for a hearing for an unwed father. The Oklahoma court concluded from the recent Supreme Court cases that the basis for constitutional protection is missing where the father seeking it has not taken on parental responsibilities commensurate with the child's best interests (*In re* Baby Boy D, 1985, p. 1088). The court stated that the Constitution ''protects only parent–child relationships of biological parents who have actually committed themselves to their children and have exercised responsibility for rearing their children.''

The judicial system appears to have taken a position that, with regard to the adoption of his child, a putative father who has not earned any rights as a parent can be legally dismissed from parenthood. There is scant analogy with the biological parents of some children in foster care, where the parents may not have had any contact with the child for years, yet their legal claim on the child remains very strong.

The Foster Care Compromise: Parents' Rights versus Children's Needs

A 1975 Iowa case (*Alsager* v. *District Court*, 1975) continues to illustrate important aspects of the situation currently surrounding foster care. The opinion takes note of the ''compelling'' nature of the State's child protection interests, but points out that ''even in a case of clear child abuse [the law] has vitiated the need for prompt termination action through its child neglect statute. That law sanctions the immediate, albeit temporary, removal of a child form the parents' home in case of maltreatment'' (*Alsager* v. *District Court*, 1975, p. 22). The opinion goes on to point out that ''once a child has been removed from the risk of harm . . . the State's child protection interests are less compelling. The State's interest in protecting a child from future harm at the hands of his or her parents is clearly less compelling in a situation where the State has already obtained temporary protective custody over the child than in those cases where the supposedly threatened child remains in the parents' home'' (*Alsager* v. *District Court*, 1975, p. 22).

This quote serves to underline an extremely important point: the rather chilling idea that once the state has taken its proper designated action—removal of the child from the parental home—then the problem has lost its immediacy. This, of course, takes no account of the immense problem posed to children who lose their parents under such circumstances, and the potential damage to the parent–child relationship done by such a removal, even should the family eventually be reunited.

A 1971 Oregon case (*State* v. *McMaster*, 1971) seeking termination of rights of neglectful parents provides a good example of the ethical and legal quagmire these cases may entail. The child had been placed with foster parents at 2 months of age. The foster parents later wished to adopt, and, when the child turned 4, the lower court effected termination of parental rights preparatory to adoption. The biological parents appealed. The Oregon Supreme Court noted that ''the parents frequently quarrelled, [the biological father] never held a job more than a month and seldom that long, they were usually on welfare, and [the biological mother] was destitute.'' Yet the court was unwilling to terminate the parental rights because this family's situation was not unusual enough to warrant such a drastic step.

> The state of the [biological] family is duplicated in hundreds of thousands of American families—transiency and incapacity, poverty and instability. . . . However, we do not believe the legislature contemplated that parental rights could be terminated because the natural parents are unable to furnish surroundings which would enable the child to grow up as we would desire all children to do. . . . The best interests of the child are paramount; however, the courts cannot sever . . . parental rights when many thousands of children are being raised under basically the same circumstances as this child. (*State* v. *McMaster*, 1971, pp. 572–573)

The court invalidated the termination but did not require transfer of custody to the biological parents. Thus the parental disabilities appeared to have justified the child's placement in foster care, but were not sufficient to warrant termination of parental rights. This impasse—judicial affirmation of parental rights coupled with judicial admission that the welfare of children may warrant custody in a foster parent—is one which significantly impairs the lives of thousands of children in foster care. To the person who is not attuned to the basics of child development, this impasse may have the appearance of a rather logical compromise between the rights of parents and the need of children not to be abused or neglected. What this author terms the foster care compromise is predicted on an egregious insensitivity to the basic issue in child development—that it takes place optimally within a secure, reciprocal relationship with a committed, caring adult. As stated by one commentator, ''the reasoning of the Alsager court is inherently deficient because it protects family autonomy at the wrong point in time'' (Hershkowitz, 1985, p. 257). In the excerpt from the dissenting opinion in *Santosky* v. *Kramer* (1982) quoted previously, Justice Rehnquist makes the same point. A recent case reflects the same rationale as the decision in the Alsager case. In rejecting a mother's contention that there was insufficient proof for removal of her child from her home, the court pointed out that there is ''a substantive difference between the quantum of adequate proof'' for purposes of termination of parental rights as opposed to mere temporary removal'' (*In re* Evans, 1986, p. 1466).

The truly momentous legal decision is the removal of the child from the home in the first place, and this juncture needs to be recognized as the critical moment it is for the child, the family, the agency, and for the decision making process itself (Derdeyn, 1977a). To the child, removal is very disruptive, for it entails a discontinuity with his or her parents, siblings, home, and school, and the child is usually plagued with feelings of helplessness, devaluation, and responsibility for the disruption. The parents are faced with a sense of loss and failure, but also may feel relief at being absolved of the responsibility of caring for the child who has been removed from the home. With the child out of the home, rehabilitative or treatment activities related to parenting skills or interactions with the child tend to lose their immediacy. For the agency, also, any sense of urgency regarding the child tends to diminish greatly when the child is placed. At this time when the adults' level of concern has diminished, the child's future with regard to stability and continuity of relationships with caretaking adults can be expected to be poor.

Santosky v. *Kramer,* with its enhanced evidentiary requirement for terminating parental rights, has tended to increase the depth and breadth of the foster care quagmire: there has been no change in how children enter foster care, but there is increased difficulty in finding a route out by way of adoption. As Hershkowitz cogently points out, "The imposition of an inflexible standard of proof interferes with the child's right to proper custody. If the state requires a preponderance of evidence to temporarily remove the child pursuant to an adjudication of dependency, the requirement of clear and convincing evidence to terminate parental rights will cause the child to languish in foster care until the state can meet the heightened standards of proof necessary to terminate parental rights" (Hershkowitz, 1985, p. 292). Some changes, however, have occurred with regard to the rights of foster parents, and these will be discussed next.

FOSTER PARENT RIGHTS

The wish to make a permanent commitment, whether in continued foster care or in adoption, to children in their care has no doubt enticed foster parents as long as the current structure of the child welfare system has existed. Attempts to do so in past decades have generally failed due to the difficulty in terminating parental rights and also due to welfare departments' policy of allowing adoption only by those persons whom the agency had designated as qualified to adopt.

Foster parents have long been considered to have a number of duties, few rights, and to be essentially employees of the agency with which they contract (Katz, 1971). Typically, when a foster parent attempts to contest removal of a child by the responsible welfare agency, or attempts to adopt a child against agency wishes, courts have upheld the sanctity of the placement contract between foster parents and the agency and the rights of biological parents (Note, 1973). These contracts generally stipulate that the making of any plans for the child, including plans for adoption, be left to the the agency. Traditionally, foster parents have not been considered to have a legally recognizable interest in their foster child. The traditional status of foster parents is reflected in the following cases.

> Foster parents appealed a lower court decision permitting a child care agency to remove from their custody a 5-year-old child who had spent 4 years in their care (*In re* Jewish Child Care Association, 1959). The foster parents had accepted the girl under the standard agency agreement that the placement would be temporary and that the foster parents were to prepare her for return to her biological mother. Before the first year ended, however, the foster parents decided to adopt the girl and actively pursued that course in direct conflict with agency policies. The court of appeals decided in favor of the agency, finding fault with the "extreme of love, affection, and possessiveness manifested by the [foster parents], together with conduct which their emotional involvement impelled." (*In re* Jewish Child Care Association, 1959, p. 70)

> A biological mother sought to gain custody of her child. The foster parents, who had cared for the child from age 3 months to 5 years, attempted to terminate the biological mother's rights preparatory to their adopting the child. The court found that the foster parents "were bound by their agreement with the Department of Public Welfare" and that the "Department . . . was entitled to the possession of the . . . child" (*Huey* v.

Lente, 1973, pp. 1087–1088). The foster parents, therefore, had no legal standing, and the child was given to the custody of her biological mother.

A New York court in 1976 disparaged the idea of a foster parent's right to custody as a notion by which "third-party custodians . . . acquire some sort of squatter's rights in another's child" (*Bennett* v. *Jeffries,* 1976, p. 552). In an earlier decision, that same court admonished that "the temporary parent substitute must keep his proper distance at all costs to himself" (*Spence–Chapin Adoption Service* v. *Polk,* 1971, p. 205).

The right to a part in decision making regarding children in their care has been increasingly sought by foster parents and foster parent organizations (*Kurtis* v. *Ballou,* 1970; Reistroffer, 1972). In 1976, a United States District Court held unconstitutional a provision of New York law that authorized the state to remove children from foster homes without affording a prior hearing to either the foster child or its foster parents. This case, which was heard by the U.S. Supreme Court as *Smith* v. *Organization of Foster Families for Equality and Reform (OFFER),* was decided in 1977.

Smith v. *Organization of Foster Families*

It was argued that when a child has lived in a foster home for one year or more, important psychological and familial ties are created (*Smith* v. *OFFER,* 1977). Therefore, foster parents possess a liberty interest in the survival of the long-term foster family sufficient to invoke Fourteenth Amendment due process clause protections. The Supreme Court conceded that

> no one would seriously dispute that a deeply loving and interdependent relationship between an adult and a child in his or her care may exist even in the absence of blood relationship. At least where a child had been placed in foster care as an infant, has never known his natural parents, and has remained continuously for several years in the care of the same foster parents, it is natural that the foster family should hold the same place in the emotional life of the foster child, and fulfill the same socializing functions, as a natural family. For this reason, we cannot dismiss the foster family as a mere collection of unrelated individuals. (*Smith* v. *OFFER,* 1977, p. 844–845)

But the court went on to identify two important distinctions between the foster family and the biological family. The first is that biological family relationships have their origin entirely apart from the power of the state, while the foster family has its source in state law and contractual arrangements. As the Supreme Court in *Smith* v. *OFFER* (1977) stated, "Whatever emotional ties may develop between foster parent and foster child have their origins in an arrangement in which the state has been a partner from the outset" (p. 845). The second major issue is that there is an unavoidable tension between protecting the liberty interests of the biological parents while also extending familial rights in favor of foster parents. The U.S. Supreme Court found it unnecessary to resolve the issue of just how much constitutional protection the foster parent-child relationship required, since the procedures utilized by the state of New York were considered by the court to be constitutionally adequate.

The Current Status of the Foster Family
The Reign of Tradition: Limited Rights

Most federal court cases subsequent to *Smith* v. *OFFER* have ruled that foster parents do not possess a constitutionally protected liberty interest in the maintenance of the foster family (*Drummond* v. *Fulton County*, 1977; *Kyees* v. *County Department of Public Welfare*, 1979). There is limited recognition of rights commensurate with or proportional to the emotional and psychological realities of the foster family.

Many of the cases coming to state courts continue to be dealt with in a manner basically indistinguishable from those prior to *Smith* v. *OFFER*. The following recent cases demonstrate this treatment. In the Pennsylvania case *Priester* v. *Fayette County Children and Youth Services* (1986), a 3-year-old boy had been placed in a foster home for the period between his first and third birthdays, at which time he was moved to another foster home where a sibling resided. In determining this ruling, the court reviewed other Pennsylvania cases to support its rationale in moving the child. The court noted that it had ruled in 1984 that foster parents have no standing to file a petition for termination of parental rights. In the earlier case, the Pennsylvania Superior Court had written, "By its very nature, the foster parent/foster child relationship implies a warning against any deep emotional involvement with the child since under the given insecure circumstances this would be judged as excessive" (*In re* Adoption of Crystal D.R., 1984, p. 1151). The opinion sums up that "we must balance the great need for stability which is an integral part of healthy human development, with the realization that foster care is, by its very nature, temporary."

In a 1986 case (*Nye* v. *Marcus*, 1986, p. 1147), it was decided that the foster parents had no legal standing regarding custody of a foster child who had been placed in their care. When the natural parents consented to termination of parental rights, the agency informed the foster parents that the child was to be removed and placed with prospective adoptive parents who had been selected by the agency. The court decided that the foster parents did "not have a liberty interest and their emotional relationship with the child, which was acquired through the temporary foster placement, is too tenuous a basis to afford [legal] standing." In response to the foster parents' argument that they should be the ones to assert the child's interests "because she does not have any natural parents to represent her and only they as foster parents are both capable of and willing to assert [her] interests," the court responded that as the "statutory parents . . . DSS provides for her welfare, which includes acting in her best interests." The court further stated that "the foster parents are not an appropriate neutral party to assert the interests of their foster child."

The major difference between these recent cases and those of twenty years ago is that the recent opinions are not as disparaging of the foster parents as were the older cases. Otherwise, little appears to have changed substantively.

Foster Parent–Child Relationships Not Created by the State

In some of the cases coming before the courts, appeals are being made on the basis of making distinctions between the case in question and those in which the foster parent–child relationship was strictly a creation of the state.

Teenage parents asked a couple to raise their daughter (*Berhow* v. *Crow*, 1982). The couple became licensed foster parents and registered as the child's parents on the consent of the mother. Shortly thereafter, the mother died, and the foster parents filed for adoption, to which the child's father agreed. The maternal grandparents then abducted the child and petitioned in another state to adopt. The court found that the foster couple had a liberty interest in preserving their relationship with the child largely because the child was placed by the natural mother and not the state. But the court also ascribed importance to the emotional ties between foster parents and child: "As the nature of the foster parent/foster child's familial relationship becomes closer and stronger, so as to approach the level of the relationship between natural parents and their offspring, so, too, do the rights of foster parents to preserve that relationship" (*Berhow* v. *Crow,* 1982, pp. 371–372).

In a situation where the rights of natural parents were not at issue, Mrs. R. was caring for her mother and two young half siblings when the mother required mental hospitalization on a permanent basis (*Rivera* v. *Marcus,* 1982). When the mother was committed to an institution, the juvenile court ordered legal custody of the children transferred to the state welfare department which arranged for Mrs. R. to serve as foster parent with compensation. Two years later, at which time the children had been living with Mrs. R. for 6 years, the welfare department notified Mrs. R. that the state had decided to remove the children, held a meeting, and 2 days later removed the children and placed them in another foster home. Under state regulations, the foster parent could not bring legal counsel to the hearing and could not confront adverse witnesses. The decision of the three-person panel was not required to be in writing or otherwise explained to the foster parent and was not appealable.

The federal appeals court found that this "extended family" was not created by the state through the foster care contract but rather was natural in origin; and, in addition, a potential for conflict between biological and foster parent was not present in this situation. The court decided that Mrs. R. possessed a liberty interest in the maintenance of her familial relationship with the children and that the procedures used by the state were constitutionally inadequate.

In a 1985 Delaware case, the court found that a long-term family relationship between a grandparent and her grandchild gave rise to a liberty interest in continued physical custody (*Alma G.* v. *Division of Child Protective Services,* 1985). When the natural mother was committed to the state hospital, the state awarded temporary custody of the child to her maternal grandmother, who had already been caring for her. The grandmother was given no compensation for foster care. In the sixth year of the existence of this family, the child remained out of school for 3 months, whereupon the state filed a neglect petition. On the basis of testimony which the grandmother had not been present to hear, the state removed the child to a foster home.

The reviewing court found that the grandmother had served as the child's psychological parent, and that she had been led to believe that the placement arrangement was permanent because of the "consent to custody" agreement signed by both the state and the grandmother. The court concluded that the grandmother had a liberty interest in the maintenance of a familial relationship with her grandchild. The state's procedures were found to be inadequate in terms of the caretaker not being informed of the state's intention, having a limited opportunity to present her case, not being apprised of the evidence being used against her, and not being able to confront witnesses or respond to the objections to her care.

The 4-month-old child of a neglectful mother was placed with a foster mother

(*Brown* v. *County of San Joaquin*, 1985). A year later, the county welfare department decided that the reunification of the child with her biological mother would never occur and invited the foster mother to apply to adopt. She did so and attended the prescribed adoption classes. A year after that, she was informed that her application had been denied. The foster mother then filed a petition to adopt the child. The county successfully moved to dismiss the petition. About a year later, the child was removed from the foster mother's custody, after having lived with her for 3¼ years. The case as it came before the superior court was that the foster mother claimed entitlement of procedural due process before the county removed the child from her home and destroyed the foster parent–child relationship.

The federal reviewing court noted that in California law the paramount goal is the reunification of children with their biological parents. But when that goal is found to be unrealistic, the focus moves to finding a permanent, stable home for a child. At that point, California law recognizes and affords protection to the interests of the foster family. Under such circumstances, the court observed, the law creates an expectation in both foster parents and foster children that a relationship of mutual love and affection will be permitted to continue and foster parents must be accorded procedural due process.

> Thus the ultimate question: is a relationship with the form and the function of a biological family entitled to the legal protections granted to a biological family despite the fact that the relationship is entirely a creature of state law? The court concludes that it is. It is artificial to treat a relationship that time and events have transformed to the most profound relationship known to mankind—mother and child—as the purely legal relationship it originally was. Reality controls: the emotional sustenance and enrichment, the very sense of self, derived from an intimate relationship with one's parent or one's child cannot be discounted by the niceties of the relationship's creation. In a series of cases . . . the Supreme Court has made it clear that the touchstone of protectible family rights is not nice legal distinctions and even simply biology, but the reality of family life. . . . In short, the court concludes that the foster family relationship is sufficiently similar to other familial relationships held by the Supreme Court to be entitled to constitutional protection. The court reaches this conclusion because the foster parent/foster child relationship has precisely the same form and content as a healthy biological parent–child relationship. . . . This court believes that to conclude that the state's role in the creation of the foster family is controlling is to sanction the triumph of form over substance. (*Brown* v. *County of San Joaquin*, 1985, pp. 664–665)

This opinion is somewhat unusual in its interpretation of the positions taken by the U.S. Supreme Court. It is, however, encouraging to see courts taking positions such as this one.

ADOPTION BY FOSTER PARENTS

It is evident that, although foster parents are making a few, circumscribed gains in their rights regarding children in their care, they are not developing appreciable rights vis-à-vis biological parents. Earlier in this chapter it was established that termination of the parental rights of biological parents, with the notable exception of uninvolved putative fathers, was more difficult to accomplish.

Yet some change has taken place with regard to adoption by foster parents. This change has come about in large part as a result of increased public awareness and interest in child abuse, neglect, and in the problems of the foster care system which became apparent in the last 25 years. The process by which this has occurred will be briefly reviewed here.

The Foster Care System in Public View

In 1959, Maas and Engler published their classic study of over 4,000 children in foster care (Maas & Engler, 1959). They predicted that more than half would remain in foster care for most of their childhoods. Kempe and associates identified the "battered child syndrome" in 1962 (Kempe et al., 1962), which stimulated the interest of members of the mental health, medical, and legal professions in the broad group of dependent, neglected, and abused children.

More disturbing reports regarding foster care came in the early 1970s. A 1973 cross-sectional study of the children in foster care in Massachusetts revealed that 60% had been in care between 4 and 8 years, with the average being 5 years (Gruber, 1973). In 1975, the Columbia University longitudinal study of children in foster care in New York City provided information regarding 467 families with one or more children entering foster care (Fanshel, 1976). Thirty percent of the original study sample of 624 children remained in foster care at the end of 5 years. Of this group remaining in care 5 years, 46% had experienced three or more placements. About two-thirds of the children remaining in care 5 years had lost contact with their parents (Fanshel, 1975).

One response to this type of information regarding foster care has been the development of various schemes to review cases in care (Festinger, 1975; Ten Broeck & Barth, 1986). The purpose of review is to stimulate permanency planning and activity in order to return the child to the parental home or make the child available for adoption. Foster care review reached the federal legislative level with the Adoption Assistance and Child Welfare Funding Act of 1980, which requires a reporting and tracking system for children in foster care (Hartley, 1984).

Another important event that brought attention to children in foster care was a class action suit brought against the entire foster care system of Jackson County, Missouri, which encompasses Kansas City. The issues raised which are most pertinent to this study are the following: 29% of the children were placed in four or more homes in less than 5 years; and the longer a child remained in care, the more likely he or she was to experience movement from home to home (Mushlin, Levitt, & Anderson, 1986). In *G. L.* v. *Zumwalt* (1983), a federal court approved a consent decree mandating specific and widespread improvements in the policies and practices of the entire foster care system of that major metropolitan area. A key doctrine of importance in determining the outcome of *G. L.* v. *Zumwalt* had been developed previously in the 1973 case concerning the Willowbrook State School for the Mentally Retarded in Staten Island, New York (*New York State Association for Retarded Children* v. *Rockefeller,* 1973). In that case, a "right to freedom from harm" was enunciated. In a consent judgment in the Willowbrook State School case, the judge elaborated: "Protection from harm requires relief more extensive than this court originally contemplated, because harm can result not only from neglect but from conditions which cause regression or which prevent development of an individual's capa-bilities" (*New York State Association for Retarded Children* v. *Rockefeller*, 1975, p. 718). The "right to freedom from harm" doctrine seems quite appropriate for foster children, whose care has been taken over by government as parent and protector in its role of *parens patriae*.

Agencies' Changing View of Foster Parent Adoption

A definite change has occurred in the attitude of welfare departments concerning foster parent adoption. In a 1974 article (Festinger, 1974), the author reported on the wording of agreements state agencies entered into with foster parents. Of the 44 states reported on, the agreement in 27 of them stated specifically that the child was not being placed for adoption and that the foster parents agreed not to attempt to adopt. A survey reported in 1981 asked the adoption specialist in the state public child welfare agency in every state and the District of Columbia the following ques-tion: "In general, are foster parents given preference to adopt a child who has been in their care as a foster child and who is free for adoption?" (Proch, 1981). Re-sponses were received from 46 states. It was found that preference for adoption by current foster parents existed in 43 states. In 9 states and in Washington, D.C., the preference was by legislation. Typical legislation is that of Virginia's current law, which states: "When a foster parent, who has a child placed in the foster parents' home by a child-placing agency, desires to adopt the child and (i) the child has resided in the home of such foster parent continuously for at least 18 months and (ii) the natural parents' rights to the child have been terminated, the court shall accept the petition filed by the foster parent and shall order a thorough investigation of the matter. . . ." In 15 states, there was reported to be preference for adoption by foster parents by agency regulation, and in 9 states, there was reported to be preference given in practice. The 1978 revision of the Child Welfare League of America Stan-dards for Adoption Service (1978) conservatively states that "the possibility of de-veloping some foster homes into adoptive homes should be explored" (p. 71).

From the above, it can be seen that the studies of children's experience in foster care and the adverse publicity regarding various aspects of the public child care system have led to a significant change in the attitude of social service professionals toward foster parents' becoming adoptive parents (Coyne & Brown, 1986). But this raises problems for child welfare agencies, which ordinarily have quite different re-quirements for foster and adoptive parents (Proch, 1981). Historically, agencies have had stringent requirements for adoptive parents. Additionally, the demand for chil-dren to adopt has made the pool of prospective adoptive parents a large one, while persons willing to take in foster children have never been in great supply. Therefore, many foster parents do not fulfill the criteria an agency requires of its prospective adoptive parents. Another development, which has grown out of the new attitude toward foster parents and has had major effects on child welfare agencies, is foster care/adoption or "risk adoption" (Lee & Hull, 1983).

Risk Adoption

In an effort to prevent multiple placements, some agencies are placing children who are not legally free for adoption, but for whom adoption appears to be a likely outcome, with families who have made a commitment to provide permanence for the child prior to the placement (Gill & Amadio, 1983; Lee & Hull, 1983). The commitment involves provision of foster care, for as long as the child needs it, and adoption, should parental rights be terminated. A commitment is also made by the agency to resolve the child's impermanent situation. Generally, risk adoption is currently being carried out in small model or pilot programs (Brodzinsky, 1987). Children thought to be appropriate for risk adoption are involved in the types of situations listed below (Gill & Amadio, 1983).

1. A child has been relinquished by the mother and the identity of the father is unknown.
2. A child has been relinquished by one parent and a diligent search has been made in an attempt to locate the absent parent, but the latter's whereabouts continue to be unknown.
3. The child has been relinquished by one parent. The identity and whereabouts of the other parent are known and it appears that this parent might also relinquish the child.
4. The child has been abandoned in circumstances in which there was indication of the parents' intent to give up the child permanently, and the identity and whereabouts of the parents are unknown.
5. Termination of parental rights has been granted by the trial court but the case is on appeal to a higher court.
6. The child comes from a family in which other children have been freed for adoption, and it seems feasible that adoption may become the eventual plan for this child.
7. The child lives in a state where courts formally or informally require that the child be in an adoptive family before considering a petition for involuntary termination of parental rights.
8. The child's parent is mentally ill or developmentally disabled and unlikely ever to be able to parent the child.

The changes in the ability of foster parents to adopt children who have been in their care as a way to maintain stability and continuity of relationship–child relationships clearly is beneficial to the children involved. The immense problems in terminating the rights of biological parents to their children have seen very little change, however.

CONCLUSION

Increased recognition of the importance of the psychological parent–child relationship has led to considerable efforts with regard to permanency planning for children in foster care. This action has led in turn to development of some rudimentary rights for the foster parent–child relationship, acceptance of adoption by foster parents, and new initiatives like risk adoption. But these developments, as positive as they are to the children who benefit from them, pale in comparison to the central issue of parental rights.

Parental Rights as the Dominant Issue

In spite of the changes that have occurred over the last several decades, the major issue affecting adoption of children by committed foster parents of long standing remains the difficulty with which parental rights are terminated. For judges to decide to end the legal relationship between biological parent and child (again, this almost always becomes an issue only years after that unit has already broken apart functionally), there usually has to be an element of culpability on the part of the parents. In one case, previously described, the court acknowledged that there was no relationship between biological father and son but felt that to terminate the father's rights would be a "terrible punishment" for him (In the Matter of the Adoption of Blumenthal, 1965, p. 788). In a case involving abandonment, a court held that "even where the flame of parental interest is reduced to a flicker the court may not properly intervene to dissolve the parentage" (*W. v. G.,* 1974, p. 38).

The sense of termination of parental rights as a punishment, for which parents must be deserving, is not limited to the lower levels of our judicial system. In *Lassiter* v. *Department of Social Services,* decided in 1981, the Supreme Court's majority opinion described termination of parental rights as a "unique kind of deprivation" (p. 27) for the parent. In the dissent, Justice Rehnquist wrote, "It is hardly surprising that this forced dissolution of the parent–child relationship has been recognized as a punitive sanction by courts, Congress, and commentators" (Lassiter, 1981, pp. 39–40).

In contrast, where parents suffer mental illness and mental retardation courts can relatively effectively terminate the rights of parents (*In re* D. N., 1983; *In re* William, Susan, and Joseph, 1982). Perhaps because of these markedly incapacitating conditions, the tendency to identify with these parents is minimized.

On the whole, the situation regarding termination of parental rights is unchanged from that found by Derdeyn and Wadlington in 1977, who observed that courts

> cannot make an objective finding that a child is abandoned, is in need of an adoptive home, or is in fact already a member of a family which does not include his biological parents. The court's attention is first directed to terminating parental rights, and the evident reluctance to do so has an important relation to the fact that parental intent and fault are integral to findings of abandonment and unfitness. The courts must be concerned with the *intent* of the parents, and often will not find an intent to abandon in spite of demonstrated lack of care and concern on the part of the biological parents and, more importantly, in spite of well-developed relationships of the child with the prospective adoptive parents. (Derdeyn & Wadlington, 1977, p. 248)

The increased evidentiary burden imposed by *Santosky* v. *Kramer* probably substantially increases the impediments to termination of parental rights. A more benign interpretation is that, after Santosky, the courts are now more clearly doing what they say they are doing (protecting parents' rights) than was previously the case, and that Santosky has not made a practical difference.

In sum, the greatest judicial impediment to acknowledging and securing by adoption long-standing, committed relationships between foster parents and children remains the great reluctance to terminate parental rights. However, should such a child become available for adoption, child care agencies have dropped some of their immense resistance in the past to the possibility of adoption by foster parents (Derdeyn, 1986).

Child Removal: The Momentous Event

It does not appear likely that our society and our courts are apt to appreciably redesign priorities regarding children's needs and parental rights and needs. It is not likely that parental rights will be terminated in the interests of children any more readily in the year 2000 than currently, in the opinion of this observer. The path from foster care to adoption, for the most part, is not likely to change very much in the foreseeable future.

The decision to remove the child for all but brief and carefully planned separations has important implications for the child's emotional life and, as mentioned before, for the level of motivation for rehabilitation of abusing and neglectful parents, and for the effective functioning of agencies and individuals attempting to help these parents. The decision to remove a child should be the critical one, and the one in which the burden should properly rest on the state to prove that removal is absolutely necessary for the well-being of the child. It is at the time of removal that the weight of parental rights should be exerted, in order to allow the parents to keep their child if the state cannot establish that they (the parents) are unable to care for their child adequately. Once the child is removed, however, the burden should shift to the parent or parents to establish that they are capable of caring for the child. In the latter case, the child should, as soon as possible, be returned to the home and be followed under careful supervision. If there is little potential for rehabilitation of parents, or if the child's timely return home is not possible, then a permanent placement with a person willing to make a long-term commitment to the child must be secured with mimimum delay.

Providing for Children in the Shadow of Their Parents' Rights

Given the implacable resistance to terminating parental rights, perhaps a place for innovation is in providing a legal framework for permanent custody with foster parents without terminating parental rights. Some years ago, this author wondered if permanent foster care without termination of parental rights might be an achievable arrangement to optimally serve some children (Derdeyn, 1977b; Derdeyn, Rogoff, & Williams, 1978). This idea has again been raised by legal scholars (Bartlett, 1984; Smith, 1986); one such article has the comprehensive title "Rethinking Parenthood as an Exclusive Status: The Need for Legal Alternatives When the Premise of the Nuclear Family Has Failed" (Bartlett, 1984).

The problems of loyalty conflicts for the children and of legal wrangling between biological and foster parents would admittedly be immense in an arrangement which would place permanent custody with foster parents. It does, however, appear to this observer that the tension between the rights of biological parents and society's concerns for the children that some parents are incapable of caring for adequately will result in experimentation in new custodial alternatives. These forces might result in the evolution of new custodial forms, such as has happened in the divorce custody field, where divorce mediation and joint custody have developed as new compromises for old problems (Derdeyn & Scott, 1984).

References

Abend, S. M. (1974). Problems of identity: Theoretical and clinical applications. *Psychoanalytic Quarterly, 43,* 606–637.

Abend, S. M. (in press). Identity. In B. Moore & B. Fine (Eds.), *Psychoanalysis: The major concepts.* New Haven, CT: Yale University Press.

Abramson, L. Y., Seligman, M. E. P., & Teasdale, J. P. (1978). Learned helplessness in humans: Critique and reformulation. *Journal for Abnormal Psychology, 87,* 49–74.

Achenbach, T. M., & Edelbrock, C. S. (1983). *Manual for the child behavior checklist and revised child behavior profile.* Burlington, VT: Queen City Printers.

Addis, R. S., Salzburger, F., & Rabel, E. (1954), *A survey based on adoption case records.* London: Association of Mental Health.

Aigner, H. (1968). *Adoption in America: Coming of age.* Greenbrae, CA: Paradigm Press.

Ainsworth, M. D. S. (1973). The development of infant–mother attachment. In B. M. Caldwell & H. N. Ricciuti (Eds.), *Review of child development research* (Vol. 3). Chicago: University of Chicago Press.

Ainsworth, M. D. S., Blehar, M. C., Waters, E., & Wall, S. (1978). *Patterns of attachment: A psychological study of the strange situation.* Hillsdale, NJ: Erlbaum.

Ainsworth, M. D. S. (1979). Infant–mother attachment. *American Psychologist, 34,* 932–937.

Alcohol, Drug Abuse, and Mental Health Administration (1986). *Journal of American Medical Association, 256,* 3201.

Aldgate, J., & Hawley, D. (1986). Helping foster families through disruption. *Adoption and Fostering, 10,* 44–49.

Alexy, W. D. (1982). Dimensions of psychological counseling that facilitate the grieving process of bereaved parents. *Journal of Counseling Psychology, 29,* 498–507.

Allen, E. C. (1983). *Mother, can you hear me?* New York: Dodd, Mead.

Alma G. v. Division of Child Protective Services, 11 FLR 1415 (1985).

Almqvist, F. (1986). Psychiatric hospital treatment of young people. *Acta Psychiatrica Scandinavica, 73,* 289–294.

Alsager v. District Court, 406 F. Supp. 10 (1975).

Amatruda, C., & Baldwin, J. V. (1951). Current adoption practices. *Journal of Pediatrics, 38,* 208–212.

American Academy of Pediatrics. (1971). Identity development in adopted children. *Pediatrics, 47,* 948–949.

American Academy of Pediatrics, Committee on Adoption and Dependent Care. (1973). *Adoption of children.* Evanston, IL: American Academy of Pediatrics.

American Civil Liberties Union. (1975). Sealed adoption records vs. the adoptees right to know the identity of the birth parents. *Children's rights report* (Vol. 3). New York: Author.

American Psychiatric Association. (1980). *Diagnostic and statistical manual of mental disorders* (3rd ed.), Washington, DC: Author.

Anderson, C. W. (1977). The sealed record in adoption controversy. *Social Service Review, 51,* 141–154.

Anderson, R. (1987) Envy and jealousy. *Journal of College Student Psychotherapy, 1,* 49–81.

Andrews, R. G. (1979). A clinical appraisal of searching. *Public Welfare, 37,* 15–21.

Archer, S. L. (1985). Career and/or family: The identity process for adolescent girls. *Youth and Society, 6,* 289–313.

Arend, R., Gove, F. L., & Sroufe, L. A. (1979). Continuity of individual adaptation from infancy to kindergarten: A predictive study of ego-resiliency and curiosity in preschoolers. *Child Development, 50,* 950–959.

Argent, H. (1984). *Find me a family.* London: Souvernir Press (Educational and Academic).

Aumend, S., & Barrett, M. (1984). Self-concept and attitudes toward adoption: A comparison of searching and non-searching adult adoptees. *Child Welfare, 63,* 251–259.

Austad, C. C., & Simmons, T. L. (1978). Symptoms of adopted children presenting to a large mental health clinic. *Child Psychiatry and Human Development, 9,* 20–27.

Auth, R. J., & Zaret, S. (1986). The search in adoption: A service and a process. *Social Casework, 67,* 560–568.

Backhaus, K. A. (1984, Nov.–Dec.). Life books: Tool for working with children in placement. *Social Work,* 551–554.

Bachrach, C. A. (1986). Adoption plans, adopted children, and adoptive mothers. *Journal of Marriage and the Family, 48,* 243–253.

Band, E. V., & Weisz, J. R. (1988). How to feel better when it feels bad: Children's perspective on coping with everyday stress. *Developmental Psychology, 24,* 247–253.

Baran, A., Pannor, R., & Sorosky, A. (1975). Secret adoption records: The dilemma of our adoptees. *Psychology Today, 9,* 38–42, 96–98.

Baran, A., Pannor, R., & Sorosky, A. (1976). Open adoption. *Social Work, 21,* 97–105.

Baran, A., Pannor, R., & Sorosky, A. (1977). The lingering pain of surrendering a child. *Psychology Today, 11,* 58–60, 88.

Barber, D. (1975). *Unmarried fathers.* London: Hutchinson.

Barinbaum, L. (1974). Identity crisis in adolescence: Problems of an adopted girl. *Adolescence, 9,* 547–554.

Barnes, M. J. (1953). The working–through process in dealing with anxiety around adoption. *American Journal of Orthopsychiatry, 23,* 605–620.

Barth, R. P., Berry, M., Yoshikami, R., Goodfield, R. K., & Carson, M. L. (1988). Predicting adoption disruption. *Social Work, 33,* 227–233.

Bartlett, K. T. (1984). Rethinking parenthood as an exclusive status: The need for legal alternatives when the premise of the nuclear family has failed. *Virginia Law Review, 70,* 879–963.

Bass, C. (1975). Matchmaker–matchmaker: Older-child adoption failures. *Child Welfare, 54,* 505–512.

Baumrind, D. (1967). Child care practices anteceding three patterns of preschool behavior. *Genetic Psychology Monographs, 75,* 43–83.

Baumrind, D. (1971). Current patterns of parental authority. *Developmental Psychology Monograph, 4* (1, Pt. 2).

Beavers, W. R. (1977). *Psychotherapy and growth: A family systems perspective.* New York: Brunner/Mazel.

Becker, W. C. (1964). Consequences of different kinds of parental discipline. In M. L. Hoffman and L. W. Hoffmann (Eds.), *Review of child development research* (Vol. 1). New York: Russell Sage Foundation.

Beebe, B., & Sloate, P. (1982). Assessment and treatment of difficulties in mother–infant attunement in the first three years of life. *Psychoanalytic Inquiry, 1,* 601–623.

Belsky, J. (1981). Early human experience: A family systems perspective. *Developmental Psychology, 17,* 3–23.

Benet, M. K. (1976). *The politics of adoption.* New York: Free Press.

Bennett v. Jeffries, 40 N.Y. 2d 453, 552 (1976).

Bental, V. (1965). Psychic mechanism of the adoptive mother in connection with adoption. *Israel Annals of Psychiatry and Related Disciplines, 3,* 24–34.

Benton, B. B., Kaye, E., & Tipton, M. (1985). *Evaluation of state activities regard to adoption disruption.* Washington, DC: Urban Systems Research & Engineering.

Berger, M. (1979). Preliminary report of the study group on the problems of adopted children. *Bulletin of the Hampstead Clinic, 2,* 169–176.

Berger, M. (1980). Second report on problems of adopted children. *Bulletin of the Hampstead Clinic, 3,* 247–256.

Berger, M. (1981) Study group on the problems of adopted children. *Bulletin of the Hampstead Clinic, 4,* 292.

Berger, M., & Hodges, J. (1982). Some thoughts on the question of when to tell the child that he is adopted. *Journal of Child Psychotherapy, 8,* 67–88.

Berhow v. Crow, 423 So. 2d 371 (1982).

Berlin, I. N. (1978). Anglo adoptions of native Americans: Repercussions in adolescence. *Journal of the American Academy of Child Psychiatry, 17,* 387–388.

Berlin, R. (1982). The role of reality in child and adult analysis. *Psychoanalytic Association of New York Bulletin, 19,* 9–10.

Berlin, R. J. (1986, March). *The analysis of an adopted boy.* Paper presented at the annual meeting of the Association for Child Psychoanalysis, Seattle.

Berman, L. B. (1987). *Running away: A prediction study of adolescent psychiatric inpatients.* Unpublished master's thesis, Goddard College.

Berman, L. B., Fullerton, C. S., Goodrich, W., & Yates, B. T. (1986). *Running away: Chestnut Lodge Hospital 1975–1986.* Paper presented at the annual meeting of the American Academy of Child and Adolescent Psychiatry, Los Angeles.

Bernard, V. W. (1953). Application of psychoanalytic concepts to adoption agency practice. In M. Heimann (Ed.), *Psychoanalysis and social work.* New York: International Universities Press.

Bernard, V. W. (1974). Adoption. In S. Arieti (Ed.), *American handbook of psychiatry* (2nd ed., Vol. 1). New York: Basic Books.

Bernstein, R. (1963). Are we still stereotyping the unmarried mother? In R. Roberts (Ed.), *The unwed mother.* New York: Harper & Row.

Bernstein, S. B. (1983). Treatment preparatory to psychoanalysis. *Journal of the American Psychoanalytic Association, 31,* 363–390.

Berry, J. (1975). *Daily experience in residential life.* London: Routledge & Kegan Paul.

Bertocci, D., & Schechter, M. D. (1987). *Adopted adults' perception of their need to search: An informal survey.* Unpublished study.

Bibring, G. L. (1959). Some considerations of the psychological processes in pregnancy. *Psychoanalytic Study of the Child, 14,* 113–121.

Bibring, G. L., Dwyer, T. F., Huntington, D. S., & Valenstein, A. F. (1961). A study of the psychological processes in pregnancy and of the earliest mother–child relationship. *Psychoanalytic Study of the Child, 16,* 9–72.

Bieder, J. (1971). Reflections on those who adopt and adoption. *Annals Medico-Psychologiques, 1,* 552–557.

Bleiberg, E., Jackson, L., & Ross, J. L. (1986). Gender identity disorder and object loss. *Journal of the American Academy of Child Psychiatry, 25,* 58–67.

Block, J. (1961). Ego identity, role variability and adjustment. *Journal of Consulting Psychology, 25,* 392–397.

Bloom-Feshbach, J., & Bloom-Feshbach, S. (1987). Psychological separatenesss and experiences of loss. In J. Bloom-Feshbach & Bloom-Feshbach (Eds.), *The psychology of separation and loss: Perspectives on development, life transitions and clinical practice.* San Francisco: Jossey-Bass.

Blos, P. (1970). *The young adolescent, clinical studies.* New York: Free Press.

Blos, P. (1978). The case of Frank, the laborer. In E. Rexford (Ed.), *A development approach to problems in acting out.* New York: International Universities Press.

Blotcky, M. J., Looney, J. G., & Grace, K. D. (1982). Treatment of the adopted adolescent: Involvement of the biologic mother. *Journal of the American Academy of Child Psychiatry, 21,* 281–285.

Blum, H. P. (1969). A psychoanalytic view of *Who's afraid of Virginia Woolf? Journal of the American Psychoanalytic Association, 17,* 888–903.

Blum, H. P. (1983). Adoptive parents: Generative conflict and generational continuity. *Psychoanalytic Study of the Child, 38,* 141–163.

Blum, L. H. (1959). Sterility and the magic power of the maternal figure: A case of pregnancy after the decision to adopt. *Journal of Nervous and Mental Disease, 128,* 401–408.

Blum, L. H. (1976). When adoptive families ask for help. *Primary Care, 3,* 241–249.

Blum R. W., & Resnick, M. D. (1982). Adolescent sexual decision making: Contraception, pregnancy, abortion, motherhood. *Pediatrics Annals, 11,* 797–805.

Bohman, M. (1970). *Adopted children and their families: A follow-up study of adopted children, their background environment, and adjustment.* Stockholm: Proprius.

Bohman, M. (1971). A comparative study of adopted children, foster children and children in their biological environment born after undesired pregnancies. *Acta Paediatrica Scandinavica* (Suppl. 221), 1–38.

Bohman, M. (1972). A study of adopted children, their background environment and adjustment. *Acta Paediatrica Scandinavica, 61,* 90–97.

Bohman, M. (1978). Some genetic aspects of alcoholism and criminality. *Archives of General Psychiatry, 35,* 269–276.

Bohman, M. (1981). The interaction of heredity and childhood environment: Some adoption studies. *Journal of Child Psychology and Psychiatry, 22,* 195–200.

Bohman, M. (1983). Alcoholism and crime: Studies of adoptees. *Substances and Alcohol Actions/Misuse, 4,* 37–147.

Bohman, M., Cloninger, C. R., Sigvardsson, S., et al. (1982). Predisposition to petty criminality in Swedish adoptees: I. Genetic and environmental heterogeneity. *Archives of General Psychiatry, 39,* 1233–1241.

Bohman, M., Cloninger, C. R., von Knorring, A. L. et al. (1984). An adoption study of somatoform disorders: III. Cross-fostering analysis and genetic relationship to alcoholism and criminality. *Archives of General Psychiatry, 41,* 872–878.

Bohman, M., & Sigvardsson, S. (1978). An 18-year prospective, longitudinal study of adopted boys. In E. J. Anthony, C. Koupernik, & C. Chiland (Eds.), *The child in his family: Vol. 4. Vulnerable children.* New York: Wiley.

Bohman, M., & Sigvardsson, S. (1979). Long-term effects of early institutional care: A prospective longitudinal study. *Journal of Child Psychology and Psychiatry, 20,* 111–117.

Bohman, M., & Sigvardsson, S. (1980). A prospective, longitudinal study of children registered for adoption: A 15-year follow-up. *Acta Psychiatrica Scandinavica, 61,* 339–355.

Bohman, M., & Sigvardsson, S. (1982). Adoption and fostering as preventative measures. In E. J. Anthony & C. Chiland (Eds.), *The child in his family: Vol. 7. Children in turmoil: Tomorrow's parents.* New York: Wiley.

Bohman, M., & Sigvardsson, S. (1985). A prospective longitudinal study of adoption. In A. R. Nicol (Ed.), *Longitudinal studies in child psychology and psychiatry.* New York: Wiley.

Bohman, M., & Sigvardsson, S., & Cloninger, C. R. (1981). Maternal inheritance of alcohol abuse. *Archives of General Psychiatry, 38,* 965–969.

Bohman, M., & von Knorring, A. L. (1979) Psychiatric illness among adults adopted as infants. *Acta Paediatrica Scandinavica, 60,* 106–112.

Boneh, C. (1979). *Disruptions in adoptive placements: A research study.* Boston: Department of Public Welfare, Office of Research Evaluation.

Borgatta, E. F., & Fanshel, D. (1965). *Behavioral characteristics of children known to psychiatric outpatient clinics.* New York: Child Welfare League of America.

Borgman, R. (1981). Antecedents and consequences of parental rights termination for abused and neglected children. *Child Welfare, 60,* 391–404.

Borgman, R. (1982). The consequences of open and closed adoption for older children. *Child Welfare, 61,* 217–230.

Boswell, J. (1988). *The kindness of strangers.* New York: Pantheon Books.

Bourne, E. (1978a). The state of research on ego identity: A review and appraisal. Part I. *Journal of Youth & Adolescence, 7,* 223–251.

Bourne, E. (1978b). The state of research on ego identity: A review and appraisal. Part II. *Journal of Youth & Adolescence, 7,* 371–392.

Bowen, M. (1978). *Family therapy in clinical practice.* New York: Jason Aronson.

Bowlby, J. (1951). *Maternal care and mental health.* (Monograph Series 2) Geneva: World Health Organization.

Bowlby, J. (1961). Childhood mourning and its implications for psychiatry. *American Journal of Psychiatry, 118,* 481–498.

Bowlby J. (1963). Pathological mourning and childhood mourning. *Journal of the American Psychoanalytic Association, 11,* 500–541.

Bowlby, J. (1969). *Attachment and loss: Vol. 1. Attachment.* New York: Basic Books.

Bowlby, J. (1973). *Attachment and loss: Vol. 2. Separation.* New York: Basic Books.

Bowlby, J. (1980). *Attachment and loss: Vol. 3. Loss: Sadness and depression.* New York: Basic Books.

Bowlby, J., Ainsworth, M. D. S., Boston, M., & Rosenbluth, D. (1956). The effects of mother–child separation: A follow-up study. *British Journal of Medical Psychology, 49,* 211–247.

Boyne, J. Denby, L., Kettenring, J. R., & Wheeler, W. (1984). *The shadow of success: A statistical analysis of outcomes of adoptions of hard-to-place children.* Westfield, NJ: Spaulding for Children.

Boys and Girls Aid Society of Oregon (1975). Survey of adoption of black children. *Opportunity Newsletter.* Portland: Author.

Boys and Girls Aid Society of Oregon (1976). Survey of adoption of black children. *Opportunity Newsletter.* Portland: Author.

Brace, C. L. (1872). *The dangerous classes in New York and twenty years' work among them.* New York: Wynkoop & Hallenbeck.

Breuer, J., & Freud, S. (1955). Studies in hysteria. In J. Strachey (Ed. and Trans.), *The standard edition of the complete psychological works of Sigmund Freud* (Vol. 2). London: Hogarth Press. (Original work published 1895).

Brinich, P. M. (1980). Some potential effects of adoption on self and object representations. *Psychoanalytic Study of the Child, 35,* 107–133.

Brinich, P. M. (1986, January). *Adoption, ambivalence, and mourning.* Paper presented at the meeting of the Northern California Regional Organization of Child and Adolescent Psychiatry, Carmel, CA.

Brinich, P. M., & Brinich, E. B. (1982). Adoption and adaptation. *Journal of Nervous and Mental Disease, 170,* 489–493.

Brodzinsky, D. M. (1984). New perspectives on adoption revelation. *Adoption and Fostering, 8,* 27–32.

Brodzinsky, D. M. (1987). Adjustment to adoption: A psychosocial perspective. *Clinical Psychology Review, 7,* 25–47.

Brodzinsky, D. M., Braff, A. M., & Singer, L. M. (1980, January). *Adoption revelation: A cognitive–development perspective.* Paper presented at the conference on Piagetian Theory and the Helping Professions, University of Southern California, Los Angeles.

Brodzinsky, D. M., & Huffman, L. (1988). Transition to adoptive parenthood. *Marriage and Family Review, 12,* 267–286.

Brodzinsky, D. M., & Jackiewicz, D. (1987). *Family life-cycle differences in adoptive parents coping styles.* Unpublished manuscript.

Brodzinsky, D. M., Radice, C., Huffman, L., & Merkler, K. (1987). Prevalence of clinically significant symptomatology in a nonclinical sample of adopted and nonadopted children. *Journal of Clinical Child Psychology, 16,* 350–356.

Brodzinsky, D. M., & Reeves, L. (1987). *The relationship between parental coping strategies and children's adjustment to adoption.* Unpublished manuscript.

Brodzinsky, D. M., Schechter, D. E., Braff, A. M., & Singer, L. M. (1984). Psychological and academic adjustment in adopted children. *Journal of Consulting and Clinical Psychology, 52,* 582–590.

Brodzinsky, D. M., Schechter, D. E., & Brodzinsky, A. B. (1986). Children's knowledge of adoption: Developmental changes and implications for adjustment. In R. Ashmore & D. Brodzinsky (Eds.), *Thinking about the family: Views of parents and children.* Hillsdale, NJ: Erlbaum.

Brodzinsky, D. M., Singer, L. M., & Braff, A. M. (1984). Children's understanding of adoption. *Child Development, 55,* 869–878.

Brown, A., Bransford, J., Ferrara, R., & Campione, J. (1983). Learning, remembering and understanding. In P. Mussen (Ed.), *Handbook of child psychology: Vol. 3. Cognitive development.* New York: Wiley.

Brown, F. (1963). Supervision of the child in the adoptive home. In I. E. Smith (Ed.), *Readings in adoption.* New York: Philosophical Library.

Brown, F. (1973). An unusual therapeutic alliance with an adopted child. *Reiss-Davis Clinic Bulletin, 10,* 52–64.

Brown, G. W., & Harris, T. (1978). *Social origins of depression: A study of psychiatric disorder in women.* London: Tavistock.

Brown, M., & Madge, N. (1982). *Despite the welfare state.* London: Heinemann.

Brown v. County of San Joaquin, 601 F. Supp. 653 (1985).

Buchanan, E. (1984). The constitutional rights of unwed fathers before and after Lehr v. Robertson. *Ohio State Law Journal, 45,* 313–382.

Burgess, L. J. (1976). *The art of adoption.* Washington, DC: Acropolis Books.

Burnell, G., & Norfleet, M. (1979). Women who place their infant up for adoption: A pilot study. *Patient Counselling and Health Education, 16,* 169–176.

Buss, A. H., & Plomin, R. (1984). *Temperament: Early developing personality traits.* Hillsdale, NJ: Erlbaum.

Byng-Hall, J. (1988). Scripts and legends in families and family therapy. *Family Process, 27,* 167–169.

Caban v. Mohammed, 441 U.S. 380 (1979).

Cadoret, R. J. (1978) Evidence for genetic inheritance of primary affective disorder in adoptees. *American Journal of Psychiatry, 135,* 463–466.

Cadoret, R. J. (1978). Psychopathology in adopted-away offspring of biologic parents with antisocial behavior. *Archives of General Psychiatry, 35,* 176–184.

Cadoret, R. J. (1982). Editorial: Genotype–environmental interaction in antisocial behavior. *Psychological Medicine, 12,* 235–239.

Cadoret, R. J. (1985). Genes, environment and their interaction in the development of psychopathology. In J. Sakai & T. Tsubio (Eds.). *Genetic aspects of human behavior.* Tokyo and New York: Aino Hospital Foundation, Igaku-Shoin.

Cadoret, R. J. (1986). Adoption studies: Historical and methodological critique. *Psychiatric Developments, 4,* 45–64.

Cadoret, R. J., & Cain, C. A. (1981). Environmental and genetic factors in predicting adolescent antisocial behavior in adoptees. *Psychiatric Journal of the University of Ottawa, 6,* 220–225.

Cadoret, R. J., & Cain, C. A. (1982). Genetic–environmental interaction in adoption studies of antisocial behavior. *Proceedings of the Third World Congress on Biological Psychiatry.* Amsterdam: Elsevier/North Holland.

Cadoret, R. J., Cain, C. A., Crowe, R. R. (1983). Evidence for gene–environment interaction in the development of adolescent antisocial behavior. *Behavior Genetics, 13,* 301–310.

Cadoret, R. J., Cunningham, L., Loftus, R., et al. (1976). Studies of adoptees from psychiatrically disturbed biological parents: III. Medical symptoms and illnesses in childhood and adolescence. *American Journal of Psychiatry, 133,* 1316–1318.

Cadoret, R. J., & Gath, A. (1978). Inheritance of alcoholism in adoptees. *British Journal of Psychiatry, 132,* 252–258.

Cadoret, R. J., & Gath, A. (1980). Biological correlates of hyperactivity: Evidence for a genetic factor. In S. B. Sells, R. Crandall, M. Roff, et al. (Eds.), *Human functioning in longitudinal perspective.* Baltimore: William & Wilkins.

Cadoret, R. J., O'Gorman, T. W., Heywood, E., et al. (1985). Genetic and environmental factors in major depression. *Journal of Affective Disorders, 9,* 155–164.

Cadoret, R. J., O'Gorman, T. W., Troughton, E., et al. (1985). Alcoholism and antisocial personality: Interrelationships, genetic and environmental factors. *Archives of General Psychiatry, 41,* 161–167.

Cadoret, R. J., Troughton, E., O'Gorman, T. W., et al. (1986). An adoption study of genetic and environmental factors in drug abuse. *Archives of General Psychiatry, 43,* 1131–1136.

Cadoret, R. J., Troughton, E., & O'Gorman, T. W. (1987). Genetic and environmental factors in alcohol abuse and antisocial personality. *Journal of Studies on Alcohol, 48,* 1–8.

Campbell, L. H. (1979). The birthparent's right to know. *Public Welfare, 22,* 11–14.

Campbell, L., & Patti, P. (1964). The postadoption experience of surrendering mothers. *American Journal of Orthopsychiatry, 54,* 271–280.

Campbell, R. J. (1981). *Psychiatric dictionary* (5th ed.) New York: Oxford University Press.

Cantwell, D. (1975). Genetics of hyperactivity. *Journal of Child Psychology and Psychiatry and Allied Disciplines, 16,* 261–264.

Cantwell, D. (1978). Hyperactivity and antisocial behavior. *Child Psychiatry, 2,* 252–262.

Caplan, G. (1974). *Support systems and community mental health.* New York: Behavioral Publications.

Carey, W. B., Lipton, W. L., & Myers, R. A. (1974). Temperament in adopted and foster babies. *Child Welfare, 53,* 352–359.

Carroll, J. (1968). *The acceptance or rejection of differences between adoptive and biological parenthood by adoptive applicants as related to various indices of adjustment/maladjustment.* Unpublished doctoral dissertation, Temple University, Philadelphia.

Cattell, J. P. (1954). Psychodynamic and clinical observations in a group of unmarried mothers. *American Journal of of Psychiatry, 3,* 337–342.

Chambers, D. (1970). Willingness to adopt atypical children. *Child Welfare, 49,* 275–279.

Child Welfare League of America. (1960). *Standards for services to unmarried parents.* New York: Author.

Child Welfare League of America. (1968). *Standards for adoption practice.* New York: Author.

Child Welfare League of America. (1978). *Standards of adoption service* (rev.). New York: Author.

Child Welfare League of America. (1988). *Standards for adoption service* (rev.). New York: Author.

Child Welfare League of America. (1988). Standards for services for pregnant adolescents and young parents (rev. ed.). Washington, DC: Author.

Clarke, A. M., & Clark, A. D. B. (1976). *Early experience: Myth and evidence.* New York: Free Press.

Cleveland Board of Education v. LaFleur, 414 U.S. 632 (1973).

Cloninger, C. R., Bohman, M., & Sigvardsson, S. (1981). Inheritance of alcohol abuse: Cross-fostering analysis of adopted men. *Archives of General Psychiatry, 38,* 861–868.

Cloninger, C. R., Reich, T., & Guze, S. (1975). The multifactorial model of disease transmission: II. Sex differences in the familial transmission of sociopathy (antisocial personality). *British Journal of Psychiatry, 127,* 11–22.

Cloninger, C. R., Rue, J., Reigh, T. (1979). Multifactorial inheritance with cultural transmission and assortative mating: II. A general model of combined polygenic and cultural inheritance. *American Journal of Human Genetics, 31,* 176–198.

Cloninger, C. R., Sigvardsson, S., Bohman, M., et al. (1982). Predisposition to petty criminality in Swedish adoptees: II. Cross-fostering analysis of gene–environment interaction. *Archives of General Psychiatry, 39,* 1242–1247.

Cloninger, C. R., Sigvardsson, S., von Knorring, A. L., et al. (1984). An adoption study of somatoform disorders: II. Identification of two discrete somatoform disorders. *Archives of General Psychiatry, 41,* 863–871.

Clothier, F. (1939). Some aspects of the problem of adoption. *American Journal of Orthopsychiatry, 9,* 598–615.

Clothier, F. (1942). Placing the child for adoption. *Mental Hygiene, 26,* 257–274.

Clothier, F. (1943a). Psychological implications of unmarried parenthood. *American Journal of Orthopsychiatry, 13,* 531–549.

Clothier, F. (1943b). The psychology of the adopted child. *Mental Hugiene, 27,* 222–230.

Cobb, S. (1976). Social support as a moderator of life stress. *Psychosomatic Medicine, 38,* 300–314.

Cohen, J. S. (1981). *Adoption breakdown with older children.* Toronto: University of Toronto.

Cohen, S., & Wills, T. A. (1985). Stress, social support and the buffering hypothesis. *Psychological Bulletin, 98,* 310–357.

Colarusso, C. A. (1987). Mother, is that you? *Psychoanalytic Study of the Child, 42,* 223–237.

Cole, E. (1979). Director's Report. (Vol. 4) *Adoption Report.* (New York: Child Welfare League of America.

Cole, E. (1984, April). *Permanency Report.* New York: Child Welfare League of America.

Cole, E. (1985). Adoption: History, policy, and program. In J. Laird & A. Hartman (Eds.), *A handbook of child welfare.* New York: Free Press.

Cominos, H. (1971). Minimizing the risks of adoption through knowledge. *Social Work, 16,* 73–79.

Condon, J. T. (1986). Psychological disability in women who relinquish a baby for adoption. *Medical Journal of Australia, 144,* 117–119.

Conklin, E. S. (1920). The foster–child fantasy. *American Journal of Psychology, 31,* 59–76.

Coppolillo, H. P., Horton, P. C. & Haller, L (1981). Secrets and the secretive mode. *Journal of the American Academy of Child Psychiatry, 20,* 71–83.

Costello, C. G. (1982). Loss as a source of stress in psychopathology. In R. Neufeld (Ed.), *Psychological stress and psychopathology.* New York: McGraw-Hill.

Costin, L. B. (1963). Implications of psychological testing for adoption placements. In E. Smith (Ed.), *Readings in adoption.* New York: Child Welfare League of America.

Costin, L. (1972). *Child welfare: Policies and practices.* New York: McGraw-Hill.

Cotton, N. S. (1979). The familial incidence of alcoholism: A review. *Journal of Studies on Alcohol, 40,* 89–116.

Coyne, A., & Brown, M. E. (1985). Developmentally disabled children can be adopted. *Child Welfare, 64,* 607–615.

Coyne, A., & Brown, M. E. (1986). Relationship between foster care and adoption units serving developmentally disabled children. *Child Welfare, 65,* 189–198.

Crowe, R. R. (1974). An adoption study of antisocial personality. *Archives of General Psychiatry, 31,* 785–791.

Crowe, R. R., Noyes, R., Jr., Pauls, D. L., et al. (1983). A family study of panic disorder. *Archives of General Psychiatry, 40,* 1065–1069.

Crown, S., & Crisp, A. H. (1966). A short clinical diagnostic self-rating scale for psychoneurotic patients. The Middlesex Hospital Questionnaire (MHQ). *British Journal of Psychiatry, 112,* 917–923.

Cunningham, L., Cadoret, R. J., Loftus, R., et al. (1975). Studies of adoptees from psychiatrically disturbed biological parents: Psychiatric conditions in childhood and adolescence. *British Journal of Psychiatry, 126,* 534–549.

Curry, S., & Russ, A. (1985). Identifying coping strategies in children. *Journal of Clinical Psychology, 14,* 61–69.

Cutright, P., & Jaffe, F. S. (1977). *Impact of family planning programs on fertility: The U.S. experience.* New York: Praeger.

Dalby, J. T., Fox, S. L., & Haslam, R. H. (1982). Adoption and foster care rates in pediatric disorders. *Developmental and Behavioral Pediatrics, 3,* 61–64.

Daunton, E. (1973a). Helping an adopted child with persistent separation difficulties. A case of treatment via the mother. *Bulletin of the Philadelphia Association for Psychoanalysis, 23,* 8–32.

Daunton, E. (1973b). *The opening phase of treatment in an adopted child with a symptom of encopresis.* Paper presented at the meeting of the Association for Child Psychoanalysis, Ann Arbor, MI.

Davidson, D. (1985). An adolescent in search of her identity. *Journal of Analytical Psychology, 30,* 339–346.

Day, C., & Leeding, A. (1980). *Access to Birth Records: The Impact of Section 26 of the Children Act 1975* (Research Series No. 1). London: Association of British Adoption and Fostering Agencies.

Day, D. (1979). *The adoption of black children: Counteracting institutional discrimination,* Lexington, MA: Lexington Books.

DeLongis, A., Coyne, J. C., Dakof, G., Folkman, S., & Lazarus, R. S. (1982). Relationship of daily hassles, uplifts, and major life events to health status. *Health Psychology, 1,* 119–136.

DeMoss, R. (1984). Adoption: The rights of the putative father. *Oklahoma Law Review, 37,* 583–605.

Depp, C. H. (1982). After reunion: Perceptions of adult adoptees, adoptive parents, and birth parents. *Child Welfare, 61,* 115–119.

Derdeyn, A. P. (1977a). Child abuse and neglect: The rights of parents and the needs of their children. *American Journal of Orthopsychiatry, 47,* 377–387.

Derdeyn, A. P. (1977b). A case for permanent foster placement of dependent, neglected, and abused children. *American Journal of Orthopsychiatry, 47,* 604–614.

Derdeyn, A. P. (1979). Adoption and the ownership of children. *Child Psychiatry and Human Development, 9,* 215–226.

Derdeyn, A. P. (1986). Foster children: Continuity of relationships and the law. *International Journal of Family Psychiatry, 7,* 303–317.

Derdeyn, A. P., Rogoff, A. R., & Williams, S. W. (1978). Alternatives to absolute termination of parental rights after long-term foster care. *Vanderbilt Law Review, 31,* 1165–1192.

Derdeyn, A. P., & Scott, E. (1984). Joint custody: A critical analysis and appraisal. *American Journal of Orthopsychiatry, 54,* 199–209.

Derdeyn, A. P., & Wadlington, W. J. (1977). Adoption: The rights of parents versus the best interests of their children. *Journal of the American Academy of Child Psychiatry, 16,* 238–255.

deShazer, S. (1982). *Patterns of brief family therapy.* New York: Guilford.

deShazer, S. (1985). *Keys to solution in brief therapy.* New York: Norton.

deShazer, S., Berg, I., Lipchick, E., Nunnally, E., Molnar, A., Gingrich, W., & Weiner-Davis, M. (1986). Brief therapy: Focused solution development. *Family Process, 25,* 207–221.

deShazer, S., & Molnar, A. (1984). Four useful interventions in brief family therapy. *Journal of Marital & Family Therapy, 10,* 297–304.

Deutsch, D. K., Swanson, J. M., Bruell, J. H., Cantwell, D. P., Weinberg, F., & Baren, M. (1982). Overrepresentation of adoptees in children with the attention deficit disorder. *Behavior Genetics, 12,* 231–238.

Deutsch, H. (1945). *The pychology of women: A psychanalytic interpretation* (Vol. 2). New York: Grune & Stratton.

Deutsch, H. (1967). *Selected problems of adolescence with special emphasis on group formation.* New York: International Universities Press.

Deykin, E. Y., Campbell, L., & Patti, P. (1984). The postadoption experience of surrendering parents. *American Journal of Orthopsychiatry, 54,* 271–280.

Deykin, E. Y., Patti, P., & Ryan, J. (1988). Fathers of adopted children: A study of the impact of child surrender on birthfathers. *American Journal of Orthopsychiatry, 58,* 240–248.

Dignan, M. H. (1965). Ego identity and maternal identification. *Journal of Personality and Social Psychology, 1,* 476–483.

Dix, T. H. (1984). *Social cognitive processes during parent–child disciplinary episodes.* Paper presented at the meeting of the American Psychological Association, Toronto.

Dix, T. H., & Grusec, J. E. (1986). Parent attribution processes in the socialization of children. In I. Sigel (Ed.), *Parental belief systems: Psychological consequences for children.* Hillsdale, NJ: Erlbaum.

Donley, K. S. (1978). The dynamics of disruption. *Adoption and Fostering, 92,* 34–39.

Donley, K. S. (1978). Observations on disruption. In U.S. Department of Health and Human Services (Ed.), *Adoption disruptions.* Washington, DC: Editor.

Douvan, E., & Adelson, J. (1966). *The adolescent experience.* New York: Wiley.

Draeger, J. H. (1983). The problem of truth in psychotherapy: A phenomenological approach to treatment. *Social Science and Medicine, 17,* 371–378.

Dreyfus, E. A. (1967). The search for intimacy. *Adolescence, 2,* 25–40.

Drummond v. Fulton County, 563 F.2d 1200 (1977).

Dryfoos, J. G., & Lincoln, R. (1981). *Teenage pregnancy: The problem that hasn't gone away.* New York: Alan Guttmacher Institute.

Dukette, R. (1962, February). Discussion of thoughts regarding the etiology of psychological difficulties in adopted children. *Child Welfare,* 66–71.

Dunning, R. W. (1962). A note on adoption among the Southamptom Island Eskimo. *Man, 53,* 163–168.

Easson, W. (1973, July). Special sexual problems of the adopted adolescent. *Medical Aspects of Human Sexuality,* 92–105.

Egeland, B., & Farber, E. A. (1984). Infant–mother attachment: Factors related to its development and changes over time. *Child Development, 55,* 753–771.

Eiduson, B. T., & Livermore, J. B. (1953). Complications in therapy with adopted children. *American Journal of Orthopsychiatry, 23,* 795–802.

Elias, M., & Ubriaco, M. (1986). Linking parental beliefs to children's social competence: Toward a cognitive-behavioral assessment model. In R. Ashmore & D. Brodzinsky (Eds.), *Perspectives on the family: Views of parents and children.* Hillsdale, NJ: Erlbaum.

Elonen, A. S., & Schwartz, E. M. (1969). A longitudinal study of emotional, social and academic functioning of adopted children. *Child Welfare, 48,* 72–78.

Emmerich, W. (1969). The parental role: A functional–cognitive approach. *Monographs of the Society for Research in Child Development, 34,* 1–71.

Endicott, J., Spitzer, R. L., Fleiss, J. L., & Cohen J. (1976). The Global Assessment Scale: A procedure for measuring overall severity of psychiatric disturbance. *Archives of General Psychiatry, 33,* 766–771.

Erikson, E. H. (1950). *Childhood and society.* New York: Norton.

Erikson, E. H. (1959). *Identity and the life cycle: Selected papers by Erik H. Erikson: Vol. 1. Psychological Issues.* New York: International Universities Press.

Erikson, E. H. (1968). *Identity: Youth and crisis.* New York: Norton.

Erlich, H. (1977). *A time to search.* New York and London: Paddington Press.

Everett, R., & Schechter, M. (1971). A comparative study of prenatal anxiety in the unwed mother. *Child Psychiatry and Human Development, 2,* 84–91.

Eysenck, H. J. (1982). *Personality, genetics and behavior.* New York: Praeger.

Fahlberg, V. (1979). *Attachment and separation.* Lansing: Michigan Department of Social Services.

Fairbairn, W. R. D. (1952). *Psychoanalytic studies of the personality.* London: Tavistock.

Fairweather, M. E. (1952). Early placement in adoption. *Child Welfare, 31,* 3–8.

Fanshel, D. (1972). *Far from the reservation: The transracial adoption of American Indian children.* Metuchen, NJ: Scarecrow Press.

Fanshel, D. (1975). Parental visiting of children in foster care: Key to discharge? *Social Services Review, 49,* 493–514.

Fanshel, D. (1976). Status changes of children in foster care: Final results of the Columbia University longitudinal study. *Child Welfare, 55,* 143–171.

Fanshel, D., & Shinn, E. B. (1978). *Children in foster care.* New York: Columbia University Press.

Farber, S. (1977). Sex differences in the expression of adoption ideas: Observations of adoptees from birth to latency. *American Journal of Orthopsychiatry, 47,* 639–650.

Feder, L. (1974). Adoption trauma: Oedipus myth/clinical reality. *International Journal of Psychoanalysis, 55,* 491–493.

Figelman, W., & Silverman, A. R. (1983). *Chosen children.* New York: Praeger.

Fein, E., Davies, L. J., & Knight, G. (1979). Placement stability in foster care. *Social Work, 24,* 156–157.

Feinsilver, D. B. (1986). Chestnut Lodge Case Conference Discussion. Chestnut Lodge, Rockville, MD.

Fellner, I. (1968). Recruiting adoptive applicants. *Social Work, 13*, 37–45.

Fenichel, O. (1945). *The psychoanalytic theory of neurosis.* New York: Norton.

Festinger, L. (1957). *A theory of cognitive dissonance.* Stanford, CA: Stanford University Press.

Festinger, T. (1974). Placement agreements with boarding homes. *Child Welfare, 53*, 643–652.

Festinger, T. (1975). The New York review of children in foster care. *Child Welfare, 54*, 211–245.

Festinger, T. (1983). *No one ever asked us: A postscript to foster care.* New York: Columbia University Press.

Festinger, T. (1986). *Necessary risk: A study of adoptions and disrupted adoptive placements.* Washington, DC: Child Welfare League of America.

Fischer, N. (1974). Multiple induced abortions: A psychoanalytic case study. *Journal of the American Psychoanalytic Association, 22*, 394.

Fisher, F. (1973). *The search for Anna Fisher.* New York: Arthur Fields.

Fisher, F. (1988). President, Adoptees Liberty Movement Association. Personal communication.

Fitzgerald, J. (1979). After disruption. *Adoption and Fostering, 98*, 11–16.

Fitzgerald, J. (1983). *Understanding disruption.* London: British Agencies for Adoption and Fostering.

Foster, H. H. (1973). Adoption and child custody: Best interests of the child. *Buffalo Law Review, 22*, 1–16.

Frazier, E. F. (1939). *The Negro family in the United States.* Chicago: University of Chicago Press.

Freedman, B. A. (1987). *Ego identity status and family and career priorities in college women.* Unpublished doctoral dissertation, Bryn Mawr College, Bryn Mawr, PA.

Freedman, J. (1977). Notes for practice: An adoptee in search of identity. *Social Work, 22*, 227–229.

Freud, A., & Burlingham, D. T. (1944). *Infants without families: The case for and against residential nurseries.* New York: International Universities Press.

Freud, S. (1953). The interpretation of dreams. In J. Strachey (Ed. and Trans.), *The standard edition of the complete psychological works of Sigmund Freud* (Vols. 4 and 5) London: Hogarth Press. (Original work published. 1900)

Freud, S. (1955). Beyond the pleasure principle. In Strachey (Ed. and Trans.), *The standard edition of the complete psychological works of Sigmund Freud* (Vol. 18). London: Hogarth Press. (Original work published 1920)

Freud, S. (1957). Mourning and melancholia. In J. Strachey (Ed. and Trans.), *The standard edition of the complete psychological works of Sigmund Freud* (Vol. 14) London: Hogarth Press. (Original work published 1917).

Freud, S. (1957). On narcissism. In J. Strachey (Ed. and Trans.), *The standard edition of the complete psychological works of Sigmund Freud* (Vol. 14). London: Hogarth Press. (Original work published 1914)

Freud, S. (1959). Family romances. In J. Strachey (Ed. and Trans.), *The standard edition of the complete psychological works of Sigmund Freud* (Vol. 9) London: Hogarth Press. (Original work published 1909)

Freud, S. (1959). The question of lay analysis. In J. Strachey (Ed. and Trans.), *The standard edition of the complete psychological works of Sigmund Freud* (Vol. 20). London: Hogarth Press. (Original work published 1926).

Freud, S. (1964). An outline of psychoanalysis. In J. Strachey (Ed. and Trans.), *The standard* edition of the complete psychological works of Sigmund Freud (Vol. 23) London: Hogarth Press. (Original work published 1940)

Freud, S. (1986). Paradoxes of parenthood: On the impossibility of raising children perfectly. In P. J. Davis & D. Park (Eds.), No way: The nature of the impossible. New York: Freeman.

Fricke, H. (1965). Interracial adoption: The little revolution. Social Work, 10, 92–97.

Friedman, R., Goodrich, W., Fullerton, C. S. (1985–1986). Locus of control and severity of illness in the residential treatment of adolescents. Residential Group Care and Treatment, 3, 3–13.

Frieze, I. H., Parsons, J. E., Johnson, P. B., Ruble, D. N., & Zellman, G. L. (1978). Women and sex roles: A social psychological perspective. New York: Norton.

Frisk, M. (1964). Identity problems and confused conceptions of the genetic ego in adopted children during adolescence. Acta Paedo Psychiatrica, 31, 6–12.

Fuller, R. (1977). The adopted child and the family romance. In R. C. Simons & H. Pardes (Eds.), Understanding human behavior in health and illness. Baltimore: Williams & Wilkins.

Fullerton, C. S., Goodrich, W., & Berman, L. B. (1986). Adoption predicts psychiatric treatment resistances in hospitalized adolescents. Journal of the American Academy of Child Psychiatry. 25, 542–551.

Furman, E. (1985). On fusion, integration and feeling good. Psychoanalytic Study of the Child, 40, 81–110.

Gallagher, U. M. (1972). Adoption in a changing scene. Children Today, 1, 2–6.

Garber, R. (1988). Faculty of Social Work, University of Toronto. Personal communication.

Garmezy, N. (1974). The study of competence in children at risk for severe psychopathology. In E. J. Anthony and C. Koupernik (Eds.), The child in his family: Vol. 3: Children at psychiatric risk. New York: Wiley.

Garmezy, N., & Rutter, M. (1983). Stress, coping, and development in children. New York: McGraw-Hill.

Gedo, J. E. (1965). Unmarried motherhood: A paradigmatic single case study. International Journal of Psychoanalysis, 45, 352–357.

Gelman, R., & Baillargeon, R. (1983). A review of some Piagetian concepts. In P. Mussen (Ed.), Handbook of child psychology: Vol. 3: Cognitive development. New York: Wiley.

Gergen, K., & Gergen, M. (1983). Narratives of the self. In T. R. Sarbin and K. E. Scheibe (Eds.), Studies in social identity. New York: Praeger.

Gill, M. M., & Amadio, C. M. (1983). Social work and law in a foster care/adoption program. Child Welfare, 62, 455–467.

Gill, O., & Jackson, B. (1983). Adoption and race: Black, Asian and mixed race children in White families, New York: St. Martin's Press.

Ginsberg v. New York, 390 U.S. 629 (1969).

Glatzer, H. T. (1955). Adoption and delinquency. Nervous Child, 11, 52–56.

G. L. v. Zumwalt, 564 F. Supp. 1030 (1983).

Glenn, J. (1974). The adoption theme in Edward Albee's Tiny Alice and The American Dream. Psychoanalytic Study of the Child, 29, 413–429.

Glenn, J. (1985–1986). The adopted child's self and object representations. International Journal of Psychoanalytic Psychotherapy, 11, 309–313.

Gochros, H. (1967). Not parents yet: A study of the post-placement period in adoption. Child Welfare, 46, 317–349.

Goebel, B., & Lott, S. L. (1986, August). Adoptees' resolution of the adolescent identity crisis: Where are the taproots? Paper presented at the meeting of the American Psychological Association, Washington, DC.

Goffman, E. (1963). *Stigma: Notes on the management of spoiled identity.* London: Prentice-Hall.

Goldberg, D. P. (1972). *The detection of psychiatric illness by questionnaire.* (Maudsley Monograph No. 21). London: Oxford University Press.

Goldberg, D. P., Cooper, B., Eastwood, M. R., Kedward, H. B. & Shepherd, M. (1970). A standardized psychiatric interview for use in community surveys. *British Journal of Preventive and Social Medicine, 24,* 18–23.

Goldfarb, W. (1945). Psychological privation in infancy and psychological adjustment. *American Journal of Orthopsychiatry, 15,* 247–255.

Goldstein, J., Freud, A., & Solnit, A. (1973). *Beyond the best interests of the child.* London: Free Press.

Goldstein, J., Freud, A., & Solnit, A. (1979). *Before the best interests of the child.* New York: Free Press.

Goodacre, I. (1966). *Adoption policy and practice.* London: Allen and Unwin.

Goodman, J. D., & Magno-Nora, R. (1975). Adoption and its influence during adolescence. *Journal of Medical Sociology, 72,* 922–928.

Goodman, J., Silberstein, M. R., & Mandel, W. (1963). Adopted children brought to psychiatric clinics. *Archives of General Psychiatry, 9,* 451–456.

Goodrich, W. (1984). Symbiosis and individuation: The integrative process for residential treatment of adolescents. *Current Issues in Psychoanalytic Practice, 1,* 23–45.

Goodrich, W. (1987). Long-term psychoanalytic hospital treatment of adolescents. *Psychiatric Clinics of North America, 10,* 273–287.

Goodrich, W., & Boomer, D. S. (1958). Some concepts about therapeutic interventions with hyperaggressive children. *Social Casework, 39,* 207–213.

Goodrich, W., & Fullerton, C. (1984). Which adolescent borderline in residential treatment will run away? *Residential Group Care and Treatment, 2,* 3–14.

Goodwin, D. W., Schulsinger, F., & Hermansen, L. (1973). Alcohol problems in adoptees raised apart from alcoholic biological parents. *Archives of General Psychiatry, 28,* 238–243.

Goodwin, D. W., Schulsinger, F., & Moller, N. (1974). Drinking problems in adopted and nonadopted sons of alcoholics. *Archives of General Psychiatry, 31,* 164–171.

Gossett, J. T., Lewis, J. M., & Barnhart, F. D. (1983). *To find a way: The outcome of hospital treatment of disturbed adolescents.* New York: Brunner/Mazel.

Grotevant, H. D., McRoy, R. G., & Jenkins, V. Y. (1988). *Emotionally disturbed adopted adolescents: Early patterns of family adaptation.* Manuscript submitted for publication.

Grow, L. J., & Shapiro, D. (1974). *Black children–white parents.* New York: Child Welfare League of America.

Gruber, A. (1973). *Foster home care in Massachusetts.* Commonwealth of Massachusetts Governor's Commission on Adoption and Foster Care.

Gruen, W. (1960). Rejection of false information about oneself as an indication of ego identity. *Journal of Consulting Psychology, 24,* 231–233.

Guesella, J. F., Wexler, N. S., Conneally, P. M., et al. (1983). A polymorphic DNA marker genetically linked to Huntington's disease. *Nature, 306,* 234–238.

Haimes, E. (1987), "Now I know who I really am." Identity change and redefinitions of the self in adoption. In T. Honess & K. Yardley (Eds.), *Self and identity.* London: Routledge & Kegan Paul.

Haimes, E., & Timms, N. (1985). *Adoption, identity, and social policy: The search for distant relatives.* Aldershot, Eng.: Gower.

Haley, J. (1980). *Leaving home.* New York: McGraw-Hill.

Harmon, R. J., Wagonfeld, S., & Emde, R. N. (1982). Anaclitic depression: A follow-up from infancy to puberty. *Psychoanalytic Study of the Child, 37,* 67–94.

Harrington, J. D. (1980). The courts contend with sealed adoption records. *Public Welfare, 38*, 29–43.

Harrington, J. (1986, Spring). Adoption and the state legislatures 1984–1985. *Public Welfare,* 18–25.

Harrington, J. (1988). Personal communication.

Hartley, E. K. (1984). Government leadership to protect children from foster care "drift." *Child Abuse and Neglect, 8*, 337–342.

Hartman, A. (1979). *Finding families.* Beverly Hills: CA: Sage.

Hartman, A. (1984). *Working with adoptive families beyond placement.* New York: Child Welfare League of America.

Hartman, A. (n.d.). *Making connections.* [Videotaped interview with an adult adoptee]. Ypsilanti: Eastern Michigan University.

Hartman, A., & Laird, J. (1983). *Family-centered social work practice.* New York: Free Press.

Hastings, J. (1908). *Encyclopedia of religion and ethics.* New York: Scribner.

Hazen, N., & Durrett, M. E. (1982). Relationship of security of attachment to exploration and cognitive mapping abilities in 2-year-olds. *Developmental Psychology, 18,* 751–759.

Hechtman, L., Weiss, G., Perlman, T., et al. (1984) Hyperactives as young adults: Initial predicators of adult outcome. *Journal of the Academy of Child Psychiatry, 23,* 250–260.

Heider, F. (1958). *The psychology of interpersonal relations.* New York: Wiley.

Heilbrun, A. B. (1964). Conformity to masculinity–femininity stereotypes and ego identity in adolescents. *Psychological Reports, 14,* 351–357.

Heiman, M., & Levitt, E. G. (1960). The role of separation and depression in out-of-wedlock pregnancy. *American Journal of Orthopsychiatry, 30,* 166–174.

Herman, J. L. (1981). *Father–daughter incest.* Cambridge, MA, and London: Harvard University Press.

Hershenson, D. B. (1967). Sense of identity, occupational fit and enculturation. *Journal of Counseling Psychology, 14,* 319–324.

Hershkowitz, S. B. (1985). Due process and the termination of parental rights. *Family Law Quarterly, 19,* 245–296.

Herzog, E., Sudia C., Harwood, J. (1971). Some opinions on finding homes for Black children. *Children, 18,* 143–148.

Heston, L. L. (1966). Psychiatric disorders in foster home reared children of schizophrenic mothers. *British Journal of Psychiatry, 112,* 819–825.

Heston, L. L., Denny, D. D., & Pauly, I. B. (1966). The adult adjustment of persons institutionalized as children. *British Journal of Psychiatry, 112,* 1103–1110.

Hill, R. (1971). Modern systems theory and the family: A confrontation. *Social Science Information, 10,* 7–26.

Hirschberg, J. C. (1972). The role of education in the treatment of emotionally disturbed children through planned ego development. In G. H. Weber & B. J. Haberlein (Eds.), *Residential treatment of emotionally disturbed children.* New York: Behavioral Publications.

Hodges, J. (1983). Oedipus was adopted. *Bulletin of the Hampstead Clinic, 6,* 171–174.

Hodges, J. (1984). Two crucial questions: Adopted children in psychoanalytic treatment. *Journal of Child Psychotherapy, 10,* 47–56.

Hodges, J., Bolletti, R., Salo, F., & Oldeschulte, R. (1985). "Remembering is so much harder": A report on work in progress from the research group on adopted children. *Bulletin of the Anna Freud Centre, 8,* 169–179.

Hoffman, L. (1982). *Foundations of family therapy.* New York: Basic Books.

Holland, J. L. (1973). *Making vocational choices. A theory of careers.* Englewood Cliffs, NJ: Prentice-Hall.

Holland, J. L. (1985). *Making vocational choices: A theory of vocational personalities and work environments* (2nd ed.). Englewood Cliffs, NJ: Prentice Hall.

Holmes, T. H., & Rahe, R. H. (1967). The social readjustment rating scale. *Journal of Psychosomatic Research, 11,* 213–218.

Hoopes, J. L. (1982). *Prediction in child development: A longitudinal study of adoptive and nonadoptive families.* New York: Child Welfare League of America.

Hoopes, J. L., Sherman, E. A., Lawder, E. A., Andrews, R. G., & Lower, K. D. (1970). *A follow-up study of adoptions: II. Post-placement functioning of adopted children.* New York: Child Welfare League of America.

Horn, J. M. (1983). The Texas adoption project: Adopted children and their intellectual resemblance to biological and adoptive parents. *Child Development, 54,* 268–275.

Horn, J. M., Green, M., Carney, R., & Erickson, M. (1975). Bias against genetic hypotheses in adoption studies. *Archives of General Psychiatry, 32,* 1365–1367.

Horn, J. M., Loehlin, J. C., & Willerman, L. (1982). Aspects of the inheritance of intellectual abilities. *Behavioral Genetics, 12,* 479–516.

Horn, J. M., & Turner, R. G. (1976). Minnesota multiphasic personality inventory profiles among subgroups of unwed mothers. *Journal of Consulting & Clinical Psychology, 44,* 25–33.

Howard, A., Royse, D., & Skerl, J. (1977). Transracial adoption: The Black community perspective. *Social Work, 22,* 184–189.

Huessy, H. R. (1987). Personal communication.

Huey v. Lente, 514 P.2d 1081 (1973).

Humphrey, J., & Ounsted, C. (1963). Adoptive families referred for psychiatric advice: Part I. *British Journal of Psychiatry, 109,* 599–608.

Hunt, J. McV. (1961). *Intelligence and experience.* New York: Ronald Press.

Hutchings, B., & Mednick, S. A. (1974). Registered criminality in the adoptive and biological parents of regesterd male adoptees. In S. A. Mednick, F. Schulsinger, J. Higgins, et al. (Eds.,) *Genetics, environment and psychopathology.* Amsterdam: Elsevier/North Holland.

Ijams, M. N. (1976). Personality adjustment of adopted children in early adulthood. *Dissertation Abstracts International, 37,* 1488B. (University Microfilms No. 76–21, 108).

In re Adoption of Crystal D. R., 480 A. 2nd. 1146 (1984).

In re Baby Boy D, 12 FLR 1088 (1985).

In re D. N., 9 FLR 2681 (1983).

In re Evans, 12 FLR 1466 (1986).

In re Jewish Child Care Association, 156 N.E. 2nd 700 (1959).

In re William, Susan and Joseph, 448 A. 2d 1250 (1982).

In the Matter of the Adoption of Blumenthal, 346 F.2d 783 (1965).

Jackson, L. (1968). Unsuccessful adoptions. *British Journal of Medical Psychology, 41,* 389–398.

Jaffee, B., & Fanshel, D. (1970). *How they fared in adoption.* New York: Child Welfare League of America.

Jameson, G. K. (1967). Psychiatric disturbances in adopted children in Texas. *Texas Medicine, 63,* 83–88.

Jenkins, S., & Norman, E. (1974). *Beyond placement: Mothers view foster care.* New York: Columbia University Press.

Jewett, C. L. (1978). *Adopting the older child,* Harvard, MA: Harvard Common Press.

Jewett, C. L. (1982). *Helping children cope with separation and loss.* Harvard MA: Harvard Common Press.

Jones, E. E., & Davis, K. E. (1965). From acts to dispositions: The attribution process in person perception. In L. Berkowitz (Ed.), *Advances in experimental social psychology* (Vol. 2). New York: Academic Press.

Jones, M. A. (1976). *The sealed adoption record controversy: Report of a survey of agency policy, practice, and opinions.* New York: Child Welfare League of America.

Josselson, R. E. (1980). Ego development in adolescence. In J. Adelson (Ed.), *Handbook of adolescent psychology.* New York: Wiley.

Josselyn, I. M. (1956). A psychiatrist looks at adoption. In M. Schapiro (Ed.), *A study of adoption practice* (Vol. 2). New York: Child Welfare League of America.

Jungmann, J. (1980a). Adoption unter vorbehalt? Zur psychischen problematik von adoptivkindern [Adoption with reservations? A contribution to the psychic problem of adoptive children]. *Praxis der Kinderpsychologie und Kinderpsychiatrie, 29,* 225–230.

Jungmann, J. (1980b). Forschungsergebnisse zur entwicklung von adoptivkindern [Research results on the development of adopted children]. *Zeitschrift für Kinder- und Jugendpsychiatrie, 8,* 184–219.

Kadushin, A. (1962). A study of adoptive parents of hard-to-place children. *Social Casework, 53,* 227–233.

Kadushin, A. (1967). A follow-up study of children adopted when older. *American Journal of Orthopsychiatry, 37,* 530–539.

Kadushin, A. (1970). *Adopting older children.* New York: Columbia University Press.

Kadushin, A. (1974). *Child welfare services.* New York: Macmillan.

Kadushin, A. (1980). *Child welfare services* (3rd ed.). New York: Macmillan.

Kadushin, A., & Seidl, F. W. (1971). Adoption failure: A social work postmortem. *Social Work, 16,* 32–38.

Kagan, R. M., & Reid, W. J. (1986). Critical factors in the adoption of emotionally disturbed youths. *Child Welfare, 65,* 63–73.

Kantor, D., & Lehr, W. (1975). *Inside the family: Toward a theory of family process.* New York: Harper & Row.

Kaplan, A. (1982). Growing up in foster care: One boy's struggles. *Journal of Child Psychotherapy, 8,* 57–66.

Katan, A. (1937). The role of "displacement" in agoraphobia. *International Journal of Psychoanalysis, 32,* 41–50.

Katz, S. (1971). Legal aspect of foster care. *Family Law Quarterly, 5,* 283–302.

Kaye, K. (1982). *The mental and social life of babies: How parents create persons.* Chicago: University of Chicago Press.

Kaye, K. (1985). Toward a developmental psychology of the family. In L. L'Abate (Ed.), *Handbook of family psychology and psychotherapy.* Homewood, IL: Dorsey.

Kaye, K., & Warren, S. (1988). Discourse about adoption in adoptive families. *Journal of Family Psychology, 1,* 406–433.

Kelley, H. H. (1971). *Attribution in social interaction.* Morristown, NJ: General Learning Press.

Kelley, H. H. (1972). *Causal schemata and the attribution process.* Morristown, NJ: General Learning Press.

Keltie, P. (1969). *The adjustment of Korean children adopted by couples in the Chicago area.* Unpublished MSW thesis, Jane Addams School of Social Work, University of Chicago.

Kempe, C. et al. (1962). The battered child syndrome. *Journal of the American Medical Association, 181,* 17–24.

Kendler, K. S., Gruenberg, A. M. (1984). An independent analysis of the Danish adoption study of schizophrenia: VI. The relationship between psychiatric disorders as defined by DSM-III in the relatives and adoptees. *Archives of General Psychiatry, 41*, 555–564.

Kendler, K. S., Gruenberg, A. M., & Strauss, J. S. (1981). An independent analysis of the Copenhagen sample of the Danish adoption study of schizophrenia: II. The relationship between schizotypal personality disorder and schizophrenia. *Archives of General Psychiatry, 38*, 982–984.

Kenny, T., Baldwin, R., & Mackie, J. B. (1967). Incidence of minimal brain injury in adopted children. *Child Welfare, 46*, 24–29.

Kent, K., & Richie, J. (1976). Adoption as an issue in casework with adoptive parents. *Journal of the American Academy of Child Psychiatry, 15*, 510–522.

Kernberg, O. (1984). *Severe personality disorders: Psychotherapeutic strategies*. New Haven, CT: Yale University Press.

Kernberg, P. F. (1985–1986). Child analysis with a severely disturbed adopted child. *International Journal of Psychoanalytic Psychotherapy, 11*, 277–299.

Kety, S. S., Rosenthal, D., Wender, P., et al. (1971). Mental illness in the biological and adoptive families of adopted schizophrenics. *American Journal of Psychiatry, 128*, 82–86.

Kety, S. S., Rosenthal, D., Wender, P., et al. (1978). The biological and adoptive families of adopted individuals who became schizophrenic: Prevalence of mental illness and other characteristics. In L. C. Wynne, R. L. Cromveel, & S. Mathysse (Eds.), *The nature of schizophrenia*. New York: Wiley.

Khlentzos, M. T., & Pagliaro, M. A. (1965). Observations from psychotherapy with unwed mothers. *Journal of Orthopsychiatry, 35*, 779–786.

Kim, T., & Reid, E. (1970). *After a long journey*. Unpublished MSW thesis, School of Social Work, University of Minnesota, Minneapolis.

Kinney, D. K., & Jacobson, B. (1978). Environmental factors in schizophrenic: New adoption study evidence. In W. C. Wynne, R. L. Cromwell, & S. Mathysse (Eds.), *The nature of schizophrenia*. New York: Wiley.

Kirk, H. D. (1953). *Community sentiments in relation to child adoption*. Unpublished doctoral dissertation, Cornell University, Ithaca, NY.

Kirk, H. D. (1964). *Shared fate*. New York: Free Press.

Kirk, H. D. (1981). *Adoptive kinship—A modern institution is in need of reform*. Toronto: Butterworth.

Kirk, H. D. Jonassohn, K., & Fisch, A. (1966). Are adopted children especially vulnerable to stress? *Archive of General Psychiatry, 14*, 291–298.

Kirk, H. D., & McDaniel, S. (1984). Adoption policy in Great Britain and North America. *Journal of Social Policy, 13*, 75–84.

Klaus, M. H., & Kennell, J. H. (1976). *Maternal–infant bonding*. St. Louis, MO: Mosby.

Klein, M. (1932). *The psychoanalysis of children*. London: Hogarth Press.

Klein, M. (1961). *Narratives of a child analysis: The conduct of psycho-analysis of children as seen in the treatment of a ten-year-old boy*. London: Hogarth Press.

Kogan, N. (1983). Stylistic variation in childhood and adolescence: Creativity, metaphor, and cognitive style. In P. Mussen (Ed.), *Handbook of child psychology: Vol. 3. Cognitive development*. New York: Wiley.

Kohut, H. (1971). *The analysis of the self*. New York: International Universities Press.

Kopp, C. B. (1983). Risk factors in development. In P. Mussen (Ed.), *Handbook of child psychology: Vol. 2. Infancy and developmental psychology*. New York: Wiley.

Kornitzer, M. (1971). The adopted adolescent and the sense of identity. *Child Adoption, 66*, 43–48.

Kowal, K. A., & Schilling, K. M. (1985). Adoption through the eyes of adult adoptees. *American Journal of Orthopsychiatry, 55*, 354–362.

Kral, R., & Schaffer, J. (1988). Treating the adoptive family. In C. Chilman, F. Cox, & E. Nunnally (Eds.), *Families in trouble: related to alternative lifestyles*. Milwaukee: Sage Press.

Kral, R., Schaffer, J., & deShazer, S. (1989). Adoptive families: More of the same and different. *Journal of Strategic & Systemic Family Therapy, 8*, 36–49.

Kramer, S. (1986). Identification and its vicissitudes as observed in children: A developmental approach. *International Journal of Psychoanalysis, 67*, 161–172.

Kronick, J. C. (1966). An assessment of research knowledge concerning the unmarried mother. In R. Roberts (Ed.), *The unwed mother*. New York: Harper & Row.

Krugman, D. C. (1968). A new home for Liz: Behavioral changes in a deviant child. *Journal of American Academy of Child Psychiatry, 7*, 398–420.

Kurtis v. Ballou, 308 NYS 2d 770 (1970).

Kyees v. County Department of Public Welfare, 600 F.2d 693 (1979).

Lachman, F. M., Beebe, B., & Stolorow, R. D. (1987). Increments of separation in the consolidation of the self. In J. Bloom-Feshbach & S. Bloom-Feshbach (Eds.), *The psychology of separation and loss: Perspectives on development, life transitions and clinical practice*. San Francisco: Jossey-Bass.

Lahti, J. (1982). A follow-up study of foster children in permanent placements. *Social Service Review, 56*, 556–571.

Laird, J. (1989). Women and stories: Restorying women's self-constructions. In M. Mc-Goldrick, F. Walsh, & C. Anderson (Eds.), *Women and families*. New York: Norton.

Lamb, M. E., & Gilbride, K. E. (1985). Compatibility in parent–infant relationships: Origins and processes. In W. Ickes (Ed.), *Compatible and incompatible relationships*. New York: Springer-Verlag.

Lassiter v. Department of Social Services, 452 U.S. 18, 27 (1981).

Laufer, M., & Laufer, M. E. (1984). *Adolescence and developmental breakdown*. New Haven, CT: Yale University Press.

Lawder, E. A., Lower, K., Andrews, R., Sherman, E., & Hill, J. (1969). *A follow-up study of adoptions: Post-placement functioning of adoption families* (Vol 1). New York: Child Welfare League of America.

Lawson v. Registrar General, 106 L.J. 204, (1956).

Lawton, J., & Gross, S. (1964). Review of the psychiatric literature on adopted children. *Archives of General Psychiatry, 11*, 663–644.

Lazarus, R. S., DeLongis, A., Folkman, S., & Gruen, R. (1985). Stress and adaptational outcomes: The problem of confounded measures. *American Psychologist, 40*, 770–779.

Lazarus, R. S., & Folkman, S. (1984). *Stress, appraisal, and coping*. New York: Springer.

Learner, E. (1986). Social issues common to adoption and the new reproductive technologies. *Australian Journal of Early Childhood, 11*, 37–42.

Lee, R. (1963). *North Carolina family law* (Vol. 3). Charlottesville, VA.: Michie.

Lee, R. E., & Hull, R. K. (1983). Legal, casework, and ethical issues in "risk adoption." *Child Welfare, 62*, 450–454.

Lehr v. Robertson, 103 S.Ct. 2985 (1983).

Leitch, D. (1984). *Family secrets: A writer's search for his parents and his past*. New York: Delacorte Press.

Lerner, H. D., & Lerner, P. M. (1987). Separation, depression and object loss: Implications for narcissism and object relations. In J. Bloom-Feshbach & S. Bloom-Feshbach (Eds.), *The psychology of separation and loss. Perspectives of development, life transitions, and clinical practice*. San Francisco: Jossey-Bass.

Lerner, R. (1985). *On the origins of human plasticity*. Cambridge: Cambridge University Press.

Levin, M. A. (1979). The adoption trilemma: The adult adoptee's emerging search for his ancestral identity. *University of Baltimore Law Review, 8*, 496–518.

Levy, D. (1955). A follow-up study of unmarried mothers. *Social Casework, 36*, 27–33.

Lewin, K. (1940). Bringing up the Jewish child. *Menorah Journal, 28*, 29–45.

Lewis, D. O., Balla, D., Lewis, M., & Gore, R. (1975). The treatment of adopted versus neglected delinquent children in the court: A problem of reciprocal attachment? *American Journal of Psychiatry, 132*, 142–145.

Lewis, H. D. (1971). The psychiatric aspects of adoption. In J. H. Howells (Ed.), *Modern perspectives of child psychiatry*. New York: Brunner/Mazel.

Lewontin, R. C., Rose, S., & Kamin, L. (1986). *Not in our genes*. New York: Pantheon.

Lifshitz, M., Baum, R., Balgur, I., & Cohen, C. (1975). The impact of the social milieu upon the nature of adoptees' emotional difficulties. *Journal of Marriage and the Family, 37*, 221–228.

Lifton, B. J. (1975). *Twice born: Memoirs of an adopted daughter*. New York: McGraw-Hill.

Lifton, B. J. (1979). *Lost and found: The adoption experience*. New York: Dial Press.

Lifton, R. J. (1973). *Home from the war: Vietnam veterans, neither victims nor executioners*. New York: Basic Books.

Lifton, R. J. (1979). *The broken connection*. New York: Simon and Schuster.

Lifton, R. J. (1986). Imagining the real: Beyond the nuclear evil. In L. Arinspoon (Ed.), *The long darkness*. New Haven, CT: Yale University Press.

Lindemann, E. (1944). Symptomatology and the management of acute grief. *American Journal of Psychiatry, 101*, 141–148.

Lindholm, B. W., & Touliatos, J. (1980). Psychological adjustment of adopted and non-adopted children. *Psychological Reports, 46*, 307–310.

Lindsay, J. W. (1987). *Open adoption: A caring option*. Buena Park, CA: Morning Glory Press.

Lindstrom, C. (1986). *Communication and interaction patterns in normal adoptive families*. Unpublished doctoral dissertation, Union Graduate School, Cincinnati, OH.

Lion, A. (1976). *A survey of 50 adult adoptees who used the rights of the Israeli "open file" adoption law*. Paper presented at the annual meeting of the International Forum on Adolescence, Jerusalem.

Little, P. (1986). Finding the defective gene. *Nature, 321*, 558–559.

Littner, N. (1956a). *The child's need to repeat his past: Some implications for placement*. New York: Child Welfare League of America.

Littner, N. (1956b). Discussion of H. Fradkin & D. Krugman, "A program of adoptive placement for infants under three months." *American Journal of Orthopsychiatry, 26*, 590–593.

Littner, N. (1956c). The natural parents. In M. Schapiro (Ed.), *A study of adoption practice* (Vol. 2). New York: Child Welfare League of America.

Littner, N. (1956d). *Some traumatic effects of separation and placement*. New York: Child Welfare League of America.

Livermore, J. (1961). *Some identification problems in adopted children*. Paper presented at the annual meeting of the American Orthopsychiatric Association, New York.

Loehlin, L. C., Willerman, L., & Horn, J. M. (1982). Personality resemblances between unwed mothers and their adopted-away offspring. *Journal of Personality and Social Psychology, 42*, 1089–1099.

Loehlin, J. C., Willerman, L., & Horn, J. M. (1985). Personality resemblances in adoptive families when the children are late-adolescent or adult. *Journal of Personality and Social Psychology, 48*, 376–392.

Loevinger, J. (1970). *Measuring ego development* (Vols. 1–2). San Francisco: Jossey-Bass.

Lopez, T. (1981). Psychoanalytic observations of foster care [An interdisciplinary seminar of the American Psychoanalytic Association]. *Journal of Preventive Psychiatry, 1,* 37–45.

Losbough, B. (1965). Relationship of E. E. G., neurological and psychological findings in adopted children. *Journal of E. E. G. Technology, 5,* 1–4.

Lowe, C. (1927). The intelligence and social background of the unmarried mother. *Mental Hygeine, 11,* 783–794.

Lowie, R. (1930). Adoption-primitive. *Encyclopedia of the Social Sciences* (Vol. 1). New York: Macmillan.

Lyle, I., Coyle, N., Mooney, S. (1983). Psychotherapy with children to be adopted: Two cases. *Residential Group Care and Treatment, 2,* 73–100.

Maas, H. (1960). The successful adoptive parent applicants. *Social Work, 5,* 14–20.

Maas, H., & Engler, R. (1959). *Children in need of parents.* New York: Columbia University Press.

Macaskill, C. (1985). Post-adoption support: Is it essential? *Adoption and Fostering, 9,* 45–49.

Maccoby, E., & Martin, J. (1983). Socialization in the context of the family: Parent–child interaction. In P. Mussen (Ed.), *Handbook of Child psychology. Vol 4: Socialization, personality, and social development.* New York: Wiley.

MacFarlene, J. W., Allen L., & Honzik, M. P. (1954). *A development study of the behaviour problems of normal children between twenty-one months and fourteen years.* Berkeley: University of California Press.

Magnusson, D., Duner, A., & Zetterblom, G. (1975). *Adjustment: A longitudinal study.* Stockholm: Almqvist & Wiksell.

Mahler, M. S. (1967). On human symbiosis and the vicissitudes of individuation. *Journal of the American Psychoanalytic Association, 15,* 740–763.

Mahler, M. S., Pine, F., & Bergman, A. (1975). *The psychological birth of the human infant: Symbiosis and individuation.* New York: Basic Books.

Mahon, E. (1986, March). *Discussion of Dr. Robert Berlin's "The analysis of an adopted child."* Paper presented at the annual meeting of the Association for Child Psychoanalysis, Seattle.

Main, M., Kaplan, N., & Cassidy, J. (1985). Security in infancy, childhood, and adulthood: A move to the level of representation. In T. Bretherton & E. Walters (Eds.), *Growing points of attachment theory and research. Monographs of the Society for Research in Child Development, 50* (Serial No. 209), 66–104.

Marcia, J. E. (1966). Development and validation of ego-identity status. *Journal of Personality and Social Psychology, 3,* 551–558.

Marcia, J. E. (1967). Ego identity status: Relationship to change in self-esteem, "general maladjustment" and authoritarianism. *Journal of Personality, 35,* 119–133.

Marcia, J. E. (1980). Identity in adolescence. In J. Adelson (Ed.), *Handbook of adolescent psychology.* New York: Wiley.

Marcia, J. E., & Friedman, M. L. (1970). Ego-identity status in college women. *Journal of Personality, 38,* 249–263.

Marcus, C. (1981). *Who is my mother?* Toronto: Macmillan.

Marmor, J. (1964). Psychodynamic aspects of trans-racial adoptions. In *Social work practice: Selected papers from the proceedings of the National Conference on Social Welfare.* New York: Columbia University Press.

Marquis, K. S., & Detweiler, R. A. (1985). Does adoption mean different? An attributional analysis. *Journal of Personality and Social Psychology, 48,* 1054–1066.

Masterson, J. F. (1976). *Psychotherapy of the borderline adult: A developmental approach.* New York: Brunner/Mazel.

Masterson, J., & Costello, J. (1980). *From boderline adolescent to functioning adult*. New York: Brunner/Mazel.

Matas, L., Arend, R. A., & Sroufe, L. A. (1978). Continuity of adaptation in the second year: The relationship between quality of attachment and later competence. *Child Development, 49*, 547–556.

Maxtone-Graham, K. (1983). *An adopted woman*. New York: Remi Books.

May v. Anderson, 345 U.S. 528 (1953).

McCausland, C. L. (1976). *Children of circumstance*. Chicago: Donnelly.

McClure, W. E., & Goldberg, B. (1929). Intelligence of unmarried mothers. *Psychological Clinic, 20*, 154–157.

McConnell, N. F. & Dore, R. (1983). *1883–1983 Crittendon services: The first century*. Washington, DC: Florence Crittendon Mission.

McCullough, P., & Rutenberg, S. (1988). Launching children and moving on. In B. Carter and M. McGoldrick (Eds.), *The changing family life cycle: A framework for family therapy*. (2nd ed.). New York: Gardner Press.

McKuen, R. (1976). *Finding my father: One man's search for identity*. Los Angeles: Cheval Books/Coward, McCann and Geoghegan.

McGillicuddy–Delisi, A., Sigel, I., & Johnson, J. (1979). The family as a system of mutual influences: Parental beliefs, distancing behaviors and children's representational thinking. In M. Lewis & L. Rosenblum (Eds.), *The child and its family*. New York: Plenum Press.

McRoy, R. & Zurcher, L. (1983). *Transracial and inracial adoptees*. Springfield IL: Charles C. Thomas.

McRoy, R., Zurcher, L., Lauderdale, M., & Anderson, R. (1982). Self-esteem and racial identity in transracial and inracial adoptees. *Social Work, 27*, 522–526.

McRoy, R. G., & Grotevant, H. D. (1988). Open adoptions: Practice and policy considerations. *Journal of Social Work and Human Sexuality, 6*, 119–132.

McRoy, R. G., Grotevant, H. D., & Zurcher, L. A. (1988). *The development of emotional disturbance in adopted adolescents*. New York: Praeger.

McRoy, R. G., & Zurcher, L. A. (1983). *Transracial adoptees: The adolescent years*. Springfield, IL: Charles C. Thomas.

McWhinnie, A. M. (1967). *Adopted children and how they grow up*. London: Routledge & Kegan Paul.

McWhinnie, A. M. (1969). The adopted child in adolescence. In G. Caplan & S. Lebovice (Eds.), *Adolescence*. New York: Basic Books.

Mead, G. H. (1934). *Mind, self and society*. Chicago: University of Chicago Press.

Mech, E. V. (1973). Adoption: A policy perspective. In B. Caldwell & H. N. Ricciuti (Eds.), *Review of child development research* (Vol. 3). Chicago: University of Chicago Press.

Mednick, S. A., & Christiansen, S. A. (1977). *Biosocial bases of criminal behavior*. New York: Gardner Press.

Mednick, S. A., Gabrielli, W. F., Jr., & Hutchings, B. (1984). Genetic influences in criminal convictions: Evidence from an adoption cohort. *Science, 224*, 891–894.

Meezan, W., Katz, S., & Russo, E. M. (1978). *Adoption without agencies: A study of independent adoptions*. New York: Child Welfare League of America.

Meezan, W., & Shireman, J. F. (1982). Foster parent adoption: A literature review. *Child Welfare, 61*, 525–535.

Meilman, P. W. (1977). Crisis and commitment in adolescence: A development study of ego-identity status. *Dissertation Abstracts International, 38*, 6B. (University Microfilms No. 2870–2871)

Melina, L. R. (1986). *Raising adopted children*. New York: Harper & Row.

Mendlewicz, J., & Rainer, J. (1977). Adoption study supporting genetic transmission in manic-depressive illness. *Nature, 268,* 327–329.

Menlove, F. L. (1965). Aggressive symptoms in emotionally disturbed adopted children. *Child Development, 36,* 519–532.

Meyer, H. J., Jones, W., & Borgatta, E. F. (1956). The decision by unmarried mothers to keep or surrender their babies. *Social Work, 1,* 103–109.

Meyer v. Nebraska, 262 U.S. 390 (1922).

Mikawa, J. K., & Boston, J. A. (1968). Psychological characteristics of adopted children. *Psychiatry Quarterly Supplement, 42,* 274–281.

Miles, M. B., & Huberman, A. M. (1984). *Qualitative data analysis.* Beverly Hills, CA: Sage.

Millen, L., & Roll, S. (1985). Solomon's mothers: A special case of pathological bereavement. *American Journal of Orthopsychiatry, 55,* 411–418.

Miller, D. (1980). Treatment of the seriously disturbed adolescent. *Adolescent Psychiatry, 8,* 469–481.

Minuchin, S. (1974). *Families and family therapy.* Cambridge, MA: Harvard University Press.

Moore, K. A., & Burt, M. R. (1982). *Private crisis, public costs: Policy perspectives on teenage childbearing.* Washington, DC: Urban Institute Press.

Moore, K. A., Hofferth, S. L., Worthheimer, R. (1979, Sept.–Oct.). Teenage motherhood, its social and economic costs. *Children Today, 8,* 12–16.

Moore v. East Cleaveland, 431 U.S. 494 (1977).

Morrison, H. (1950). Research study in an adoption program. *Child Welfare, 29,* 7–13.

Mushlin, M. B., Levitt, L., & Anderson, L. (1986). Court-ordered foster family care reform: A case study. *Child Welfare, 65,* 141–154.

Munsinger, H. (1975). The adopted child's IQ: A critical review. *Psychological Bulletin, 82,* 623–659.

Napier, A., & Whitaker, C. (1978). *The family crucible.* New York: Harper & Row.

National Center for Social Statistics. (1975). Social and Rehabilitation Service. In *Adoptions in 1975.* Washington, DC: U.S. Department of Health, Education, and Welfare.

National Committee for Adoption. (1985). *Adoption factbook: U.S. data, issues, regulations and resources.* Washington, DC: Author.

Nelson, K. A. (1985). *On the frontier of adoption: A study of special needs adoptive families.* Washington, DC: Child Welfare League of America.

Nemovicher, J. A. (1960). A comparative study of adopted boys and nonadopted boys in respect to specific personality characteristics (Doctoral Dissertation, New York University, 1960). *Dissertation Abstracts International, 20,* 4722.

New York State Association for Retarded Children v. Rockefeller, 357 F. Supp. 752 (1973).

New York State Association for Retarded Children v. Rockefeller, 357 F. Supp. 715 (1975).

Nickman, S. L. (1985). Losses in adoption: The need for dialogue. *Psychoanalytic Study of the Child, 40,* 365–398.

Nieden, M. Z. (1951). The influence of constitution and environment upon the development of adopted children. *Journal of Psychology, 31,* 91–95.

Nordlie, E. B., & Reed, S. C. (1962). Follow-up on adoption counseling for children of possibly racial admixture. *Child Welfare, 41,* 297–327.

Norton, R. (1983). Measuring marital quality: A critical look at the dependent variable. *Journal of Marriage and the Family, 45,* 141–151.

Norvell, M., & Guy, R. F. (1977). A comparison of self-concept in adopted and nonadopted adolescents. *Adolescence, 12,* 443–448.

Nospitz, J. D. (Ed.), (1979). *Basic handbook of child psychiatry* (Vol. 1). New York: Basic Books.

Note. (1973). The rights of foster parents to the children in their care. *Chicago–Kent Law Review, 50*, 86–102.

Nottingham, R. D. (1937). A psychological study of forty unmarried mothers. *Genetic Psychology Monographs, 19*, 155–228.

Nowicki, S., & Strickland, B. (1973). A locus of control scale for children. *Journal of Consulting and Clinical Psychology, 40*, 148–154.

Nurnberger, J. I., Jr., Goldin, L. R., & Gershon, E. S. (1986). Genetics of psychiatric disorders. In G. Winokur & P. Clayton (Eds.), *The medical basis of psychiatry*. Philadelphia: Saunders.

Nutt, T. A., & Snyder, J. (1973). *Transracial adoption*. Unpublished monograph, Massachussets Institute of Technology, Department of Sociology, Cambridge, MA.

Nye v. Marcus, 12 FLR 1146 (1986).

Offer, D. (1969).*The psychological world of the teenager—a study of normal adolescent boys*. New York: Basic Books.

Offer, D. (1973). *The Offer Self-Image Questionnaire*. Chicago: Michael Reese Medical Center, Department of Psychiatry.

Offer, D., Ostrov, E., & Howard, K. I. (1981). *The adolescent: A psychological self-portrait*. New York: Basic Books.

Offord, D. R., Aponte, J. F., & Cross, L. A. (1969). Presenting symptomatology of adopted children. *Archives of General Psychiatry, 20*, 110–116.

O'Hanlon, W. (1987). *Taproots*. New York: Norton.

O'Leary, K. M., Shore, M. F., & Wilder, S. (1984). Contacting pregnant adolescents: Are we missing cues? *Social Casework, 65*, 297–305.

Olson, L. (1980). Social and psychological correlates of pregnancy resolution among adolescent women: A review. *American Journal of Orthopsychiatry, 50*, 432–445.

Pannor, R., & Baran, A. (1984). Open adoption as standard practice. *Child Welfare, 43*, 245–250.

Pannor, R., & Evans, B. (1975). The unmarried father revisited. *Journal of School Health, 5*, 286–290.

Pannor, R., Massarik, F., & Evans, B. W. (1971). *The unmarried father*. New York: Springer.

Pannor, R., Sorosky, A., & Baran, A. (1974). Opening the sealed record in adoption—the human need for continuity. *Journal of Jewish Communal Service, 51*, 188–196.

Parkes, C. M. (1972). *Bereavement: Studies of grief in adult life*. New York: International Universities Press.

Parsons, T. (1955). Family structure and socialization of the child. In T. Parsons, & R. F. Bales (Eds.), *Family socialization and interaction process*. Glencoe, IL: Free Press.

Partridge, S., Hornby, H., & McDonald, T. (1986). *Legacies of loss—visions of gain: An inside look at adoption disruptions*. Portland: University of Southern Maine, Center for Research and Advanced Study.

Pastor, D. L. (1981). The quality of mother–infant attachment and its relationship to toddlers' initial sociability with peers. *Developmental Psychology, 17*, 326–335.

Paton, J. M. (1954). *The adopted break silence*. Action, CA: Life History Study Center.

Paton, J. M. (1960). *Three trips home*. Action, CA: Life History Center.

Paton, J. (1968). *Orphan voyage*. New York: Vintage.

Pearson, K. (1914). *The life, letters and labours of Francis Galton*. Cambridge: Cambridge University Press.

Pederson, D. R., & Gilby, R. L. (1986). Children's concepts of the family. In R. Ashmore & D. Brodzinsky (Eds.), *Thinking about the family: Views of parents and children*. Hillsdale, NJ: Erlbaum.

Peller, L. (1961). About "telling the child" of his adoption. *Bulletin of the Philadelphia Association for Psychoanalysis, 11,* 145–154.

Peller, L. (1963). Further comments on adoption. *Bulletin of the Philadelphia Association for Psychoanalysis, 13,* 1–14.

Phipps-Yonas, S. (1980). Teenage pregnancy and motherhood: A review of the literature. *American Journal of Orthopsychiatry, 50,* 403–431.

Piaget, J. (1954). *The construction of reality in the child.* New York: Basic Books.

Piaget, J. (1964). *Judgment and reasoning in the child.* Paterson, NJ: Littlefield, Adams.

Picton, C. (1980). *Persons in question: Adoptees in search of origins.* Unpublished manuscript, Monash University, Melbourne, Australia.

Pierce v. Society of Sisters, 268 U.S. 5510 (1925).

Pierce, W. (1988). Personal communication.

Plomin, R. (1981). Heredity and temperament: A comparison of twin data for self-report questionnaires, parental ratings, and objectively assessed behavior. In L. Gedda, P. Parisi, & W. E. Nance (Eds.), *Progress in clinical and biological research: Vol. 69B. Twin Research 3, Part B: Intelligence, personality and development.* New York: Alan R. Liss.

Plomin, R., & DeFries, J. (1985). *Origins of individual differences in infancy. The Colorado Adoption Project.* Orlando, FL: Academic Press.

Plomin, R., DeFries, J. C., & Loehlin, J. C. (1977). Genotype-environment interaction and correlation in the analysis of human behavior. *Psychological Bulletin, 84,* 309–327.

Pollock, G. H. (1978). Process and affect: Mourning and grief. *American Journal of Psychoanalysis, 59,* 255–276.

Polsby, G. K. (1986). Adoption and relinquishment as experiences in loss and mourning (abstract). *American Journal of Orthopsychiatry, 38,* 257–258.

Pope, H. (1967, August). Unwed mothers and their sex partners. *Journal of Marriage and the Family,* pp. 555–567.

Powdermaker, H. (1968). *After freedom: A cultural study in the deep South.* New York: Atheneum.

Prentice, C. S. (1940). *An adopted child looks at adoption.* New York: Appleton–Century.

President's task force says transracial adoption should be permitted. (1987, Dec. 5). *Los Angeles Times,* p. 21.

Presser, S. B. (1972). The historical background of the American law of adoption. *Journal of Family Law, 11,* 443–516.

Price, R. A., Cadoret, R. J., Stunkard, A. J., et al. (1987). Genetic contributions to human fatness. *American Journal of Psychiatry, 144,* 1003–1008.

Priester v. Fayette County Children and Youth Services, 12 FLR 1512 (1986).

Prince v. Massachusetts, 321 U.S. 158 (1943).

Pringle, M. L. K. (1967). *Adoption facts and fallacies: A Review of research in the United States, Canada and Great Britain between 1948 and 1965.* London: Longman.

Proch, K. (1981). Foster parents as preferred adoptive parents: Practice implications. *Child Welfare, 60,* 617–625.

Provence, S. (1978). Application of psychoanalytic principles to treatment and prevention in infancy. In J. Glenn (Ed.), *Child analysis and therapy.* New York: Jason Aronson.

Quilloin v. Walcott, 434 U.S. 246 (1978).

Raphael, B. (1983). *The anatomy of bereavement.* New York: Basic Books.

Rasmussen, J. E. (1964). The relationship of ego identity to psychological effectiveness. *Psychological Reports, 15,* 815–825.

Raynor, L. (1980). *The adopted child comes of age.* London: George Allen and Unwin.

Redl, F. (1972). The concept of a "Therapeutic Milieu." In G. H. Weber & B. J. Haberlein

(Eds.), *Residential Treatment of Emotionally Disturbed Children*. New York: Behavioral Publications.

Redl, F., & Wineman, D. (1952). *Controls from within*. Glencoe, IL: Free Press.

Reece, S., & Levin, B. (1968). Psychiatric disturbances in adopted children: A descriptive study. *Social Work, 13*, 101–111.

Reed, R. (1934). *The illegitimate family in New York City*. New York: Columbia University Press.

Reeves, A. C. (1971). Children with surrogate parents: Cases seen in analytic therapy and an aetiological hypothesis. *British Journal of Medical Psychology, 44*, 155–171.

Reid, J. (1957). Principles, values, and assumptions underlying adoption practice. In E. Smith (Ed.), *Readings in adoption*. New York: Child Welfare League of America.

Reiss, D. (1981). *The family's construction of reality*. Cambridge, MA: Harvard University Press.

Reistroffer, M. (1972). Participation of foster parents in decision making: The concept of collegiality. *Child Welfare, 51*, 25–29.

Resnick, M. D. (1984). Studying adolescent mothers' decision making about adoption and parenting. *Social Work, 29*, 5–10.

Resnick, M. D., & Blum, R. W. (1985). Developmental and personological correlates of adolescent sexual behavior and outcome. *International Journal of Adolescent Medicine and Health, 1*, 293–313.

Reynolds, W. F., Chiappise, D., & Danzl, R. (1975). *The search by adopted persons for their natural parents: A research project comparing those who search and those who do not—preliminary data*. Paper presented at the meeting of the American Psychology-Law Society, Chicago, IL.

Reynolds, W. F., Eisnitz, M. F., Chiappise, D., & Walsh, M. (1976, August). *Personality factors differentiating searching and non-searching adoptees*. Paper presented at the 84th Annual Convention of the American Psychological Association, Washington, DC.

Reynolds, W. F., Levey, C., & Eisnitz, M. F. (1977, September). *Adoptees' personality characteristics and self-ratings of adoptive family life*. Paper presented at the annual convention of the American Psychological Association, San Francisco.

Riben, M. (1988). *Shedding light on the dark side of adoption*. Detroit: Harlow.

Richards, A. D. (1987, July). *Self-mutilation and father–daughter incest: A psychoanalytic case report*. Paper presented at the 35th Congress of the International Psychoanalytic Association, Montreal.

Richardson, L. F. (1912–1913). The measurement of mental "nature" and the study of adopted children. *Eugenics Review, 4*, 391–394.

Rickarby, G. A., & Egan, P. (1980). Issues of preventive work with adopted adolescents. *Medical Journal of Australia, 1*, 470–472.

Rillera, M. J., & Kaplan, S. (1984). *Cooperative adoption: A handbook*. Westminster, CA: Triadoption Publications.

Rinsley, D. B. (1980). *Treatment of severely disturbed adolescents*. New York: Jason Aronson.

Ripple, L. (1968). A follow-up of adopted children. *Social Service Review, 42*, 479–497.

Rivera v. Marcus, 696 F. 2d 1016 (1982).

Roberts, B. (1980). *Adoption project for handicapped children: Ohio District 11*. Washington, DC: Office of Human Development Services.

Rochlin, G. (1965). *Griefs and discontents: The forces of change*. Boston: Little, Brown.

Roe, A. (1944). Adult adjustment of children of alcoholic parents raised in foster homes. *Quarterly Journal of Studies on Alcohol, 5*, 378–393.

Rogers, R. (1969). The adolescent and the hidden parent. *Comprehensive Psychiatry, 10*, 296–301.

Roiphe, H. (1983). Precocious anal zone arousal: A developmental variant in the differentiation process. In J. D. Call, E. Galenson, & R. L. Tyson (Eds.), *Frontiers of infant psychiatry.* New York: Basic Books.

Rosenberg, M. (1979). *Conceiving the self.* New York: Basic Books.

Rosenthal, D. (1970). *Genetic theory and abnormal behaviour.* New York: McGraw-Hill.

Rosenthal, D. (1975). The spectrum concept in schizophrenic and manic-depressive disorders. In D. X. Dreedman (Ed.), *Biology of the major psychoses.* New York: Raven Press.

Rosenthal, D., & Kety, S. S. (1968). *Transmission of schizophrenia.* Oxford: Perdgamon Press.

Rosenthal, D., Wender, P. H., & Kety, S. S. (1971). The adopted-away offspring of schizophrenics. *American Journal of Psychiatry, 128,* 307–311.

Rotter, J. B. (1975). Some problems and misconceptions related to the construct of internal vs. external control of reinforcement. *Journal of Consulting and Clinical Psychology, 48,* 56–67.

Rowe, J., Cain, H., Hundleby, M., & Keane, A. (1984). *Long term foster care.* London: Batsford.

Rutter, M. (1979). Protective factors in children's responses to stress and disadvantage. In M. W. Kent & J. E. Rolf (Eds.), *Primary Prevention of Psychopathology: Vol. 3. Social Competence in Children.* Hanover, NH: University Press of New England.

Rutter, M., Quinton, D., & Liddle, C. (1983). Parenting in two generations. In N. Madge (Ed.), *Families at risk.* London: Department of Health and Social Security.

Rynearson, E. K. (1981). Relinquishment and its maternal complications. *American Journal of Psychiatry, 139,* 338–340.

Sabalis, R. F., & Burch, E. A. (1980). Comparisons of psychiatric problems of adopted and non-adopted patients. *Southern Medical Journal, 73,* 867–868.

Sambrano, S. (1987). Social Science Researcher, Department of Health and Human Services, Washington, DC. Personal communication.

Santosky v. Kramer, 455 U.S. 745 (1982).

Sants, H. J. (1964). Genealogical bewilderment in children with substitute parents. *British Journal of Medical Psychology, 37,* 133–141.

Scarr, S. (1981). *Race, social class, and individual differences in IQ.* Hillsdale, NJ: Erlbaum.

Scarr, S., & Kidd, K. K. (1983). Developmental behavior genetics. In M. M. Haith & J. J. Campos (Eds.), *Handbook of child psychology: Vol. 2. Infancy and developmental psychobiology.* New York: Wiley.

Scarr, S., Scarf, E., & Weinberg, R. A. (1980). Perceived and actual similarities in biological and adoptive families: Does perceived similarity bias genetic inferences? *Behavior Genetics, 10,* 445–458.

Scarr, S., & Weinberg, R. A. (1983). The Minnesota adoption studies: Genetic differences and malleability. *Child Development, 54,* 260–267.

Schafer, R. (1980). Narration in the psychoanalytic dialogue. *Critical Inquiry 7,* 29–53.

Schaffer, J., & Kral, R. (1988). Adoptive families. In C. Chilman, F. Cox, & E. Nunnally (Eds.), *Families in trouble: Families with problems related to alternative lifestyles.* Milwaukee: Sage Press.

Schaffer, J., & Lindstrom, C. (1989). *How to raise an adopted child.* New York: Crown Publishers.

Schechter, M. D. (1960). Observations on adopted children. *Archives of General Psychiatry, 3,* 21–32.

Schechter, M. D. (1967). Psychoanalytic theory as it relates to adoption (Report of a panel). *Journal of the American Psychoanalytic Association, 15,* 695–708.

Schechter, M. D. (1970). About adoptive parents. In E. J. Anthony & T. Benedek (Eds.), *Parenthood: Its psychology and psychopathology.* Boston: Little, Brown.

Schechter, M. D. (1973). A case study of an adopted child. *International Journal of Child Psychotherapy, 2,* 202–223.

Schechter, M., Carlson, P. V., Simmons, J. Q., & Work, H. H. (1964). Emotional problems in the adoptee. *Archives of General Psychiatry, 10,* 37–46.

Schenkel, S., & Marcia, J. E. (1972). Attitudes toward premarital intercourse in determining ego identity status in college women. *Journal of Personality, 3,* 472–482.

Schmidt, D. M. (1986). Presentation of research findings on prevention of adoption disruption. In D. M. Schmidt (Ed.), *Special needs adoption: A positive perspective.* Denver: Colorado State Department of Social Services.

Schneider, J. (1984). *Stress, loss and grief.* Baltimore: University Park Press.

Schoenberg, C. (1974). On adoption and identity. *Child Welfare, 53,* 549.

Schulsinger, F. (1977). Psychopathy: Heredity and environment. In S. A. Mednick & K. O. Christiansen (Eds.), *Biosocial bases of criminal behavior.* New York: Gardner Press.

Schumacher, H. C. (1927). The unmarried mother: A socio-psychiatric viewpoint. *Mental Hygiene, 11,* 775–782.

Schwartz, A. D. (1986). *Early parental attitudes and adopted adolescent self-esteem.* Unpublished master's thesis, Bryn Mawr College, Bryn Mawr, PA.

Schwartz, E. M. (1975). Problems after adoption: Some guidelines for pediatrician involvement. *Pediatrics, 87,* 991–994.

Sears, R. R., Maccoby, E. E., & Levine, H. (1957). *Patterns of child rearing.* Evanston, IL: Row, Peterson.

Seglow, J., Pringle, M. L. K., & Wedge, P. (1972). *Growing up adopted.* Windsor, Eng.: National Foundation for Educational Research in England and Wales.

Seligman, M. E. P. (1975). *Helplessness.* San Francisco: Freeman.

Selye, H. (1950). *The physiology and pathology of exposure to stress.* Montreal: Acta.

Selye, H. (1976). *The stress of life* (rev. ed.). New York: McGraw-Hill.

Senior, N., & Himadi, E. (1985). Emotionally disturbed adopted inpatient adolescents. *Child Psychiatry and Human Development, 15,* 189–197.

Shackleton, C. H. (1984). The psychology of grief: A review. *Advances in Behavioral Research and Therapy, 6,* 153–205.

Shantz, C. U. (1983). Social cognition. In P. Mussen (Ed.), *Handbook of child psychology: Vol. 3. Cognitive development.* New York: Wiley.

Shapiro, M. (1956). *A study of adoption practice: Vol 1. Adoption agencies and the children they serve.* New York: Child Welfare League of America.

Shaver, K. G. (1975). *An introduction to attribution processes.* Cambridge, MA: Winthrop.

Sherick, I. (1983). Adoption and disturbed narcissism: A case illustration of a latency boy. *Journal of the American Psychoanalytic Association, 31,* 487–513.

Shyne, A., & Schroeder, A. (1978). *National study of social services to children and their families.* Washington, DC: U.S. Department of Health and Human Services.

Siggins, L. D. (1966). Mourning: A critical survey of the literature. *International Journal of Pyschoanalysis, 47,* 14–25.

Sigvardsson, S., Bohman, M., & Cloninger, C. R. (in press). Structure and stability of childhood personality: Prediction of later social adjustment. *Journal of Child Psychology and Psychiatry and Allied Disciplines.*

Sigvardsson, S., Cloninger, C. R., Bohman, M., & von Knorring, A. (1982). Predisposition to petty criminality in Swedish adoptees: III. Sex differences and validation of the male typology. *Archives of General Psychiatry, 39,* 1248–1253).

Sigvardsson, S., von Knorring, A. L., Bohman, M., et al. (1984). An adoption study of somatoform disorders: I. The relationship of somatization to psychiatric disability. *Archives of General Psychiatry, 41,* 853–859.

Silber, K., & Speedlin, P. (1983). *Dear birthmother.* San Antonio, TX: Corona.

Silver, L. B. (1970). Frequency of adoption in children with the neurological learning disability syndrome. *Journal of Learning Disabilities, 3,* 11–14.

Silverman, A. R. (1980). The assimilation and adjustment of transracially adopted children in the United States. Unpublished doctoral dissertation, University of Wisconsin-Madison.

Silverman, A., & Weitzman, D. (1986). Nonrelative adoption in the United States. In R. A. C. Hoksbergen (Ed.), *Adoption in worldwide perspective: A review of programs, policies and legislation in 14 countries.* Lisse: Swets & Zeitlinger; Berwyn: Swets North America.

Silverman, M. A. (1985–1986). Adoptive, anxiety adoptive rage, and adoptive guilt. *International Journal of Psychoanalytic Psychotherapy, 11,* 301–307.

Silverman, M. A. (1985). *Termination of the analysis of an adopted child.* Panel presentation to the Psychoanalytic Association of New York.

Silverman, P. R. (1981). *Helping women cope with grief.* Beverly Hills, CA: Sage.

Simenauer, E. (1985). Identification in the theory and technique of psychoanalysis. *International Journal of Psychoanalysis, 66,* 171–184.

Simmons, D. (1970). Development of an objective measure of identity achievement status. *Journal of Projective Techniques and Personality Assessment, 34,* 241–244.

Simmons, W. W. (1980). A study of identity formation in adoptees. *Dissertation Abstracts International, 40,* 12-B Part I, 5832.

Simon, N. M., & Senturia, A. G. (1966). Adoption and psychiatric illness. *American Journal of Psychiatry, 122,* 858–867.

Simon, R. J., & Altstein H. (1977). *Transracial adoption.* New York: Wiley.

Simon, R., & Altstein, H. (1981). *Transracial adoption: A follow-up.* Lexington, MA: Lexington Books.

Simon, R., & Altstein, H. (1987). *Transracial adoptees and their families: A study of identity and commitment.* New York: Praeger.

Simpson, M., Timm, H., & McCubbin, H. (1981). Adoptees in search of their past: Policy induced strain on adoptive families and birth parents. *Family Relations, 30,* 427–434.

Singer, L. M., Brodzinsky, D. M., & Braff, A. M. (1982). Children's belief about adoption: A developmental study. *Journal of Applied Developmental Psychology, 3,* 285–294.

Singer, L. M., Brodzinsky, D. M., Ramsay, D., Steir, M., & Waters, E. (1985). Mother–infant attachment in adoptive families. *Child Development, 56,* 1543–1551.

Skeels, H. M. (1936). Mental development of children in foster homes. *Journal of Genetic Psychology, 49,* 91–106.

Skeels, H. M. (1938). Mental development of children in foster homes. *Journal of Consulting and Clinical Psychology, 2,* 33–43.

Skeels, H. M. (1966). Adult status of children with contrasting early life experiences. *Monographs of the Society for Research in Child Development, 31* (3, Whole No. 105).

Skodak, M. (1939). Children in foster homes: A study of mental development. *University of Iowa Studies in Child Welfare, 16,* 1–156.

Skodak, M., & Skeels, H. M. (1949). A final follow-up study of one hundred adopted children. *Journal of Genetic Psychology, 75,* 85–125.

Slaytor, P. (1986). Reunion and resolution: The adoption triangle. *Australian Social Work, 39,* 15–20.

Small, J. W. (1979). Discrimination against the adoptee. *Public Welfare, 37,* 38–43.

Small, J. (1987, April). *Empowering post-adoptive families in family therapy.* Workshop presentation, 64th Annual Meeting of the American Orthopsychiatric Association, Washington, DC.

Smith, E. (Ed.). (1963). *Readings in adoption.* New York: Philosophical Library.

Smith, L. F. (1986). Adoption—the case for more options. *Utah Law Review, 495*, 495–557.

Smith, R. (1976). The sealed adoption record controversy and social agency response. *Child Welfare, 55*, 73–74.

Smith v. Organization of Foster Families for Equality and Reform, 431 U.S. 816 (1977).

Sobol, M., & Cardiff, J. 91983). A sociopsychological investigation of adult adoptees search for birth parents. *Family Relations, 32*, 477–483.

Sokoloff, B. (1977). Should the adopted adolescent have access to his birth records and to his birthparents? Why? When? *Clinical Pediatrics, 16*, 975–977.

Sorich, C. J., & Siebert, R. (1982). Toward humanizing adoption. *Child Welfare, 61*, 207–213.

Sorosky, A. D., Baran, A., & Pannor, R. (1975). Identity conflicts in adoptees. *American Journal of Orthopsychiatry, 45*, 18–27.

Sorosky, A., Baran, A., & Pannor, R. (1977). Adoption and the adolescent: An overview. In S. C. Feinstein & P. Giovacchini (Eds.), *Adolescent Psychiatry* (Vol. 5). New York: Jason Aronson.

Sorosky, A., Baran, A., & Pannor, R. (1978, rev. 1984). *The adoption triangle*. New York: Doubleday.

Soule, M. (1968). Contribution clinique a la comprehension de l'imaginaire des parents: À propos de l'adoption ou le roman de Polybe et Merope [Clinical contribution to the comprehension of the imaginary as regards parents: Apropos of adoption or the story of Polybus and Merope]. *Revue Française de Psychanalyse, 32*, 419–464.

Soule, M. (1972). L'imaginaire des parents et al structuration de la dynamique familiale: Exemplarite clinique de la famille adoptive [Parental fantasies and the structuring of family dynamics: The adoptive family as a clinical example]. *Revue de Neuropsychiatrie Infantile et D'Hygiene Mentale de L'Enfance, 20*, 5–7.

Speece, M. W., & Brent, S. B. (1984). Children's understanding of death: A review of three components of a death concept. *Child Development, 55*, 1671–1686.

Spence–Chapin Adoption Service v. Polk, 29 N.Y. 2d 296, 205 (1971).

Spitz, R. A. (1945). Hospitalism: An inquiry into the genesis of psychiatric conditions in early childhood. Psychoanalytic Study of the Child, 1, 53–74.

Spivak, G., & Swift, M. (1975). *The Hahnemann Elementary School Behavior Rating Scale Manual*. Philadelphia: Hahnemann Medical College and Hospital.

Sroufe, L. A., & Fleeson, J. (1986). Attachment and the construction of relationships. In W. W. Hartup & Z. Rubin (Eds.), *Relationships and development*. Hillsdale, NJ: Erlbaum.

Sroufe, L. A., & Waters, E. (1977). Attachment as an organizational construct. *Child Development, 48*, 1184–1199.

Stanley v. Illinois, 405 U.S. 645 (1972).

State v. McMaster, 486 P.2d 567 (1971).

Stein, L. M., & Hoopes, J. L. (1985). *Identity formation in the adopted adolescent*. New York: Child Welfare League of America.

Steinhauer, P. D. (1983). Issues of attachment and separation: Foster care and adoption. In P. Steinhauer & Q. Rae–Grant (Eds.), *Psychological problems of the child in the family* (2nd ed.). New York: Basic Books.

Stephenson, P. (1973). Working with 9 to 12-year-old children. *Child Welfare, 52*, 18–27.

Stern, D. N. (1985). *The interpersonal world of the infant: A view from psychoanalysis and developmental psychology*. New York: Basic Books.

Stone, F. H. (1972). Adoption and identity. *Child Psychiatry and Human Development, 2*, 120–128.

Stunkard, A. J., Thorkild, S. I. A., Harris, C., et al. (1986). An adoption study of human obesity. *New England Journal of Medicine, 314*, 193–198.

Summers, F., & Walsh, F. (1977). The nature of the symbiotic bond between mother and schizophrenic. *American Journal of Orthopsychiatry, 47,* 484–494.

Sweeney, D. M., Gasbarro, D. T., & Gluck, M. R. (1963). A descriptive study of adopted children seen in a child guidance center. *Child Welfare, 42,* 345–349.

Swigar, M. E., Bowers, M. B., & Fleck, S. (1976). Grieving and unplanned pregnancy. *Psychiatry, 39,* 72–80.

Taichert, L. C., & Harvin, D. D. (1975). Adoption and children with learning and behavior problems. *Western Journal of Medicine, 122,* 464–470.

Talen, M., & Lehr, M. (1984). A structural developmental analysis of symptomatic children and their families. *Journal of Marital & Family Therapy, 10,* 381–391.

Tan, A. L., Kendis, R. F., Fine, J. T., & Porac, J. (1977). A short measure of Eriksonian ego identity. *Journal of Personality Assessment, 41,* 279–284.

Tec, L., & Gordon, S. (1967). The adopted children's adaptation to adolescence. *American Journal of Orthopsychiatry, 37,* 402.

Ten Broeck, E., & Barth, R. P. (1986). Learning the hard way: A pilot permanency planning program. *Child Welfare, 65,* 281–294.

Ternay, M., Wilborn, R., & Day, H. D. (1985). Perceived child–parent relationships and child adjustment in families with both adopted and natural children. *Journal of Genetic Psychology, 146,* 261–272.

Tetlow, C. (1955). Psychoses of childbearing. *Journal of Mental Science, 101,* 629–639.

Thoburn, J., Murdoch, A., & O'Brien, A. (1986). *Permanence in child care.* Oxford: Blackwell.

Thomas, A., & Chess, S. (1977). *Temperament and development.* New York: Brunner/Mazel.

Thomas, A., & Chess, S. (1984). Genesis and evolution of behavioral disorders: From infancy to early adult life. *American Journal of Psychiatry, 141,* 1–9.

Thompson, J., Stoneman, L., Webber, J., & Harrison, D. (1978). *The adoption rectangle: A study of adult adoptees search for birth family history and implications for adoption service.* Unpublished Project Report of the Children's Aid Society of Metropolitan Toronto.

Thurston, H. W. (1930). *The dependent child: A story of changing aims and methods in the care of dependent children.* New York: Columbia University Press.

Tienari, P., Sorri, A., Lahti, I., et al. (1985). Interaction of genetic and psychosocial factors in schizophrenia. *Acta Psychiatrica Scandinavica, 71,* 19–30.

Tizard, B. (1977). *Adoption: A second chance.* London: Open Books.

Tooley, K. M. (1978). The remembrance of things past: On the collection and recollection of ingredients useful in the treatment of disorders resulting from unhappiness, rootlessness, and the fear of things to come. *American Journal of Orthopsychiatry, 48,* 174–182.

Torgerson, S. (1983). Genetic factors in anxiety disorders. *Archives of General Psychiatry, 40,* 1085–1089.

Toussieng, P. W. (1962). Thoughts regarding the etiology of psychological difficulties in adopted children. *Child Welfare, 41,* 59–65.

Tremitiere, B. S. (1984). *Disruption: A break in commitment.* Paper presented at the Ninth North American Council of Adoptable Children Conference, Chicago.

Triseliotis, J. (1973). *In search of origins.* London: Routledge & Kegan Paul.

Triseliotis, J. (1980). *Growing up in foster care and after.* London: Social Science Research Council.

Triseliotis, J. (1983). Identity and security in adoption and long-term fostering. *Adoption and Fostering, 7,* 22–31.

Triseliotis, J. (1984). Obtaining birth certificates. In P. Bean (Ed.), *Adoption.* London: Tavistock.

Triseliotis, J., & Russell, J. (1984). *Hard to place*. London: Gower.

Tyson, R. L. (1983). Some narcissistic consequences of object loss: A developmental view. *Psychoanalytic Quarterly, 52*, 205–224.

Unger, C., Dwarshuis, G., & Johnson, E. (1977). *Chaos, madness, and unpredictability . . . placing the child with ears like Uncle Harry's*. Ann Arbor, MI: Spaulding for Children.

U.S. Congress. Senate. (1975). *Adoption and foster care*. Hearings before the Subcommittee for Children and Youth of the Committee on Labor and Public Welfare. Washington, DC: Government Printing Office.

VanBuskirk, D. (1983). Clinical illustrations of the regulation of self-esteem. In J. E. Mack & S. L. Ablon (Eds.), *The developmental and sustaining of self-esteem in childhood*. Madison, CT: International Universities Press.

van Eerdewegh, M. M., Gershon, E. S., & van Eerdewegh, P. M. (1980). X-chromosome threshold models of bipolar manic depressive illness. *Journal of Psychiatry Research, 15*, 215–238.

VanPutten, R., & LaWall, J. (1981). Postpartum psychosis in an adoptive mother and in a father. *Psychosomatics, 22*, 1087–1089.

Vilardi, E. M. (1988). Executive Chairman, International Soundex Reunion Registry. Personal communication.

Vincent, C. (1961). *Unmarried mothers*. New York: Free Press.

Volkan, V. D. (1984) *What do you get when you cross a dandelion with a rose?* New York: Jason Aronson.

Volkan, V. D. (1984–1985). Complicated mourning. *Annals of Psychoanalysis, 12–13*, 323–348.

von Knorring, A. L., Cloninger, C. R., Bohman, M., et al. (1983). An adoption study of depressive disorders and substance abuse. *Archives of General Psychiatry, 40*(9), 943–950.

W. v. G., 356 NYS 2d 24 (1974).

Wallerstein, J. S. (1983). Children of divorce: Stress and developmental tasks. In N. Garmezy & M. Rutter (Ed.), *Stress, coping, and development in children*. New York: McGraw-Hill.

Wallerstein, J. S., & Kelly, J. B. (1980). *Surviving the breakup: How children and parents cope with divorce*. New York: Basic Books.

Walsh, E. D., & Lewis, F. S. (1969, December). A study of adoptive mothers in a child guidance clinic. *Social Casework*, 587–594.

Walsh, F. (1982). *Normal family process*. New York: Guilford.

Washington, A. (1982). A cultural and historical perspective on pregnancy related activity among U.S. teenagers. *Journal of Black Psychology, 9*, 1–28.

Wasson, V. P. (1939). *The chosen baby*. Philadelphia: Lippincott.

Waterman, A. S. (1982). Identity development from adolescence to adulthood: An extension of theory and a review of research. *Development Psychology, 18*, 341–358.

Waterman, A. S., Geary, P., & Waterman, C. K. (1974). A longitudinal study of changes in ego identity status from the freshman to senior year in college. *Development Psychology, 10*, 387–392.

Waterman, A. S., & Goldman, J. A. (1976). A longitudinal study of ego identity development at a liberal arts college. *Journal of Youth & Adolescence, 5*, 361–369.

Waterman, A. S., & Waterman, C. K. (1971). A longitudinal study of changes in ego identity status during the freshman year at college. *Development Psychology, 5*, 167–173.

Watson, K. W. (1979). Who is the primary client? *Public Welfare, 37*, 11–14.

Webber, J., Thompson, J., & Stoneman, L. (1980). *Adoption reunion: A struggle in uncharted relationships*. Unpublished study for the Children's Aid Society of Metropolitan Canada.

Weckler, J. E. (1953). Adoption on Mokil. *American Anthropologist, 55.*

Weidell, R. C. (1980). Unsealing sealed birth certificates in Minnesota. *Child Welfare, 59,* 113–119.

Weil, R. H. (1984). International adoption: The quiet migration. *International Migration Review, 18,* 280–281.

Weiss, A. (1984). Parent–child relationships of adopted adolescents in a psychiatric hospital. *Adolescence, 19,* 77–88.

Weiss, A. (1985). Symptomatology of adopted and nonadopted adolescents in a psychiatric hospital. *Adolescence, 20,* 763–774.

Wender, P. H., Rosenthal, D., Kety, S. S., et al. (1974). Cross-fostering: A research strategy for clarifying the role of genetic and experimental factors in the etiology of schizophrenia. *Archives of General Psychiatry, 30,* 121–128.

Wender, P. H., Rosenthal, D., Rainer, J. D., et al. (1978). Schizophrenics' adopting parents' psychiatric status. *Archives of General Psychiatry, 34,* 777–784.

Wertlieb, D., Weigel, C., & Feldstein, M. (1987). Measuring children's coping. *American Journal of Orthopsychiatry, 57,* 548–560.

Whan, M. (1979). Accounts, narrative, and case history. *British Journal of Social Work, 9,* 489–499.

Whitaker, D. (1984). *The experience of residential care from the perspectives of children, parents and care-givers.* Final Report to the ESRC.

Whitbourne, S. K., & Waterman, A. S. (1979). Psychosocial development during the adult years: Age and cohort comparisons. *Development Psychology, 15,* 373–378.

Wieder, H. (1977a). On being told of adoption. *Psychoanalytic Quarterly, 46,* 1–22.

Wieder, H. (1977b). The family romance fantasies of adopted children. *Psychoanalytic Quarterly, 46,* 185–200.

Wieder, H. (1978a). On when and whether to disclose about adoption. *Journal of the American Psychoanalytic Association, 26,* 793–811.

Wieder, H. (1978b). Special problems in the psychoanalysis of adopted children. In J. Glenn (Ed.), *Child analysis and therapy.* New York: Jason Aronson.

Wilson, M. R. (1985). *Long-term inpatient psychiatric treatment of adolescent adopted children, a population at risk.* Paper presented at the seminar of the San Diego Society for Adolescent Psychiatry.

Wiltse, K. T. (1985). Foster care: An overview. In J. Laird & A. Hartman (Eds.), *A handbook of child welfare: Context, knowledge and practice.* New York: Free Press.

Wimberly, T. (1981). The making of a Munchausen. *British Journal of Medical Psychology, 54,* 121–129.

Winkler, R. C., Brown, D. W., Van Keppel, M., & Blanchard, A. (1988). *Clinical practice in adoption.* New York and Oxford: Pergamon Press.

Winkler, R. C., & Midford, S. (1986). Biological identity in adoption, artificial insemination by donor (A.I.D.) and the new birth technologies. *Australian Journal of Early Childhood, 11,* 43–48.

Winkler, R., & van Keppel M. (1984). *Relinquishing mothers in adoption: Their long-term adjustment* (Monograph No. 3). Melbourne: Institute of Family Studies.

Winnicott, D. W. (1953). Transitional objects and transitional phenomena: A study of the first "not-me" possession. *International Journal of Psychoanalysis, 34,* 89–97.

Winnicott, D. W. (1953). *Two adopted children.* Paper presented to the Association of Child Care Officers (S. E. Area).

Winnicott, D. W. (1954). Pitfalls in adoption. *Medical Practice, 232,* 23.

Winnicott, D. W. (1955). Adopted children in adolescence. *Report of the residential conference held at Roehampton, July 13–15, 1955.* London: Standing Committee of Societies Registered for Adoption.

Winnicott, D. W. (1956). Primary maternal preoccupation. In D. W. Winnicott, *Collected papers*. London: Tavistock.

Winnicott, D. W. (1957). On adoption. In D. W. Winnicott, *Mother and child: A primer of first relationships*. New York: Basic Books.

Winnicott, D. (1965). *The maturational process and the facilitating environment*. New York: Basic Books.

Winokur, G., Clayton, P., & Reich, T. (1969). *Manic depressive illness*. St. Louis, MO: Mosby.

Witmer, H. L., Herzog, E., Weinstein, E. A., & Sullivan, M. E. (1963). *Independent adoptions*. New York: Russell Sage Foundation.

Wittenborn, J. R., et al. (1956). A study of adoptive children. *Psychological Monographs, 70* (nos. 1–2).

Work, H. H., & Anderson, H. (1971). Studies in adoption: Requests for psychiatric treatment. *American Journal of Psychiatry, 127*, 984–950.

W. R. I. (1978). *Evaluation of the test of regional planning in adoption*. Albany, NY: Welfare Research, Inc.

Yarrow, L. J. (1964). Separation from parents during early childhood. In M. Hoffman & L. Hoffman (Eds.), *Review of child development research* (Vol. 1). New York: Russell Sage Foundation.

Yarrow, L. J., & Goodwin, M. S. (1973). The immediate impact of separation: Reactions of infants to a change in mother figure. In L. J. Stone, H. T. Smith, & L. B. Murphy (Eds.), *The competent infant*. New York: Basic Books.

Yarrow, L. J., Goodwin, M. S., Manheimer, H., & Milowe, I. D. (1973). Infancy experiences and cognitive and personality development at 10 years. In L. J. Stone, H. T. Smith, & L. B. Murphy (Eds.), *The competent infant*. New York: Basic Books.

Young, L. (1954). *Out of wedlock*. New York: McGraw-Hill.

Zachler, J., & Brandstadt, W. (Eds.). (1975). *The teenage pregnant girl*. Springfield, IL: Charles C. Thomas.

Zeilinger, R. (1979). The need vs. the right to know. *Public Welfare, 37*, 44–47.

Ziatek, K. (1974). Psychological problems of adoption. *Psychological Wychowawcza* (Warsaw), *17*, 63–76.

Zill, N. (1985, April). *Behavior and learning problems among adopted children: Findings from a U.S. national survey of child health*. Paper presented at the meeting of the Society for Research in Child Development, Toronto.

Zisook, S., & DeVaul, R. (1977). Grief-related facsimile illness. *International Journal of Psychiatry in Medicine, 7*, 329–336.

Zisook, S., & DeVaul, R. (1985). Unresolved grief. *American Journal of Psychoanalysis, 45*, 370–379.

Zwimpfer, D. M. (1983). Indicators of adoption breakdown. *Social Casework, 64*, 169–177.

Subject Index

Name Index